Quattro Pro 2 Companion

Quattro Pro 2 Companion

Douglas Cobb
Mark W. Crane
with Stephen L. Nelson

PUBLISHED BY
Microsoft Press
A Division of Microsoft Corporation
One Microsoft Way, Redmond, Washington 98052-6399

Copyright © 1991 by Douglas Ford Cobb

All rights reserved. No part of the contents of this book
may be reproduced or transmitted in any form or by any means
without the written permission of the publisher.

Library of Congress Cataloging-in-Publication Data
Cobb, Douglas Ford.
    Quattro Pro companion / Douglas Cobb, Mark W. Crane, Stephen L.
  Nelson.
       p.   cm.
    Includes index.
    ISBN 1–55615–358–9
    1. Quattro pro (Computer program) 2. Business—Computer programs.
  3. Electronic spreadsheets. I. Crane, Mark W. II. Nelson, Stephen
  L., 1959– . III. Title.
  HF5548.4.Q39C6 1991
   005.369—dc20   90–26593
                                                   CIP

Printed and bound in the United States of America.

1 2 3 4 5 6 7 8 9   RDC   5 4 3 2 1

Distributed to the book trade in Canada by Macmillan of Canada, a division of Canada
Publishing Corporation.

Distributed to the book trade outside the United States and Canada by Penguin Books Ltd.

Penguin Books Ltd., Harmondsworth, Middlesex, England
Penguin Books Australia Ltd., Ringwood, Victoria, Australia
Penguin Books N.Z. Ltd., 182-190 Wairau Road, Auckland 10, New Zealand

British Cataloging-in-Publication Data available.

Quattro® is a registered trademark of Borland International, Inc. IBM® and PS/2® are registered trademarks of International Business Machines Corporation. Intel® is a registered
trademark of Intel Corporation. Lotus® is a registered trademark of Lotus Development
Corporation. Microsoft® and MS-DOS® are registed trademarks of Microsoft Corporation.

Acquisitions Editor: Marjorie Schlaikjer
Project Editor: Casey D. Doyle
Editing and Technical Review: Sakson & Taylor, Inc.

Contents

Preface   *ix*

Acknowledgments   *xiii*

CHAPTER 1

Quattro Pro Basics   1

Hardware considerations ■ Starting Quattro Pro ■ A tour of the Quattro Pro worksheet ■ The Quattro Pro function keys ■ Moving the cell selector using keys ■ Moving the cell selector using a mouse ■ Making entries in your Quattro Pro worksheet ■ Editing existing cell entries ■ Quattro Pro commands ■ Undoing your mistakes ■ Memory management ■ Recalculation ■ Naming cells and blocks ■ Exiting from Quattro Pro

CHAPTER 2

Formatting a Worksheet   45

Using formats ■ Improving your worksheet by hiding zeroes ■ Alignment of labels and values ■ Changing the default label prefix

CHAPTER 3

Editing Your Worksheet   59

Adjusting column widths ■ Erasing the worksheet ■ Erasing entries in cells and blocks ■ Inserting rows and columns ■ Deleting rows and columns ■ Moving cell entries ■ Copying cell entries ■ Making special copies

CHAPTER 4

Functions   85

Function basics ■ Mathematical functions ■ Statistical functions ■ Financial functions ■ Lookup functions ■ Logical functions ■ String functions ■ Numeric conversion functions ■ Other Quattro Pro functions

CHAPTER 5
Worksheet Commands 141
Filling blocks ■ Computing frequency distributions ■ Building what-if tables ■ Computing linear regression ■ Manipulating matrices in your worksheets ■ Solving optimization problems ■ Using Solve For ■ Protecting your worksheets ■ Using the Edit Search And Replace command ■ Creating input forms ■ Word processing your worksheet

CHAPTER 6
Dates and Times 185
Dates ■ Times ■ Combined date and time entries ■ Converting labels to dates and times

CHAPTER 7
Printing 205
Hardware setup ■ Printing basics ■ Previewing your worksheets before printing ■ Formatting reports using print settings ■ Adding headers and footers ■ Printing column and row headings ■ Improving worksheets using line drawing, shading, and fonts ■ Manual page breaks ■ Using setup strings ■ Listing a worksheet ■ Using the Print Layout Reset command to return print defaults

CHAPTER 8
File Management 243
Saving worksheets ■ Retrieving worksheets ■ Changing the default directory ■ Stacking worksheets in memory ■ Using Quattro Pro's File Manager ■ The File Utilities DOS Shell command ■ Using the Tools Xtract command ■ Combining worksheets ■ Linking spreadsheets using formulas

CHAPTER 9
Working With Windows 285
Freezing labels in view ■ Splitting the screen ■ More about worksheet windows

CHAPTER 10
Creating Graphs 299
The basics of creating graphs ■ Quattro Pro's graph types ■ Enhancing graphs ■ Printing graphs ■ Using the Annotate feature

CHAPTER 11
Database Management 349
What is a database? ■ Sorting ■ Querying ■ Database statistical functions ■ Accessing external databases from Quattro Pro

CHAPTER 12
Macro Basics 381
Macro fundamentals ■ Editing macros ■ Documenting your macros ■ Executing macros ■ Debugging macros ■ Saving and retrieving macros ■ Macro libraries ■ Using Transcript to record keystrokes and commands

CHAPTER 13
Programming Command Basics 413
Programming command basics ■ Descriptions of programming commands ■ Advanced macro techniques

APPENDIX A
Exchanging Data with Other Programs 459
Importing data ■ Exporting data

APPENDIX B
Customizing Quattro Pro 481
Changing Quattro Pro's default hardware settings ■ Changing default screen colors ■ Configuring international settings ■ Display mode ■ Startup defaults ■ Changing the mouse palette ■ Other customization options

APPENDIX C
Using Special Characters 503

Index 505

Preface

Quattro Pro 2 Companion was written to make Quattro Pro version 2 easier to learn and use. No matter what your level of expertise, you'll find a great deal of useful information in this book. The book begins with the basics, such as moving the cell selector and making cell entries, and builds up to more advanced topics, such as Quattro Pro's macro command language. *Quattro Pro 2 Companion* does not simply tell you what to do—it explains in detail how Quattro Pro operates. You should be able to find the answers to most of your Quattro Pro questions between these covers.

About this book

How you use this book depends on your level of experience. If you are new to spreadsheet applications, you can use the book as a tutorial, beginning with Chapter 1, "Quattro Pro Basics," and reading straight through to the end. If you are an experienced spreadsheet user, you will probably want to keep this book near your computer so that you can use it as a reference guide. When you have a question or encounter a problem, you can scan the table of contents and the index to find an answer quickly.

The organization of this book

Quattro Pro 2 Companion is organized functionally, rather than by command name. As a result, you can find the answer to "how-to" questions quickly and easily. This book has 13 chapters and 3 appendixes. Chapters 1 through 6 cover the Quattro Pro worksheet. Chapter 1, "Quattro Pro Basics," covers all the fundamentals: moving the cell selector, making entries, and so forth. This chapter also covers the concept of worksheet recalculation and tells you how Quattro Pro manages memory. Chapter 2, "Formatting a Worksheet," shows you how to format and align the entries in your worksheets. Chapter 3, "Editing Your Worksheet," explains how to copy, move, and erase entries; how to insert and delete rows and columns; and how to change the widths of columns. Chapter 4, "Functions," shows you how to use all of Quattro Pro's functions, except the date and time functions (which are covered in Chapter 6) and the database statistical functions (which are covered in Chapter 11). Chapter 5, "Worksheet Commands," explains the commands you can use to manipulate data within a worksheet, including the Frequency, What-If, Advanced Math Regression, Math Optimization, and Solve For commands in the Tools menu. Chapter 6, "Dates and Times," shows you how to enter and manipulate dates and times within Quattro Pro.

Chapters 7, 8, and 9 cover general system topics. Chapter 7, "Printing," covers the Print command. This chapter shows you how to create, format, and print reports. Chapter 8, "File Management," shows you how to save and retrieve worksheets, erase files, extract a portion of a worksheet into a file, and combine one worksheet with another. Chapter 9, "Working with Windows," describes how to manage the windows that Quattro Pro uses to display worksheets on the screen by adding titles, moving windows, changing window sizes, and so forth.

Chapters, 10, 11, 12, and 13 describe three of Quattro Pro's special features that extend the functionality of the Quattro Pro worksheet. Chapter 10, "Creating Graphs," describes how you can use worksheet data to create graphs. This chapter also explains how to print and enhance graphs, and use Quattro Pro's Annotator. Chapter 11, "Database Management," covers Quattro Pro's database commands and functions, teaching you how to create, sort, and query a database, and how to use the database statistical functions. Chapters 12 and 13 explain one of Quattro Pro's most powerful features—macros. Chapter 12, "Macro Basics," starts by teaching you what macros are and how to create them. Chapter 13, "Programming Commands," covers Quattro Pro's programming commands, as well as some advanced programming concepts.

Quattro Pro 2 Companion also has three appendixes. Appendix A, "Exchanging Data with Other Programs," shows you how to transfer information from Quattro Pro to other programs and how to import data from those programs into Quattro Pro. Appendix B, "Customizing Quattro Pro," shows you how to change Quattro Pro's default settings, use another menu tree structure, and create your own menu tree structure. Appendix C, "Using Special Characters," explains how to enter special characters (such as the Japanese yen symbol) in a Quattro Pro worksheet.

Using this book with Quattro Pro version 1

This book was written for version 2 of Quattro Pro. However, you can use it with Quattro Pro version 1 if you ignore discussions and examples that relate to new features. (You also might want to learn more about the newest features if you are considering upgrading.)

Quattro Pro version 2 includes several significant features. The Tools Solve For command, described in Chapter 5, "Worksheet Commands," is new. Version 2 also provides several enhancements related to graphs. Quattro Pro now has three-dimensional graphing capabilities, lets you export graphs in file formats that service bureaus can make into 35mm slides, lets you import clip art files and use them in graphs, and lets you use mouse buttons with displays of graphs that, when clicked, display another graph or start a macro. Quattro Pro version 2 also is capable of 132-column screen display so that you can pack more information on a screen, as explained in Appendix B, "Customizing Quattro Pro." Users can now switch between Paradox version 3.5 and Quattro Pro version 2 simply by choosing a command. Finally, on a network, Quattro Pro version 2 saves disk space by sharing fonts and menu trees.

Conventions

Throughout *Quattro Pro 2 Companion* you'll find certain conventions designed to make this book easier to use. A string within text is enclosed within quotation marks (" ") and a label in text is preceded by a single quotation mark ('). Screen messages, entries the user types, and function arguments are shown in italic.

Acknowledgments

Thanks to Nan Borreson, Books Department Manager, and Spencer Leyton, Senior Vice President of Business Development, at Borland International for their help in completing this book.

Thanks also to the folks at Sakson & Taylor Inc., including Carol Taylor, Robert Boiko, Joseph Anderson, Lise Kreps, Ward Webber, and Barbara Browne, to David Blatner and Valerie Brewster for Parallax Productions, and to the people at Microsoft Press, particularly Casey Doyle, Sally Brunsman, Marjorie Schlaikjer, Mary DeJong, and Jeff Hinsch for their important contributions.

1

Quattro Pro Basics

This chapter starts you on the road to using Quattro Pro. After a discussion of hardware and a few basics of the program, you'll take a tour of the Quattro Pro worksheet. You'll learn how to move around in the worksheet, how to make and edit entries, and how to choose and cancel commands and undo mistakes. You'll also discover how Quattro Pro manages memory and recalculates a worksheet and how you can name cells. Finally, you'll learn how to end your Quattro Pro session after a hard day's work.

Hardware considerations

Quattro Pro runs on the IBM Personal Computer family (including the IBM XT, AT, and PS/2) and all 100% PC compatibles, under the MS-DOS or PC-DOS operating system (version 2.0 or later).

Quattro Pro requires at least one floppy disk drive and a hard disk drive with at least 3 megabytes (MB) of disk space. (4 MB is preferred.) Quattro Pro also requires at least 512 KB memory. If you use Quattro Pro with only 512 KB memory, however, you will not be able to take full advantage of its capabilities. Instead, consider installing a full 640 KB in your computer.

To use Quattro Pro, you must have a monitor and (if you intend to use Quattro Pro's powerful graphics capabilities) a graphics display adapter. Quattro Pro supports almost every display adapter available, including IBM's CGA, EGA, VGA, and MCGA (Model 30) display adapters; the Hercules Graphics card; AT&T's 6300 640×400 adapter; and the IBM 8514 graphics adapter.

To print your Quattro Pro worksheets and graphs, you also need a printer. Quattro Pro supports a wide range of dot matrix, daisy-wheel, laser, and PostScript printers, including the Epson FX-80 and the Hewlett-Packard LaserJet Series II.

Hardware options

Like most application programs, Quattro Pro supports several optional hardware devices. One of these is the Intel 8087 (or 80287) math coprocessor. A math coprocessor is a special microprocessor that enables your computer to perform arithmetic more efficiently, sometimes from 2 to 300 times faster than is possible without a coprocessor. If speed is important to you, you should buy an Intel 8087 or 80287.

Quattro Pro also supports the Lotus/Intel/Microsoft Expanded Memory Specification 3.2 or 4.0, the bank-switching memory scheme that makes it possible to install and use more than the normal maximum of 640 KB memory in your computer. You'll read more about this topic in "Memory Management" later in this chapter.

Using Quattro Pro with a mouse

Quattro Pro supports any mouse that is compatible with the Microsoft Mouse interface, such as the Microsoft Mouse, the Mouse Systems Mouse, and the Logitech Mouse. Later in this chapter, "Moving the Cell Selector Using a Mouse" explains the mechanics of working with a mouse.

Starting Quattro Pro

After you install Quattro Pro, you can start the program and begin your first Quattro Pro session. To start Quattro Pro, access the drive and directory in which you installed Quattro Pro's program files. If you installed Quattro Pro in a directory named QPRO, for example, type *CD QPRO* to change to the QPRO directory. Then type *Q* at the DOS prompt, and press the Enter key. After a few moments, your screen looks like the one shown in Figure 1-1.

You can also start Quattro Pro with a menu that is compatible with Lotus 1-2-3 and a worksheet that uses default settings for Lotus 1-2-3. To do so, type *Q123* at the DOS prompt instead of *Q*. To switch a Quattro Pro that's already started, choose the Options Startup Menutree command and choose 123. Later in this

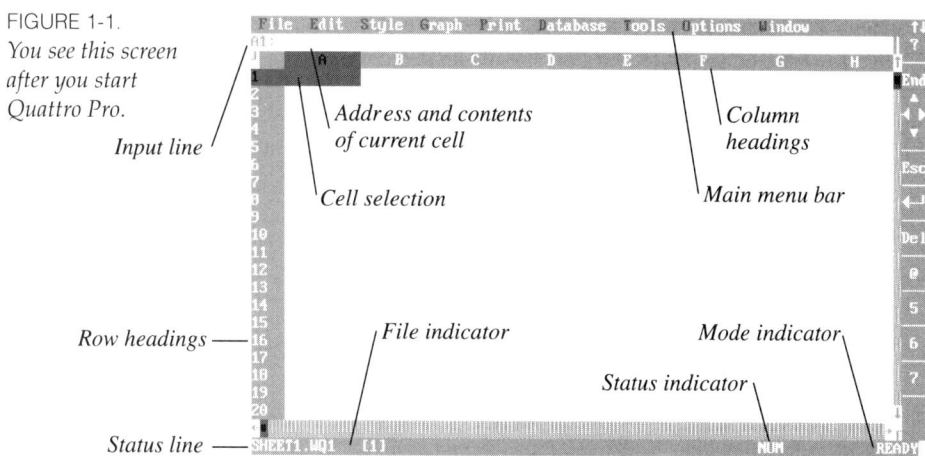

FIGURE 1-1.
You see this screen after you start Quattro Pro.

chapter, "Quattro Pro Commands" explains how to use the program's menus and commands.

A tour of the Quattro Pro worksheet

The Quattro Pro worksheet is like a huge sheet of the kind of columnar paper that accountants use. The worksheet has 256 columns and 8192 rows. The columns are labeled with letters from A to IV, and the rows are labeled with numbers from 1 to 8192. As shown in Figure 1-1, the column and row headings appear in reverse video immediately above and to the left of the worksheet area.

Worksheet cells

The intersection of each column and row in the Quattro Pro worksheet is called a cell, and the location of each cell is identified by its column and row coordinates. This location is referred to as the cell address. For example, the cell at the intersection of column A and row 1 is called cell A1. Similarly, the cell at the intersection of column BB and row 200 is called cell BB200.

Cells are the basic building blocks for all Quattro Pro worksheets. Cells hold the labels, values, formulas, and functions that you enter in your worksheets. In addition, many commands operate on cells or blocks of cells. Every Quattro Pro worksheet contains over 2 million individual cells. The maximum usable area of your worksheet, however, is limited by the amount of memory available on your computer.

The cell selector

The highlighted block that appears in cell A1 in Figure 1-1 is called the cell selector. Use the cell selector to point to the cell in which you want to make an entry or to the cell or block that you want to affect with a command. When you first start Quattro Pro the cell selector appears in cell A1, but as you use Quattro Pro you move the cell selector throughout the worksheet.

Worksheet windows

Although every Quattro Pro worksheet contains 256 columns and 8192 rows, Quattro Pro can display only a small portion of the worksheet—about 20 rows and 8 columns—on your screen at one time. Of course, you can move the cell selector around on the worksheet and bring different areas into view. Still, at any given time only a small area is in view. In effect, your computer screen is a "window" into your entire Quattro Pro worksheet. In most cases, you use only one window to view your worksheet. Quattro Pro has the ability, however, to split your screen into two separate windows, making it possible to view two different areas of the worksheet on your screen at the same time. You'll see how to create and work with additional windows in Chapter 9, "Working with Windows."

Main menu bar, input line, and status line

The first two lines on your screen are called the main menu bar and the input line. The main menu bar displays the name of each of the menus, from which you can choose commands. The input line displays the address and contents of the current cell (the cell that contains the cell selector). For example, the label A1: in the upper-left corner of Figure 1-1 shows that the cell selector is currently positioned in cell A1.

The last line on your screen is called the status line. The status line contains the file indicator, the status indicators, and the mode indicator. The file indicator, which is at the left side of the status line, displays the name of the current worksheet file. For example, the file indicator in Figure 1-1 displays the filename SHEET1.WQ1. The file indicator is replaced with a command description, or a descriptor line, when you select a menu or command. The mode indicator, which is at the right side of the status line, tells you about Quattro Pro's current mode. The word READY that appears in Figure 1-1, for example, tells you that Quattro Pro is ready for your next action. Status indicators tell you about the status of the worksheet or the keyboard. For example, the status indicator in Figure 1-1 shows the word NUM, which means that the Num Lock key is activated. Table 1-1 lists Quattro Pro's status indicators and gives a brief description of what they mean.

Indicator	Meaning
CALC	At least one formula in the worksheet needs to be recalculated. Press the F9 key to recalculate.
CAP	The Caps Lock key has been pressed.
CIRC	A formula in the worksheet contains a circular reference (refers to itself).
DEBUG	The macro debug window is displayed or a macro is being debugged, or both.
END	The End key has been pressed and the next direction key you press will move the cell selector to the cell at the next boundary between a blank cell and a cell that contains an entry.
MACRO	A macro is being executed.
NUM	The Num Lock key is active.
OVR	Quattro Pro is in the Overwrite mode. (Text will be overwritten as you type.)

TABLE 1-1. *Status indicators tell you about the status of the worksheet.*

A look at the mouse palette

If your computer has a mouse, Quattro Pro displays a mouse palette at the right side of the screen as shown in Figure 1-2. The mouse palette has rectangular buttons that you can click to do tasks equivalent to those tasks you can accomplish by pressing keys. For example, clicking the Esc button on the mouse palette is equivalent to pressing the Esc key on the keyboard. Later in this chapter, "Moving the Cell Selector Using a Mouse" explains more about the mechanics of using a mouse and the mouse palette.

The scroll bars

Immediately above the status line, Quattro Pro displays a horizontal scroll bar and at the right edge of the screen, a vertical scroll bar, as shown in Figure 1-2. Scroll bars are important because they give mouse users another way to move the cell selector and because they show where the cell selector is in the worksheet's active rectangle. (The active rectangle is a block that includes every entry and formatted cell in the worksheet.)

To see how the scroll bars show the location of the cell selector, look at the scroll bars shown in Figure 1-2. At the left end of the horizontal scroll bar, next to the small arrow is a small rectangle, which is the horizontal scroll bar marker. In Figure 1-2, the horizontal scroll bar marker shows that the cell selector is in the extreme left column of the worksheet. The vertical scroll bar marker is at the top of the vertical scroll bar, showing that the cell selector is in the top row of the worksheet. As you build bigger worksheets, the two scroll bar markers become valuable indicators of the cell selector's relative position.

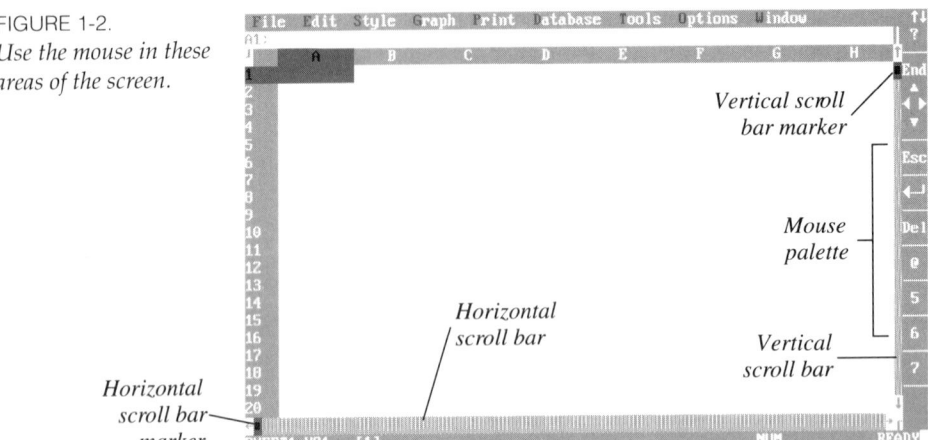

FIGURE 1-2.
Use the mouse in these areas of the screen.

Error messages

If an error occurs while you use Quattro Pro, an error message appears in the center of the screen, and the mode indicator changes from READY to ERROR. When this happens, press the Enter or Esc key to acknowledge the error and then retry your last action.

The Quattro Pro function keys

Quattro Pro assigns special tasks to the function keys on your keyboard. Use these function keys to perform such tasks as accessing Help, displaying a graph, or recalculating a worksheet. Some function keys work only under certain conditions. For example, F2 works only when the cell selector is active on the worksheet, and not when the menu bar is active. Table 1-2 lists each function key's name and purpose.

[Expand] and [Contract] menu keys

In addition to the 10 function keys on your keyboard, Quattro Pro has assigned special functions to the plus (+) and minus (-) keys on your keyboard's numeric keypad (but not to the plus and minus keys on the alphanumeric keypad). These keys are called the [Expand] (+) and [Contract] (-) keys. The [Expand] key enlarges Quattro Pro's menus so that you can view the current menu's settings, and the [Contract] key suppresses display of the current menu's settings. This book shows Quattro Pro's expanded menus. This book also uses Quattro Pro's names for special keys whenever they're referred to. The names of the function keys appear in brackets. For instance, the F2 key is referred to as the [Edit] key.

Function key	Quattro Pro name	Use
F1	[Help]	Access Help.
F2	[Edit]	Edit contents of current cell.
Alt-F2	[Macro Menu]	Display the macro menu.
Shift-F2	[Debug]	Enter the single-step mode for macro debugging.
F3	[Choices]	Display a list of block names when Quattro Pro prompts you for a block name.
Alt-F3	[Functions]	Display a list of Quattro Pro functions.
Shift-F3	[Macros]	Display a list of Quattro Pro macro commands and menu-equivalent commands.
F4	[Abs]	Change the address of the cell to the left of the selector from relative to absolute and mixed references.
F5	[Go To]	Move the cell selector to a specified cell.
Alt-F5	[Undo]	Undo the effect of an erasure, edit, deletion, or file retrieval. (Available only when the undo feature is enabled.)
Shift-F5	[Pick Window]	Display a list of open windows from which you can choose one window to activate.
F6	[Pane]	Jump the cell selector from window to window.
Shift-F6	[Next Window]	Activate the next open window.
Alt-F6	[Zoom]	Expand or shrink the active window.
F7	[Query]	Repeat the last Query command.
Alt-F7	[All Select]	Select all files in the active File Manager file list. Or if some files are already selected, unselect all files.
Shift-F7	[Select]	When in the worksheet, switch to EXT mode to select a block of text. When in the File Manager, select the highlighted file from the active file list.
F8	[Table]	Repeat the last Tools What-If command.
Shift-F8	[Move]	Remove the files marked in the active File Manager file list and store them in temporary memory so that they can be inserted elsewhere.
F9	[Calc]	Recalculate the worksheet.
Shift-F9	[Copy]	Copy the files marked in the active File Manager file list to temporary memory so that they can be inserted elsewhere.
F10	[Graph]	Display the last graph created.
Shift-F10	[Paste]	Paste the files stored in temporary memory into the directory indicated in the active File Manager file list.
Ctrl-F10	[Pdx Access]	When using Paradox Access, switch from Paradox to Quattro Pro.

TABLE 1-2. *Quattro Pro uses special function keys to perform a number of important tasks.*

Moving the cell selector using keys

Quattro Pro's cell selector lets you make entries in the worksheet. When you first start Quattro Pro, the cell selector is in cell A1, or the "home" position. To make an entry in another cell, you have to move the cell selector to that cell. You can move the cell selector using either the keys or the mouse. This section explains how to move the cell selector around in the worksheet using keys. The mouse method is explained in "Moving the Cell Selector Using a Mouse," later in this chapter.

Using the direction keys to move the cell selector

You can use your computer's direction keys—Up direction, Down direction, Left direction, and Right direction—to move the cell selector by one cell in any direction. For example, if you press the Down direction key when the cell selector is in cell A1, the cell selector moves to cell A2. As the cell selector moves down, the input line changes to reflect the cell selector's new position in the worksheet. You can press the direction keys multiple times and in any order to move the cell selector in any direction. Holding down a direction key is equivalent to pressing the key repeatedly.

The direction keys are labeled with arrows pointing up, down, left, and right. Some keyboards have arrow keys only on the numeric keypad located to the right of the alphanumeric keys. Other keyboards have a second set of direction keys in addition to those on the numeric keypad. Later in this chapter, "Using the Num Lock Key to Move the Cell Selector" describes how to use the numeric keypad.

Moving beyond the edge of the window

You can see only as many rows and columns of a worksheet as will fit on your screen. To see a part of the worksheet that is not currently in view, move the cell selector beyond the edge of the window; Quattro Pro shifts the window so that the cell selector remains in view. For example, suppose that the cell selector is in cell H20. If you press the Down direction key, the cell selector moves to cell H21, and Quattro Pro brings row 21 into view. As a result, row 1 moves off the screen. If you press the Right direction key while the cell selector is in cell H21, Quattro Pro moves the cell selector to cell I21. To bring cell I21 into view, Quattro Pro shifts the window one column to the right, bringing column I into view and moving column A off the screen, as shown in Figure 1-3.

You cannot move the cell selector beyond the edge of the worksheet. That is, you cannot move up from row 1, down from row 8192, left from column A, or right from column IV. If you try to move beyond these borders, Quattro Pro beeps and the cell selector remains in its original position.

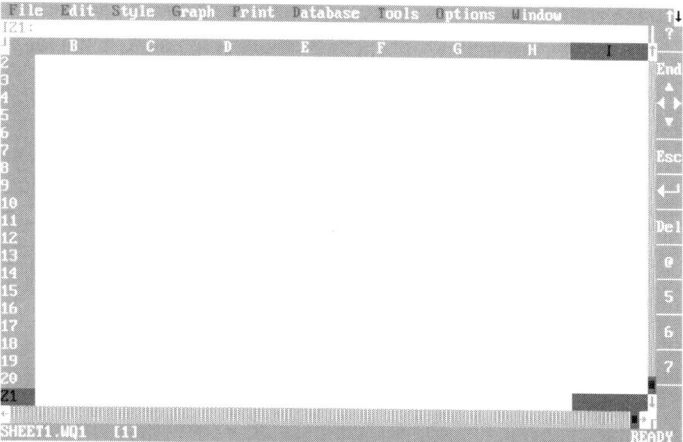

FIGURE 1-3.
When you move the cell selector beyond the edge of the window, Quattro Pro shifts the window so that the cell selector remains in view.

Using the Num Lock key to move the cell selector

The keys in the numeric keypad of the IBM PC and most compatible computers perform two functions: You can use them as direction keys to move the cell selector or as a numeric keypad to enter numbers. When your keypad is in READY mode, you can use the four direction keys, plus the Home, End, PgUp, and PgDn keys, to move the cell selector. If you want to use the keypad to type numbers, you must press the Num Lock key. From then on, you can use the numeric keypad to type numbers but not to move the cell selector, although you can press the Shift key in combination with the direction keys to move the cell selector while Num Lock is active. The Num Lock key remains active until you press it again or until you turn off your PC.

If your keyboard has a separate set of direction keys in addition to the direction keys on the numeric keypad, you might want to use the numeric keypad to enter numbers in the worksheet and the other set of direction keys to move the cell selector. If your keyboard does not have a second set of direction keys, however, you might want to use the number keys at the top of the keyboard to enter numbers.

Using the End key to move the cell selector

The End key lets you move the cell selector to the end of a group, or block, of cells. This key is especially useful when selecting a block of cells; for example, when you are defining a block of the worksheet for the Block Move command. After you understand how the End key works, you'll likely find it one of Quattro Pro's most helpful tools.

Pressing the End key followed by a direction key moves the cell selector in the indicated direction. It moves to the cell at the next boundary between a blank cell and a cell that contains an entry. The cell selector always lands on a cell that contains an entry (if such a cell exists in the indicated direction). If no cells contain entries in the indicated direction, the cell selector moves to the end of the worksheet—to a cell in row 1 or row 8192, or in column A or column IV.

Although this rule might sound complicated, in practice it is easy to put to use. For example, assume that you have a blank worksheet and that the cell selector is in cell A1. If you press the End-Right direction keys, the cell selector moves to cell IV1. If you then press the End-Down direction keys, the cell selector moves to cell IV8192. Pressing the End-Left direction keys from cell IV8192 moves the cell selector to cell A8192, and then pressing the End-Up direction keys returns the cell selector to cell A1 where you started.

Now consider a worksheet that contains a few entries, like the one shown in Figure 1-4. As you can see, the cell selector is in cell A5, which contains an entry. Pressing the End-Right direction keys moves the cell selector to cell C5, the cell at the next boundary between a blank cell (D5) and a cell that contains an entry (C5). Pressing the End-Right direction keys again moves it to cell E5, the cell at the next boundary between a blank cell (D5) and a cell that contains an entry (E5). Notice that the cell selector always lands on a cell that contains an entry. Pressing the End-Right direction keys a third time moves the cell selector to cell G5.

Moving the cell selector by full windows

The direction keys are the most useful for moving the cell selector around the visible portion of a worksheet. But for moving a long distance, Quattro Pro offers four keys: PgUp, PgDn, Ctrl-Right direction key (or Tab), and Ctrl-Left direction key (or Shift-Tab). Use these keys to move through a worksheet a full window at a time in any direction.

The PgUp and PgDn keys move the cell selector up or down one window at a time. Because the window that appears on your screen when you first start Quattro Pro is 20 rows deep, pressing PgUp or PgDn usually moves the cell selector 20 rows up or down. If you have split your window horizontally using the Windows Options Horizontal command, however, pressing PgUp or PgDn moves the cell selector up or down only by the number of rows in the current window.

FIGURE 1-4.
Pressing the End key and a direction key moves the cell selector in the indicated direction to the cell at the next boundary.

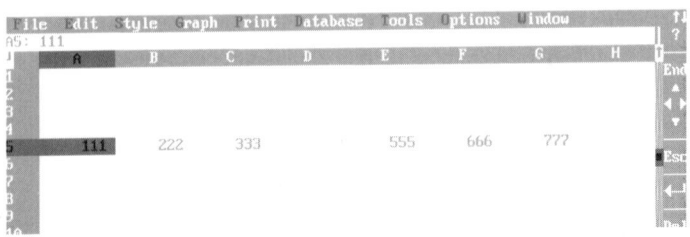

You'll see how to split your screen into two windows in Chapter 9, "Working with Windows."

The Ctrl-Left direction keys and Ctrl-Right direction keys move the cell selector left or right one window at a time. Exactly how far the cell selector moves depends on the widths of the columns in the worksheet and the number of columns in the window. If you have not split the screen or changed the widths of any columns, the cell selector moves a maximum of seven columns to the right or left when you press one of these combinations. If you have split the screen vertically using the Windows Options Vertical command, pressing the Ctrl-Right direction keys or Ctrl-Left direction keys moves the cell selector right or left only by the number of columns in the current window. If you have used the Style Column Width command to change the widths of the columns in the worksheet, pressing the Ctrl-Right direction keys or the Ctrl-Left direction keys may move the cell selector more or less than the maximum seven columns. (In Chapter 3, "Adjusting Column Widths" explains how to change column widths.)

TIP: *Instead of pressing the Ctrl-Right direction keys to move the cell selector to the right, you can press the Tab key. Instead of pressing the Ctrl-Left direction keys to move the cell selector to the left, you can press the Shift-Tab keys.*

Using the Home key to move the cell selector

Pressing the Home key moves the cell selector directly to cell A1. The Home key provides a handy shortcut for moving the cell selector "home" from any location in the worksheet.

Using the End-Home combination to move the cell selector

Pressing the End key followed by the Home key moves the cell selector to the lower-right corner of the worksheet's active area (the area containing entries). This key combination comes in handy when you are defining print blocks and other full-worksheet blocks.

The [Go To] key

The [Go To] key (F5) lets you move the cell selector directly to any cell in the worksheet. Press [Go To] and Quattro Pro responds with the prompt *Enter address to go to*, followed by the address of the current cell. Type the address of the cell you want to go to, and press the Enter key. Quattro Pro moves the cell selector to that address.

When you use the [Go To] key and specify a cell address that is not in view, Quattro Pro shifts the screen, placing that cell in the upper-left corner. If the cell you want to move to is in view when you use the [Go To] key, Quattro Pro simply moves the cell selector to that cell without shifting the screen. You can also specify a block name instead of a cell address at the Go To prompt. Later in this chapter, the section titled "Naming Cells and Blocks" explains block names.

Moving the cell selector using a mouse

If you have a mouse, you can also move the cell selector around the worksheet by pointing and clicking, and by using the scroll bar and the mouse palette.

Clicking on cells to move the cell selector

If the cell to which you want to move the cell selector shows in the window, you can point to that cell with the mouse pointer and then click the left mouse button. The cell selector moves to the cell you chose. In this book, this process is described simply as "clicking."

Using the scroll bar to move the cell selector

Clicking on cells works well as long the cell shows in the Quattro Pro window. If the cell to which you want to move the cell selector does not show in the window, use the scroll bar arrows, the scroll bar markers, and the scroll bar itself to move the cell selector.

The scroll bar arrows

When you click the scroll bar arrows, they work like the direction keys. The arrows at the top and bottom of the vertical scroll bar correspond to the Up and Down direction keys. If you click on an arrow, the cell selector moves up or down by one cell. Similarly, the arrows at the ends of the horizontal scroll bar correspond to the Left and Right direction keys. Clicking on the left or right arrow moves the cell selector one cell left or right.

The scroll bar markers

You can also use the scroll bar markers to move the cell selector. The scroll bar markers are the small rectangles located in the scroll bars. To move the cell selector left or right, click on the horizontal scroll bar marker but continue to hold down the left mouse button. Then drag the scroll bar marker in the direction you want to move the cell selector and release the mouse button when you reach where you want to go. This process is called "dragging." Similarly, to move the cell selector up or down, drag the vertical scroll bar marker in the direction you want. Remember that the scroll bars correspond roughly to the active area of the worksheet. So, for example, if you drag the horizontal scroll bar marker to the middle of the horizontal scroll bar, the cell selector moves to the middle column of the active area.

Chapter 1: Quattro Pro Basics

Clicking on the scroll bar

Just as you can click on cells to move the cell selector, you can also click on the scroll bar. To move the cell selector by one full window to the right, click on the horizontal scroll bar to the right of the horizontal scroll bar marker. Or to move the cell selector by one full window to the left, click on the horizontal scroll bar to the left of the horizontal scroll bar marker. Clicking on the vertical scroll bar works in the same way to move the cell selector by one full window up or down.

Using the mouse palette to move the cell selector

The mouse palette provides another method of moving the cell selector. The second box from the top (labeled End) gives you four options for moving the cell selector. Clicking on the arrow that points to the left (it looks like a triangle) is equivalent to pressing the End-Left direction keys. Clicking on the arrow that points right is the same as pressing the End-Right direction keys. Similarly, clicking on the arrow that points up is equivalent to pressing the End-Up direction keys. Clicking on the arrow that points down is equivalent to pressing the End-Down direction keys.

Making entries in your Quattro Pro worksheet

Quattro Pro uses three types of cell entries: labels, numbers, and formulas. Labels and numbers are simple text and number entries. Formulas are entries that perform both simple and complex calculations.

Locking in an entry

As you type a new cell entry, it first appears in the input line, not in the current cell itself. After you finish typing the entry, lock the entry into the cell, which stores the entry in the current cell. To lock in an entry, press the Enter key or click on the Enter button on the mouse palette (the arrow between [Esc] and [Del]). The characters you type now show both in the current cell and in the input line.

NOTE: *If you have a mouse, the input line shows [Enter][Esc] followed by your entry, after you type the entry but before you lock it in. [Enter] indicates that you can lock in your entry by pressing the Enter key. [Esc] indicates that you can cancel your entry by pressing the Esc key (a topic that the next section explains). You can also click [Enter] or [Esc] in the input line to perform these actions.*

You can also lock in an entry by pressing any of the cursor-movement keys, including the Up, Down, Left, and Right direction keys, the Home, End, Tab, and Shift-Tab keys, the Ctrl-Right direction keys, the Ctrl-Left direction keys, and the PgUp and PgDn keys. You can also lock in an entry by clicking on the equivalent buttons on the mouse palette or on the scroll bar. Either of these approaches locks the entry into the current cell and moves the cell selector at the same time. If you need to make a series of entries (for example, a series of numbers down a column or a group of labels across a row) save keystrokes by using the cursor-movement keys or the mouse to lock in your entries instead of pressing the Enter key.

Canceling an entry

If you begin typing an entry but then decide you don't want to lock it in, you can press the Esc key or click on the Esc button on the mouse palette to cancel the entry. The Esc key erases all of the characters you have typed and returns the worksheet to the READY mode.

Entering labels and numbers in a worksheet

To enter a label or a number in a worksheet cell, move the cell selector to that cell, type the label or number, and press the Enter key. For example, suppose you want to enter the number 456 in cell C2 in a blank worksheet. To do so, move the cell selector to cell C2, type 456, and press the Enter key, as shown in Figure 1-5.

Quattro Pro uses the first character in an entry you type to determine whether the entry is a value or a label. If that first character is a numeral (0 to 9) or one of the symbols +, -, (, $, #, ., or @, Quattro Pro considers the entry a value (a number or a formula). As soon as you type the first character of a value entry, the mode indicator changes from READY to VALUE. If the first character is not a value, Quattro Pro considers the entry a label, and the mode indicator changes to LABEL.

Numbers

Number entries are simply numerical values that you have entered in the cells of a worksheet. Numbers have two important characteristics. First, numbers can be used as the objects of mathematical formulas. You can add, subtract, multiply, divide, and "exponentialize" numbers. Second, number entries can be formatted in several ways. For example, you can format the number 6543.21 to display as $6,543.21, 6,543.21, or 6.54E+3. In Chapter 2, the section "Using Formats" explains formats in detail.

FIGURE 1-5.
To enter a label or a number in a cell, move the cell selector to that cell, type the label or number, and press the Enter key.

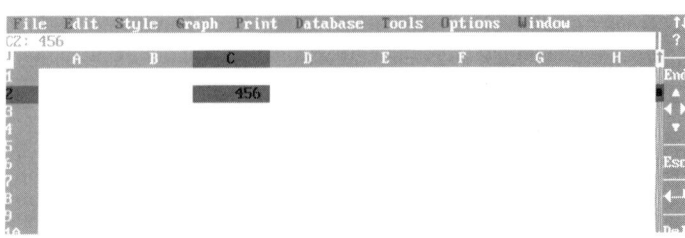

Value characters. Normally, numbers begin with a value character—a numeral, a minus sign, or a decimal point. (The other value characters are typically used only in formulas and functions.) If you begin a number with a minus sign, Quattro Pro interprets the entry as a negative number and retains the minus sign. If you begin a number with a decimal point, Quattro Pro interprets the entry as a decimal value.

Numbers cannot contain commas, spaces, or any alphabetic characters. (The only exception is the letter E, which can be used to designate exponential notation.) If you try to include one of these characters in an entry that begins with a value character, Quattro Pro does not accept the entry. When you press the Enter key to lock in the entry, Quattro Pro beeps and displays an error message.

Long numbers. Although most number entries will be only a few characters long, number entries can include up to 240 characters. If you enter a long number in a cell, however, you probably will not be able to view the entry in full. Quattro Pro displays such long numbers in scientific notation. For example, if you enter the number 1234567890 in cell C4, which is nine characters wide, Quattro Pro displays it in scientific notation (1.23E+09), as shown in Figure 1-6.

The number of digits that Quattro Pro displays depends on the width of the column. If you change the width of a column that contains a long entry, Quattro Pro increases or decreases the number of digits displayed accordingly, as illustrated in Figure 1-7. In Chapter 3, the section "Adjusting Column Widths" explains how to change the width of a column.

Cell contents and display. Notice in Figure 1-6 the difference between the contents of cell C4 (as displayed in the input line) and the appearance of the cell. Although cell C4 actually contains the number you entered, 1234567890, it displays the value

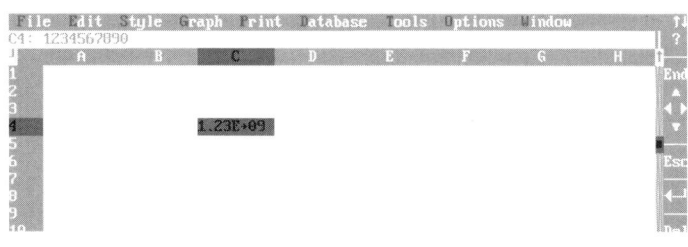

FIGURE 1-6.
A long number is displayed in scientific notation.

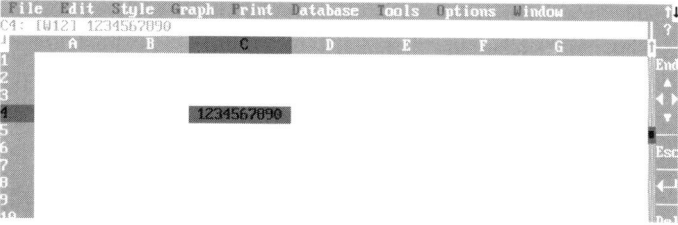

FIGURE 1-7.
This figure displays a long number in a wider column.

as 1.23E+09. Quattro Pro has changed the appearance of the entry in cell C4 but the actual contents of cell C4 are still the same. You can control the display of your number entries by assigning formats to cells, as described in "Using Formats" in Chapter 2.

Precision of numeric values. When you enter a number in a cell, Quattro Pro normally remembers the actual number you enter, even if the number is changed for display purposes. If you enter a very large number, however, or a very small number, Quattro Pro stores only an abbreviated version of the number. Quattro Pro stores any value greater than 99999999999999 or smaller than .0001 in scientific notation.

For example, if you enter a number like 12345678901234567890 in a cell, Quattro Pro stores the number in scientific notation as 1.23456789012345E+19. Scientific, or exponential, notation shortens the entry without changing its value significantly. The character E in this entry means "times 10 raised to the power of." The entire entry can be interpreted as "1.23456789012435 times 10 raised to the power of 19."

Similarly, if you enter a value that is very small, Quattro Pro also stores that number in scientific notation. For example, if you enter the value .00000000001234 in a cell, Quattro Pro stores the value as 1.234E-11.

Entering labels

Labels are simply text: for example, column headings, row labels, worksheet titles, or notes. Because Quattro Pro considers any entry that does not begin with a value character to be a label, characters such as letters, spaces, or punctuation marks are considered the beginnings of labels.

There is an important difference between labels and values: Labels are text entries, while values are entries that display a value (number entries and formulas). Although Quattro Pro lets you create formulas that link values to values or labels to labels, it does not allow you to create a formula that links a value to a label. If you try to link values to labels in a formula, Quattro Pro displays an error message.

Label prefixes. In Quattro Pro, every label must begin with a character called a label prefix. The label prefix controls the alignment of the label in the cell. Quattro Pro offers the label prefixes shown in Table 1-3.

Prefix	Meaning
'	Left aligned
"	Right aligned
^	Centered
\	Repeated to fill cell

TABLE 1-3. *Label prefixes.*

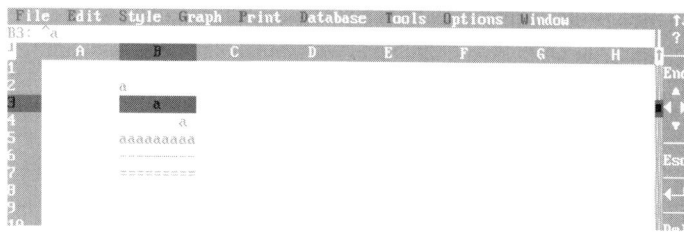

FIGURE 1-8.
Different label prefixes change the label alignment.

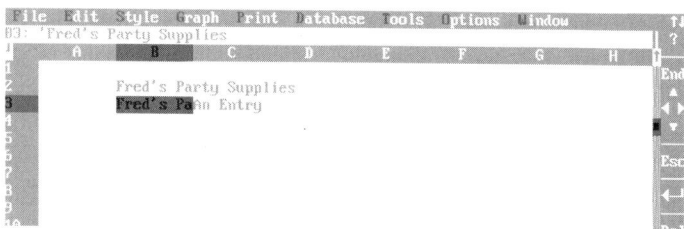

FIGURE 1-9.
Quattro Pro cuts off a long label if you make entries in adjacent cells.

Quattro Pro has one other label prefix (|) which is used only in special situations, as described in "Using Setup Strings" in Chapter 7. The left-aligned label prefix (') is the default label prefix.

If you enter a label without first typing a label prefix, Quattro Pro places the default label prefix in front of the label, and the label is left-aligned in the cell. In Chapter 2, the section "Changing the Default Label Prefix" explains how to change this default.

In Figure 1-8, cells B2 through B5 show how the different label prefixes affect the label *a*. For example, the label in cell B3 is displayed in the center of the cell, and the label in cell B4 is aligned with the right side of the cell. (Labels with the " label prefix are actually offset one character from the right side of the cell.)

Repeating labels. The \ label prefix tells Quattro Pro to repeat the label you specify enough times to fill the current cell. Repeating a label comes in handy when you need to draw lines and dividers in worksheets. For example, the label in cell B5 in Figure 1-8 uses the label prefix \, which repeats the label *a* to fill the cell.

Long labels. Labels, like numbers, can be up to 240 characters long in Quattro Pro. But if you enter a label that is too long to fit in a cell, Quattro Pro allows the label to spill over into the adjacent cells. For example, suppose you enter the label *'Fred's Party Supplies* in cells B2 and B3 in a blank worksheet, as shown in Figure 1-9. Notice that the label in cell B2 spills over into cells C2 and D2. Even though it seems that the label is stored in three cells, the entire label is actually stored in cell B2.

Quattro Pro allows a long label to spill over into adjacent cells, however, only if the adjacent cells are empty. If the adjacent cells contain entries, Quattro Pro

FIGURE 1-10.
Formulas use the operators +, -, *, /, and ^ to perform numeric calculations.

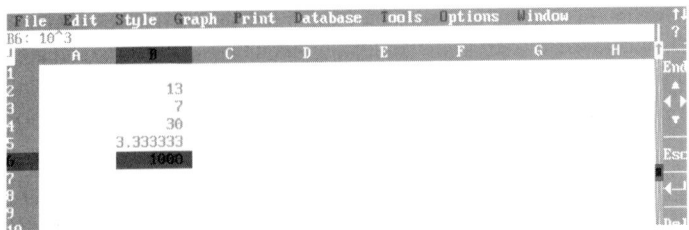

simply cuts off the long label. For example, if you enter the label *'An entry* in cell C3 as shown in Figure 1-9, Quattro Pro cuts off the label in cell B3. Quattro Pro does not change the label itself; it merely changes the way the label is displayed.

Numeric labels. To enter a label that begins with a value character (such as the address *123 Main Street*) you must begin the entry with a label prefix. Otherwise, when you type the first character in the label, which is a numeral, Quattro Pro assumes that the entry is a value.

Entering formulas

Formulas are entries that perform calculations. Some formulas use mathematical operators (+, -, *, /, and ^) to make numeric calculations, and others use the string operator (&) to link labels. Still other formulas use special, preconstructed functions, as described in Chapter 4, "Functions." Some formulas are simple; others are complex and can be up to 254 characters long. Quattro Pro's most exciting feature is probably its capability to understand and evaluate formulas.

Examples of formulas

To look at some examples of formulas, begin by moving the cell selector to cell B2 in a blank worksheet. Now, type *10+3* and press the Enter key. Quattro Pro displays the value *13,* the result of the simple formula 10+3, in cell B2, as shown in Figure 1-10. If you look at the input line, however, you see that cell B2 actually contains the formula that you entered.

Now move to cell B3, type *10-3,* and press the Enter key. Quattro Pro displays the value *7* in cell B3. Now enter the formula *10*3* in cell B4, the formula *10/3* in cell B5, and the formula *10^3* in cell B6. Quattro Pro displays the values shown in Figure 1-10.

Each of the formulas in Figure 1-10 uses one of Quattro Pro's mathematical operators. The plus sign (+) tells Quattro Pro to add, the minus sign (-) tells Quattro Pro to subtract, the asterisk (*) tells Quattro Pro to multiply, the slash (/) tells Quattro Pro to divide, and the caret (^) tells Quattro Pro to raise a number to a specified power.

Formula	Value
3*4-12/6+2	12
(3*4)-12/(6+2)	10.5
3*(4-12)/6+2	-2
(3*4-12)/6+2	2
3*(4-(12/6+2))	0

TABLE 1-4. *Quattro Pro's precedence of operators.*

Precedence of operators

As your formulas become more complex, you need to understand the precedence that Quattro Pro assigns to the mathematical operators, that is, the order in which Quattro Pro performs the calculations in complex formulas. Here's the rule: Quattro Pro multiplies and divides before it adds and subtracts. For example, the formula 5+3*2 returns the result 11 after Quattro Pro first performs the multiplication 3*2 and then adds 5 to that value.

When a formula becomes long, you might be unable to predict how Quattro Pro is going to calculate it. To avoid confusion, use parentheses to control the order in which you want the elements of your formula to be evaluated. For example, each of the formulas in Table 1-4 uses the same values and the same operators; only the parentheses are different. Notice that the different groupings of parentheses produce completely different results. Always be sure, however, that you provide a closing parenthesis for each opening parenthesis in a formula. An unmatched parenthesis causes Quattro Pro to beep and reject the entry when you try to lock it in.

Using cell references in formulas

Most of the time, your formulas operate on values that are stored in other cells of the worksheet. When you include a reference to a cell in a formula, you create a link between the cell that contains the formula and the cell to which the formula refers. The result of the formula is thus dependent on the values in the cell or cells to which it refers. Changing the values in any of the cells that are referenced by a formula changes the result of the formula, one of the features that make Quattro Pro such a powerful tool.

To enter a formula that contains a cell reference, begin the formula with a value character, such as +, -, or (. If you forget to type the value character, Quattro Pro stores your formula as a label because the first character in a cell reference, a letter, is not a value character.

Figure 1-11 provides an example of a formula that contains a cell reference. Cells B2, B3, and B4 in Figure 1-11 contain the values 10, 25, and 50. Let's enter a few formulas in this worksheet that refer to these three cells. First, move the

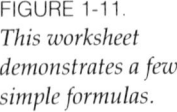

FIGURE 1-11.
This worksheet demonstrates a few simple formulas.

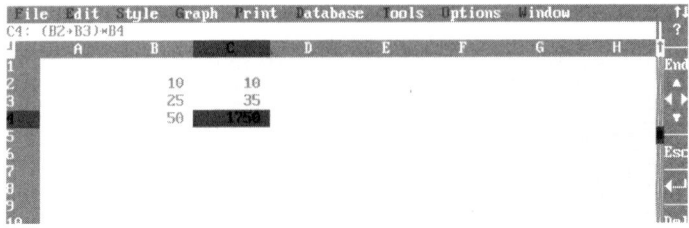

cell selector to cell C2, type +*B2* and press the Enter key. As Figure 1-11 shows, this formula returns the value 10, which is the value of cell B2. The formula links cell C2 to cell B2 so that the value of cell C2 will always be equal to the value of cell B2.

Next, enter the formula +*B2*+*B3* in cell C3. As you can see in Figure 1-11, the result of this formula is 35, the sum of the values in cells B2 and B3. This formula thus links cell C3 to cells B2 and B3.

Finally, move the cell selector to cell C4 and enter the formula *(B2+B3)*B4*. This formula adds the values in cells B2 and B3 and then multiplies the result by the value in cell B4, returning the value 1750. The parentheses in this formula tell Quattro Pro to add before it multiplies.

If you change the value in a cell to which a formula refers, the value of the formula also changes. For example, if you change the value in cell B2 as shown in Figure 1-11, the values in cells C2, C3, and C4 also change.

Defining formulas by pointing

So far, you've created formulas by typing cell addresses. Quattro Pro also allows you to define a formula by pointing to the cells to which the formula refers. You can save time and avoid making critical typing mistakes by pointing to create a formula. Pointing simplifies the whole process of creating formulas, whether you use the keyboard or the mouse to point.

For example, suppose you want to enter a formula in cell B6 (Figure 1-12) that adds the values you entered in cells B2, B3, and B4. To do so, move the cell selector to cell B6 and type a plus sign (+). Now, press the Up direction key to move the cell selector to cell B2; the formula in the input line changes to reflect the position of the cell selector (from +B6 to +B5 and so on). Also, notice that the mode indicator at the bottom of the screen changes to POINT as you are pointing.

When the cell selector reaches cell B2, type another +. The cell selector jumps back down to cell B6 and the formula in the input line reads +B2+. Now, press the Up direction key to move the cell selector to cell B3, and type another +. Finally, press the Up direction key again to move the cell selector to cell B4, and then press the Enter key. As you can see in Figure 1-12, the completed formula is +B2+B3+B4; it returns the value 85.

You can use any of Quattro Pro's direction keys to point to cells as you define a formula. These keys have the same effect in POINT mode as they do in READY

FIGURE 1-12.
Quattro Pro allows you to define formulas by pointing to the cells to which the formula refers.

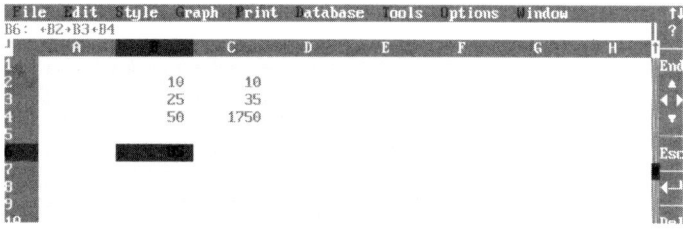

mode: They move the cell selector around on the worksheet. In addition, you can use the mouse to point to the cells you want to use in a formula, simply by clicking on the cells you want.

You might have noticed that Quattro Pro does not place a cell reference in a formula until you type a mathematical operator or press the Enter key. If you begin pointing and then realize you've made a mistake, you can press the Esc key one time to return the cell selector to the cell that contains the formula and to remove from the formula the reference to the cell you were pointing to.

Absolute and relative references

Quattro Pro uses three kinds of cell references: relative, absolute, and mixed. All of the cell references that you've used so far have been relative cell references. The difference between these kinds of references is important only when you use the Edit Copy command to copy formulas. When you copy a formula that contains relative cell references, the references in the copied formula change to reflect the location of the copy. When you copy a formula that contains absolute cell references, the references do not change. When you copy a formula that contains a mixed reference, which is half relative and half absolute, part of the reference changes and part remains fixed. In Chapter 3, the section "Copying Cell Entries" explains relative, absolute, and mixed cell references in detail.

String formulas

Although most formulas are numeric equations, Quattro Pro allows you to create string formulas, which are formulas that refer to cells containing labels. Quattro Pro also offers an operator (&) that you can use in string formulas to concatenate labels and strings.

An example of a string formula. Cell B5 in Figure 1-13 contains an example of a string formula. As you can see, cell B2 contains the label 'Pensacola and cell B3 contains the label 'FL. In cell B5, the formula returns the string "Pensacola, FL".

Concatenation in formulas. Quattro Pro's concatenation operator (&) links labels and strings. For example, the formula in cell B5 in Figure 1-13, +B2&", "&B3, returns the string "Pensacola, FL" by linking the labels in cells B2 and B3.

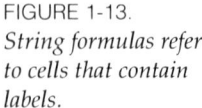

FIGURE 1-13.
String formulas refer to cells that contain labels.

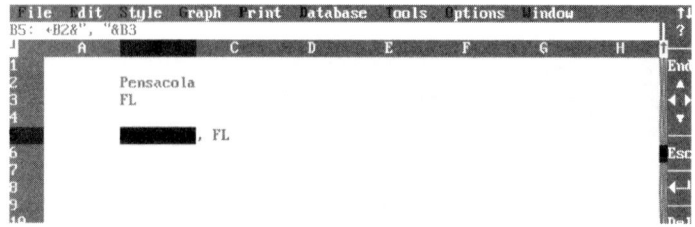

Notice that the formula in cell B5 also contains what's called a literal string: In this case, it's a comma followed by a space, with both enclosed in quotation marks. A literal string tells Quattro Pro that you want the characters that are enclosed in quotes to appear exactly (literally) as is, instead of interpreting them as special characters. For example, if you type a comma in a formula without using the quotes, Quattro Pro gives you an error message. You can include any literal string you want in a string formula as long as you enclose it in quotation marks.

You can use the concatenation operator only on strings; it does not work on numeric values. Attempting to concatenate numeric values makes no more sense than does attempting to multiply or divide one label by another. If you enter a formula that links a label to a value, that formula returns an error (ERR), as explained in the next section.

Error values in formulas

Sometimes your formulas return error messages (ERR) instead of numbers. The ERR message is displayed in the cell that contains the formula. Many situations can cause a formula to return an error, including an attempt to divide a number by zero. For instance, the formula +123/B3 returns ERR either if cell B3 is blank or if cell B3 contains the value 0.

You also create errors if you delete a row or column that contains cells that are referred to by a formula. For example, if you enter the formula +B1+B2 in cell B3 and delete row 2 from the worksheet, the formula changes to +B1+ERR, and the cell containing the formula returns ERR. "Deleting Rows and Columns" in Chapter 3 explains the Edit Delete Rows and Edit Delete Columns commands which delete rows and columns in worksheets.

Adding a Note to a cell

You can add a Note to cells that contain values, formulas, and dates. Notes appear only in the input line and not in the cell itself. To add a Note to a cell, type a semicolon (;) followed by the text of the Note at the end of the cell entry. For example, the Note in the entry *+B2+B3+B4;total amount* reminds you that this value is the total amount.

Editing existing cell entries

Quattro Pro offers tools that make it easy to edit existing cell entries. If you make a mistake while you are typing an entry, you can correct it in one of two ways before you lock in the entry. If your error is minor and you catch it quickly, use the Backspace key to erase the error and then retype the corrected portion. If you make several mistakes while you are typing an entry, or if the entry is fairly short, you are probably better off canceling the entry and starting over rather than editing the mistakes. To cancel an entry before you've locked it in, press the Esc key, then retype the entry from scratch. Correcting mistakes after you lock in an entry requires a different approach, as the following sections explain.

Editing after you lock in an entry

If you need to correct a mistake after you have locked in an entry, you can correct it either by replacing the entry with a new entry or by using the [Edit] key (F2) to edit the entry.

Replacing a short entry

If you've locked in an entry that you want to correct and it is fairly short, the easiest way to make the correction is to replace the entry with a new entry. To do so, move the cell selector to the cell that contains the incorrect entry, type the new entry, and press the Enter key. Quattro Pro deletes the old entry and locks in the new one.

The [Edit] key

If you've locked in an entry that you want to correct and it is long or complex, it is probably easier to edit the entry than it is to replace it. To edit an entry, move the cell selector to the cell that contains the entry, and then press the [Edit] key (F2). Quattro Pro enters the EDIT mode. Edit the entry in the input line, where the cell contents are displayed. A flashing cursor appears at the end of the entry in the input line. When editing the entry, you can use a number of the cursor movement keys, as the next section explains.

Moving the cursor while editing an entry. After you press the [Edit] key (F2), you can use the Left direction key, Right direction key, Home key, End key, Ctrl-Left direction keys, and Ctrl-Right direction keys to position the cursor on the portion of the entry that you want to edit. Pressing the Left direction key or Right direction key moves the cursor one space to the left or right, and pressing the Home key moves the cursor to the beginning of the entry. Pressing the End key moves the cursor to the end of the entry, and pressing the Ctrl-Left direction keys or the Ctrl-Right direction keys moves the cursor five spaces to the left or five spaces to the right.

If you press any of the other cursor movement keys (including the Up direction key, Down direction key, PgUp key, or PgDn key) while you are editing a cell entry, Quattro Pro locks in the entry and moves the cell selector the indicated distance in the appropriate direction.

If you have a mouse, you can use it to move the cursor after you press [Edit] by clicking on the character in the input line where you want to locate the cursor, on the horizontal scroll bar, or on the Left and Right End direction buttons on the mouse palette. However, if you click on the vertical scroll bar, or the Up and Down End direction buttons on the mouse palette, Quattro Pro locks in the entry you are editing and moves the cell selector. If you are a mouse user, you might have noticed the words *[Enter]* and *[Escape]* in the input line when you're in EDIT mode. You can also click on *[Enter]* to select the Enter key, and you can click on *[Esc]* to select the Esc key.

Inserting, deleting, and replacing characters while editing an entry. After you have positioned the cursor, you can insert, delete, or replace existing characters. To insert characters, position the cursor where you want the characters to appear, then type. In insert mode, the characters you type are inserted between the existing entry characters. The insert mode is Quattro Pro's default mode, and you may find that in most situations it best suits your needs.

To delete characters, position the cursor to the right of the characters you want to delete and press the Backspace key. Or, position the cursor on the characters you want to delete and press the Del key.

Instead of adding or deleting characters, you can choose to replace existing characters. Position the cursor at the beginning of the group of characters you want to replace, press the Ins key to switch from insert mode to overwrite mode (OVR), and type over the characters you want to replace. In overwrite mode, the indicator OVR appears in the status line at the bottom of the screen. When you press the Ins key again to return to insert mode, the OVR mode indicator disappears.

Locking in the change after editing an entry. After you have changed an entry, you must lock it in. To do so, press the Enter key; or press the Up direction key, PgUp key, PgDn key, or use the mouse to move the cell selector. Unlike when you create new entries, you cannot lock in editing changes to existing entries by pressing the Left direction key, Right direction key, Home key, End key, Ctrl-Left direction keys, or Ctrl-Right direction keys. Pressing any of these keys or key combinations merely moves the cursor around on the input line.

Canceling the change after editing an entry. If you want to undo the changes you've made to an entry and you have not yet locked in the entry, simply press the Esc key, which tells Quattro Pro to ignore the changes you have made and restore the original entry to the cell. This technique works only if you press the Esc key before you lock in your changes. If you have already locked in your changes, you must re-create the original entry from scratch. Or, if Quattro Pro's Undo feature is enabled, you can choose the Edit Undo command. Later in this chapter, "Undoing Your Mistakes" explains how to undo actions.

Editing formulas

You edit formulas in the same ways that you edit labels. Keep in mind that if the formula you want to change is long or complex, you might be better off editing the existing formula. Of course, you can add cell references to existing formulas. Simply edit the cell containing the formula, move the cursor to the point in the formula where you want to add the reference, type an operator (+, -, *, /, or ^), and then type the cell reference. To add a cell reference to the end of a formula, define that reference by pointing: Type an operator, then use either the Up direction key, Down direction key, PgUp key, or PgDn key to move the cell selector to the cell you want to reference. You can also click on a cell using the mouse.

Quattro Pro commands

Quattro Pro offers a set of commands that you can use to copy, move, and erase entries; to insert and delete rows and columns; to format cells; to print a worksheet; to split the screen; and to perform various other editing and housekeeping chores. You'll see how to use these commands later in this book. For now, take a look at the Quattro Pro menus and learn how to choose and cancel commands.

Activating the main menu

To activate the main menu shown at the top of the screen, press the forward slash key (/). Be sure not to confuse the forward slash key (/) with the backslash key (\). The forward slash key activates the main menu, and the backslash key is the repeat label prefix. The menu to the extreme left, File, is highlighted as shown in Figure 1-14. Notice that the mode indicator changes to MENU.

Each word on the main menu (File, Edit, Style, and so on) is the name of a submenu that you can choose from the main menu. In Figure 1-14, the File command is highlighted, and the status line at the bottom of the screen contains a description of the commands you'll see on the File menu, *File Operations*, which include saving a worksheet and retrieving a previously saved worksheet.

Using the main menu

To choose a submenu from the main menu, point to the menu name and press the Enter key, type the first letter of the menu name, or click on the menu name. When choosing a submenu by pointing, use the direction keys to move the highlight to the menu you want. If you press the Right direction key when the highlight is on

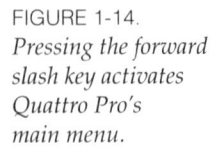

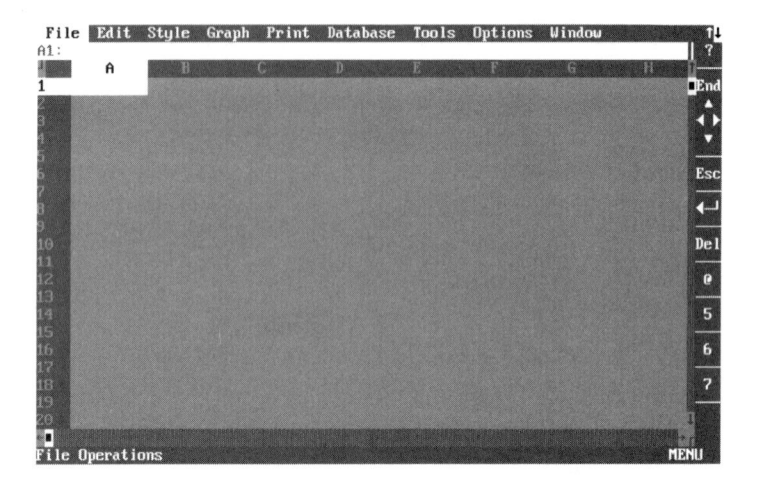

FIGURE 1-14.
Pressing the forward slash key activates Quattro Pro's main menu.

the last menu (Window) or the Left direction key when the highlight is on the first menu (File), the highlight wraps around to the other end of the main menu. You can also use the Home and End keys to move the highlight around the main menu. Pressing the Home key moves the highlight to the File menu, and pressing the End key moves the highlight to the Window menu. When choosing a menu by typing, keep in mind that Quattro Pro ignores capitalization. You can type either an uppercase or lowercase letter.

NOTE: *You can press Esc at any time to cancel the main menu and return to READY mode.*

Using submenus

After you choose File, Edit, Style, Graph, Print, Database, Tools, Options or Window from the main menu, Quattro Pro displays a submenu that contains commands. For example, if you choose File from the main menu, Quattro Pro displays the menu shown in Figure 1-15. To choose a command from a submenu, use the same techniques as when you choose a menu: Point to the command and press Enter, type the letter associated with the command, or click on the command. Because submenus list their commands vertically, use the Up and Down direction keys to move the cursor up and down the list of commands, rather than using the Left and Right direction keys. If you press the Up direction key when the highlight is on the first command, or the Down direction key when the highlight is on the last command, the highlight wraps around to the other end of the menu. You can use the Home and End keys to move the highlight to the first and last commands. If you press the Left or Right direction keys when a submenu is displayed, Quattro Pro displays the submenu that's to the left or right of the current submenu. For

FIGURE 1-15.
When you choose a menu name from the main menu, Quattro Pro displays a submenu that contains commands.

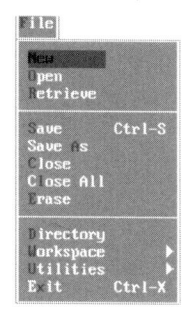

example, if the File submenu is displayed, pressing the Right direction key displays the Edit submenu.

In the File menu, two of the menu commands are followed by the word *Ctrl* and a letter, as shown in Figure 1-15. The Save command, for example, is followed by *Ctrl-S*. These control key combinations represent shortcuts that you can use to choose commands. Instead of pressing /, choosing the File menu, and then choosing the Save command, simply press the Ctrl-S keys.

Many of Quattro Pro's submenus have associated settings. These settings can be either the current default or the value that was last specified for the command. When you first start Quattro Pro, the submenus do not display the current menu settings. To view these settings along with the submenus, display a submenu and press the [Expand] key (the plus key on the numeric keypad). To remove these settings from the screen, press the [Contract] key (the minus key on the numeric keypad) while the menu is in view. Figure 1-16 shows the expanded File submenu.

Some commands that you want to choose appear on menus that are three or four levels down in the menu structure. For example, to set a worksheet for manual recalculation, press /, choose the Options menu from the main menu, choose the Recalculation command from the Options menu, choose the Mode command from the Recalculation menu, and then choose the Manual command from the Mode menu. In other words, choose the Options Recalculation Mode Manual command. Pressing the Esc key lets you back up one menu to the preceding menu.

NOTE: *You can press the Ctrl-Break keys at any time to cancel a command from any menu level and return to the READY mode.*

Defining blocks of cells

Some Quattro Pro commands, such as Edit Move or Edit Erase Block, operate on blocks of cells. For example, when you choose the Edit Erase Block command, Quattro Pro asks you to specify the block of cells you want to erase. A block is a rectangular group of adjacent cells. It can be as small as a single cell or as large as the entire worksheet. For example, cells A1, A2, B1, and B2 could be defined as a block. Cells B1, B2, and C1 could not be defined as a block because this group of

FIGURE 1-16.
The expanded File submenu

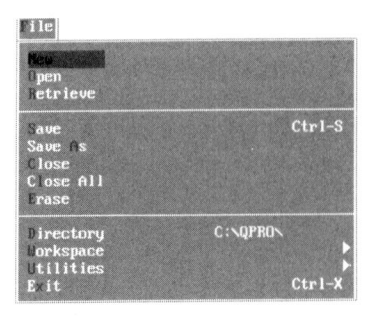

cells is not rectangular. Cells B1, B2, D1, and D2 could not be defined as a block because they are not adjacent.

Quattro Pro uses the addresses of the cells in the upper-left and lower-right corners of a block to designate the block. For example, Quattro Pro designates the block that contains cells A1, A2, B1, and B2 with the notation A1..B2. Similarly, the block A1..Z50 contains all of the cells in the rectangular area that begins at cell A1 and ends at cell Z50.

When Quattro Pro prompts you to specify a block of cells, you can choose from several ways to define a block. One way is to type the upper-left and lower-right addresses of the cells, separated by a period (.), and press the Enter key. Another way is to point to a corner cell, type a period, point to the opposite corner cell, and press the Enter key. For example, to define the block A1..Z50, you could type *A1.Z50* and press the Enter key; or point to cell A1, type a period, point to cell Z50, and press the Enter key.

When you define a block by pointing, only the lower-right corner of the block is movable: Pressing the Right and Down direction keys expands the block, and pressing the Left and Up direction keys contracts the block. You can change the movable corner, however, by pressing the period (.) key. Pressing the period key one time makes the lower-left corner of the block movable. Pressing the period key again makes the upper-left corner of the block movable. Pressing the period key a third time makes the upper-right corner of the block movable. Finally, pressing the period key a fourth time makes the lower-right corner of the block movable. Quattro Pro accepts either one or two periods between cells when you are defining a block. If you supply only one, Quattro Pro adds a second period for you. You'll get a chance to work more with blocks in "Naming Cells and Blocks" later in this chapter.

Mouse users can define a block by clicking on a corner cell of the block and then (while holding down the left mouse button) dragging the cursor to the opposite corner of the block. For example, to define the block A1..Z50, click on cell A1, drag the cursor to cell Z50, and then click the Enter button on the mouse palette.

Undoing your mistakes

Quattro Pro offers an Undo feature that lets you reverse the effect of most, but not all, actions. For instance, if you erase or edit a cell entry by mistake, you can use Undo to return the worksheet to the condition it was in before your action. Undo acts as a kind of safety net that minimizes or eliminates the negative consequences of mistakes you make.

Enabling Undo

You cannot undo an action unless the Undo feature was enabled, or turned on, prior to the action. By default, however, Undo is not enabled when you install Quattro Pro because Undo, for all of its benefits, uses up memory and slows down Quattro Pro; a potential problem discussed in the upcoming section, "Memory Management." To enable Undo when you need it, choose the Options Other Undo Enable command. Choosing this command enables Undo for the current session of Quattro Pro; that is, until you quit the program. If you want to enable Undo permanently, however, update Quattro Pro's current settings so that Undo is enabled for future sessions. To update the current settings after you've chosen the Options Other Undo Enable command, choose the Update command from the Options menu.

To leave the Options menu after enabling Undo and updating any current settings, choose Quit from the Options menu, press the Esc key, or click the Esc button on the mouse palette.

Undoing mistakes

After Undo is enabled, you can reverse the effects of many things you do to the worksheet either by pressing the [Undo] function key combination (Alt-F5) or by choosing the Edit Undo command. As you work with Undo, keep in mind that it doesn't matter how long it's been since the last action you performed. For example, if you incorrectly edit a formula in the morning, leave your computer for several hours, and then discover later in the afternoon that you have made a mistake, you can undo the edit, as long as it was the last action and Quattro has been running on your computer during the interval. Also keep in mind that Undo always undoes the last action *that can be undone*, which may not actually be the last action. As you recall, some actions can be undone and others cannot. Finally, remember that Undo has a powerful cousin, the Transcript Utility. Using the Transcript Utility, you can undo actions you performed at any time during the current session, even if you have performed other actions since. The section "Using Transcript to Record Keystrokes and Commands" in Chapter 12 explains Transcript.

Memory management

The topic of your computer's memory might seem to be esoteric. But as you begin constructing larger and more elaborate worksheet models, you need to consider memory management problems and solutions.

For example, Quattro Pro and DOS 3.3 consume about 340 KB of your computer's Random Access Memory (RAM). Subtracting this number from the total memory capacity of your computer yields the amount of memory that is available to hold the labels, formulas, and functions that you want to use in a worksheet. If your computer has 640 KB of memory, you have about 300 KB of memory available for your worksheets. If your computer has 512 KB of memory, you have about 172 KB of memory available. Those free memory figures might sound expansive, but consider that almost everything you add to a worksheet consumes memory. The precise amount of memory a given entry consumes depends on its type and length. Some types of entries, such as functions, consume more memory than other types do. In addition, long entries use more memory than short entries do, and decimal values consume more memory than integers do.

Even the location of a cell entry can determine how much memory it consumes. In general, the farther away an entry is from the home position (cell A1), the more memory the entry requires. For this reason, keep your worksheet in as small a rectangle as possible. Don't waste memory by allowing the worksheet to grow unnecessarily large in either a vertical or horizontal direction. Also, cell entries aren't the only items that use memory. Each block name you define consumes memory, and every blank cell you format consumes memory. In most cases, however, block names and cell formats do not consume enough memory to be of concern.

You can determine how much memory is free at any time by choosing the Options Hardware command. After you choose this command, Quattro Pro displays a menu like the one shown in Figure 1-17, which lists the current status of many of Quattro Pro's default settings as well as the amount of memory that is currently free. The third line of the Hardware menu shows the normal (as opposed to expanded) memory that is currently free. The fourth line shows the amount of expanded memory that is available if you have installed an expanded memory specification (EMS) device, such as the Intel Above Board, in your computer.

When you work with a large worksheet, you should keep track at all times of the amount of memory available. If the amount drops below 25,000 bytes, trim

FIGURE 1-17.
The Options Hardware command checks available memory.

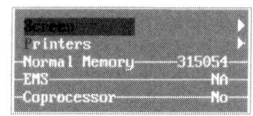

down the size of the worksheet before you make any additional entries. After you check the amount of free memory, press the Esc key to return to the Options menu, and then choose the Quit command from the Options menu to return to the worksheet.

Memory-full errors

Although Quattro Pro allocates memory efficiently, you could possibly create a worksheet that consumes all of your computer's available memory. When the amount of available memory drops to 0 or when you attempt some operation that requires more memory than is free, Quattro Pro beeps and displays an error message alerting you to the problem. If you get this message, press the Enter key to acknowledge the error. Then, before you take any other actions, choose the File Save command to save the worksheet on disk. After you save the worksheet, trim down the size of the worksheet or close the worksheet and resume your work with a different worksheet.

Recovering memory

To free up memory, you can search for any blank cells that have been formatted and use the Style Numeric Format Reset command to unformat those cells. Each cell you unformat will recover about 9 bytes of memory. You can also look for cells that contain only label prefixes or label prefixes made up of blank spaces and then use the Edit Erase Block command to erase those cells. You recover about 5 bytes of memory for each null label you erase. In addition, if your worksheet contains formulas you no longer need, you can recover memory by converting unneeded formulas to literal values with the Edit Values command. You recover about 52 bytes for each formula you convert. You'll learn about how to convert formulas to values in "Making Special Copies" in Chapter 3.

Although you often realize memory savings immediately after you begin erasing entries, removing formats, and converting formulas to values, you do not fully recover the newly released memory until you save and then retrieve the worksheet with the File Retrieve command.

If you have other memory-resident programs (programs that are loaded into memory before you use them, such as Sidekick) that are consuming memory, you might consider removing these. To do so, first exit from Quattro Pro, and then unload the other programs (while referring to the other software's user manuals if needed). Then start Quattro Pro again. The savings you realize depend on how much memory the other memory-resident programs were consuming.

Finally, if you've enabled the Undo feature, you might consider disabling it by choosing the Options Other Undo Disable command.

If the techniques explained here do not free up enough memory, you can use the Tools Xtract command to break up the worksheet into several smaller worksheets which you can then link. You'll read about how to use the Tools Xtract command and how to create and use file links in "Using the Tools Xtract Command" in Chapter 8.

Expanded memory

Another solution to the problem of inadequate memory is to increase your computer's available memory. Quattro Pro supports the Lotus/Intel/Microsoft Expanded Memory Specification (LIM/EMS), which allows Quattro Pro to use up to 8 MB of memory to store worksheets. To take advantage of the LIM/EMS, you must install an expanded memory board, such as the Intel AboveBoard, the AST RAMpage! board, or the Quadram Liberty PC board, in your computer. Each of these boards comes with a program that activates expanded memory. Run this program before you start Quattro Pro.

Recalculation

In Quattro Pro, the word "recalculation" describes the process of updating the values of the formulas in a worksheet. Understanding how Quattro Pro recalculates worksheet, and how you can control the process of recalculation, is an important part of mastering Quattro Pro.

Controlling recalculation

Like most spreadsheet programs, Quattro Pro offers a command that allows you to control the mode of recalculation (automatic, manual, or background) and the order of recalculation (natural, in columns, or in rows) in your worksheets. The command is Options Recalculation. The following sections describe both the mode and order of recalculation.

The mode of recalculation

The Options Recalculation Mode command offers three recalculation mode options: Automatic, Manual, and Background. When the recalculation mode is set to Background (the default setting), Quattro Pro recalculates the worksheet in its spare time between keystrokes so that your work is not interrupted. When the recalculation mode is set to Automatic, Quattro Pro automatically recalculates the worksheet each time you make an entry. When the recalculation mode is set to Manual, Quattro Pro recalculates the worksheet only when you press the [Calc] key (F9). When recalculating, Quattro Pro updates the necessary formulas in the worksheet to reflect the entries and changes you've made since the last recalculation.

To set the mode of recalculation to Automatic or Manual, choose the Options Recalculation Mode command. Then, when the Options Recalculation Mode submenu appears with its three options (Automatic, Manual, and Background) select the one you want. If you select Manual, remember that when you want Quattro Pro to recalculate the worksheet, you must press the [Calc] key (F9). When the mode of recalculation is set to Manual and you make or edit an entry in the worksheet, the indicator CALC appears in the status line to remind you that you've made a change in the worksheet but have not yet recalculated. Unfortunately, the CALC indicator is not very discriminating. If you make any change in the worksheet, even if the change has no effect on any formula in the worksheet, the indicator appears.

The order of recalculation

The Options Recalculation Order command lets you control the order of recalculation in a worksheet and offers you three options: Natural, Columnwise, and Rowwise. When recalculation is set to Natural (the default recalculation order), Quattro Pro begins by recalculating the most basic cells in the worksheet; that is, the cells to which formulas in the other cells refer. These basic cells must be recalculated first if the others are to be recalculated correctly. Next, Quattro Pro recalculates cells that reference those basic cells, and then the cells referencing cells that refer to basic cells, and so on until the entire worksheet has been recalculated.

For example, suppose you enter the following formulas in cells D2, D3, and D4 in a worksheet:

D2: 100+50+25+25

D3: .081 * D2

D4: +D2+D3

When recalculating the worksheet, Quattro Pro recalculates the formula in cell D2 first because the other cells in the worksheet depend on its value. After recalculating cell D2, Quattro Pro recalculates cell D3, and then cell D4. If Quattro Pro didn't recalculate cells using this order, you couldn't be sure the values returned by the worksheet formulas were correct.

The Options Recalculation Order command lets you change the order of recalculation from Natural to Columnwise or Rowwise. These options tell Quattro Pro to recompute the worksheet either column by column or row by row, beginning with cell A1, and are throwbacks to the days when spreadsheets did not offer natural recalculation. Although they are seldom used and are not recommended, Columnwise and Rowwise are maintained as options in Quattro Pro. The disadvantage of using Columnwise or Rowwise recalculation is that Quattro Pro does not recalculate correctly if your worksheet includes formulas with forward references. A forward reference refers to a cell that references another cell that is not recalculated until after the cell that contains the reference.

Circular references

A circular reference occurs when a cell contains a formula that refers to itself, usually as the result of an error. Because circular references make it difficult or impossible for Quattro Pro to recalculate a worksheet correctly, they create significant problems for your worksheets. You will undoubtedly encounter a circular reference in your work with Quattro Pro, so the following sections explain how to identify and correct circular references.

The CIRC indicator

When you enter a formula that contains a circular reference, Quattro Pro displays the indicator CIRC in the status bar. If the method of recalculation is Background or Automatic, this indicator appears as soon as you lock in the entry. If you select Manual recalculation, the CIRC indicator is not displayed until you press the [Calc] key (F9) to recalculate the worksheet.

Finding and fixing circular references

Because some circular references are unsolvable, and because almost all circular references are accidental, watch for the presence of the CIRC indicator. When you see it, immediately locate and correct the circular reference.

The Options Recalculation command makes it easy to find circular references. The menu that appears when you choose this command contains a line, Circular Cell, that shows the location of the circular reference in the worksheet. For example, Figure 1-18 shows the screen that appears when you choose the Options Recalculation command after entering the circular reference +D1-D2 in cell D2. Notice the cell reference to D2 on the Circular Cell line of the menu.

After you locate a circular reference, you must correct it. In the example in Figure 1-18, for instance, you can correct the error by editing cell D2 and removing the reference to cell D2 from that formula. After you make the correction, press the Enter key to lock in the new entry, and then press the [Calc] key (F9) to recalculate the worksheet.

Circular references are not always easy to find and correct, however. They can involve several cells, each of which makes one link in the circle, that are widely separated in the worksheet. Although a worksheet might contain more than one circular reference, the Options Recalculation command produces the address of only one of the cells that contain a circular reference. Therefore, after correcting one circular reference, you must choose the Options Recalculation command again

FIGURE 1-18.
The Options Recalculation command makes it easy to find circular references.

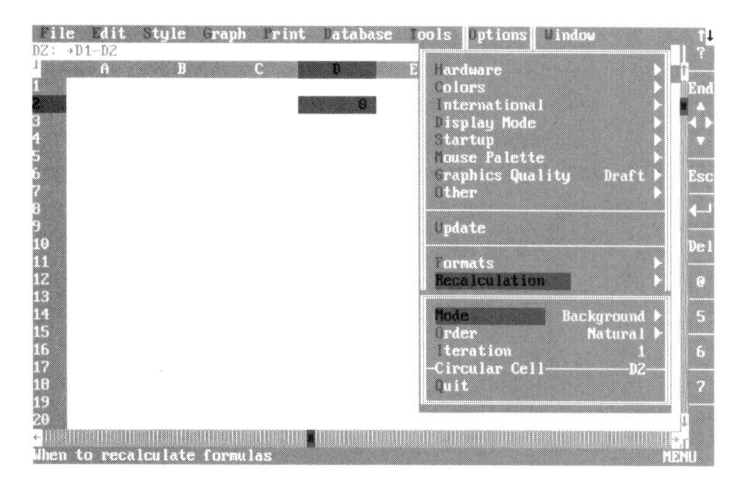

to verify that no others exist. Repeat this process until you've corrected all the circular references.

Solvable circular references

Some circular references can be recalculated correctly. In fact, you can sometimes use a circular reference to solve a problem that would otherwise be unsolvable.

For example, suppose you need to calculate the maximum contribution you can make to your pension and that, by law, the maximum contribution is set to 15 percent of your income minus the contribution. This calculation can be expressed as Contribution = .15 * (Income – Contribution). By definition, then, the calculation is circular because you cannot calculate the contribution until you know the contribution (unless you want to work out the problem algebraically). To solve the formula in Quattro Pro, you inevitably create a circular reference. For example, if your income is $10,000, entering the formula .15*(10000-A1) in cell A1 creates a circular reference. The CIRC indicator appears as soon as you enter the formula.

Quattro Pro offers a command called Options Recalculation Iteration that you can use to solve this sort of circular reference. It lets you set the number of times that Quattro Pro will recalculate the worksheet each time you press the [Calc] key (F9). After you choose the Options Recalculation Iteration command, Quattro Pro presents the prompt *Number of times to re-evaluate circular references (1..255): 1*. When you see this prompt, type a number between 1 and 255 to tell Quattro Pro how many recalculations you want when you press the [Calc] key. When you change the Iteration setting from its default of 1 to a new value, Quattro Pro recalculates the worksheet that number of times each time you press the [Calc] key.

To resolve the problem in our pension contribution example, choose the Options Recalculation Iteration command, type *10*, and then press the Enter key. Then, press the [Calc] key (F9) to recalculate the worksheet. Quattro Pro recalculates the worksheet repeatedly, each time getting closer to the correct contribution amount. Quattro Pro eventually converges on the contribution that equals 15 percent of the income after subtracting the contribution.

Such iterative recalculation can provide a handy tool, but it can also be a very slow process. If your worksheet contains several formulas and the iteration count is set to 10 or more, for example, Quattro Pro might take several minutes to recalculate the worksheet. It's best to leave the iteration setting at 1 and change it only when you need to solve a circular reference problem. You should also set the recalculation method to Manual when you are solving problems that use circular references.

Naming cells and blocks

All of the examples so far have referred to cells in the worksheet by their addresses: A1, D4, and so on. Quattro Pro also lets you assign names to cells and blocks of cells and use those names in place of cell addresses in your formulas and commands.

Creating block names

Use the Edit Names Create command to assign names to cells and blocks. After you choose this command, Quattro Pro displays the prompt *Enter name to create/ modify*, asking you to supply the name you want to give a block. The name can be up to 15 characters long and can include any character (but the first character should be a letter). Quattro Pro makes no distinction between uppercase and lowercase letters in block names. The names Total, TOTAL, and total are all identical to Quattro Pro. (For clarity, however, all block names in this book are presented in uppercase form.)

After you type the name and press the Enter key, Quattro Pro displays the address of the current cell as the default block in the input line. For example, if the cell selector is on cell B3 when you choose the Edit Names Create command, Quattro Pro displays *B3..B3*. You can press the Enter key to name the current cell. Or you can press the Enter key after you do one of the following: use the cursor-movement keys to expand the block to include several cells; click or drag the mouse to identify the block; or press the Esc key to unanchor the block reference, and then either point to a different block or type a different block reference. In most cases, you'll want to move the cell selector to the cell you want to name (or, if you plan to name a block, to the upper-left corner of the block) before you choose the Edit Names Create command. "Defining Blocks of Cells," appearing earlier in this chapter, provides more information on selecting blocks.

Rules for block names

As mentioned, block names can be up to 15 characters long and can use any character—including spaces, punctuation marks, and special ASCII characters like π and £. For example, the names JULY 88, GROSS PROFIT, N!, and DALLAS,TX are all acceptable. (For more on using special ASCII characters in Quattro Pro, see Appendix C, "Using Special Characters.") You will almost always want to begin block names with a letter. Although you can begin a block name with a number, in formulas you can use only block names that begin with letters. You should also avoid names that look like cell addresses. For example, don't create block names like A1, AA25, or FE1988. Although Quattro Pro allows you to assign such a name to a cell or block, you cannot use that name in formulas or commands. If you try to use such a name, Quattro Pro assumes you are supplying a cell address instead of a block name.

A particular block name can appear only one time in a worksheet. If you try to assign the same name to two different blocks, Quattro Pro reassigns the name from the old block to the new one. However, you can assign more than one name to a single cell in a worksheet. For example, you can give cell E10 in Figure 1-19 the names TOTAL and QTR1 TOTAL. If a cell has more than one name, you can refer to it by any of its names.

Examples of creating block names

Suppose you want to assign the name PRODUCT 1 to the block B5..D5 in Figure 1-19. To begin, move the cell selector to cell B5 and choose the Edit Names Create command. When Quattro Pro prompts you for the name you want to create, type PRODUCT 1 and press the Enter key. Quattro Pro displays the block name *B5..B5* in the input line. Press the Right direction key two times to select the block B5..D5 and press the Enter key, or type *B5.D5* and press the Enter key, or click cell B5 and drag the cursor to cell D5.

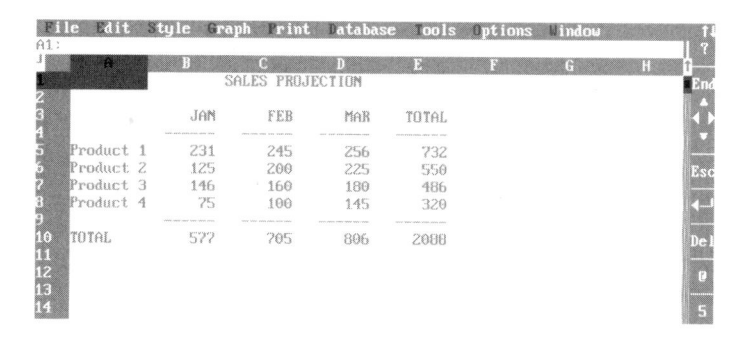

FIGURE 1-19.
Use this worksheet to create block names.

Now, suppose you want to assign the name TOTAL to cell E10 in Figure 1-19. To do so, move the cell selector to cell E10, choose the Edit Names Create command, type *TOTAL*, and press the Enter key. When Quattro Pro suggests *E10..E10* as the block to be named, press the Enter key to assign the name to cell E10.

Using block names

Use block names in the same way that you use cell references in your formulas, functions, and commands. For example, if cell E10 has the name TOTAL then the formula +TOTAL is identical to the formula +E10. In fact, Quattro Pro uses block names instead of cell references in your formulas whenever possible. For example, suppose that cell E5 in a worksheet contains the formula +E10. If you then use the Edit Name Create command to assign the name TOTAL to the cell E10, Quattro Pro changes the formula +E10 to +TOTAL .

You can also use block names whenever a command asks you to specify a block. For example, suppose you want to move the cell selector to cell E10, which has the name TOTAL. To do so, press the [Go to] key (F5), type TOTAL, and press the Enter key. Quattro Pro then moves the cell selector to cell E10. If the block name you supply includes more than one cell, Quattro Pro moves the cell selector to the upper-left corner of the named block.

Using the [Choices] key to remember block names

If you create many block names in a worksheet, you might have a difficult time remembering them all. Fortunately, Quattro Pro provides a tool, the [Choices] key (F3), that helps you remember your block names. Whenever Quattro Pro asks you to identify a block of cells (such as after you press the [Go To] key (F5) or after you choose any of the commands that prompt you for a block) press the [Choices] key to display an alphabetic list of all the block names in the worksheet.

For example, suppose you want to use the [Go To] key (F5) to move the cell selector in the Figure 1-19 example to cell B5, which is the first cell in the block named PRODUCT 1. To do so, press the [Go To] key. When you see the prompt *Enter address to go to* in the input line, press the [Choices] key (F3). At this point, your screen looks like Figure 1-20. The names that appear in the window are all the block names that exist in this worksheet. Now use the direction keys or the mouse to point to the name PRODUCT 1 and press the Enter key. Quattro Pro moves the cell selector to the first cell in the block named PRODUCT 1, cell B5.

Quattro Pro can display a maximum of 16 block names at a time. If your worksheet contains more than 16 names, you see only the first 16 names when you press the [Choices] key (F3). You can then use the Up direction key, Down direction key, Home key, End key, PgUp key, and PgDn key to move the cell selector through the list and bring more names into view. Mouse users can also use the vertical scroll bar that appears in the list window.

FIGURE 1-20.
After you press the [Choices] key (F3), Quattro Pro displays a list of all the block names in the worksheet.

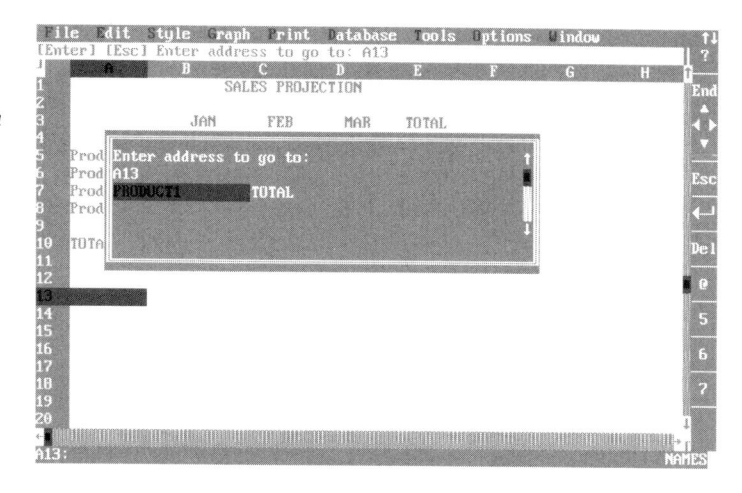

Creating a table of block names

Quattro Pro's Edit Names Make Table command creates a table of all the block names in a worksheet. This command comes in handy whenever you want to see all the names you have created and the blocks to which those names apply. After you choose this command, Quattro Pro prompts you to indicate where in the worksheet you want the table to be located and displays the address of the current cell as the default location. For example, if the cell selector is in cell B3 when you choose the Edit Names Make Table command, Quattro Pro displays the prompt *Enter block: B3..B3* in the input line. You can press the Enter key to accept Quattro Pro's default. You can also press the Esc key to unanchor the block reference, point to a different cell or block of cells, and then press the Enter key. Or you can type a different cell or block reference and press the Enter key. Quattro Pro begins the block name table at the cell you specify. If you specify a block, rather than a single cell, Quattro Pro begins the block name table in the cell in the upper-left corner of the block.

In most cases, you will want to move the cell selector to the cell in which you want the table to begin before you choose the Edit Names Make Table command.

An example of creating a block name table

Let's create a table of block names beginning at cell A13 in the worksheet shown in Figure 1-21. First, move the cell selector to cell A13, and choose the Edit Names Make Table command. When Quattro Pro prompts you for the location of the table, press the Enter key to accept the current cell address. The resulting table is shown in Figure 1-21.

FIGURE 1-21.
Use the Make Table command to create a table of named blocks.

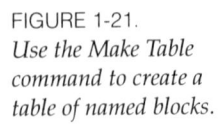

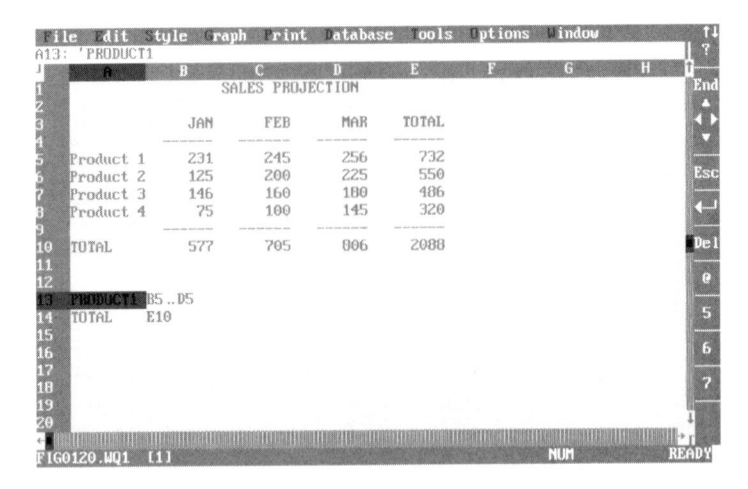

As you can see, Quattro Pro creates a table that lists the two block names used in the example worksheet. The first column of the table contains the names, and the second column contains the addresses of the blocks to which the names apply. The first name appears in cell A13, the cell you selected.

A few notes about block name tables

When creating a block name table on a worksheet, Quattro Pro overwrites any existing entries in that block of cells. Consequently, you should always select a block in your worksheet that does not contain any important cell entries.

Quattro Pro's block name tables are static; that is, they do not change as block names are added to and deleted from the worksheet. If you define a new block name after you choose the Edit Names Make Table command, Quattro Pro does not add that name to the table automatically. To add the name to the table, repeat the Edit Names Make Table command.

Deleting block names

Use the Edit Names Delete command when you want to delete block names from your worksheets. After you choose this command, Quattro Pro presents the prompt *Enter name to delete* and displays a list of the existing block names in the worksheet. To delete a name, point to the name in the list and press the Enter key or click on the name. That's all there is to it! But be careful, because Quattro Pro does not give you a chance to change your mind after you press the Enter key or click; the name is deleted immediately. Once you have deleted a block name, the only way to restore it is to rename the block. After you delete a block name, Quattro Pro changes every formula in which the name appears, so that instead of referring to the block by name, all the formulas refer to the block by its cell coordinates.

You can use the Edit Names Delete command to delete only one block name at a time. To delete several names, choose the command one time for each name. You can delete every name in the worksheet by choosing the Edit Names Reset command. After you choose this command, Quattro Pro displays the prompt *Delete all named blocks?* which gives you two options: No and Yes. If you select Yes, Quattro Pro deletes every block name from the worksheet and adjusts every formula in which the names appear.

Changing block coordinates

After you create a block name, you can change the block to which that name refers. To do so, you must choose the Edit Names Create command, select the name you want to change from the list, and then specify a new block for that name.

For example, suppose you want to change the block to which the name PRODUCT 1 refers in Figure 1-21 from B5..D5 to B5..E5. To do so, choose the Edit Name Create command, select the name *PRODUCT 1* from the list, and then press the Enter key. Quattro Pro highlights cells B5..D5, which is the block to which the name PRODUCT 1 currently applies. Adjust the block to include B5..E5 using the direction keys or mouse and press the Enter key.

Although you can easily change the block to which a name refers, it is generally not a good idea to do so. Changing the block can disrupt any formulas that use the name. Instead of changing the block to which a name refers, you're usually better off using the Edit Names Delete command to delete the name, and then redefining that name using the Edit Names Create command. This method adds an extra step to the process, but ensures that your formulas will continue to work correctly.

Using labels to name cells

The Edit Names Labels command lets you use the labels in a block of a worksheet to name the cells that are adjacent to that block. This is convenient for entering a whole sequence of names at one time. After you choose the Edit Names Labels command, Quattro Pro presents a menu that has four options: Right, Down, Left, and Up. The option you choose tells Quattro Pro which cells you want to name. For example, if you choose the Right option, Quattro Pro assigns names to the cells that are to the right of the labels in the block you specify.

After you choose an option from the Edit Names Labels menu, Quattro Pro displays a message that prompts you to designate the block that contains the labels you want to use as block names. Quattro Pro displays the address of the current cell as the default block. You can press the Enter key to accept the default. Or before you press the Enter key, you can use the direction keys to adjust the size

FIGURE 1-22.
The Edit Names Labels command lets you use labels in the worksheet to name adjacent cells.

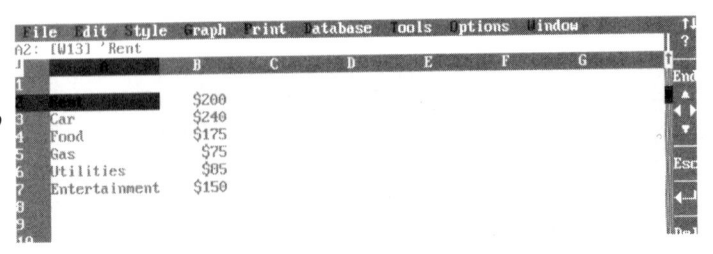

of the block, press the Esc key to unanchor the block reference and then point to a different block, type the coordinates of a different block, or click and drag to identify the coordinates of a different block.

An example of using labels to name cells

Suppose you want to use the labels in the block A2..A7 in Figure 1-22 to name the cells in the block B2..B7. First, move the cell selector to cell A2 and choose the Edit Names Labels command. Because you want to name the cells to the right of the labels, choose the Right option from the Edit Names Labels menu. Quattro Pro prompts you in the input line to define the block that contains the labels: Press the Down direction key five times to highlight the entire block A2..A7, and then press the Enter key. (You can also type the block coordinates, press Esc to unanchor the block, or use a mouse to click and drag.) Quattro Pro then uses the labels in the block A2..A7 to name each of the cells in the block B2..B7, assigning the name RENT to cell B2, the name CAR to cell B3, and so forth.

A few notes about using labels to name cells

The Edit Names Labels command can name only one cell for each label in the label block. Also, the command can name only cells that are adjacent to the label block. For example, you cannot use the labels in the block A2..A7 in Figure 1-22 to name the block B2..E7. If any of the cells in the label block are blank or contain values, Quattro Pro will not name the cells adjacent to those cells. If the label block you specify contains duplicate labels, Quattro Pro names only the cell adjacent to the last (bottom or extreme right) duplicate label. Quattro Pro does not name the cell adjacent to any of the other duplicates. If one of the labels in the label block duplicates a block name elsewhere in the worksheet, Quattro Pro transfers the name to the cell that's next to the label.

Although you can use any character in a block name, the name can be no longer than 15 characters. If any of the labels in the label block are more than 15 characters long, Quattro Pro uses only the first 15 characters to define the block name for the adjacent cell. "Rules for Block Names," appearing earlier in this chapter, provides more information on naming conventions used for blocks.

Exiting from Quattro Pro

After you finish working in Quattro Pro, you'll want to exit the program. But before exiting from Quattro Pro, you should save the current worksheet. To do so, choose the File Save command, type a name for the file, and press the Enter key.

After you save your work, use the File Exit command to leave Quattro Pro and return to DOS. After you choose this command, Quattro Pro checks to see whether you have made any changes to the worksheet since you last saved it. If you have not made any changes, Quattro Pro returns you to DOS. If you try to exit from Quattro Pro before you save your work, Quattro Pro displays the prompt *Lose your changes and Exit?* followed by the options No, Yes, and Save&Exit. To cancel the command and remain in Quattro Pro, choose the No option. You might choose this option if you forgot to save your work or if you chose the File Exit command by accident. To exit Quattro Pro without saving your changes, choose the Yes option. (Choose this option cautiously. As soon as you choose Yes, any changes you made to the worksheet are erased, your screen goes blank, and the DOS prompt appears.) To save the file and exit in one step, choose the Save&Exit option. When you choose this option, Quattro Pro asks you to specify a filename if you have never saved the file before. Type the name and press Enter. If the file already has a name, Quattro Pro notifies you and gives you the option to cancel the save operation, replace the file with the new changes, or create a backup copy of the original file and save the new changes. You'll learn more about saving files in "Saving Worksheets" in Chapter 8.

2
Formatting a Worksheet

In Chapter 1, you saw how to make entries in the cells of a worksheet. This chapter explains how to improve the appearance of your worksheets by formatting the entries in individual cells, specifying global formatting rules for the entire worksheet, changing the alignment of labels, and setting the alignment of values.

Using formats

You can use formats to change the way that Quattro Pro displays the values in a worksheet. For example, suppose that you entered the value 2345.67 in a cell. If you assign the Currency format with two decimal places to that cell, the value is displayed as $2,345.67. But if you assign the Fixed format with no decimal places to that cell, the value is displayed as 2346.

Quattro Pro offers seven value formats: Fixed, Scientific, Currency, Comma (,), General, +/- (Bar Graph), and Percent. In addition, Quattro Pro offers the Text format, which controls the display of formulas, and the Hidden format, which applies to both values and labels and lets you hide the entries in selected cells. All of these formats are explained in this chapter. Quattro Pro also offers date and time formats which control the display of dates and times. Explanations of date and time formats are in "Dates" and "Times" in Chapter 6.

Quattro Pro's global format

Every Quattro Pro worksheet has a global format. When you open a new worksheet all of the cells are in the global format. Like other formats, the global format determines how the contents of a cell will be displayed on the worksheet. Unless you assign a different format to one or more cells in a worksheet, every value in the worksheet remains in the global format.

Quattro Pro's default global format is the General format. In this format, the appearance of a cell matches the contents of the cell exactly, without any alteration in the format. If the cell contains a formula, for example, the result of the formula is displayed exactly as computed by Quattro Pro. Figure 2-1 shows a worksheet in which column B contains several values, each of which is displayed in the General format. Cell B3 contains the value 33, which is displayed as 33. Similarly, cell B4 contains the value 187.5, which is displayed as 187.5. Cell B13 contains the formula +B8+B9+B10+B11. The result of this formula, 1012.47, is displayed in the General format.

Provided that a value (or the result of a formula) is short enough to be displayed in full, the General format displays that value as entered. If the value is too long, Quattro Pro displays as much of the value as possible. If the integer portion

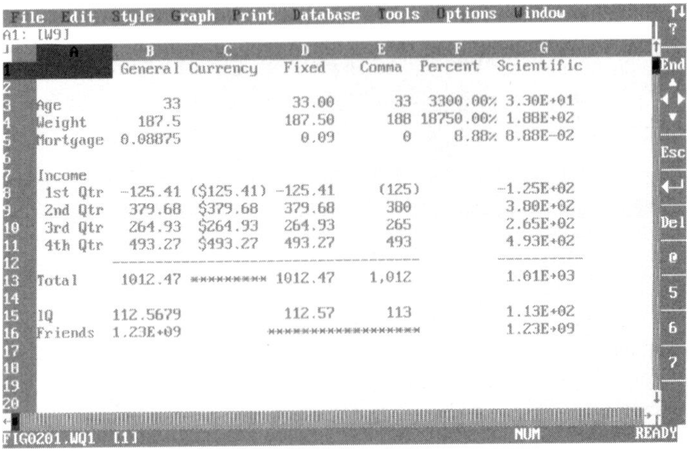

	A	B	C	D	E	F	G
1		General	Currency	Fixed	Comma	Percent	Scientific
2							
3	Age	33		33.00	33	3300.00%	3.30E+01
4	Weight	187.5		187.50	188	18750.00%	1.88E+02
5	Mortgage	0.08875		0.09	0	8.88%	8.88E-02
6							
7	Income						
8	1st Qtr	-125.41	($125.41)	-125.41	(125)		-1.25E+02
9	2nd Qtr	379.68	$379.68	379.68	380		3.80E+02
10	3rd Qtr	264.93	$264.93	264.93	265		2.65E+02
11	4th Qtr	493.27	$493.27	493.27	493		4.93E+02
12							
13	Total	1012.47	*********	1012.47	1,012		1.01E+03
14							
15	IQ	112.5679		112.57	113		1.13E+02
16	Friends	1.23E+09		******************			1.23E+09

FIGURE 2-1. *This worksheet and its contents illustrate several of Quattro Pro's more common formats.*

of the value will fit in the cell, Quattro Pro displays the value's integer portion and truncates the decimal portion. For example, cell B15 in Figure 2-1 contains the value 112.56789, which is too long to be displayed in full in a column that's nine characters wide. Quattro Pro displays this value as 112.5679.

If the integer portion of a value does not fit in a cell, Quattro Pro displays the value in scientific notation. For example, cell B16 in Figure 2-1 contains the 10-digit value 1234567890. Because column B is only nine characters wide, Quattro Pro cannot display the integer portion of this value in full, and instead displays the value in scientific notation as 1.23E+09.

You can change the global format of any worksheet from General to one of Quattro Pro's other formats, as described later in this chapter in "Changing the Global Format."

Formatting cells and blocks

Although the global format determines how every value in a worksheet is displayed initially, Quattro Pro also allows you to format individual cells and blocks of cells in your worksheets to display entries in different ways. When you format a cell or a block, the format you assign to that cell or block overrides the global format, and the values in the formatted cells are displayed differently from other values in the worksheet.

Use the Style Numeric Format command to format cells or blocks. This command's menu is shown in Figure 2-2, which lists the formats that you can assign to a cell or block.

If you choose the Fixed, Scientific, Currency, Comma (,), or Percent format from this menu, Quattro Pro prompts you to specify the number of decimal places you want displayed in the formatted values. Either press the Enter key to accept the default setting of two decimal places, or type a number from 0 to 15 and press the Enter key.

When you select a format and specify the number of decimal places, Quattro Pro displays the prompt *Block to be modified* in the input line followed by a reference to the cell that contains the cell selector. Press the Enter key to accept the current cell, or press the cursor-movement keys to expand the block, press the Esc

FIGURE 2-2.
The Style Numeric Format command lists the formats that you can assign.

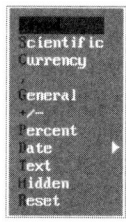

key to unanchor the block and then select a different block, type the coordinates of the block you want to format, or specify the block by clicking and dragging, and then press the Enter key.

Quattro Pro uses the address of the cell selector as the default block to be modified, so you'll usually want to select the cell that you want to format. Or, if you want to format a block of cells, first select a cell in the corner of the block before you choose the Style Numeric Format command.

An example of formatting

Suppose you've created the worksheet shown in Figure 2-1, and you want to assign the Currency format with two decimal places to the block C8..C13. To do so, move the cell selector to cell C8 and choose the Style Numeric Format command. Choose the Currency format from the menu and, when Quattro Pro prompts you for the number of decimal places, press the Enter key to accept the default, 2. When you're prompted for the block to be modified in the input line, press the Down direction key five times to select C8..C13. Finally, press the Enter key to to apply the Currency format to the block you've selected. Column C in Figure 2-1 shows the result.

A closer look at formatting

Changing the format of a cell never changes the value stored in the cell. Although the appearance of the value changes, the value itself stays the same. If you replace the value in a formatted cell with a new value, the new value is displayed in the format already assigned to the cell. For example, if you replace the value in cell C8 in Figure 2-1, -125.41, with the value 14.95, the new entry is displayed as $14.95. Negative numbers formatted in the Currency format are enclosed in parentheses.

The Style Numeric Format command does not affect the appearance of labels. If you use this command to format a cell that contains a label, the appearance of the label does not change. If you later replace the label with a value, however, the value is displayed in the format you have assigned to the cell.

You can use the Style Numeric Format command to format any block, from a single cell to the entire worksheet. Although you typically format a single cell or a small block of cells, you might occasionally want to format a large block of cells. To accomplish the same task an easier way, use the Options Formats command to change the worksheet's global format, as described later in this chapter in "Changing the Global Format."

Formats and column widths. Sometimes formatting a value makes the value too wide to be displayed in full. When this happens, Quattro Pro displays a series of asterisks in the cell. For example, cell C13 in Figure 2-1, which calculates a value of 1263.29, displays asterisks because column C is too narrow to display the formatted entry ($1,263.29). Quattro Pro can display a formatted value as long as the column that contains the value is one character wider than the formatted value.

When you see asterisks in a cell indicating that the cell is too narrow, you can either use the Style Column Width command to increase the width of the column or select a format that requires fewer characters for the value. In Chapter 3, "Adjusting Column Widths" explains how to use the Style Column Width command.

The format indicator. When the cell selector is on a formatted cell, Quattro Pro displays a format indicator in the input line that describes the cell's format. If the cell selector is positioned on a cell with a Currency format using two decimal places, for example, the input line contains the format indicator *(C2)*. In Figure 2-3, for example, the cell selector is positioned on cell C8. If more than one cell is selected, the input line displays the format of the last cell selected in the block.

Unformatting blocks

The Style Numeric Format Reset command unformats a block. After you choose this command, the cells in the block you select revert to the global format. For example, suppose you want to unformat the cells in the block C8..C13 in Figure 2-3. Move the cell selector to cell C8 and choose the Style Numeric Format Reset command. When Quattro Pro prompts you for the block to unformat in the input line, press the Down direction key five times to select the block C8..C13 (or type *C8..C13)* and press the Enter key. Quattro Pro returns the display of the values in the block C8..C13 to the General format.

Of course, you can also change the format of a block simply by reformatting it. To do so, choose the Style Numeric Format command, choose a different format that is not necessarily General, and specify the block you want to format.

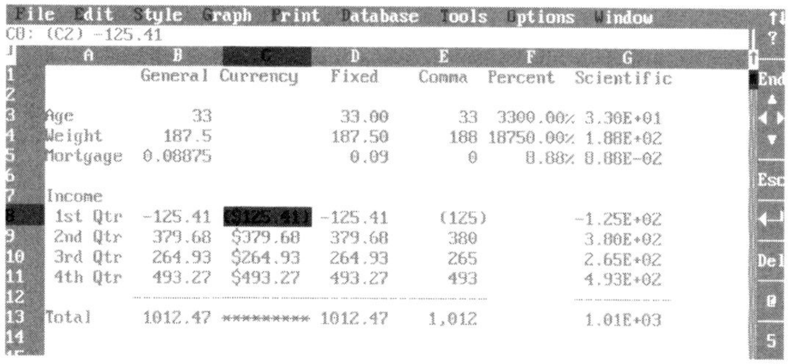

FIGURE 2-3.
The input line displays a format indicator that describes the cell's format.

Quattro Pro's format options

Now that you've seen the basic technique for formatting a cell or block and taken a look at the currency formats, you're ready to examine Quattro Pro's seven remaining formats: Fixed, Comma (,), Percent, Scientific, +/- (Bar Graph), Hidden, and Text.

The Fixed format

The Fixed format lets you specify the number of decimal places that Quattro Pro displays in a formatted value. When you assign the Fixed format to a cell or block, you can instruct Quattro Pro to display the values in that block using 0 to 15 decimal places. To see examples of the Fixed format, look at column D in Figure 2-3, which holds all the same values as column B.

The Comma format

The Comma (,) format inserts commas between hundreds and thousands, thousands and millions, and so on, in formatted values. Like the Fixed format, the Comma format allows you to specify the number of decimal places that Quattro Pro displays. In addition, this format encloses negative numbers in parentheses. For examples of the Comma format with no decimal places, see column E in Figure 2.3. Notice that cell E8, which contains the value -125.41, shows as *(125)*. Cell E13, which contains the value 1012.47, shows as *1,012*.

The Percent format

Use the Percent format to display decimal values as percentages. Like the Comma, Currency, and Fixed formats, the Percent format allows you to choose the number of decimal places that you want Quattro Pro to display. Quattro Pro expects values in cells with the Percent format to be decimal values; for example, .7 and .95. For such a value, Quattro Pro moves the decimal point two places to the right and appends a percent sign (%) to the formatted value. When you apply this format to a value greater than 1, the result is a percentage over 100%. Column F in Figure 2-1 shows examples of the Percent format. Cell F5, which contains the only decimal value, .08875, displays that value as 8.88%. Cell F3, which contains the whole number 33, displays that value as 3300.00%.

The Scientific format

The Scientific format displays values in scientific (or exponential) notation. Like most of the other formats we have explained so far in this chapter, this format allows you to control the number of decimal places that Quattro Pro includes in the formatted value. Use the Scientific format whenever the numbers you present are very large or very small. In Scientific format, Quattro Pro represents numbers as powers of 10. For example, the value 2222222222 is represented as 2.22E+9 in Scientific format with two decimal places. The letter E in this formatted value represents "10 to the power of," so this value can be read as 2.22 times 10 to the power of 9. The value 10 raised to the power of 9 is 10*10*10*10*10*10*10*10*10, or 1000000000.

You also use the Scientific format for very small values. For example, Quattro Pro displays the number .000007 as 7.00E-6 in the Scientific format with two decimal places. The expression E-6 in this example display stands for 10 raised to the -6 power, or .000001. The cells in column G in Figure 2-3 show an example of the Scientific format.

The +/- (Bar Graph) format

When you use the +/- format, Quattro Pro displays values as a series of plus (+) and minus (-) signs. This format, which is sometimes called the Bar Graph format, essentially creates simple bar graphs in the cells of your worksheet. Although you might never use this format, some interesting things can be done with it.

Column B in Figure 2-4 shows in thousands of dollars a company's net profit. Cells B3..B7 contain the income values. Cells C3..C7 actually hold the same values, but this block is formatted with the +/- format. In the +/- format, Quattro Pro displays positive numbers as a series of plus signs, and negative numbers as a series of minus signs. Quattro Pro displays the value 0 as a decimal point in +/- format, as you can see in cell C4.

For display purposes, the +/- format rounds values to the nearest integer. For example, in Figure 2-4 the value 5.5 in cell C6 is displayed as a series of six plus signs. Like Quattro Pro's other numeric formats, the +/- format displays a value as a series of asterisks when the formatted value is too wide to fit in its cell. For example, because column C is only nine characters wide, the value 12 in cell C7 is displayed as a series of asterisks.

You can widen a column to display the additional plus and minus signs, but because the Quattro Pro screen is only 76 characters wide, the largest number you can fully display in the +/- format is 75. To display a number this wide, you must

FIGURE 2-4.
This worksheet demonstrates the +/- format.

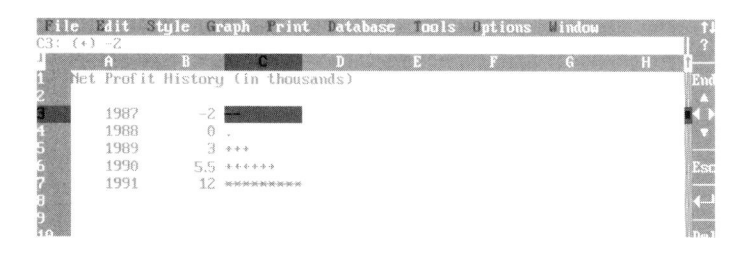

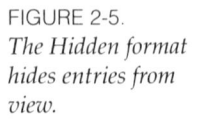

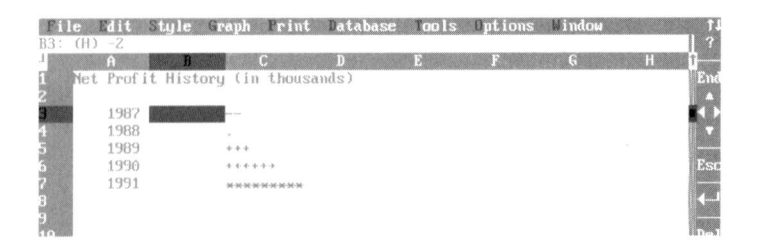

FIGURE 2-5.
The Hidden format hides entries from view.

use the Style Column Width command to increase the width of the column to 76 characters.

To display a large number properly in the +/- format, factor that number down until it is small enough to be displayed within the 76-character limitation. For example, notice that the numbers in column B and C in Figure 2-4 represent thousands of dollars. Because it is not practical to display a value such as -2,000 in +/- format, the example shows each number divided by 1,000.

Because the bar graphs produced by the +/- format are not nearly as attractive or useful as those you can create by using the Graph command, you will probably not use this very often. In Chapter 10, the section "Quattro Pro's Graph Types" shows you how to create bar graphs.

The Hidden format

Unlike Quattro Pro's other formats, the Hidden format affects both values and labels. Use the Hidden format when you want to hide cell entries from view. Of course, the entries are not gone; they are simply hidden. Suppose you want to hide the entries in cells B3..B7 as shown in Figure 2-4. To do so, move the cell selector to cell B3, choose the Style Numeric Format Hidden command, select the block B3..B7, and press the Enter key. Figure 2-5 shows that all the entries in the selected block are now hidden.

To "unhide" the cell entries, choose the Style Numeric Format Reset command and select the desired block. When you press the Enter key, Quattro Pro brings the hidden cells back into view.

Be aware that you can still see the contents of a hidden cell by selecting it and looking at the input line. For instance, the value in cell B3 disappeared when you assigned the Hidden format to that cell. But you can see the contents of that cell next to the cell address in the input line.

Why would you use the Hidden format? You might use this format to hide comments or notes that you've embedded in a worksheet. Or you might use the Hidden format to hide proprietary and confidential worksheet data. Remember, however, that someone can still view the contents of a cell in the input line.

Quattro Pro also provides the Style Hide Column command, which you can use to hide entire columns from view. In Chapter 3, the section "Adjusting Column Widths" explains how to use this command.

FIGURE 2-6.
The Text format tells Quattro Pro to display the actual formulas in cells rather than the results of those formulas.

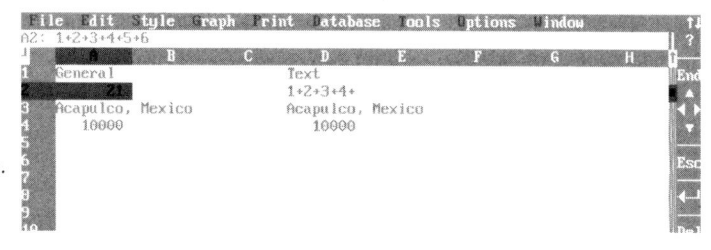

The Text format

When you enter a formula in a cell, Quattro Pro displays the result of the formula rather than the formula itself. The Text format lets you tell Quattro Pro to display the actual formula in a cell, as illustrated in Figure 2-6. The two blocks A2..A4 and D2..D4 contain the same entries. The cells in row 2 contain the formula *1+2+3+4+5+6*, and the cells in row 3 contain the label *Acapulco, Mexico*. The cells in row 4 contain the number 10000. The Text format has no effect on cells that contain labels or literal values. It affects only cells with formulas.

Formulas in cells to which the Text format has been assigned are displayed in the same way that labels are, with one exception: Long formulas will not overlap from one cell into the adjacent cells even when those cells are empty. For example, notice that the formula in cell D2 in Figure 2-6 only shows *1+2+3+4+*, even though the complete formula is 1+2+3+4+5+6. To view such entries in their entirety, increase the width of the column in which they're contained.

Changing the global format

Although Quattro Pro's default global format, General, is appropriate in most cases, you might occasionally want to choose a different format as the global format. Fortunately, Quattro Pro makes it easy to use any of the formats discussed so far in this chapter as the global format. The Options Formats Numeric Format command lets you change the global format. After you choose this command, Quattro Pro displays the same menu that you see when you choose the Style Numeric Format command. To change the global format from General to one of the other formats, simply choose the format you want from this menu. If you choose the Fixed, Scientific, Currency, Comma, or Percent format, Quattro Pro asks you to specify the number of decimal places to include in the format. Either press the Enter key to accept the default number of decimals, which is 2, or type the desired number of decimals and press the Enter key.

The formats you assign to cells and blocks by using the Style Numeric Format command override the worksheet's global format. As a result, the formats of any cells to which you assign a specific format do not change when you change a worksheet's global format. Changing the worksheet's global format, however, affects every cell that does not have a specific format. Also, if you reset the format of a block by using the Style Numeric Format Reset command, Quattro Pro displays the values in that block in the new global format.

To change the global format back to General or to any other format, choose the Options Formats Numeric Format command again, and then choose the desired format from the menu.

Improving your worksheet by hiding zeros

The Options Formats Hide Zeros command allows you to improve the appearance and clarity of your worksheets by hiding extraneous zeros. When you choose this command, Quattro Pro prompts you with two choices: Yes and No. If you choose Yes, Quattro Pro suppresses the display of every zero in the worksheet. If you choose No, Quattro Pro displays the contents of the cells than contain zeros. This command affects cells that contain literal zeros as well as cells that contain formulas and functions that return zero values.

An example of hiding zeros

Figure 2-7 shows a worksheet that posts checks into expense categories. As you can see, each check is posted to only one account. Quattro Pro displays a zero in every other cell of each row. These zeros clutter the worksheet and make it difficult to interpret. (The formulas in this worksheet use the @IF function, which you'll read about in Chapter 4 in "Logical Functions.")

To remove these unwanted zeros, choose the Options Formats Hide Zeros command, and then choose the Yes option. Figure 2-8 shows the result. The zeros that clutter the worksheet in Figure 2-7 are hidden in Figure 2-8.

A closer look at zero suppression

Although the Options Formats Hide Zeros command can affect the appearance of a worksheet significantly, it has no effect on the substance of the worksheet.

FIGURE 2-7.
This worksheet is cluttered with zeros that make it hard to read.

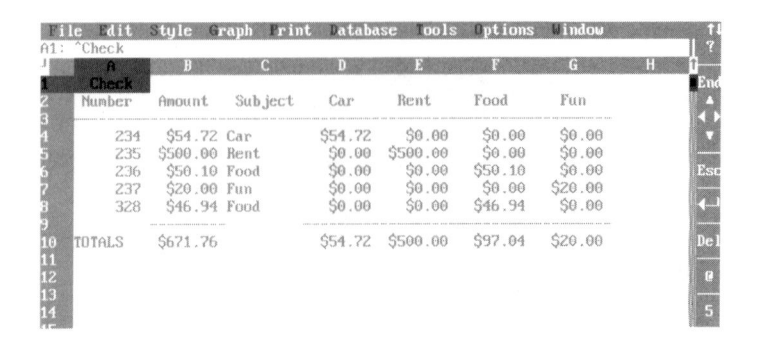

Check Number	Amount	Subject	Car	Rent	Food	Fun
234	$54.72	Car	$54.72	$0.00	$0.00	$0.00
235	$500.00	Rent	$0.00	$500.00	$0.00	$0.00
236	$50.10	Food	$0.00	$0.00	$50.10	$0.00
237	$20.00	Fun	$0.00	$0.00	$0.00	$20.00
328	$46.94	Food	$0.00	$0.00	$46.94	$0.00
TOTALS	$671.76		$54.72	$500.00	$97.04	$20.00

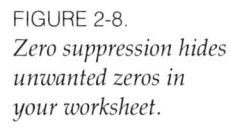

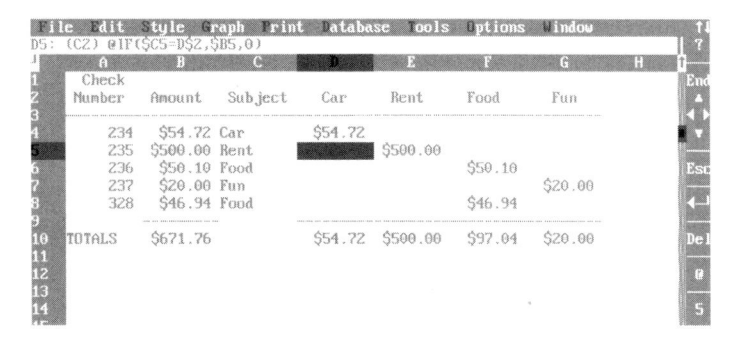

FIGURE 2-8.
Zero suppression hides unwanted zeros in your worksheet.

Choosing the Options Formats Hide Zeros command does not erase zeros from cells; it merely hides the zeros from view. Similarly, this command does not affect the format of any cell in a worksheet.

The disadvantage of using zero suppression is that you cannot easily tell which cells contain zeros and which cells are blank, which means you might erase or damage contents without realizing it. For this reason, pay particular attention to the input line because it shows the contents of cells, including those that contain hidden zeros. In Figure 2-8, for example, the cell selector is in cell D5, which contains hidden zeros. The contents of this cell are visible in the input line.

NOTE: *Quattro Pro does not save a worksheet's zero-suppression setting with the worksheet. If you save a worksheet in which you have suppressed the display of zeros, exit from Quattro Pro, start Quattro Pro again, and then retrieve the file, the zeros are visible. Of course, you can hide the zeros again by choosing the Options Formats Hide Zeros command and then choosing the Yes option.*

To make Quattro Pro display all of the zeros in any worksheet after you've hidden them, choose the Default Formats Hide Zeros command and then choose the No option. Quattro Pro brings every zero in the worksheet back into view.

Alignment of labels and values

As explained in Chapter 1, every label you enter in a worksheet must begin with one of Quattro Pro's four label prefixes: ' (left aligned), " (right aligned), ^ (centered), or \ (repeating). The label prefix you use determines how the label is aligned in its cell. Quattro Pro also provides menu commands that you can use to control how labels will be aligned in cells. These menu commands do not affect only labels; they affect the alignment of values as well.

Label prefixes and alignment

Although every label must begin with a label prefix, you usually do not need to type the prefix when you enter a label. If you make an entry that begins with a letter and you do not type a label prefix, Quattro Pro assumes that the entry is a label and provides a default prefix for it: the left alignment label ('), assuming you have not changed the default. To enter a label that has an alignment other than the default, precede that label with the appropriate prefix.

Realigning a block of labels

The Style Alignment command provides four alignment choices: General, Left, Right, or Center. General is the default alignment setting. It right-aligns values and dates and aligns labels using the default label prefix. Left, Right, and Center work as you might expect: Left alignment left-aligns labels and values, Right alignment right-aligns labels and values, and Center alignment center-aligns labels and values. Figure 2-9 shows the alignment options available with the Style Alignment command.

After you choose the Style Alignment command, Quattro Pro presents a menu that lists the four alignment choices. Choose from this menu, and Quattro Pro prompts you to define the block you want to modify, suggesting the cell that contains the cell selector. Press the Enter key to accept Quattro Pro's default. Or, press the Esc key and specify a different block to realign, or type the block coordinates of the block you want to realign, and then press the Enter key.

When you use the Style Alignment command to realign a block of labels, Quattro Pro actually changes the label prefixes of those labels. As a result, you can use the command only to change the alignment of labels that are already in place in the worksheet; you cannot use it to predefine the label alignment for a block of empty cells.

Quattro Pro treats value alignments differently from label alignments, however. In effect, Quattro Pro memorizes the alignments you assign with the Style Alignment command and uses the memorized settings to determine the correct alignment. If you assign an alignment with the Style Alignment command when the

FIGURE 2-9.
The Style Alignment command lets you choose from four alignments for labels and values.

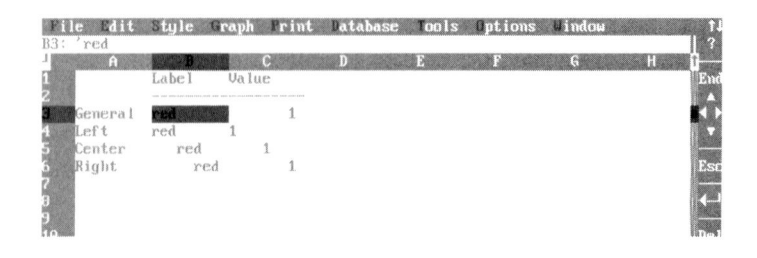

cell holds a value, the command will not apply to a label you enter subsequently. However, if you assign an alignment with the Style Alignment command when the cell holds a label, the command will apply to a value you enter subsequently.

Changing the default label prefix

As a rule, it's easier not to type label prefixes. Instead, enter labels in the worksheet using the ' (left aligned) default label prefix, and then use the Style Alignment command to change the alignment of the labels. Quattro Pro allows you to change the default label prefix from ' (left aligned) to " (right aligned) or ^ (centered). You cannot choose the \ (repeating) prefix as the default label prefix. To change the default label prefix, choose the Options Formats Align label command. Quattro Pro presents a menu with three choices: Left, Right, and Center. Choose the option that you want to use as your default label prefix. Changing the default label prefix has no effect on the labels that are already in place in a worksheet. Those labels keep the prefixes that were assigned to them when they were entered in the worksheet. The new default prefix affects only new labels that you enter.

3
Editing Your Worksheet

Quattro Pro offers 14 commands that you can use to edit a worksheet. They let you change the widths of columns, hide columns, erase an entire worksheet or individual cells, insert and delete rows and columns, and move or copy cell entries.

Adjusting column widths

You will need to change the widths of the columns in your Quattro Pro worksheets often to adjust for the amount of information you have. As discussed earlier in the book, the width of a column determines how Quattro Pro displays the contents of the cells in that column. In addition, you can clean up the appearance of your worksheet by changing the widths of certain columns. For example, you might want to increase the width of a column to separate the information in that column from the information in an adjacent column. Or, you might want to decrease the width of a column to bring more columns into view on the screen.

You can use Quattro Pro's Style Column Width, Style Block Widths, and Option Formats Global Width commands to adjust the widths of the columns in a worksheet. The Style Column Width command allows you to change the width of one column at a time. The Style Block Widths command allows you to change the widths of all the columns in a block. The Options Formats Global Width command, however, allows you to adjust the default width of every column in a worksheet.

Changing the width of a single column

Use the Style Column Width command when you want to change the width of any single column in a worksheet. You can specify a column width ranging from as few as 1 character to as many as 254 characters.

To change the width of a column, move the cell selector to any cell in the column you want to change. Choose the Style Column Width command and specify the new column width in one of three ways. You can type a new width, which works best when you know precisely how wide you want the column to be. You can press the Left direction and Right direction keys to change the width of the column: Pressing the Left direction key decreases the column width by one character, and pressing the Right direction key increases the column width by one character. This second method works best when you are not sure how wide to make the column in order to display long labels or formatted values. You can also drag the column letter with the mouse. After you use one of these methods to specify the new width, press the Enter key.

An example of changing column width

Suppose you want to widen column A in Figure 3-1 so that the labels in block A5..A8 are not truncated. Because column A is only nine characters wide (Quattro Pro's default width), and cells A5..A8 contain entries that are longer than nine characters, Quattro Pro can display only the first nine characters of these labels.

To make column A wider, position the cell selector anywhere in column A and choose the Style Column Width command. Quattro Pro displays the prompt *Alter the width of the current column (1..254)* in the input line with the current width of column A (9 characters) as the default.

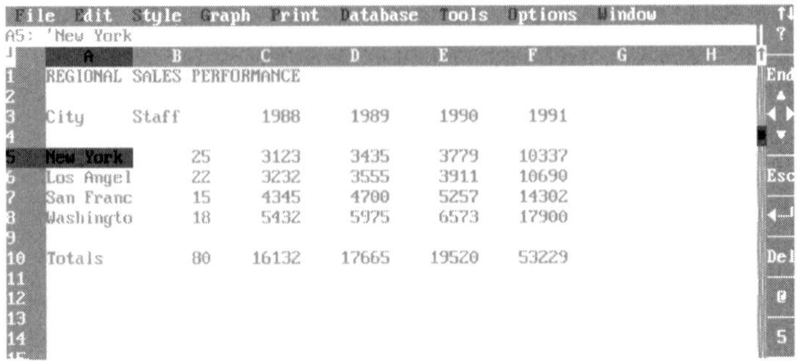

FIGURE 3-1.
The labels in column A of this worksheet are truncated, so column A should be widened using the Style Column Width command.

Because you want to increase the width of column A so that the labels are in view, use the Right direction key to widen the column one character at a time. As you continue to press the Right direction key, more letters appear in the labels in cells A6, A7, and A8. To see every character in the labels in column A, widen the column to 16 characters. You can also type 16, and then press the Enter key. You can also drag the column letter with the mouse. The worksheet now looks like the one shown in Figure 3-2.

The indicator *W16* in the input line tells you that the width of column A has been set to 16 characters. You see an indicator like this whenever the cell selector is in a column whose width has been changed.

Resetting the width of a column

After you use the Style Column Width command to change the width of a column, you might want to return the column to its original width. To do so, move the cell selector to the column and choose the Style Reset Width command. Quattro Pro resets the width of the current column to the global column width. The global column width is the default size used for all columns in the worksheet, except those that have been adjusted with the Style Column Width command. Unless you have already changed the global column width, the current width is nine spaces. The upcoming section, "Changing the Global Column Width," explains how to set the global column width to a new value.

Changing the widths of all columns in a block

Although the Style Column Width and Style Reset Width commands allow you to change or reset the width of only one column at a time, the Style Block Widths command lets you change and reset all of the columns in a block.

When you choose the Style Block Widths command, Quattro Pro displays a submenu listing three choices: Set Width, Reset Width, and Auto Width. To set the column widths for an entire block, choose the Set Width option. Quattro Pro

FIGURE 3-2.
Using the Style Column Width command to increase or decrease the widths of columns.

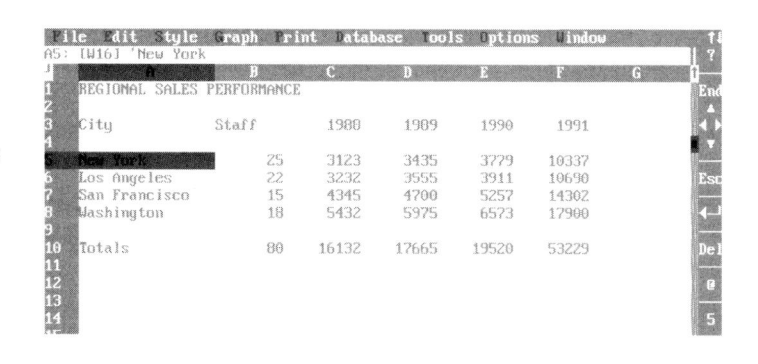

prompts you in the input line to specify the block of columns for which you want to set column widths. When you specify a block of columns and press the Enter key, Quattro Pro displays the prompt *Alter the width of columns [1..245]* and shows the current default global width (9) as the default. Specify this block as you do any other: by pointing with the direction keys, by clicking and dragging, or by typing the block coordinates. Change the width of columns in a block in the same way you change the width of an individual column: Use the Left and Right direction keys, drag the column letter with the mouse, or type the width and then press the Enter key. Quattro Pro adjusts each of the column widths in the block.

Resetting the widths of all columns in a block

Just as with individual columns, you can use the Style Block Widths command to reset column widths in a block. When you choose the Style Block Widths command, Quattro Pro displays a submenu listing three choices: Set Width, Reset Width, and Auto Width. Choose the Reset Width option. Quattro Pro prompts you in the input line to enter the block of columns for which you want to reset column widths. Specify the block by pointing with the direction keys, by clicking and dragging, or by typing the block coordinates. After you specify the block, press the Enter key, and Quattro Pro returns all the columns in the block to the global column width. "Changing the Global Column Width," appearing later in this chapter, tells you how to adjust the global column width.

Increasing the widths of selected columns

The Style Block Widths command's third choice is Auto Width. The Auto Width option adjusts the widths of selected columns so that they are wide enough for the longest entry in the column. To use this option, choose the Style Block Widths command and then choose the Auto Width option from the submenu. Quattro displays the prompt *Enter extra space between columns [0-40]*, which includes the default extra space setting (1). Using the default means that the longest entry in the column is still one character shorter than the column's width. You can, however, specify a different extra space setting ranging from 0 to 40. After you type the setting, press the Enter key. Quattro Pro prompts you in the input line to specify the block; do so by pointing with the direction keys, by clicking and dragging, or by typing the block coordinates. After you have specified the block, press the Enter key, and Quattro Pro adjusts each of the column widths in the blocks.

Changing the global column width

Quattro Pro also gives you the ability to change the widths of every column in the worksheet at one time by changing the global column width with the Options Formats Global Widths command. When you choose this command, Quattro Pro displays the prompt *Set the default column width to a new value (1..254)* in the input line, followed by the current default column width. (Unless you have changed it, the current global column width is nine characters.) To specify a new global column width, type the new width, press the Left and Right direction keys, or drag the column letter with the mouse to adjust the global column width visually, and then press the Enter key.

A closer look at the global column width

When you use the Options Formats Global Widths command, Quattro Pro sets the width of every column in the worksheet to the new default width, except columns that you have modified using the Style Column Width command. If you find, after choosing this command, that you've changed the widths of some columns that you would rather not have changed, you can use the Style Column Width command to restore the widths of those columns individually.

As mentioned earlier, the Style Reset Column command resets the width of the current column to the current global width for the worksheet; not to that column's original width. For instance, suppose that you change the width of an individual column from 9 to 15 and then change the global column width to 10. If you then use the Style Reset Column command to reset the width of that one column, Quattro Pro sets the width of that column to the new global width of 10, and not the column's previous width of 9.

Hiding columns

The Style Hide Column command lets you hide a column, or a group of columns, by reducing the column width to zero characters. When you hide a column using this command, Quattro Pro prevents that column from being displayed on the screen and prevents the column entries from being printed.

When you choose the Style Hide Column command, Quattro Pro displays a menu with two choices: Hide and Expose. When you choose the Hide option, Quattro Pro displays the prompt *Hide columns from view* in the input line, followed by the address of the current cell. Press the Enter key to accept Quattro Pro's default and hide the current column. Alternatively, point to another column and press the Enter key to hide that column; or type a period to anchor the cell selector, expand the block with the direction keys to include several columns, and then press the Enter key to hide those columns. Keep in mind that you can point to a cell or cells in any row of the columns that you want to hide.

After you hide a column (or columns), it disappears from the screen, and the columns on either side of the hidden column appear side by side in the worksheet.

An example of hiding columns

Suppose you want to hide column B of the worksheet shown in Figure 3-2. First, move the cell selector to any cell in column B, choose the Style Hide Column command, and choose the Hide option. Quattro Pro displays the prompt *Hide columns from view* in the input line, followed by the address of the current cell. Press the Enter key to hide column B. Figure 3-3 shows column B hidden from view.

A closer look at hiding columns

Hiding a column from view is not the same as deleting a column from the worksheet. Hiding a column merely prevents Quattro Pro from displaying that column on the screen and from printing it—it does not remove the column from the worksheet. As a result, any formulas or functions that refer to hidden cells are still valid.

In general, you cannot move the cell selector into a hidden column. When Quattro Pro is in POINT mode, however, all hidden columns are revealed temporarily in the worksheet. (Quattro Pro enters POINT mode whenever you choose a command that requires that you specify a block, such as the Edit Move or Edit Names commands, or whenever you press a direction key while defining a formula or function.) While Quattro Pro is in POINT mode, it displays an asterisk next to the column letter of any hidden column, as shown in Figure 3-4. When Quattro Pro leaves POINT mode, the hidden columns disappear from view. Because Quattro Pro reveals hidden columns while in POINT mode, you can choose commands that affect cells in those columns. You can also create formulas and functions that refer to cells in hidden columns.

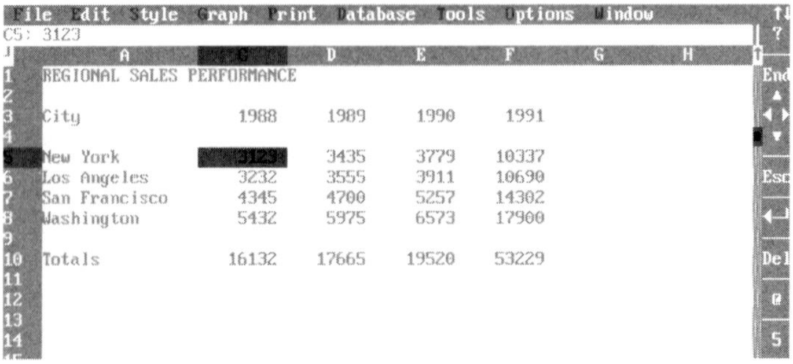

FIGURE 3-3.
The Style Hide Column Hide command has hidden column B from view.

Chapter 3: Editing Your Worksheet

FIGURE 3-4.
When Quattro Pro is in POINT mode, all hidden columns in the worksheet are temporarily revealed.

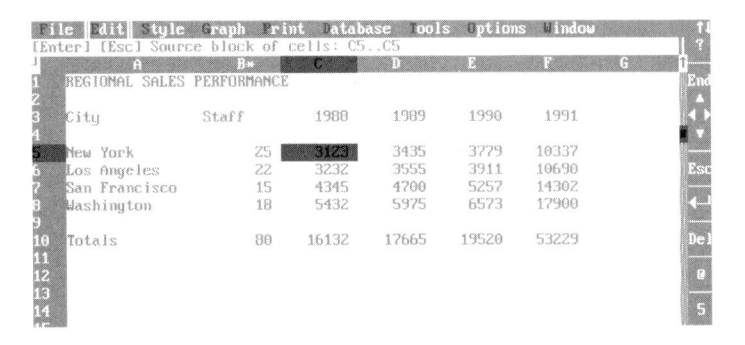

Revealing hidden columns

The Style Hide Column command also lets you unhide, or expose, hidden columns. When you choose this command, Quattro Pro displays a submenu that has two options: Hide and Expose. Choose the Expose option. Quattro Pro enters POINT mode, brings all of the hidden columns into view, and displays the prompt *Expose hidden columns* followed by the address of the current cell. To expose a hidden column, point to that column and press the Enter key. To expose more than one column, point to any cell in the extreme left or extreme right column that you want to expose, press the period (.) key, point to any cell in the column at the opposite side of the block, and press the Enter key.

Using the Expose option of the Style Hide Column command has no effect on unhidden columns. Consequently, the block you define can include columns that are not hidden; Quattro Pro simply reveals any hidden columns in the selected block.

Erasing the worksheet

The File Erase command erases a worksheet, including all of your cell entries, block names, cell formatting, and graphs, and then resets the worksheet to its original condition. When you choose this command, Quattro Pro checks to see whether you have made any changes to the current worksheet since you last saved it. If you have not made any changes, Quattro Pro erases the entire worksheet. If you have made some changes that you have not yet saved and you try to erase the worksheet, Quattro Pro displays the prompt *Lose your changes?* followed by the options No and Yes. If you choose Yes, Quattro Pro erases the entire worksheet. If you choose No, however, Quattro Pro returns to READY mode without erasing the worksheet. To save the worksheet, choose the File Save command, type a name for the file if this is the first time you have saved it, and press the Enter key.

Use the File Erase command with extreme caution. After you erase a worksheet, you cannot easily retrieve it. Quattro Pro, however, has an add-in program called Transcript that allows you to reconstruct an erased worksheet. For more information on Transcript, see the section "Using Transcript to Record Keystrokes and Commands" in Chapter 12.

Erasing entries in cells and blocks

You can use Quattro Pro's Edit Erase Block command to erase entries from the cells in a worksheet. Because you'll need to erase cells often, to correct mistakes or to remove entries that are no longer needed, the Edit Erase Block command will probably be one of your most frequently used commands.

When you choose the Edit Erase Block command, Quattro Pro displays the prompt *Block to be modified* in the input line, followed by a block reference to the current cell. Press the Enter key to accept the default and erase the contents of the current cell. Or, select several cells, or press the Esc key and point to a different cell or block, or type a reference to a different block, and then press the Enter key.

Although the Edit Erase Block command removes the contents of a cell or block, unlike the File Erase command it does not remove any formats that have been assigned to those cells.

An example of erasing the contents of a cell

Suppose you want to erase cell B5, as shown in Figure 3-2. To do so, move the cell selector to cell B5 and choose the Edit Erase Block command. When you see the prompt *Block to be modified: B5..B5* in the input line, press the Enter key. Quattro Pro erases the contents of cell B5.

After you erase the contents of a cell that is referenced by a formula or a function elsewhere in the worksheet, Quattro Pro assigns the value 0 to the empty cell and changes the result of the formula or function in the other cells that reference it in the worksheet to reflect this new value.

An example of erasing the contents of a block

You can also use the Edit Erase Block command to erase the contents of a block of cells. Position the cell selector at one of the corners of the block you want to erase, and then choose the Edit Erase Block command. When Quattro Pro prompts you in the input line to define the block you want to erase, use the direction keys to point to the opposite corner of the selected block. Press the Enter key to erase the contents of the selected cells.

For example, suppose you want to erase the contents of cells B5..D8, shown in Figure 3-2. To begin, position the cell selector on cell B5 or on any of the other three corners of the block (B8, D5, or D8), and then choose the Edit Erase Block command. Quattro Pro presents the prompt *Block to be modified: B5..B5* in the input line. Select the block B5..D8 with the direction keys and press the Enter key to erase the contents of the block.

Inserting rows and columns

Use the Edit Insert Rows or Edit Insert Columns command when you want to insert new rows or columns in a worksheet.

Inserting rows

Use the Edit Insert Rows command to insert one or more rows in a worksheet. To begin, choose the Edit Insert Rows command. Quattro Pro displays the prompt *Enter row insert block*, followed by a block reference to the current cell. Specify a block that includes cells in each of the rows that you want to insert, and then press the Enter key. Press the Enter key to accept the default block. Or, use the direction keys to modify the default to include several rows, or press the Esc key and specify a different block, and then press the Enter key.

Quattro Pro inserts a row above the row that contains the cell selector. If you select a block that spans more than one row, Quattro Pro inserts one row in the worksheet for each row in the block. All of these rows are inserted above the first row in the block. At the same time, Quattro Pro pushes the entries in the rows below the inserted row down one row.

An example of inserting rows

Suppose you want to insert a blank row between rows 6 and 7 of the worksheet shown in Figure 3-2. To do so, move the cell selector to any cell in row 7 (the row above which you want to insert the new row), choose the Edit Insert Rows command, and then press the Enter key. Figure 3-5 shows the result: Quattro Pro inserts a blank row immediately above the row that contained the cell selector (row 7), pushes all the entries in rows 7 through 8192 down one row, and pushes row 8192 off the edge of the worksheet. (Quattro Pro would not push row 8192 off the worksheet if it contained entries.)

You can use the Edit Insert Rows command to insert more than one row in a worksheet at one time. First, move the cell selector to the row above which you want to insert the rows, and then choose the Edit Insert Rows command. When Quattro Pro prompts you for the block of rows to insert, use the Down direction key to select a block that contains the number of rows you want to insert, and then

FIGURE 3-5.
The Edit Insert Rows command lets you insert rows in a worksheet.

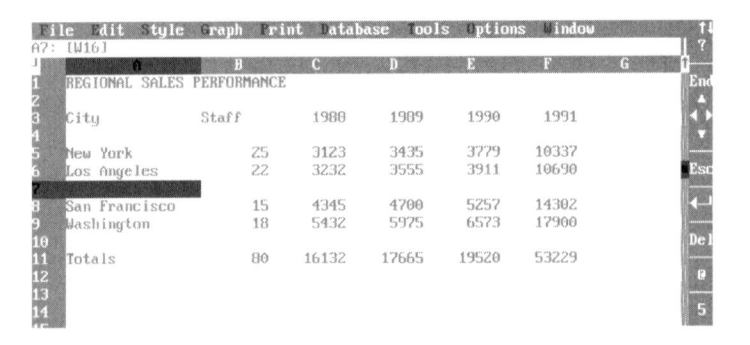

```
File Edit Style Graph Print Database Tools Options Window
A7: [W16]
                A              B         C       D       E       F       G
1   REGIONAL SALES PERFORMANCE
2
3   City               Staff       1988    1989    1990    1991
4
5   New York              25        3123    3435    3779   10337
6   Los Angeles           22        3232    3555    3911   10690
7
8   San Francisco         15        4345    4700    5257   14302
9   Washington            18        5432    5975    6573   17900
10
11  Totals                80       16132   17665   19520   53229
12
13
14
```

press the Enter key. Quattro Pro inserts rows above the topmost row in the specified block. You can include as many cells in each row of the block as you want. Quattro Pro always inserts one row in the worksheet for each row in the block you define, no matter how many cells in each row are selected.

Inserting columns

Inserting new columns in a Quattro Pro worksheet is similar to inserting new rows. To insert one or more blank columns, choose the Edit Insert Columns command; Quattro Pro displays the prompt *Enter column insert block,* followed by a block reference to the current cell. Specify a block that includes cells in each of the columns you want to insert, and then press the Enter key. Press the Enter key to accept the default block. Or, press the direction keys to modify the default to include several columns, or press the Esc key and specify a different block, and then press the Enter key.

Quattro Pro inserts a column to the left of the column that contains the cell selector. If you select a block that spans more than one column, Quattro Pro inserts one column in the worksheet for each column in the block. All of these columns are inserted to the left of the first column in the block. At the same time, Quattro Pro pushes the entries in the columns to the right of the inserted column one column to the right.

An example of inserting columns

Suppose you want to insert two columns between columns D and E in a worksheet you are building. To do so, move the cell selector to any cell in column E, and then choose the Edit Insert Columns command. When Quattro Pro prompts you for the insert block, press the Right direction key one time to expand the highlight one cell into column F, and then press the Enter key. Quattro Pro inserts two blank columns in the appropriate place.

How inserting rows and columns affects references

As mentioned, inserting a row in a worksheet pushes all the rows beneath it down by one row. Inserting a new column pushes all the columns to the right of it to the right by one column. Quattro Pro adjusts formulas or references to cells that are relocated by the insertion of a row or column to reflect the cells' new locations.

If you insert a row or a column within the boundaries of a referenced block, the block definition changes to include the appropriate cells in that new row or column. For example, suppose you gave the name Sales to the block B5..B8. If you then insert a row between rows 6 and 7, the block definition of Sales changes to B5..B9. If you insert three more rows between rows 8 and 9, the block definition of Sales changes to B5..B12.

Deleting rows and columns

The Edit Delete Rows and Edit Delete Columns commands let you delete rows and columns from a worksheet. Unlike the Edit Erase Block command, which only empties the contents of cells, these two commands actually remove entire rows and columns from your worksheet.

Deleting rows

Use the Edit Delete Rows command when you want to delete a row or a group of adjacent rows from a Quattro Pro worksheet. When you choose this command, Quattro Pro presents the prompt *Enter block of rows to delete* in the input line, followed by a block reference to the current cell. Press the Enter key to accept the default and delete the current row. Or, press the Up direction and Down direction keys to modify the default block to include several rows, or press the Esc key and specify a different block, and then press the Enter key.

An example of deleting rows

Suppose you want to delete rows 7, 8, and 9 from the worksheet shown in Figure 3-5. To do so, move the cell selector to any cell in row 7, and then choose the Edit Delete Rows command. When you see the prompt *Enter block of rows to delete* in the input line, press the Down direction key two times to highlight cells in rows 8 and 9, and then press the Enter key. Quattro Pro deletes rows 7, 8, and 9 from the worksheet, as shown in Figure 3-6. As you can see, Quattro Pro filled the space vacated by rows 7, 8, and 9 by shifting the contents of rows 10 through 8192 up three rows. In addition, Quattro Pro added three new blank rows at the bottom of the worksheet so that the worksheet still contains 8192 rows. The old row 10 is now row 7, the old row 11 is now row 8, and the old row 12 is now row 9.

FIGURE 3-6.
The Edit Delete Rows command lets you delete rows from a worksheet.

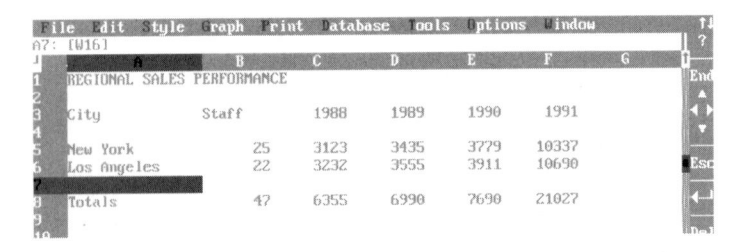

	A	B	C	D	E	F
1	REGIONAL SALES PERFORMANCE					
2						
3	City	Staff	1988	1989	1990	1991
4						
5	New York	25	3123	3435	3779	10337
6	Los Angeles	22	3232	3555	3911	10690
7						
8	Totals	47	6355	6990	7690	21027

To delete the three rows in this example, only one cell in each of the rows was highlighted. You can, however, include as many cells in each row of the block as you want. Quattro Pro always deletes every row that is included in the block that you highlight, no matter how many cells in each row are highlighted.

Deleting columns

Quattro Pro's Edit Delete Columns command lets you delete columns from a worksheet. When you choose this command, Quattro Pro displays the prompt *Delete one or more columns* in the input line, followed by a block reference to the current cell. Press the Enter key to accept the default and delete the current column. Or, press the Left and Right direction keys to modify the default block to include several columns, or press the Esc key and specify a different block, and then press the Enter key.

An example of deleting columns

Suppose you want to delete columns E and F from the worksheet shown in Figure 3-6. To begin, move the cell selector to any cell in column E, and then choose the Edit Delete Columns command. When you see the prompt *Delete one or more columns* in the input line, press the Right direction key one time to expand the block reference to include one cell from column F in the block, and then press the Enter key. Quattro Pro deletes columns E and F and shifts the contents of columns G through IV by two columns to the left to fill the gap, as shown in Figure 3-7.

How deleting rows and columns affects references

Deleting a row from a worksheet pushes all the rows beneath it up one row. Deleting a column pushes all the columns to the right of it to the left by one column. Quattro Pro adjusts all references to blocks of cells that were shifted as a result of the deletion. Quattro Pro also contracts a block when you delete rows or columns that fall within the boundaries of that block. For example, suppose you gave the name Sales to the block B5..B12. If you delete rows 9, 10, and 11, the block definition of Sales changes to B5..B9.

FIGURE 3-7.
The Edit Delete Columns command lets you delete columns from a worksheet.

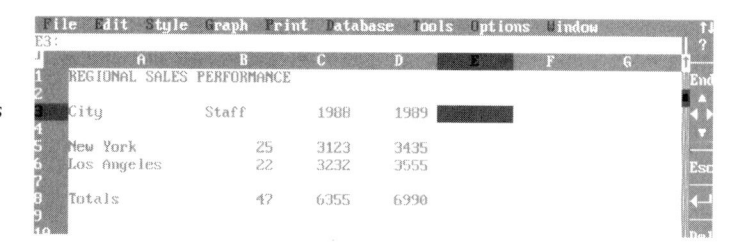

You'll run into problems, however, if you delete a row or column containing a cell that is referenced by a formula. For example, suppose that cell G9 in a worksheet that you are constructing contains the formula +B9+C9+D9. If you use the Edit Delete Column command to delete column B, C, or D from the worksheet, this formula will return the value ERR, because deleting column B, C, or D deletes one of the cells upon which the formula depends. Whenever you delete a cell that is referenced by a formula or function in another cell, the reference to that cell will be replaced with the value ERR, and the formula or function will return the value ERR. For example, with the formula +B9+C9+D9, deleting column B would change the formula to +ERR+C9+D9. Obviously, you want to avoid this type of situation, so be sure that any columns or rows you delete do not contain cells referenced by other cells that no longer exist in your worksheet.

Moving cell entries

The Edit Move command allows you to move the contents of a cell or block to another location in a worksheet, making Edit Move one of Quattro Pro's most useful and frequently used commands.

To move the contents of a cell or block, choose the Edit Move command. Quattro Pro displays the prompt *Source block of cells* in the input line, followed by a block reference to the current cell. Press the Enter key to accept the current cell as the source block. Alternatively, press the direction keys to expand the default block, press the Esc key and specify a different source block, or type a different block reference, and then press the Enter key.

Quattro Pro presents the prompt *Destination for cells* in the input line, followed by the address of the current cell, which is the default. At this point you can press the Enter key to accept the default. Or you can either type the address of the cell or block to which you want to move, point to the destination with the direction keys, or click on the destination. Because the cell selector is not anchored at this point, you do not have to press the Esc key before you begin pointing. After you define

FIGURE 3-8.
Use this worksheet to experiment with the Edit Move command.

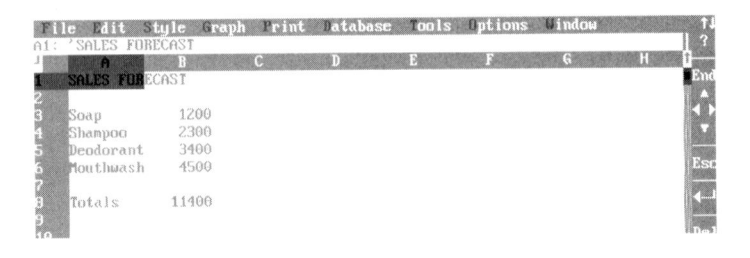

FIGURE 3-9.
The Edit Move command lets you move the contents of cells and blocks.

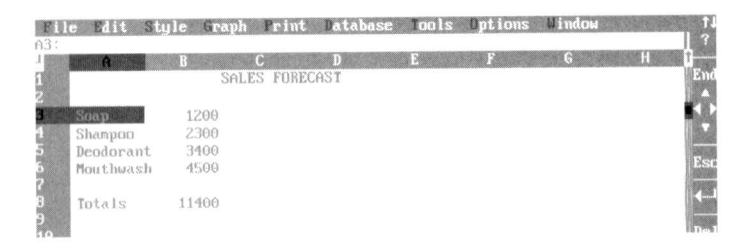

the destination block, press the Enter key. The contents of the source block moves from the original location to the destination you specified.

An example of moving the contents of a single cell

This example uses the worksheet shown in Figure 3-8 to demonstrate the Edit Move command. Suppose you want to move the label *SALES FORECAST* from cell A1 to cell C1. To do so, move the cell selector to cell A1 and choose the Edit Move command. When you see the prompt *Source block of cells: A1..A1* press the Enter key to accept the current cell as the source block. When you see the next prompt *Destination for cells: A1*, press the the Right direction key two times to point to cell C1 (or type the reference C1), and then press the Enter key. Quattro Pro moves the label from cell A1 to cell C1. Figure 3-9 shows the result. Following these same steps, you can also use the Edit Move command to move values and formulas.

An example of moving more than one cell

Quattro Pro's Edit Move command also allows you to move the contents of a block of cells of any size. For example, suppose you want to move the contents of the block A3..B8 as shown in Figure 3-9 to block C3..D8. First, move the cell selector to cell A3 (one of the endpoints of the block you want to move), and then choose the Edit Move command. When Quattro Pro prompts you for the source

FIGURE 3-10.
You can use the Edit Move command to move blocks of cells.

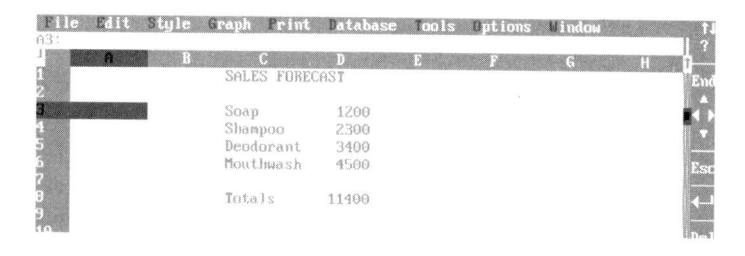

block, define the block and press Enter. When Quattro Pro prompts you for the destination block, define it either by pointing to block C3..D8 or by pointing to the single cell C3. Then press the Enter key to complete the move. Figure 3-10 shows the result.

When you are moving a block of cells in a worksheet, you do not have to specify the full dimensions of the destination block. Because the size and shape of the destination block will be identical to the size and shape of the source block, you need only identify the cell in the upper-left corner of the destination block. Quattro Pro then moves the entries from the source block into the cell you identify and into the cells below it and to its right. Of course, you can identify the entire destination block if you prefer.

A closer look at moving entries

The Edit Move command moves both the contents and the formats of the cells in the source block to the cells in the destination block. After you use the Edit Move command, all the cells in the source block are blank and unformatted. On the other hand, the cells in the destination block include the contents of the cells in the source block, along with any formats that were assigned to those cells.

If the cells in the destination block contain entries or have been assigned formats, Quattro Pro overwrites those entries and assigns new formats when performing the move, which can cause some problems if you are not careful. You might need to use the Edit Insert Rows or Edit Insert Columns command to insert a few blank rows or columns at the destination before you choose the Edit Move command. If you take this precaution, you will avoid overwriting information that is already contained in the worksheet.

How moving entries affects references

When you use the Edit Move command to move the contents of a cell or block, any formula that refers to a cell in the source block is adjusted to account for the new location of that cell. For example, suppose cell B5 in your worksheet contains the formula 1900+A2. After you move the contents of cell A2 to cell E1, this formula is changed to 1900+E1. On the other hand, when you use the Edit Move command to move a formula that contains cell references, that formula or function does not change. For example, if you move the formula in cell B5 in a worksheet you are constructing to cell B4, the formula in cell B4 would still be 1900+A2.

A potential problem with moving entries

As mentioned earlier, when you move a cell or block of cells, Quattro Pro overwrites the cell or cells in the destination block. For this reason, you'll have a problem if you move an entry into a cell that is referenced by a formula elsewhere in the worksheet. For example, suppose you use the Edit Move command to move the contents of cell B6 (or any other cell) to cell C6, in a worksheet you're constructing. After using the Edit Copy command, you see that all the formulas in the worksheet that depend on cell C6 (either directly or indirectly) return the value ERR. This problem occurs because you replaced the contents of cell C6 with the contents of cell B6. Because the formulas that depend on cell C6 cannot locate the original contents of cell C6, the references to cell C6 in those cells change to ERR. This problem arises whenever you move the contents of one cell into a cell that is referenced by a formula or function.

How moving entries affects block names

If you move the contents of a cell that has been assigned a name, that name moves with the contents of the cell. For example, suppose you have assigned the name TITLE to cell A1. If you move the contents of cell A1 to cell C1, the name TITLE refers to cell C1.

If the cell that contains the entry you want to move is at one of the corners of a named block, Quattro changes the definition of the named block to adjust for the move. For example, suppose the block A1..B2 of your worksheet has been assigned the name TEST. If you move the contents of cell A1 to cell C1, the block name TEST then refers to the block C1..B2. As you can see, moving the corner cell of a named block means it no longer refers to the correct block.

If the destination block you specify has been assigned a block name, or is one of the corner cells of a named block, the move destroys the block name. For example, suppose you assigned the block name TEST to the block C6..C9 in a worksheet. If you move the contents of cell B6 to cell C6, the block name TEST no longer applies to a block in the worksheet. Although the name TEST continues to exist, it does not apply to any cells.

Copying cell entries

The Edit Copy command lets you copy the contents of any cell or block of cells to other cells in the same worksheet. The difference between copying and moving is that with copying, the block remains in its original position and a copy is inserted in the destination block. Because the process of copying an entry or a block of entries can be tricky, the following sections discuss one at a time the different methods for copying. First, you'll look at various combinations of sources and destinations by copying simple values and labels. Then, you'll learn how Quattro Pro copies formulas.

Basics of copying

To copy the contents of one block to another, choose the Edit Copy command. Quattro Pro displays the prompt *Source block of cells* in the input line, followed by a block reference to the current cell. Press the Enter key to accept the default and use the current cell as the source block. Alternatively, press the direction keys to expand the default block, press the Esc key and point to a different source block, or type a different block reference, and then press the Enter key.

Next, Quattro displays the prompt *Destination for cells* followed by the address of the cell selector. Press the Enter key to accept the current cell as the destination. Or, type the address of the cell or block to which you want to copy, use the direction keys to point to that block, or click on that block, and then press the Enter key. Because the cell selector is not anchored, you do not have to press the Esc key before you point.

When you are copying a block of cells, you do not have to specify the full dimensions of the destination block. Because the size and shape of the destination block will be identical to the size and shape of the source block, you need only identify the cell in the upper-left corner of the destination block. Quattro Pro then copies the entries from the source block into the cell you identify and into the cells below it and to its right. Of course, you can identify the entire destination block if you prefer.

A simple copy

Suppose you want to copy the dashed line label (- - - - - -) from cell B6 (as shown in Figure 3-11) to cell B9 (as shown in Figure 3-12). First, move the cell selector to cell B6 and choose the Edit Copy command. When Quattro Pro prompts you for

FIGURE 3-11.
The Edit Copy command lets you copy an entry from one cell to another.

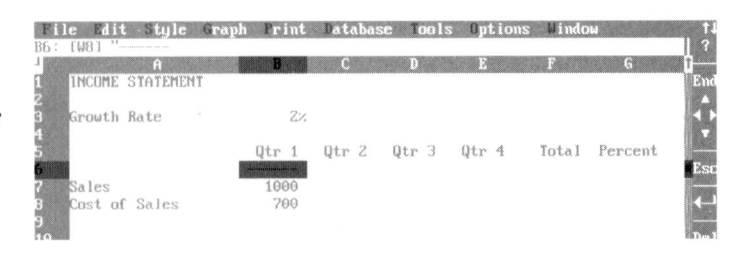

FIGURE 3-12.
This is what the worksheet looks like after using the Edit Copy command.

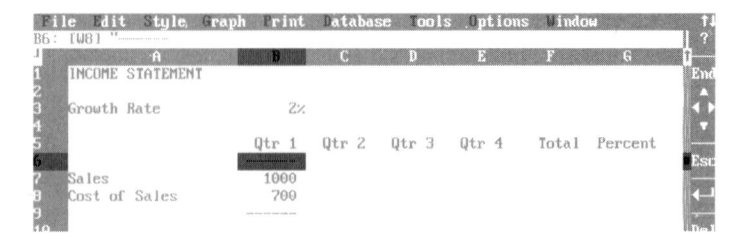

the source block in the input line, press the Enter key to accept the default. When Quattro Pro prompts you for the destination block, point to cell B9, or type *B9*, and then press the Enter key. Quattro Pro copies the label from cell B6 to cell B9, as shown in Figure 3-12. As you can see, Quattro Pro has placed an exact copy of the label from cell B6 into cell B9.

You can also use the Edit Copy command to copy a value. In fact, you copy values in the same way that you copy labels: Choose the Edit Copy command, define the source block, press the Enter key, define the destination block, and then press the Enter key again. When you copy an entry from a cell that has been assigned a format, Quattro Pro also copies that format to the destination block.

In the preceding example, both the source block and the destination block are single cells. You can choose from six other possible combinations, however, of source and destination blocks. Table 3-1 summarizes these combinations.

Source block	Destination block	Example
Single cell	Single cell	A1 to B1
Single cell	Multiple cells	A1 to B1..E1
Single row	Single row	A1..E1 to A2..E2
Single column	Single column	A1..A5 to B1..B5
Single row	Multiple rows	A1..E1 to A2..E5
Single column	Multiple columns	A1..A5 to B1..E5
Rectangular block	Rectangular block	A1..E5 to H1..L5

TABLE 3-1. *Use the Edit Copy command to copy from different types of source blocks to different types of destination blocks.*

Copying entries from one cell to more than one cell

Use the Edit Copy command to copy the contents of a single cell to several cells. For example, suppose you want to copy the contents of cell B6, shown in Figure 3-12, to cells C6..G6 in order to form a line. To do so, move the cell selector to cell B6, choose the Edit Copy command, and then press the Enter key to define cell B6 as the source block. When Quattro Pro asks for the destination block, point to cell C6, press the period (.) key to anchor the cell selector, and then press the Right direction key four times to select block C6..G6. Press the Enter key, and Quattro Pro copies the label from cell B6 into each of the cells in the block C6..G6.

Copying from a single row to a single row

The Edit Copy command also copies cell entries from one row to another or information to a new block within that row. Suppose, for example, you want to copy the labels you copied in the previous example from block C6..F6 into block C9..F9. Move the cell selector to cell C6, choose the Edit Copy command, press the Right direction key three times to highlight C6..F6, and then press the Enter key to define C6..F6 as the source block. When Quattro Pro prompts you for the destination block, move the cell selector to cell C9 and press the Enter key. Again, when you are copying a block of cells in a worksheet, you need only identify the upper-left corner of the destination block; in this case, cell C9.

Copying from a single column to a single column

Copy information from one column to another or to a new block within that column by using the same technique used for copying information from one row to another. For example, suppose you want to copy the entries in block A7..A10 into cells A15..A18. Move the cell selector to cell A7, choose the Edit Copy command, and then press the Down direction key three times to select cells A7..A10 as the source block. After you press the Enter key, define the destination block by pointing to cell A15 (the upper-left cell in the block) and pressing the Enter key. Quattro Pro copies the entries from cells A7..A10 into cells A15..A18.

Copying from a single row to multiple rows

The Edit Copy command copies the entries from a single row into a span of two or more rows. To do so, choose the Edit Copy command, specify the source block, and then press the Enter key. Then, specify a block that spans two or more rows as the destination block and press the Enter key; you can select the entire block that will be filled by the copy, or only the leftmost cell in each row of the block. You'll see an example of this kind of row-to-row copy below in "Copying Formulas and Functions."

Copying from a single column to multiple columns

Copy information from a single column into multiple columns in the same way that you copy from a single row into multiple rows. First, choose the Edit Copy command, specify the source block, and then press the Enter key. Then, select a block that spans two or more columns as the destination block and press the Enter key; you can select the entire block that will be filled by the copy or only the top cell in each column of the block. Again, you will see an example of this kind of column-to-column copying in "Copying Formulas and Functions."

Copying from a block to a block

The Edit Copy command also copies a two-dimensional block into another block. For example, suppose you want to copy the entries in block B5..E6 into B13..E14. To do so, move the cell selector to cell B5, choose the Edit Copy command, select block B5..E6, and then press the Enter key to define the source block. When Quattro Pro prompts you for the destination block, you need only specify the upper-left cell of the destination block; for this example, cell B13. Press the Enter key, and Quattro Pro copies the entries in cells B5..E6 into cells B13..E14.

Copying formulas and functions

In addition to labels and values, Quattro Pro lets you copy formulas and functions. Because formulas and functions usually contain cell references, copying these entries is a more complex process than copying values and labels. When you copy a formula that contains a cell reference, Quattro Pro must decide whether to maintain all the cell references exactly as they appear in the original formula, or adjust the cell references to reflect the new location of the formula.

As explained in Chapter 1, "Quattro Pro Basics," Quattro Pro recognizes three types of cell references: relative, absolute, and mixed. How Quattro Pro handles the cell references in the formulas you copy depends on what types of references those formulas use. An understanding of these different types of references is crucial to understanding how Quattro copies formulas and functions. You'll learn more about functions in Chapter 4, "Functions."

Relative references

Quattro's default reference type is a relative reference. Nearly all of the references used so far in this book have been relative references. For example, the formula +B3+2 includes a relative reference to cell B3. When you copy a formula that contains a relative reference, the new formula no longer refers to the same cell as the original formula does. Instead, Quattro adjusts the cell reference in the new formula to reflect its new position relative to the worksheet. The copy of the formula refers to the same relative cell but not to the same absolute cell. You'll see how this works in the example that follows.

An example of copying formulas that include relative references. Quattro Pro's ability to adjust the relative references used in formulas has some powerful applications. Suppose, for example, that you want to enter the following formulas in block B10..F10 of a worksheet:

    B10   +B7-B8

    C10   +C7-C8

    D10   +D7-D8

    E10   +E7-E8

    F10   +F7-F8

Notice that the formulas have some similarity. In each cell, the formula subtracts the value in the cell two rows above it from the value in the cell three rows above the cell containing the formula. You can simply enter one of the formulas and then copy the formula to the other cells. To do so, enter the formula +B7-B8 into cell B10, choose the Edit Copy command, press the Enter key to designate cell B10 as the source block, designate block C10..F10 as the destination block, and then press the Enter key.

Because the formula in cell B10 contains relative references to cells B7 and B8, the formulas in cells C10..F10 would differ from the formula in cell B10. Cell C10 would contain the formula +C7-C8, cell D10 would contain the formula +D7-D8, cell E10 would contain the formula +E7-E8, and cell F10 would contain the formula +F7-F8. Because the references to cells B7 and B8 in cell B10 are relative, Quattro Pro adjusts the formulas when performing the copy.

Absolute references

Most of the time, you'll want to use relative references in your formulas and functions. You'll encounter times, however, when you will not want the cell references in a formula to change as you copy the formula. In those situations, you'll need to use absolute references. Unlike relative references, which change as you copy them, absolute references are fixed; they do not change as they're copied.

To define an absolute reference, include a dollar sign ($) in front of the column and row coordinates of the cell reference. For example, to enter an absolute reference to cell A1 in cell A2, type *+$A$1*. If you copy this formula from cell A2 to cell B2, the result of the copy is the formula +$A$1, the same formula that is in cell A2. Because the reference to cell A1 is an absolute reference, it does not change when you copy it.

Defining absolute references. In absolute references, you can either type the dollar signs manually or use the [Abs] key (F4) to insert them. You can also use the [Abs] key to change any reference to an absolute reference while you are pointing to a cell to define a reference, typing a reference, or editing a formula that contains a reference.

For example, suppose you want to enter an absolute reference to cell A1 in cell A2. Move the cell selector to cell A2, type +, and point to cell A1. Quattro Pro displays the formula +A1 on the input line. Press the [Abs] key (F4) to change the relative reference +A1 to the absolute reference +$A$1. You can also use the [Abs] key while you type an entry. To do so, type the entry and then press the [Abs] key to change the relative reference to an absolute reference. You can also use the [Abs] key while editing an entry. Move the cell selector to the cell that contains the entry you want to edit, and then press the [Edit] key (F2) to enter EDIT mode. Then, position the cursor under the reference you want to change (or under the character following that reference), and then press the [Abs] key.

Mixed references

In addition to relative and absolute references, Quattro Pro offers mixed references, which contain a mix of relative and absolute references. Either the column or the row portion of a mixed reference is absolute; the other portion is relative. When you copy a mixed reference, the absolute portion of the reference remains constant, and the relative portion changes.

Like absolute references, mixed references are designated by dollar signs. The portion of a mixed reference that is preceded by a dollar sign is the absolute portion. For example, the reference +$A1 is a mixed reference that will always refer to column A, no matter where it is copied. If you enter this formula in cell A2, and then copy it into cell B3, the formula reads +$A2. If you then copy the formula into cell D4, it reads +$A3. Notice that as you copy the formula around the worksheet, the column portion of the reference remains fixed and the row portion is adjusted relative to the position of the copy. If you place a dollar sign in front of the row portion of the mixed reference, the row portion of the entry remains fixed.

Defining mixed references. Use the same techniques to define mixed references that you use to define absolute references. You can either type dollar signs in the appropriate places while you are typing the formula, or use the [Abs] key (F4). To define a mixed reference using the [Abs] key, however, you have to press [Abs] two or three times. The first time you press the [Abs] key, the reference becomes absolute. Pressing the [Abs] key again makes the row portion of the entry absolute and the column portion relative. Pressing the [Abs] key a third time makes the column portion of the entry absolute and the row portion relative. Pressing the [Abs] key a fourth time makes the reference relative again. For example, suppose you are entering the formula +A1 into cell A2. Pressing the [Abs] key one time changes the formula to +$A$1. Pressing the [Abs] key a second time changes the reference to +A$1. Pressing the [Abs] key a third time changes it to +$A1.

Making special copies

Quattro Pro offers two commands that allow you to make special kinds of copies: Edit Values, which converts formulas to their current values as it copies them, and Edit Transpose, which copies a row of entries into a column or a column of entries into a row.

Using the Edit Values command to copy formula values

The Edit Values command copies the current values of formulas, not the formulas themselves. In every other way, the Edit Values command is identical to the Edit Copy command.

To copy the current values of the formulas in a block, choose the Edit Values command. Quattro Pro displays the prompt *Source block of cells* in the input line, followed by a block reference to the current cell. Press the Enter key to accept the default and use the current cell as the source block. Alternatively, press the direction keys to expand the default block, press the Esc key and point to a different source block, or type a different source block, and press the Enter key.

Next, Quattro Pro displays the prompt *Destination for cells* followed by the address of the cell selector. Either type the address of the cell or block to which you want to copy, use the direction keys to point to that block, or click on the block. Because the size and shape of the destination block will be identical to the size and shape of the source block, you need only identify the upper-left corner of the destination block. Also, because the cell selector is not anchored, you do not have to press the Esc key before you point. After you have selected the destination block, press the Enter key. You'll notice that the input line for the new entry now displays the value of the formula rather than the formula itself.

An example of copying the current value of a formula

Suppose you want to copy the current value of a formula in cell B10 into cell C10. Cell B10 contains the formula +5+10. First, move the cell selector to cell B10 and choose the Edit Values command. When you see the prompt *Source block of cells: B10..B10* in the input line, press the Enter key to designate this block as the source block. Next, Quattro Pro displays the prompt *Destination for cells: B10*. To define the destination block, press the Right direction key to select cell C10, and then press the Enter key. The value of the formula in the cell B10 (15) will now appear in cell C10, and in the input line when you move the cell selector to cell C10.

A closer look at the Edit Values command

The Edit Values command works exactly like the Edit Copy command when you use it on values or labels. If you include any values or labels in the source block of the Edit Values command, Quattro Pro simply copies those entries into the appropriate cell of the destination block. Like the Edit Copy command, the Edit Values command overwrites any existing entries in the destination block.

Uses for the Edit Values command

You can find practical uses for the Edit Values command, such as freezing the current results of a formula so that you can compare those results to the same formula's updated results. After you freeze the results in the new location, you can change certain key assumptions, recalculate the worksheet, and then compare the new results with the frozen results.

Because formulas require more memory than do values and labels, you can save memory by using the Edit Values command to convert formulas to values once you no longer need to update them. To do so, choose the Edit Values command and specify identical source and destination blocks. Quattro Pro replaces the formulas in the specified block with their current values. Because this technique destroys the formulas in the destination block, you should be careful when you use it.

Using Edit Transpose to rotate a block as you copy it

The Edit Transpose command lets you rotate a block 90 degrees as you copy it; that is, it lets you copy the information from a row into a column or a column into a row.

When you choose the Edit Transpose command, Quattro Pro displays the prompt *Source block of cells* in the input line, followed by a block reference to the current cell. Press the Enter key to accept the default and use the current cell as the source block. Alternatively, press the direction keys to expand the default block, press the Esc key and point to a different source block, or type a different block reference, and then press the Enter key.

Next, Quattro Pro displays the prompt *Destination for cells*, followed by the address of the cell selector. Either type the address of the cell or block to which you want to copy, or point to that block. Because the size and shape of the destination block will be determined by the size and shape of the source block, you need only identify the upper-left corner of the destination. Also, because the cell selector is not anchored, you do not have to press the Esc key before you point. After you select the destination block, press the Enter key.

An example of rotating a block

Suppose you began creating a worksheet by entering the labels JAN, FEB, MAR, and so forth in cells A3..A14, as shown in Figure 3-13. Now, suppose you decide that you would rather place these entries across row 3 of the worksheet in cells A3..L3. First, move the cell selector to cell A3 and choose the Edit Transpose command. When you see the prompt *Source block of cells: A3..A3* in the input line, press the Down direction key 11 times to select the block A3..A14, and then press the Enter key. Quattro Pro then displays the prompt *Destination for cells*, followed by the address of the current cell. Point to cell A3, then press the Enter key. Quattro Pro copies the entries in the block A3..A14 to the block A3..L3, as shown in Figure 3-14. Quattro Pro copied the entry from the first cell in the source block (A3) to the first cell in the destination block (A3), the entry from the second cell in the source block (A4) to the second cell in the destination block (B3), and so forth. Because you specified a single column as the source block, Quattro Pro copied the entries into a single row.

A closer look at the Edit Transpose command

As you can see, the Edit Transpose command did not erase the entries in the source block after it transposed them. Because the Edit Transpose command is a special form of the Edit Copy command, Quattro Pro does not erase the entries in its source block. If you want to remove the entries in the source block after they have been transposed, use the Edit Erase Block command to erase them.

You can also use the Edit Transpose command to transpose a row of entries into a column. Transposing a single row of entries always copies those entries into a single column.

Transposing formulas

Although you'll usually use the Edit Transpose command to transpose a single row or column of entries, you can also use it to transpose an entire block of cells that contains several rows and several columns. When you do this, Quattro Pro copies the entries from the first row of the source block into the first column of the destination block, the entries from the second row of the source block into the second column of the destination block, and so forth.

FIGURE 3-13.
This is what the worksheet looks like before the Edit Transpose command.

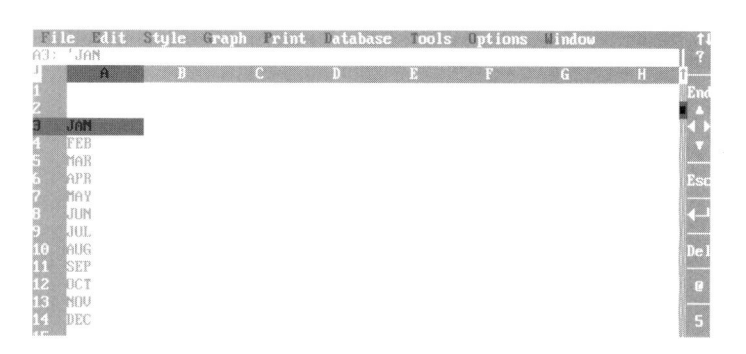

FIGURE 3-14.
The Edit Transpose command allows you to copy the information from a row into a column or from a column into a row.

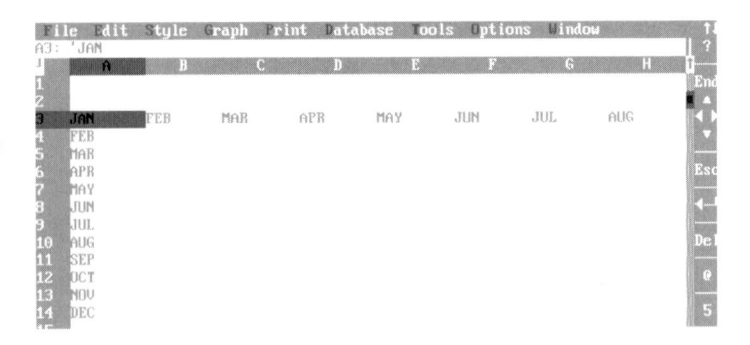

You can use the Edit Transpose command to transpose blocks whose cells contain formulas, but this is generally not a good idea. If the formula you transpose contains relative references, Quattro Pro adjusts the references exactly as if you had copied them using the Edit Copy command. The references will not be transposed, however, so they will probably not refer to the cells to which you want them to refer. If the formulas contain absolute references, those references will not change when you transpose the block, and your formulas will still refer to the same cells as do the original formulas. In most cases, however, you will still find these results unsatisfactory.

4

Functions

*F*unctions are preconstructed formulas that you can use to perform complex calculations quickly and efficiently. Functions in Quattro Pro are like the function keys on a business calculator; they simplify operations that would be difficult or impossible to perform with conventional formulas. For example, Quattro Pro offers a function called @AVG that lets you calculate the average value of a list of values.

This chapter explains most of Quattro Pro's functions except for date and time functions and database functions. Date and time functions are covered in Chapter 6 and database functions in Chapter 11.

Function basics

All of Quattro Pro's functions have the same basic form: a short, descriptive name that identifies what the function does and, for most functions, one or more arguments that define what the function should act upon. For example, consider the following function:

@SUM(D3..D9)

The function name is @SUM and the argument is (D3..D9). This function tells Quattro Pro to sum, or add, the values in the block D3 to D9.

Function names

The name of a function is usually an abbreviation or an acronym that describes the function's purpose. For example, the function @AVG calculates the average of several values, and the function @FV computes the future value of a stream of cash flows. Quattro Pro function names always begin with the @ character, which tells Quattro Pro that the entry is a function and not a label. If you type SUM(D3..D9) instead of @SUM(D3..D9), for example, Quattro Pro will record your entry as the label 'SUM(D3..D9). So, don't forget the @.

Function arguments

Most Quattro Pro functions require one or more arguments to tell Quattro Pro what the function is to act upon. A function's arguments always follow the function's name and are enclosed in parentheses. For example, the argument to the function @SUM(D3..D9) is the block reference D3..D9. This argument defines the values that should be summed; in this case, the values in cells D3, D4, D5, D6, D7, D8, and D9.

Although most functions require only one argument, some functions require two or more. Separate additional arguments with a comma. For example, the function @ROUND(A3,2) has two arguments; the first (A3) identifies the value you want to round, and the second (2) specifies the number of decimal places to which you want to round the first argument. Notice that the function's two arguments are enclosed in a single set of parentheses and are separated by a comma.

Several of Quattro Pro's financial functions have both required arguments and optional arguments. To clearly identify optional arguments, this book shows them enclosed in angle brackets <> in the function syntax. For example, later in this chapter the @PVAL function syntax is shown as follows:

@PVAL(RATE,TERM,PAYMENT,<FUTURE VALUE>,<TYPE>)

A few Quattro Pro functions require no argument at all. For example, the function @PI, which returns the value pi, requires no argument; nor does the function @NOW, which returns the values for the current date and time.

Types of function arguments

Function arguments can be literal values, references to cells or blocks, block names, formulas, other functions, strings and labels, or conditional tests. For example, in the function @ROUND (A3,2), the first argument is a cell reference and the second argument is a literal value. The single argument of the function @SQRT(9) is the literal value 9. Many of the examples in this chapter use literal values as function arguments to make the arguments easier for you to understand. In your actual worksheets, you'll probably use cell references more often as arguments.

Block names can be useful arguments to Quattro Pro functions. For instance, suppose that you give the name SALES to the block D3..D9 in a worksheet and that you want to sum the values in that block. You can use the function @SUM(SALES) to sum the values in those cells. Of course, you can also use the function @SUM(D3..D9) to compute the sum.

When a function uses a block reference as an argument, the block reference should be absolute. For example, the function @SUM($D$3..$D$9) contains an absolute reference to the block D3..D9. Make a block name reference absolute by putting a dollar sign in front of it; for example, @SUM($SALES). The reason for using absolute rather than relative references in a function is the same as for any other formula: When the function is copied, Quattro Pro will not adjust the references.

Although you will usually use literal values and references to cells or blocks as the arguments for your functions, you can also use formulas and other functions as arguments. For example, consider the following @INT function:

@INT(@SQRT(10))

This function uses another function, @SQRT, as its argument. The @INT function returns the integer portion of the square root of 10, which is 3. The technique of using one function as the argument to another function is called nesting.

Although most functions operate on values, a few functions, called string functions, operate on strings and labels. For example, the single argument to the function @UPPER (which converts a string to all uppercase letters) must be a reference to a cell that contains a label, or a formula or function that returns a string. Later in this chapter, you'll find more information about this topic in "String Functions."

Quattro Pro uses one other type of argument: a conditional test. The first argument to the @IF function, for example, must be a conditional test. Later in this chapter, "Logical Functions" explains the uses of conditional tests and the @IF function.

Entering functions in a worksheet

You can enter functions in a worksheet cell just like labels, numbers, or formulas: Select the cell, type the entry, and then press the Enter key. If you type a function name incorrectly, omit an argument, include an extra argument, or include an argument that is not acceptable, Quattro Pro displays an error message.

You can also enter functions by selecting them from a list. Selecting functions from the function list is convenient if you cannot remember the name for a function. To display a list of functions to choose from, press the Alt-F3 keys. Then use the direction keys or mouse to select the function you want to insert and press Enter. Quattro Pro adds the function name to the input line, where you can enter any arguments for the function. After you've entered the arguments, press Enter to lock in and perform the function.

Whenever a function uses a block reference as an argument, you can specify the block as you do in formulas by either typing the block reference or selecting the block with the direction keys or the mouse. "Quattro Pro Commands" in Chapter 1 describes how to specify a block of cells.

Mathematical functions

Mathematical functions perform common mathematical computations. Quattro Pro has 19 mathematical functions: @ABS, @MOD, @RAND, @SQRT, @ROUND, @INT, @PI, @RADIANS, @DEGREES, @SIN, @COS, @TAN, @ASIN, @ACOS, @ATAN, @ATAN2, @LOG, @LN, and @EXP. The arguments to these functions must be values. In turn, these functions all return values.

The @ABS function

The @ABS function returns the absolute (positive) value of the number specified by its argument. The form of this function is shown below:

@ABS(value)

For example, @ABS(-37) returns the value 37. @ABS(37) also returns the value 37. If cell C3 contains the value -37 or the value 37, @ABS(C3) also returns the value 37.

The @MOD function

The @MOD function computes the modulus, or remainder, that results from dividing one value by another. The form of this function is shown below:

@MOD(dividend,divisor)

The result of this function is the remainder that results from dividing *dividend* by *divisor*. For example, 4 divided by 2 leaves no remainder, so @MOD(4,2) returns the value 0. Also 5 divided by 2 leaves a remainder of 1, so @MOD(5,2) returns the value 1. Of course, you can also use cell references as arguments. If cell B3 contains the value 5 and cell B4 contains the value 2, @MOD(B3,B4) returns the value 1. @MOD is particularly helpful in calculations that involve dates, as further discussed in Chapter 6, "Dates and Times."

The @RAND function

The @RAND function provides a way to generate random numbers in Quattro Pro worksheets. This function is useful for generating sample data to simulate situations. It takes no arguments and always returns a random value between 0 and 1. Every time you recalculate the worksheet, @RAND returns a new value.

The @SQRT function

Quattro Pro's @SQRT function computes the square root of the value referred to by its argument. The form of this function is as follows:

@SQRT(value)

The result of the function is the square root of *value*. For example, the function @SQRT(100) returns the value 10. If cell C3 contains the value 16, @SQRT(C3) returns the value 4. Although the @SQRT function computes square roots, Quattro Pro does not offer functions to compute other roots. You can use the ^ operator, however, to compute any root of a number. For example, the formula 8^(1/3) returns the value 2, the cube root of 8.

The @ROUND function

The @ROUND function rounds the value specified by its first argument to the number of decimal places specified by its second argument. The form of this function is shown below:

@ROUND(value,number of decimal places)

The *number of decimal places* is a number from -15 to 15 that specifies the number of decimal places to which the *value* argument should be rounded. The @ROUND function follows the same rules about rounding that one learns in grade school: Digits greater than or equal to 5 are rounded up (away from 0), and digits less than 5 are rounded down (toward 0). For example, @ROUND(3451.8574,3) returns the value 3451.857, @ROUND(3451.8574,2) returns the value 3451.86, and @ROUND(3451.8574,1) returns the value 3451.9.

Although the *number of decimal places* argument is usually positive, it can be negative. A negative *number of decimal places* argument merely rounds to the left of the decimal point. For example, the function @ROUND(3451.8574,-2) returns the value 3500. You can also use the @ROUND function to round negative numbers. For instance, the function @ROUND(-3451.8574,2) returns the value -3451.86.

The @INT function

Like the @ROUND function, the @INT function adjusts the number of decimal places in a value. Unlike @ROUND, which rounds values to the number of decimal places you specify, @INT simply truncates decimal values into integers. The form of this function is as follows:

@INT(value)

The result of the function is the integer portion of *value*. For example, the function @INT(3451.8574) returns the integer portion of the argument value, 3451. You can also use the @INT function to remove the decimals from negative values. For example, the function @INT(-3451.8574) returns the value -3451.

Using the @ROUND function to round a value to 0 decimal places is different from using the @INT function to extract the integer portion of a value. The @ROUND function rounds the value to the nearest integer, but the @INT function simply discards the decimal portion of the value and returns its integer portion. For example, the result of the function @ROUND(3451.8574,0) is 3452, but the result of the function @INT(3451.8574) is 3451.

Trigonometric functions: @PI, @RADIANS, @DEGREES, @SIN, @COS, @TAN, @ASIN, @ACOS, @ATAN, @ATAN2

Trigonometric functions allow you to compute common trigonometric values, such as the sine or cosine of an angle. Ten functions fall in this group: @PI, @RADIANS, @DEGREES, @SIN, @COS, @TAN, @ASIN, @ACOS, @ATAN, and @ATAN2.

The @PI function

The most basic trigonometric function is @PI, which returns the value of the constant pi, accurate to 12 decimal places. The form of this function is simply @PI. Whenever you enter this function in a cell, it returns the value 3.1415926535898.

The @RADIANS and @DEGREES functions

Quattro Pro's @RADIANS and @DEGREES functions allow you to convert angle measurements from degrees to radians and from radians to degrees. The forms of these functions are shown below:

@RADIANS(angle in degrees)
@DEGREES(angle in radians)

The single argument, *angle in degrees* or *angle in radians*, is the measure of an angle you want to convert. @RADIANS converts an angle measurement from degrees to radians, and @DEGREES converts an angle measurement from radians to degrees. The function @RADIANS(180) returns the value 3.141593, which is the radian measure of a 180-degree angle. The function @DEGREES(3.141593) returns the value 180, which is the degrees measure of a 3.141593-radian angle.

The @SIN, @COS, and @TAN functions

The @SIN, @COS, and @TAN functions compute the basic trigonometric values sine, cosine, and tangent. The forms of these functions are as follows:

@SIN(angle)

@COS(angle)

@TAN(angle)

The argument, *angle*, is the measure of an angle (in radians) whose sine, cosine, or tangent you want Quattro Pro to compute. This angle measurement must be stated in radians, and not in degrees. (Use the @RADIANS function to convert an angle to radians.) For example, suppose you want to construct a worksheet to calculate the sine, cosine, and tangent of the value 1.047198, which is the radian measure of a 60-degree angle. The function @SIN(1.047198) returns the value 0.866026, which is the sine of a 60-degree angle. The function @COS(1.047198) returns the value 0.5, which is the cosine of a 60-degree angle. Finally, the function @TAN(1.047198), returns the value 1.732053, which is the tangent of a 60-degree angle.

Inverse trigonometric functions: @ASIN, @ACOS, @ATAN, and @ATAN2

As you have just seen, the @SIN, @COS, and @TAN functions return the sine, cosine, and tangent of the angles specified by their arguments. Quattro Pro also features four functions that have the opposite effect: They return the measurement of an angle (in radians), given its sine, cosine, or tangent. These four functions—@ASIN, @ACOS, @ATAN, and @ATAN2—are called arc functions. For example, the function @ASIN(.866026) returns the value 1.047199, the measurement of the angle (in radians) whose sine equals the function's argument. In the same manner, the function @ACOS(.866026) returns the value .523598, the angle whose cosine equals the function's argument. Finally, the function @ATAN(.866026) returns the value .713725, the angle whose tangent is equal to the function's argument.

The @ATAN2 function computes a four-quadrant arctangent. Like the other three arc functions, this function returns an angle value measured in radians. Unlike the other arc functions, however, the @ATAN2 function requires two arguments. The function has the following form:

@ATAN2(x-coordinate,y-coordinate)

The function's arguments specify the absolute position of a point in relation to the x and y axes. For example, suppose you want to find the four-quadrant arctangent defined by a point with an x-coordinate of 2 and a y-coordinate of -1. Use the function @ATAN2(2,-1), which returns the value -0.46365.

Logarithmic functions: @LOG, @LN, and @EXP

Quattro Pro's logarithmic functions, @LOG, @LN, and @EXP, make it easy to work with base 10 and natural logarithms in Quattro Pro worksheets. These functions are useful to scientists, engineers, and others who work with logarithms.

The @LOG function

Quattro Pro's @LOG function computes the base 10 logarithm of a value, which is the power of 10 that equals that value. For instance, because 10^3 equals 1000, the base 10 logarithm of 1000 is 3. The form of the @LOG function is shown below:

@LOG(value)

The result of this function is the base 10 log of *value*. For example, the function @LOG(234) returns the value 2.369216.

The @LN function

Quattro Pro's @LN function calculates the natural logarithm of a value. The natural (base *e*) logarithm of a value is the power of the constant *e* (2.71828) that equals the value. This function's form is shown below:

@LN(value)

The result of this function is the natural logarithm of *value*. For example, the function @LN(234) returns the natural logarithm of the value 234, which is 5.455321.

The @EXP function

Quattro Pro's @EXP function raises the constant *e* (2.71828) to the power specified by its argument, and is the inverse of the @LN function. The form of this function is as follows:

@EXP(value)

The result of this function is equal to the constant *e* raised to the power specified by *value*. For example, the function @EXP(5.455321) returns the value 234, which is the value of *e* raised to the 5.455321 power.

Statistical functions

Quattro Pro's 10 statistical functions allow you to calculate statistics, such as sums, averages, and standard deviations, using the values in your worksheets. These functions are: @SUM, @SUMPRODUCT, @COUNT, @AVG, @MIN, @MAX, @STD, @STDS, @VAR, and @VARS.

The form of statistical functions

All of Quattro Pro's 10 statistical functions have the general form @FUNCTION(list), where *list* is a list of cell and block references that identify the cells that contain the values for which you want to compute statistics. To calculate statistics on a block of adjacent cells, you would enter the address of that block as the argument to the function. For example, to sum the values in cells A1 through A4, enter the function @SUM(A1..A4) in a cell. The argument A1..A4 tells the function to sum the values in cells A1, A2, A3, and A4. You'll use this form of Quattro Pro's statistical functions most often.

Instead of using a block reference, you can list as a separate argument each of the cells to which you want the function to refer. For example, use the function @SUM(A1,A2,A3,A4) to sum the values in cells A1..A4. You can even use a mixture of block and cell references as the arguments to a statistical function. For instance, the functions @SUM(A1..A3,A4) and @SUM(A1,A2..A4) return the same result as the function @SUM(A1..A4). Generally, you use multiple arguments only to calculate statistics on the values in discontinuous blocks. For example, use the function @SUM(A1,B2,C3) to sum the values in cells A1, B2, and C3.

The @SUM function

Quattro Pro's @SUM function sums, or adds, a list of values. This function offers an alternative to the + operator, which is used in conventional formulas to add values. This function's form is shown below:

@SUM(list)

The argument *list* is the list of cells whose values you want to sum. The result of the function is the sum of the values in the list. @SUM provides a much more efficient means of adding values than does the familiar + operator. For example, use the following formula to total the values in the block C5..C14:

+C5+C6+C7+C8+C9+C10+C11+C12+C13+C14

On the other hand, you can also enter the function @SUM(C5..C14). As you can see, the function is much shorter and less cumbersome than the formula.

In addition to saving you time, the @SUM function offers one other significant advantage over the + operator. As explained in "Inserting Rows and Columns" in Chapter 3, when you insert or delete rows or columns from within the block specified by a function, the block shrinks or grows to adjust for the insertion or deletion. For example, suppose you use the Edit Insert Rows command to insert a new row between rows 13 and 14 in a worksheet with the function @SUM (C5..C14). As a result of the insertion, the @SUM function changes to @SUM (C5..C15); the argument block expands to include the new cell.

The argument block of a @SUM function can refer to both cells that contain labels and cells that contain values. If the function's argument block includes a cell that contains a label, that cell is assigned the value 0. For that reason, including label cells in the argument block of a @SUM function will not affect the @SUM function's result.

TIP: *To take advantage of the @SUM function's flexibility, always include an extra cell at either end of the @SUM function's argument block. Then, if you insert a row immediately below the last item in the list or immediately above the first item in the list, the @SUM function's argument block adapts to the change. Usually, the cells at either end of the block contain labels.*

The @SUMPRODUCT function

The @SUMPRODUCT function multiplies the values in one block by the values in a second block and then sums the products. This function's form is shown below:

@SUMPRODUCT(block1,block2)

The *block1* and *block2* arguments are two worksheet blocks whose values you want to multiply together. You then want to sum their products. Suppose, for example, that you want to multiply block A1..A5 by the block B1..B5 as shown in Figure 4-1. To do so, use the function @SUMPRODUCT(A1..A5,B1..B5), which returns the result 30.

The @SUMPRODUCT function as used in the worksheet shown in Figure 4-1 multiplies A1 by B1, A2 by B2, A3 by B3, A4 by B4, and A5 by B5 and then sums these products. The @SUMPRODUCT function shown in Figure 4-1, therefore, is equivalent to the following formula:

(A1*B1)+(A2*B2)+(A3*B3)+(A4*B4)+(A5*B5)

FIGURE 4-1.
You can use the @SUMPRODUCT function to multiply two worksheet blocks and display the sum of their products.

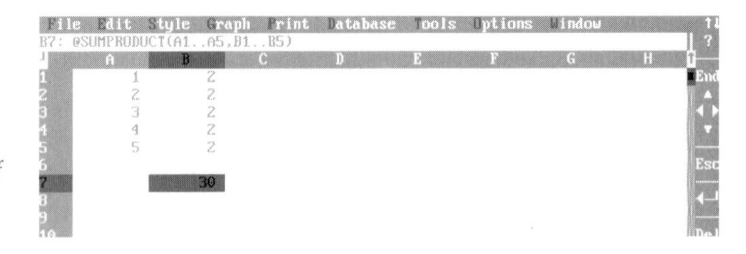

The @COUNT function

The @COUNT function counts the number of nonblank cells in the block specified by its argument. The form of this function is as follows:

@COUNT(list)

The *list* argument is the list of cells whose nonblank cells you want to count. The result of this function is the number of nonblank cells in the list. For example, the function @COUNT(C5..C14) counts the number of entries in block C5..C14. If all the cells in this 10-cell block contain entries—either values or labels—this function returns the value 10.

The @COUNT function has one peculiarity that needs explanation: @COUNT always returns the value 1 if the block specified by its argument is a single cell, regardless of whether that cell is blank.

The @AVG function

Quattro Pro's @AVG function computes the average (arithmetic mean) of a list of values. This function's form is as follows:

@AVG(list)

The argument *list* is the list of cells whose values you want to average. The result of this function is the average of the values in the list. The function @AVG computes the average of a list of values in the same way you would: It sums the values in the list and then divides the sum by the number of items in the list. For example, the function @AVG(1,2,3,4,5) computes the average of the values 1, 2, 3, 4, and 5 and returns the value 3. This is the same result you would have obtained by using the formula @SUM(1,2,3,4,5)/@COUNT(1,2,3,4,5).

Be careful not to include any cells that contain labels in the argument block of an @AVG function. If you do, the function's result will be incorrect. When the @AVG function computes the sum of the values in the argument block, it assigns the value 0 to each label in that block. When computing the count of the items in the block, however, the @AVG function treats each label as another item. When the function divides the sum by the count, the count will be too high and the average too low.

The @MIN function

The @MIN function returns the lowest value from the list specified by its argument. The function's form is as follows:

@MIN(list)

The argument *list* is the list of cells whose values you want to analyze. The result of the @MIN function is the lowest value in *list*. For example, the function @MIN(C5..C14) returns the lowest value in the block C5..C14.

When evaluating a @MIN function, Quattro Pro assigns the value 0 to any cell in the argument block that contains a label or string. For this reason, any @MIN function that operates on a block that contains a label or string returns the value 0 (unless that block also contains a negative value).

The @MAX function

The @MAX function returns the highest value from the list specified by its argument. The function's form is as follows:

@MAX(list)

The argument *list* is the list of cells whose values you want to analyze. The result of the @MAX function is the largest value in *list*. For example, the function @MAX(C5..C14) returns the largest value in block C5..C14.

The @STD and @STDS functions

The @STD function computes the population standard deviation of the values in the list specified by its argument. The form of this function is shown below:

@STD(list)

The argument *list* is the list of cells whose values you want to analyze. The result of this function is the population standard deviation of the values in *list*.

The @STDS function computes the sample standard deviation of the values in the list specified by its argument. The form of this function is as follows:

@STDS(list)

The argument *list* is the list of cells or values you want to analyze. The result of the @STDS function is the sample standard deviation of the values in *list*.

As examples of the @STD and @STDS functions, suppose block A1..A10 contains the values 1, 2, 3, 4, 5, 6, 7, 8, 9, and 10. The function @STD(A1..A10) returns the value 2.872281, and the function @STDS(A1..A10) returns the value 3.02765.

The standard deviation of a group of values is a measure of the extent to which the values in that group are dispersed from the mean for that group. In general, a low standard deviation indicates that values in the block are clustered closely about the mean, and a high standard deviation means that the values are widely dispersed. About 68 percent of the individuals in a normally distributed group will be within one standard deviation from the mean, and about 95 percent will be within two standard deviations from the mean.

Typically, you use the @STDS function when you do not have all the values in the population in your list. In effect, the @STDS function estimates the standard deviation of the entire population's values based on a random sample, or subset, of the population's values. (The @STDS function makes this adjustment by dividing the sum of the values by *n*-1 rather than by *n*, with *n* being the number of values in the list.)

The @VAR and @VARS functions

The @VAR function computes the population variance of the values in the list specified by its argument. This function's form is shown below:

@VAR(list)

The argument *list* is the list of cells whose values you want to analyze. The result of this function is the variance of the values in *list*.

The @VARS function computes the sample variance of the values in the list specified by its argument. The form of this function is as follows:

@VARS(list)

The argument *list* is the list of cells whose values you want to analyze. The result of the function is the sample variance of the values in *list*.

As an example of the @VAR and @VARS functions, suppose block A1..A10 contains the values 1, 2, 3, 4, 5, 6, 7, 8, 9, and 10. The function @VAR(A1..A10) returns the value 8.25, and the function @VARS(A1..A10) returns the value 9.166667.

Like the standard deviation, the variance measures the dispersion of the values in the specified block. The standard deviation and the variance are closely related because the standard deviation is merely the square root of the variance.

Financial functions

Quattro Pro offers 18 financial functions—@PV, @PVAL, @NPV, @IRR, @PMT, @PAYMT, @IPAYMT, @PPAYMT, @FV, @FVAL, @TERM, @CTERM, @NPER, @RATE, @IRATE, @SLN, @DDB, and @SYD. You can use these functions to perform sophisticated financial computations without constructing complex formulas.

The @PV function

The @PV function calculates the present value of a stream of cash flows of constant interval and amount. Its form is shown below:

@PV(payment,rate,term)

The *payment* argument specifies the amount of each cash flow you will receive, and the *rate* argument specifies the discount rate you want to use to discount the stream of cash flows. The last argument, *term*, specifies the number of cash flows you will receive. The @PV function's three arguments can be literal values, references to cells that contain literal values, or formulas or functions that return values.

You can use the present value of an investment to determine the attractiveness of that investment. In general, if the present value of an investment is greater than its cost, the investment is attractive.

An example of @PV

Suppose you want to calculate the present value of an investment that will pay you 10 equal yearly payments of $500 beginning one year from today. Because you know that you can earn a 10 percent rate of return from another investment you are considering, you decide to use 10 percent as the discount rate. The function @PV(500,.1,10) calculates the present value of the investment, $3,072.28.

A closer look at @PV

The @PV function assumes that the first cash flow of the stream of cash flows you are analyzing occurs precisely one period from the current date; this situation is usually called an "ordinary annuity" or "payments in arrears." In some cases, however, the first cash flow occurs not one period in the future but immediately. These cash flow streams are usually called "annuity due" or "payments in advance." Quattro Pro's @PV function normally does not calculate the present value of an annuity due or payments in advance investment. For that calculation, use the @PVAL function, which is described in the following section.

The @PV function can be used only to analyze investments that follow a strict set of rules. The amount of each cash flow generated by the investment must be the same, and the interval between each of the cash flows must be constant. Although the interval between the cash flows generated by the investment you are analyzing must be constant, the interval does not have to be one year. You can use the @PV function to compute the present value of an investment that makes payments daily, weekly, monthly, or at any other regular interval. If you analyze an investment that has an interval other than one year, however, you need to be careful to state the discount rate argument so that it matches the interval between the cash flows. For instance, if the interval between the cash flows of an investment is monthly, the discount rate should be stated as a monthly rate.

The @PVAL function

The @PVAL function is an improved version of the @PV function. Like @PV, the @PVAL function calculates the present value of a stream of cash flows of constant interval and amount. The @PVAL function, however, works for both ordinary annuity investments and annuity due investments. What's more, the @PVAL function can include a future value argument—an amount that's in addition to the regular payment amounts—in the present value function. The form of the @PVAL function is shown below:

@PVAL(rate,term,payment,<future value>,<type>)

The argument *rate* specifies the discount rate you want to use to discount the stream of cash flows, *term* specifies the number of periods over which payments will be made, and *payment* specifies the amount of each cash flow you will receive. The <*future value*> and <*type*> arguments are optional. The <*future value*> argument specifies an additional cash flow you will receive at the end of the term. The <*type*> argument specifies whether the cash flows constitute an ordinary annuity or an annuity due. A <*type*> equal to 0 indicates an ordinary annuity, and a <*type*> equal to 1 indicates an annuity due. (If you omit an optional argument, Quattro Pro assumes the value is 0.)

An example of @PVAL

Suppose you want to calculate the present value of an investment that will pay you 10 equal payments of $500 beginning today. Also suppose that in addition to the 10 equal payments, you will receive a single $1000 payment at the end of the 10th year. Because you know that you can earn a 10 percent rate of return from another investment you are considering, you decide to use 10 percent as the discount rate. The function @PVAL(.1,10,500,1000,1) calculates the present value of this investment, -$3765.06.

A closer look at @PVAL

The @PVAL function assumes that positive values represent cash inflows and negative values represent cash outflows. When the @PVAL function arguments that represent cash flow amounts are positive, @PVAL assumes that you are analyzing an investment that's generating positive cash flows. The @PVAL function assumes that the price, or present value, of the investment is a cash outflow—indicated by a negative value. If you enter the cash flow arguments as negative values, the @PVAL function returns a positive value.

The <*future value*> and <*type*> arguments are optional when you use the @PVAL function. You can, for example, use the function @PVAL(.1,10,500). You can also use only the <*future value*> argument; for example, @PVAL(.1,10,500,1000). But, if you want to specify a <*type*> argument, you must include the <*future value*> argument even if it's 0.

Like the @PV function, the @PVAL function requires that the payments and the intervals between payments be constant; although, as noted for the @PV function, the interval between payments need not be equal to one year. The interval can be daily, weekly, or monthly. The discount rate, however, needs to match the interval. Annual intervals require an annual discount rate, monthly intervals require a monthly discount rate, and so on.

The @NPV function

The @NPV function also calculates the present value of a stream of cash flows of a constant interval. Unlike the @PV function, however, @NPV can compute the present value of a series of unequal cash flows. The form of this function is shown below:

@NPV (rate,block of cash flows,<type>)

The first argument, *rate*, specifies the discount rate you want to use to discount the stream of cash flows. This argument can be a literal value, a reference to cells that contain literal values, or a formula or function that returns a value. The second argument, *block of cash flows*, refers to a block that contains the cash flows that occur at the end of each period during the term of the investment. The *block of cash flows* argument must be a contiguous block, such as C3..C9. The values in this block do not have to be equal. Typically, the first cash flow in the block will be negative. This cash flow represents the payment you have to make to buy the cash flows generated by the investment.

The third argument, <type>, is optional. It indicates whether the cash flows start at the beginning of the first period or at the end of the first period. A <type> equal to 0 indicates that the cash flows start at the end of the first period. A <type> equal to 1 indicates that the cash flows start at the beginning of the first period. If you omit the <type> argument, the @NPV function assumes cash flows start at the end of the first period (0).

You can use the net present value of an investment to determine the attractiveness of that investment. In general, if the net present value of an investment is greater than 0, the investment is attractive.

An example of @NPV

Suppose you want to calculate the net present value of an investment that will cost you $1500 one year from now and pay you $250 at the end of year two, $500 at the end of year three, $750 at the end of year four, and $1000 at the end of year five. Because you know that you can earn a 10 percent rate of return from another investment, you decide to use 10 percent as the discount rate. Figure 4-2 shows a worksheet that's set up to make this calculation. Cells C6 through C10 in the worksheet contain the cash flows associated with the investment, and cell C3 contains the annual discount rate of 10%. The function in cell C13, @NPV(C3,C6..C10), computes the net present value of this investment—assuming the cash flows begin in one year—and produces the result $351.81. The function in cell C14, @NPV(C3,C6..C10,1), computes the net present value of this investment—assuming the cash flows begin immediately—and produces the result $387.00.

FIGURE 4-2.
The @NPV function also calculates the present value of a stream of cash flows of constant interval.

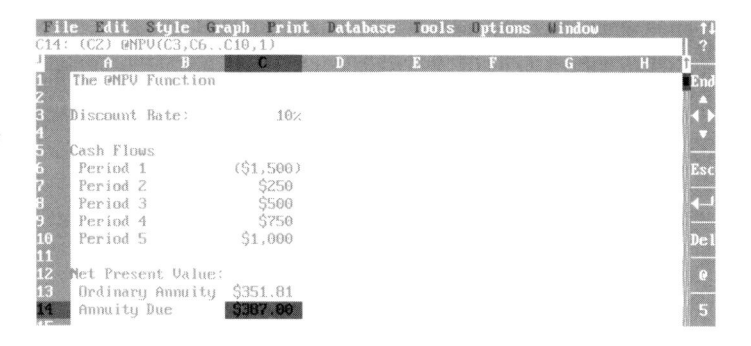

```
C14: (C2) @NPV(C3,C6..C10,1)
         A              B              C
1   The @NPV Function
2
3   Discount Rate:               10%
4
5   Cash Flows
6       Period 1              ($1,500)
7       Period 2                 $250
8       Period 3                 $500
9       Period 4                 $750
10      Period 5               $1,000
11
12  Net Present Value:
13      Ordinary Annuity      $351.81
14      Annuity Due           $387.00
```

A closer look at @NPV

The @NPV function can be used only to analyze investments in which the interval between each of the cash flows is constant. As with the @PV and @PVAL functions, however, the interval need not be one year. You can use the @NPV function to compute the present value of an investment that makes payments daily, weekly, monthly, or at any other regular interval. You need to be careful to match the period of the discount rate to the interval between the cash flows.

The @IRR function

The @IRR function computes the internal rate of return on an investment, which is the rate of return implied by its stream of cash outflows and inflows. The form of the @IRR function is as follows:

@IRR(guess rate,block of cash flows)

The argument *guess rate* approximates the internal rate of return, and *block of cash flows* refers to a block of the worksheet that contains the cash flows you want to analyze. The *guess rate* argument can be a literal value, a reference to a cell that contains a literal value, or a formula or function that returns a value. The *block of cash flows* argument must be a contiguous block, such as C3..C9. The first value in this block should be a negative number that represents the cost of the investment.

A closer look at @IRR

The concepts of internal rate of return and net present value are closely related. This is because the internal rate of return is the rate that makes the present value of the cash inflows from the investment exactly equal to the initial cash outflow. In other words, the internal rate of return of an investment is that rate at which the net present value of the investment is 0.

Quattro Pro calculates an @IRR function using an iterative process, beginning by calculating the net present value of the cash flows and using the *guess rate* argument as the discount rate. If the result is greater than 0, Quattro Pro chooses a higher rate and recalculates the net present value. If the result is less than 0,

Quattro Pro chooses a lower rate and recalculates the net present value. Quattro Pro continues this iterative process until the rate that produces a net present value of 0 is pinpointed. You can determine the attractiveness of an investment by comparing the internal rate of return on that investment to the best alternative rate. Assuming equal risk, the alternative with the higher internal rate of return is the best investment.

You need to be careful when using the @IRR function because of some mechanical difficulties related to the actual mathematics used to compute the @IRR function. Because of their cash flows, some investments do not produce a unique internal rate of return. Rather, they might actually produce several rates of return. In these cases, picking the internal rate of return measure to use in your investment decisionmaking becomes difficult. To mitigate this problem, the @IRR function allows you to specify the *guess rate* argument as @NA. The @NA function, described in more detail later in this chapter in "Other Quattro Pro Functions," stands for "not available." When you use the @NA function as the *guess rate* argument, the @IRR function returns a value only if a single internal rate of return is used. If the investment uses multiple rates of return, using @NA for the *guess rate* argument causes the @IRR function to return an error (ERR). If you do use a *guess rate* argument other than @NA in the @IRR function and the investment has more than one internal rate of return, the @IRR function returns the internal rate of return closest to your *guess rate*.

An example of @IRR

Suppose you want to calculate the internal rate of return of an investment that will cost you $1500 and pay you $250 at the end of year two, $500 at the end of year three, $750 at the end of year four, and $1000 at the end of year five. If cells C6 through C10 in the worksheet contain the cash flows, the function @IRR(@NA,C6..C10) returns the value 19.194 percent; the internal rate of return of the investment.

The @PMT function

The @PMT function computes the periodic payment necessary to amortize (pay off) a loan. This function's form is shown below:

@PMT(amount,rate,term)

The *amount* argument is the amount borrowed, *rate* is the periodic interest rate, and *term* is the number of periods over which the loan will be paid. The @PMT function's three arguments can be literal values, references to cells that contain literal values, or formulas or functions that return values.

Chapter 4: Functions

An example of @PMT

Suppose you want to calculate the monthly payment required to pay off a $10,000 installment loan. The loan has a term of four years and carries an interest rate of 11.7 percent. The function @PMT(10000,.117/12,4*12) computes the loan's monthly payment, which is $261.87. (Notice that the interest rate argument and the term argument are both formulas. The formula .117/12 converts the annual interest rate into a monthly interest rate, and the formula 4*12 calculates the number of monthly payments made over four years.)

A closer look at @PMT

The @PMT function has a trap that you'll want to keep in mind when you use it. Although most loans require monthly payments, the interest rate that you'll pay is usually stated as an annual rate. When you use the @PMT function to compute the payment on a loan, you must be certain that the *rate* and *term* arguments agree; that is, if the term of the loan is stated in months, the rate argument should specify a monthly rate. The preceding example divided the annual interest rate by 12 to obtain a monthly interest rate and multiplied the term of the loan by 12 to convert the number of years to the number of months. The result was the correct monthly payment for the loan.

Be careful also that you do not confuse the annual percentage rate, which is required by the truth-in-lending laws, with the annual interest rate. The annual percentage rate includes all the costs of obtaining a loan, including such items as the interest, loan origination fee, escrow expenses, and credit report costs. The annual interest rate, which is what you want, is the percentage used to calculate the actual interest costs.

The @PMT function assumes that the first payment you'll make will occur one period from the date of analysis and that the other payments will occur at the end of each period thereafter. This assumption is correct for most installment loans, such as home mortgages and auto loans. Some loans, however, might require that the first payment be made immediately. When this is the case, use the @PPAYMT function, which is described later in this chapter.

The @PAYMT function

The @PAYMT function is an improved version of the @PMT function. @PAYMT also computes the periodic payment necessary to amortize a loan. The @PAYMT function, however, lets you make the calculation for ordinary annuities (when you make the payment at the end of the period) and for annuities due (when you make the payment at the beginning of the period). The @PAYMT function also lets you calculate payments for loans that include a balloon payment. The form of this function is shown below:

@PAYMT(rate,term,amount,<future value>,<type>)

The *rate* argument is the periodic interest rate, *term* is the number of periods over which the payments will be made, and *amount* is the amount borrowed. The <*future value*> and <*type*> arguments are optional; <*future value*> is the balloon payment made with the final payment, and <*type*> indicates whether payments are made at the beginning or end of the period. A <*type*> of 0 indicates an ordinary annuity with payments made at the end of the period. A <*type*> of 1 indicates an annuity due with payments made at the beginning of the period. (If you omit an optional argument, Quattro Pro assumes the value is 0.) Any of the five arguments can be literal values, references to cells that contain literal values, or formulas or functions that return values.

An example of @PAYMT

Suppose you want to calculate the monthly payment required to pay off a $10,000 loan on which you'll make monthly payments over the next four years. Also suppose the last monthly payment includes a $3,000 balloon payment, the annual interest rate is 11.7 percent, and the payments will be made at the beginning of each month. The function @PAYMT(.117/12,4*12,10000,-3000,1) computes the loan's monthly payment, which is shown as -$210.51.

Like the @PVAL function, the @PAYMT function differentiates between cash inflows and cash outflows. Cash inflows show as positive values and cash outflows as negative values, which is why Quattro Pro displays the balloon payment amount and the monthly payment amount as negative values. For the same reason, Quattro Pro displays the actual loan amount that you receive as a positive value.

A closer look at @PAYMT

As with the @PMT function, be careful when you use the @PAYMT function that you state the interest rate as the interest rate per payment period and the term as the number of payment periods. For example, to calculate a monthly payment, use a monthly interest rate and the number of monthly payments. The <*future value*> and <*type*> arguments are optional. You can use only the <*future value*> argument. But if you want to specify a <*type*> argument, you must include a <*future value*> argument, even if it's 0.

The @IPAYMT and @PPAYMT functions

The @IPAYMT and @PPAYMT functions calculate the interest and principal portions of a particular loan payment. The @IPAYMT function calculates the interest portion of a payment. Its form is shown below:

@IPAYMT(rate,period,term,amount,<future value>,<type>)

The @PPAYMT function calculates the principal portion of a payment; its form is as follows:

@PPAYMT(rate,period,term,amount,<future value>,<type>)

The *rate* argument is the periodic interest rate, *period* is the payment number (1 is the first payment, 2 is the second payment and so forth), *term* is the number of periods over which payments will be made, and *amount* is the amount borrowed. The optional *<future value>* argument is the balloon payment amount. The optional *<type>* argument indicates whether payments are made as an ordinary annuity, which is shown with a 0, or as an annuity due, which is shown with a 1. (If you omit an optional argument, Quattro Pro assumes the *<type>* value is 0.)

An example of @IPAYMT and @PPAYMT

Suppose you want to calculate the interest and principal portions of the first monthly payment required to pay off the same $10,000 described earlier for the @PAYMT function. That loan has a term of four years, an 11.7 percent annual interest rate, a $3,000 balloon payment, and payments made at the beginning of the month. The preceding example calculated this loan's monthly payment as -$210.50.

The function @IPAYMT(.117/12,1,4*12,10000,-3000,1) returns the value -$98.61, which is the interest portion of the first payment. The function @PPAYMT(.117/12,1,4*12,10000,-3000,1) returns the value -$111.89, which is the principal portion of the first payment. Adding the results of the @IPAYMT and @PPAYMT functions, -$98.61 and -$111.89, gives the total payment amount, which is -$210.50. (The @IPAYMT and @PPAYMT functions, like the @PAYMT function, show cash inflows as positive values and cash outflows as negative values.)

The *<future value>* and *<type>* arguments are optional. If you want, you can use only the *<future value>* argument. But if you want to specify a *<type>* argument, you must include the *<future value>* argument, even if it's 0.

The @FV function

The @FV function calculates the future value that will result from investing a specified amount at regular intervals at a specified rate of return, across a specified period of time. The future value of an investment is its value at some future time, including all the interest it has earned up to that point. The form of this function is shown below:

@FV(payment,rate,term)

The *payment* argument specifies the amount you'll invest at the end of each period, *rate* specifies the interest rate that the investment will earn, and *term* specifies the number of investments that will occur. These three arguments can be literal values, references to cells that contain literal values, or formulas or functions that return values.

An example of @FV

For example, suppose you want to calculate the future value of your Individual Retirement Account (IRA). You plan to contribute $1500 each year for 30 years and think your investment will earn a 13 percent annual rate of interest. The function @FV(1500,.13,30), computes the value of this investment 30 years from now, and returns the value $439,798.80.

A closer look at @FV

Like many of the other financial functions, the @FV function assumes that your first investment occurs one period in the future. For instance, in the example IRA calculation Quattro Pro assumes that the first contribution of $1500 occurs not today but one year from now. In some circumstances, however, you'll want to compute the future value of an investment that will begin immediately. To do so, use the @FVAL function, which is described in the next section.

The @FVAL function

The @FVAL function is an improved version of the @FV function. Like @FV, the @FVAL function calculates the future value of a stream of cash flows of constant interval and amount. The @FVAL function, however, works for both ordinary annuities and annuities due, and includes a present value amount that's in addition to the regular payments. The form of this function is as follows:

@FVAL(rate,term,payment,<present value>,<type>)

The *rate* argument specifies the interest rate you want to use to compound the stream of cash flows, *term* specifies the number of periods over which payments will be made or interest compounded, and *payment* specifies the amount of the period payment. The *<present value>* and *<type>* arguments are optional. The *<present value>* argument specifies the lump sum cash you have already accumulated, and the *<type>* argument specifies whether cash flows represent an ordinary annuity (because they will be made at the ends of the periods) or an annuity due (because they will be made at the beginnings of the periods). A *<type>* equal to 0 indicates an ordinary annuity. A *<type>* equal to 1 indicates an annuity due. (If you omit an optional argument, Quattro Pro assumes the value is 0.)

An example of @FVAL

Again, suppose that you want to calculate the future value of your IRA, that you plan to contribute $1500 a year for 30 years, and that your investment will earn a 13 percent annual interest rate. Further, suppose that you've already accumulated $10,000 in your IRA and that, rather than making payments at the end of the year, you will make payments at the beginning of the year. The function @FVAL(.13,30,1500,10000,1) performs this calculation, returning the value -$888,132. The function returns a negative value, representing a cash outflow from the IRA, because the *payment* and *present value* arguments are positive values, representing cash inflows to the IRA.

A closer look at @FVAL

As noted earlier, the <*future value*> and <*type*> arguments are optional. You can use only the <*future value*> argument. But if you want to specify a <*type*> argument, you must include the <*future value*> argument, even if it's 0.

The @TERM function

The @TERM function calculates the number of periods required for a series of investments of equal amounts and constant intervals to compound to a specified target amount, given a constant rate of interest. This function's form is shown below:

   @TERM(payment,rate,target value)

The *payment* argument is the amount of each equal periodic investment, *rate* is the periodic interest rate, and *target value* is the amount you want to have at some point in the future. The three arguments to the @TERM function can be literal values, references to cells that contain literal values, or formulas or functions that return those values.

An example of @TERM

Suppose you want to know how many years it would take to accumulate an IRA worth $1,000,000 if you deposit $1500 per year, assuming a 13 percent rate of interest. The function @TERM(1500,.13,1000000) makes this calculation and returns the value 36.603. This result indicates that it will take between 36 and 37 years for annual contributions of $1500 to compound to $1,000,000 at an annual rate of 13 percent.

A closer look at @TERM

The @TERM function assumes that the first cash flow occurs one period from the date of analysis and that all additional cash flows occur at the end of each additional period thereafter. In cases in which the first cash flow occurs today, the second flow one year from today, and so on, use the @NPER function, which is described in the upcoming section, "The @NPER Function."

The @CTERM function

The @CTERM function computes the number of periods required for a lump-sum investment to compound to a specified target amount at a specified rate of interest.

Notice how this function differs from the @TERM function, which computes the number of periods necessary for a series of payments to compound to a target amount. The form of the @CTERM function is:

@CTERM(rate,target amount,starting amount)

The *rate* argument specifies the fixed periodic rate of interest. The *target amount* argument specifies the desired future value of the investment, and *starting amount* specifies the amount invested. The arguments can be literal values, references to cells that contain literal values, or formulas or functions that return values.

An example of @CTERM

Suppose you want to calculate the number of years it will take for $1500 to grow to a value of $5000 at an annual interest rate of 8.7%. The function @CTERM(.087,1500,5000) computes the number of years required for the initial amount to grow to the target, and returns the value -14.4324.

The @NPER function

The @NPER function is an improved, hybrid version of the @TERM and @CTERM functions. @NPER calculates such items as the number of periods required to pay off a loan given a certain payment and the number of periods required for a present value and stream of payments to grow into a future value amount. The form of this function is shown below:

@NPER(rate,payment,present value,<future value>,<type>)

The *rate* argument specifies the periodic interest rate, *payment* specifies the amount of each equal periodic payment, and *present value* specifies the initial amount you invest. Like the @PVAL, @FVAL, @PAYMT, @IPAYMT, and @PPAYMT functions, @NPER differentiates between cash inflows and cash outflows by their signs. Inflows should be positive values, and outflows negative values. The <*future value*> and <*type*> arguments are optional. The <*future value*> is the desired future value of the investment, and the <*type*> designates the payments as being an ordinary annuity or an annuity due; a 0 designates the ordinary annuity, and a 1 designates annuity due.

Examples of @NPER

Suppose you want to calculate how long it will take to pay off a $10,000 loan bearing an annual interest rate of 12 percent if you make a $300 payment each month. The function @NPER(.12/12,-300,10000) makes this calculation and returns the value 40.7489. This result indicates that you will need to make more than 40 monthly payments of $300 to pay off the loan.

As another example of the @NPER function, suppose you want to calculate how long it will take for your IRA to grow to $1,000,000. Also suppose that you have already saved $10,000, that you will contribute $2,000 at the beginning of each year, and that your money will earn 12 percent interest annually. The function @NPER(.12,2000,10000,-1000000,1) makes this calculation and returns the value 31.5058. This result indicates that it will take between 31 and 32 years for your IRA balance to reach $1,000,000.

A closer look at @NPER

The *<future value>* and *<type>* arguments are optional. If you want, you can also use only the *<future value>* argument. But if you want to specify a *<type>* argument, you must include the *<future value>* argument, even if it's 0.

The @RATE function

The @RATE function computes the periodic rate of interest required to compound a lump-sum investment to a target amount over a specified number of periods. The form of this function is as follows:

@RATE(target amount,initial amount,term)

The *target amount* argument is the desired future value of the investment, *initial amount* is the lump sum invested, and *term* is the number of periods over which the investment will compound. These three arguments can be literal values, references to cells that contain literal values, or formulas or functions that return values.

An example of @RATE

Suppose you want to know the rate of return that would be required to make $10,000 grow into $1,000,000 in 30 years. The function @RATE (1000000,10000,30) makes this calculation and returns the value 0.165914. This result indicates that the investment will have to earn an annual return of nearly 16.6 percent to total $1,000,000 in 30 years.

The @IRATE function

The @IRATE function is an improved version of the @RATE function. Like @RATE, the @IRATE function computes the periodic rate of interest required to compound a lump-sum investment to a target amount, or future value, over a specified number of periods. Unlike @RATE, however, the @IRATE function also lets you include a stream of payments you will make to move the balance toward the target amount. The @IRATE function also lets you calculate the implied interest rate on a loan given the loan term, the loan payment, and the loan amount. This function's form is shown below:

@IRATE(term,payment,initial amount,<future value>,<type>)

The *term* argument is the number of periods over which interest will compound or payments will be made, *payment* is the payment amount, and *initial amount* is the lump sum either invested or borrowed. The optional <future value> argument specifies the future target amount. The optional <type> argument specifies whether payments constitute an ordinary annuity or an annuity due. Like the @PVAL, @FVAL, @PAYMT, @IPAYMT,@PPAYMT, and @NPER functions, @IRATE differentiates between cash inflows and cash outflows by their signs. Inflows should be positive values, and outflows should be negative values.

Examples of @IRATE

Suppose you want to calculate the implied annual interest rate on a $7,500 loan with $87.08 monthly payments made over a 10-year term. The function @IRATE(10*12,-87.08,7500)*12 makes this calculation, returning the value 0.069996, or 7 percent. Notice that because the payments and the interest rate are monthly, the @IRATE function actually returns the monthly interest rate, which is multiplied by 12 to produce the annual interest rate.

As another example, suppose you want to calculate the implied annual interest rate on an investment on which you make annual $1,000 payments for 25 years and then receive $100,000 at the end of the 25th year. Suppose also that you will make these payments at the beginning of each year. The function @IRATE (25,-1000,0,100000,1) makes this calculation and returns the result 0.095054, indicating that the implied annual interest rate equals 9.5 percent.

A closer look at @IRATE

The <future value> and <type> arguments are optional for the @IRATE function. You can also use only the <future value> argument. But if you want to specify a <type> argument, you must include the <future value> argument, even if it's 0.

Depreciation functions

Quattro Pro offers a group of three financial functions—@SLN, @DDB, and @SYD —that you can use to compute depreciation. Each of these calculates depreciation according to a different scheme: The @SLN function calculates straight-line depreciation, the @DDB function calculates depreciation by the double-declining balance method, and the @SYD function calculates depreciation by the sum-of-the-years' digits method. The worksheet in Figure 4-3 demonstrates these functions. As you can see, cell C3 contains the value 2000 (the depreciable value of the asset), cell C4 contains the value 200 (the salvage value of the asset), and cell C5 contains the value 5 (the life of the asset).

Chapter 4: Functions 111

FIGURE 4-3.
Quattro Pro's three depreciation functions —@SLN, @DDB, and @SYD—compute depreciation using the straight-line, double-declining balance, and sum-of-the-years' digits methods.

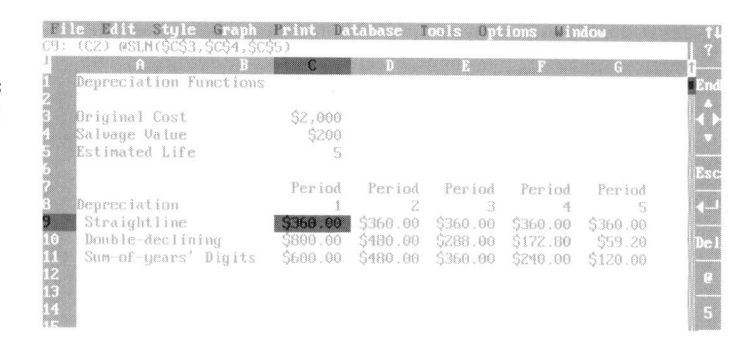

The @SLN function

The @SLN function calculates depreciation using the straight-line method. The form of this function is as follows:

@SLN(cost of asset,salvage value,life of asset)

The *cost of asset* argument specifies the depreciable value of the asset, *salvage value* specifies the value of the asset at the end of its depreciable life, and *life of asset* specifies the number of years in the asset's life. These three arguments can be literal values, references to cells that contain literal values, or formulas or functions that return values.

Cells C9 through G9 of the worksheet shown in Figure 4-3 contain examples of the @SLN function. The function in cell C9, @SLN($C$3,$C$4,$C$5), calculates the first-year, straight-line depreciation for the example asset. As you can see, this function returns the result $360.00. Because the depreciation expense for each year in the life of an asset is handled using the same straight-line method, the functions in cells D9 through G9 return the same result.

The @DDB function

The @DDB function calculates depreciation for an asset using the double-declining balance method. This function's form is as follows:

@DDB(cost of asset,salvage value,life of asset,current period)

The *cost of asset* argument specifies the depreciable value of the asset, *salvage value* specifies the value of the asset at the end of its depreciable life, and *life of asset* specifies the number of years in the asset's life. The fourth argument in this function, *current period*, specifies the particular period in the asset's life for which you want to calculate the depreciation. This argument is required because the double-declining balance method of depreciation produces a different depreciation expense for each period. The four arguments can be literal values, references to cells that contain literal values, or formulas or functions that return values.

Cells C10 through G10 of the worksheet shown in Figure 4-3 contain examples of the @DDB function. The function in cell C10, @DDB($C$3,$C$4,$C$5,C8), calculates the first-year double-declining balance depreciation for the example asset. Notice that the cell reference C8 is used to specify the period for which depreciation is to be calculated. As you can see, this function returns the result $800.00. The function in cell E10, @DDB($C$3,$C$4,$C$5,D8), calculates the second-year depreciation for this asset and returns the result $480.00. The function in cell E10 computes the third-year depreciation, and so on.

The @SYD function

The @SYD function computes depreciation using the sum-of-the-years' digits method, and has the following form:

@SYD(cost of asset,salvage value,life of asset,current period)

The *cost of asset* argument specifies the depreciable value of the asset, *salvage value* specifies the value of the asset at the end of its depreciable life, *life of asset* specifies the number of years in the asset's life, and *current period* specifies the period in the asset's life for which you want to calculate the depreciation. Cells C11 through G11 shown in Figure 4-3 contain examples of the @SYD function. The function in cell C11, @SYD($C$3,$C$4,$C$5,C8), calculates the first-year depreciation for a $2000 asset with a salvage value of $200 and a five-year life. This function returns the result $600.00. The function in cell D11, @SYD($C$3,$C$4,$C$5,D8), calculates the second-year depreciation expense for this asset and returns the result $480.00. The function in cell E11 computes the third-year depreciation, and so on.

Lookup functions

Quattro Pro offers a group of four functions—@CHOOSE, @INDEX, @VLOOKUP, and @HLOOKUP—that are called lookup functions. These functions look up a value or string from a block or list. They're handy when you need to choose a value from a list or a table or make calculations that involve tables, such as tax tables.

The @CHOOSE function

The @CHOOSE function allows Quattro Pro to select a value or string from a list, based on the position of that value or string in the list. The form of this function is as follows:

@CHOOSE(offset,item 1,item 2,item 3,..item n)

The arguments *item 1, item 2, item 3,..item n* make up the list of possible results from which Quattro Pro will choose, and *offset* specifies the position in that list of the item that you want to choose. The items in the list can be literal values, literal strings, cell references, functions, formulas, or a mixture of these types of entries. Separate the individual items in the list with commas.

The *offset* argument must be a literal value, a reference to a cell that contains a value, or a formula or function that returns a value; *offset* specifies the offset of the item in the list that you want the function to return. The offset of an item is its position relative to the first item in the list; the first item has an offset of 0, the second an offset of 1, and so on. In other words, if you specify an offset of 0, Quattro Pro chooses the first item from the list, and if you specify an offset of 1, Quattro Pro chooses the second item, and so on. The *offset* argument must specify a value between 0 and *n*-1, where *n* is the number of items in the list. If you specify an offset value outside this block, the function returns the result ERR.

An example of @CHOOSE

Suppose that in a worksheet cells E3 through E7 contain the values from which you want to choose and that cell B3 contains the value 2. In this case, the function @CHOOSE(B3,E3,E4,E5,E6,E7) returns the contents from cell E5 because the *offset* argument to this function refers to cell B3, which contains the value 2. Quattro Pro selects the item from the list with an offset of 2, which is E5. It wouldn't matter whether cell E5 showed a value or a label; the @CHOOSE function returns both labels and values. For example, the function @CHOOSE(2,11,22,3333,44,55) returns the value 3333. The function @CHOOSE(B3,"Milt","Pervis","Herbert","Billy","Jeff") returns the string "Herbert".

The @INDEX function

The @INDEX function looks up a value or label from a rectangular block of cells, based on the row and column position of that value or label in the block. This function's form is shown below:

    @INDEX(block,column offset,row offset)

The *block* argument specifies the rectangular block of cells that contains the entries from which Quattro Pro will choose. This argument can be either a block reference (like A1..E4) or a block name (like VALUES). The *column offset* argument specifies the column of the block that contains the result, and the *row offset* argument specifies the row of the block that contains the result. These arguments can be literal values, references to cells that contain literal values, or formulas or functions that return values. These arguments specify the offset, or the position relative to the upper-left corner of the block, of the item you want to look up. The first column and the first row in the block have an offset of 0.

The worksheet shown in Figure 4-4 contains an example of the @INDEX function; notice the table of data in cells D2 through H6. Cell B6 contains the function

FIGURE 4-4.
The @INDEX function looks up a value or label from a block based on the row and column position of that value or label in the block.

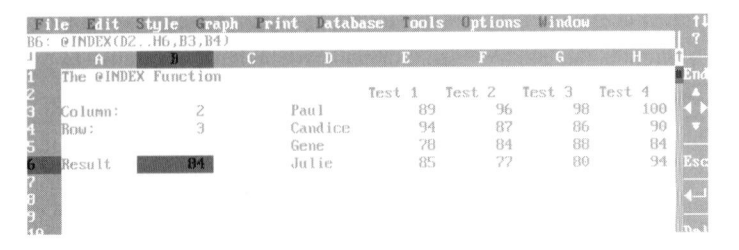

@INDEX(D2..H6,B3,B4), which returns 84—the value from cell F5, which has a column offset of 2 and a row offset of 3 in the block D2..H6. The @INDEX function can also look up labels and strings. For example, if you change the values in cells B3 and B4 in Figure 4-4 to 0 and 1 respectively, the function in cell B6 returns the string "Paul".

The @VLOOKUP and @HLOOKUP functions

The @VLOOKUP and @HLOOKUP functions are perhaps Quattro Pro's most useful lookup functions; they allow you to use a key value or a string to look up an entry from a table. Because these functions are so similar, this section uses the @VLOOKUP function to discuss general principles of table lookups. An explanation of the @HLOOKUP function follows the discussion of the @VLOOKUP function.

The @VLOOKUP function

The form of the @VLOOKUP function is as shown below:

@VLOOKUP(key entry,table block,offset)

The *key entry* argument specifies the value or string that Quattro Pro will use to locate the function's result. The *table block* argument specifies the location of the table entries that you want to look up. And the *offset* argument specifies the column of the table that contains the desired result.

Lookup tables. The @VLOOKUP function looks up values or labels from a table you have built in the worksheet. The location of the table is defined by the function's table block argument, and the lookup table must include at least two partial columns. The entries in the table can be literal values or labels, references to cells that contain values or labels, or formulas or functions that return values or labels. For example, block D3..F7 in Figure 4-5 contains a simple lookup table.

When calculating a @VLOOKUP function, Quattro Pro compares the function's *key entry* argument with the entries in the leftmost column of the lookup table, which is sometimes called the index column. The entries in this column, sometimes called the index entries, can be either values or labels. The type of the *key entry* argument, however, must match the type of the index entries. If the index

FIGURE 4-5.
The @VLOOKUP function looks up values or labels from a table you have built in a worksheet.

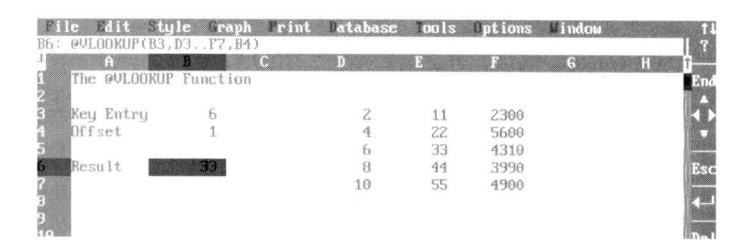

column contains values, *key entry* must also be a value, and if the index column contains labels, *key entry* must be a label; you cannot mix values and labels in the index column of a lookup table. If the entries in the index column are values, they must be arranged in ascending order, and if the entries in the index column are labels, then they can be arranged in any order. For example, in the lookup table shown in Figure 4-5, column D is the index column, and the entries in this column are values arranged in ascending order.

Quattro Pro evaluates a @VLOOKUP function differently depending on whether the *key entry* argument is a value or a label, so the following sections discuss these two cases separately.

Numeric lookups. When processesing a @VLOOKUP function with a numeric *key entry* argument, Quattro Pro searches the index column (the first column in the table) for the first value that is greater than or equal to the value of *key entry*. If Quattro Pro finds an exact match for *key entry*, the function uses the row that contains the matching index entry. If Quattro Pro finds no exact match, the function uses the row directly above the row that contains the first index entry that is greater than *key entry*. After identifying the row that contains the result, Quattro Pro uses the *offset* argument to identify the column that contains the result. The first column of the table (the index column) has an offset of 0, the second column an offset of 1, and so on. The function's result is the entry in the cell that's at the intersection of the row identified by the *key entry* argument and the column that's identified by the *offset* argument.

An example of @VLOOKUP

Cell B6 in the worksheet shown in Figure 4-5 contains an example of the @VLOOKUP function. This function, @VLOOKUP(B3,D3..F7,B4), returns the value 33; the value from cell E5. Here's how the function works. The *key entry* argument to this function is a reference to cell B3, which contains the value 6. Quattro Pro uses this value to pinpoint the row that contains the function's result. To do so, Quattro Pro searches the lookup table's index column (block D3..D7) until it finds an index entry that's greater than or equal to 6. Because the value in cell D5, which is 6, equals the value of *key entry*, Quattro Pro determines that row 5 contains the function's result.

Next, Quattro Pro uses the *offset* argument to pinpoint the column that contains the function's result. In this case, the offset of 1 (referenced by B4) tells Quattro Pro that the second column in the table, column E, contains the result. Having now determined the row (5) and column (E) locations of the result, the @VLOOKUP function returns the value from cell E5.

Now, suppose you replace the value in cell B3 with the value 7. Once again, the @VLOOKUP function in cell B6 returns the value 33; the value from cell E5. As before, Quattro Pro uses the value in cell B3, which is 7, to pinpoint the row that contains the function's result by searching the index column for an index entry greater than or equal to 7. The value in cell D6, which is 8, is the first value in this column that is greater than 7. Consequently, Quattro Pro determines that row 5, the row directly above cell D6, contains the function's result. Next, Quattro Pro uses the *offset* argument to pinpoint the column that contains the function's result. As before, the offset of 1 tells Quattro Pro that column E contains the result. The function therefore returns the value from cell E5.

A closer look at @VLOOKUP with a value argument

Because the @VLOOKUP function searches the index column for the first value that is greater than or equal to the value of *key entry*, it is important that the values in the index column appear in ascending order, and that no index entry appear twice in the index column. Although it is still possible for @VLOOKUP to operate on a table that breaks these rules, the results of the function are likely to be incorrect.

The index entries in your lookup tables are usually positive, but you can use negative values in the index column. As always, the index entries should be arranged in ascending order; negative values first, followed by positive values. If the *key entry* argument to a @VLOOKUP function is less than the first value in the index column, the function returns ERR. For example, if you enter a value that's less than 2 in cell B3 in Figure 4-5, the @VLOOKUP function in cell B6 returns ERR. If the *key entry* argument to a @VLOOKUP function is greater than the last value in the index column, the function assumes that its result is in the last row of the lookup table. For example, if you enter the value 11 in cell B3 in Figure 4-5, the function in cell B6 returns the value 55 from cell E7.

The @VLOOKUP function returns ERR if the offset you specify is not in block 0 to *n*-1, where *n* is the number of columns in the lookup table. For example, the @VLOOKUP function in cell B6 returns ERR if the value in B4 is changed to any number greater than 2 or less than 0. If a @VLOOKUP function with a numeric *key entry* value has an *offset* value of 0, the function returns the appropriate value from the index column. For example, if you change the value in cell B4 to 0 in Figure 4-5, the function in cell B6 returns the value 6 from cell D5.

Using the @VLOOKUP function to look up text

So far, you've seen @VLOOKUP functions that return values. The @VLOOKUP function, however, can also look up labels and strings from a table. For example, the worksheet shown in Figure 4-6 contains a modified version of the lookup table shown in Figure 4-5. As you can see, column E now contains the labels 'Jeff, 'Matt, 'Mark, 'Robbie, and 'Cameron. The function in cell B6, @VLOOKUP(B3,D3..G7,B4), returns the string "Mark". To return this result, Quattro Pro uses the value of *key entry* from cell B3, which is 6, to determine that the result lies in row 5 and the value of *offset* from cell B4, which is 1, to determine that the result lies in column E. Because cell E5 contains the label 'Mark, the result of this function is the string "Mark".

Using a string as a *key entry* argument. Instead of using a numeric value as the *key entry* argument to a @VLOOKUP function, you can use a string. Of course, if the *key entry* argument is a string, the entries in the index column must be labels. When evaluating a @VLOOKUP function that has a string as a *key entry* argument, Quattro Pro searches the index column for a label that is identical to the string in *key entry*. After identifying the row that contains the result, Quattro Pro uses the *offset* argument to identify the column that contains the result. The function's result is the entry in the cell that's at the intersection of the row identified by the *key entry* argument and index entries and the column identified by the *offset* argument. If Quattro Pro finds no exact match, the function returns ERR.

An example of @VLOOKUP with a string argument

The worksheet shown in Figure 4-7 contains an example of a @VLOOKUP function that has a string *key entry* argument. The function in cell B6, @VLOOKUP(B3,D3..G7,B4), compares the string in the *key entry* in cell B3, which is "Robbie", with the labels in the index column of the lookup table. Because the label in cell D6 is identical to the string in *key entry*, Quattro Pro determines that row 6 contains the function's result. Quattro Pro then uses the *offset* argument, which is 1, to determine that the result lies in column E; the column that's one column to the right of the index column. Consequently, this function returns 44, the value from cell E6.

FIGURE 4-6.
The @VLOOKUP function can look up labels and strings as well as values.

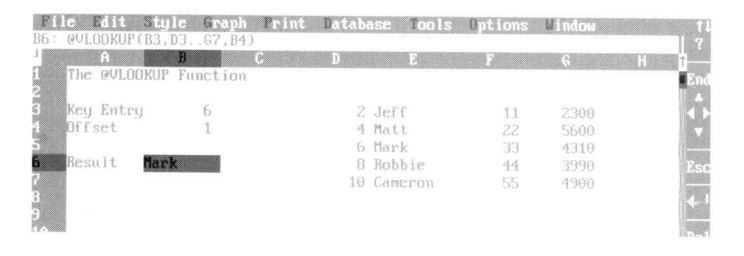

FIGURE 4-7.
You can use a string as the key entry *argument of a @VLOOKUP function.*

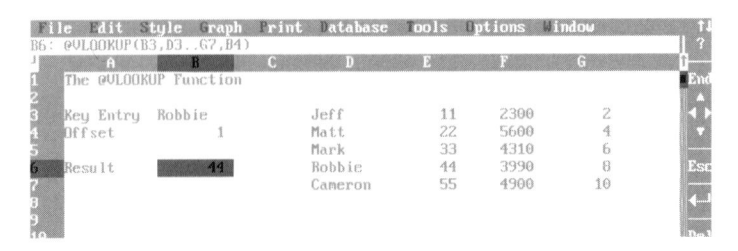

A closer look at @VLOOKUP with a string argument

If a @VLOOKUP function with a string as a *key entry* argument cannot find an exact match for the string in *key entry* in the index column, the function returns ERR. It also returns ERR if you specify an offset of less than 0 or greater than the number of columns in the table block, minus 1.

Surprisingly, if you specify an offset of 0 in a @VLOOKUP function with a string *key entry*, the function does not return a string. Instead, it returns a value that indicates the offset of the row that contains the index entry and that matches the string in *key entry*. For example, if you change the value of *offset* in cell B4 from 1 to 0, the function in cell B6 returns the value 3; the offset of the row in the table that contains the entry 'Robbie.

The @HLOOKUP function

The @HLOOKUP function is the same as the @VLOOKUP function, with one exception: @HLOOKUP looks up entries from horizontal lookup tables. In a horizontal lookup table, the index values are in the top row, and the items to be looked up are in the following rows. The form of this function is as follows:

@HLOOKUP(key entry,table block,offset)

The *key entry* argument specifies the value Quattro Pro will look up in the index row, *table block* specifies the block of entries that contain the values you want to look up, and *offset* specifies the row of the table that contains the function's result.

Like @VLOOKUP, @HLOOKUP looks up values or labels from a table you have built in the worksheet. The location of the table is defined by the function's *table block* argument, and the lookup table must include at least two partial rows. The entries in the table can be literal values or labels, references to cells that contain literal values or labels, or formulas or functions that return values or labels. For example, block C9..G11 in Figure 4-8 contains a horizontal lookup table.

When calculating an @HLOOKUP function, Quattro Pro compares its *key entry* argument with the entries in the top row of the lookup table, which is the index row. The entries in this row, the index entries, can be either values or labels. As with vertical lookup tables, the type of the *key entry* value must match the type of the index entries. If the entries in the index row are values, they must be arranged in ascending order from left to right, with no repeating entries, in order to get the

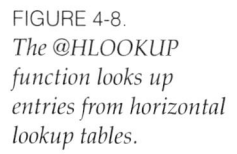

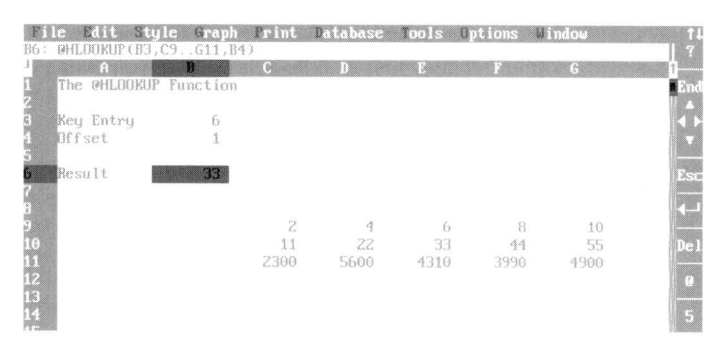

FIGURE 4-8.
The @HLOOKUP function looks up entries from horizontal lookup tables.

correct result. If the entries in the index row are labels, they can be arranged in any order. Note that in the example, the index values are in row 9, and the entries to be looked up are in rows 10 and 11.

Numeric lookups. When processing an @HLOOKUP function with a numeric *key entry* value, Quattro Pro searches the index row (the first row in the table) for the first value that is greater than or equal to the value of *key entry*. If Quattro Pro finds an exact match for the *key entry* value in the index row, then the function uses the column that contains the matching index entry. If Quattro Pro finds no exact match, the function uses the column immediately to the left of the column that contains the first index entry whose value is greater than that of *key entry*. After identifying the column that contains the result, Quattro Pro uses the *offset* argument to identify the row that contains the result. The first row of the table, the index row, has an offset of 0, the second row an offset of 1, and so on. The function's result is the entry in the cell at the intersection of the column that's identified by the *key entry* argument and the row that's identified by the *offset* argument.

Cell B6 of the worksheet shown in Figure 4-8 contains the function @HLOOKUP (B3,C9..G11,B4). This function uses the *key entry* value from cell B3 and the *offset* value from cell B4 to look up the result in cell E10, which is 33. (Notice that this function is the horizontal equivalent of the vertical lookup function shown in cell B6 of Figure 4-5.) To evaluate this function, Quattro Pro searches the index row (C9..G9) for the first value that is greater than or equal to the value of *key entry*, which is 6. Because the value in cell E9 (6) is equal to that of *key entry*, Quattro Pro determines that column E contains the function's result. The *offset* value of 1 then selects the second row of the table block (row 10), and the function returns the value in cell E10, which is 33.

If the value of the *key entry* you specify is less than the first value in the index table or if you specify an offset that is less than 0 or greater than the number of rows minus 1, the @HLOOKUP function returns the value ERR. If you specify a value for *key entry* that is greater than the last value in the index row, @HLOOKUP assumes that the result lies in the last row of the table. If the *offset* argument to a numeric @HLOOKUP function is 0, the function returns a value from the index row.

Text lookups. As with @VLOOKUP, you can use a string as the *key entry* argument of an @HLOOKUP function. If the *key entry* argument is a string, the entries in the index row must also be strings. When evaluating an @HLOOKUP function that has a string as *key entry*, Quattro Pro searches the index row for a label that is identical to the *key entry* string. After identifying the column that contains the result, Quattro Pro uses the *offset* argument to identify the row that contains the result. The function's result is the entry in the cell at the intersection of the column that's identified by the *key entry* argument and the row that's identified by the *offset* argument. Text lookups return the value ERR if no match for the *key entry* argument can be found in the index row. If you specify an offset of 0 with a string *key entry*, the @HLOOKUP function returns a value that indicates the offset of the column that contains the index entry matching the *key entry*. If Quattro Pro finds no exact match, the function returns ERR.

Logical functions

Quattro Pro offers eight logical functions that allow you to build decision-making capabilities into your worksheets: @IF, @ISERR, @ISNA, @ISNUMBER, @ISSTRING, @FILEEXISTS, @TRUE, and @FALSE.

The @IF function

The @IF function allows Quattro Pro to make decisions based on the results of conditional tests. This function's form is shown below:

@IF(conditional test,true result,false result)

Quattro Pro will deem the *conditional test* argument true or false. The *true result* and *false result* arguments can be literal values, literal strings, or formulas or functions that return values or strings. If *conditional test* is true, the function returns a true result. If *conditional test* is false, the function returns a false result.

Conditional tests

A conditional test is an expression that makes a comparison between two values, labels, formulas, or functions or that tests the contents of a particular cell or block for some characteristic. For example, the following expressions are all conditional tests:

B3<5

B3=C3

(B3+C3)>=D3

@SUM(SALES)>B3

B3="David Jones"

Operator	Definition
<	Less than
>	Greater than
=	Equal to
<>	Not equal to
<=	Less than or equal to
>=	Greater than or equal to

TABLE 4-1. *The simplest conditional tests use one of Quattro Pro's six conditional operators to make comparisons.*

The simplest conditional tests use one of Quattro Pro's six conditional operators to make comparisons. Table 4-1 lists these conditional operators.

Any expression that uses one of the six conditional operators to make a comparison must be either true or false. For example, the conditional test B3<5 is false if cell B3 contains a value that is greater than or equal to 5 and is true if cell B3 contains a value that is less than 5. Quattro Pro always represents *true result* and *false result* with the values 1 and 0. If you enter a conditional test in a cell, Quattro Pro evaluates the condition and returns 1 if the conditional test is true and 0 if the conditional test is false.

Examples of conditional tests

The worksheet shown in Figure 4-9 contains several examples of the @IF function. In cell C5 the first function, @IF(B5<100,0,0.05), compares the value in cell B5 with the value 100. The function says, "If the value in cell B5 is less than 100, return the value 0; otherwise, return the value 0.05." Because the value in cell B5 (34.32) is less than 100, this function returns the value 0; the true result.

Notice that the @IF function in cell C6, @IF(B6<100,0,0.05), compares the entry in cell B6 with the value 100. Because the value in cell B6 (100.78) is greater than 100, this function returns the value 0.05; the false result. Similarly, the function in cell B7, @IF(B7<100,0,0.05), tests to see whether the value in cell B7 is less than 100. Because the value in that cell, 100, is not less than 100 (they are equal), this function returns the value 0.05; the false result.

Using strings as the true and false results

In most cases, an @IF function's true result and false result arguments will be values. The arguments to an @IF function, however, can also be strings or references to cells that contain labels. For example, the function @IF(F5>70,"Pass","Fail") compares the value in cell F5 with the value 70. If cell F5 holds a value that is greater than 70, the function returns the string "Pass"; if cell F5 holds a value that is equal to or less than 70, the function returns the string "Fail".

FIGURE 4-9.
The @IF function allows Quattro Pro to make decisions based on the results of conditional tests.

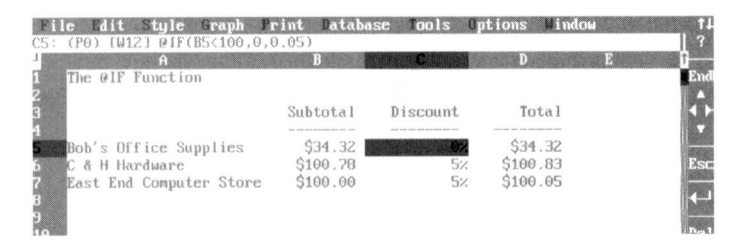

Using strings in the conditional test

You can also use labels or strings in an @IF function's conditional test. For example, the function @IF(A1='YES, B1, C1) says, "If cell A1 holds the label 'YES, return the contents of cell B1; otherwise, return the contents of cell C1." By the way, when you use the @IF function to compare labels, capitalization does matter: 'Yes does not equal 'YES or 'yes.

Complex logical operators

Quattro Pro offers three complex logical operators—#AND#, #OR#, and #NOT#—that let you join simple conditional tests to make compound conditional tests.

The #AND# operator. You can use the #AND# operator to join two simple conditional tests to make a single complex test. For a complex conditional test that uses #AND# to be true, each individual conditional test must be true. If any or all of the simple conditional tests that make up the complex test are false, the complex conditional test is also false.

For example, with the function @IF(F5>70#AND#E5>70,"Pass","Fail"), the conditional test F5>70#AND#E5>70 will be true only when both F5 and E5 contain values that exceed 70. If the conditional test is true, the function returns the result "Pass". If the result in cell E5 is less than 70, if the value in cell F5 is less than 70, or if both are less than 70, the combined conditional test is false, and the function returns the result "Fail".

The #OR# operator. You also can use the #OR# operator to join two simple conditional tests to make a single complex test. A complex conditional test that uses the #OR# operator returns the true condition as long as any one of the simple conditional tests that it contains is true. The complex conditional test returns the false condition only if all of the simple conditional tests that it contains are false.

For example, suppose that you have used Quattro Pro to create last year's income statement for your company and that you've decided to throw a party either if sales for the year exceed $100,000 or if net income exceeds $20,000. Assuming that these values are in cells C1 and C20, you can use the function @IF (C1>100000#OR#C20>20000,"Party time!","Get to work!") to test your company's results. This function returns the false condition, which is the string "Get to work!", only if both conditions (C1>100000 and C20>20000) are false.

The #NOT# operator. You can use Quattro Pro's #NOT# operator to negate a conditional test. For example, the function @IF(#NOT#B3=0,"Nonzero","Zero") returns the string "Nonzero" if cell B3 contains any value other than 0 and the string "Zero" if cell B3 contains the value 0.

In most cases, you can obtain the same result achieved by the #NOT# operator without using the operator. For example, the functions @IF(B3=0,"Zero","Nonzero") and @IF(B3<>0,"Nonzero","Zero") return the same results as does the function @IF(#NOT#B3=0,"Nonzero","Zero").

Nesting @IF functions

In some cases, you'll need to use two or more @IF functions in a single formula to express a certain condition correctly. Using one @IF function within another is called nesting. By nesting @IF functions, you create a hierarchy of conditional tests in a single formula that allows Quattro Pro to take different actions based on the combined results of the different tests. For example, suppose you want to compute the letter grades A, B, C, D, or F for the students in a class you teach. Suppose also that you will assign grades based on the final test scores and that the first student's final test score is stored in cell F5. To compute the first student's letter grade you can use the formula

@IF(F5<60,"F",@IF(F5<70,"D",@IF(F5<80,"C",@IF(F5<90,"B","A"))))

This formula says, "If the value in cell F5 is less than 60, return an F; or, if the value in cell F5 is less than 70, return a D; or, if the value in cell F5 is less than 80, return a C; or, if the value in cell F5 is less than 90, return a B; otherwise, return an A." As you can see, each @IF function in this formula is nested within the previous @IF function. For the formula to return the last result, "A", the results of the conditional tests of all four previous @IF functions must be false.

Other logical functions

In addition to the basic conditional operators (<, >, =, <>, <=, >=) and the complex conditional operators (#AND#, #OR#, and #NOT#) discussed so far, Quattro Pro also provides seven special functions: @ISERR, @ISNA, @ISNUMBER, @ISSTRING, @FILEEXISTS, @TRUE, and @FALSE. You can use any of these functions as the conditional test of an @IF function; they test conditions that would be impossible to test using traditional formulas.

The @ISERR function

Quattro Pro's @ISERR function determines whether a formula or function returns the special value ERR indicating an error. The form of this function is shown below:

@ISERR(argument)

The *argument* argument is the formula or function you want to test, or it is a reference to a cell that contains that formula or function. The @ISERR function is true when its argument returns the value ERR and is false when its argument returns any other result. A formula or function returns the value ERR whenever Quattro Pro is unable to evaluate the formula or function due to incorrect syntax, illogical cell references, division by 0, and so forth.

To see how this function works, suppose cell B3 contains the value 1 and cell B4 contains the value 0. Because division by 0 is an error, the formula +B3/B4 returns the value ERR. Consequently, the function @ISERR(B3/B4) is true, and the function @IF(@ISERR(B3/B4),"Error","No Error") returns the string "Error".

The @ISNA function

The @ISNA function determines whether a formula or function returns the special value NA; its form is shown below:

@ISNA(argument)

The *argument* argument is the formula or function you want to test, or it is a reference to a cell that contains that formula or function. The @ISNA function is true only when its argument returns the value NA. The value NA stands for Not Available and usually results from the use of the @NA function. The @NA function is explained later in this chapter in "Other Quattro Pro Functions."

For example, suppose cell Q50 contains a formula or function that returns the value NA. The function @ISNA(Q50) is true, and the function @IF(@ISNA(Q50), "Assumption missing",Q50) returns the string "Assumption missing".

The @ISNUMBER and @ISSTRING functions

Quattro Pro's @ISNUMBER and @ISSTRING functions allow you to determine whether a cell contains a value or a label. The forms of these functions are as follows:

@ISNUMBER(argument)

@ISSTRING(argument)

The *argument* argument refers to the cell you want to test. The @ISNUMBER function returns the value 1 (True) when the cell specified by its argument either contains a value (including a literal value or a formula or function that returns a value) or is empty; otherwise, @ISNUMBER returns the value 0 (False). Similarly, the @ISSTRING function returns the value 1 (True) when the cell referenced by its argument contains a label or string (or a formula or function that returns a string) and otherwise returns the value 0 (False).

For example, suppose cell B3 contains the value 100. As you might guess, the function @ISNUMBER(B3) returns the value 1 (True) and the function @ISSTRING(B3) returns the value 0 (False). If cell B3 contains the label 'Sales instead, @ISNUMBER(B3) returns False and @ISSTRING(B3) returns True. If cell B3 is empty, however, @ISNUMBER(B3) returns True, and @ISSTRING(B3) returns False. Remember that @ISNUMBER returns True even when the cell referenced by its argument is empty.

The @FILEEXISTS function

Quattro Pro's @FILEEXISTS function lets you determine whether a specified file exists on your disk drive. The form of this function is as follows:

@FILEEXISTS(filename)

The *filename* argument is the name of the file whose existence you want to verify, and must be a literal string enclosed in quotation marks or a formula or function that returns a string. The string specified by *filename* must be in the form of a legal DOS filename, including the filename extension. To search for a file in a directory other than the default directory, you must precede *filename* with the file's full directory path. The @FILEEXISTS function returns the value 1 (True) if the file specified exists and the value 0 (False) otherwise. For example, suppose you want to determine whether the file SALES.WQ1 exists in the current directory. To do so, use the function @FILEEXISTS("SALES.WQ1"), which returns the value 1 (True) if the file exists or the value 0 (False) otherwise. If you want to test for the existence of SALES.WQ1 in the directory C:\QPRO\DATA, use the function @FILEEXISTS("C:\QPRO\DATA\SALES.WQ1").

The @FILEEXISTS function is used mostly in Quattro Pro macros, which are explained in Chapter 12, "Macro Basics."

The @TRUE and @FALSE functions

Quattro Pro's @TRUE and @FALSE functions simply return the logical values True (the value 1) and False (the value 0); they accept no arguments. Most users will rarely, if ever, use these functions.

String functions

Quattro Pro offers a wide variety of functions that allow you to manipulate string entries: @CODE, @CHAR, @FIND, @EXACT, @REPLACE, @LEFT, @RIGHT, @MID, @LENGTH, @UPPER, @LOWER, @PROPER, @STRING, @VALUE, @REPEAT, @TRIM, and @CLEAN.

The @CODE and @CHAR functions

All personal computers use a code system called ASCII, or American Standard Code for Information Interchange, to represent the characters—letters, numbers, and symbols—that appear on your computer's screen. The ASCII system uses a three-digit code to represent each of the 256 characters in its system. For example, your computer knows the character E as code 69, the number 3 as code 051, and the symbol & as code 038. (The Quattro Pro manual contains a complete listing of the characters that the ASCII codes represent.) Quattro Pro offers two functions—@CODE and @CHAR—that you can use to convert a character to its three-digit ASCII code or to convert an ASCII code to a character.

The @CODE function

Quattro Pro's @CODE function returns the ASCII code of the character specified by its argument. This function's form is shown below:

@CODE(character)

The single argument *character* specifies the character whose ASCII code you want to determine. The argument must be either a literal string enclosed in quotation marks or a reference to a cell that contains a label. For example, the function @CODE("G") returns the value 71, indicating that the character G has the ASCII code 71. Similarly, if cell B5 contains the label '#, the function @CODE(B5) returns the value 35; the ASCII code for the symbol character #. Likewise, if cell B6 contains the label '3, the function @CODE(B6) returns the value 51; the ASCII code for the character 3. (As you may have noticed, leading zeros are usually omitted for low-level ASCII codes.)

If a @CODE function's argument consists of more than one character, @CODE returns the ASCII code of only the first character in the string. If the argument is a value, the function returns the result ERR.

The @CHAR function

Although the ASCII character set contains exactly 256 characters, you can enter only about 100 of these using your computer's keyboard. To enter the remaining characters, you must use either the Alt key, which is discussed in Appendix C, "Using Special Characters," or the @CHAR function. @CHAR returns the character specified by the ASCII code you supply as the function's argument. The form of this function is shown below:

@CHAR(value)

The *value* argument is an integer from 000 to 255 that specifies the ASCII code value of the character you want Quattro Pro to return. For example, the function @CHAR(68) returns the character D; the character represented by ASCII code 68. Similarly, if cell A5 contains the value 156, the function @CHAR(A5) returns the character £ (ASCII code 156). And if cell C6 contains the value 159, the function @CHAR(C6) returns the character ƒ (ASCII code 159).

The @FIND function

The @FIND function allows you to locate a substring within a string; its form is shown below:

@FIND(substring,string,offset)

The *substring* argument specifies the group of characters that you want to locate within *string*. The third argument, *offset*, tells Quattro Pro where in *string* you want to begin the search. If *offset* is 0, Quattro Pro begins searching with the first character in *string*, if *offset* is 1, Quattro Pro begins with the second character, and so on. You'll usually want to specify an offset of 0 to have Quattro Pro begin searching at the beginning of *string*. The result of the function is a number that specifies the offset of the first character of *substring* within *string*. If Quattro Pro cannot find the substring within the string, it returns the value ERR.

The *offset* argument makes it possible to search for multiple occurrences of the same substring within a specified string. For example, suppose you want to locate the second comma in the string "John said, 'Get out, and stay out!'" The function @FIND(",","John said, 'Get out, and stay out!'",10) returns the correct result, which is 19. The *offset* argument to this function tells Quattro Pro to skip to the 10th character in the string before beginning the search. Consequently, the function skips the first occurrence of the comma and finds the second.

The @EXACT function

The @EXACT function allows you to compare one string to another. The form of this function is as follows:

@EXACT(string1,string2)

The *string1* and *string2* arguments are the two strings you want Quattro Pro to compare. If the two strings are identical, including capitalization, the @EXACT function returns the value 1 (True). If the two strings are not identical, the @EXACT function returns the value 0 (False). The string can also be a reference to a cell that returns a string.

Suppose you want to know whether cell B3 contains the label 'xyz. To find out, enter the function @EXACT(B3,"xyz"). This function returns the value 1 (True) if cell B3 contains the label 'xyz, "xyz, or ^xyz, or any cell reference, formula, or function that returns the string "xyz." If cell B3 contains any other string—even a string such as "Xyz" that varies from the string "xyz" only in capitalization—this function returns the value 0 (False). If you want to compare two strings but are not concerned about differences in capitalization, you should use the = operator instead of the @EXACT function. For example, the function @EXACT(B3,"xyz") is true only if cell B3 contains the string "xyz" (with any label prefix). On the other hand, the equation B3="xyz" will be true if cell B3 contains any of the following strings: "xyz", "Xyz", "xYz", "xyZ", "XyZ", "XYz", "xYZ", or "XYZ".

Because the @EXACT function returns either a 1 (True) or a 0 (False), it can be used as the conditional test argument to an @IF function or the macro command {IF}. For example, the following function uses the @EXACT function to compare the contents of cell C1 with the string "Smith":

@IF(@EXACT(C1,"Smith"),@VLOOKUP(B3,D1..G150,2),0)

The @REPLACE function

The @REPLACE function allows you to replace a group of characters in a string with another group of characters. The form of this function is as follows:

@REPLACE(original string,starting point,number of characters to replace, replacement string)

The *original string* argument specifies the string in which you want to replace characters. The next two arguments, *starting point* and *number of characters to replace*, tell Quattro Pro where to start and how many characters to replace. A *starting point* of 0 specifies the first character, a *starting point* of 1 specifies the second character, and so forth. When executing this function, Quattro Pro removes the number of characters specified by the *number of characters to replace* argument from *original string* beginning at *starting point*. The last argument, *replacement string*, specifies the string that Quattro Pro will insert in *original string* in place of the removed characters.

For example, suppose cell B3 on a worksheet contains the label 'John said that you should get out. Suppose also that you want to replace the word "said" with the word "suggested." Using the function in cell B5, @REPLACE(B3,5,4,"suggested"), would do that. This function's first argument tells Quattro Pro to replace some characters in the string in cell B3. The second argument tells Quattro Pro to start replacing with the character whose offset is 5 (the sixth character in the string; in this case, the letter "s" in "said"). The third and fourth arguments tell Quattro Pro remove four characters from the string and replace them with the characters "suggested." Consequently, when evaluating this function, Quattro Pro replaces the characters "said" with the characters "suggested" to produce the string "John suggested that you should get out."

The @LEFT, @RIGHT, and @MID functions

Quattro Pro offers three string functions—@LEFT, @RIGHT, and @MID—that extract groups of characters from a string, based on the position of those characters within that string. Use these functions when you want to break strings into smaller strings that can be manipulated individually.

The @LEFT function

You can use Quattro Pro's @LEFT function to extract a specified number of characters from a string, starting with the first character of that string. This function's form is shown below:

@LEFT(string,number of characters)

The *number of characters* argument specifies the number of characters you want to extract from *string*. The @LEFT function extracts the number of characters specified in *number of characters* from *string*, beginning with the first (leftmost) character. If *number of characters* specifies more characters than are contained in the string, Quattro Pro returns the entire string. For example, the function @LEFT("Moe, Larry, and Curly",3) returns the first three characters from the string, "Moe".

The @RIGHT function

The @RIGHT function extracts a specified number of characters from the end of a string. The form of this function is as follows:

@RIGHT(string,number of characters)

The *number of characters* argument specifies how many characters you want to extract from *string*. The @RIGHT function extracts the number of characters specified in *number of characters* from *string*, beginning with the last (rightmost) character. If *number of characters* specifies more characters than are contained in the string, Quattro Pro returns the entire string. For example, suppose you want to extract the name "Curly" from the string "Moe, Larry, and Curly". Because the characters you want to extract are the last five characters in the string, you can use the function @RIGHT("Moe, Larry, and Curly",5) to return that string.

The @MID function

The @MID function extracts a specified number of characters from any position in a string. The form of this function is shown below:

@MID(string,starting point, number of characters)

The *string* argument specifies the string from which you want to extract characters. The *starting point* argument specifies the offset of the first character you want to extract. A *starting point* value of 0 specifies the first character, a *starting point* value of 1 specifies the second character, and so forth. The final argument, *number of characters*, tells Quattro Pro how many characters you want to extract, starting with and including the character you pinpointed with the *starting point* argument.

Suppose you want to extract the name "Larry" from the string "Moe, Larry, and Curly". The function @MID("Moe, Larry, and Curly",5,5) tells Quattro Pro to extract five characters from the string, beginning with the character whose offset is 5.

The @LENGTH function

Quattro Pro's @LENGTH function measures the length of a string. Its form is as follows:

@LENGTH(string)

The result of the function is the number of characters in *string*, including any leading or trailing spaces or spaces between parts of the string. The *string* argument must be a literal string enclosed in quotation marks or a formula or function that returns a string. For example, if cell B3 contains the five-character label 'Sales, the function @LENGTH(B3) returns the value 5. Similarly, if cell B4 contains the label 'Net Income, the function @LENGTH(B4) returns the value 10. If the string argument is a value, the function returns ERR.

The @UPPER, @LOWER, and @PROPER functions

Quattro Pro's @UPPER, @LOWER, and @PROPER functions allow you to modify the capitalization of strings. The forms of these functions are shown below:

@UPPER(string)

@LOWER(string)

@PROPER(string)

The @UPPER function converts *string* to all uppercase characters. The @LOWER function converts *string* to all lowercase characters. The @PROPER function converts the first letter after each space in *string* to uppercase and converts the remaining letters to lowercase. To illustrate these three functions, suppose cell B3 contains the string "tHe quick BRown Fox jumps OvEr thE LaZY dog". Note the random capitalization. The function @UPPER(B3) returns the string "THE QUICK BROWN FOX JUMPS OVER THE LAZY DOG". The function @LOWER(B3) returns the string "the quick brown fox jumps over the lazy dog". The function @PROPER(B3) returns the string "The Quick Brown Fox Jumps Over The Lazy Dog".

The @STRING and @VALUE functions

Quattro Pro provides two special string functions, @STRING and @VALUE, that convert values to strings and strings to values. To understand the usefulness of these functions, remember that Quattro Pro recognizes two types of entries: labels (or strings) and values. Although you can create formulas that operate on strings and formulas that operate on numeric values, you cannot create a formula that refers to a mix of strings and values. Any formula that attempts to mix strings and values returns the value ERR. The primary purpose of @STRING and @VALUE is to convert an entry from one type to the other (that is, from a value to a string or from a string to a value) so that the entry can be used with other entries of that type in a formula.

The @STRING function

The @STRING function converts a value to a string. The form of the @STRING function is shown below:

@STRING(value,decimals)

The *value* argument specifies the value you want to convert, and the *decimals* argument tells Quattro Pro how many decimal places to include in the resulting string. The *value* argument can be a literal value or a formula or function that returns a value.

The @STRING function rounds the value to a specified number of decimal places and then converts that rounded value to a string. For example, the function @STRING(6666.66,0) returns the string "6667". Notice that Quattro Pro rounds the value 6666.66 to 0 decimal places before converting it to a string. The function @STRING(6666.66,1) returns the string "6666.7". Similarly, the functions @STRING(6666.66,2) and @STRING(6666.66,3) return the strings 6666.66 and 6666.660, respectively.

The @VALUE function

The @VALUE function converts a numeric string to a value. Its form is shown below:

@VALUE(numeric string)

The *numeric string* argument specifies the string (or label) that you want to convert. A numeric string is a string that looks like a value. Numeric strings can contain only numerals (0, 1, 2, and so forth) and special numeric symbols such as dollar signs, percent signs, commas, periods, and parentheses. The *numeric string* argument can be in the form of either a value that has been assigned any of the Quattro Pro formats, or a fraction (such as ½) or mixed number (such as 1½). The result of the @VALUE function is a value.

Cells C5 through C10 in Figure 4-10 contain examples of the @VALUE function. The function in cell C5, @VALUE(B5), converts the label in cell B5, which is '1234.56, to the value 1234.56, and the function in cell C6, @VALUE(B6), converts the label in cell B6, which is '$1,234.56, to the value 1234.56. The function in cell C7, @VALUE(B7), converts the label in cell B7, which is '12.3%, to the value 0.123. The function in cell C8, @VALUE(B8), converts the label in cell B8, which is '1.2E+3, to the value 1200, and the function in cell C9, @VALUE(B9), converts the label in cell

B9, which is '½, to the value 0.5. Finally, the function in cell C10, @VALUE(B10), converts the label in cell B10, which is '1¾ into the value 1.75.

The @VALUE function comes in handy when you need to convert data that has been imported from another program as numeric strings to values that can be manipulated mathematically. For instance, if you import numeric data from a word processing file, you need to convert the numeric strings using the @VALUE function before you can perform any calculations on the data.

The @REPEAT function

The @REPEAT function returns a string that repeats the character or characters you specify the number of times you specify. The form of the function is as follows:

@REPEAT(string,number of repeats)

The *string* argument is the group of characters you want to repeat, and the *number of repeats* argument is the number of times you want those characters repeated. *String* can be a literal string or formula or a function that returns a string. If *string* is a literal string, it must be enclosed in quotation marks. For example, the function @REPEAT("-",25) would return a series of 25 consecutive dashes.

The @TRIM function

Quattro Pro's @TRIM function removes unwanted spaces from a label or string. This function's form is shown below:

@TRIM(string)

The *string* argument is the string from which you want spaces removed. If *string* is a literal string, it must be enclosed in quotation marks. The result of the function is *string* without any leading or trailing spaces and with only one space between words. For example, if cell B3 contains the 30-character label 'get   your act   together (notice all the extra spaces), the function @TRIM(B3) returns the 21-character string "get your act together".

FIGURE 4-10.
The @VALUE function converts a numeric string to a value.

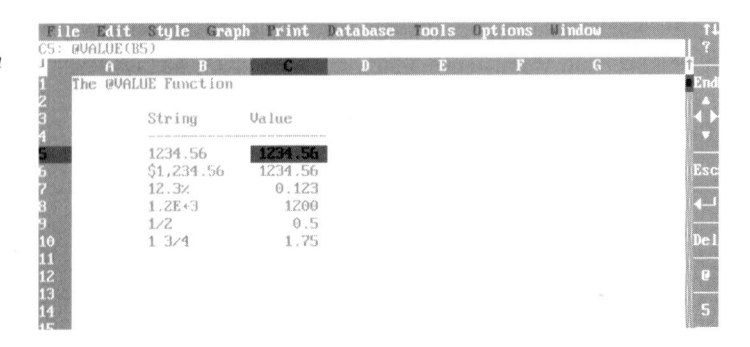

The @CLEAN function

The @CLEAN function strips control characters, which are characters with ASCII codes from 0 to 31, from strings. The form of this function is shown below:

@CLEAN(string)

The *string* argument is the string you want to clean up. If *string* is a literal string, it must be enclosed in quotation marks. If you import data from other programs, the text you import might contain some control characters. For example, if the label in cell B3 contains some control characters, the function @CLEAN(B3) returns the label without those characters.

Numeric conversion functions

Quattro Pro offers two functions—@HEXTONUM and @NUMTOHEX—that allow you to convert numbers from base 16 to base 10, and vice versa. These two functions are especially useful to programmers who need to work with numbers in both their decimal and hexidecimal forms.

The @HEXTONUM function

The @HEXTONUM function converts a hexadecimal (base 16) number to its corresponding decimal value. The form of the @HEXTONUM function is shown below:

@HEXTONUM(hexadecimal string)

The *hexadecimal string* argument is the hexadecimal (base 16) number you want to convert; *hexadecimal string* must be a literal string enclosed in quotation marks or a formula or function that returns a string. The result of this function is the decimal value that corresponds to *hexadecimal string*. For example, the function @HEXTONUM("A") returns the value 10, and the function @HEXTONUM("10") returns the value 16.

The @NUMTOHEX function

The @NUMTOHEX function converts a decimal number to its corresponding hexadecimal string. The @NUMTOHEX function's form is shown below:

@NUMTOHEX(decimal value)

The *decimal value* argument is the decimal number you want to convert; *decimal value* must be a value or formula or a function that returns a value. The result of this function is the hexadecimal string that corresponds to *decimal value*. For example, the function @NUMTOHEX(10) returns the string "A", and the function @NUMTOHEX(16) returns the string "10".

Other Quattro Pro functions

All of the functions covered so far in this chapter can be easily classified into distinct categories: mathematical functions, statistical functions, string functions, numeric conversion functions, and so forth. Quattro Pro offers an additional 14 other functions, however, that are not easily categorized, and so are covered here. They are: @CELLPOINTER, @CELL, @CELLINDEX, @CURVALUE, @ROWS, @COLS, @MEMAVAIL, @MEMEMSAVAIL, @ERR, @NA, @N, @S, @VERSION and @@.

The @CELLPOINTER, @CELL, and @CELLINDEX functions

@CELLPOINTER, @CELL, and @CELLINDEX are functions that return information about the status of a cell. The @CELLPOINTER function returns information about the cell on which the cell selector is positioned when you recalculate the worksheet. The @CELL function returns information about the cell you specify. And, the @CELLINDEX function returns information about the cell with a specified row and column offset in a specified block.

The @CELLPOINTER function

The simplest of these three functions is @CELLPOINTER, which always acts upon the cell over which the cell selector is positioned. This function has the following form:

@CELLPOINTER(code)

The *code* argument is a string that tells Quattro Pro what you want to know about the current cell. Table 4-2 shows the nine possible *code* arguments and the information that each code returns. The @CELLPOINTER function *code* argument must be one of these nine literal strings.

Code	Returns
address	The absolute address of the specified cell
col	The column number of the specified cell
contents	The contents of the specified cell
format	The format code of the specified cell
prefix	The label prefix of the specified label-containing cell
protect	The protection status of the specified cell
row	The row number of the specified cell
type	The type of entry in the specified cell
width	The width of the specified cell

TABLE 4-2. *Use the code argument in the @CELLPOINTER, @CELL, and @CELLINDEX functions to obtain information about the cells in a worksheet.*

The @CELL function

The @CELL function returns information about a specific cell; its form is shown below:

@CELL(code,cell)

The *code* argument is one of the codes listed in Table 4-2 and the *cell* argument is the address of the cell you want to analyze. Although the @CELL function operates only on a single cell, *cell* must be stated as a block reference (for example, A1..A1). If you supply a *cell* that references only a single cell, Quattro Pro converts it to a block reference when you press the Enter key to lock in the function. If you specify a multiple-cell block (such as A1..C4), the function operates on the upper-left cell of that block. The *cell* argument can also be a block name.

Examples of the @CELL function

Figure 4-11 contains several examples of the @CELL function. As you can see, cell C3 contains the value 1000, which has been assigned the Currency format with 0 decimal places ($1,000). The @CELL functions in the block C5..C13 all refer to this cell. The function in cell C5, @CELL("address",C3..C3), returns the string $C$3; the absolute address of cell C3. The function in cell C6, @CELL("col",C3..C3), returns the value 3 because column C is the third column in the worksheet. Similarly, the function in cell C11, @CELL("row",C3..C3), returns the value 3; the row number of cell C3. The function in cell C13, @CELL("width",C3..C3), returns the width of column C, which is 9.

The function in cell C7, @CELL("contents",C3..C3), returns the value 1000, the contents of cell C3. If the entry in cell C3 were a function or formula, the @CELL function would return the result of that entry, not the entry itself. If cell C3

FIGURE 4-11.
The @CELLPOINTER, @CELL, and @CELLINDEX functions return information about the status of a cell.

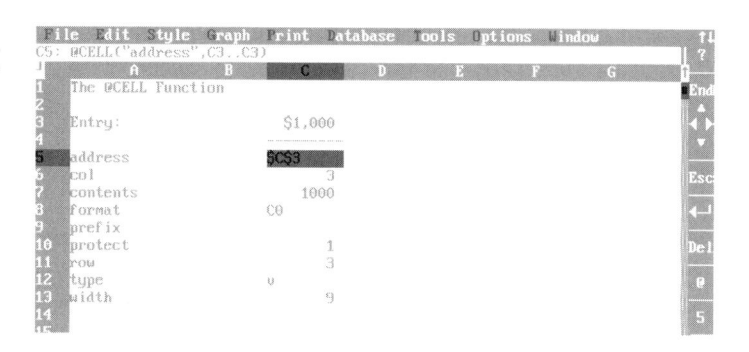

contained a label, the function would simply return that label. The function in cell C8, @CELL("format",C3..C3), returns the string "C0," which means that cell C3 has been assigned the Currency format with 0 decimal places. If the cell had been assigned another format (regardless of the entry in the cell), the function would have returned the first letter of the name of that format, followed by a number indicating the number of decimal places that the cell would display.

The function in cell C9, @CELL("prefix",C3..C3), returns an empty string because cell C3 contains a value instead of a label. If cell C3 had contained a left-aligned label, this function would have returned the label prefix '. If the entry in cell C3 had been a right-aligned label or a centered label, this function would have returned the label prefix " or ^, respectively. The function in cell C10, @CELL("protect",C3..C3), returns the value 1, indicating that cell C3 is protected. If cell C3 were unprotected, this function would have returned the value 0. The function in cell C12, @CELL("type",C3..C3), returns the string "v", indicating that cell C3 contains a value. This function would also return "v" if cell C3 contained a formula or function that returned a value. If cell C3 contained a label instead of a value, this function would have returned the string "l". And, if cell C3 were blank, this function would have returned the string "b".

The @CELLINDEX function

The @CELLINDEX function returns information about the cell with a specified row and column offset in a specified block. The form of the @CELLINDEX function is as follows:

@CELLINDEX(code,block,column offset,row offset)

The *block* argument specifies the rectangular block of cells that contains the cell you want to analyze, and the *column offset* argument specifies the column in *block* that contains the desired cell. The *row offset* argument specifies the row in *block* that contains the desired cell. These arguments specify the offset, or position relative to the upper-left corner of *block*, of the cell whose attributes you want to obtain. Quattro Pro considers the first column and the first row in the block to have an offset of 0. The *block* argument can be either a block reference (such as A1..E4) or a block name (such as VALUES). The *column offset* and *row offset* arguments can be literal values, references to cells that contain literal values, or formulas or functions that return values. For examples of how the *block*, *column offset,* and *row offset* arguments work, see "The @INDEX Function" earlier in this chapter.

The @CURVALUE function

Quattro Pro's @CURVALUE function allows you to determine the current value of any command setting; its form is shown below:

@CURVALUE(general category,specific item)

The *general category* argument specifies a general menu category, and the *specific item* argument specifies a menu item that requires a setting. Both of these arguments must be surrounded by quotation marks; taken together, they should create one of the menu-equivalent commands listed in documentation that comes with Quattro Pro.

Consider an example of the @CURVALUE function that supposes you want to determine the current setting of the print block for your current worksheet. To do so, first find Quattro Pro's menu equivalent command for the Print Block command; it is {/ Print Block}. Next, supply the appropriate arguments in the @CURVALUE function. Because the menu equivalent command for the Print Block command is {/ Print Block}, use "print" for the *general category* argument and "block" for the *specific item* argument, like this: @CURVALUE("print","block"). After you enter this function in a worksheet, it returns the current setting of the print block.

You might be wondering why you would ever want to determine the current menu setting using the @CURVALUE function. Although this function seems to serve little purpose by itself, it allows you to create intelligent and efficient worksheet macros. Chapter 12, "Macro Basics" discusses in detail macros and their applications.

The @ROWS and @COLS functions

Quattro Pro's @ROWS and @COLS functions measure the number of rows or columns in a block. The forms of these functions are shown below:

@ROWS(block)

@COLS(block)

The @ROWS function returns the number of rows in the block specified by *block*, and the @COLS function returns the number of columns in *block*. For example, suppose you have assigned the block name TABLE to the block A1..H50 in your worksheet. The function @ROWS(TABLE) returns the value 50, which indicates that the block TABLE encompasses 50 rows. Similarly, the function @COLS(TABLE) returns the value 8, which indicates that the block TABLE includes eight columns.

The @MEMAVAIL and @MEMEMSAVAIL functions

Quattro Pro offers two functions, @MEMAVAIL and @MEMEMSAVAIL, that help you figure out how much of your computer's memory is free. The @MEMAVAIL function returns the number of bytes of conventional memory available. The @MEMEMSAVAIL function, on the other hand, returns the number of bytes of expanded memory available. These functions accept no arguments. If expanded memory has not been installed on your computer, the @MEMEMSAVAIL function returns the value NA. Like the @CURVALUE function, these two functions are used primarily in macros rather than in worksheet formulas.

The @ERR function

Quattro Pro's @ERR function lets you enter the error value ERR in a cell. This function accepts no arguments. After you enter this function in a cell, that cell displays the result ERR, which is the same result you'll see whenever you attempt to make Quattro Pro do something impossible, such as divide a value by 0, add a value to a label, or use incorrect function syntax. Any cell that contains a reference to a cell that contains the @ERR function also returns the result ERR.

The most common use of the @ERR function is for signalling errors in your worksheets. For example, the function @IF(B1<0,@ERR,B1) returns the value ERR if cell B1 contains a value less than 0.

The @NA function

Quattro Pro's @NA function lets you enter the value NA, which stands for Not Available, in a worksheet. Like @ERR, this function accepts no arguments. After you enter the @NA function in a cell, that cell displays the value NA. In addition, any cell that contains a formula that refers to the cell with the @NA function also displays the value NA.

@NA is most commonly used as a placeholder in incomplete worksheets. If you do not yet have the correct entry for a cell in a worksheet, you can enter the function @NA in that cell. After you recalculate the worksheet, every cell that refers to the cell with the @NA function also returns the result NA, reminding you that your worksheet is incomplete.

The @N and @S functions

The @N and @S functions are rarely used functions that return the contents of the upper-left cell of a block. The forms of these functions are as follows:

@N(block)

@S(block)

FIGURE 4-12.
The @@ function lets you make indirect references to cells and blocks.

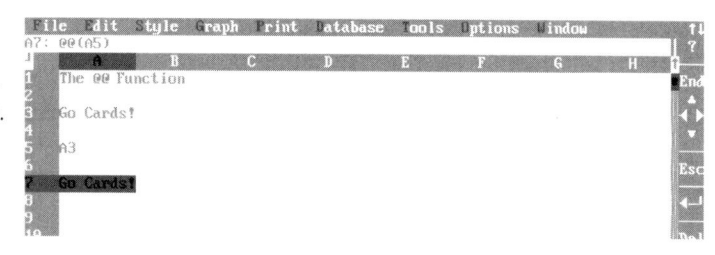

The *block* argument specifies the block of cells on which you want the function to operate. If the upper-left cell of *block* contains a value or formula or a function that returns a value, the @N function returns that value. If the upper-left cell of *block* contains a label or formula or a function that returns a string, the @N function returns the value 0. On the other hand, if the upper-left cell of *block* contains a label or formula or a function that returns a string, the @S function returns the string. But if the upper-left cell of *block* contains a value or formula or a function that returns a value, the @S function returns a blank string.

The @VERSION function

The @VERSION function returns the version number of the copy of Quattro Pro you're using. For example, if you're using version 2.02 of Quattro Pro, @VERSION returns the value 2.02. The function accepts no arguments.

The @@ function

The @@ function lets you make an indirect reference to a cell or block. Like @CELLPOINTER, the @@ function is primarily used in advanced macros. The form of this function is shown below:

   @@(cell reference)

The *cell reference* argument is the address or name of a cell (the first cell) that contains the address or name of another cell (the second cell). The address stored in the first cell must be a label. The @@ function uses the label in the first cell to locate the second cell, and then returns the contents of the second cell.

The worksheet in Figure 4-12 contains an example of the @@ function. Cell A3 contains the label 'Go Cards!, and cell A5 contains the label 'A3. As you can see, the function in cell A7, @@(A5), returns the label 'Go Cards!; the contents of cell A3. When evaluating this function, Quattro Pro looks in cell A5 (the cell specified by the function's argument) for the address or name of another cell. In this case, cell A5 contains the label 'A3, so Quattro Pro returns the contents of cell A3.

5

Worksheet Commands

You've already read about the Edit Names Create command, the Style Numeric Format command, and the cut-and-paste editing commands. This chapter covers the rest of Quattro Pro's worksheet commands you use to enter and manipulate data in the worksheet.

Filling blocks

Quattro Pro includes a command called Edit Fill that lets you create a series of evenly spaced values. You might need, for instance, to use Edit Fill to number the records in a Quattro Pro database or to create a series of dates.

After you choose the Edit Fill command, Quattro Pro displays the prompt *Destination for cells* in the input line, followed by the address of the current cell. Specify the block you want Quattro Pro to fill, and then press the Enter key. Next, Quattro Pro prompts you to supply the start value, the number you want Quattro Pro to place in the block's first cell. You can press the Enter key to accept Quattro Pro's default value. Or, you can type any value you want (including a formula or function), and then press the Enter key. Quattro Pro then prompts you to supply the step value, the interval you want between each value in the series. You can press the Enter key to accept Quattro Pro's default value. Or, you can type any value (including a negative value), and press the Enter key. Finally, Quattro Pro prompts you to supply the stop value, which specifies the largest (or the smallest) value you want Quattro Pro to include in the series. Type this value and press the Enter key. Quattro Pro fills the selected block with the series you have defined.

An example of filling blocks

Suppose you want to fill the block A1..A10 in a new worksheet with a series of numbers, with the first value in the series 10, the interval between the numbers in the series 10, and the last value in the series 100. To begin, press the Home key to move the cell selector to cell A1, and then choose the Edit Fill command. At the *Destination for cells* prompt, select block A1..A10, and press the Enter key. When you see the prompt *Start Value*, type 10 and press the Enter key. Then, when you see the prompt *Step Value*, type 10 and press the Enter key. Finally, when you see the prompt *Stop Value*, specify a value that is greater than or equal to the last value you want Quattro Pro to include in the series (in this case, 100), and press the Enter key. Figure 5-1 shows the result.

A closer look at Edit Fill

You can use the Edit Fill command to generate a series of evenly spaced values. But if you want to generate a series of numbers that are unevenly spaced, you'll have to use a series of formulas instead of values.

You can also use Edit Fill to fill a block of cells with the same number. Type the number you want as the start and stop values and 0 as the step value.

Defaults

The first time you choose the Edit Fill command, Quattro Pro supplies its own default values for the fill block and the start, step, and stop values. The default fill block is simply a reference to the current cell. Move the cell selector to the first cell in the block before you choose the Edit Fill command to take advantage of this

FIGURE 5-1.
The Edit Fill command fills a block of a worksheet with an evenly spaced series of values.

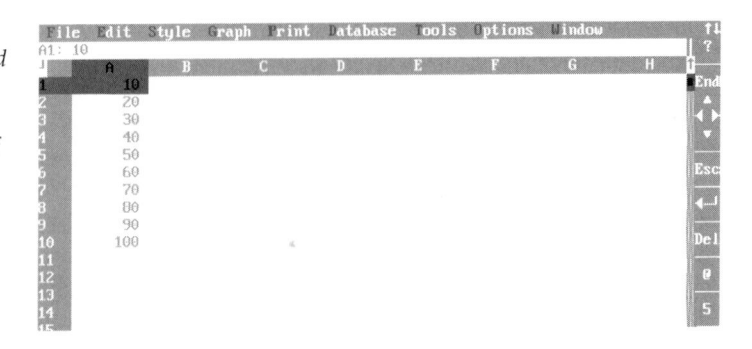

default. The default start value is 0, the default step value is 1, and the default stop value is 8192.

After you use the Edit Fill command in a worksheet, Quattro Pro remembers the settings you have defined for the fill block and the start, step, and stop values, and uses those settings as the new defaults the next time you choose the Edit Fill command before you exit from the program. You'll find this feature handy if you want to fill the same block with a different series.

The fill block

Although the fill block will usually be a one-column or one-row block, the Edit Fill command also lets you fill a rectangular block of cells. If the fill block you specify includes more than one column and more than one row, Quattro Pro fills the block in order by columns.

The stop value

Use the stop value to tell Quattro Pro to stop filling the fill block after the numbers in the series exceed a certain value. Quattro Pro stops filling after it reaches the end of the fill block or after the numbers exceed the stop value, whichever comes first.

For example, suppose you want to fill block A1..A10 with numbers that begin with 10 and have an interval of 1, stopping when the numbers in the block reach 15. Choose the Edit Fill command, select block A1..A10 as the fill block, and press the Enter key; type 10 as the start value, and press the Enter key. Type 1 as the step value and press the Enter key, then type 15 as the stop value and press the Enter key. Figure 5-2 shows the result of this command. Notice that Quattro Pro has filled only part of the fill block, stopping when the numbers in the fill block reached the stop value of 15 in cell A6.

The stop value comes in handy when you are filling a large block with a series that has a definite end point. Instead of guessing at the exact dimensions of the fill block, you can define it to be larger than it needs to be, and then use the stop value to stop the series when it reaches the end value. In most cases, however, you only need to be sure that the stop value is large enough not to interfere with the series you are creating. If you specify a stop value that is less than the start value, Quattro Pro will not fill any cells in the fill block. If your step value is positive, you

FIGURE 5-2.
The stop value lets you tell Quattro Pro when to stop filling the fill block with values.

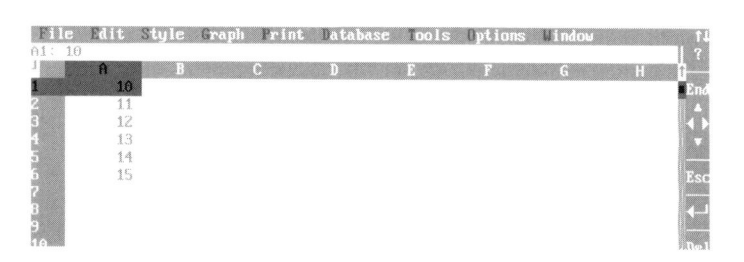

should make sure that the stop value is greater than the largest value you want Quattro Pro to place in the fill block.

The start, step, and stop values can be positive or negative and can be integer, decimal, or mixed numbers. Be careful, however, when you specify a negative value. Whenever the step value is less than 0, you need to specify a stop value that is less than the start value. Of course, if the step value is less than 0 and the start value is negative, then the stop value must also be negative.

Using formulas and functions

The start, step, and stop values will usually be literal numbers. Quattro Pro also allows you, however, to use formulas and functions to specify those values. For example, in Chapter 6, "Dates and Times," you'll see how to create a series of dates by using a @DATE function as the start value. To use a formula or function as the start, step, or stop value, type that formula or function when Quattro Pro prompts you for those values.

If you use a formula or function as the start, step, or stop value, Quattro Pro converts that formula or function to a value while generating the values in the series. If you choose the Edit Fill command again after specifying a formula or function as the start, step, or stop value, Quattro Pro presents the result of the formula or function (instead of the formula or function itself) as the new default setting.

Computing frequency distributions

The Tools Frequency command allows you to compute a frequency distribution for a set of values. A frequency distribution is a table that groups a series of values into ranges that you specify. For example, you might use a frequency distribution to group the students in a class according to the scores they received on a test. The distribution could include categories for scores below 70, scores between 70 and 80, scores between 80 and 90, and scores of 90 or above.

To compute a frequency distribution in Quattro Pro, enter two sets of numbers in the worksheet. The first is the set of numbers you want to distribute. This block is called the values block. The second set defines the groups into which you want to distribute the numbers in the values block. Because this group defines the "bins" into which you will group the numbers, it is called the bin block. The bin block must be entered in a single column.

After you enter both sets of numbers in the worksheet, choose the Tools Frequency command to generate the frequency distribution. Quattro Pro displays the prompt *Specify Values block* in the input line, followed by a reference to the current cell. Specify the block that contains the values you want to group, and press the Enter key. Next, Quattro Pro presents the prompt *Specify Bin block*, followed by a reference to the current cell. Specify the block that contains the bin values, and press the Enter key. Quattro Pro computes a frequency distribution and displays it in the cells directly to the right of the bin block, overwriting any information contained in these cells.

An example of computing frequency distribution

The worksheet shown in Figure 5-3 is set up for a frequency distribution. Block B1..B10 contains the salaries of a number of people, and the values in block D1..D4 define the bins into which you want to group the salaries. Suppose you want to compute a frequency distribution that tells you how many people earn a salary of $20,000 or less, how many earn between $20,000 and $30,000, how many earn between $30,000 and $40,000, and so forth.

To compute the distribution, choose the Tools Frequency command. When Quattro Pro prompts you for the values block, select block B1..B10, which contains the values you want to group, and press the Enter key. After Quattro Pro prompts you for the bin block, select block D1..D4, which contains the values that define the bin, and press the Enter key. Quattro Pro computes the distribution, as shown in Figure 5-4.

The values in column E of Figure 5-4 are the number of items from the values block that fall within the bins defined by the numbers in column D. The number 2 in cell E1 indicates that two people have a salary of $20,000 or less, and the number

FIGURE 5-3.
Use the data in this worksheet to create a frequency distribution.

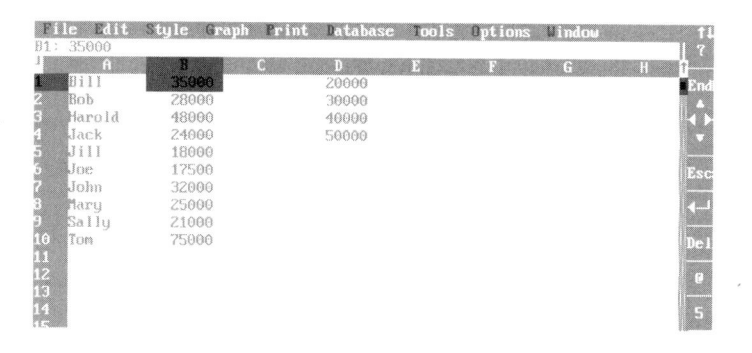

FIGURE 5-4.
The Tools Frequency command distributes values into the bins you define.

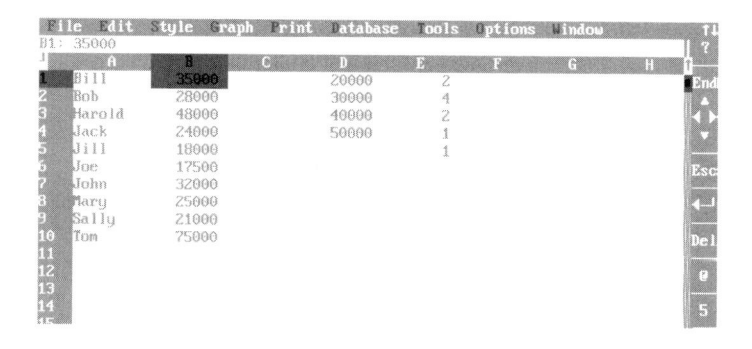

4 in cell E2 indicates that four people have a salary between $20,000 and $30,000, and so on.

A closer look at Tools Frequency

Notice that the values in the bin block in column D of Figure 5-4 are arranged in ascending order. Always place the lowest bin value in the top cell of the bins block and arrange the values in ascending order. The values in the bin block represent the upper limit for each bin. In other words, each bin contains the values that are less than or equal to the bin value, but greater than the next lowest bin value. If a value is exactly equal to one of the values in the bin block, it will be placed in the bin with that value. For example, the number 1 in cell E5 tells you that one person has an income of over $50,000.

Quattro Pro always includes one more value in the frequency distribution than there are entries in the bin block. This additional entry tells you how many values are greater than the last bin value. You can place the values block and bin block anywhere in your worksheet, including nonadjacent locations. You will, however, typically want to keep the values and bin blocks adjacent in the worksheet. Fortunately, Quattro Pro imposes no limits on the number of values you can include in the values or bin blocks, or on the size of those values. You cannot, however, include labels in either of these blocks; only values are allowed.

After you use the Tools Frequency command one time in a worksheet, Quattro Pro remembers your settings for the values and bin blocks. The next time you choose this command, Quattro Pro offers your previous settings as the new defaults. If you want to recompute the distribution, choose the Tools Frequency command and press the Enter key two times to accept your previous values and bin blocks settings. Of course, if you want to define different values or bin blocks, you must redefine these blocks when you choose the command again.

Building what-if tables

Perhaps the most important benefit of spreadsheet software is its ability to perform what-if analysis. For example, suppose you are considering setting up an Individual Retirement Account (IRA) to which you will deposit $1,000 each year, and you want to know how much the IRA will be worth in 25 years. Of course, the value of the investment is directly affected by the rate of interest that your IRA earns, and a what-if analysis helps you look at the affects of those varying rates.

To analyze the future value of this IRA, you could create a simple two-column table like the one shown in Figure 5-5. As you can see, the left column of this table contains several different interest rates, and the right column contains the future

FIGURE 5-5.
You might use a simple table like this one to perform a what-if analysis manually.

Interest Rate	25 Year FV of IRA
5.5%	$51,153
8.0%	$73,105
10.5%	$106,052
13.0%	$155,620
15.5%	$230,260

value of the IRA at each of those interest rates. (You would need to use either a financial calculator or a future value table to calculate the future values.)

Quattro Pro's Tools What-If command allows you to build this kind of what-if table in your Quattro Pro worksheets. The Tools What-If command lets you compute the result of a formula or function using a series of values, and creates a table that shows the result generated by each value.

Basics of what-if tables

Before you can use the Tools What-If command in a worksheet, you must first set up the framework of a what-if table. The what-if table must include one or two sets of values and at least one formula: the table formula. The exact form of the table depends on whether it is a one-variable or two-variable table and how many formulas you want to compute. In either case, enter the values or formulas in the left column or the top row of the table, or both; Quattro Pro fills in the rest of the table with the results.

When you choose the Tools What-If command, Quattro Pro presents a menu that allows you to define the type of table you want to set up and offers four choices: 1 Variable, 2 Variables, Reset, and Quit. The 1 Variable option lets you create a one-variable table, the 2 Variables option lets you create a two-variable table, the Reset option allows you to reset the blocks you have previously defined using the Tools What-If command, and the Quit option cancels the command and returns Quattro Pro to the READY mode. When you choose the type of table you want to set up, Quattro Pro displays the prompt *Block of cells to use as Data Table* in the input line, followed by a reference to the current cell. Specify the table block and press the Enter key. The table block is the smallest rectangular block that includes the table formula and all of the table's variables. You'll learn more about the different types of tables in later sections of this chapter.

Next, Quattro Pro prompts you for the input cell (or cells if you're working with a two-way table, which is explained shortly), which is a cell that is referred to, either directly or indirectly, by the table formula. This is a temporary working cell Quattro Pro uses while performing the calculations for the table. Quattro Pro places a value from each cell in the table in the input cell one at a time, recalculating the table formula each time. The result of each calculation is stored next to the corresponding value in the table. Quattro Pro remembers the entries you have made for the table block and the input cell (or cells). The next time you choose the Tools What-If command, Quattro Pro displays these settings as the new defaults. If you want to remove any previous settings you have entered, choose the Tools What-If Reset command.

One-variable tables

What-if tables that contain one variable let you compute the results of a formula as the variable changes. One-variable tables can include one or more formulas. A one-variable table has a specific form: The values of the variable must be entered vertically in a single column, and the table formulas must be entered horizontally one row above and one column to the right of the column that contains the variables. The table's results appear below the table formula. Each result appears next to the value with which it is associated.

An example of a one-formula table

Suppose you want Quattro Pro to compute the future value of an IRA at five different interest rates: 5.5 percent, 8 percent, 10.5 percent, 13 percent, and 15.5 percent. To build this table, first enter these interest rates, which will be the values of the variables for the what-if table, in block A3..A7. Next, enter the function @FV(1000,B1,25), the table formula, in cell B2. At this point, your screen looks like the one shown in Figure 5-6.

After you have set up the what-if table, move the cell selector to cell A2 and choose the Tools What-If command. Because this will be a one-variable what-if table, choose 1 Variable from the menu. Next, Quattro Pro displays the prompt *Block of cells to use as Data Table*. Select block A2..B7, the smallest rectangular block that contains all of the values and the table formula, and press the Enter key. Quattro Pro now displays the prompt *Input Cell from column*. The input cell of a what-if table is a cell that is referred to by the table formula. Because the table formula (in cell B2) refers to the blank cell B1, you should select cell B1 as the input cell and then press the Enter key to complete the command.

FIGURE 5-6.
Before you can use the Tools What-If command, you must build the framework of a what-if table in your worksheet.

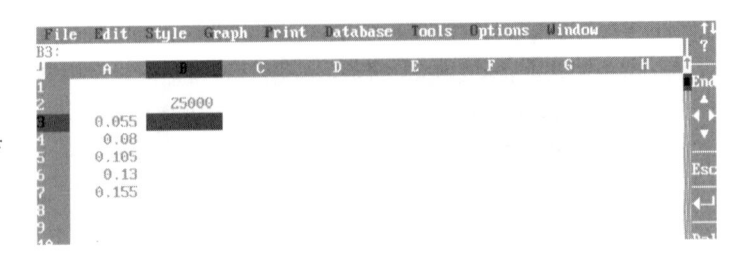

Quattro Pro now computes the table results, displaying the five results of the table formula (one result for each substitution value) in block B3..B7, as shown in Figure 5-7.

How the what-if table works

Here's how the what-if table works: After you press the Enter key to lock in the input cell, Quattro Pro substitutes the first value from the list, .055, in the input cell, B1. At this point, Quattro Pro calculates the table formula in cell B2 and places the result of the formula in cell B3. Because the table formula refers to cell B1, it returns a different result every time a new value is substituted in cell B1. When cell B1 contains the value .055, the table formula in cell B2 returns the value 51152.59. Quattro Pro places the result of the formula in cell B3, next to the value .055. After computing the result for the first value, Quattro Pro substitutes the second value, .08, in cell B1 and recalculates the table formula. Because the value in cell B1 has changed, the result of the table formula also changes. Quattro Pro then enters the new result, 73105.94, in the table in cell B4, next to the value .08.

This process of substitution and recalculation continues until Quattro Pro uses the last value. Quattro Pro then erases the last value from the input cell and stops recalculating the table. This whole process of substitution and recalculation takes place so quickly that you probably notice only a slight pause while Quattro Pro does its work.

A table with two equations

You can include more than one table formula in a one-variable what-if table. You must enter the second formula in the cell immediately to the right of the first formula, and you must enter any additional formulas in the same row to the right of the second formula. Again, all of the table formulas must refer, directly or indirectly, to the table's input cell.

For example, suppose you want to determine the future value of the IRA account assuming a contribution of $2,000 each year. You can modify the table shown in Figure 5-7 to make the additional calculations by entering the function @FV(2000,B1,25) in cell C2. After you add the formula to the table, redefine the table block by choosing the Tools What-If command and then choosing the

FIGURE 5-7.
Quattro Pro presents the results of the table formula next to the values in the what-if table.

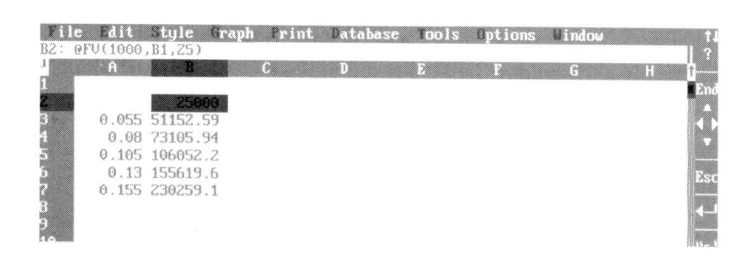

1 Variable option. Quattro Pro displays the prompt *Block of cells to use as Data Table*. (Notice that Quattro Pro uses the current table block as the default block for the command.) Press the Right direction key one time to change this block to A2..C7 and then press the Enter key. Quattro Pro displays the prompt *Input Cell from column*. Because the input cell for this new table is also B1, you can simply press the Enter key to accept the default setting.

Now, Quattro Pro recalculates the entire table and enters the new results. The results for the second table formula appear below that formula, as shown in Figure 5-8. As before, Quattro Pro calculates this table by substituting the variables in block A3..A7 into the input cell, B1. After each substitution, Quattro Pro calculates both table formulas and enters the results in the table.

Two-variable tables

All of the examples considered so far in this chapter have been one-variable what-if tables. Quattro Pro also lets you create two-variable what-if tables, in which Quattro Pro calculates the results of the table formula for two different variables. A two-variable what-if table has a specific form: The values of the first variable must be entered in adjacent cells of a single column, and the values of the second variable must be entered in adjacent cells of the row immediately above the first variable in the first set. This forms a grid with one set of values in the column on the left side and another in the row along the top. Quattro Pro fills in values for each unique combination of the two variables in the empty grid. In addition, the table formula must be entered in the cell at the intersection of the row and the column containing the two sets of values.

Quattro Pro allows you to enter only one formula in a two-variable what-if table; you cannot test two formulas at one time, as you can in one-variable what-if tables. To test the second and subsequent formulas, you must change the formula and recalculate the table repeatedly.

An example of a two-variable table

Suppose that you want to build a table that will calculate the future value of an IRA using a variety of term and interest rate assumptions, and that you plan to

FIGURE 5-8.
You can include more than one table formula in a one-variable table.

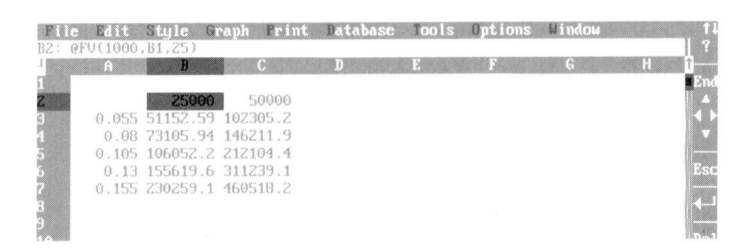

make an annual IRA contribution of $1,000. You want to compute the future value of the IRA after 20, 25, 30, and 35 years at interest rates of 5.5 percent, 8 percent, 10.5 percent, 13 percent, and 15.5 percent.

First, enter the five interest rates you want to test in block A3..A7 of a blank worksheet. Next, enter the different terms (20, 25, 30, and 35 years) in block B2..E2. Then, enter the table formula @FV(1000, B1, C1) in cell A2. Notice that this formula is located in the cell at the intersection of the row and column containing the two sets of values. Also notice that this formula refers to the two blank cells B1 and C1. You'll define cells B1 and C1 as the input cells for the table. Figure 5-9 shows the screen at this point.

After you have set up the new table, move the cursor to cell A2, choose the Tools What-If command, and then choose the 2 Variables option. Quattro Pro displays the prompt *Block of cells to use as Data Table*. Select block A2..E7, the smallest rectangular range that includes the table formula and both sets of values, and press the Enter key.

Next, Quattro Pro prompts you for the table's input cells. Because this is a two-variable table, you must define two input cells: one for the values in the table's first column and one for the values in the table's first row. When calculating the table, Quattro Pro substitutes the values from the table's first column in the first input cell you specify, and substitutes the variables from the table's first row into the second input cell you specify. It is important to keep the order straight in a two-way table. If you reverse the substitution values, Quattro Pro uses the wrong input values in the table formula, and your results are meaningless. You will recall that the table formula in cell A2 refers to cells B1 and C1. After Quattro Pro displays the prompt *Input Cell from column*, select cell B1 and press the Enter key. When you see the prompt *Input Cell from top row*, select cell C1 and press the Enter key.

As soon as you lock in the second input cell, Quattro Pro computes the table; Figure 5-10 shows the result. The numbers that you see throughout this table are the future values of the IRA at each combination of interest rates and terms. For example, the number in cell E6, 546680.8, is the future value of the IRA at an interest rate of 13 percent and a term of 35 years.

FIGURE 5-9.
A two-way table includes two sets of values and one table formula.

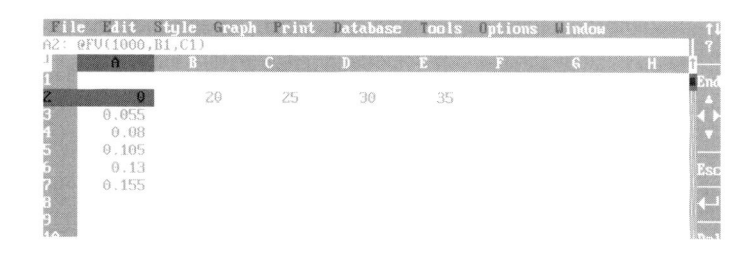

FIGURE 5-10.
Quattro Pro places the results of a two-way table formula in the appropriate rows and columns of the table.

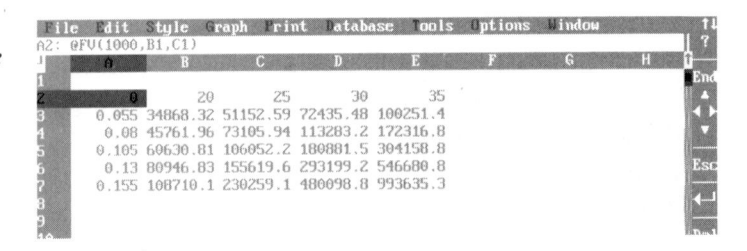

How the two-way table works

Quattro Pro computes this table using a process of substitution and recalculation, substituting the first value from column A, which is 0.055, in cell B1, and the first value from row 2, which is 20, in cell C1. Then, Quattro Pro computes the table formula and stores the result, 34868.32, in cell B3. Notice that Quattro Pro stores the result next to the value 0.055 in column A and below the value 20 in row 3. After making the first calculation and storing the result in the table, Quattro Pro substitutes the second value from column A, which is 0.08, into cell B1; substitutes the first value from the row 3 list, which is 20, into cell C1 again; recalculates the table formula in cell A2, and stores that result in cell B4. The same process of substitution and recalculation continues until each pair of substitution values has been used.

Using the [What-If] key to recompute

After you build a what-if table and define the table block and the input cell, you can easily recompute the table with a different set of substitution values or a different formula. To recompute the table, simply change the substitution values or the table formula (or both), and then press the [What-If] key (F8). Quattro Pro immediately recomputes the active what-if table and displays the new results in the table.

A closer look at what-if tables

The examples used in this chapter placed the what-if tables in the upper-left corner of the worksheet. You can, however, position a table anywhere in the worksheet; no restrictions on its position apply. Similarly, the examples used cells B1 and C1 as the input cells, but you can position the input cells anywhere you want. The only rule concerning input cells is that the table formula must refer to them either directly or indirectly. The examples use a formula that refers to the input cells directly, but you can also create what-if tables that have formulas that refer to the input cell indirectly. In other words, the table formula can refer to a cell or cells that contain formulas that refer to the input cell. As long as a link exists between the table formula and the input cell(s), the table will work. In addition, although the input cells used in the examples were empty, you can define input cells that contain entries. In fact, your what-if tables will often refer to input cells that contain entries. When the input cell you define contains an entry, Quattro Pro stores that entry temporarily while performing substitution and recalculation. After the table calculation is finished, Quattro Pro returns the original entry to the input cell.

The results Quattro Pro enters in the what-if table are pure values, and not formulas or functions. For example, the entry in cell B3 of Figure 5-10 contains the value 34868.32. Because these entries are pure values, they can be copied easily to other areas of the worksheet without fear of confusing absolute or relative references.

Computing linear regression

Quattro Pro's Tools Advanced Math Regression command allows you to perform linear regression in your Quattro Pro worksheets. Linear regression is a statistical technique that measures the extent to which one characteristic of a population (the dependent variable, y) is related to another characteristic (the independent variable, x). For example, you can use regression analysis to measure the extent to which the number of houses sold is determined by interest rates.

After you choose the Tools Advanced Math Regression command, you see the menu shown in Figure 5-11. To compute the regression statistics, define the Independent data block, the Dependent data block, and the Output block, and then choose Go. The Independent block is a block that contains the values for the independent variable. The Dependent block is a block that contains the values for the dependent variable. The Output block should be a blank area of your worksheet in which Quattro Pro can place the results of the command. You need only specify the address of the upper-left corner of the Output block. If you want to cancel the command and return Quattro Pro to READY mode, choose the Quit option.

You can use the Tools Advanced Math Regression command in a number of ways: to plot a regression line (which is explained shortly), to predict the value of the dependent variable (y) that corresponds to a given value of the independent variable (x), and to measure the degree of certainty to which you can predict values of the dependent variable from values of the independent variable.

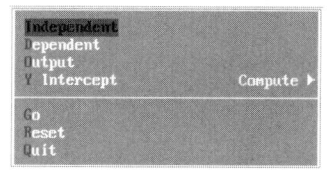

FIGURE 5-11.
Quattro Pro's Tools Advanced Math Regression command lets you perform linear regression.

An example of computing linear regression

The worksheet shown in Figure 5-12 contains age, height, and weight data for nine men. These men were selected randomly from a large group of men, which we'll call the population. The group of nine men is called a sample of the population.

Now, suppose you want to perform linear regression on this data. To begin, you can measure the extent to which the weight of these men is dependent upon their height. Because it's assumed that weight is to some extent dependent on height, height is the independent (or x) variable and weight is the dependent (or y) variable.

To begin computing the regression, choose the Tools Advanced Math Regression command. From the Regression menu shown in Figure 5-11, choose the Independent option. Then, select block C2..C10 and press the Enter key. Next, choose the Dependent option from the menu, select block D2..D10, and press the Enter key. Now, choose the Output option from the menu, select cell A12, and press the Enter key. Finally, choose Go from the menu to compute the regression statistics. Figure 5-13 shows the results. Notice the small table that Quattro Pro has created in block A12..D20 to display the regression results.

Using the results of linear regression

The most useful regression statistics are the constant and the x coefficient. The constant is the y-axis intercept value of the regression line that describes the relationship between the dependent (y) and independent (x) variables, and the x coefficient is the slope of that line. In the example shown in Figure 5-13, the constant for the regression line, -536.858, appears in cell D13. This value is the y-axis intercept of the regression line that describes the relationship between height and weight. The x coefficient for the regression, 9.933628, appears in cell C19. The x coefficient predicts how much the dependent variable will change for a change of one unit in the independent variable. Because the x coefficient in the example is 9.933628, you can predict that the value of the dependent variable (weight) will

FIGURE 5-12.
Use this worksheet to demonstrate the Tools Advanced Math Regression command.

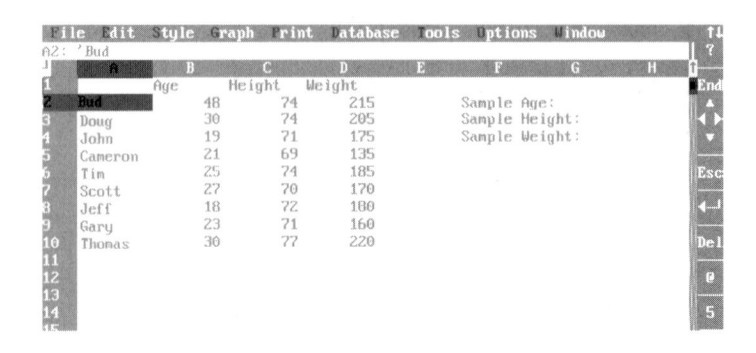

FIGURE 5-13.
The Tools Advanced Math Regression command computes statistics that describe the relationship between two variables.

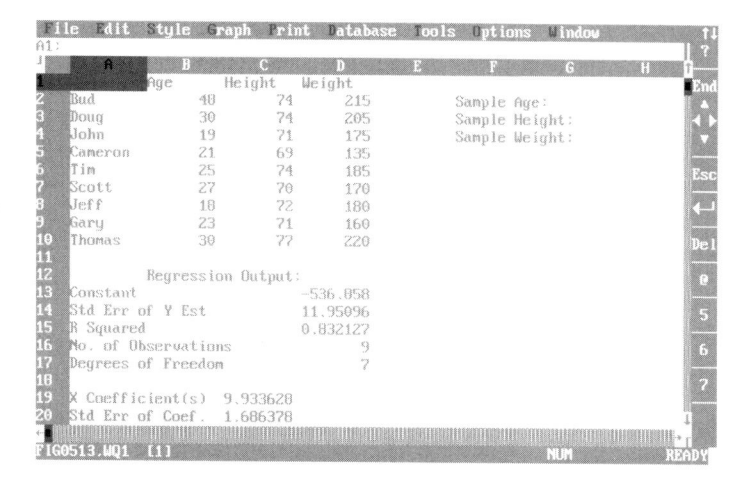

```
File Edit Style Graph Print Database Tools Options Window
A1:
       A         B         C         D         E         F         G         H
              Age     Height    Weight
2   Bud        40        74       215              Sample Age:
3   Doug       30        74       205              Sample Height:
4   John       19        71       175              Sample Weight:
5   Cameron    21        69       135
6   Tim        25        74       185
7   Scott      27        70       170
8   Jeff       18        72       180
9   Gary       23        71       160
10  Thomas     30        77       220
11
12              Regression Output:
13  Constant                     -536.058
14  Std Err of Y Est              11.95096
15  R Squared                      0.832127
16  No. of Observations                  9
17  Degrees of Freedom                   7
18
19  X Coefficient(s)   9.933620
20  Std Err of Coef.   1.686378

FIG0513.WQ1  [1]                                              NUM      READY
```

increase 9.93 for each increase of 1 in the independent variable (height). For example, you can predict that if Jeff grows 1 inch, he will gain 9.93 pounds.

Making predictions. You can predict the value of the dependent variable (y) for any given value of the independent variable (x) by using the constant and the x coefficient in an equation, as shown below:

y= (x coefficient*x)+constant

You might recognize this formula as the standard mathematical formula $y=mx+b$. After the equation is written in this form, m represents the x coefficient, or slope, and b represents the constant, or y-axis intercept. As an example, suppose you want to predict the weight (y value) for someone who has a height (x value) of 73. To do so, move the cell selector to cell H3 and enter the value 73. Next, move to cell H4, enter the formula ($C$19*H3)+$D$13, and press the Enter key. Quattro Pro returns the predicted y value for an x value of 73, which is 188.2965. In other words, the regression formula predicts that a person who is 73 inches tall will weigh 188.3 pounds.

Creating the regression line. You can also use y=(x coefficient*x)+constant to create a regression line that illustrates the relationship between the dependent and independent variables. For example, suppose you want to create a regression line that describes the relationship between height and weight in the sample worksheet. To begin, move the cell selector to cell E2 and enter the formula ($C$19*C2)+$D$13. (Notice that this formula is almost identical to the one in cell H4). Now, use the Edit Copy command to copy this formula from cell E2 to block E3..E10. Figure 5-14 shows the resulting worksheet.

The values in column E of Figure 5-14 predict the weight for men who are the same height as the men in the sample. For example, the value in cell E2 predicts

FIGURE 5-14.
You can use the Constant, X Coefficient, and X values to create a regression line in a worksheet.

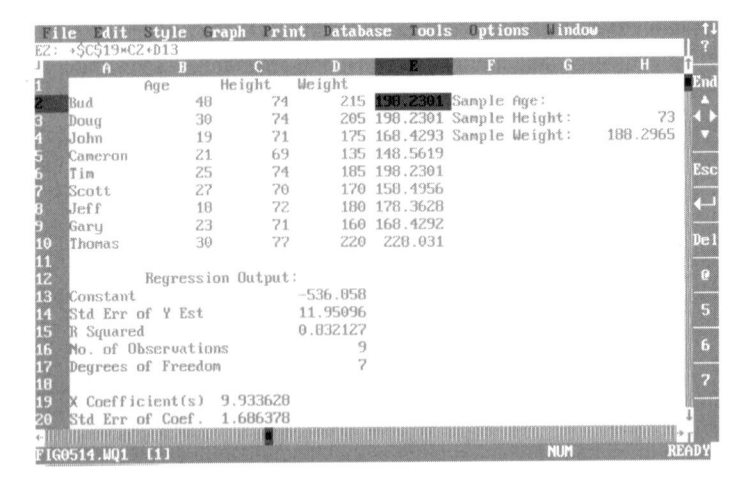

that a man who is 74 inches tall will weigh approximately 198 pounds. The predicted values in column E are close to, but not equal to, the actual values of the dependent variables shown in column D. The regression line merely estimates the relationship between the dependent and independent variables. Although the values predicted by the regression are seldom identical to the actual values of the dependent variable, the predicted values illustrate the basic relationship between the independent and dependent variables. In the example, the regression line predicts that a man's weight will increase by 9.93 pounds for each 1-inch increase in his height.

After you have created the regression line, you'll probably want to plot it on an XY graph, which is explained in Chapter 10 in "Quattro Pro's Graph Types."

Interpreting the results of a regression

So far, we have assumed that the constant and x coefficient generated by the Tools Advanced Math Regression command predict the relationship between the dependent and independent variables. You should be aware, however, that this is not always the case; sometimes the results of a regression do not accurately depict the relationship between the independent and dependent variables. Fortunately, the Tools Advanced Math Regression command computes several statistics that help you measure the reliability of a regression. These statistics are called the standard error of y Estimate, the r squared, the number of observations, the degrees of freedom, and the standard error of coefficient.

Cell D14 in Figure 5-14 contains the standard error of y estimate (abbreviated Std Err of y Est) for the regression line, which is 11.95096. This value helps you determine the certainty with which the dependent variable can be predicted from the independent variable. As a rule, the larger the standard error of y estimate is relative to the predicted y values, the less certain you can be about the prediction.

Cell D15 contains the *r* squared value (sometimes called the coefficient of determination) for the regression, which is 0.832127. The *r* squared value tells you what percentage of the variation in the dependent variable is explained by the variation in the independent variable. The value ranges from 1 (a strong relationship between the dependent and independent variables) to 0 (no relationship between the variables). As a rule, the larger the *r* squared value, the better the chances are that the independent variable explains the variation in the dependent variable. In this example, the *r* squared value in cell D15 means that in about 83 percent of the cases, the variation in weight is explained by the variation in height.

Cell D16 contains the number of observations, which is 9. This number is simply the total number of values in the *x* or *y* block. Cell D17 contains the degrees of freedom, which is 7. For a simple example like this one, the degrees of freedom is calculated by subtracting 2 from the number of observations.

Finally, cell C20 contains the standard error of coefficient (abbreviated Std Err of Coef): 1.686378. This value is an estimate of the standard deviation of the sampling distribution of the *x* coefficient. In general, the larger the standard error of coefficient is in relation to the *x* coefficient, the less certain you can be about the prediction. As a rule, the larger the sample, the smaller the standard error of coefficient will be. Because this sample is small, the standard error of coefficient is rather large.

A closer look at linear regression

In the example, you computed a regression using a sample of only nine men, but you can perform regression on much larger data sets; up to 8,192 values in both the dependent and independent blocks. As in the example, the values for the independent variable must be arranged in a single column; so must the values for the dependent variable. Although the values for the two variables do not have to be in adjacent columns, it is more convenient to set up the worksheet so that they are adjacent. In addition, a one-to-one correspondence must exist between the values in the dependent and independent blocks. In other words, no blanks should be included in either the independent or dependent blocks.

Multiple regression

In the first example, you perform a simple linear regression in which you measured the relationship between one independent variable and one dependent variable. You can also use the Tools Advanced Math Regression command to perform a multiple linear regression, in which you measure the relationship between two or more independent variables and a dependent variable.

FIGURE 5-15.
Multiple regression uses two or more independent variables to explain the variation in the dependent variable.

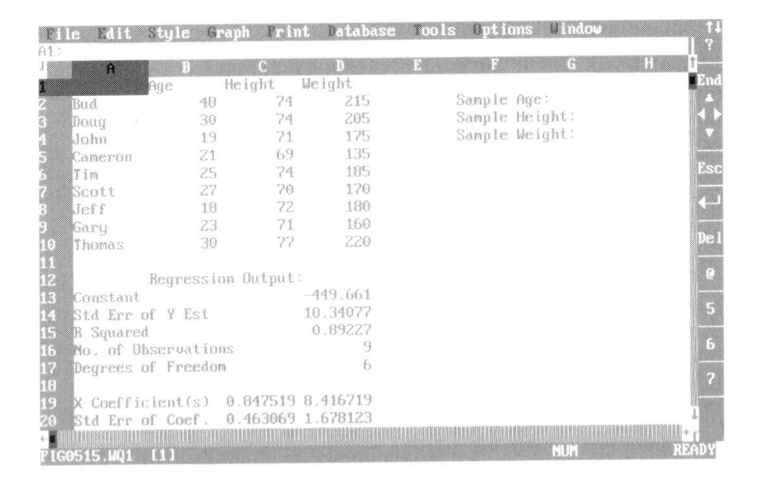

```
 A1:
      A         B        C         D         E        F         G         H
 1              Age     Height   Weight
 2    Bud        48       74       215              Sample Age:
 3    Doug       30       74       205              Sample Height:
 4    John       19       71       175              Sample Weight:
 5    Cameron    21       69       135
 6    Tim        25       74       185
 7    Scott      27       70       170
 8    Jeff       18       72       180
 9    Gary       23       71       160
10    Thomas     30       72       220
11
12             Regression Output:
13    Constant                    -449.661
14    Std Err of Y Est             10.34077
15    R Squared                     0.89227
16    No. of Observations                9
17    Degrees of Freedom                 6
18
19    X Coefficient(s)   0.847519  8.416719
20    Std Err of Coef.   0.463069  1.678123
```

An example of multiple regression

Suppose you want to measure the relationship among the ages, heights, and weights of the men in the sample. In this analysis, age and height are the independent variables, and weight is the dependent variable. To begin, choose the Tools Advanced Math Regression command, choose the Independent option, and select block B2..C10. Notice that this block includes all of the independent variables (age and height) for each person. Next, choose the Dependent option and select block D2..D10. Now, choose the Output option and select cell A12. Finally, choose Go to calculate the new regression. Figure 5-15 shows the resulting worksheet. Notice that Quattro Pro has calculated an *x* coefficient and the standard error of coefficient for each independent variable. Also notice that the confidence statistics were improved by using a second independent variable.

A closer look at multiple regression

In the example shown in Figure 5-15, you computed a multiple regression using two independent variables, but you can perform a multiple regression using three, four, or more independent variables. The values for all of the independent variables must be arranged in adjacent columns. In addition, no blanks should be included in the independent or dependent blocks.

The results of a multiple regression are as useful as the results of a simple regression. For example, suppose you want to predict the weight of a man who is 74 inches tall and 48 years old. To do so, enter the value 48 in cell H2 and the value 74 in cell H3. Next, enter the formula ($C$19*H2)+($D$19*H3)+$D$13 in cell H4. This formula predicts the value of the dependent variable (weight) quite accurately by using both of the independent variables (age and height). Of course, you can use a similar formula to create the regression line by using both *x* coefficients.

The Y Intercept option

The Y Intercept option in the Advanced Regression menu allows you to compute a linear regression with a preset constant (y-intercept) of 0. In other words, this option tells Quattro Pro to set the y-intercept of the regression line to 0 and to adjust the other regression statistics (including the x coefficient, or slope, of the regression line) to compensate. When you choose the Y Intercept option, Quattro Pro presents a menu with two choices: Compute and Zero. If you choose the Compute option, Quattro Pro computes the constant as usual. If you choose the Zero option, however, Quattro Pro does not compute the constant but sets the constant to 0.

You might want to set the constant to 0 if a constant of anything other than 0 would be illogical. For example, you might recall that the constants used in the examples are -536.858 and -449.661. These constants indicate that a man with a height of 0 inches weighs -537 or -450 pounds. It is somewhat more realistic to assume that a person who is 0 inches tall weighs 0 pounds, so you might want to use the Intercept option to set the Y Intercept option to 0.

Manipulating matrices in your worksheets

The Tools Advanced Math menu provides two options that let you manipulate matrices in your Quattro Pro worksheets: Multiply and Invert. You can use these commands to solve systems of simultaneous linear equations, perform linear programming, and compute expected values from a set of probabilities and a set of possible outcomes. Although you might never use these commands, you will find them invaluable if you need to perform any of these tasks. The Tools Advanced Math Multiply command allows you to multiply two matrices. The Tools Advanced Math Invert command is used to invert a matrix. We'll look at the Multiply option first.

The Tools Advanced Math Multiply command

The Tools Advanced Math Multiply command lets you multiply one matrix by another. When you choose this command, Quattro Pro displays the prompt *Specify 1st matrix* in the input line, followed by a reference to the current cell. Specify the block that contains the first matrix you want to multiply, and press the Enter key. Next, Quattro Pro displays the prompt *Specify 2nd matrix*, followed by a reference to the current cell. Again, specify the block that contains the second matrix you want to multiply, and press the Enter key. Finally, Quattro Pro displays the prompt *Destination for cells*, followed by a reference to the current cell. Specify the block in which you want Quattro Pro to place the resulting matrix, and press the Enter key. Quattro Pro multiplies the two matrices and places the result in the specified block.

An example of computing expected outcomes

You can use the Tools Advanced Math Multiply command to forecast the outcome of an event, given a set of possible outcomes and the probability of each of those outcomes occurring. For example, suppose you're preparing to throw a huge Labor Day party for your company that could attract a huge crowd (150 people), a large crowd (100 people), a good crowd (50 people), a fair crowd (30 people), a small crowd (15 people), or a pitiful crowd (5 people). You expect a 5 percent chance of a huge crowd, a 20 percent chance of a large crowd, a 30 percent chance of a good crowd, a 25 percent chance of a fair crowd, a 15 percent chance of a small crowd, and a 5 percent chance of a pitiful crowd, and you want to estimate the turnout.

Figure 5-16 shows a worksheet that's set up to do this estimate. Notice that each of the possible outcomes is entered in block B7..B12 and the probabilities of each of those outcomes in block A3..F3. To compute the expected number of attendees, multiply the percentage probabilities for each of the possible outcomes by the number of attendees expected if that outcome occurs. The sum of those products is the estimated number of attendees.

To make this computation, choose the Tools Advanced Math Multiply command. When Quattro Pro prompts you to specify the first matrix, select block A3..F3 and press the Enter key. Then, when Quattro Pro prompts you to specify the second matrix, select block B7..B12 and press the Enter key. Finally, after Quattro Pro prompts you for the Output block, point to cell D14 and press the Enter key. Quattro Pro multiplies the matrix A3..F3 by the matrix B7..B12 and stores the result, 52.5, in cell D14. This result indicates that you should expect a turnout of about 52 or 53 people for your party.

Rules for computing expected outcomes

You must follow a few strict rules when you use the Tools Advanced Math Multiply command. First, you can multiply two matrices only if the number of

FIGURE 5-16.
The Tools Advanced Math Multiply command computes the product of two matrices.

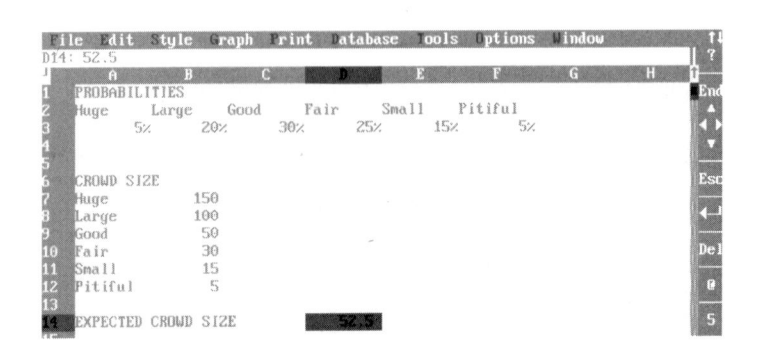

rows in the first matrix is equal to the number of columns in the second matrix, or vice-versa. (In a matrix, the number of rows precedes the number of columns.) This rule means that you can use this command to multiply two square matrices of the same size (for example, to multiply a 3×3 matrix by another 3×3 matrix) or to multiply a row vector by a column vector with the same number of elements (for example, a 4×1 matrix by a 1×4 matrix).

In addition, the product of the number of columns in the first matrix multiplied by the number of rows in the second matrix must be less than 8192. This rule means that you can multiply a 90×90 matrix by another 90×90 matrix (resulting in 8100); you cannot, however, multiply a 100×100 matrix by another 100×100 matrix (resulting in 10000).

The matrix that results from multiplying two matrices always has the same number of rows as does the first matrix and the same number of columns as the second matrix. In the example, you multiplied a 1×6 matrix by a 6×1 matrix. The result was a 1×1 matrix. If you multiply a 6×1 matrix by a 1×6 matrix, the result is a 6×6 matrix. If you multiply a 4×4 matrix by a 4×4 matrix, the result is a 4×4 matrix.

If the Output block you specify contains entries, the Tools Advanced Math Multiply command overwrites them. You need to be sure that the Output block you select is at least as large as the matrix produced by the multiplication.

Like the numbers generated by the Tools What-If command, the results of Tools Advanced Math Multiply are literal values. Also, as with Tools What-If, Quattro Pro remembers the first and second matrices and the Output blocks you define. The second time you choose the Tools Advanced Math Multiply command, Quattro Pro presents your previous selections as the new defaults.

The Invert option

Quattro Pro's Tools Advanced Math Invert command allows you to compute the inverse of a matrix, which is another matrix that, when multiplied by the original matrix, produces the identity matrix. All of the elements in an identity matrix are 0, except for the elements in the diagonal (the first element in the first row, the second element in the second row, the third element in the third row, and so forth). The diagonal elements are all 1. An inverse matrix is always the same size as its original matrix.

When you choose the Tools Advanced Math Invert command, Quattro Pro displays the prompt *Source block of cells* in the input line, followed by a reference to the current cell. Specify the block that contains the matrix you want to invert, and press the Enter key. Next, Quattro Pro presents the prompt *Destination for cells*, followed by a reference to the current cell. Specify the destination block for the resulting inverse matrix, and press the Enter key.

An example of linear programming

Although you will almost never use the Tools Advanced Math Invert command by itself, you can use it in conjunction with the Tools Advanced Math Multiply command to perform linear programming in your worksheets. Linear programming is a technique that allows you to figure out how to achieve an optimal outcome, given a set of constraints. Although a full discussion of linear programming is beyond the scope of this book, we can introduce you to linear programming techniques by showing you how to use the Tools Advanced Math Invert and Multiply commands to solve a simple linear programming problem.

Suppose you own a company that produces two products: Wonkas and Womnuts. Producing a Wonka consumes 2 hours of time and 6 pounds of raw material. Making a Womnut requires 3 hours of time and 4 pounds of raw material. Each Wonka you make earns you $5, and each Womnut earns you $7. You have 24 hours of time and 62 pounds of raw material at your disposal. What is the most efficient way to utilize these scarce resources? To solve this problem, you must define the following set of equations:

2*Wonkas+3*Womnuts=24 hours

6*Wonkas+4*Womnuts=62 pounds of raw material

These two equations summarize the relationship between Wonkas, Womnuts, and the amount of available resources. By solving these equations simultaneously, you can determine the number of Wonkas and Womnuts you should produce to make the most efficient use of your resources.

To use linear programming and the Tools Advanced Math Invert and Multiply commands to solve this problem, begin by entering as a matrix the coefficients of the variables and constants from the above equations in the worksheet. Figure 5-17 shows a worksheet with these values in place. Next, choose the Tools Advanced Math Invert command. After Quattro Pro prompts you for the block to invert, select block B2..C3, the block that contains the coefficients of the variables from the equations, and press the Enter key. Next, Quattro Pro asks you where to place the result. Select a blank cell (for this example, use cell B6) and press the Enter key. The result is shown in Figure 5-18. As you can see, Quattro Pro has calculated the inverse matrix of the matrix in cells B2..C3, and placed it in cells B6..C7.

FIGURE 5-17. This worksheet contains the coefficients of the variables and constants in the simultaneous equations.

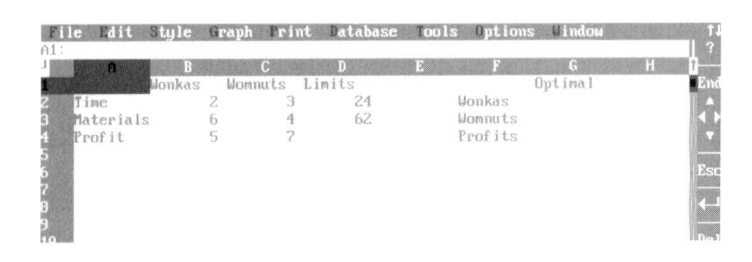

FIGURE 5-18.
The Tools Advanced Math Invert command computes the inverse of a matrix.

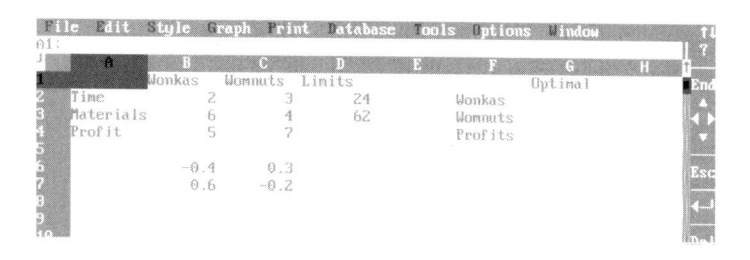

FIGURE 5-19.
The Tools Advanced Math Invert and Multiply commands allow you to perform linear programming in your Quattro Pro worksheets.

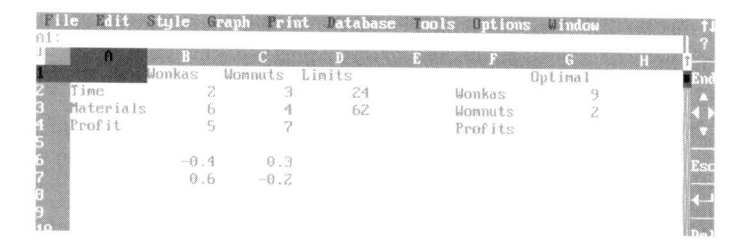

You can now solve the problem by multiplying the inverse matrix by the matrix that contains the constants from the original formula (24 and 62). The result will be a 2 × 1 matrix that contains the optimal number of Wonkas and Womnuts that you should produce. To perform the multiplication, choose the Tools Advanced Math Multiply command, select cells B6..C7 as the first block to multiply, and press the Enter key. Now, select cells D2..D3 as the second block to multiply, press the Enter key, select G2 as the destination cell, and press the Enter key to complete the command. Figure 5-19 shows the result. The numbers in cells G2 and G3 (9 and 2) are the number of Wonkas and Womnuts you should produce to use your resources most efficiently.

Now you can figure out how much profit you'll make after performing at the highest level of efficiency. The amount of profit is expressed by the equation 5*Wonkas+7*Womnuts=Profit. Enter the equation +B4*G2+C4*G3 in cell G4 of your worksheet, and press the Enter key. The result, 59, is the profit you will make at the optimal level of production.

Rules for linear programming

Like the Multiply option, the Invert option requires that you follow a few strict rules: You can invert only square matrices; that is, matrices that have the same number of rows as columns; you can invert matrices with no more than 90 columns and 90 rows; and the determinant of the matrix you want to invert cannot be 0. Don't worry too much about these rules; they seldom come into play.

Always be sure that the Output block you specify is large enough to hold the inverted matrix. If you specify an Output block that contains entries, the Tools Advanced Math Invert command overwrites them. Quattro Pro remembers the

FIGURE 5-20.
The Tools Advanced Math Optimization menu lets you solve optimization problems using linear programming techniques.

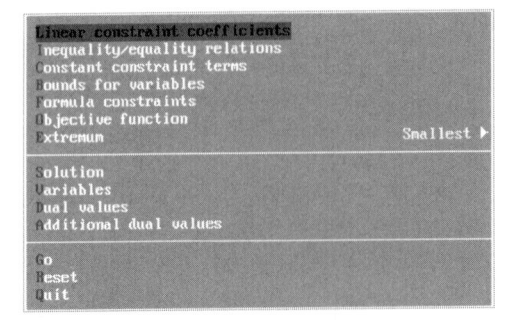

Invert and Output blocks you select when you choose the Tools Advanced Math Invert command. The next time you choose the command, Quattro Pro presents those blocks as the command's new defaults.

Solving optimization problems

The Tools Advanced Math Optimization menu, shown in Figure 5-20, provides a series of commands that let you solve optimization problems using linear programming techniques. In most cases, you'll find the Optimization menu commands an easier method for solving linear programming than the method described earlier in "Manipulating Matrices in Your Worksheets."

The linear programming problem described earlier works well to illustrate the mechanics of an optimization problem. To refresh your memory, suppose you own an imaginary company that produces Wonkas and Womnuts. Your total profit, which of course you want to maximize, can be calculated using the following formula because you make $5 on each Wonka and $7 on each Womnut:

($5*Number of Wonkas)+(7$*Number of Womnuts)

Your time and raw materials, however, are limited. You have only 24 hours of time and 62 pounds of raw material. Each Wonka requires 2 hours of time, and each Womnut requires 4 pounds of raw material. The constraints can be expressed by using the following two equations:

(2*Number of Wonkas)+(3*Number of Womnuts)≤24 hours

(6*Number of Wonkas)+(4*Number of Womnuts)≤62 pounds

In the earlier description of this linear programming problem, the constraint equation used equal signs, which would actually indicate that you must use all of the available time and all of the available raw materials. You wouldn't actually have to use all of the resources; you simply wouldn't be able to use more than are

Chapter 5: Worksheet Commands

FIGURE 5-21.
Use this worksheet to illustrate optimization.

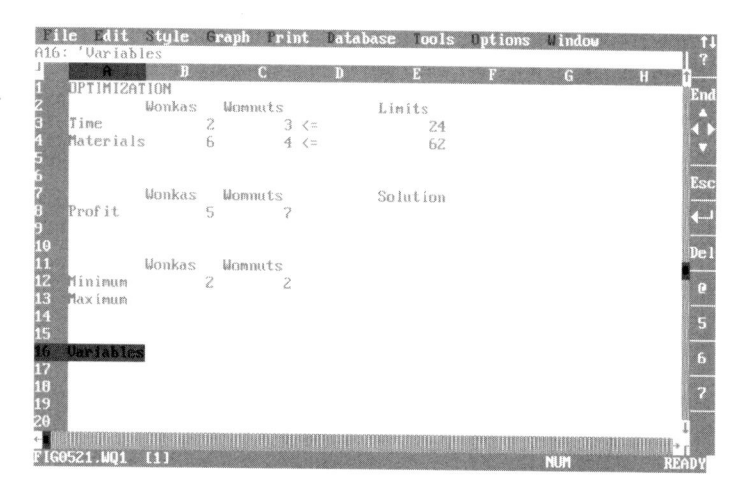

available. As a result, the constraint equations are shown here using less-than-or-equal-to signs. Further suppose that in order to maintain the skills that are necessary, you must always produce at least two Wonkas and at least two Womnuts.

To solve this optimization problem, start with a worksheet similar to the one created for Figure 5-21. Column B in this figure represents Wonkas, and column C represents Womnuts. Block B3..C4, which contains the coefficients for the resource constraints, quantifies the resources used in the production of Wonkas and Womnuts.

Time(2*Wonkas+3*Womnuts)

Materials(6*Wonkas+ 4*Womnuts)

In Figure 5-21, block D3..E4 contains the inequality symbols and the maximum resource limits for the two resources. The inequality symbol consists of a left angle bracket and the equal sign (<=). It indicates less than or equal to. The values in cells E3 and E4 contain the maximum resource limits for time, 24, and for the pounds of raw materials, 62. If you use the greater-than or greater-than-or-equal-to inequality symbols, the resource limits would be minimums instead of maximums.

Block B8..C8 contains the coefficients of the objective function; the formula you want to maximize or minimize. Remember that because column B represents Wonkas and column C represents Womnuts, block B8..C8 actually quantifies the objective profit function:

($5*Wonkas+$7*Womnuts)

Finally, block B12..C13 identifies the minimum and maximum values allowed for Wonkas and Womnuts. Block B12..C12 holds the minimum values: two Wonkas and two Womnuts. Block B13..C13 holds the maximum values; blanks indicate infinity.

Defining the inputs to an optimization problem

Use the first seven options in the Optimization menu to define the inputs to an optimization. The sections that follow describe how to use each of these menu options except the Formula Constraint option, which is described later in the chapter in "Formula Constraints Option."

Linear Constraints Coefficients option

To define the resource constraints in an optimization problem, choose the first option, Linear Constraints Coefficients, from the Optimization menu shown in Figure 5-20. Quattro Pro displays the prompt *Row(s) with the constraints* in the input line, followed by the current address of the cell selector. Define the block that contains the resource constraints. For example, in the case of the Wonka and Womnut optimization problem shown in Figure 5-21, you define block B3..C4. Note that you cannot include nonlinear resource constraints in an optimization problem.

Inequality/Equality Relations option

To indicate whether the resource constraints must be equal to, less than, less than or equal to, greater than, or greater than or equal to a resource, choose the Inequality/Equality Relations option from the Optimization menu shown in Figure 5-20. Quattro Pro displays the prompt *Column with the labels* in the input line, followed by the current address of the cell selector. Define the block that contains the inequality or equality symbols for the resource constraints. For the optimization problem shown in Figure 5-21, define block D3..D4.

Constant Constraint Terms option

To specify the maximum or minimum amount of a resource, choose the Constant Constraint Terms option from the Optimization menu shown in Figure 5-20. Quattro Pro displays the prompt *Column with the constants* in the input line, followed by the current location of the cell selector. Define the block that contains the resource available. For example, for the optimization problem shown in Figure 5-21, define block E3..E4.

Bounds For Variables option

A variable in an optimization problem often must fall within a certain upper or lower boundary. In the example problem using Wonkas and Womnuts, you must produce at least two Wonkas and two Womnuts. In real-life optimization problems, you might also have upper bounds, such as an export quota or a legal limit. To indicate bounds in an optimization problem, choose the Bounds For Variables option from the Optimization menu shown in Figure 5-20. Quattro Pro displays the prompt *Block (2 rows) to hold the bounds for the variables*, followed by the current address of the cell selector. Define the two-row block that contains the lower and upper bounds. Quattro Pro considers the first row in the block you define the lower bound, and the second row the upper bound. If your optimization problem has only one bound, as in the case of the Wonkas and Womnuts, leave the row that would ordinarily contain the unneeded bound blank. For example, in the Wonkas and Womnuts optimization, you indicate the bounds B12..C13. Quattro Pro restricts the possible variable values to non-negative real numbers.

Objective Function option

The equation or formula you want to optimize is called the objective function. Sometimes the objective function is a profit formula that you want to maximize; other times it is a cost formula that you want to minimize. In the Wonkas and Womnuts example optimization problem, the optimization function is shown in block B8..C8. To indicate that the values contained in this block make up the objective function, choose the Objective Function option from the Optimization menu shown in Figure 5-20. When Quattro Pro displays the prompt *Row with the coefficients,* define block B8..C8.

Extremum option

After you identify the objective function's coefficients, you still need to specify whether the function should be maximized or minimized. To do so, choose the Extremum option from the Optimization menu shown in Figure 5-20. Quattro Pro then displays a menu with two options. Choose Smallest if the objective function should be minimized or Largest if the objective function should be maximized. In the Wonka and Womnut optimization problem, you choose Largest because you want to maximize the profit function.

Identifying the output areas

After you define the inputs to the optimization problem, you're ready to indicate where you want the solution outputs placed. You need to locate two sets of outputs: solution and variables. In addition, you can also specify dual values and additional dual values to test the sensitivity of the first two options; this is described a little later in this chapter in "Working with Dual Values" and "Working with Additional Dual Values."

Solution option

The Solution option in the Optimization menu lets you locate the value for the solved objective function. In other words, if your objective function quantifies profits, you want to maximize the solution value so that it equals the maximum profit value, given any constraints and any lower or upper bounds. Or, if the objective function quantifies costs, you want to minimize the solution value so that it equals the minimum cost value, given any constraints and any lower or upper bounds.

To locate the solution value, choose the Solution option from the Optimization menu shown in Figure 5-20. Quattro Pro displays the prompt *Enter the cell where the computed value is placed* followed by the current location of the cell selector. Point to the appropriate cell location (E8 in this example) and then press the Enter key.

Variables option

The Variables option lets you locate the optimal values for the variables. In the Wonkas and Womnuts example, you use the Variables option to locate the optimal number of Wonkas and Womnuts you should produce. To locate the variables values, choose the Variables option from the Optimization menu shown in Figure 5-20. Quattro Pro displays the prompt *Enter the row* followed by the current address of the cell pointer. Define the block in which you want the optimal variable values located (in this example, B16..C16) and press the Enter key.

Solving the optimization problem

After you define the inputs and have identified where you want the output values located, you're ready to solve the optimization problem. To do so, choose the Go option from the Optimization menu shown in Figure 5-20. The mode indicator briefly flashes WAIT and then Quattro Pro redisplays the worksheet; this time with the solution and variables values shown. For example, Figure 5-22 shows the same worksheet as does Figure 5-21, after you have defined the optimization problem's inputs and outputs and after you have chosen Go. The variables output block, B16..C16, shows that given the resource constraints and bounds, the optimal variable values are nine Wonkas and two Womnuts. Given these variables, the solution output cell, E8, shows the resulting profit, 59.

FIGURE 5-22.
The optimization problem solution, nine Wonkas and two Womnuts, means $59 in profits.

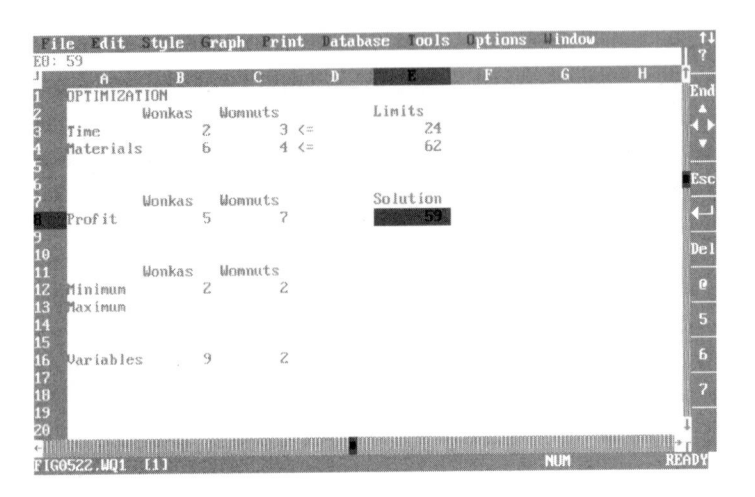

Changing the inputs and outputs

To see the effect of changing one of the inputs, generally you edit the coefficient that needs to change. Suppose, for example, that in the Wonkas and Womnuts example you want to change the minimum number of Wonkas and Womnuts that must be produced to 1. To make this change, simply replace the 2 in cells B12 and C12 with 1. Then, choose the Go option again from the Optimization menu to recalculate the optimal solution and variables. The Optimization function places literal values in the output areas.

To change one of the input or output blocks, choose the menu option used to define the input or output block. Then, when Quattro Pro displays the appropriate prompt and the current block setting, press the Esc key to redefine the block.

To change all the input and output settings (because you're solving a new problem, for instance) you'll probably find it easier simply to choose the Reset option from the Optimization menu. Doing so clears all of the input and output settings.

Working with dual values

Dual value outputs test the sensitivity of the objective function's solution to changes in resource constraints. Dual values show how much the solution value changes if you change the resource limit; when a resource limit is a maximum limit, the dual values show the effect of decreasing the minimum resource. For example, in the Wonkas and Womnuts optimization example, you can use dual values to test the effect of increasing the available time and pounds of raw material. To do so, choose the Dual Values option from the Optimization menu shown in Figure 5-20. Quattro Pro displays the prompt *Column to hold the computed dual values*, followed by the current location of the cell selector. Define a one-column block that contains as many rows as there are resource constraints and then press the Enter key. For example, Figure 5-23 shows the dual values placed in block F3..F4.

The 2.2 in cell F3 indicates that the objective function solution value of 59 increases by 2.2 to 61.2 if the available time increases by 1 to 25. The 0.1 in cell F4 indicates that the objective function solution value of 59 increases by 0.1 to 59.1 if the number of pounds of raw material available increases by 1 to 63. In the Wonkas and Womnuts example, then, you would know that increasing the available time by a unit has a much larger input than does increasing the number of pounds of raw material available.

Working with additional dual values

Additional dual value outputs indicate the sensitivity of the objective function's solution to changes in an upper or lower bound. Similar to dual values, additional dual values show how much the solution value changes if you relax a lower bound or an upper bound. What's tricky about bound dual values is that the

FIGURE 5-23.
Dual values let you test an objective function's sensitivity to changes in resource constraints.

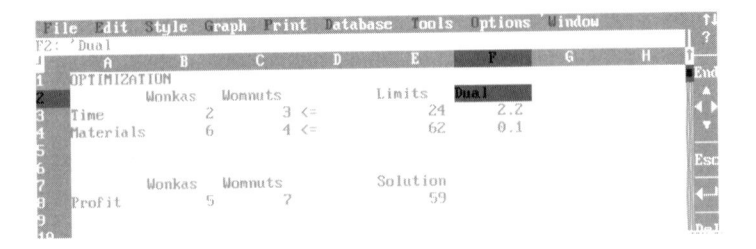

```
F2: 'Dual
         A         B         C         D         E         F         G    H
1  OPTIMIZATION
2            Wonkas    Womnuts              Limits    Dual
3  Time         2         3    <=            24       2.2
4  Materials    6         4    <=            62       0.1
5
6
7            Wonkas    Womnuts              Solution
8  Profit       5         7                   59
9
```

output value shows the change in the relevant bound, which means that if you have both an upper and a lower bound, you must first identify which bound is coming into play. To tell if a bound is affecting the solution value, you can compare the optimal variable values with the values at the bounds. If the optimum value is close to a bound, the bound probably affects the solution. In the Wonkas and Womnuts optimization example, if the lower bound of the Womnut production equals 2 and the optimal value equals 2, you know that the lower bound might be affecting the solution and that the upper bound is definitely not affecting the solution.

To solve for additional dual values, use the Additional Dual Values option on the Optimization menu shown in Figure 5-20. For example, to solve for the additional dual values in the Wonkas and Womnuts example, choose the Additional Dual Values option from the Optimization menu. Quattro Pro displays the prompt *Row to hold the computed dual value* in the input line, followed by the current location of the cell selector. Define a one-row block that contains as many columns as variables. Press the Enter key and then choose Go to recalculate the optimization problem. Figure 5-24 shows another version of the familiar Wonkas and Womnuts example with a lower bound of three units for Wonkas and Womnuts. The additional dual values show in block B18..C18.

Because the example shown in Figure 5-24 includes no upper bound constraints, the additional dual values apply to the lower bounds. The 0 in cell B18 indicates that relaxing the minimum Wonka value of 3 has no effect on the solution value, which you could also have ascertained by comparing the optimal value for Wonkas in cell B16, (7.5), to the minimum, or lower, bound in cell B12 (3). If the optimal value is 7.5, a minimum value of 3 is not a relevant bound. The situation differs, however, with regard to the minimal Womnut value. The -0.5 in cell C18 indicates that you could increase your optimal solution value by 0.5 if you relaxed your Womnut production by one unit.

Formula Constraints option

One option on the Optimization menu hasn't yet been described: the Formula Constraints option. This option lets you quantify resource constraints as formulas rather than as a matrix of coefficients, which is the approach illustrated earlier. To

Chapter 5: Worksheet Commands

FIGURE 5-24.
Additional dual values show the sensitivity of the objective function to changes in the bounds.

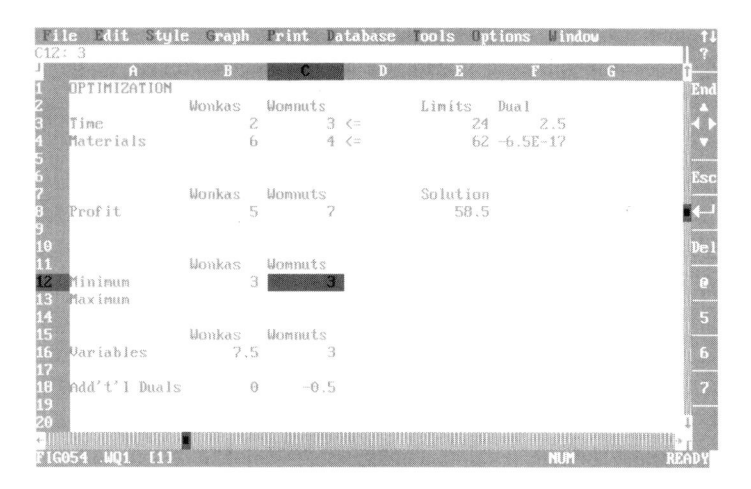

use the formula constraints approach, you must first arrange the resource constraint equations so that they express the resource constraints as formulas that are greater than or equal to 0. For example, consider the following formulas:

2*Wonkas+3*Womnuts<=24

6*Wonkas+4*Womnuts<=64

These formulas must be rearranged as shown below:

24-(2*Wonkas+3*Womnuts)>=0

64-(6*Wonkas+4*Womnuts)>=0

Figure 5-25 shows an optimization problem worksheet constructed using formula constraints, which appear in block B3..B4. (These cells are formatted as text in the example so you can see both equations.) Notice that the Wonka and Womnut variables are represented by cell references. The cells referenced must be the same ones you use to locate the optimal variable values.

To identify the cells that contain the formulas, choose the Formula Constraints option from the Optimization menu shown in Figure 5-20. When Quattro Pro displays the prompt *Block of formulas constrained to be >=0*, define the block that contains the constraint formulas; in Figure 5-25, this block is B3..B4. You must also define the objective function location, the extremum, the solution value location, and the optimal variables value location as described earlier in this chapter. In Figure 5-25, the objective function location is B8..C8, the extremum is Largest, the solution value location is cell E8, and the variables value location is B11..C11.

FIGURE 5-25.
Formula constraints represent an alternative method for quantifying resource constraints.

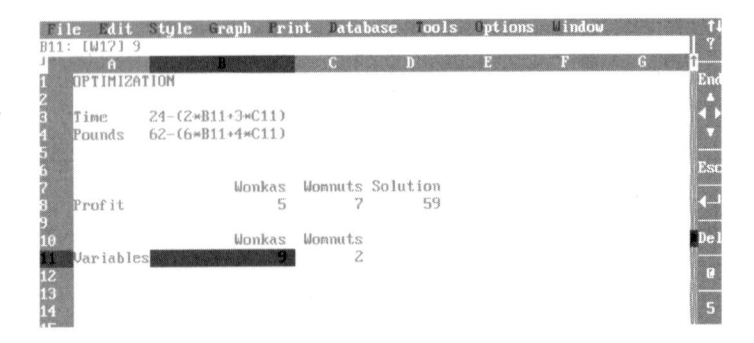

Rules for optimization

The examples described here illustrate the basics of using Quattro Pro's optimization feature. But if you want to use optimization to solve more complicated problems, you need to keep several rules in mind.

The output values that the optimization feature calculates are literal values. Accordingly, if you change a resource constraint or object function coefficient, you cannot simply recalculate the worksheet to get the updated optimal variable values and solution. Instead, you must use the Optimization menu's Go option.

Quattro Pro has a limit on the size of the coefficient matrix you can use to define the resource constraints. The maximum size is 90 rows by 254 columns. Because rows hold constraints and columns represent variables, your optimization problems can have up to 90 constraints and 254 variables.

You need not actually specify the inequality/equality relations if the resource constraints are all equal to a specific amount because the default inequality/equality relations symbol is an equal sign. For example, in the Wonkas and Womnuts optimization example, if you must use all 24 hours of time and all 64 pounds of raw materials, the actual resource constraints are the following:

2*Wonkas+3*Womnuts=24

6*Wonkas+4*Womnuts=64

You also do not need to specify the block that contains the inequality/equality relations symbols.

Using Solve For

The last option on the Tools menu, Solve For, lets you solve a formula by iteratively changing one of its variables until the formula equals a certain target result. For example, you can calculate how many years you need to contribute $2,000 to a savings account earning 12 percent interest to accumulate $1,000,000.

First enter the formula that you want Solve For to calculate. To calculate the number of years you would need to put $2,000 in a savings account earning 12 percent to accumulate $1,000,000, use the @FV function. Enter the formula, @FV(2000,0.12,A2) in cell A1. Solve For will substitute values for cell A2 (the @FV term argument) until it calculates a future amount.

Next, choose the Tools Solve For command. Quattro Pro presents a menu listing the seven Tools Solve For options: Formula Cell, Target Value, Variable Cell, Parameters, Go, Reset, and Quit. To identify cell A1 as the location of the formula you want to solve, select Formula Cell from the Solve For menu, specify cell A1 at the *Formula Cell* prompt in the input line, and press Enter. To identify cell A2 as the substitution value, select Variable Cell from the Solve For menu, specify A2 at the *Variable Cell* prompt, and press Enter. To give Quattro the value you want the formula cell to equal, select the Target Value, type the number 1000000 at the *Target value* prompt, and press Enter.

The Parameters option on the Solve For menu lets you control certain characteristics of Solve For's iterative calculations. The Parameters option displays a submenu listing two options: Max Iterations and Accuracy. By default, the maximum number of iterations is five, which means that Solve For recalculates the formula up to five times in an effort to solve the equation. It will take about 50 iterations to solve this equation. To change the maximum number of iterations, select the Max Iterations option, enter 50, and press Enter. By default, the accuracy is set to .005, which means Solve For attempts to get within .005 of the specified target value. In the example of solving for the $1,000,000 target value, this would mean half a penny (probably more precision than you need). Within $500 of $1,000,000 might be close enough. To change the accuracy to $1,000,000 plus or minus $500, select Accuracy, enter 500, and press Enter.

When you're ready to start Solve For, select the Go option from the Solve For menu. Quattro will iteratively substitute values in the variable cell the specified number of times until it finds a value that causes the formula to equal the target value. If Quattro Pro can't find a solution of specified accuracy within the maximum number of iterations, it displays the message *Maximum iterations reached*.

To clear the current formula cell, target value, and variable cell settings and return the parameters to their default values, choose the Reset option from the Solve For menu. When you're ready to leave the Solve For menu, choose Quit.

Protecting your worksheets

Sooner or later, you'll feel the need to protect your worksheet entries against unwanted changes or to protect whole worksheets against commands chosen accidentally; commands such as the Edit Erase Block or Edit Delete Columns.

Anytime you create a worksheet that contains formulas or data that you do not want to lose, you should consider using worksheet protection.

Each cell in every Quattro Pro worksheet has its own protection attribute: unprotected or protected. The Style Protection Unprotect and Style Protection Protect commands allow you to change the protection attributes of cells and blocks. In addition, each Quattro Pro worksheet has a global protection setting: Enable or Disable. The Options Protection command controls the worksheet's protection setting.

The cell protection attributes and the worksheet's protection setting work together to determine which cells are protected. The Options Protection Disable command is the master switch for protection. When the worksheet protection is set to Disabled, the worksheet is unprotected. When the worksheet protection is set to Enabled, every cell in the worksheet that has the Protected attribute is protected, and you cannot make any changes to the contents of those cells. Any cell that has the Unprotected attribute is unprotected, and you can change its contents.

Every cell in a new Quattro Pro worksheet is protected, but the global worksheet protection is set to Disabled in a new worksheet. As a result, you can make entries in a new worksheet and choose commands that are not affected by protection. But as soon as you choose the Options Protection Enable command, every cell in the worksheet is protected, which prevents you from making cell entries, making changes to existing cell entries, and choosing commands that could erase or overwrite cell entries. To make changes to cells or blocks after you enable worksheet protection, you first use the Style Protection Unprotect command to unprotect those cells.

Protecting a worksheet

Because every cell in a new Quattro Pro worksheet has the Protected attribute, you can protect the entire worksheet by choosing the Options Protection Enable command; Quattro Pro will no longer let you make any changes to the worksheet. After you enable global protection, Quattro Pro displays the letters PR in the input line next to the cell indicator whenever you point to a cell whose protection is enabled. You can use the PR indicator to identify the protection status of each cell in your worksheet.

To check the protection status of a worksheet, simply choose the Options Protection command and look at the setting on the right side of the Protection menu. (If you do not see the setting, press the [Expand] key (+) on your keyboard's numeric keypad to expand the menus.)

The Style Protection Unprotect command

You will seldom want to protect every cell in a worksheet because you cannot do anything except look at the cell entries if every cell is protected. To be able to make changes in some cells in a protected worksheet, use the Style Protection Unprotect command. When you choose the Style Protection Unprotect command, Quattro Pro displays the prompt *Block to be modified* in the input line, followed by a block reference to the current cell. Define the block you want to unprotect and press the Enter key. Quattro Pro unprotects every cell in that block.

After you move the cell selector to an unprotected cell while worksheet protection is enabled, Quattro Pro displays the letter U (for Unprotected) in the input line and modifies the appearance of the entries in unprotected cells. A monochrome monitor shows unprotected cells in high intensity, and a color monitor displays the unprotected cells in a different color from the rest of the cells in the worksheet.

Protection effects

When a cell is protected and the worksheet protection setting is enabled, any attempt to make an entry in a protected cell, including any blank cells, makes Quattro Pro beep and display an error message. In addition, you cannot use the Edit Erase Block command to erase the contents of a protected cell, or the Edit Delete Rows or Edit Delete Columns commands to delete a row or column that contains a protected cell. Similarly, you cannot move or copy cell entries into a protected cell.

Note, however, that there is one exception to the protection rule: Quattro Pro's File Erase command erases all cell entries, protected and unprotected, in a protected worksheet. After you choose the File Erase command and choose the Yes option, the entire worksheet, including the protected cells, is erased.

Reprotecting unprotected cells

To reprotect a cell or block that you have previously unprotected, choose the Style Protection Protect command. Quattro Pro prompts you for the block of unprotected cells that you want to protect. Specify the block and press the Enter key. Quattro Pro reprotects all of the previously unprotected cells in the block. You can unprotect the entire worksheet at one time by choosing the Options Protection Disable command, which turns off master protection for the whole worksheet, disabling the protection attribute of every cell. Keep in mind, however, that this command does not affect the protection attributes of any individual cells. When you use the Options Protection Enable command to reprotect a previously unprotected worksheet, the cell protection attributes of every cell will be exactly as you left them.

Using the Edit Search And Replace command

The Edit Search And Replace command is among Quattro Pro's most exciting features. This command lets you search through a block of cells for a string of characters that you've specified. You can also tell Quattro Pro to replace each occurrence of the specified string with a new string. The Edit Search And Replace command comes in handy in many situations. For example, you might use this command to correct a word that you have consistently misspelled throughout a worksheet or to find all of the formulas that refer to a particular cell.

The basics of Edit Search And Replace

After you choose the Edit Search And Replace command, Quattro Pro presents the menu shown in Figure 5-26. The first three options in this menu let you define the block you want to search through, the string you want to search for, and the string you want to use as the replacement. The Next and Previous options tell Quattro Pro to begin searching for the string you specified in the block you defined. The Next option tells Quattro Pro to look forward to the next row or column in the defined block. The Previous option tells Quattro Pro to look backward to the previous row or column in the defined block.

Choose the Block option from the menu and define the block you want to search. Next, choose the Search String option and define the search string you want to search for. To replace some or all occurrences of the search string, choose the Replace String option and define the replace string. Finally, choose the Next or Previous option to begin searching. The command searches the actual contents of the cells in the block, not the values displayed in those cells. For example, suppose cell C10 contains the formula SALES-COSTS and that this formula returns the value 100. If you use the Edit Search And Replace command to search a block that contains this cell, Quattro Pro looks for a match for the search string in the contents of the cell, the formula SALES-COSTS, and not in the formula's result. Because Quattro Pro searches the contents of cells, you can find and replace strings in formulas and functions as well as in labels.

When Quattro Pro finds a match, it displays a screen like the one shown in Figure 5-27. The area on the left side of the status line at the bottom of the screen shows the entire contents of the cell that contains the match and the address of the matching cell. Also on the screen is the Replace This String menu, which contains five options: Yes, No, All, Edit, and Quit. This menu asks what you want to do with the matching string that Quattro Pro has found.

FIGURE 5-26.
Quattro Pro's Edit Search And Replace command lets you search for strings or replace strings in your worksheet cells.

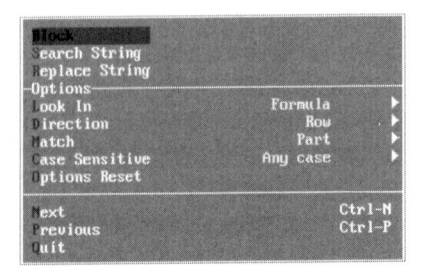

FIGURE 5-27.
Quattro Pro offers five options after it locates a matching string.

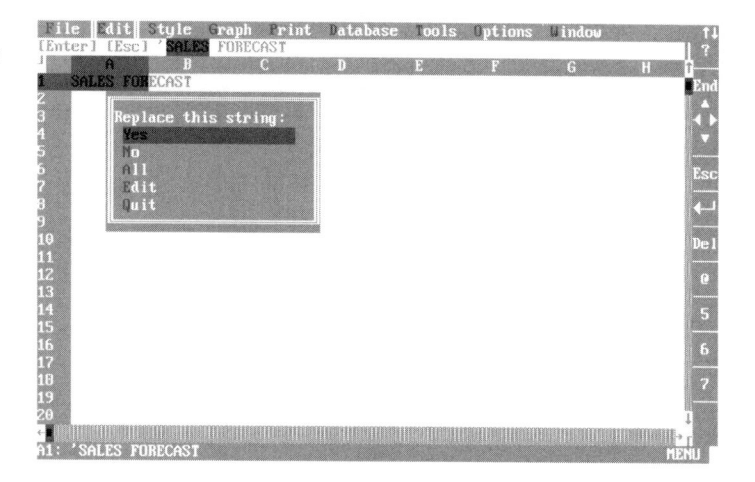

The Yes option tells Quattro Pro to replace the matching string with the replace string and to continue searching for another match. The No option tells Quattro Pro to ignore the match it has found but to continue searching for more matches. The All option tells Quattro Pro to replace every occurrence of the search string with the replace string without further prompting. The Edit option displays the label, value, or formula in the input line and changes Quattro Pro to EDIT mode so that you can modify the string. Finally, the Quit option tells Quattro Pro to stop searching and to return to READY mode.

NOTE: *The search block you define can be as large as the entire worksheet or as small as a single cell. The search string and replace string can be up to 60 characters long and can contain any character you can type on your computer's keyboard. After you define a block, a search string, and a replace string, Quattro Pro remembers those settings until you change them, cancel them, or open another worksheet. If you save the worksheet after defining these settings, Quattro Pro remembers them the next time you open the worksheet.*

An example of Edit Search And Replace

The worksheet shown in Figure 5-28 contains all four types of cell entries: labels, values, formulas, and functions. Perform search and replace operations on this worksheet to demonstrate the power and flexibility of the Edit Search And Replace command.

Suppose you want to replace all occurrences of the string "Product" with the string "Package." To begin, choose the Edit Search And Replace command. When the menu shown in Figure 5-26 appears, choose the Block option, select cells A1..G15, and press the Enter key. Next, choose the Search String option, type *Product* (capitalization is not important), and press the Enter key. Then, choose the

FIGURE 5-28.
Use this worksheet to demonstrate the Edit Search And Replace command.

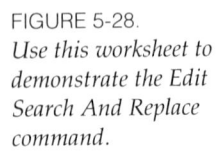

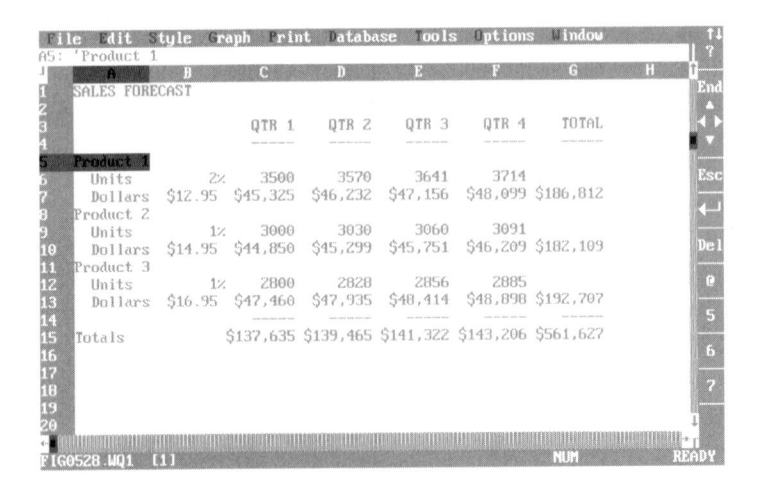

Replace String option, type *Package*, and press the Enter key. Finally, choose the Next option. Figure 5-29 shows the screen at this point.

Quattro Pro finds the first match for the search string in cell A5. To replace all occurrences of the string "Product" with "Package," choose the All option in the Replace This String menu. Quattro Pro replaces all occurrences of "Product" in cells A5, A8 and A11 with the string "Package" and returns to the Search And Replace menu.

Search And Replace command options

By default, the Edit Search And Replace command looks at the actual formulas or labels in cells, searches row by row, searches for partial cell entries and whole cell entries, and ignores capitalization. You can change these default search settings, however, using the Search And Replace menu's Look In, Direction, Match, Case Sensitive, and Options Reset options.

Look In option

The Look In option determines where Quattro Pro looks when searching. When you choose the Look In option, Quattro Pro presents a submenu with three choices: Formula, Value, and Condition. The default setting, Formula, tells Quattro Pro to search the actual cell contents, including labels, values, formulas, and functions. Value tells Quattro Pro to search for the values displayed. With Look In set to Value, for example, Quattro Pro finds a cell with the formula 10+10 if the search string equals 20. Condition tells Quattro Pro to search for cells that show values that meet a certain condition. For example, to find cells that contain values equal to 100, specify the search argument as ?=100 and set the Look In option to Condition. With these search settings, Quattro Pro finds cells in the search block that contain the value 100.

Chapter 5: Worksheet Commands

FIGURE 5-29.
The Edit Search And Replace command displays this screen after it finds the first occurrence of the search string.

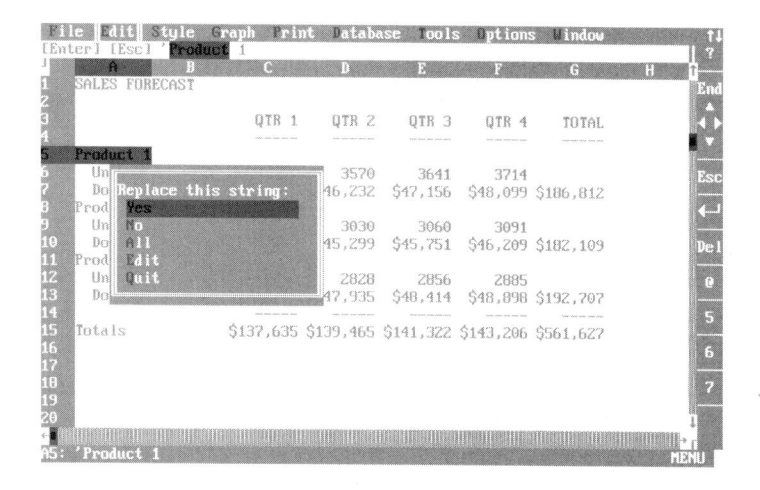

Direction option

Again, Quattro Pro searches a block row by row. Suppose, for example, that you define A1..D5 as the search block. Quattro Pro searches row 1 first, starting with cell A1 and continuing through cell D1. Next, Quattro Pro searches row 2, starting with cell A2 and continuing through cell D1. The Direction option lets you change this order. When you choose the Direction option, Quattro Pro presents a submenu with two choices, Row and Column, that you can use to specify whether Quattro Pro should search row by row or column by column. If you choose Column and then search block A1..D5, for example, Quattro Pro searches column A first, starting with cell A1 and continuing through cell A5. Next, Quattro Pro searches column B, starting with cell B1 and continuing through cell B5, and so on.

Match option

The Match option controls whether the search string must be the whole cell entry or whether it may be only part of the cell entry. If you choose the Match option, Quattro Pro presents a submenu with the two choices, Part and Whole, that you use to control the match setting. The default match setting is Part. With a match setting of Part and a search string of "war", Quattro Pro finds "war", "warehouse", and "hardware". With a match setting of Whole and a search string of "war", however, Quattro Pro finds only "war".

Case Sensitive option

Quattro Pro by default ignores the capitalization of the strings it looks for. "War", "wAR", and "war" can all be found using the search string "WAR", even though the cases of the letters do not match. You can use the Case Sensitive option to change Quattro Pro's insensitivity to case. If you choose Case Sensitive from the

Search And Replace menu, Quattro Pro presents a menu with two choices: Any Case and Exact Case. Any Case tells Quattro Pro to ignore capitalization.

Options Reset option

To return to the default search option settings, choose the Options Reset option from the Search And Replace menu. Quattro Pro sets Look In to Formula, Direction to Row, Match to Part, and Case Sensitive to Any Case.

Creating input forms

You can use Quattro Pro's Database Restrict Input command to transform the cells of your worksheet into a simple input form. You can use these forms to help inexperienced users make cell entries and to clean up the appearance of your Quattro Pro applications. These forms are almost always used with a macro that controls the entry of information through the form.

Basics of input forms

Before you choose the Database Restrict Input command, you must set up a simple form in an unused portion of your worksheet. Next, you can use the Style Protection Unprotect command to unprotect the cells in which you want to make entries. Then, you're ready to choose the Database Restrict Input command. When you do, Quattro Pro displays the prompt *Block to be modified* followed by a reference to the current cell. Define the appropriate block and press the Enter key.

After you define the input block, Quattro Pro restricts the cell selector to only the unprotected cells in the specified block. You can then use the Left, Right, Up, and Down direction keys, and the Home and End keys, to move the cell selector around the unprotected cells in the input form. You can make entries in the unprotected cells or edit existing entries as you move through the form. The cell selector continues to be restricted to the input block until you press the Esc or Enter key, which returns the cell selector to its previous location.

An example of an input form

As an example of the Database Restrict Input command, suppose you've created the simple check template shown in Figure 5-30, and you want to use the Database Restrict Form Input command to make entries in this form.

To begin, unprotect the cells in which you want to make cell entries by choosing the Style Protection Protect command, defining block A1..G13, and pressing the Enter key. This step ensures that the protection attribute is turned on for all cells in the form. Now, move the cell selector to cell B1, choose the Style Protection Unprotect command, and press the Enter key. Repeat this procedure for cells G1,

FIGURE 5-30.
Use the Database Restrict Input command to create simple input forms in your worksheets.

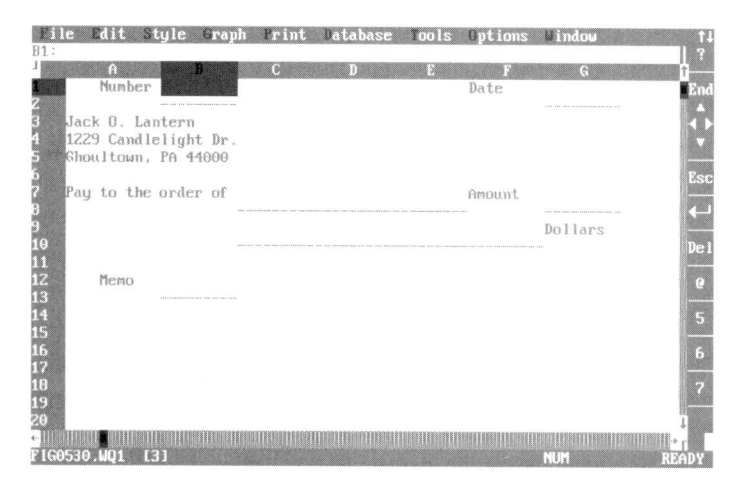

C7, G7, C9, and B12, the cells you'll want to be able to move to after you activate the form. To specify that cell G1 (the check data input field) accepts only dates, move the cell selector to cell G1 and choose the Database Data Entry Dates Only command. When Quattro Pro prompts you for the block, press the Enter key to accept G1..G1. Next, move the cell selector to cell A1 and choose the Database Restrict Input command. After Quattro Pro prompts you for the block, choose block A1..G13, and press the Enter key. Quattro Pro moves the cell selector to cell B1, the first unprotected cell in the input block. Quattro Pro is now in the INPUT mode.

Moving the cell selector

At this point, you can use the Left, Right, Up, and Down direction keys, as well as the Home and End keys, to move the cell selector through the unprotected cells in the input block. (Pressing any other cursor-movement key simply causes Quattro Pro to beep.) For example, if you press the Right direction key, the cell selector moves to the next unprotected cell in the block, which in this example is cell G1. Pressing the Right direction key again moves the cell selector to cell C7. If you press the Right or Down direction key when the cell selector is in the last unprotected cell in the input block, the cell selector wraps around to the first cell. Similarly, pressing the Left or Up direction key when the cell selector is in the first unprotected cell in the input block wraps the cell selector to the last unprotected cell.

Making entries in a form

As you move around in a form, you can make entries in it. For example, enter the information into the sample input form as shown in Figure 5-31. To make these entries, press the Home key to move the cell selector to cell B1, type *101*, and press the Right direction key to lock in this entry and move the cell selector to cell G1, the next cell in the input block. Type the date as MM/DD/YY. (For example, type *08/01/92* to indicate August 1, 1992.) Press the Right direction key to move to the

FIGURE 5-31.
The Database Restrict Input command restricts the cell selector to the cells in the entry form.

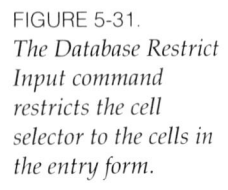

next cell, and type *John Smith*. Continue in this manner until you have filled in the form. Then press the Escape key to leave the INPUT mode. Figure 5-31 shows an example of a completed form.

If you make an error while typing an entry, simply move the cell selector back to that cell and retype or edit the entry. To edit an entry, press the [Edit] key (F2), use the direction keys to insert or delete characters, press the Enter key, and press a direction key to move to the next cell.

A closer look at the Database Restrict Input command

You can use either the Enter key or the direction keys to lock in your entries while you are in INPUT mode. If you press the Enter key for any reason other than to lock in an entry, however, Quattro Pro returns to READY mode. Similarly, if you press the Esc key after you begin typing an entry, Quattro Pro cancels that entry but stays in INPUT mode. If you press the Esc key at any other time, Quattro Pro leaves INPUT mode. Don't forget that the [Help] key (F1) is always available for you while Quattro Pro is in INPUT mode.

Quattro Pro pays no attention to the order in which you unprotect the cells in the form. The cell selector always starts at the upper-left corner of the form and moves down or to the right as you press the Down and Right direction keys.

As mentioned, the Database Restrict Input command is most commonly used in conjunction with macros. For example, the following simple macro statement allows a macro to use the form in Figure 5-30 to accept user input:

    {/Block,Input}A1..g20{cr}

When processing this command, Quattro Pro activates the form and pauses the macro while you enter information. After you press the Enter key to exit from INPUT mode, the macro continues with the next command. The commands that follow can then operate on the entries you made in the form. For example, the macro might print the check or deduct its amount from the current balance. Chapters 12 and 13 explain macros.

Word processing your worksheet

The Tools Reformat command allows you to perform limited word processing in a Quattro Pro worksheet. In essence, this command lets you break up one or more long labels into several smaller labels, simulating the wordwrap effect common to most word processors. When you choose the Tools Reformat command, Quattro Pro displays the prompt *Block to be modified* followed by a block reference to the current cell. Define the block that contains the long label you want to break up. The block sets the margins for the labels the command will create after it breaks up the original labels. Then, press the Enter key to complete the command. Quattro Pro breaks the long labels into several smaller labels and places those labels in the block you defined.

An example of the Tools Reformat command

Suppose you have created the worksheet shown in Figure 5-32, which is a short memo from Billy to Mark. The label in cell A5 forms the body of the memo. Cell A5 contains a long label that begins *As you can see below, we are falling further and further behind in our e....* Because the label in this cell is so long, only a portion of it is visible on the screen. To view the entire label at one time, use the Tools Reformat command to break it into a series of smaller labels.

To begin, move the cell selector to cell A5 and choose the Tools Reformat command. Quattro Pro displays the prompt *Block to be modified* followed by a block

FIGURE 5-32.
Use this memo to demonstrate the Tools Reformat command.

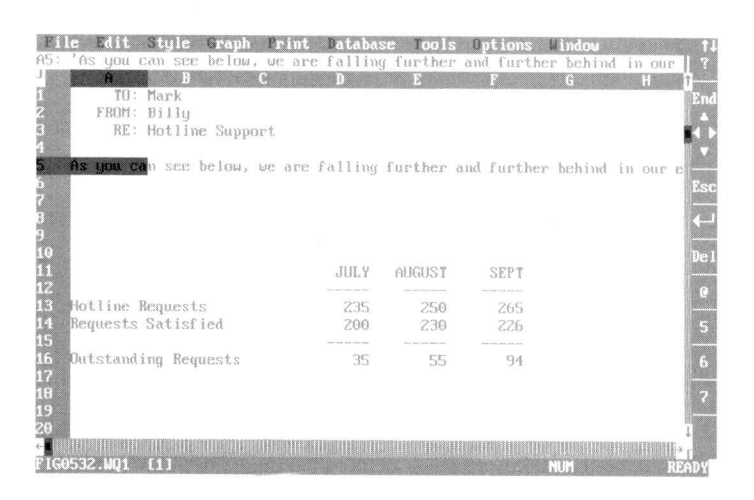

FIGURE 5-33.
The Tools Reformat command breaks up a long label into a series of several smaller labels.

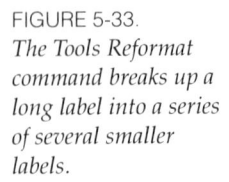

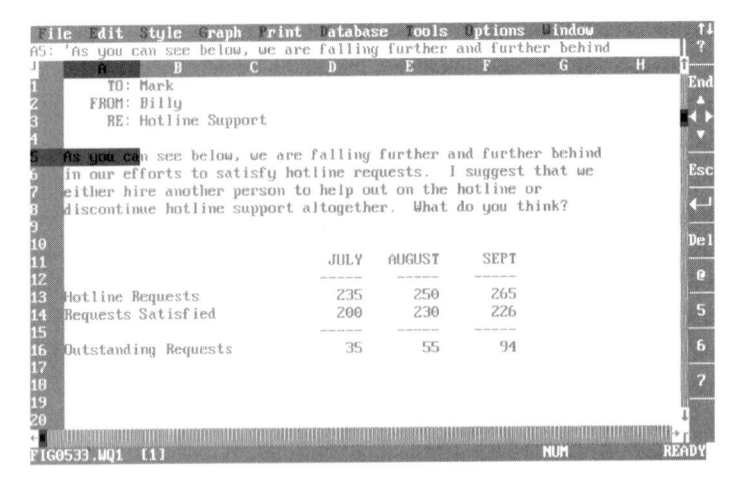

reference to the current cell; in this case, A5..A5. Use the Right and Down direction keys to select block A5..G8. This block defines the maximum length of the short labels the command will create after it breaks up the long label. In other words, this block sets up the margins for the body of the memo. Now, press the Enter key. Figure 5-33 shows the resulting worksheet, in which Quattro Pro has used the label from cell A5 to create four shorter labels in cells A5, A6, A7, and A8. Notice that each of these labels is short enough to fit in the column.

Reformatting blocks

You can also use the Tools Reformat command to reformat a series of labels, combining several small labels into one or more longer labels. For example, suppose you want to reformat the labels in block A5..A8 shown in Figure 5-33. To do so, move the cell selector to cell A5 and choose the Tools Reformat command. When Quattro Pro asks for the block to be modified, define block A5..X8 (column X defines the maximum length of the new labels), and press the Enter key. Quattro Pro then reformats the labels in block A5..A8 to make two labels in cells A5 and A6; the label in cell A5 extends to cell X5, and the label in cell A6 extends to cell D6.

A closer look at defining a reformat block

When you define the reformat block, you must be sure that the block you specify is large enough to hold the labels. If you specify a reformat block that is too small, Quattro Pro displays the message *Reformat block is full*. Also, remember that the width of the labels created by the Tools Reformat command is determined by the widths of the individual columns in the reformat block. To adjust the width of the reformat block to a specific size (for instance, to 75 characters), you'll have to adjust the widths of individual columns in the block.

6

Dates and Times

*L*ike Lotus 1-2-3 and many other popular spreadsheet programs, Quattro Pro can keep time. Quattro Pro's ability to manipulate dates and times lets you perform date and time arithmetic in your worksheets. You can also use dates and times to sort worksheets and databases into date and time order. This chapter explains how to take full advantage of Quattro Pro's timekeeping capabilities.

Dates

A date in Quattro Pro is represented internally by a value that equals the number of days that have elapsed from Quattro Pro's "zero" date, December 30, 1899, to the date in question. This integer value is called a serial date value. For example, the date January 1, 1900, has a serial date value of 2 because it falls two days after the zero date. January 2, 1900, has a value of 3; January 1, 1901, has a value of 367, and so on. Of course, the integer values that represent recent dates are much larger. For instance, the date April 5, 1991, is represented by the value 33333.

Because dates are represented as integer values, Quattro Pro can easily perform date arithmetic. For example, you can use Quattro Pro to calculate the interval between two dates or to determine which date is a specified number of days after a given date. Serial date values also make it possible for Quattro Pro to sort dates. (Chapter 11, "Database Management," explains sorting.)

Unfortunately, the serial date values Quattro Pro uses to represent dates do not look like dates. Most users would have a difficult time figuring out exactly what date is represented by a particular value, such as 28765. Fortunately, Quattro Pro provides two tools that make it easy to work with serial dates: date functions and date formats. The following sections demonstrate how to use these special functions and formats to enter dates in your worksheets.

Entering dates

Quattro Pro gives you two ways to enter serial date values: using date entry mode and using the @DATE function, as described in the following sections.

Entering dates using the date entry mode

The easiest way to enter a serial date value in a cell is by using date entry mode. In date entry mode you can enter dates between March 1, 1800 (-36463) and December 31, 2099 (73050). When you're in date entry mode, Quattro Pro interprets the value or string you enter as a date if it is in one of Quattro Pro's date formats. For example, 1-Jan-92 and 1/1/92 are both interpreted as dates, so if you type either of those dates, Quattro Pro converts your entry to the serial value 33604.

To change to the date entry mode, press Ctrl-D when Quattro Pro is in READY mode. The mode indicator changes to DATE, indicating you're in date entry mode, and you can then enter the date you want. Quattro Pro converts your entry to the appropriate serial date value. Quattro Pro displays the date as you type it, but shows the serial date value in the input line. Quattro Pro leaves date mode when you lock in your entry.

Entering dates using the @DATE function

The @DATE function also allows you to enter dates in a Quattro Pro worksheet. The form of this function is shown below:

@DATE(year,month,day)

The *year* argument specifies the year of the date you want to enter, *month* specifies the month, and *day* specifies the day. The arguments can be literal values, references to cells that contain values, or formulas or functions that return values. The result of a @DATE function is the serial date value of the date specified by the function's arguments. For example, if the function @DATE(92,9,25) represents the date September 25, 1992, Quattro Pro returns the serial value 33872 and displays it in the cell containing the function.

The @DATE function can handle dates ranging from January 1, 1900 (serial value 2) to December 31, 2099 (serial value 73050). In other words, the year argument can range from 0 (for the year 1900) to 199 (for the year 2099). If you try to use the @DATE function with a year argument outside this range, the function returns the value ERR.

Quattro Pro will not allow you to enter dates that do not exist. If you try to use the @DATE function to enter a nonexistent date, the function returns the value ERR. For example, because the month of April has only 30 days, the function @DATE(88,4,31) returns the value ERR.

Formatting dates

If Quattro Pro displayed dates only as serial values like 23523, working with dates would be difficult. Fortunately, Quattro Pro offers a set of date formats that let you display serial date values in a more recognizable form. When you use the Style Numeric Format Date command to assign a date format to a cell that contains a serial date value, Quattro Pro displays that date in a form such as 26-May-91 or 5/26/91. Table 6-1 gives examples of each of Quattro Pro's date formats. (As mentioned, you can use any of these formats to enter dates only after you have changed to the date entry mode.)

You assign date formats to cells in the same way that you assign other formats. To assign a date format to a cell, choose the Style Numeric Format Date command. Quattro Pro presents the menu shown in Figure 6-1. The first five options on this menu represent the five date formats that you can assign to a cell. The last option, Time, allows you to assign time formats, as explained later in this chapter.

Format	Code	Form	Example
1	D1	DD-MMM-YY	23-Sep-91
2	D2	DD-MMM	23-Sep
3	D3	MMM-YY	Sep-91
4 (Long Intl)	D4	MM/DD/YY	09/23/91
5 (Short Intl)	D5	MM/DD	09/23

TABLE 6-1. *Quattro Pro's five date formats let you display date values in various forms.*

FIGURE 6-1.
The Style Numeric Format Date command displays this menu.

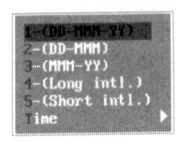

FIGURE 6-2.
Using the Style Numeric Format Date command to format a date makes the date value easy to understand and manipulate.

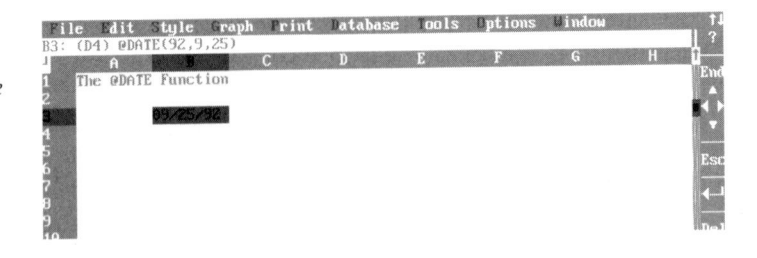

To assign one of these formats to a cell, choose that format from the menu. Quattro Pro then displays the prompt *Block to be modified,* followed by a block reference to the current cell. Specify the block you want, and then press the Enter key.

An example of formatting a date

Suppose you want to assign date format 4 (MM/DD/YY) to cell B3, which contains a serial date value. To do so, move the cell selector to cell B3 and choose the Style Numeric Format Date command, choose Format 4 (Long International), and press the Enter key. Figure 6-2 shows the resulting example worksheet.

Notice the format code D4, which now appears in the input line. When the cell selector is positioned on a cell to which you've assigned a date format, Quattro Pro displays the format code that describes that cell's format.

Column widths and date formats

Quattro Pro displays a formatted value as a series of asterisks (*) if the column that contains the value is not at least one character wider than the number of characters in the value. If you assign the D1 format to a date value in a standard-width column, Quattro Pro displays that date value as a series of asterisks because date values with the D1 format are nine characters long, and the default column width is only nine characters.

You can solve this problem by increasing to at least 10 characters the width of the column that contains the formatted date value. Or, you can use the D4 format instead of the D1 format. As Table 6-1 shows, the D4 format supplies the same information as does D1 in a slightly different format. The D4 format, however, requires only eight characters instead of nine. As a result, Quattro Pro can display dates in the D4 format in standard nine-character columns.

FIGURE 6-3.
The Options International Date command displays this menu.

```
A. MM/DD/YY (MM/DD)
B. DD/MM/YY (DD/MM)
C. DD.MM.YY (DD.MM)
D. YY-MM-DD (MM-DD)
```

Option	Long International	Short International
A	06/07/91	06/91
B	07/06/91	07/06
C	07.06.91	07.06
D	91.06.07	06.07

TABLE 6-2. *You can choose from among these alternative forms for the D4 and D5 formats.*

Changing the Long International and Short International date formats

Most of Quattro Pro's date formats cannot be altered. Quattro Pro gives you some choice, however, about the form of the D4 (Long International) and D5 (Short International) date formats, which you can change using the Options International Date command. When you choose this command, Quattro Pro presents the menu shown in Figure 6-3. The four options in this menu represent the alternative forms of the D4 and D5 formats. Table 6-2 illustrates the different forms of the Long and Short International date formats.

To change the active form of the D4 and D5 formats, choose one of the options shown in Table 6-2. When you do, the appearance of any date value in a cell that has been assigned the D4 or D5 format changes to the new form, and any cells to which you subsequently assign the D4 or D5 format also display date values in the new form. If you want to make your changes to the D4 and D5 formats permanent, choose the Options Update command, and Quattro Pro uses the new D4 and D5 formats until you change the defaults again. Otherwise, your format changes affect only the current Quattro Pro session.

To determine which forms of the D4 and D5 formats are active, choose the Options International command and look at the settings area to the right of the commands on the International menu. If you do not see the settings on this menu, press the Expand key (+) on the numeric keypad while the International menu is on the screen.

Working with date values

After you have entered a date in a worksheet, you can use it in a number of ways. To manipulate a date, you can use Quattro Pro's mathematical operators, mathematical functions, or one of the three special functions that work on dates.

Using mathematical operators and functions on dates

You can manipulate the results of a @DATE function using any of Quattro Pro's mathematical operators (such as + or -) or functions (such as @AVG or @MOD). These operators and functions allow you to perform tasks like calculating the days or weeks between two dates or calculating the date that is a specified number of days before or after a given date.

To calculate the interval between two dates, subtract one date from the other. For example, suppose you want to calculate the number of days between May 27, 1991 (Memorial Day), and September 2, 1991 (Labor Day). You can use the formula @DATE(91,9,2)-@DATE(91,5,27), which gives the result 98.

To determine how many weeks there are between two dates, divide the difference between the two date values by 7. For example, consider the following formula:

(@DATE(91,9,2)-@DATE(91,5,27))/7

This formula returns the value 14, which indicates that there are 14 weeks between Memorial Day and Labor Day, 1991.

To determine which date is a specified number of days before or after another date, add or subtract that number of days to or from the date. For example, suppose you want to figure out what date falls 90 days after November 16, 1992. To do so, you can use the formula @DATE(92,11,16)+90. If you assign a date format to the result, 34014, you'll see that the date February 14, 1993 falls 90 days after November 16, 1992.

You can also operate on serial date values by using any of Quattro Pro's mathematical functions. For instance, you can determine the day of the week of September 5, 1994, with the formula @MOD(@DATE(94,9,5),7). This formula, which uses the @MOD function, returns the remainder of dividing the serial date value for September 5, 1994, which is 34582, by 7. The result, 2, indicates that September 5, 1994, is a Monday. If you use the @MOD function to compute the remainder of dividing a date value by 7 and the result is 0, you know the date is a Saturday. Likewise, if the remainder of dividing a date value by 7 is 1, you know the date is a Sunday. You can use this rule to create a formula that returns the day of the week of any date value:

@CHOOSE(@MOD(@DATE(YY,MM,DD),7),"Saturday","Sunday",
   "Monday","Tuesday","Wednesday","Thursday","Friday")

If you replace *yy*, *mm*, and *dd* in this formula with a year, month, and day, the formula returns the day of the week (Sunday, Monday, and so on) of the date.

Special date functions

Quattro Pro offers three special date functions (@DAY, @MONTH, and @YEAR) that you can use to determine the day, month, or year term of any date. These functions have the following form:

@DAY(serial date value)

@MONTH(serial date value)

@YEAR(serial date value)

@DAY returns the day component of the *serial date value* argument; @MONTH returns the month component of the argument; and @YEAR returns the year component of the argument. The *serial date value* argument can be a literal date value, a reference to a cell that contains date values, or a formula or function that returns a date value.

The @DAY function. The @DAY function returns a value between 1 and 31 that represents the day of the month of the date referred to by its argument. For example, if the function @DATE(92,5,26) is in cell B3, @DAY(B3) returns a value of 26 for May 26, 1992.

The @MONTH function. The @MONTH function returns the month of the year in which the date referred to by its argument falls. @MONTH returns a value from 1 to 12. Assuming the function @DATE(92,5,26) is entered in cell B3, @MONTH(B3) returns the value 5, the month number of the date May 26, 1992.

The @YEAR function. The @YEAR function returns a value from 0 to 199 that specifies the year in which the date referred to by its argument falls. If cell B3 contains the function @DATE(92,5,26), the function @YEAR(B3) returns the value 92, which indicates that the date in cell B3 falls in the year 1992.

Creating date series

A date series is a sequence of date entries that have a constant time interval; usually a day, a week, a month, or a year. You can create these series in your worksheets.

Daily and weekly date series. Use the Edit Fill command to create daily and weekly date series. For example, suppose you want to enter a series of dates in block A1..A20 of a blank worksheet. The series begins with the date January 1, 1992, and each date in the series is one day greater than the prior date. To begin, choose the Edit Fill command, and define A1..A20 as the fill block. Enter the function *@DATE(92,1,1)* as the start value, *1* as the step value, and *100000* as the stop value. Press the Enter key, and Quattro Pro fills block A1..A20 with the values

FIGURE 6-4.
You can use the Edit Fill command to create a date series, and the Style Numeric Format Date command to display the values in a date format.

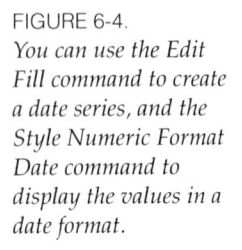

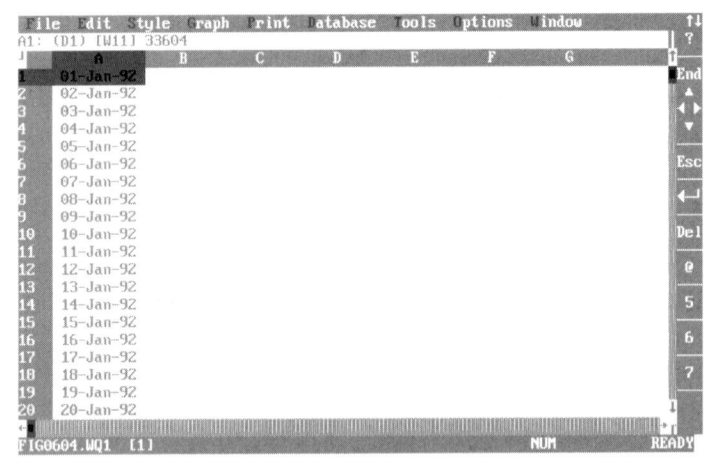

33604, 33605, 33606, and so on. After the series is in place, you can display these values in a date format by choosing the Style Numeric Format Date command. Figure 6-4 shows the result when column A is 11 characters wide.

You might have noticed that 100000 was used as the stop value for this command, which is because of the relatively large numbers that are used to represent dates. Actually, any number greater than about 40000 could have been used as the stop value.

You can vary the interval between dates in a series simply by changing the step value of the Edit Fill command. A step value of 7 will create a weekly series. For example, suppose that you want to create a date series in block A1..A20 that begins with September 5, 1994 (a Monday), and that you want the interval between the dates to be seven days so that every date in the series is a Monday. To create this series, choose the Edit Fill command, and define A1..A20 as the fill block. Enter the function @DATE(94,9,5) as the start value, the value 7 as the step value, and the value *100000* as the stop value. Press the Enter key, and Quattro Pro fills block A1..A20 with the values 34582, 34589, and so on, which are exactly seven days apart. Then, use the Style Numeric Format Date command to format the dates.

Monthly and yearly date series. The Edit Fill command maintains a constant interval between each item in a data series. Because all months and years do not contain the same number of days, Edit Fill is not as good at creating monthly and yearly series as it is at creating daily and weekly series. If you want the interval in your series to be a month or a year, you'll have to use a formula.

You can create two kinds of monthly series in Quattro Pro: imprecise series and precise series. Imprecise series are easy to create but are not accurate to the day. Precise series are much harder to create, but are accurate to the day.

FIGURE 6-5.
You can use the Edit Fill command to create an imprecise monthly series.

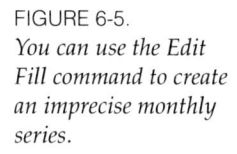

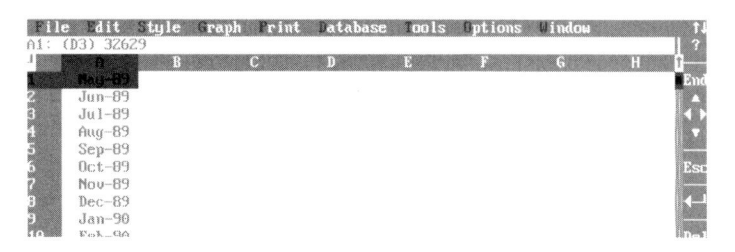

To create an imprecise monthly series, use the Edit Fill command. For example, suppose you want to create an imprecise monthly series that begins on May 1, 1989, in block A1..A20 of a blank worksheet. To do so, choose the Edit Fill command and define A1..A20 as the fill block. Enter the function @DATE(89,5,1) as the start value, the value *31* as the step value, and the value *100000* as the stop value. Press the Enter key, and Quattro Pro fills block A1..A20 with the values 32629, 32660, and so on. Then, choose the Style Numeric Format Date command, choose date format 3, and specify block A1..A20. The result is shown in Figure 6-5. As you can see, the Edit Fill command has produced what appears to be an accurate monthly series. Although the underlying date values are not exactly one month apart, the MMM-YY format still displays an evenly spaced monthly series.

Precise monthly series are accurate to the day. These series are important in cases in which some event occurs on the same day, month after month. For example, suppose that you have borrowed money to buy a new car, and that you must make a payment on this loan on the first day of every month, beginning on July 1, 1991. You want to create a schedule that shows the date, amount, and so forth, of each payment. The interval between each of the dates on the payment schedule is exactly one month; dates will appear in column A. To create this monthly series, enter the function @DATE(91,7,1) into cell A1. Next, enter the following formula in cell A2:

+A1+@CHOOSE(@MONTH(A1)-1,31,@IF(@MOD(@YEAR(A1),4)=0,29,28),
31,30,31,30,31,31,30,31,30,31)

This complicated formula uses the @MONTH function to compute the month of the date in cell A1 and then adds the appropriate number of days to that date to arrive at the same date in the next month. The function @IF(@MOD(@YEAR(A1),4)=0,29,28) adjusts for leap years.

Next, use the Style Numeric Format Date command to display the result in a date format. Then use the Edit Copy command to copy it down column A. Figure 6-6 shows the result when the column is enlarged to 11 characters. You can use

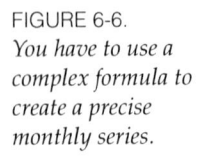

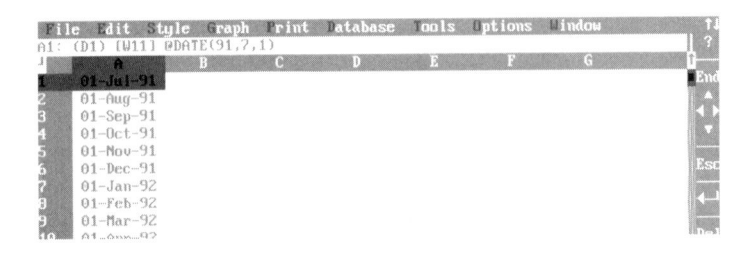

FIGURE 6-6.
You have to use a complex formula to create a precise monthly series.

this formula to create any precise monthly series that begins on a date that falls between the first and twenty-eighth day of the month. Computing a monthly series that begins after the twenty-eighth day of the month is a topic beyond the scope of this book.

You can also create a yearly series in Quattro Pro. For example, suppose you want to create a yearly series that begins on May 1, 1992, in block A1..A20. You begin by entering the function @DATE(92,5,1) in cell A1. Next, enter the following formula in cell A2:

+A1+@IF(@MOD(@YEAR(A1),4)=3,@IF(@MONTH(A1)>2,366,365),@IF(@MOD (@YEAR(A1),4)=0,@IF(@MONTH(A1)>2,365,366),365))

This formula adds the appropriate number of days to the prior date in the series to arrive at the same date in the next year. Then, use the Style Numeric Format Date command to display the result in a date format, and the Edit Copy command to copy it down column A. The result is a series of dates exactly one year apart.

Times

The base unit of time in Quattro Pro is a day. Quattro Pro represents the time as fractions of a day called decimal time values. For example, 12:00 noon is represented by the decimal time value .5 because 12:00 noon marks exactly half the day. Similarly, 6:00 AM is represented by the value .25, and 6:00 PM is represented by the value .75. In most cases, however, the time values you see will be much more complicated than these simple examples. For instance, the value .4791666666 represents 11:30 AM.

Just as it is difficult to interpret the serial values Quattro Pro uses to represent dates, it is also difficult to understand the decimal values that Quattro Pro uses to represent times. Fortunately, Quattro Pro provides a function called @TIME that makes it easy to enter time values in your worksheets. Quattro Pro also offers a set of formats that display time values in meaningful forms.

Entering times

Quattro Pro gives you two ways to enter decimal time values: using the date entry mode explained earlier in this chapter and using the @TIME function as described in the following sections.

Entering times using the date entry mode

The easiest way to enter a decimal time value is by using the date entry mode. When you're in date entry mode, Quattro Pro interprets your entry as a time if its format looks like one of Quattro Pro's time formats. For example, 3:50 PM and 12:00:00 are both interpreted as times, so if you type either of those times, Quattro Pro converts the entry to a decimal time.

To change to the date entry mode, press Ctrl-D when Quattro Pro is in READY mode. The mode indicator changes to DATE. Enter the time you want and press the Enter key. Quattro Pro displays the time as you typed it in the cell, but displays the decimal time value in the input line.

Entering times using the @TIME function

You can use the @TIME function to enter a time value in a worksheet. The form of this function is shown below:

@TIME(hours,minutes,seconds)

The *hours* argument specifies the hour of the time you want to enter, *minutes* specifies the minutes, and *seconds* specifies the seconds. The *hours*, *minutes*, and *seconds* arguments can be literal values, references to cells that contain values, or formulas or functions that return values. The result of a @TIME function is the decimal time value of the time specified by its arguments. For example, the function @TIME(5,43,0) returns the value 0.238194, which is the decimal time value of 5:43 AM.

Like the @DATE function, @TIME accepts only arguments that identify real times. The *hours* argument can range from 0 to 23, where 0 is midnight, 12 is 12:00 noon, 18 is 6:00 PM, and so on. The *minutes* and *seconds* arguments can range from 0 to 59. If you specify an *hours* argument that is less than 0 or greater than 23, or a *minutes* or *seconds* argument that is less than 0 or greater than 59, the @TIME function returns the result ERR.

Formatting times

Quattro Pro offers a set of four time formats that you can apply to cells that contain decimal time values. Table 6-3 illustrates each of Quattro Pro's time format options.

To format a cell that contains a decimal time value, choose the Style Numeric Format Date command, and then choose the Time option. Quattro Pro then displays the menu shown in Figure 6-7. After you choose a format, Quattro Pro

Format	Code	Form	Example
1	D6	HH:MM:SS AM/PM	3:18:48 PM
2	D7	HH:MM AM/PM	3:18 PM
3 (Long Intl)	D8	HH:MM:SS (24-hr)	15:18:48
4 (Short Intl)	D9	HH:MM (24-hr)	15:18

TABLE 6-3. *Quattro Pro's time formats let you display decimal time values in meaningful forms.*

FIGURE 6-7.
The Style Numeric Format Date Time command displays this menu.

```
1-(HH:MM:SS AM/PM)
2-(HH:MM AM/PM)
3-(Long intl.)
4-(Short intl.)
```

prompts you to define the block to be formatted and offers the address of the current cell as the default. Specify the block you want and press the Enter key.

An example of formatting a time

Suppose you want to assign Time Format 2 (HH:MM AM/PM) to cell B3, which contains the decimal time value 0.238194. To do so, move the cell selector to cell B3, choose the Style Numeric Format Date Time command, choose Time Format 2, and press Enter. The result appears as 05:43 AM in cell B3.

Notice the format code D7, which now appears in the input line. When the cell pointer is positioned on a cell to which you've assigned a time format, Quattro Pro displays a format code describing the cell's format. Because Quattro Pro considers the four time formats as extensions of its set of date formats, Quattro Pro assigns the format code D6 to time format 1, the code D7 to time format 2, and so forth.

Column widths and time formats

Items formatted with Time Format 1 (HH:MM:SS AM/PM) are too long for standard nine-character columns and are displayed as a series of asterisks (*). You can overcome this problem by using the Style Column Width command to increase to at least 12 characters the width of the column that contains the time value. Alternatively, you can display the times in one of Quattro Pro's other time formats (such as Time Format 2). Because the other time formats create time values that are eight or fewer characters long, Quattro Pro can display times with these formats in standard-width columns. Since you usually won't need to display the seconds portion of a time anyway, you can save yourself some work by choosing Time Format 2.

FIGURE 6-8.
The Option International Time command displays this menu.

```
A. HH:MM:SS (HH:MM)
B. HH.MM.SS (HH.MM)
C. HH,MM,SS (HH,MM)
D. HHhMMmSSs (HHhMMm)
```

Option	Long Intl form	Short Intl form
A	15:30:23	15:30
B	15.30.23	15.30
C	15,30,23	15,30
D	15h30m23s	15h30m

TABLE 6-4. *You can choose from among these alternative forms for the D8 and D9 formats.*

Changing the Long and Short International time formats

Quattro Pro lets you change the form of the D8 (Long International) and D9 (Short International) time formats using the Options International Time command. When you choose this command, Quattro Pro presents the menu shown in Figure 6-8. The four choices in this menu represent the different forms of the D8 and D9 formats. Table 6-4 illustrates each of these four options. Notice that the international formats use the 24-hour (or military) format.

To change the active form of the D8 and D9 formats, choose one of these options. When you do so, the appearance of any date value in a cell that has been assigned the D8 or D9 format changes to the new format, and any cells to which you subsequently assign the D8 or D9 format also display time values in the new form. If you want to make your changes to the D8 and D9 formats permanent, choose the Options Update command. Quattro Pro uses the new D8 and D9 formats until you change the defaults again. Otherwise, your format changes affect only the current Quattro Pro session.

To determine which forms of the D8 and D9 formats are active, choose the Options International command and look at the settings area to the right of the commands on the International menu. If you do not see the settings on this menu, press the Expand key (+) on the numeric keypad while the International menu is on the screen.

Working with time values

After you enter time values in a Quattro Pro worksheet, you operate upon those values with Quattro Pro's mathematical operators (such as + and -) or manipulate them with Quattro Pro's three special time functions.

Manipulating time values using mathematical operators

You can manipulate the results of a @TIME function using any of Quattro Pro's mathematical operators. For instance, you can compute the time between two times simply by subtracting the smaller time value from the larger one. For example, the following formula calculates the amount of time between 12:47 PM and 2:30 PM:

@TIME(14,30,0)-@TIME(12,47,0)

The result, .071528, represents the fraction of a day that falls between the two times. Formatting the cell that contains this result with the D8 or D9 format reveals that there is 1 hour and 43 minutes between these two times.

You can also add time values. For example, the formula @TIME(18,42,56) +@TIME(3,38,23) adds 3 hours, 38 minutes, and 23 seconds to the time 6:42:56 PM. The result, .931470, is the decimal time value of the sum of these times. Formatting the result reveals that 10:21:19 PM is 3 hours, 38 minutes, and 23 seconds after 6:42:56 PM.

Special time functions

Quattro Pro offers three special time functions that can manipulate time values: @HOUR, @MINUTE, and @SECOND. The functions have the following form:

@HOUR(decimal time value)

@MINUTE(decimal time value)

@SECOND(decimal time value)

@HOUR returns the hour component of *decimal time value*; @MINUTE returns the minute component of *decimal time value*; and @SECOND returns the second component of *decimal time value*. The *decimal time value* argument can be a literal time value, a reference to a cell that contains time values, or a function or formula that returns a time value.

The @HOUR function. The @HOUR function returns a value from 0 to 23 that represents the hours portion of the time referred to by its argument. For example, if cell B3 contains the decimal time value for 17:34:16, the function @HOUR(B3) returns the value 17.

The @MINUTE function. The @MINUTE function returns a value from 0 to 59 that represents the minutes portion of the time referred to by its argument. For example, if cell B3 contains the decimal time value for 17:34:16, @MINUTE(B3) returns the value 34.

The @SECOND function. The @SECOND function returns a value from 0 to 59 that represents the seconds portion of the time referred to by its argument. For example, if cell B3 contains the decimal time value for 17:34:16, @SECOND(B3) returns the value 16.

Combined date and time entries

Up to this point, date and time values have been discussed separately. Quattro Pro also allows you, however, to create combined date/time entries. A date/time entry is represented by a mixed number that has both an integer and a decimal portion. The integer portion of the date/time entry represents a date, and the decimal portion represents a time. For example, the entry 33817.5 represents the date/time August 1, 1992, 12:00 noon. The integer portion of this entry, 33817, represents the date August 1, 1992, and the decimal portion, .5, represents the time 12:00 noon.

The @NOW function

Quattro Pro's @NOW function allows you to enter the current date and time in the worksheet. The form of this function is simply @NOW; the function accepts no arguments. When you enter this function in a worksheet, Quattro Pro retrieves the current date and time from your computer's clock and uses those values to create a date/time value. For example, if you entered the function @NOW in a worksheet at exactly 10:25:32 AM on October 1, 1991, Quattro Pro returns the value 33512.43440. The integer portion of this value, 33512, specifies the date October 1, 1991. The decimal portion, .43440, specifies the time 10:25:32 AM. In effect, the entry 33512.43440 represents the date and time that is 33512.43440 days after Quattro Pro's zero date.

As with all other functions, Quattro Pro updates any @NOW functions in a worksheet each time you recalculate that worksheet. If Quattro Pro is set for manual recalculation, it updates the value of @NOW when you press the [Calc] key (F9). For this reason, you might notice a discrepancy between the result of @NOW and the system clock at the bottom of the screen until you recalculate. Because @NOW is updated every time you recalculate your worksheet, the value of the @NOW function changes constantly. If you want to lock in the result of the @NOW function, position the cell selector on the cell that contains the value, choose the Edit Values command, and press the Enter key two times.

Because the @NOW function gets its value from your computer's system clock, the result of @NOW will be wrong if your system clock is wrong. You may find this limitation troublesome if your computer does not have a battery-powered clock. To set the system clock, you must exit from Quattro Pro to DOS (using either the File Exit or File Utilities DOS Shell command), and then run DOS's DATE and TIME utilities.

Formatting date/time entries

Unfortunately, Quattro Pro does not offer a format that displays both the date and time components of a date/time entry. You can display a date/time entry as a date or as a time, but not as both. For example, suppose you enter the function @NOW in a worksheet at precisely 9:00 AM on June 1, 1991 so that the function returns the date/time value 33390.375. If you use the Style Numeric Format Date command to assign Date Format 4 to that cell, Quattro Pro displays the date/time entry as 06/01/91. If you use the Style Numeric Format Date Time command to assign Time Format 8 to the same cell, Quattro Pro displays the value as 09:00 AM. There is no format that displays both the date and the time together. Accordingly, to display both the date and the time components of a serial date value in a worksheet, you must enter the value in two different cells, and then assign a date format to one cell and a time format to the other.

Creating your own date/time entries

You can also create combined date/time entries simply by adding the result of a @DATE function to the result of a @TIME function. For example, suppose you want to create a single entry that represents the time 5:30 PM on January 1, 1992. To do so, you use the following formula:

@DATE(92,1,1)+@TIME(17,30,0)

The result of this formula, 33604.729167, is the date/time value that represents the time 5:30 PM on January 1, 1992.

Working with date/time entries

You can use Quattro Pro's mathematical operators to perform math with combined date/time values. For example, if you want to know what date and time falls four days and nine hours after 8:00 PM on February 21, 1990, the following formula returns the correct result of 32930.21:

(@DATE(90,2,21)+@TIME(20,0,0))+(4+@TIME(9,0,0))

This value represents the date February 26, 1990 and the time 5:00 AM; the date and time four days and nine hours after 8:00 PM on February 21, 1990. Now, suppose you want to know the date and time that is four days and nine hours before 8:00 PM on February 21, 1990. You can use the following formula to compute the result of 32921.46:

(@DATE(90,2,21)+@TIME(20,0,0))-(4+@TIME(9,0,0))

The result represents the date February 17, 1990 and the time 11:00 AM. You can also determine the interval between two date/time values by subtracting one value from the other. For example, the following formula computes the interval between 8:00 PM on February 21, 1990, and 11:00 AM on February 17, 1990:

(@DATE(90,2,21)+@TIME(20,0,0))-(@DATE(90,2,17)+@TIME(11,0,0))

The result of this function is the date/time value 4.375, which indicates that the interval is four days and nine hours.

Converting labels to dates and times

You'll usually enter dates and times in your worksheets using the functions @DATE, @TIME, and @NOW, which return date or time values that Quattro Pro can manipulate mathematically. Occasionally, when you import data into Quattro Pro from another program or when someone with less experience with Quattro Pro enters dates and times in a worksheet as labels, the worksheet contains label entries that are in the form of dates or times. Because Quattro Pro can manipulate values only mathematically, labels in the form of dates and times are not useful. Fortunately, Quattro Pro offers two functions, @DATEVALUE and @TIMEVALUE, that convert labels in the form of dates and times to date and time values.

The @DATEVALUE function

The @DATEVALUE function converts labels in the form of dates to serial date values. The form of this function is shown below:

@DATEVALUE(date label)

The *date label* argument is a label (or string) in the form of any of Quattro Pro's standard date formats. (See Table 6-1.) The result of this function is the serial date value of the date specified by *date label*. Figure 6-9 contains several examples of the @DATEVALUE function. The functions in cells B3..B9 convert the date labels in block A3..A9 to serial date values. As an example, the function in cell B3, @DATEVALUE(A3), converts the label in cell A3, '26-May-92, to the serial date value 33750.

If the argument of a @DATEVALUE function is in a short form that omits some information, like '26-May or 'May-92, Quattro Pro guesses at the missing component. If the day is missing, Quattro Pro returns the serial date value for the first

FIGURE 6-9.
The @DATEVALUE function converts labels in date form to serial date values.

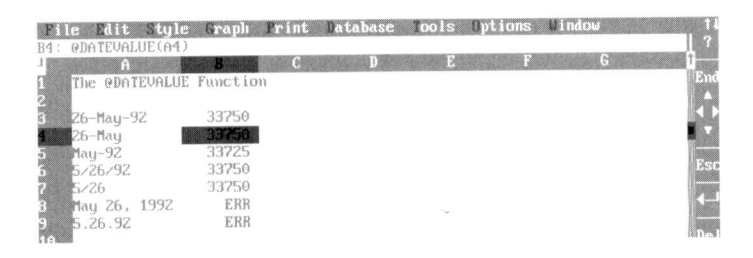

FIGURE 6-10.
The @TIMEVALUE function converts labels in time form to time values.

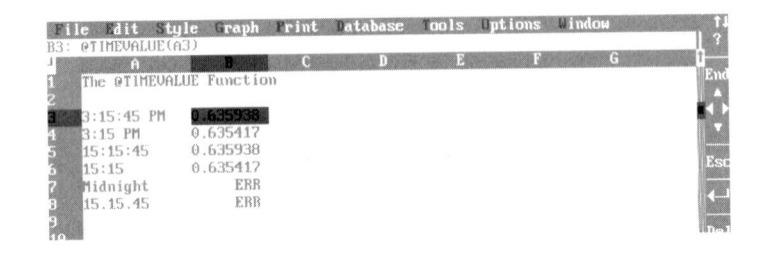

day in the specified month. For example, the date label in cell A5 in Figure 6-9 is 'May-92. The function in cell B5, @DATEVALUE(A5), returns the value 33725, which is the serial date value for May 1, 1992.

If the year term of a date label is missing, @DATEVALUE will assume that the date falls in the current year. For example, cell A4 in Figure 6-9 contains the label '26-May. If the system clock shows that the current year is 1992, the function in cell B4, @DATEVALUE(A4), returns the value 33750; the serial date value for May 26, 1992. If the argument of a @DATEVALUE function is not in a form that Quattro Pro can recognize (including a Long or Short International form that is not currently active), the function returns ERR. For example, Quattro Pro cannot recognize the form of the date in cell A8, so the function in cell B8, @DATEVALUE(A8), returns the value ERR. The function in cell B9, @DATEVALUE(A9), also returns ERR, even though the label in cell A9 is in one of Quattro Pro's International date formats. The problem is that the format MM.DD.YY is not the currently active Long International date format.

The @TIMEVALUE function

The @TIMEVALUE function converts labels in the form of times to time values; its form is shown below:

@TIMEVALUE(time label)

The *time label* argument is a label in the form of any of Quattro Pro's standard time formats. (See Table 6-3.) The result of this function is the time value of the time represented by *time label*. Figure 6-10 contains several examples of the @TIMEVALUE function. The functions in block B3..B8 convert the time labels in block A3..A8 to time values. For example, the function in cell B3, @TIMEVALUE(A3), converts the label in cell A3, '3:15:45 PM, to the time value .635938.

If the @TIMEVALUE function's argument is not in the form of one of Quattro Pro's time formats (including a Long or Short International form that is not currently active), the function returns ERR. For example, because the time label in cell A7 is not in one of Quattro Pro's standard forms, the function in cell B7 in Figure 6-10, @TIMEVALUE(A7), returns the value ERR. The function in cell B8, @TIMEVALUE(A8), also returns ERR. Although HH.MM.SS is a valid International time format, it is not the active Long International time format.

7

Printing

You'll find that it is easy to make printed copies of your Quattro Pro worksheets. This chapter shows you how to use the Print command to define, format, and print Quattro Pro worksheets as reports. It also shows you how to use Quattro Pro's print options and the Style Shading, Style Font, and Style Insert Break commands to embellish reports.

Several additional printing topics are covered later in this book. Chapter 10, "Creating Graphs," explains the process of printing graphs. Appendix A, "Exchanging Data with Other Programs," covers the Print Destination File and Print Destination Binary File commands. These commands allow you to "print" worksheets as files, which can then be imported into other programs, including word processors and database managers.

Hardware setup

Before you print for the first time, you must give Quattro Pro some information about your printer or printers. Typically, you will already have done so as part of the installation. If you have, skip ahead to "Printing Basics" later in this chapter. If you haven't, or if you buy a new printer, you must indicate which interface your printer uses and whether to send a carriage return or line feed, or both, to the printer after each line. If you use a serial printer, you also must indicate the baud rate, number of stop bits, and parity that Quattro Pro should use to communicate with your printer. The baud rate specifies the speed at which information is sent to your computer, the stop bits specify the format of the information, and the parity specifies how to check the information for transmission errors.

To configure your printer in Quattro Pro, choose the Options Hardware Printers command. Quattro Pro displays the Printers menu shown in Figure 7-1. Use the first three options in the Printers menu to identify the printers you use with Quattro Pro and, if you use more than one, which printer you use most often.

Defining a printer

If you did not define a printer when you installed Quattro Pro, you must do so now before you can begin printing worksheets and graphs. To define a printer, choose the 1st Printer or 2nd Printer option from the Printers menu. Quattro Pro then displays a submenu like the one shown in Figure 7-2. Use this menu to identify a printer and the way in which the printer connects to your computer.

The first option in the Printer submenu, Type Of Printer, lets you identify a printer make, model, and mode. (If you identified a printer during the installation of Quattro Pro, a printer make and model may already be shown.) Choose the Type Of Printer option. Quattro Pro first displays a box that lists printer manufacturers, as shown in Figure 7-3. Choose the make of printer you want, and then press the Enter key. Not all the printer manufacturers fit in the list box at one time, so use the PgUp and PgDn keys or the mouse with the scroll bar to see the next or previous portion of the list.

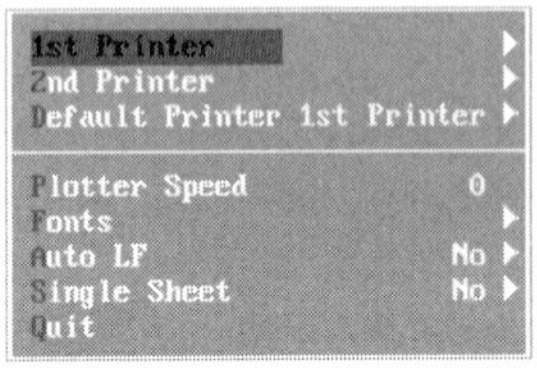

FIGURE 7-1.
When you choose the Options Hardware Printers command, Quattro Pro displays the Printers menu.

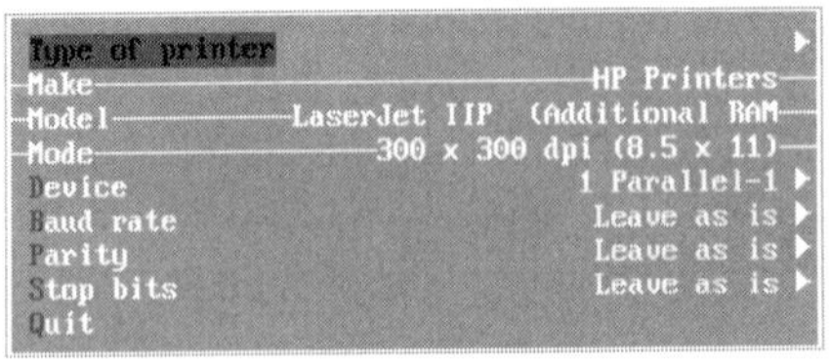

FIGURE 7-2.
The Printer submenu provides options for identifying your printer and how it connects to your computer.

FIGURE 7-3.
This list shows printer manufacturers.

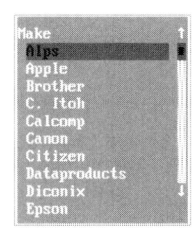

FIGURE 7-4.
This list shows the Hewlett-Packard printer models supported by Quattro Pro.

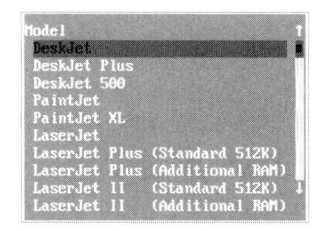

FIGURE 7-5.
This list shows the modes available for your printer.

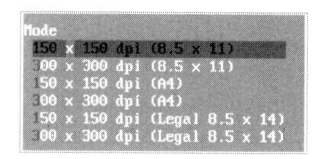

After you choose the make of the printer, Quattro Pro displays a list of the printer models that the manufacturer supplies. For example, if you choose HP Printers, which stands for Hewlett-Packard printers, you see a list of printer models like the one shown in Figure 7-4.

After you choose the printer model you have, Quattro Pro displays the Mode menu, as shown in Figure 7-5. Your printer's manual should provide information about the available modes. Once you choose a mode from the menu, Quattro Pro displays the Printer submenu again, but this time with the printer make, model, and mode showing on the submenu, as Figure 7-2 illustrates.

The Printer submenu includes five other options: Device, Baud Rate, Parity, Stop Bits, and Quit. These options describe how your printer connects to your computer and how information will be passed between your printer and computer.

Telling Quattro Pro where to send printed output

Before you can print, Quattro Pro must know where to send the printed output. Your printer is connected to your computer through one of your computer's printer ports—the sockets on the back of a computer where you plug in a printer cable. There are two types of printer ports: parallel and serial. The vast majority of printers use a parallel port. One notable exception is Hewlett-Packard's original

LaserJet printer, which uses a serial port. Because most printers use a parallel port, Quattro Pro's default device setting is Parallel-1. If you plan to use only one parallel printer, you probably will not need to adjust this setting. But if your printer uses a serial port or if you have more than one printer connected to your computer, choose the appropriate device setting before you begin printing.

To specify the printer port where your computer connects to your printer, choose the Device option from the Printer submenu. Quattro Pro presents a menu that has nine options: Parallel-1 (the default), Serial-1, Parallel-2, Serial-2, LPT1, LPT2, LPT3, LPT4, and EPT. The four LPT devices are used only to print through a network to remote output devices. Unless your printer is connected to a network, you need not be concerned with these options.

As mentioned, if you use a single parallel printer, you should leave the Device option set at Parallel-1 (the default). If you use anything other than a single parallel printer, choose the option that corresponds to the interface used by your printer.

The last option on the Device menu, EPT, tells Quattro Pro that you are using IBM's Pageprinter, which is a PostScript printer that requires a special interface card inside your computer. The EPT interface works only with IBM's Pageprinter; you cannot use this option to print to other PostScript printers.

Setting Baud Rate, Stop Bits, and Parity options

If you use a serial printer (options 2 or 4 in the Device menu), you must also be sure that the Baud Rate, Stop Bits, and Parity settings in the Printer submenu match those defined for your printer. (Parallel printers do not require that you specify these settings.) Your printer's manual should describe the settings your printer uses.

If you used DOS's MODE command to define these three parameters for your serial port before you started Quattro Pro, the settings you've defined are used as the defaults and you do not need to set them again inside of Quattro Pro.

If you have not used the MODE command to set up your computer's serial port, or if you want to override the defaults, you need to use the Baud Rate, Stop Bits, and Parity options in the Printer submenu to define the parameters your computer will use to communicate with your printer. When you choose any of these options, you see a menu that lists the various options that are available for that setting. After the menu is presented, choose the option you want to use (or choose the Leave As Is option to retain the current setting) and press the Enter key.

Working with two printers

If your computer connects to two printers, step through the same process described in the preceding sections to define both printers. The only difference is that you choose the 2nd Printer option rather than the 1st Printer option from the Printers menu.

If you do define two printers, you'll want to identify one as the default printer (the one that Quattro Pro uses until you tell it otherwise). To do so, choose the Default Printer option from the Printers menu. Quattro Pro presents a menu that has two choices: 1st Printer and 2nd Printer. Choose the printer you want as the default, and press the Enter key. To specify a printer as the permanent default printer—not only for the current session, but for future sessions as well—you must also choose the Options Update command.

Setting plotter speeds

If you want to use a plotter with Quattro Pro, set it up just like a printer; by choosing it from the Printer list. You can control the plotter's drawing speed from Quattro Pro. Why might you want to control speed? Some types of paper and transparencies need to be drawn slowly to ensure good quality plotting. To set the plotter speed, choose the Options Hardware Printers Plotter Speed command. Quattro Pro displays a box with the prompt *Speed used to run a plotter (0..9, 0 = fastest or current)*. Type the speed setting you want, and press the Enter key. The default plotter speed setting is 0, which indicates the plotter's fastest speed or whatever speed it is already set to. To override the default speed, use a speed setting from 1 to 9. (For plotting on transparencies, try a plotter speed of 2.)

Identifying laser font cartridges

The Fonts option in the Printers menu presents a submenu that has two options: LaserJet Fonts and Autoscale Fonts. The Autoscale Fonts option is for printing graphs, which is described in "Creating Graphs" in Chapter 10. The LaserJet Fonts option is for printing spreadsheets. This option gives you a way to identify which font cartridges to use in your laser printer.

To specify the fonts your laser printer uses, choose the Options Hardware Printers Fonts Laserjet Fonts command. Quattro Pro presents a submenu that has two options: Left Cartridge and Right Cartridge. If you have a font cartridge in the left cartridge slot, choose the Left Cartridge option. If you have a font cartridge in the right cartridge slot, choose the Right Cartridge option. Quattro Pro displays a list of font cartridges from which you can choose.

Specifying line feeds

The Auto LF option in the Printers menu tells Quattro Pro how your printer responds to carriage-return codes. The default setting for Auto LF is No, which tells Quattro Pro to send both a carriage return and a line feed at the end of each printed line. A carriage return tells the printer to move the print head to the left edge of the paper, and a line feed tells the printer to scroll the paper up one line so that the next line of print will appear on a new line. Of course, the Auto LF setting you should choose depends on the type of printer you have. Some printers issue a line feed automatically when they receive a carriage return, and others require you to send both a carriage return and a line feed after each line of print. If your printer interprets a carriage return as a carriage return plus a line feed, Quattro Pro's default Auto LF setting inserts an extra line after each printed line in your report.

If your printed worksheets always come out double spaced, change the Auto LF option to Yes. To do so, choose the Options Hardware Printers Auto LF command, and then choose the Yes option. This setting tells Quattro Pro to send only a carriage return after printing each line, allowing your printed reports to come out single spaced.

Printing basics

After you have told Quattro Pro about your printer, you're ready to print. The Print command is the tool you use to print reports in Quattro Pro. A report is a portion of your worksheet that you choose to print as a unit. When you choose the Print command, Quattro Pro presents the Print menu shown in Figure 7-6. The commands on this menu allow you to define the area of the worksheet you want to print, specify whether to print column and row headings on each page, specify formatting options, advance the paper in the printer, and print.

To print a report, choose the Print Block command, select the block of cells you want to see in the report, align the paper in the printer, choose the Print Adjust Printer Align command, and then choose the Print Spreadsheet command. The other options in the Print menu let you customize your reports in a number of ways, as explained in the upcoming sections.

FIGURE 7-6.
Use the commands on the Print menu to print reports from your Quattro Pro worksheets.

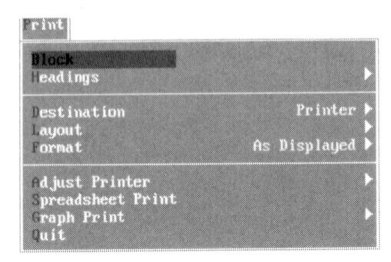

FIGURE 7-7.
Use this worksheet to demonstrate Quattro Pro's printing capabilities.

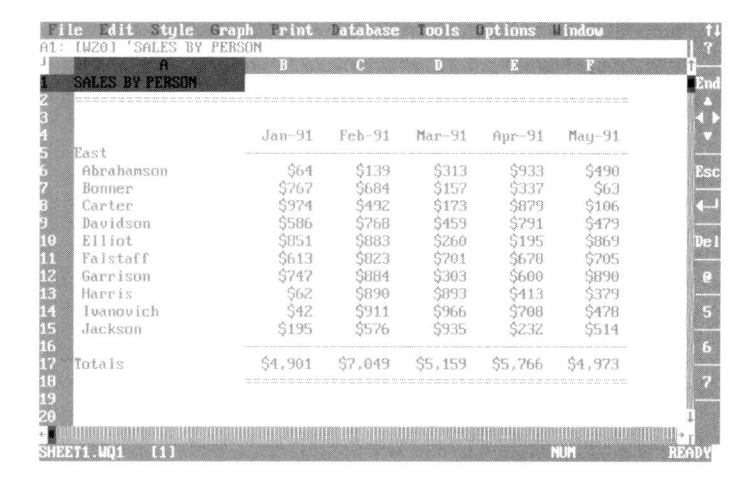

An example of printing

Figure 7-7 shows part of a worksheet that contains a sales forecast for a fictitious company. The worksheet shows the expected level of sales for the first five months of 1991. To improve the appearance of the worksheet, the width of column A has been changed to 20 characters.

To print this worksheet, first choose the Print command and choose the Block command from the Print menu. When Quattro Pro prompts you to specify the block of the worksheet you want to print, select block A1..F18 and press the Enter key. Next, check your printer to be sure that it contains paper, that the "on line" light is on, and that the paper in the printer is properly aligned. Then, choose the Print Adjust Printer Align command to tell Quattro Pro that the printer is positioned at the top of a new page. Finally, print the report by choosing the Spreadsheet Print command from the Print menu. Figure 7-8 shows the worksheet printed on a Hewlett-Packard Laserjet printer on 8½-by-11-inch paper. (If you're printing on a laser printer, choose the Adjust Printer option from the Print menu and select the Form Feed option to eject the last page of the report.)

The print block

Before you can print a worksheet, you must use the Print Block command to define the block you want to print. When you choose the Block option, Quattro Pro displays the prompt *The block of the spreadsheet to print*, followed by the address of the current cell. Specify the block of cells you want to print and press the Enter key. Quattro Pro returns you to the Print menu, where you can use the other Print menu options to format and print the report. As a reminder, you specify a block of cells either by typing the block's range (for example A1..C10) or by pressing the period key (.) to anchor the cell selector and using the direction keys to extend the selection.

FIGURE 7-8.
This is a printout of the worksheet shown in Figure 7-7.

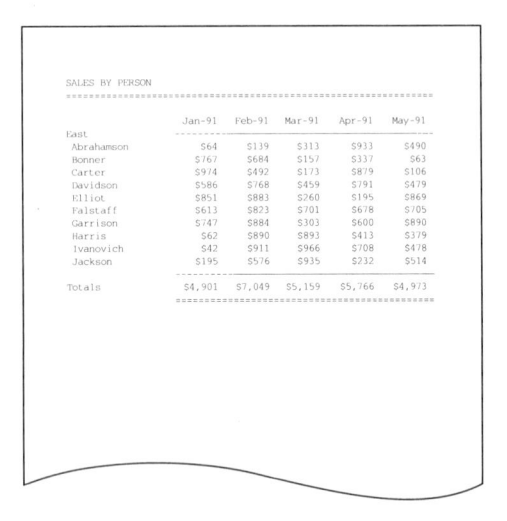

```
SALES BY PERSON
=================================================================

              Jan-91   Feb-91   Mar-91   Apr-91   May-91
East          ------   ------   ------   ------   ------
Abrahamson      $64     $139     $313     $933     $490
Bonner         $767     $684     $157     $337      $63
Carter         $974     $492     $173     $879     $106
Davidson       $586     $768     $459     $791     $479
Elliot         $851     $883     $260     $195     $869
Falstaff       $613     $823     $701     $678     $705
Garrison       $747     $884     $303     $600     $890
Harris          $62     $890     $893     $413     $379
Ivanovich       $42     $911     $966     $708     $478
Jackson        $195     $576     $935     $232     $514
              ------   ------   ------   ------   ------
Totals       $4,901   $7,049   $5,159   $5,766   $4,973
=================================================================
```

If you try to print without first defining a print block, Quattro Pro displays the error message *No block defined.* When you see this message, press the Enter key, choose the Print Block command again, and define the block you want to print. Quattro Pro then prints that block of the worksheet.

Changing a print block

You'll often need to change the print block you've defined. For instance, you might need to change the print block to include more or less of the worksheet or to include a different part of the worksheet. To change the print block, choose the Print Block command. Quattro Pro displays the prompt *The block of the spreadsheet to print,* followed by the coordinates of the current print block. In addition, Quattro Pro expands the cell selector to include the entire print block. The upper-left corner of the block is anchored, and the lower-right corner is free.

At this point, you can specify the new print block in one of several ways. If you want to redefine the block entirely, press the Esc key to cancel the current print block. Then select the block of cells you want to print. If you want to expand the print block to include a few more rows or columns, use the Right and Down direction keys to expand the selection, and then press the Enter key to lock in the new block. Pressing these keys shifts the lower-right corner of the print block, the unanchored corner, one cell in the indicated direction. If you want to contract the block by a few rows or columns, press the Left and Up direction keys, and then press the Enter key.

If you want to change the unanchored corner of a print block, press the period key (.), which shifts the unanchored corner from the lower-right corner of the block to the lower-left corner. Pressing the period key again shifts the unanchored corner to the upper-left corner, pressing it again shifts the unanchored corner to the upper-right corner, and pressing it one more time shifts the unanchored corner back to the lower-right corner. After moving the unanchored corner, you can press the Left, Right, Up, or Down direction keys to expand or shrink the print block. Then, press the Enter key to lock in your changes.

Quattro Pro automatically changes the print block if you insert or delete rows or columns within the current print block. If you delete one of the rows or columns that contains a corner cell of the print block, however, the block is no longer referenced, and you'll have to redefine the block again.

Resetting a print block

You might also encounter times when, instead of modifying the current print block, you want to completely reset a print block you've defined. For instance, to define a brand new print block, you're probably better off resetting the block and then defining the new block from scratch. To reset the print block, choose the Print Layout Reset Print Block command. Quattro Pro then discards the previous print block and will not print the worksheet until you define a new print block.

Aligning the paper in the printer

Before you begin printing a report, it is important to align the paper properly in your printer. Which aligning techniques you use depends on the type of printer you have. The three most popular types of printers are dot matrix, daisy wheel, and laser.

Dot-matrix and daisy-wheel printers

If you use a dot-matrix or daisy-wheel printer, be sure that the print head or typing element is aligned with the top of a new page before you begin printing. Then, choose the Print Adjust Printer Align command, which tells Quattro Pro that the printer is ready to start printing at the top of a new page. It is important to use the Print Adjust Printer Align command; it lets Quattro Pro insert page breaks correctly when printing a report. After you choose the Print Adjust Printer Align command, you should not adjust the paper manually in the printer because Quattro Pro might insert page breaks incorrectly in your report. To avoid this problem, you can use Quattro Pro's paper scrolling commands instead of the printer's manual controls to adjust the position of the paper in your printer. To scroll the paper one line at a time, choose the Print Adjust Printer Skip Line command. Each time you choose this command, Quattro Pro advances the paper one line. To advance the printer to the top of the next page, choose the Print Adjust Printer Form Feed command. Quattro Pro advances the printer to the top of the next page. Alternatively, you can align the paper in the printer manually and choose the Print Adjust Printer Align command each time you print. If you get into the habit of choosing this command each time before you print, you will seldom have problems with misaligned page breaks.

Laser printers

As with dot-matrix and daisy-wheel printers, you must align the paper in a laser printer before you print. To align paper in a laser printer, press the "form feed" key on the printer's control panel to eject the current page, and then choose the Print Adjust Printer Align command. This command tells Quattro Pro that the laser printer is ready to begin printing on a new sheet of paper. If you do not align your paper, Quattro Pro might insert page breaks in the wrong places.

You can also use the Print Adjust Printer Form Feed command instead of the controls on the printer to eject the current page from a laser printer. This command does essentially the same thing for laser printers as it does for other types of printers; it tells the printer that the current page is finished and should be ejected. You cannot use the Print Adjust Printer Skip Line command to advance the paper one line at a time in a laser printer.

How Quattro Pro divides a report into pages

Quattro Pro divides a report into several pages if it is too large to fit on a single page. The number of lines and characters that can fit on each page is determined by the Margin and Page Length settings. Quattro Pro always uses the same technique for breaking a worksheet into multiple pages. The first page always contains as many rows and columns, beginning in the upper-left portion of the worksheet, as Quattro Pro can fit on one page. For example, it might print the information from the cells in columns A–H and rows 1–20. If there are additional rows, they are printed on the following pages. These pages contain information from the same columns that appeared on the first page. For example, Quattro Pro might print the information from columns A–H and rows 21–40.

After printing all the rows in the leftmost columns of the print block, Quattro Pro begins printing another group of columns, starting with the top row of the print block. For example, it might print the information from columns I through P and rows 1 through 20. If the worksheet is more than two pages wide, Quattro Pro prints all the rows in the second set of columns, and then goes back to the top of the worksheet and prints another group of columns. Quattro Pro continues printing in this fashion until the entire print block is printed. Figure 7-9 shows the printing order for a worksheet that contains four report pages of information.

If you want to see how many columns will fit on each page of a report before you print it, subtract the left margin setting from the right margin setting to compute the report's page width. Next, if all the columns in the worksheet are the same width, divide the page width by the column width to determine how many columns will fit on each page.

When dividing a report into pages, Quattro Pro never divides a column between two pages; it always divides a report between columns. For example,

FIGURE 7-9.
Quattro Pro prints all the information from the leftmost columns first before printing the information from the columns to the right.

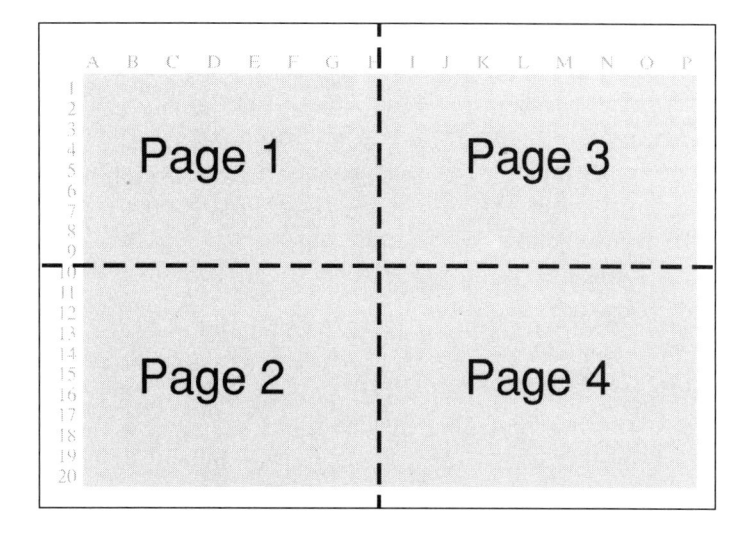

suppose your left and right margin settings are 4 and 76, respectively, to yield a page width of 72 characters. If all the columns in the worksheet are 10 characters wide, Quattro Pro can fit 7.2 columns on each page. Because Quattro Pro never divides a column between two pages, however, only seven full columns are printed on each page of this report.

When your worksheet contains columns of varying widths, it's a little trickier to calculate the number of columns that will fit on each page. In this situation, you must add the widths of the individual columns and then compare the running sum to the page width to determine which columns fit on each page. The Print Destination Screen Preview command described later in this chapter provides another way of determining where pages will break.

In addition to changing the margin and page length settings to control the way the report is divided into pages, you can insert page breaks in your worksheets using the Style Insert Break command. Both of these techniques are demonstrated later in this chapter.

Forcing the printer to pause between pages

Quattro Pro is able to handle both continuous-feed paper and single sheets of paper. Unless you tell it otherwise, Quattro Pro assumes that you are using continuous-feed paper. After printing each page in a report, Quattro Pro tells the printer to advance to a new page and continue printing the report. If you want to print on single sheets of paper, such as on company letterhead, you must tell Quattro Pro to pause after it prints each page in the report while you insert a new sheet of paper. To do so, choose the Option Hardware Printers Single Sheet command, and then choose the Yes option from the menu. (The default setting is No.)

When you print a report with the Yes option turned on, Quattro Pro pauses after printing each page of the report, and presents a submenu that has two choices: Continue and Abort. While Quattro Pro waits, you can insert a new sheet of paper in the printer. When you are ready, choose the Continue option from the menu to resume the printing process. If you want to abort single-sheet printing and return to READY mode, choose the Abort option from the menu. If, after changing the single-sheet setting from No to Yes, you decide to use continuous-feed paper again, choose the Options Hardware Printers Single Sheet command again, and choose the No option.

Aborting printing

If you are like most Quattro Pro users, you will occasionally choose the Print Spreadsheet Print command to begin printing a worksheet and then discover that you forgot to include something in the report. Rather than wait for the entire worksheet to print, you can press the Ctrl-Break keys to stop printing. Quattro Pro pauses briefly, and then returns to READY mode. Because the printer's buffer might still contain a few characters, it might continue to print for a little while after you press Ctrl-Break.

Previewing your worksheets before printing

You don't have to actually print a worksheet to see what it will look like. Instead, you can use the Print Destination Screen Preview command to display an on-screen version of the actual printed report. To use this command, define your print block and any print settings you want, choose the Print Destination Screen Preview command, and then choose the Spreadsheet Print option from the Print menu. Quattro Pro creates the printed report and sends it to the screen rather than to the default printer. Figure 7-10 shows an example of a report "printed" on the screen.

At the top of the screen, Quattro Pro lists commands unique to the Preview feature, which are described in the following sections. In the middle of the screen, Quattro Pro displays a representation of the first page of the printed report, although the report's numbers and letters will probably be too small to read. At the bottom of the page, Quattro Pro identifies how much of the printed page is shown on the screen and which page of the report is displayed.

Paging through the on-screen version of a report

When you choose the Print Spreadsheet Print command, the first page of the printed report is shown on the screen. The Next and Previous options let you flip back and forth through the pages of the on-screen version of the report. To see the

FIGURE 7-10.
Quattro Pro can "print" a report on the screen rather than on paper.

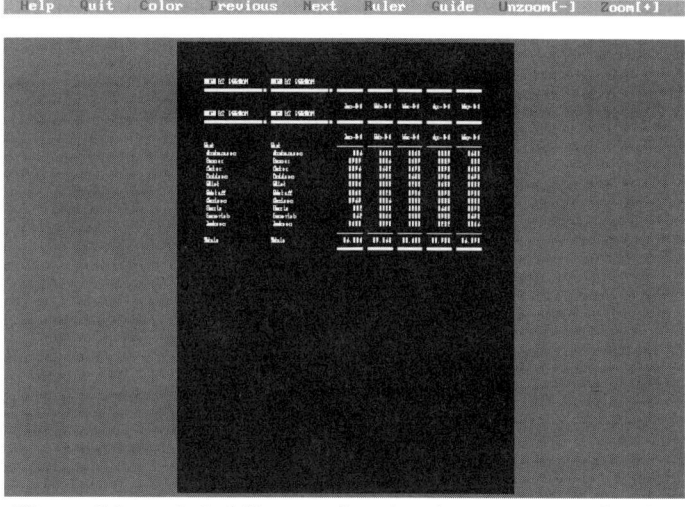

next page of the report, press N, /-N (the slash key and then the N key), or the PgDn key. To see the previous page of the report, press P, /-P, or the PgUp key.

Getting help

To see a list of the commands available on the Preview screen and a brief description of what each command does, choose the Help command by pressing H, /-H, or the [Help] key (F1). To get more information select one of the commands in the list and press the Enter key. When you're finished getting help, press the Esc key to remove the on-screen help.

Changing the color of the preview screen

On a color monitor, Quattro Pro displays the Preview screen using white pages on a blue background. You can also display white pages on a black background and black pages on a white background using the Color command, which you choose by pressing C or /-C. Repeatedly pressing C or /-C toggles you through these color scheme combinations. On a monochrome monitor, the Color command toggles back and forth between black pages on a white background and white pages on a black background.

Using a page ruler

The Ruler command, which you choose by pressing R or /-R, draws vertical and horizontal lines at 1-inch intervals across the on-screen version of the report. If you want to compare the positions of the different parts of the printed report, you might find these ruler lines helpful. To remove the ruler lines when they are already showing, choose the Ruler command again.

Zooming and unzooming

The Zoom command magnifies the top half of the displayed report page. Choose the Zoom command by pressing Z, /-Z, or the Plus key (+). To further magnify this already magnified portion of the report, choose the Zoom command a second time; the screen shows the top-left quarter of the top half of the report page. To display different portions of the magnifed page, use the Up, Down, Left, and Right direction keys to move your view. You can also press the Home key to view the top of the zoomed page, and the End key to view the bottom of the zoomed page.

When the report page is zoomed, Quattro Pro displays a page guide in the upper-right corner of the screen, as shown in Figure 7-11. It shows part of the printed page you're looking at. If you find the guide more of a hindrance than a help, you can remove it; choose the Guide command by typing G or /-G. To display the guide display again if you previously removed it, choose the Guide command again. You can also press the Del key to remove the guide and the Ins key to display it again.

The Unzoom command reverses the effect of a previous Zoom command, unmagnifying the report. To choose the command, press U or /-U, or the Minus key (-). If you choose the Zoom command two times to double-magnify the page, you need to choose the Unzoom command two times to again display the entire page on the preview screen.

Quitting the preview screen

To return to the Quattro Pro worksheet, choose the Quit command from the Preview screen. You can do so by pressing Q, by pressing /-Q, or by pressing the Esc key.

Formatting reports using print settings

It's easy to print a report using Quattro Pro's default print settings, which in many situations will meet your printing needs. Quattro Pro offers several print settings, however, that you can use to improve the appearance and clarity of your reports. You can change a report's margins, define a header and footer, change the page length setting, define a setup string, and designate certain rows and columns in your report as headings. The default print settings apply to any new

FIGURE 7-11.
The page guide shows you which portion of a report is currently zoomed.

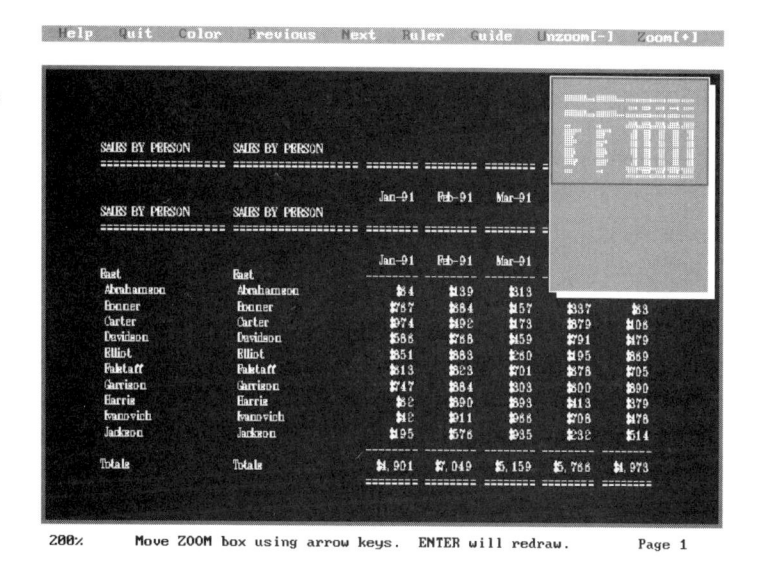

worksheet you create unless you adjust those settings. The following sections explain how to change the settings for individual worksheets and how to adjust the default settings.

Adjusting margins

Unless you change the default margin settings, your reports will have a left margin of four characters, a right margin of 76 characters, a top margin of two lines, and a bottom margin of two lines. If you want, you can use the Print Layout Margins command to change the print margin settings for any worksheet. After you choose this command, Quattro Pro displays the Margins menu shown in Figure 7-12.

Changing the left margin

The left margin setting tells Quattro Pro how many blank spaces to indent the lines in a printed report. For example, if your left margin is four characters (the default), Quattro Pro indents the first character in each line by four spaces. If your left margin setting is 0, Quattro Pro begins each line as far to the left as your printer will go.

You can use the Print Layout Margins Left command to change the left margin setting. After you choose this command, Quattro Pro displays the prompt *Left margin (number of characters from left edge [0..254]*, followed by the current left margin setting. When you see this prompt, type the left margin setting you want to use and then press the Enter key. You need not erase the old setting before you type a new one. Quattro Pro replaces the old setting with the number you type. As

FIGURE 7-12.
The Margins menu gives you options for changing the default margin settings.

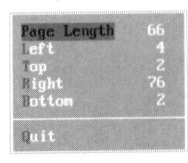

Page Length	66
Left	4
Top	2
Right	76
Bottom	2
Quit	

the prompt indicates, you can enter a left margin setting ranging from 0 to 254 characters, but the left margin setting must always be less than the right margin setting. You will usually use a left margin setting of less than 10 characters. If you want to fit as much information as possible onto each page, use a left margin setting of 0.

Changing the right margin

The right margin setting tells Quattro Pro how long to make each line in your report. For example, a right margin of 76 characters (the default) tells Quattro Pro to make each line in the report 76 characters long. The total line length includes any spaces that are reserved for the left margin. For instance, if you set your right margin to 80 and your left margin to 0, Quattro Pro can fit 80 characters on each line.

To change the right margin setting, choose the Print Layout Margins Right command. This command tells Quattro Pro to display the prompt *Right margin (number of characters from right edge [0..254]*, followed by the current right margin setting. When you see this prompt, type the new right margin setting and press the Enter key. The right margin setting can range from 0 to 254 and must be larger than the left margin setting. In fact, the difference between the right margin and left margin settings must be at least equal to or greater than the widest column in your print block. If the right margin setting is less than the left margin setting, Quattro Pro is not able to print any data.

You should always use a right margin setting that is consistent with the width of the paper in your printer and with the setup string you have specified (if any). If you specify a right margin setting that is greater than the maximum number of characters your printer can print on one line, each line of the report wraps around to the next line, which makes a confusing mess of the printout and disrupts Quattro Pro's page breaks. If you use a narrow-carriage printer (one that accepts paper up to 8½ inches wide), the maximum line length is about 80 characters. If you print in compressed type, the maximum length increases to about 136 characters. If you have a wide-carriage printer, the maximum line length is about 130 characters. If you use compressed print and wide paper the maximum length increases to about 200 characters.

Changing the top and bottom margins

The top and bottom margin settings tell Quattro Pro how many blank rows to insert at the top and bottom of each page. As mentioned, the default top and bottom margin settings are both two lines. To change the top margin setting, choose the Print Layout Margins Top command. Quattro Pro displays the prompt *Top margin (number of lines from top edge [0..32]*, followed by the current top margin setting. When you see this prompt, type the new top margin setting and then press the Enter key. Change the bottom margin setting in the same way: Choose the Print Layout Margins Bottom command, type the new bottom margin setting, and then press the Enter key. Although you can specify top and bottom margin settings ranging from 0 lines to 32 lines, you will rarely use a setting greater than 5 or 6 lines. If you want to fit as much information as possible on each page, set the top margin and the bottom margin to 0.

As you may recall, Quattro Pro reserves three blank lines at the top and bottom of each page for a header and a footer, in addition to the top and bottom margins. As a result, the effective default top and bottom margins are five lines. If you change the top margin setting to 4, Quattro Pro inserts seven lines at the top of each page. If you set both the top and bottom margin settings to 0, Quattro Pro still reserves three blank lines at the top and bottom of each page. The only way you can remove all blank lines from the top and bottom of each page is to choose the Print Layout Break Pages No command. Unfortunately, Quattro Pro cannot print a report with only one or two blank lines at the top or bottom (or both the top and bottom) of each page. Quattro Pro always reserves at least three blank lines or no blank lines at all.

Changing the page length

The number of lines that Quattro Pro can print on each page of a report is determined by the page length setting. To calculate the number of lines that will fit on each printed page, subtract the top and bottom margins and the header and footer lines from the page length setting. The default page length setting is 66 lines, so Quattro Pro can print 56 lines per page for a report that uses the default settings (66-2-2-3-3 = 56).

Because the page length setting determines where Quattro Pro will place page breaks in a report, it is very important that you specify an appropriate page length. The default page length setting assumes that you are printing on 11-inch-long paper and that the printer prints six lines per inch. If your paper and printer match these assumptions, the default page length setting will suit them. But if you change the number of lines per inch or if you use paper that is longer or shorter than 11 inches (including mailing labels or special forms), you must adjust the page length setting accordingly. To change this setting, choose the Print Layout Margins Page Length command. Quattro Pro displays the prompt *The number of lines on a page [1..100]*, followed by the current page length setting. When you see this prompt, type the new page length setting and press the Enter key.

You can specify any page length setting from 1 line to 100 lines. You must be sure, however, that the page length you specify is at least as long as the sum of the top and bottom margins, the header and footer spaces, and one line of data. For example, if the top and bottom margin settings are both 2, the minimum page length setting must be at least 11 (2+3+2+3+1 = 11). If you enter a page length setting that is too short, Quattro Pro displays the error message *Print parameter errors* when you try to print the report.

If you have defined a page length other than 66 lines and you find that you are getting double page breaks at unpredictable intervals, check your printer manual. Some printers, including most laser printers, print only 60 lines per page, and other printers have switches that control the default page length. Unless the default page length for your printer matches Quattro Pro's page length setting, you will not be pleased with the page breaks in your reports.

If you choose the Print Layout Break Pages command and choose the No option, Quattro Pro ignores the page length setting. For more information about the Print Layout Break Pages command, see "Printing Reports Without Page Breaks" later in this chapter.

Changing dimensions

Quattro Pro by default measures the top and bottom margins of a worksheet in lines and the left and right margins in characters. You can change the method Quattro Pro uses to measure, however, by using the Print Layout Dimensions command. Quattro Pro gives you two other ways to calibrate the dimensions of a spreadsheet you're printing: inches and centimeters. To use one of the these methods, choose the Print Layout Dimensions command. Quattro Pro presents a menu with three choices: Lines/Characters (the default), Inches, and Centimeters. Choose the method you want to use and then press the Enter key. If you change measurement methods, Quattro Pro converts the existing margin and page length settings to the equivalent settings in the new measurement method.

Changing the orientation

Quattro Pro by default prints worksheets using a portrait orientation, which means that on $8\frac{1}{2}$-by-11-inch paper, for example, Quattro Pro prints columns from left to right across the $8\frac{1}{2}$-inch width of the page and rows down the 11-inch length. With a graphics printer, Quattro Pro can also print reports using the landscape orientation, which means that on 8½-by-11-inch paper, Quattro Pro prints columns across the 11-inch width of the page and rows down the 8½-inch length. Which orientation you use depends on the organization of your worksheet. It's often more convenient, however, to print reports in a landscape orientation. Figure 7-13 illustrates the difference between portrait and landscape orientation.

To print a report in Landscape orientation, choose the Print Layout Orientation command. Quattro Pro presents a menu that has two choices: Portrait and Landscape. Choose the Landscape option. Next, quit the Layout menu and choose the Destination option from the Print menu to display the Destination submenu, which has five choices: Printer, File, Binary File, Graphics Printer, and Screen Preview. Choose the Graphics Printer option. If you then choose the Print Spreadsheet Print command, Quattro Pro prints the worksheet using the landscape orientation.

Default layout settings

You might have noticed that Quattro Pro added a top, bottom, left, and right margin to the report shown in Figure 7-8. Because no special print settings were specified before this report was printed, Quattro Pro used its default settings to determine margin sizes and page length.

Default margins

The default left margin setting is four characters, which means that Quattro Pro adds four blank spaces to the beginning of each line of the reports you print. The default right margin setting is 76 characters, which means that each line of the

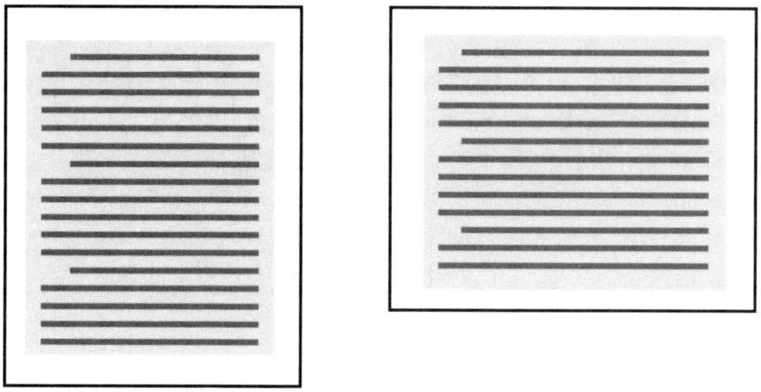

FIGURE 7-13.
Portrait orientation prints columns across the short dimension of the page and landscape orientation prints columns across the long dimension of the page.

report will be 76 characters long. Because the left margin takes up 4 characters, however, Quattro Pro can fit only 72 printed characters on each line.

The default setting for the top and bottom margins is two lines. This setting tells Quattro Pro to print two blank lines at the top and bottom of each page. The page shown in Figure 7-8, however, contains five blank rows at the top. The extra three lines are reserved for a header and footer, even if you have not defined a header or footer for the report. These lines are inserted between the top and bottom margin and the printed data. Consequently, the effective top and bottom margin on each page of the report is 5 lines. You can force Quattro Pro to release the three reserved lines at the top and the bottom of the page by choosing the Print Page Layout Break Pages No command, which turns off all page formatting for the report.

Default page length

The default setting for Page Length is 66 lines per page. The 66 lines include two lines for the top and bottom margins and three lines each for the header and footer. As a result, a report that uses default margins and page length can have up to 56 rows of data per page (66-2-2-3-3 = 56).

Changing the layout defaults

If you change the default print settings in a worksheet, those changes apply only to that worksheet. When you choose the File Save command, your print settings are saved along with the worksheet. The next time you open that worksheet using the File Retrieve command, any print settings you have defined for that worksheet will be loaded along with the worksheet.

If you want to change the default page layout settings (margins, page length, page breaks, setup string, header, and footer) for every worksheet, first choose the Print Layout command and use the menu options to define each of the settings. Next, choose the Print Layout Update command to save the current values of the layout settings as the new layout defaults. These defaults will be in effect the next time you print a new worksheet.

When you choose the Print Layout Update command, Quattro Pro updates the default values for all of the layout settings. Be sure that you've set each of the page layout settings correctly before you choose the Update option. Otherwise, you might change a default value accidentally.

Restoring the defaults

After you change the default page layout settings for a worksheet, you might want to return some or all of those settings to their default values. The quickest way to do so is to choose the Print Layout Reset All command. This command restores all the settings on the Layout menu to their original value except for the header and footer.

Printing reports without page breaks

Quattro Pro normally inserts a page break after each page in a printed report. Quattro Pro also offers you the option, however, of printing a report without page breaks. To print such an unformatted report, Quattro Pro ignores the top and bottom margin settings, the page length setting, and any header or footer you have defined. Instead of inserting blank lines at the top and bottom of each page, Quattro Pro begins printing on the first line of the page and continues to the bottom of the page. At the end of a page in an unformatted report, Quattro Pro ignores the page break and continues printing, leaving no space between the bottom of one page and the top of the next.

To specify that a report is unformatted, choose the Print Layout Break Pages command, and choose the No option. To turn pagination back on, choose the Print Layout Break Pages command again, and choose the Yes option. Although choosing the No option tells Quattro Pro to ignore the headers, footers, and manual page breaks, it does not affect your left and right margins or any other formatting. The left and right margin settings still determine where the vertical page breaks in the report should occur, and the printer will use whatever other formatting you have defined.

If you define column headings before you print an unformatted report, those headings appear on each vertical section of the report. Because an unformatted report has no horizontal page breaks, however, the row headings appear only one time at the top of the report.

Adding headers and footers

Quattro Pro lets you define a header, a footer, or both for your printed reports. A header is a line of text that is printed at the top of every page in a report, while a footer is a line of text that is printed at the bottom of every page. You can use headers and footers in a variety of ways. For instance, you can use headers and footers to title a report, or you can include special characters in headers and footers to date and number the pages in a report.

The Print Layout Header command lets you create a header. When you choose this command, Quattro Pro displays the prompt *A line of text to be printed at the top of each page.* When you see this prompt, type the characters that you want to appear at the top of each page and then press the Enter key. In the same way, you can specify a footer using the Print Layout Footer command.

An example of using headers and footers

Suppose you want to include the header "Sales History for 1991" at the top of each page of the report shown in Figure 7-8. To create this header, choose the Print

Layout Header command, type *Sales History for 1991*, and then press the Enter key. When you print the report, this header line appears at the upper-left edge of each page, as shown in Figure 7-14.

A closer look at headers and footers

As explained, Quattro Pro reserves three lines at the top of each page for the header and three lines at the bottom of each page for the footer, even if you have not defined a header or footer. If you have defined a header, Quattro Pro prints it on the first of these three lines, with two blank lines between the header and the first line of the report. Similarly, if you have defined a footer, Quattro Pro prints it on the third line at the bottom of the page, with two blank lines between the footer and the last line of the report. Notice that the first character in the header line is aligned at the report's left margin. The left margin setting determines the position of the first character in both the header and footer.

Although headers and footers can contain up to 254 characters, the left and right margin settings determine the number of characters that can actually fit on the page. If your header or footer is too long to fit within your left and right margins, Quattro Pro cuts off the end of the header or footer. The default left margin (4) and right margin (76) allow Quattro Pro to print a header or footer that is up to 72 characters long.

Editing Headers and Footers

After you define a header or footer, you might want to change it. To do so, choose the Print Layout Header or Print Layout Footer command. Quattro Pro displays the existing header or footer, and you can either press the Esc key to erase the

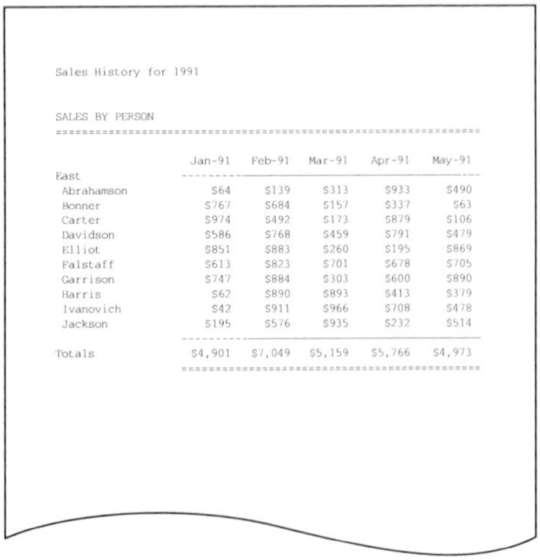

Sales History for 1991

SALES BY PERSON

	Jan-91	Feb-91	Mar-91	Apr-91	May-91
East					
Abrahamson	$64	$139	$313	$933	$490
Bonner	$767	$684	$157	$337	$63
Carter	$974	$492	$173	$879	$106
Davidson	$586	$768	$459	$791	$479
Elliot	$851	$883	$260	$195	$869
Falstaff	$613	$823	$701	$678	$705
Garrison	$747	$884	$303	$600	$890
Harris	$62	$890	$893	$413	$379
Ivanovich	$42	$911	$966	$708	$478
Jackson	$195	$576	$935	$232	$514
Totals	$4,901	$7,049	$5,159	$5,766	$4,973

FIGURE 7-14.
The Print Layout Header command lets you define a one-line header to appear at the top of each page of your report.

existing header and type a new one, or edit the existing entry in the same way you edit the contents of a cell.

Controlling the alignment of headers and footers

The vertical bar character (|) is the tool you use to control the alignment of your headers and footers. If you omit this symbol from your header or footer, Quattro Pro assumes that the entire header or footer should be left aligned. If you include one vertical bar in the header or footer, Quattro Pro centers the text following the vertical bar. If the header or footer includes two vertical bars, Quattro Pro left aligns the text to the left of the first bar, centers the text following the first bar, and right aligns the text following the second bar.

For example, suppose you want to create the header shown in Figure 7-15. To do so, choose the Print Layout Header command, and change the existing header to the following:

Sales History for 1991 | INTERNAL USE ONLY | Pork Chops, Inc.

The part of the header to the left of the first vertical bar will be left aligned, the part between the two | characters will be centered, and the part to the right of the second | character will be right aligned.

You do not have to include text in every part of a header or footer. If you leave one part of a header or footer blank, Quattro Pro skips that part of the header or footer and prints the text following the next vertical bar with the proper alignment. For example, suppose you want to center the header "Sales History for 1991" at the top of each page of your report. To do so, choose the Print Layout Header command and change the header to look like the following:

| Sales History for 1991

Because no text is included to the left of the first vertical bar in this header, Quattro Pro skips the left-aligned portion of the header and prints the text after the vertical bar in the center of the header line.

To print a heading on the right at the top of each page of your report, you might change the header to the following:

| | Pork Chops, Inc.

Quattro Pro skips the left-aligned and centered portion of the header and prints the text after the second vertical bar on the right end of the header line.

Numbering pages

You can also print page numbers in the headers and footers of your reports by including the pound symbol (#) in that header or footer. When you print the report, Quattro Pro substitutes the current page number for the # symbol throughout the

FIGURE 7-15.
The two | characters in this header tell Quattro Pro to divide the header into left-aligned, centered, and right-aligned sections.

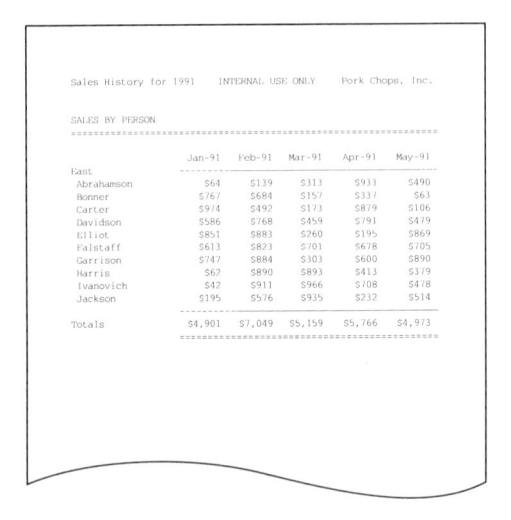

```
Sales History for 1991    INTERNAL USE ONLY    Pork Chops, Inc.

SALES BY PERSON
================================================================

                  Jan-91   Feb-91   Mar-91   Apr-91   May-91
East
  Abrahamson        $64     $139     $313     $933     $490
  Bonner           $767     $684     $157     $337      $63
  Carter           $974     $492     $171     $879     $106
  Davidson         $586     $768     $459     $791     $479
  Elliot           $851     $883     $260     $195     $869
  Falstaff         $613     $823     $701     $678     $705
  Garrison         $747     $884     $303     $600     $890
  Harris            $62     $890     $893     $413     $379
  Ivanovich         $42     $911     $966     $708     $478
  Jackson          $195     $576     $935     $232     $514

  Totals         $4,901   $7,049   $5,159   $5,766   $4,973
================================================================
```

report. For example, suppose you want to print the word *Page* followed by the current page number in the lower-left corner of each page in a report. To do so, choose the Print Layout Footer command, type *Page #*, and press the Enter key. When you print the report, each page will contain the word *Page* followed by the correct page number.

After printing a report that has numbered pages, Quattro Pro does not reset the first page number to 1. For example, suppose you print a four-page report that has the page numbers in the lower-left corner of the page and then, without leaving the Print menu, define a new print block and print another report that also has page numbers. Quattro Pro remembers the last page number in the first report (4) and begins with page 5 when numbering the second report. To reset the first page number to 1, either choose the Print Adjust Printer Align command to tell Quattro Pro that you are ready to print something new; or, choose Quit from the Print menu. If you want continuous page numbering between print jobs, however, be sure you do not choose Align or Quit from the Print menu.

Dating reports

You can also print the current date in the headers and footers of your reports by including the at symbol (@) in your header or footer. When you print the report, Quattro Pro substitutes the current date for the @ symbol throughout the report. For example, suppose you want to print the current date in the upper-right corner of each page in a report. Choose the Print Layout Header command, type | |@, and press the Enter key. When you print the report, the date will appear in the upper-right corner of each page.

Deleting a header or footer

To delete the current header or footer, choose the Print Layout Header (or Footer) command. When you see the existing header (or footer) in the Edit line, press the Esc key to delete it, and then press the Enter key. As mentioned earlier, removing the header or footer line simply removes the text from the header or footer lines in the report. Quattro Pro still inserts three blank lines at the top and bottom of each page of the printed report.

Alternatively, you can use the Print Layout Reset command to restore the current header and footer to their default values. Because this command resets all of your other current layout options (page length, margins, and setup string) to their default settings, however, it's best to use this command with extreme care.

Printing column and row headings

Across the top and down the left side of a worksheet, you usually enter labels that describe the entries in the worksheet's rows and columns. The labels in the first few rows and columns of a large worksheet disappear from view when you scroll down or right. You'll experience a similar problem when you print a large worksheet: When Quattro Pro divides a large report into pages, some of the pages will not contain the necessary explanatory labels.

Fortunately, Quattro Pro offers two commands—Print Headings Left Heading and Print Headings Top Heading—that you can use to print selected rows and columns on every page of a report. These commands are similar to Quattro Pro's Window Options Locked Titles command, which is explained in "Creating Titles" in Chapter 9. The Print Headings Left Heading command lets you define the row headings that you want Quattro Pro to print on the left edge of each page. When you choose this command, Quattro Pro displays the prompt *Row headings to print on the left of each page* in the input line. When you see this prompt, define a block that includes at least one cell from each of the columns that contain the row headings you want Quattro Pro to print on each page. For example, if columns A, B, and C contain the row heading you want to use, define a block that includes at least one cell from each of these columns, such as A1..C1, or A1..C3.

The Print Headings Top Heading command lets you define the rows that contain the column headings you want Quattro Pro to print across the top of each page of a report. When you choose this command, Quattro Pro displays the prompt *Column heading to print across the top of each page* in the input line. When you see this prompt, define a block that includes at least one cell from each of the rows that contain the column headings you want Quattro Pro to print on each page. For example, if rows 2 and 3 contain the column heading you want, define a block that includes at least one cell from each of these rows, such as A2..A3, or A2..B3.

Once you define heading rows or columns, you must adjust the print block to exclude them. Otherwise, Quattro Pro prints the entries in those rows or columns two times on some pages. To redefine the print block, choose the Print Block command and define the new print block.

An example of printing column and row headings

After you define your heading columns and rows and redefine your print block, you can print the report in the usual fashion. While printing the report, Quattro Pro includes on each page the appropriate sections of the heading columns and rows you selected. To illustrate the effect of headings, consider a version of the report shown previously in Figure 7-15 that is expanded to include more sales people and sales figures for the entire year. The expanded report takes four pages to print. Figure 7-16 shows page four of the report without headings. The headings on this worksheet are in column A, rows 1-4, but the data is in the block G23..M35. When you print this page, it is difficult to tell what row each cell is in. Figure 7-17 shows the same report page with the headings from column A, rows 1-4 added, which makes the report much easier to read.

Remember that Quattro Pro divides your pages differently after you add headings. For example, because Quattro Pro has printed the row headings in column A in Figure 7-17, fewer columns of data can appear on that page. Instead of showing seven columns of sales figures, as in Figure 7-16, Figure 7-17 shows five columns of figures (plus the headings in column A). The remaining columns appear on another page of the report, which increases the length of the report.

FIGURE 7-16.
This page was printed without any headings.

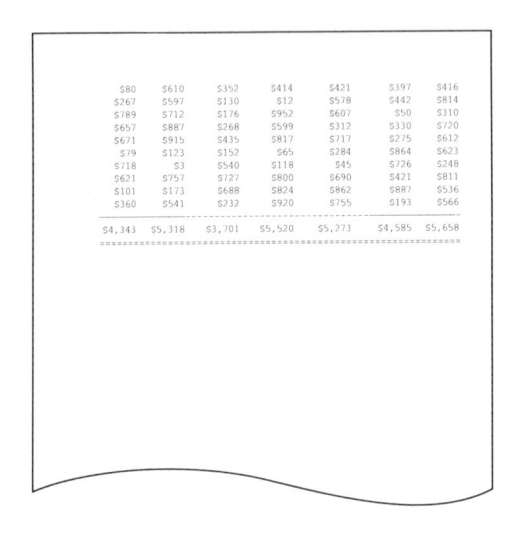

FIGURE 7-17.
This page was printed with headings, which make the report much easier to understand.

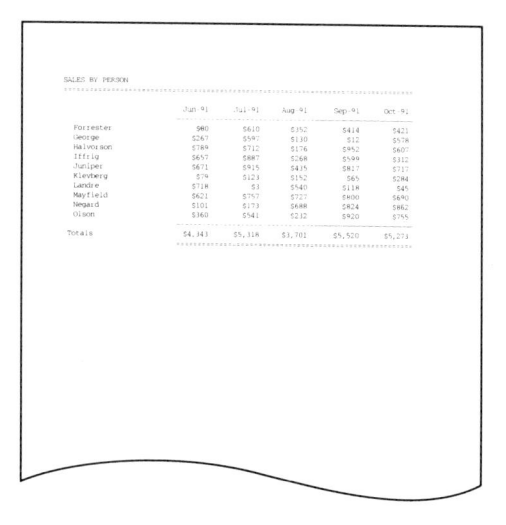

Clearing column and row headings

If, after you define headings, you decide that you do not want Quattro Pro to print them, you can delete the headings using the Print Layout Reset Headings command. This command clears both the left heading and the top heading; Quattro Pro does not allow you to clear only your left heading or only your top heading. You cannot clear headings as you can some of the other Print settings, such as the header or setup string, by choosing the Print Headings Left (or Right) Heading command and pressing the Esc key.

Improving worksheets using line drawing, shading, and fonts

Quattro Pro has a number of features that let you improve the appearance of your worksheets and printed reports. You can draw lines, change fonts and colors, and shade sections of your worksheet to create professional-looking documents. Improving the appearance of a worksheet might at first seem frivolous. But, Figure 7-19 shows how much easier it is to read the information from Figure 7-18 with lines, shading, and a well-chosen variety of fonts added.

Drawing lines

Suppose you want to improve the appearance of the worksheet shown in Figure 7-20 by first drawing lines and then adding shading and fonts. To draw lines like those shown in Figure 7-21, choose the Style Line Drawing command. Quattro Pro displays the prompt *Enter block to draw lines,* followed by the current address

FIGURE 7-18.
This report was printed without lines, shading, and fonts.

```
1992 Revenue Forecast

Eastern Region        $350,000
Midwest Region         400,000
Western Region         500,000
International          250,000
                      --------
Total              $1,500,000
```

FIGURE 7-19.
This report shows the same information as Figure 7-18, but it includes lines, shading, and fonts.

1992 Revenue Forecast	
Eastern Region	$350,000
Midwest Region	400,000
Western Region	500,000
International	250,000
Total	$1,5500,000

of the cell selector. Define the block you want to draw lines in or around. To draw a line around the outside border, for example, define block A1..E9.

After you define the block, press the Enter key. Quattro Pro then presents the Placement menu, which lists 10 options: All, Outside, Top, Bottom, Left, Right, Inside, Horizontal, Vertical, and Quit. The Quit option quits the Placement menu and returns you to READY mode. The other nine options describe different lines that you can draw in the block. The All option draws lines around the border of the block and between every cell in the block, and the Outside option draws a line around the border of the block. The Top option draws a line on the top side of every cell in the block, and the Bottom option draws a line on the bottom side of every cell in the block. Left draws a line on the left side of all cells in the block, and Right draws a line on the right side of every cell in the block. The Inside option draws lines between every cell in the block. The Horizontal option, which is a combination of Top and Bottom, draws horizontal lines between each of the rows of the block. Finally, Vertical, which is a combination of Left and Right, draws vertical lines between each of the columns in the block.

To draw a line around the border of the worksheet data, choose the Outside option. Quattro Pro presents the Line Types menu, which lists the options None, Single, Double, and Thick. The options Single, Double, and Thick determine what type of line Quattro Pro will draw. The None option erases the lines already drawn in the block using the specified line placement. Choose the type of line you want, and press the Enter key. For the example worksheet, choose Double. Quattro Pro then draws the lines and redisplays the Placement menu so that you can draw additional lines.

If you want to draw additional lines, you'll probably want to first change the defined block. To do so, press the Esc key from the Placement menu. Quattro Pro again displays the prompt *Enter block to draw lines*. Define the new block and press

FIGURE 7-20.
Use this worksheet to illustrate lines, shades, and fonts.

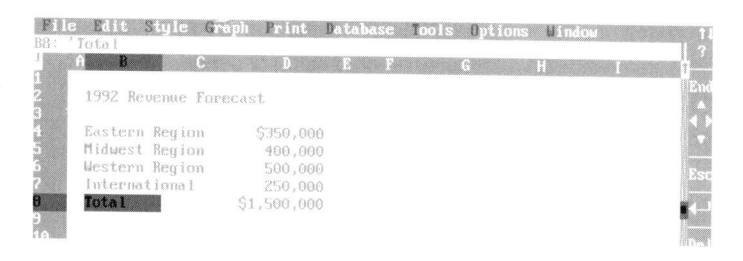

FIGURE 7-21.
This is how the worksheet looks after you have drawn several lines.

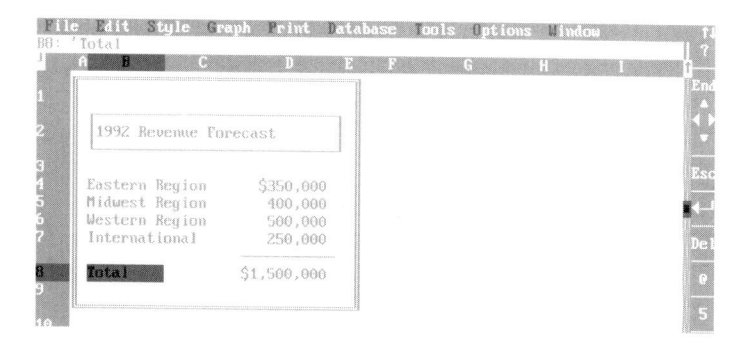

the Enter key to display the Placement menu again. Choose the placement you want from the Placement menu, and Quattro Pro presents the Line Types menu, from which you can choose the type of line you want to draw. Quattro Pro draws the lines and redisplays the Placement menu. To continue drawing lines, repeat these steps. To stop drawing lines, choose the Quit option from the Placement menu.

To print a worksheet with lines on it, you need to use the Print Destination Graphics Printer command because lines only show up if you use a graphics printer.

Adding shading

To add shading to a worksheet, choose the Style Shading command. Quattro Pro presents the Shading menu, which lists the options None, Grey, and Black. Choose the Grey option to produce a light gray shading, the Black option to produce black shading, or the None option to remove shading previously added. Quattro Pro then displays the prompt Enter block to shade, followed by the current address of the cell selector. Define the block you want to shade, and then press the Enter key. Quattro Pro redisplays the worksheet with the defined block shaded. Figure 7-22 shows an example of gray shading.

FIGURE 7-22.
This is how the worksheet looks on the screen after you have added shading.

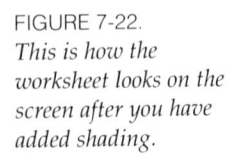

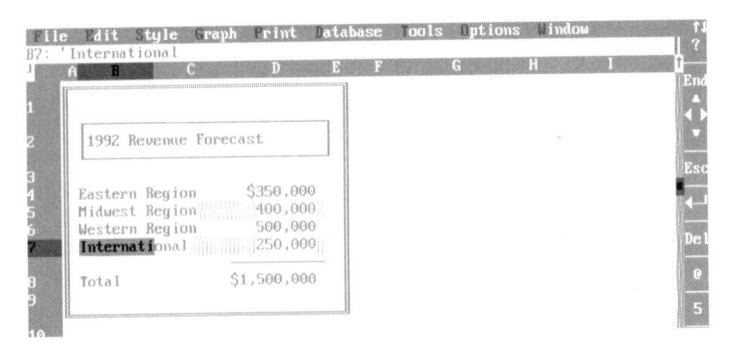

FIGURE 7-23.
This list shows examples of Quattro Pro's eight fonts.

Dutch 12-point black
Dutch 18-point black
Dutch 8-point black
Dutch 12-point black italic
Swiss 12-point black
Swiss 18-point black
Swiss 8-point black
Swiss 12-point black italic

Using different fonts

Quattro Pro has eight default fonts. Figure 7-23 shows examples of each of these fonts printed on a laser printer. Notice that the Dutch type style resembles Times Roman and that the Swiss type style resembles Helvetica.

Assigning a font to a block

To use a font other than the default font, choose the Style Font command. Quattro Pro presents the Font menu, as shown in Figure 7-24.

To assign a font to a block, choose one of the first eight options from the Font menu. Quattro Pro displays the prompt *Enter block to set font,* followed by the current address of the cell selector. Define the block in which you want to use the font, and press the Enter key. You do not see the fonts on the screen, but they appear on the printed report.

Editing the fonts

Quattro Pro by default sets the eight fonts that are available within a worksheet to the eight fonts that Quattro Pro provides. Until you tell Quattro Pro otherwise, it considers Font 1 to be Dutch 12-point black, Font 2 to be Dutch 18-point black, and so on. To edit fonts, choose the Style Font Edit Fonts command. Quattro Pro presents the Edit Font menu shown in Figure 7-25. Choose the font you want to

FIGURE 7-24.
The Font menu shows Quattro Pro's eight available fonts.

```
1 Font 1              Bitstream Dutch 12 point Black
2 Font 2              Bitstream Dutch 18 point Black
3 Font 3              Bitstream Dutch 8 point Black
4 Font 4              Bitstream Dutch 12 point Black Itlc
5 Font 5              Bitstream Swiss 12 point Black
6 Font 6              Bitstream Swiss 18 point Black
7 Font 7              Bitstream Swiss 8 point Black
8 Font 8              Bitstream Swiss 12 point Black Itlc
Edit Fonts                                           ▶
Reset
Update
```

FIGURE 7-25.
The Edit Font menu shows the fonts you can choose.

```
1 Font 1              Bitstream Dutch 12 point Black
2 Font 2              Bitstream Dutch 18 point Black
3 Font 3              Bitstream Dutch 8 point Black
4 Font 4              Bitstream Dutch 12 point Black Itlc
5 Font 5              Bitstream Swiss 12 point Black
6 Font 6              Bitstream Swiss 18 point Black
7 Font 7              Bitstream Swiss 8 point Black
8 Font 8              Bitstream Swiss 12 point Black Itlc
Quit
```

FIGURE 7-26.
The Type menu shows the four elements of a font.

```
Typeface              Bitstream Dutch ▶
Point Size                   12 point ▶
Style                                 ▶
Color                          Black  ▶
Quit
```

change and press the Enter key. For example, to change Font 1, Dutch 12-point black, choose Font 1 from the Edit Font menu.

Quattro Pro then displays the Type menu shown in Figure 7-26. Use the Type menu to specify the typeface, point size, style, and color used for a particular font selection (for example, Font 1). When you choose each of these options, another menu appears showing the available selections, as described in the following sections. When you finish specifying these four elements of a font, choose the Quit option to return to the Edit Font menu. To edit another font, choose it from the Edit Font menu.

Defining the typeface. To define the typeface, choose the Typeface option from the Type menu. Quattro Pro displays a of list all of the typefaces that Quattro Pro provides, including Bitstream Dutch, Bitstream Swiss, Bitstream Courier, Roman, Roman Length, Sans Serif, Sans Serif Light, Script, Old English, Eurostyle, and Monospace. If you have a laser printer that has font cartridges and you have identified which font cartridge your printer uses, these fonts will also be listed. Choose a typeface and press the Enter key.

Defining point size. To define the font's point size, choose the Point Size option from the Type menu. Quattro Pro displays a list of each of the available point sizes. Each point represents $1/72$ inch. The larger the point size number, therefore, the bigger the font size.

Defining style. Style refers to whether the font is bold, underlined, or italicized. When you choose the Style option from the Type menu, Quattro Pro displays a list that includes five options: Bold, Italic, Underlined, Reset, and Quit. The first three options—Bold, Italic, and Underlined—represent alternatives to the standard style. The Reset option returns the font style from Bold, Underlined, or Italic to regular text. The Quit option quits the box of options without making a change to the font style.

Defining color. For color printers, Quattro Pro also lets you specify font color. To specify the color of a font, choose the Color option from the Type menu. Quattro Pro displays a list of the available colors. Choose the color you want and press the Enter key.

Resetting fonts to the default settings

You can edit the font settings freely without having to worry that your changes will be permanent. The Reset option on the Font menu lets you return all the font settings to their default settings. To do so, choose the Style Font Reset command, and Quattro Pro returns all eight font settings to their default settings.

Changing the default font settings permanently

You might want to change the default font settings permanently. To do so, first edit the font settings so that they represent what you want for the new default font settings. Then, choose the Style Fonts Update command, and Quattro Pro makes the current font settings the default font settings.

Manual page breaks

Whenever you're not happy with the page breaks that Quattro Pro inserts in your report, you can insert manual page breaks that override the automatic ones. To insert a manual page break in a worksheet, first move the cell selector to the row above which you want to insert the page break and the first column in the print block. (This is usually column A.) Next, choose the Style Insert Break command. Quattro Pro inserts a new blank row and enters a special page-break symbol (::), which tells Quattro Pro where to break the page when printing the report. If you insert a page break anywhere other than the leftmost column of the print block, Quattro Pro ignores it.

An example of using manual page breaks

Suppose you want to place a page break between rows 48 and 49 in your example worksheet. To do so, move the cell selector to cell A49, and choose the Style Insert Break command to tell Quattro Pro to place a page-break symbol between rows 48 and 49. Quattro Pro inserts a blank row and enters the page-break symbol in the column in which the cell selector is located (usually in column A). The original row 49 is now row number 50. When you print this worksheet, Quattro Pro chooses a page break after printing row 48 and before printing row 50. Of course, the new row and page-break symbol will not appear in your printed report.

A closer look at page breaks

When Quattro Pro encounters a manual page break, it adjusts the position of all the automatic page breaks that follow. That means that Quattro Pro adjusts the location of its automatic page breaks to be sure that only full pages of data are printed.

If your printed report is more than one page wide, the manual page breaks you set apply across all the columns in the worksheet. For example, if the worksheet in the above example is two pages wide, Quattro Pro inserts a page break after row 48 on every page of the report that includes that row.

Deleting manual page breaks

To delete a manual page break, choose the Edit Delete Rows command to delete the row that contains the page-break symbol. As long as no other entries are included in the row that contains the page break, deleting that row has no effect on your worksheet; it simply removes the manual page break.

Using setup strings

Most printers by default print six lines per inch vertically and either 10 or 12 characters per inch horizontally. However, most printers also have the ability to print more lines per inch, to print in boldface and in italics, to print compressed or expanded characters, or even to print in different fonts. One way to take advantage of these features built into your printer is to send special strings of characters, called setup strings, to your printer. For example, you might want to use a setup string to use a special font supplied by your printer.

A setup string tells your printer how to print instead of what to print. By sending the correct setup string to your printer, you can instruct it to print in boldface, italic, underlined, compressed, or expanded characters. You can also change the number of lines per inch and the number of characters per inch that your printer prints.

Defining a setup string

The Print Layout Setup String command allows you to define a setup string for your printed reports. When you choose this command, Quattro Pro displays the prompt *Specify printer code to be sent to the printer*. When you see this prompt, type the setup string you want and press the Enter key. A setup string usually consists of one or more three-digit numbers, each of which must be preceded by a backslash (\). (Exceptions to this rule include the setup strings for the Hewlett-Packard LaserJet family of printers, which requires strings of other lengths and character types.) The three-digit numbers are the ASCII codes (in decimal notation) of the character sequences that activate (or deactivate) the special printing features you want to use. For example, the character sequence that activates boldface printing on Epson printers is Esc-E; the Quattro Pro setup string representation for this character sequence is \027\069. The first part of this string, 027, is the ASCII representation for Esc, and the second part, 069, is the ASCII representation for the letter E. The backslashes separate the codes from each other.

After you define a setup string, Quattro Pro sends that string to the printer each time you print a worksheet, but does not print the characters in the setup string; Quattro Pro merely looks at the setup string to see which special features to use. The printer continues to use the settings in this string until it is turned off or until another setup string changes the typeface again. Any setup string you define using the Print Layout Setup String command affects your entire worksheet, including headers and footers.

You can link several setup strings to form a single string that activates more than one special print feature. For example, the setup string \015\027\069 turns on compressed and boldface printing on an Epson LQ-1500. The longest string you can specify, however, is 39 characters (including the backslashes).

Remember that the particular print options available to you are determined entirely by your printer. The setup string does not import any special features; it merely asks the printer to use the features that are already there. For example, you cannot use a setup string to create italic type if your printer is not capable of generating italic characters. To find out what options are available with your printer, check your printer manual.

Deleting a setup string

After you enter a setup string, you might want to delete that string; for example, so that you can print a report in your printer's standard typeface. To delete a setup string, choose the Print Layout Setup String command, press Esc to delete the existing string, and then press the Enter key. You will probably find that deleting a setup string has no immediate effect on your printer. Although you've deleted the string, you still see the current special print features the next time you print. As mentioned, after you turn on a special print attribute, that attribute remains in effect until you either turn off the printer or send another control sequence that turns off the special attribute. Consequently, simply deleting a setup string is usually not enough to reverse that string's effect. To restore normal printing, you must both delete the setup string and reset the printer by turning it off and on again.

Instead of deleting a setup string, you can replace the existing setup string with a new string that resets the printer to its default condition. To determine the printer reset string for your printer, check your printer manual. After Quattro Pro sends this string to the printer, formatting options are reset.

Embedded setup strings

Any setup string you define using the Print Layout Setup String command affects your entire worksheet. To assign some special attributes to only a portion of the worksheet, you have to insert, or embed, the setup strings that control the attributes you want to use in the worksheet. When you print a report that contains an embedded setup string, only the part of the worksheet that follows the string will be printed with special attributes. If you embed a second setup string that turns off the attribute that was activated by the first setup string, only the part of the worksheet between the two strings will have the special attributes.

To embed a setup string in a report, first insert a blank row immediately above the first row that you want to print with the special attribute. Next, move the cell selector to the column to the extreme left (this will usually be column A) in the new row in the print block. Then, type two vertical bars (| |) followed by the setup string that turns on the attribute. Type the setup string exactly as you would type it after choosing the Print Layout Setup String command.

You will typically want to include a second setup string in your worksheet to turn off the attribute that is activated by the first string. To do so, move the cell selector to the row below the last row you want to print with the special attribute, insert another blank row, and move the cell selector to the leftmost cell in the print block in that row. Then, type two vertical bars (| |) followed by the setup string that deactivates the print attribute.

An example of using embedded setup strings

Suppose that you want to print the report shown in Figure 7-8, and that you want the text in row 1 of the worksheet—SALES BY PERSON—to appear in enlarged type. To begin, move the cell selector to cell A1 and choose the Edit Insert Rows command to insert one blank row above row 1. Then, move the cell selector to cell A1, type | | \027\087\049, and press the Enter key. (This setup string works for an Epson printer. If you use a different printer, check your printer manual for the equivalent string.) Now, move the cell selector to row 3 and choose the Edit Insert Rows command to insert another blank row immediately below the text you want to enlarge. Finally, move the cell selector to cell A3, type | | \027\087\048, and press the Enter key.

After the setup strings are in place, you can print the worksheet in the usual fashion by choosing the Print Block command and redefining the print block so that it includes block A1..D36. (This step is required because you inserted a row above row 1 to hold the first embedded setup string. Had you placed the string elsewhere in the report, you would not have needed to redefine the print block.) Next, align the printer paper, choose the Align option from the Adjust Printer menu, press the Esc key, and choose the Spreadsheet Print option from the Print menu. The worksheet's title in row 2—SALES BY PERSON —is printed in enlarged type; the remainder of this report is printed in normal type.

A closer look at embedded strings

The first vertical bar characters you enter are not displayed in the cells of the worksheet. The vertical bar is a special label prefix that tells Quattro Pro that the numbers in this cell are not normal values but are instead printer setup strings. As with other label prefixes, Quattro Pro never displays the | prefix.

The rows that contain the embedded setup strings do not appear in the printed report. Whenever you embed a setup string in a worksheet, Quattro Pro does not print the row that contains that string.

You must always enter embedded setup strings in the leftmost column of the print block (this is usually column A). If your setup string is not in the print block's first column, Quattro Pro ignores it.

When you use embedded setup strings in reports wider than a single page, Quattro Pro applies the special print attribute defined by the string to every character in the rows that follow the string, including entries that are not on the first page of the report.

Listing a worksheet

Instead of printing a report that looks like the worksheet on your screen, you can print a listing of the contents of each nonblank cell in the worksheet. You might use this kind of listing to document the worksheet or as a helpful tool for finding errors in a worksheet. To print a worksheet listing, choose the Print Format Cell-Formulas command. When you choose the Print Spreadsheet Print command to begin printing, Quattro Pro prints a cell-by-cell list of the entries in the print block. For example, Figure 7-27 shows a portion of the listing of cell contents for the worksheet in Figure 7-8.

As you can see in Figure 7-27, this listing shows all the information you would normally see in the input line when you select a cell: its contents, its format (if any), the column width (when the width is different from the global default), and the label prefix for label entries. As mentioned, the listing includes only nonblank cells; the only blank cells that appear are those that have been assigned a format.

The listing created by the Cell-Formulas option is useful for seeing various information about a cell. However, it is difficult to determine the relationships among the cells in the listing. Also, because Quattro Pro prints only one cell per

FIGURE 7-27.

If you choose the Print Format Cell-Formulas command before you print, Quattro Pro prints a listing of all the nonblank cells in the worksheet.

```
A1: [W20] 'SALES BY PERSON
A2: [W20] \=
B2: \=
C2: \=
D2: \=
E2: \=
F2: \=
B4: 33239
C4: 33270
D4: 33298
E4: 33329
F4: 33359
A5: [W20] 'East
B5: \-
C5: \-
D5: \-
E5: \-
F5: \-
A6: [W20] ' Abrahamson
B6: (C0) 63.570230384357
C6: (C0) 138.61289864872
D6: (C0) 312.73837026674
E6: (C0) 933.26234968845
F6: (C0) 489.58149843384
```

line, the listing for even a relatively small worksheet can be long. Finally, although the listing does include some important information, it also leaves out a few items. For instance, the listing does not provide a list of block names or of graph and database settings.

Using the Print Layout Reset command to return print defaults

After you change the default print settings for a worksheet, you might decide to return some or all of these settings to their default values. The quickest way to do so is to choose the Print Layout Reset All command.

To reset all of the print settings to their defaults, choose the Print Layout Reset All command. This command deletes your header and footer, removes any headings you have defined, and returns the settings for the setup string, margins, and page length to their defaults. It also removes the block you have defined as your print block. The only settings that are not affected by this command are the manual page breaks you have defined, embedded setup strings, and the printer settings defined using the Options Hardware Printers command.

To retain the current settings for the print block, left heading, and top heading but to reset the header, footer, margins, page length, and setup string, choose the Print Layout Reset Layout command. If you want only to clear the headings settings, choose the Print Layout Reset Headings command. Finally, to reset the print block, choose the Print Reset Print Block command.

8
File Management

After you create a worksheet, you'll probably want to save it on disk. Saving a worksheet on disk stores the worksheet permanently in a file. When you want to work with the saved worksheet again, simply retrieve it from disk.

Use the commands on Quattro Pro's File menu to save and retrieve your worksheets. In addition to letting you save and retrieve worksheets, the File menu commands allow you to perform other file management tasks, such as combining one worksheet (or part of a worksheet) with another or erasing one or more files from disk. Understanding how to create and manage files is an important step in mastering Quattro Pro.

This chapter explains all of the File menu commands except Tools Import and Tools Parse, which are discussed in Appendix A, "Exchanging Data with Other Programs."

Saving worksheets

The worksheets you create in Quattro Pro are stored temporarily in your computer's random access memory (RAM). To create a permanent copy of a worksheet, you must save it on disk, where it remains until you choose to erase it. The commands you use to transfer a worksheet from RAM to disk are File Save and File Save As. After you save a worksheet, you can continue working in Quattro Pro or exit the program.

Saving a worksheet for the first time

Use the File Save As command to save a new worksheet for the first time. When you choose this command, Quattro Pro displays the prompt *Enter save file name*, followed by the name of the default directory and the filename descriptor *.WQ1, as shown in Figure 8-1. Quattro Pro displays an alphabetical listing of all the Quattro Pro worksheet files (that is, files with a filename extension .WQ1) and subdirectories in the default directory. When you see this prompt, type the name you want to assign to the worksheet file and press the Enter key. You do not need to type the filename extension .WQ1. Quattro Pro adds it automatically to the name you type. For example, if you type the filename BUDGET, Quattro Pro saves your worksheet in a file named BUDGET.WQ1 in the default directory.

Choosing an existing name for a worksheet file

After you choose the File Save As command, Quattro Pro displays a list of all the worksheet files in your default directory. Instead of typing a new filename for your worksheet, you could choose one of the names from the list. To save a new worksheet with an existing name, choose the File Save As command, point to the filename you want to use, and press the Enter key.

If you save a worksheet with a name that is already in use, Quattro Pro replaces the current contents of the file with your worksheet. Before overwriting the existing file, however, Quattro Pro presents a menu that offers three options: Cancel, Replace, and Backup. If you choose the Cancel option, Quattro Pro cancels the command and returns to READY mode. If you choose the Replace option, Quattro Pro replaces the existing file with the current worksheet, and the contents of the original file are lost. If you choose the Backup option, Quattro Pro changes the filename extension of the existing file to .BAK before saving the current worksheet. As a result, you will have two files on your disk with the same filename but

FIGURE 8-1.
Quattro Pro displays this box when you choose the File Save As command.

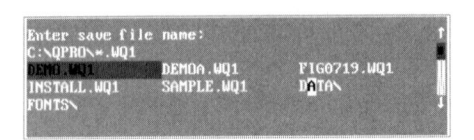

with different extensions; one with the extension .WQ1 (the current worksheet) and one with the extension .BAK (the old worksheet file).

Filename rules

You must follow a few rules when choosing names for your worksheets. First, the name you specify for a worksheet file can contain no more than eight characters. If you specify a filename that is longer than that, Quattro Pro leaves out any characters beyond the eighth character. In addition to the eight-character filename, you can supply a three-character filename extension. If you do not supply an extension, Quattro Pro automatically adds the extension .WQ1.

Filenames and extensions can include any combination of letters of the alphabet (uppercase and lowercase), the digits 0 through 9, the underline character (_), and any of the following symbols:

! @ # $ % ^ & ( ) - { } ~ ` '

Quattro Pro lets you save a file with any filename extension you want. You need only to type a period and then the extension you want to use after you type the filename.

Saving a worksheet again

If you want Quattro Pro to save a worksheet that you've saved before and you want to assign the same name to that worksheet, use the File Save command instead of File Save As. Quattro Pro presents a menu that has three choices: Cancel, Replace, and Backup. Choose the Replace option if you want to replace the version stored in the file with the version to which you've made changes. If you do not want to replace the old worksheet, choose the Cancel option to cancel the command. To save the current worksheet but keep a copy of the old one as well, choose the Backup option. Quattro Pro creates a new file with the same name and the extension .BAK. If a backup file already exists, Quattro Pro replaces it with the new backup file.

Changing a filename

Most of the time, you'll want to save your worksheets with their original filenames. You can always specify a new name, however, when you save an old worksheet, which creates a new worksheet file with the new name while keeping the old worksheet file with the old name. For example, suppose that after you make changes to a worksheet named SALES.WQ1, you decide to save the modified worksheet in a file named SALES2.WQ1. To do so, choose the File Save As command, and Quattro Pro displays the prompt *Enter save file name*, followed by the current directory and filename. Type the new name, SALES2, and press the Enter key. As soon as you start typing the new name, Quattro Pro removes the old filename from the prompt when you press Enter. Quattro Pro saves the worksheet in a new file named SALES2.WQ1. You still have an original unmodified version of the worksheet in the file SALES.WQ1.

Editing a filename

If you want to save your worksheet with a name that is slightly different from the original filename, edit the existing filename rather than typing a new name from scratch. To do so, press the Spacebar to enter EDIT mode after you choose the File Save As command. You can then use any of the cursor-movement keys, the Del key, and the Backspace key to edit the original filename. After you specify the new name, press the Enter key.

Disk-full errors

You will occasionally run into disk-full problems when you save files, especially if you save your worksheets on floppy disks. Quattro Pro beeps and display a message when your disk is too full to store the worksheet you are saving. If you encounter an error, press the Spacebar to acknowledge the error and return to READY mode. Then do whatever you can to free enough disk space to save your worksheet. You might need to erase one or two un-needed files from the disk (using the File Utilities File Manager Edit Erase command) or replace the disk with another disk that has enough space. Afterward, you can use the File Save As command to save the worksheet.

Before saving a worksheet on disk, Quattro Pro completely erases the old version of the worksheet file. If Quattro Pro then runs out of disk space before saving the worksheet, neither the old version of the file nor the new version are saved.

CAUTION: *Be careful! If you do not pay attention to the amount of space on your disk, sooner or later you may run into a situation where there is no copy of your worksheet stored on your disk and you risk losing all your work.*

Password protection

When you save a worksheet in a file, you can give that file a password to protect it. Protecting a file makes it impossible for anyone who does not know the password to retrieve the file in Quattro Pro, allowing you to protect confidential information and prevent accidental changes to the file.

Protecting a worksheet file

To protect a worksheet file, choose the File Save As command, specify a name for the worksheet file, press the Spacebar, type *p*, and then press the Enter key. Quattro Pro then displays the prompt *Enter password*. Now type the password of your choice and press the Enter key. The password can be up to 15 characters long and can include any character you can type on your keyboard. Quattro Pro then displays the prompt *Verify password.* Retype your password, exactly as you entered it the first time, and then press the Enter key again. (Quattro Pro asks you to verify your password to prevent the possibility of saving the worksheet with an incorrect, and thus unknown, password.) If the two passwords match, Quattro Pro saves your worksheet with the password. If the passwords do not match, Quattro Pro prompts you again for the filename and does not save your file.

An example of using a password. Suppose you want to assign the password Widgets to a worksheet with the filename SALES. Choose the File Save As command, type *SALES p* and press the Enter key. When Quattro Pro prompts you to assign a password, type *Widgets* and then press the Enter key again. Next, when Quattro Pro asks you to verify the password, type *Widgets* again and press the Enter key. Assuming you type the password correctly both times, Quattro Pro saves the worksheet in a file named SALES with the password Widgets.

A closer look at passwords. As you type a password in response to either of Quattro Pro's password prompts, Quattro Pro displays a small square in place of each character you type, to prevent anyone from reading the password on the screen. If you make a mistake while typing the password, press the Backspace key, and then retype the character correctly. To remove the entire entry and retype it from scratch, press the Esc key.

Quattro Pro allows you to assign a password to a worksheet any time you want (not simply the first time you save it). To give a worksheet a password after you've saved it one time, choose the File Save As command, press the Spacebar, type *p*, and press the Enter key. Quattro Pro then prompts you for a new password.

Quattro Pro recognizes the case of a password. Widgets, WIDGETS, and widgets, for example, are all recognized as different passwords by Quattro Pro. As a result, be careful about case when initially defining and later entering passwords.

Use password protection as seldom as possible; after you protect a worksheet file, it is impossible to retrieve that file without entering its password. If you forget the password, you lose the worksheet. If you decide to use password protection on any of your worksheet files, keep a written copy of the passwords in a safe location.

Compressing files as they're saved

Quattro Pro comes with SQZ!, by Turner Hall Publishing, which is a popular spreadsheet utility that squeezes, or compresses, worksheet files as they are saved. SQZ! makes it possible to save a worksheet file in as little as 5 percent of the disk space it would normally consume.

Extension	Compresses for use as
.WQ!	Quattro Pro worksheet
.WKZ	Quattro Pro .WKQ file used by earlier versions of Quattro Pro
.WK$	.WKS file used with Lotus 1-2-3, Release 1A
.WK!	.WK1 file used with Lotus 1-2-3, Release 2.0 and later

TABLE 8-1. *You can compress your worksheet as you save it by choosing the File Save As command and specifying one of these filename extensions.*

Saving worksheets in compressed form

To save a worksheet in compressed form, choose the File Save As command as usual, and then specify a filename with one of the three filename extensions shown in Table 8-1. After you press the Enter key to lock in the filename, Quattro Pro compresses the worksheet as it is saved.

Quattro Pro lets you choose one of four compressed forms in which to save your worksheet. If you supply a .WQ! extension after the filename, Quattro Pro saves your worksheet in a compressed form that can be retrieved only by Quattro Pro's File Retrieve or File Open commands. If you supply a .WKZ extension after the filename, Quattro Pro saves your worksheet in a compressed form that can be retrieved by Quattro Pro and earlier versions of Quattro Pro. If you supply a .WK$ extension, Quattro Pro saves your worksheet in a form compatible with SQZ! for Lotus 1-2-3, Release 1A. Finally, if you supply a .WK! extension, Quattro Pro saves the worksheet in a form that is compatible with SQZ! for Lotus 1-2-3, Release 2.0 and later.

Suppose, for example, that you want to save the current worksheet with the name BUDGET, and that you want to compress this worksheet as it is saved. To do so, choose the File Save As command, type *BUDGET.WQ!*, and press the Enter key. If you now compare an uncompressed version of the BUDGET.WQ1 worksheet to BUDGET.WQ!, you'll see a substantial size difference.

Retrieving a compressed worksheet

Retrieving a compressed worksheet is no different from retrieving an uncompressed worksheet. For example, to retrieve the BUDGET.WQ! worksheet you just saved, choose the File Retrieve command and then select the file BUDGET.WQ! from the list of worksheet files. Press the Enter key, and Quattro Pro uncompresses and then opens the BUDGET worksheet.

FIGURE 8-2.
The File Utilities SQZ! command displays this menu.

Remove Blanks	No
Storage of Values	Exact
Version	1 - SQZ!
Quit	

Changing the SQZ! settings

The File Utilities SQZ! command lets you control Quattro Pro's SQZ! settings. After you choose the File Utilities SQZ! command, Quattro Pro presents the menu shown in Figure 8-2. The settings in this menu (Remove Blanks, Storage of Values, and Version) control three of the methods that Quattro Pro uses to compress files.

The Remove Blanks setting lets you control whether empty cells are saved in a compressed file. An empty cell is either a blank label or a formatted cell that contains no entry. If you change the Remove Blanks setting from No (the default) to Yes before you save a worksheet, blank cells are not saved in the compressed file. The Storage of Values setting controls whether both formulas and their current values are saved in a compressed file. The three options for the Storage of Values setting are Exact, Approximate, and Remove. The Exact option tells Quattro Pro to save all formulas along with a 15-significant-digit representation of their current values. The Approximate option tells Quattro Pro to save current formula values with up to seven significant digits. The Remove option tells Quattro Pro to save only the worksheet formulas, and not those formulas' current values. Finally, the Version setting on the SQZ! menu lets you specify one of two different compression methods. The default option, 1 - SQZ!, does not save as much disk space as the does alternative option, 2 - SQZ! Plus. But, if you need to exchange data between Quattro Pro and another worksheet program that uses an older version of SQZ!, you'll probably want to choose the 1 - SQZ! setting.

Retrieving worksheets

Use Quattro Pro's File Retrieve or File Open command to retrieve a worksheet that you have saved previously on disk. The File Retrieve command replaces the current worksheet with the one you retrieve from the disk. The File Open command leaves the current worksheet in memory and simply overlays, or stacks on top, the one you retrieve from disk. (Later in this chapter, "Stacking Worksheets in Memory" describes how to change the order of stacked worksheets.) When you choose the File Retrieve or File Open command, Quattro Pro displays the prompt *Enter name of file to retrieve* or *Enter name of file to open,* followed by the default directory and the .W?? descriptor. This descriptor tells Quattro Pro to display the names of all files in the default directory with a filename extension that begins with the letter W, such as .WQ1, .WQ!, WKQ, .WK1, or .WKS. To retrieve a file from disk, select its name from the list and then press the Enter key. Quattro Pro retrieves the contents of the file and displays it on the screen.

If you choose the File Retrieve command without saving changes to the current worksheet, Quattro Pro displays the prompt *Lose your changes?* If you choose Yes, Quattro Pro discards the current worksheet and displays the prompt *Enter name of file to retrieve*. If you choose No, Quattro Pro returns to the File menu where you can choose to save your current worksheet before retrieving a new one.

An example of retrieving a worksheet

Suppose you want to retrieve the file named SALES.WQ1 from the list shown in Figure 8-3. First, choose the File Retrieve command, use the direction keys to point to SALES.WQ1 in the list, and press the Enter key. (Alternatively, choose the File Retrieve command, type *SALES*, and press the Enter key.) The screen becomes blank and the indicator WAIT appears in the status line. After a few seconds, the contents of the SALES worksheet appear on the screen.

Retrieving files that have nonstandard extensions

When you retrieve a file that has the standard filename extension .WQ1, you do not have to specify the extension when you type the filename. But, if you want to retrieve a file that has a nonstandard extension (an extension that does not begin with the letter W), your job is a little more complicated. Because Quattro Pro includes the descriptor *W?? in the prompt when you choose the File Retrieve or File Open command, Quattro Pro includes only the names of files with standard extensions in its list, so you cannot select a file with a nonstandard extension by pointing.

To retrieve a file that has a nonstandard filename extension, choose the File Retrieve or the File Open command, type the name of the file (including the filename extension), and press the Enter key. You can also choose the File Retrieve or File Open command, press the Esc key to erase the descriptor *.W??, and type a new descriptor that tells Quattro Pro to list all the files that contain the characters you specify (for example, *.TXT). After you press the Enter key to lock in the new extension, you can select the file you want to retrieve from the new list.

FIGURE 8-3.
Quattro Pro prompts you to enter the name of the file to retrieve.

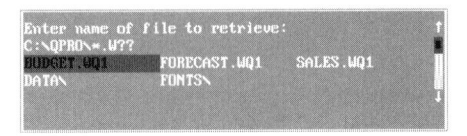

Changing the default file extension

Although Quattro Pro supplies the default file extension .WQ1, you can direct Quattro Pro to use some other file extension as the default.

To change the default file extension, choose the Options Startup File Extension command. Quattro Pro displays the prompt *Default worksheet file extension*, followed by the current default file extension. Press the Backspace key to erase the current default setting, and then type a new default file extension, such as WQ2, and press the Enter key. Now, if you do not specify a file extension when saving a file, Quattro Pro uses this new default file extension.

Retrieving protected worksheets

To retrieve a password-protected worksheet, choose the File Retrieve or the File Open command and select the name of the file you want to retrieve. Quattro Pro displays the prompt *Enter password*. Type the password that is assigned to that file and press the Enter key. If you type the correct password, Quattro Pro retrieves the file immediately. If you do not type the correct password, Quattro Pro displays an error message and aborts the File Retrieve or File Open command.

The password you supply must match the worksheet's password character for character. Every detail, including capitalization, counts. For example, if the password is Widgets, you must type *Widgets*, and not *widgets* or *WIDGETS*.

Automatic-load worksheets

If you open the same worksheet file almost every time you begin a new Quattro Pro session, you might want to make that worksheet an automatic-load (or autoload) file. Quattro Pro retrieves your autoload file each time you start Quattro Pro, allowing you to bypass the File Retrieve or File Open command.

Quattro Pro provides two ways to designate a worksheet as an autoload worksheet. Either save the worksheet with Quattro Pro's default autoload filename, which is QUATTRO.WQ1, or change the default autoload filename from QUATTRO.WQ1 to your worksheet's filename. Quattro Pro automatically opens the autoload file when you start it.

To change the default autoload filename, choose the Options Startup Autoload File command, and press the Esc key to remove the previous default filename. Then type the name of the worksheet you want Quattro Pro to load automatically (including a filename extension) and press Enter. After you specify a new autoload filename, you must choose the Quit option from the Startup menu and then from the Options menu to return to READY mode, and then choose the Options Update command to save the change.

If you store your worksheet files on floppy disks, you can have worksheets on different disks with the same filename. If you specify that filename as the autoload file, Quattro Pro retrieves the worksheet file from whichever disk is in the default directory when it starts. If you store your worksheet files on a hard disk, you can have worksheets with the same name in different subdirectories. When Quattro Pro starts, it retrieves the autoload worksheet from whichever subdirectory is the default. To retrieve an autoload file from a different directory, change the default directory, which is explained shortly.

Retrieving a file as Quattro Pro starts

When you start Quattro Pro, if you know which worksheet file you want to retrieve, you can retrieve the file and start Quattro Pro at the same time. You already know that to load Quattro Pro, you type *q* at the DOS prompt. To open a file, follow *q* with a space and then the pathname and filename. For example, to start Quattro Pro and retrieve the file SALES.WQ1 in the directory C:\QPRO, type the following at the DOS prompt:

    Q C:\QPRO\SALES

If the file you want to retrieve is in the default directory, you do not have to include the pathname. (Later in this chapter, "Changing the Default Directory" explains more about this directory.) For example, if C:\QPRO were the default directory (and it is, unless you've changed the default) you could start Quattro Pro and retrieve the file SALES.WQ1 in the directory C:\QPRO by typing the following at the DOS prompt:

    Q SALES

If the filename you specify does not exist, Quattro Pro opens a new file and gives it the name you specified.

Changing the default directory

All of Quattro Pro's File commands assume that you want to operate on files that are stored in the default directory. One way to work with files in other directories is to change the default data directory. You can choose from three methods to change the default directory. You can change the directory during the execution of a File command, such as File Save or File Retrieve. You can also use the File Directory command to change the default directory for the current Quattro Pro session. Or, you can use the Options Startup Directory and Options Update commands to change the default directory permanently. The following sections explain these three methods.

Changing the directory during a command

When you choose a File command, Quattro Pro displays a prompt such as *Enter name of file to save* or *Enter name of file to retrieve*, followed by the name of the default directory and the *.W?? filename descriptor. In addition, Quattro Pro lists the names of the worksheets in the default directory. This process works well when you want to access a file in the default directory. If you want to work with the files in another directory, however, you have to change the directory before you can continue with the command.

Pressing the Esc key to change the directory

One way to change the directory during the execution of a File command is by pressing the Esc key two times after you choose the command. Pressing Esc two times erases both the file descriptor and the name of the default directory. You can then type a new directory name (including the drive name, the pathname, and the directory name, if applicable). After you press the Enter key to lock in the new directory, Quattro Pro displays the descriptor *.W?? and lists all of the worksheet files in that directory. You can then complete the command. You can use this technique with the File Save As command to save a file in a different directory.

An alternative approach to accessing a different directory

If you have grouped your Quattro Pro files into subdirectories on your hard disk, you can use another method to access a different directory during the execution of a File command. As mentioned, when you choose a File command, Quattro Pro displays a list of all the files whose filename extensions begin with the letter W. If any subdirectories exist under the default directory, this list also includes the names of those subdirectories. To change from the current directory to one of its subdirectories, point to the name of the subdirectory and then press the Enter key. Quattro Pro displays all of the worksheet files and subdirectories in that subdirectory.

To display the files in the next highest directory while the file list is in view, press the Backspace key. Quattro Pro displays a list of the files and subdirectories that are stored in that directory. Each time you press the Backspace key, you back up another level in the directory path until you reach the root directory. By using this technique, you can browse through your directories and subdirectories until you find the file that you want.

When this technique will not work. You can use this technique with any of Quattro Pro's File commands that display a list of files. The technique just described does not work, however, unless at least one worksheet file or subdirectory exists in the default directory. If the default directory is empty, pressing the Backspace key after you choose a File command simply deletes letters in the prompt.

The effect of changing a directory

The techniques described above change the directory only while you're using a File command. The directory reverts to the previous default as soon as the command is completed. One exception to the rule, however, is that when you save a worksheet you have retrieved from a directory other than the default, Quattro Pro assumes that you want to save that worksheet in the directory from which it was retrieved.

Changing the default directory for a single session

Use the File Directory command to change the default directory for the duration of the current Quattro Pro session. This command is convenient whenever you plan to work with the files in one particular directory for most of your session. For example, suppose that the default directory is C:\QUATTRO\DATA and that you want to change it to C:\QUATTRO\DATA\COSTS for the remainder of the current session. Choose the File Directory command, type *C:\QUATTRO\DATA\COSTS*, and press the Enter key. You do not have to press the Esc or Backspace key to erase the name of the current default directory; Quattro Pro erases the name of the current directory as soon as you begin typing the new name. Unfortunately, you cannot edit the name of the current default directory when you specify the new default directory. You must type the new directory's full name.

After you change the default directory, Quattro Pro assumes whenever you choose a File command that you want to work with the files in the new default directory. For example, when you choose the File Retrieve command after changing the default directory to C:\QUATTRO\DATA\COSTS, Quattro Pro displays the following prompt along with a list of the files in that directory:

Enter name of file to retrieve:

C:\QUATTRO\DATA\COSTS*.W??

Again, the new default directory remains in effect for the duration of the current session (or until you use the File Directory command to change it again). When you exit from Quattro Pro, however, your change is not preserved. The next time you start Quattro Pro, the original default directory will be in effect.

Changing the default directory permanently

The Options Startup Directory command lets you change the default directory permanently. You might want to use this command when you make a major change in the organization of your files, such as moving the files you work with most often from one subdirectory to another. After you've used this command to change the default directory, you must use the Options Update command to save the change permanently on your disk. If you do not use the Options Update command, the default directory changes back to the previous default directory the next time you start Quattro Pro. After you choose Options Update, the new default data directory remains in effect until you change it again using the Options Startup Directory and the Options Update commands. Each time you start the program, Quattro Pro uses the new default directory you have specified.

Stacking worksheets in memory

As mentioned, the File Open command lets you retrieve another worksheet from disk without erasing the current worksheet or worksheets stored in memory. Every time you use the File Open command, you retrieve a worksheet from the disk and stack it on top of the currently displayed worksheet. You may find this feature extremely useful, because it means that you can work with more than one worksheet file at a time. Suppose, for example, that you are constructing a new worksheet for budgeting and that the sales figures are in the worksheet SALES.WQ1, the cost-of-goods-sold figures are in the worksheet COGS.WQ1, and the expense figures are in the worksheet EXPENSES.WQ1. You would probably find it helpful to be able to flip among these worksheets as you construct the new budgeting worksheet.

Changing the top worksheet

When you have more than one worksheet open, you can change which worksheet is on top. To do so, choose the Window Pick command. Quattro Pro displays a list of the worksheet files currently open in memory. To move one of the worksheet files to the top of the stack, use the direction keys to highlight the one you want on top and then press the Enter key.

Creating a new worksheet in the stack

The File Open command lets you retrieve a previously saved worksheet from disk and place it on top of the stack of worksheets in memory. When you want to construct a brand new worksheet from scratch, you need an empty worksheet; the File New command lets you place a fresh, empty worksheet at the top of the stack.

Removing a worksheet from the stack

To remove a worksheet file from the stack, use the File Close command, which closes the top worksheet in the stack. If the worksheet you want to close is not on top of the stack, you might need to use the Window Pick command first to move the worksheet to the top of the stack. After you choose the File Close command,

Quattro Pro displays the prompt *Lose your changes?* if you have not saved the worksheet file since you made the last change to it. To continue the File Close operation without saving the file, select Yes. Or, to abort the File Close operation so that you can save the file, select No and then use the File Save or File Save As command.

Removing the entire stack

To remove the entire stack of worksheets from memory, choose the File Close All command. This command is equivalent to closing each of the worksheets in a stack individually. As is the case with the File Close command, when you use File Close All, Quattro Pro removes the worksheet files from memory but not from disk.

When you choose the File Close All command, Quattro Pro begins removing worksheet files from memory starting at the top of the stack. For each worksheet file removed from the stack, Quattro Pro checks to verify that you have saved it. If you have not saved the worksheet file since you made the last change to it, Quattro Pro displays the message *Lose your changes and Close Window?* followed by three options: No, Yes, and Save & Close. The No option leaves the worksheet in the stack. The Yes option removes the worksheet file from the stack without saving your most recent changes. The Save & Close option saves the worksheet under its current filename and then removes the worksheet file from the stack.

A closer look at removing the entire stack

If you remove all the worksheets in the stack, Quattro Pro's menu changes. The main menu includes only the File command, and the File menu includes only the New, Open, Workspace, Utilities, and Exit commands. Quattro Pro removes all the other menus because they pertain only to open worksheets. Predictably, the same menu change also occurs if you use the File Close command to remove the last worksheet from memory.

Using the File Workspace commands to group worksheets

As you start working with stacks of worksheets in memory, you'll probably find yourself using certain sets of worksheet files over and over. You might, for example, use two or three particular worksheets every time you construct a budget. In such a situation, you'll find the File Workspace Save and File Workspace Restore commands useful.

An example of using the File Workspace commands

Rather than stacking worksheets by repeatedly using the File Open command, you can store a list of the stacked worksheets by using the File Workspace Save command. After you store the list, you can use the File Workspace Restore command to open all of the worksheets in the list.

Suppose, for example, that you frequently work with the same three worksheet files: SALES.WQ1, EXPENSES.WQ1, and COGS.WQ1. To store these worksheets in a list so that you can open all of them at once, first retrieve each of the worksheets using the File Open command. Then, save the list of worksheets in the stack by choosing the File Workspace Save command. Quattro Pro displays the prompt *Workspace name,* followed by the default directory and the file descriptor *.WSP. To name the stack of worksheets as a workspace, simply type a valid filename and then press the Enter key.

After you save a workspace, use the File Workspace Restore command to simultaneously open all the worksheets in a list that you've stored as a workspace. First, choose the File Workspace Restore command. Quattro Pro displays the prompt *Workspace name,* followed by the default directory and descriptor *.WSP, as well as a list of the files in the default directory with the file extension WSP. Use the direction keys to highlight the workspace you want, and then press the Enter key.

Changing the worksheets in a workspace

To change the worksheets listed in a workspace, use the File Workspace Save command. First, stack the worksheets you want in the list using the File Open command. Next, choose the File Workspace Save command. When Quattro Pro displays the *Workspace name* prompt, use the direction keys to highlight the workspace name you want, and then press the Enter key. Because the workspace already exists, Quattro Pro presents a menu that has three choices: Cancel, Replace, and Backup. Choose the Cancel option to abort the File Workspace Save command. Choose the Replace option to save the changed list of worksheets using the existing workspace name. Choose the Backup option to save the current workspace but also keep a copy of the old workspace. Both workspaces will use the same name but different file extensions. The backup file has a .BAK extension.

A closer look at the File Workspace commands

When you choose the File Workspace Save command, Quattro Pro does not save the worksheet files in the stack. Quattro Pro saves only a list of the files so that it can reconstruct the stack. To save the individual worksheet files in a stack, use the File Save and File Save As commands.

This section explained workspaces in terms of memorized lists of worksheet files. However, the workspaces can also store information about the order the worksheets were opened in. Chapter 9, "Working with Windows," describes what windows are and how you can use them.

Using Quattro Pro's File Manager

After a while you may find that you have dozens and perhaps hundreds of worksheet files. Fortunately, Quattro Pro provides a file utility called the File Manager which you can use to locate, copy, rename, and erase files; to print lists of files and directories; and even to make directories.

Opening the File Manager

To open the File Manager, choose the File Utilities File Manager command. Quattro Pro displays a new window, the File Manager window, on top of the current worksheet, as shown in Figure 8-4. This window does not replace your worksheet, but instead stacks on top of the worksheet.

Reviewing the File Manager window

At the top of the window, the File Manager identifies the specified drive, directory, and filename descriptor (called the filter). The upper part of the File Manager window is called the Control Pane.

Beneath the Control Pane, the File Manager window lists the files that match the specified drive, directory, and filter shown in the Control Pane. The subdirectories in the specified directory are also shown. This portion of the File Manager window is called the File List Pane. Files are listed alphabetically, followed by subdirectories. For each file, Quattro Pro provides the filename, extension, size in bytes, and date. If more files exist than will fit on a single page of the list, Quattro Pro displays the word "more" at the bottom of the page. To see the next page of the file list, press the PgDn key; to see the previous page of the file list, press the PgUp key. You can also press the Home key to display the first page of the file list and the End key to display the last page of the file list.

FIGURE 8-4.
The File Manager window is displayed on top of the current worksheet.

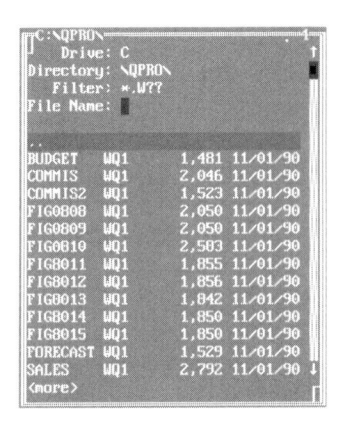

At the end of the file list, Quattro Pro shows the number of files that match the filter, the number of files in the directory, the total bytes used by the files displayed in the file list, and the total number of bytes available on the specified drive. Not all of this information shows unless you increase the File Manager window's size using the Window Zoom command. Chapter 9, "Working with Windows," describes each of the Window commands, including Zoom.

The File Manager window has a different menu from the one you see when you are working with a Quattro Pro worksheet. It includes fewer menu commands. Two of the commands, Sort and Tree, are displayed only in the File Manager. You'll read more about the File Manager menu later in this section.

Using the Control Pane to change the drive, directory, or filter

The Control Pane settings determine which files and subdirectories are listed in the File List Pane. One way to change the files listed is to change the Control Pane settings. To do so, move the cursor to the Control Pane field you want to change, and then type over the existing setting. To move to the Control Pane, press the Tab or F6 key until the cursor highlights one of the Control Pane settings. Or you can also activate the Control Pane and move the cursor to the Filename field simultaneously by pressing Shift-Tab. After the Control Pane is activated, you can use the direction keys or click the mouse to move the cursor to the field you want to change.

For example, to see the files listed on drive A instead of on drive C, move to the Control Pane using the Tab key, move the cursor to the Drive field using the Up direction key, replace the letter C with the letter A, and press Enter. To change the directory, you follow a similar sequence of steps: Move to the Control Pane, move the cursor to the Directory field, and then replace the current directory with a new one. Shortly, you'll find a description of some other methods of changing the directory as part of retrieving a file.

You can control which files are listed from the specified drive and directory by using the filter setting. Initially, the filter is set to *.W??, which lists every file whose file extension starts with the letter W. But you can also use the * and ? characters, which are DOS wildcard characters, to create other filters. For example, the filter S*.WQ1 lists every file that starts with the letter S and uses the WQ1 file extension. The ?????.* filter lists every file that has a five-letter filename. For more information about using the DOS * and ? wildcard characters, see "Using Wildards in Link Formulas" later in this chapter, the DOS manual that came with your computer, or the latest edition of *Running MS-DOS* written by Van Wolverton and also published by Microsoft Press.

You can show only files that do not match the filter by enclosing the filter in brackets. For example, the filter [*.W??] excludes any file whose extension starts with the letter W.

You can specify several filters simultaneously by separating them with commas. For example, to list all the files in the current directory that either start with the letter S or use the WQ1 file extension, you can use the filter S*.*,*.WQ1. A combination filter can include up to 62 characters and use both regular and exclude filters.

Retrieving a file from the File Manager's list

Most often, you use the File Manager to find and retrieve a worksheet file. The extra information that the File Manager window shows, such as the file date, can be helpful, for example, in locating a budget worksheet you used some time ago.

Using the Filename field in the Control Pane. If you see the file you want in the list, you can open it by typing the first few characters of the filename. As you type, Quattro Pro records your keystrokes in the Control Pane's File Name field, moves the cursor to the first file in the File List Pane that matches what you've typed, and marks the file with a check. Now, press the Enter key to open the file. Quattro Pro places the file on top of the worksheet stack. As you can see, opening a file by using the File Manager is equivalent to choosing the File Open command.

By the way, when you use the Control Pane to open a file, the file need not be displayed in the file list; it only needs to be in the current directory. Simply because the filter in the Control Pane shows *.W??, for example, does not mean you cannot retrieve a file with the extension .JAN. You will need to type the complete filename, however, in the File Name field.

Using the File List Pane. You can also retrieve a file using the File List Pane if the file appears in the list. To do so, use either the direction keys or the mouse to move the cursor so that it marks the file you want to open, and then press the Enter key.

Looking in other directories. If the file you want to find is not in the current directory, you can still use the File Manager to find it. One way to do so is to type *.* in the filter field of the Control Pane, and type a filename that describes the file as accurately as possible in the filename field. Use the DOS wildcard characters to fill in the portions you do not know. Then press the [Goto] key (F5). The File Manager then searches through every directory on the specified disk, looking for files that match the filename. If it finds one, the File Manager changes to the current directory and highlights the file that matches the name you specify. If the first directory that the File Manager finds is not the correct one, press the [Goto] key again.

Below the list of files in the File List Pane, Quattro Pro lists any subdirectories in the current directory. To see the files in a subdirectory, move the cursor to the subdirectory and press the Enter key. Quattro Pro displays a list of the files in the indicated subdirectory that match the filter. For files and directories, you also indicate the subdirectory you want to select by typing the subdirectory name. As you type, Quattro Pro marks with a check the first file or directory that matches what you type. As soon as the subdirectory you want is marked with a check, press the Enter key to display a list of the files in that directory.

Changing the specified directory using the File List Pane. In addition to using the Control Pane's Directory field, you can use another approach to change the specified directory. Notice in Figure 8-4 that the first item shown in the list of files is ".." which stands for "the next highest directory." If you move the cursor to this list entry and press the Enter key, Quattro Pro displays a list of the directories and files in the next highest level of the directory tree. For example, if the current directory is C:\QPRO\DATA, selecting the .. entry displays a list of the files and directories in the C:\QPRO directory. If the current directory is C:\QPRO, selecting the .. entry displays a list of the files and directories in the C:\ directory (root). To then see the files in one of the listed directories, move the cursor to the directory name and press the Enter key.

Using the File Manager's File menu

The File Manager uses a slightly different version of Quattro Pro's standard File menu. The menu lists several familiar commands, including New, Open, Close, Close All, Workspace, Utilities, and Exit. These commands all work the same way in the File Manager as they do when a worksheet is displayed. Two of the commands, however, are different in the File Manager version of the File menu: Read Dir and Make Dir. These commands ease the work of dealing with directories, as described in the following sections.

Reading a directory using the File Read Dir command. The File Read Dir command rereads the files in the current directory. If you've added a file to or deleted a file from the directory, you can use this command to tell the File Manager to update the information in the list of the files. To use the File Read Dir command, first verify that the directory for which you want to see files is displayed, and then choose the command.

Making a directory using the File Make Dir command. The File Make Dir command lets you add a subdirectory to the current directory. Suppose, for example, that you want to add a subdirectory named DATA to the directory C:\QPRO. To do so, first display the C:\QPRO directory, and then choose the File Make Dir command. Quattro Pro displays the prompt *Directory Name* inside a small box entitled Create a New Directory. Type the name of the subdirectory you want to create (for this example, type *DATA*) and press the Enter key. Quattro Pro creates the subdirectory C:\QPRO\DATA.

Using the File Manager's Edit menu

The File Manager's Edit menu commands differ completely from those in Quattro Pro's standard Edit menu, which makes sense. The File Manager's Edit menu commands (Select File, All Select, Copy, Move, Erase, Paste, Duplicate, and Rename) all apply to files instead of to cells in a worksheet.

Selecting files using the File Manager's Edit menu. Before you choose File Manager commands such as Open, Copy, Erase, and Rename, you must select one or more files from the list. The first two commands in the File Manager's Edit menu select and unselect files in the File Manager window. When you choose the Edit Select command (or press its equivalent key combination Shift-F7), Quattro Pro selects the highlighted file, displaying it in bold, high-intensity characters. Or, if the highlighted file is already selected, Quattro Pro unselects the file and redisplays the filename in regular, normal-intensity characters. If you choose the Edit All Select command or press its equivalent key combination Alt-F7, Quattro Pro selects all the files shown in the list, displaying the files in bold, high-intensity characters. If files are already selected, the File All Select command unselects all the selected files.

Copying files using the File Manager's Edit menu. Use the Edit Copy and Edit Paste commands to copy a worksheet file from the current directory to another directory or even to another disk. To use the Edit Copy command, select the files you want to copy, and then choose the Edit Copy command. Doing so tells Quattro Pro to store a copy of the selected file or files in what's called the paste buffer, which is a temporary storage area. Change the current directory to indicate where you want the file or files to be copied, and then choose the Edit Paste command. Quattro Pro displays a message at the bottom of the Control Pane that tells you how many files have been copied.

Moving files using the File Manager's Edit menu. When you copy a file, you end up with two identically named copies of a file in two different directories. When you move a file, you change the location of a file from one directory to another. To use the Edit Move command, select the files you want to move, and then choose the Edit Move command. Doing so tells Quattro Pro to store a copy of the selected file or files in the paste buffer. Next, change the directory to indicate where you want the file or files to be moved, and then choose the Edit Paste command. Quattro Pro displays a message at the bottom of the Control Pane to show how many files have been moved.

Erasing a file using the File Manager's Edit menu. To delete a file, use the Edit Erase command. First, select the file or files you want to delete, and then choose the Edit Erase command. Quattro Pro displays the prompt *Are you sure you want to delete this file?* followed by the options Yes and No. To delete the file, choose the

Yes option. To abort the Edit Erase command without deleting the file, choose the No option. Note that although the Edit menu does not list a shortcut key for deleting a file, one does exist; it's the [Delete] key (F9).

Duplicating a file using the File Manager's Edit Duplicate command. The Edit Duplicate command makes a duplicate copy of a selected file in the current directory. First, highlight the file you want to duplicate, and then choose the Edit Duplicate command. The File Manager displays the prompt *File Name* in a box titled Duplicate a File. Enter the filename and file extension you want to use for the new copy of the file and then press the Enter key. Quattro Pro makes a copy of the selected file using the new filename and extension.

Renaming a file using the File Manager's Edit Rename command. The Edit Rename command is equivalent to the DOS Rename command, but you should find Edit Rename easier to use. To change a file's name and extension, first select the file you want to rename. Then, choose the Edit Rename command. The File Manager displays the prompt *File Name*, followed by the current name of the file. Type the new filename and extension, and then press the Enter key. Quattro Pro renames the selected file.

Arranging files using the File Manager's Sort command

The Sort command lists five options for arranging the files in the File List Pane: Name, Timestamp, Extension, Size, and DOS Order. The default sort order setting is Name, which arranges files alphabetically by filename. To use one of the other sort order settings, however, simply choose the Sort command and then pick the sort order you want. If you pick Timestamp, the File Manager arranges files chronologically by the file dates, starting with the oldest file. Extension arranges files alphabetically by file extension, and Size arranges files by size starting with the smallest file. Finally, if you pick DOS Order, the File Manager arranges files in the same alphanumeric order that DOS uses.

Using the File Manager's Tree menu

The File Manager's Tree menu commands let you create a directory tree that shows the directories in the root directory, the subdirectories in each of the directories, the subdirectories in each subdirectory, and so on. To create a directory tree, choose the Tree Open command. Quattro Pro opens a new pane, the Tree Pane, that contains your directory tree. Figure 8-5 shows an example directory tree with the current directory highlighted. If the File Manager window is zoomed, the tree is shown to the right of the file list. If the window is not zoomed, as shown in the figure, the tree is shown below the file list. When you want to remove the directory tree later, choose the Tree Close command.

FIGURE 8-5.
Use the Tree Open command to create a directory tree.

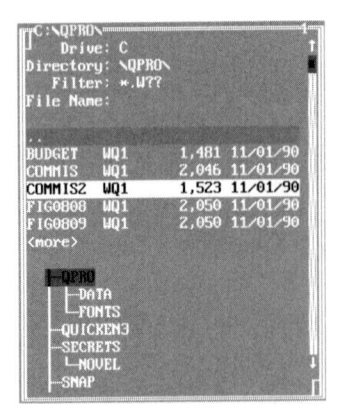

Using the Tree Pane to create a directory tree. The directory tree creates a visual map that shows the organization of your directories and subdirectories. You can also use the directory tree, however, to control the directions for which files are displayed in the File List Pane. To do so, first verify that the Tree Pane is active by checking that one of the directories in the tree is highlighted. If you need to activate the Tree Pane, press the F6 or Tab key to alternately activate the panes of the File Manager window. After the Tree Pane is active, use the Up and Down direction keys or click the mouse to move the cursor so that it marks the directory or subdirectory you want, and then press Enter. As you mark a directory using the cursor, Quattro Pro displays the files in that directory that match the filter.

Resizing the Tree Pane. Quattro Pro uses the bottom half of the File Manager window to display the Tree Pane, as Figure 8-5 shows. If you want to resize the Tree Pane, however, choose the Tree Resize command. Quattro Pro displays the prompt *Relative Tree size (10-100%)*, followed by the current Tree Pane size. The default tree pane size, which is 50, indicates that the Tree Pane occupies 50 percent of the space below the Control Pane in the File Manager window. To change the Tree Pane's portion of the File Manager window, increase the percentage. To decrease the Tree Pane's portion of the File Manager window, decrease the percentage. As the prompt indicates, you can enter a percentage as low as 10 and as high as 100.

Using the File Manager's Print menu commands

The File Manager's Print menu closely resembles the regular menu version. Five of the File Manager's Print commands (Destination, Page Layout, Reset, Adjust Printer, and Quit) are identical to the commands on the regular Print menu. The two commands that are different, Block and Go, are described briefly in the paragraphs that follow.

The Print Block command lets you indicate which information in the File Manager window you want to print. After you choose this command, the File Manager displays a submenu that has three choices: Files, Tree, or Both. If you choose the Files option, the File Manager prints the current file list. If you choose the Tree option, the File Manager prints a copy of the directory tree. If you choose the Both option, the File Manager prints both a list of the files and a copy of the directory tree.

The Print Go command, which you may recognize if you worked with earlier versions of Quattro Pro, simply prints the block you defined.

Using the File Manager's Options menu

The commands on the File Manager version of the Options menu are similar to those on the regular Options menu, with the exception of File List. The Options File List command lets you fit more files into the File List Pane by listing only filenames and extensions instead of filenames, extensions, sizes, and dates. After you choose the Options File List command, Quattro Pro presents a submenu that has two choices: Wide View and Full View. Choose the Wide View option if you want to see only the filenames and extensions, and thereby pack more files in the File List Pane. Choose the Full View option if you want to see all the file information, including the filenames, extensions, sizes, and dates.

Using the Window Pick command

As mentioned earlier in the chapter, the Window Pick command causes Quattro Pro to display a list of the worksheets stacked in memory; you can change the top worksheet in the stack by choosing the Window Pick command, selecting the worksheet you want to see, and pressing the Enter key. The Window Pick command, however, also lists any additional windows, such as the File Manager window. As a result, you can use the Window Pick command to switch between the File Manager window and any other worksheet you have on the screen.

The other commands in the File Manager's version of the Window menu are identical to those in the regular version of the Window menu.

The File Utilities DOS Shell command

Quattro Pro's File Utilities DOS Shell command allows you to exit to DOS without actually quitting Quattro Pro. If you are like most Quattro Pro users, you'll find the File Utilities DOS Shell command an indispensable tool. For instance, have you ever wanted to save a large worksheet on a floppy disk, only to find that you have no formatted disks? If so, you'll want to take advantage of the File Utilities DOS Shell command.

After you choose the File Utilities DOS Shell command, a DOS prompt is displayed on this screen. While you are in DOS, you can choose any DOS command, such as DIR, FORMAT, COPY, or ERASE. You can also move through your disk drive's directories or start another small application program.

When you finish working in DOS, simply type *EXIT*, and then press the Enter key to return to Quattro Pro, where your worksheet looks the same as it did when you left it.

The File Utilities DOS Shell command tells Quattro Pro to start a new copy of DOS in memory in the area above the first copy of DOS and Quattro Pro. If less than about 4000 bytes of memory are available when you choose the File Utilities DOS Shell command, Quattro Pro displays a message telling you it is not able to start DOS.

As mentioned earlier, you can run other programs after you are in DOS, including most of the DOS utilities. Many application programs, however, require more memory than is available after you choose the File Utilities DOS Shell command. In addition, some application programs overwrite the Quattro Pro program code and make it impossible for you to return to Quattro Pro. For these reasons, you should run only DOS utilities and small applications after you choose the File Utilities DOS Shell command. If you try to run large applications in addition to Quattro Pro, unpredictable results might occur. It is always best to save your worksheet before choosing the File Utilities DOS Shell command.

Using the Tools Xtract command

Quattro Pro's Tools Xtract command allows you to save a portion of the current worksheet in a different file. The size of the portion you extract can range from a single cell to the entire worksheet. The Tools Xtract command is especially helpful when you need to break a large worksheet into smaller pieces. It also comes in handy for extracting a block from one worksheet and combining it with another worksheet.

Tools Xtract basics

When you choose the Tools Xtract command, Quattro Pro presents a menu that has two options: Formulas and Values. These options let you tell Quattro Pro how to handle the formulas in the block you want to extract. The Formulas option tells Quattro Pro to save all the formulas in the block you extract. The Values option tells Quattro Pro to save only the current results of the formulas and functions in the extracted block, and not the formulas themselves.

The option you choose from the Tools Extract menu depends on the kinds of entries you've made in the block and what you want to do with them. If you are extracting a block that contains no formulas or functions, it makes no difference which option you choose; both obtain the same result. If the block includes formulas and functions that refer only to cells within the extracted block, you probably want to choose the Formulas option. If the block includes formulas and functions that refer to cells outside the block, choose the Values option.

After you choose the Formulas or Values option, Quattro Pro displays the prompt *Enter xtract file name,* and displays a list of all the worksheet files in the default directory. Choose one of the existing files, or type a new name, exactly as you do when use the File Save As command. Of course, if you choose an existing name, Quattro Pro overwrites the existing file with the extracted data, so you will usually want to specify a new name.

Next, Quattro Pro displays the prompt *Enter xtract block* in the input line, followed by the address of the current cell. Specify the block you want to extract, and then press the Enter key. Quattro Pro creates the extracted file and stores your extracted information in that file.

The Formulas option

The Tools Xtract command's Formulas option tells Quattro Pro to save the formulas in the extracted block to the specified file. This option reproduces the formulas in the new file. If the extracted block contains formulas and functions that refer to cells outside the extracted block, however, choosing the Formulas option can cause some problems because the formula refers to cells in a different worksheet.

An example of using the Formulas option

The worksheet shown in Figure 8-6 computes the sales commissions earned by two people, Mike Cowherd and Alice Farnsley. The cells in column F contain formulas that compute a portion of the commission for the two salespeople. Suppose you want to extract block A3..F9, which contains the commission computation for Mike Cowherd, and copy it into a separate worksheet called COMMIS.WQ1. Because you want to maintain this worksheet's ability to recalculate the commissions, you must save the formulas in the extracted block.

To begin, choose the Tools Xtract command. Because you want Quattro Pro to extract the formulas in column F, and not only the current values of those formulas, choose the Formulas option from the menu. Next, when Quattro Pro asks you to supply a name for the extracted file, type the new name *COMMIS* and then press the Enter key. When Quattro Pro prompts you for the extracted block, specify block A3..F9. Press the Enter key to lock in this block. Quattro Pro copies the formulas from cells A3..F9 to the file COMMIS.WQ1. Now, suppose you want to retrieve the file COMMIS. To do so, choose the File Retrieve command, specify

FIGURE 8-6.
Use this worksheet to demonstrate Quattro Pro's Tools Xtract command.

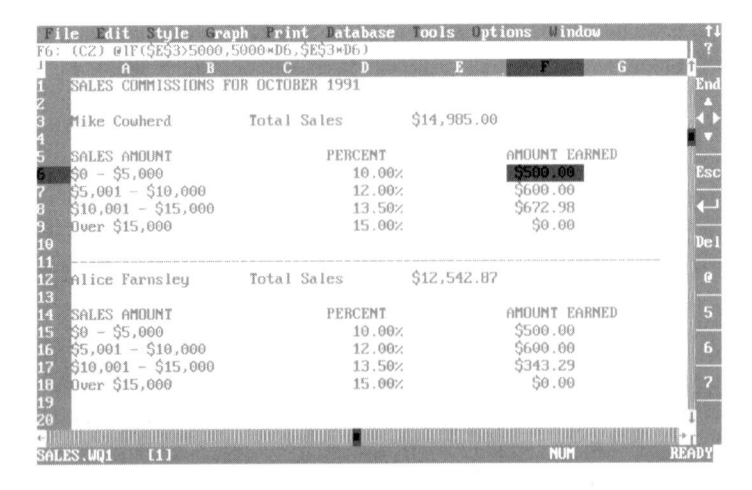

FIGURE 8-7.
When Quattro Pro extracts part of a worksheet, the information appears in the upper-left corner of the new worksheet.

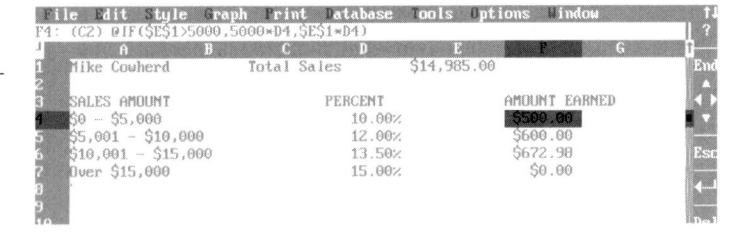

the file COMMIS.WQ1, and press the Enter key. Figure 8-7 shows the resulting worksheet.

Notice that the extracted block, which occupied cells A3..F9 in the original worksheet, now appears in the upper-left corner of the new worksheet file, shown in Figure 8-7. For instance, the label 'Mike Cowherd, which was in cell A3, appears in cell A1 of the new worksheet. Whenever you extract a block, it begins in the upper-left corner of the new worksheet.

Because you chose the Formulas option, Quattro Pro saved the formulas from the original worksheet as formulas in the new file. Quattro Pro adjusts these formulas to reflect their new positions in the extracted file. For example, in the original worksheet, cell F6 contains the following formula:

F6: @IF($E$3>5000,5000*D6,$E$3*D6)

In the extracted file, the formula appears in cell F4 and reads as follows:

F4: @IF($E$1>5000,5000*D4,$E$1*D4)

As you can see, both formulas return the same result. Whenever you extract a block that includes formulas and functions, Quattro Pro adjusts those formulas and functions to account for their new positions in the extracted file.

As you would expect, the entries in the worksheet shown in Figure 8-6 have the same format and alignment as do the entries in the extracted block shown in Figure 8-7. When you extract a block from a worksheet, the cells in the extracted worksheet retain the same format and alignment they had in the original worksheet.

When the Formulas option does not work

In the preceding example, you chose the Formulas option. Because the extracted block (A3..F9) contains all the cells that are referenced by the formulas in cells F6 through F9, choosing the Formulas option did not cause any problems. Had the extracted block included formulas that referred to cells outside the block, however, this method would not have worked as well. First of all, because some of the values on which the formulas depend are not included in the extracted block, the values of these formulas would be changed. In addition, because Quattro Pro adjusts the cell references in the formulas in the extracted block, some of the formulas might look different after they're placed in the extracted file.

The Values option

The Values option tells Quattro Pro to save only the current values of the formulas in the extracted block in the new file. Use this option when you need only the values and not the formulas, or when the extracted block includes formulas that refer to cells outside the block. For example, suppose that you want to use the Values option to extract block F6..F9 from the worksheet shown in Figure 8-6. To do so, choose the Tools Xtract Values command, type the name COMMIS2 as the extracted file, define block F6..F9, and then press the Enter key. Next, choose the File Retrieve command and retrieve the file COMMIS2.WQ1. Figure 8-8 shows the result.

As you can see in Figure 8-8, the values in block A1..A4 are identical to those in block F6..F9 in Figure 8-6. When extracting block F6..F9 from the original worksheet, however, Quattro Pro saved only the current values of the formulas in that block, and not the formulas themselves. As you can see, cell A1 in Figure 8-8 contains the literal value 500.

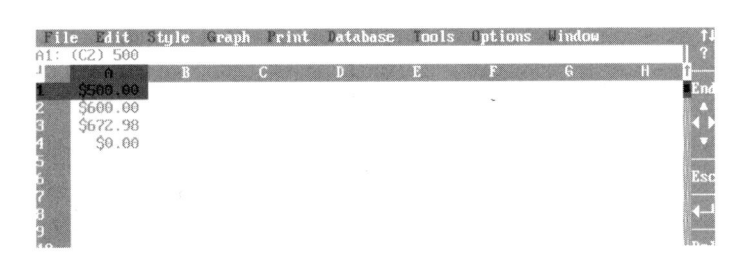

FIGURE 8-8.
When you choose the Tools Extract Values command, Quattro Pro saves only the current values of the worksheet formulas, and not the formulas.

A closer look at using the Values option

Quattro Pro does not recalculate the worksheet before saving the contents of the extracted block in the extracted file. Quattro Pro saves only the current results of the formulas in the extracted block (the results you currently see on your screen). As a result, you should recalculate the worksheet to be sure that your values are current before you choose the Tools Xtract Values command. Also, remember that no links exist between the entries in the extracted file and the entries in the original worksheet. Changing the values in the original worksheet does not affect the values in the extracted file. If you want to update the values in the extracted file, use the Tools Xtract Values command again.

Combining worksheets

Occasionally, you might need to add some or all of the information from another worksheet to your current worksheet. You can do so with the Tools Combine command. Like the Retrieve command, the Tools Combine command tells Quattro Pro to retrieve the contents of a worksheet file. Unlike File Retrieve, however, Tools Combine does not remove the current worksheet from memory before opening the new file. Instead, it combines the contents of the file you select with the current worksheet. Consequently, you can use the Tools Combine command to consolidate information from two or more worksheets into a single summary worksheet or to transfer data from one worksheet to another. You can use the Tools Combine command to produce several results, as described in the following sections.

Basics of combining worksheets

When you choose the Tools Combine command, Quattro Pro presents a menu that has three options: Copy, Add, and Subtract. These options determine how Quattro Pro combines the entries from a worksheet file with the current worksheet. The Copy option tells Quattro Pro to replace entries in the current worksheet with entries from the file you select. The Add and Subtract options tell Quattro Pro to either add or subtract the new values from the values in the current worksheet. If a value from the file you are combining falls on top of a value in the worksheet, Quattro Pro adds or subtracts those two values. Use the Add and Subtract options when you want to consolidate information from two or more similar worksheets into a single worksheet.

After you choose an option from the Tools Combine menu, Quattro Pro presents a menu that has two options: File and Block. Choosing the File option tells Quattro Pro to combine all of the values from the worksheet file with the current worksheet. Choosing the Block option tells Quattro Pro to combine only the entries from a block of the worksheet file that you specify. The block size can range from a single cell to the entire worksheet. If you choose the Block option, Quattro Pro prompts you for the coordinates or name of the block you want to add to the current worksheet. After you specify the block, press the Enter key.

After you choose either the File or Block option, Quattro Pro displays the prompt *Enter name of file to combine,* along with a list of all the worksheet files in the current directory. Choose the file you want to combine using the same techniques you use to select a filename when you choose the File Retrieve or File Open command. Quattro Pro then combines the contents of that file with the current worksheet.

It is important to position the cell selector properly before you choose the Tools Combine command. Quattro Pro always begins inserting the contents of the file at the position of the cell selector. In other words, the upper-left cell of the worksheet file or selected block writes over the cell that contains the cell selector (the active cell). The other cells in the worksheet file write over the cells below and to the right of the active cell.

Because the Tools Combine command can alter data in the current worksheet, you should always save the current worksheet before you choose the Tools Combine command. If you do so, you can always retrieve a clean copy of your original worksheet if you run into trouble.

The Copy option

When you simply want to copy information from one worksheet to another, use Quattro Pro's Tools Combine Copy command. This command allows you to copy the contents of a worksheet or selected block into the current worksheet without altering the contents of the copied worksheet.

An example of copying worksheet information

Consider the worksheets in Figures 8-9 and 8-10, which contain two sets of test scores for a small group of students. The first worksheet is saved in a file named TEST1 and the second is in a file named TEST2. Suppose you want to combine TEST1 and TEST2 into a single worksheet.

To begin, retrieve the file TEST1 and move the cell selector to A10, the upper-left cell of the block where you want the combined worksheet to appear. Next, choose the Tools Combine Copy command. Because you want to combine the entire contents of TEST2 with TEST1, choose File from the menu. Then, choose the filename TEST2 from Quattro Pro's list of worksheet files, and press the Enter key. Quattro Pro reads the file from the disk and copies its contents into the current worksheet. Figure 8-11 shows the resulting worksheet.

FIGURE 8-9.
This is the first worksheet you can use to demonstrate the Tools Combine command.

```
File Edit Style Graph Print Database Tools Options Window
A1: 'TEST SCORES FOR EXAM #1
         A          B       C      D
 1  TEST SCORES FOR EXAM #1
 2  ===================================================
 3   Name     Part 1  Part 2   Total
 4   Burt       49      50      99
 5   John       48      47      95
 6   Bobbi      45      43      88
 7   Mark       40      49      89
 8   Nancy      40      46      86
 9
```

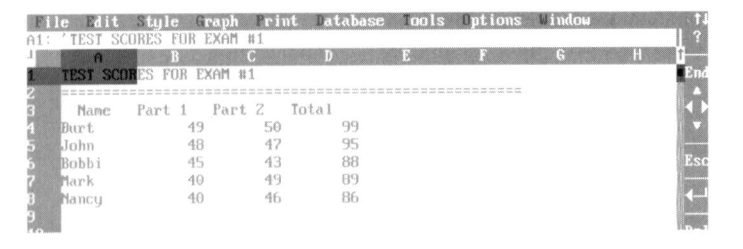

FIGURE 8-10.
This is the second worksheet you can use to demonstrate the Tools Combine command.

```
File Edit Style Graph Print Database Tools Options Window
A1: 'TEST SCORES FOR EXAM #2
         A          B       C      D
 1  TEST SCORES FOR EXAM #2
 2  ===================================================
 3   Name     Part 1  Part 2   Total
 4   Burt       45      47      92
 5   John       47      48      95
 6   Bobbi      48      43      91
 7   Mark       49      50      99
 8   Nancy      38      41      79
 9
```

A closer look at copying from one worksheet to another

The cell entries you combined in the preceding example retained their formats and alignment. Whenever you combine worksheets using the Tools Combine Copy command, Quattro Pro combines the formats and the label prefixes of the cells in the worksheet file along with the entries in those cells. Quattro Pro also copies the formulas you specify into the current worksheet and adjusts the cell references in those formulas to account for their new positions in the worksheet.

In this example, you copied the contents of the worksheet file into a blank area of the current worksheet. If the area of the worksheet had contained entries, they would have been replaced by the entries you copied. Consequently, be sure that plenty of space is available below and to the right of the cell selector before you choose the Tools Combine Copy command. You'll find one exception to this rule: Blank cells do not overwrite existing cell entries. In other words, when a blank cell from the worksheet file is combined with a cell in the current worksheet, the cell retains its entry.

You may want to save your combined worksheet under a new name, such as TEST1&2, so that you do not overwrite the original files TEST1 and TEST2.

The Add and Subtract options

Quattro Pro's Tools Combine Add and Tools Combine Subtract commands let you consolidate and unconsolidate information in different worksheets. The Add option tells Quattro Pro to add values from the worksheet file you specify to the corresponding values in the current worksheet. Similarly, the Subtract option tells Quattro Pro to subtract values in the worksheet file you specify from the corresponding values in the current worksheet.

FIGURE 8-11.
The Copy option lets you transfer information from one worksheet to another.

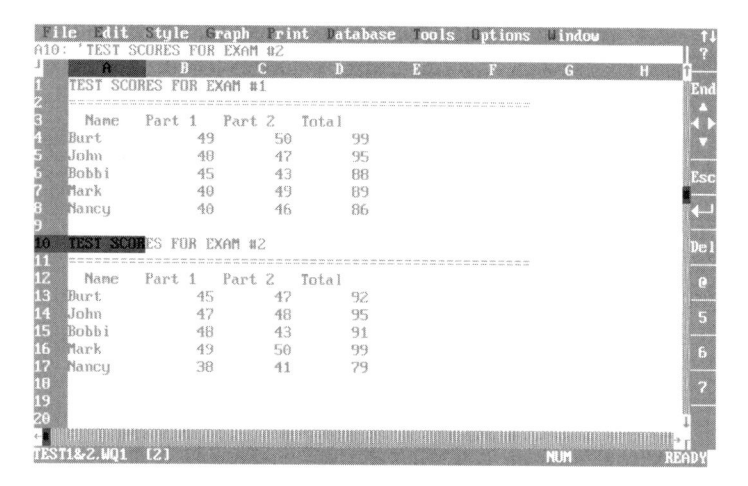

The Add option

Quattro Pro's Tools Combine Add command adds values in one worksheet to the values in the corresponding cells of another worksheet. Use this option to consolidate values in two or more worksheets. Although the Tools Combine Add command is one of Quattro Pro's most helpful tools, it has one significant limitation: The block or entire worksheet you plan to add must have the same layout as the current worksheet. Unless you design the layout of the worksheets you plan to combine carefully, this limitation can present problems.

An example of using the Add option. The worksheets in Figures 8-12 and 8-13 show the travel expenses for two salespeople. In each of these worksheets, cells B4 through B7 contain the expense information for a particular category, and cell B9 contains the function @SUM(B4..B7), which computes the total for these expenses. These worksheets are saved with the names BURT and NATALIE.

Now, suppose you want to total the travel expenses for these two salespeople in a single worksheet. First, you need to create a form worksheet like the one shown in Figure 8-14, which has the same layout as the individual worksheets shown in Figures 8-12 and 8-13 but contains no values. Use this worksheet to consolidate the other two worksheets. Although cell B9 in the form worksheet contains the function @SUM(B4..B7), this formula presently returns the value 0 because cells B4 through B7 are blank. You could combine NATALIE directly with BURT; however, to protect the data in your original worksheet it is often best to work with a separate form worksheet.

To begin the consolidation, move the cell selector to cell A1 in the form worksheet shown in Figure 8-14, and then choose the File Tools Combine Add command. Next, choose the File option, select the file BURT.WQ1 from Quattro Pro's list, and then press the Enter key. The resulting worksheet is shown in Figure 8-15.

FIGURE 8-12.
This worksheet was saved in the file BURT.

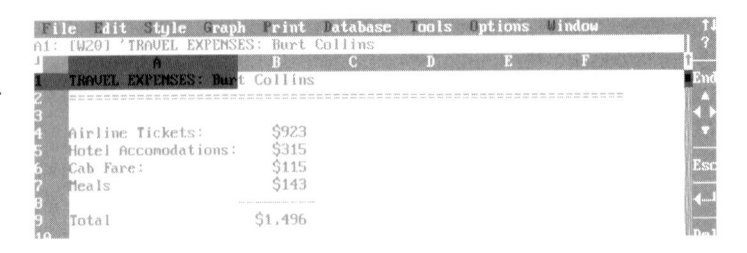

FIGURE 8-13.
This worksheet was saved in the file NATALIE.

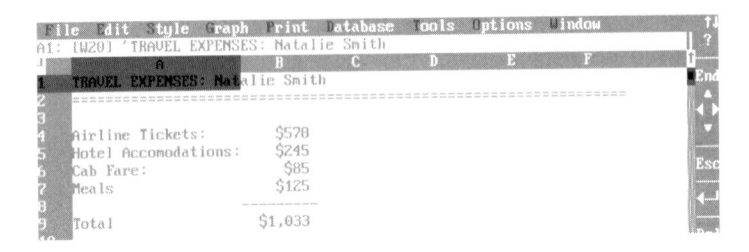

FIGURE 8-14.
Use this form worksheet to combine the BURT and NATALIE worksheets.

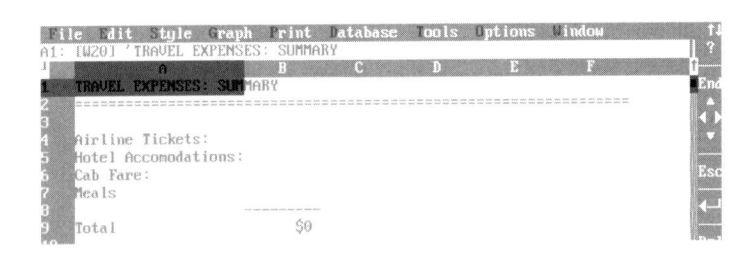

Notice that the values from block B4..B7 in the BURT file have been combined with the block B4..B7 in the form worksheet. Next, choose the Tools Combine Add File command again, select the file NATALIE.WQ1, and press the Enter key. Figure 8-16 shows the result.

When you combined the worksheet NATALIE with the form worksheet, Quattro Pro added the values in the block B4..B7 of the worksheet NATALIE to the values in the block B4..B7 in the form worksheet. The values in cells B4..B7 in Figure 8-16 contain the sums of the corresponding cells in the worksheets BURT and NATALIE. If you point to one of the cells in block B4..B7 in the form worksheet, you see that it contains a pure literal value; the result of adding the values from the two worksheets. For example, cell B4 in Figure 8-16 contains the value $1,501 ($923+$578).

How the Add option treats labels. Unlike the Tools Combine command's Copy option, the Add option does not combine the labels from the worksheet file with those of the current worksheet. For example, notice that the label in cell A1 of the BURT and NATALIE worksheets did not replace the label in cell A1 of the form worksheet.

FIGURE 8-15.
This worksheet shows the values from the BURT file combined with the form worksheet.

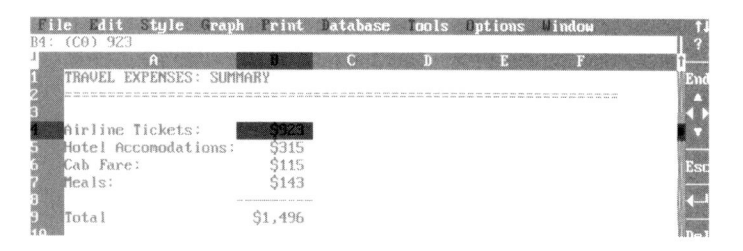

FIGURE 8-16.
This worksheet shows the combined values from the BURT and NATALIE files.

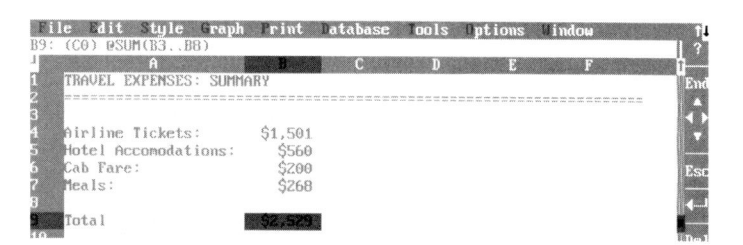

How the Add option treats formulas. Quattro Pro treats a formula in the worksheet file differently depending on what is in the corresponding cell of the current worksheet. If the corresponding cell is blank, only the results of the formula (a pure value or a pure label) are copied to the cell. If the corresponding cell contains a label, the formula does not replace the label. If the corresponding cell contains a value, Quattro Pro adds the result of the formula to the value in the worksheet. Finally, if the corresponding cell also contains a formula, the formula from the file does not replace the formula in the worksheet.

Unwanted combinations. If you use the Add option frequently, you may run into situations in which Quattro Pro adds numbers inappropriately. This problem often occurs when the worksheets you are combining contain serial date values or numbers that are supposed to remain constant. To avoid this problem, you can combine only selected blocks, which excludes the problem cells from the combination. Alternatively, you can enter dates or numbers that you do not want to be affected by the combination as labels instead of as values. Of course, if you enter dates and times as labels instead of as values, you cannot perform date and time arithmetic on them.

The Subtract option

The Subtract option lets you subtract the values in the worksheet file you specify from the corresponding values in the current worksheet. In every other respect, the Subtract option and the Add option are identical. All the rules discussed in the preceding section also apply to the Subtract option.

To see how the Subtract option works, suppose that after combining the BURT and NATALIE worksheets as shown in Figure 8-16, you discover an error in the

NATALIE worksheet. To correct the mistake, you can subtract the NATALIE worksheet from the form worksheet, fix the error in NATALIE, and then add it back to the form worksheet. To subtract the NATALIE worksheet from the consolidated worksheet shown in Figure 8-16, press the Home key to move the cell selector to cell A1, and choose the Tools Combine Subtract File command. When Quattro Pro prompts you for the name of the file you want to combine, choose NATALIE .WQ1, then press the Enter key. Quattro Pro subtracts the NATALIE values from the values in the form worksheet. The form worksheet now has only the data from BURT in it, as shown in Figure 8-15.

After you subtract the NATALIE worksheet from the form worksheet, you can retrieve the NATALIE file, make the necessary corrections, and use the File Tools Combine Add File command to add it back to the form worksheet.

Combining a block

Combining a block from a worksheet file is similar to combining the entire worksheet. Consequently, all the rules and cautions in the previous sections apply to blocks as well as to entire worksheets. To combine a block, choose the Tools Combine Add Block command. When Quattro Pro displays the prompt *Enter block name or coordinates,* type the name or cell coordinates of the block you want to combine, and then press the Enter key. Next, Quattro Pro prompts you for the name of the worksheet file that contains the specified block.

The method Quattro Pro uses to combine the block depends on whether you choose the Copy, Add, or Subtract option. If you choose the Copy option, Quattro Pro copies the block into the current worksheet at the position of the cell selector. If you choose the Add or Subtract option, Quattro Pro adds or subtracts the values in the indicated block of the worksheet file to (or from) the values in the current worksheet when combining a block.

A closer look at combining a block. If you use the Block option, you must remember the correct cell coordinates or name of the block you plan to combine. Because it's difficult to remember all of the block coordinates or names in a worksheet, write down the coordinates or names of the blocks. If you have two worksheets that you often combine, you might want to write a macro that performs the operation for you. Chapters 12 and 13 discuss macros.

Linking spreadsheets using formulas

The Tools Xtract and Tools Combine commands let you move data between worksheets by choosing commands. You can also, however, move data between worksheets continuously using formulas called spreadsheet links. A spreadsheet link creates a permanent connection between different worksheets. To create a spreadsheet link, you simply identify the spreadsheet and the cell or block from which you want to retrieve information.

Some powerful arguments exist for using spreadsheet links, particularly in place of the Tools Xtract and Tools Combine commands. Because a spreadsheet link is a formula, you do not need to choose a command to pass data; you only need to recalculate the worksheet. Spreadsheet links can also simplify the design of a worksheet or group of worksheets because it's often easier to work with several small worksheets than with one large worksheet. Finally, working with several worksheets allows you to divide work between several people, as well as reduce the risk of running out of memory.

Linking basics

All spreadsheet link formulas use the same basic format: +[filename]block. You can use the +[filename]block formula anywhere you normally use a cell reference or block reference.

Referencing a single cell in a spreadsheet link formula

Suppose, for example, that you want to retrieve the contents of cell A1 from the worksheet named SALES.WQ1, which is stored in the default directory, and place the contents in cell C25 of the current worksheet called PLAN92.WQ1. To do so, you simply move the cell selector to cell C25 in the PLAN92.WQ1 worksheet, and type the following:

+[SALES]A1

Press the Enter key, and Quattro Pro retrieves the contents from cell A1 of the SALES.WQ1 worksheet and places it in cell C25 of PLAN92.WQ1. For example, if cell A1 in SALES.WQ1 contains the value 500, the formula +[SALES]A1 returns the value 500. Or, if cell A1 of SALES.WQ1 contains the label 'Acapulco, the formula +[SALES]A1 returns the string "Acapulco".

Referencing a block in a spreadsheet link formula

Here's another example, this time referencing a block: Suppose you want to calculate the sum of the cells A1..A5 in the SALES.WQ1 worksheet and place the sum in cell C25 of the PLAN92.WQ1 worksheet. To do so, move the cell selector to cell C25 in the PLAN92.WQ1 worksheet and type the following:

@SUM([SALES]A1..A5)

Quattro Pro sums the values in cells A1..A5 of the SALES.WQ1 worksheet and displays the result in cell C25 of PLAN92.WQ1.

Specifying file extensions in a spreadsheet link formula

As shown in the preceding examples, you do not need to specify the file extension when specifying a filename if the worksheets you're linking use the same file extension. But if the worksheets have different file extensions, you need to include them. For example, if the two files were named SALES.WKQ and PLAN92.WQ1, the formulas shown above would have to be changed as follows:

+[SALES.WKQ]A1

@SUM([SALES.WKQ]A1..A5)

Specifying directories

If the file you want to specify is not in the default directory or in the stack of worksheets currently stored in memory, you need to include the drive letter and path so that Quattro Pro can locate the file. For example, if the file SALES.WQ1 is located in the C:\DATA directory, the formulas must be changed as follows:

+[C:\DATA\SALES]A1

@SUM([C:\DATA\SALES]A1..A5)

Using block names

You can use block names instead of cell or block references in spreadsheet link formulas. If cell A1 in the SALES worksheet is named BUDGET90 and block A1..A5 is named TOTSALES, you can use the formulas shown below:

+[SALES]BUDGET90

@SUM([SALES]TOTSALES)

Linking stacked worksheets

Quattro Pro offers a number of features that let you easily create links between worksheets that are stacked in memory. You can use the Edit Move command to create a link, the Edit Copy command to copy a link, and the wild card characters * and ? to create links to multiple worksheets stacked in memory.

Creating links by moving cells

When you move a cell or block to another worksheet stack in memory, Quattro Pro automatically creates link formulas whenever the cells you are moving reference cells outside the block. For example, if you move the formula @AVG(C4..L4) from the SALES.WQ1 worksheet to the PLAN92.WQ1 worksheet, Quattro Pro adjusts the new formula in PLAN92.WQ1 to @AVG([SALES]C4..L4). Quattro Pro creates a link formula to preserve the meaning the formula had in the original worksheet. As always, the Move command preserves any cell references in the block you move. In this case, to preserve the references, Quattro Pro had to create a link formula.

To move the cell or block between worksheets, use the standard move procedure. The only difference is that you have to specify the name of the worksheet you want to move as part of the destination. For example, to move a cell from the current worksheet to cell A5 of the sales worksheet, type the destination shown below:

   [SALES]A5

Because Edit Move creates link formulas, it provides a quick way to break a large worksheet into several smaller, linked worksheets.

Using wildcards in link formulas

To create spreadsheet link formulas that reference one or more worksheets stacked in memory, it is often convenient to use the wildcard characters ? and * as part of the worksheet name. A * character represents any group of characters in a filename, and a ? character represents any single character in a filename. By using these characters in the filename argument, you can refer to one or more of the worksheets in the stack.

Using the * character. Suppose, for example, that the current worksheet in the stack is named 92PLAN.WQ1, and the other worksheets in the stack are named 92SALES.WQ1, 92EXPNS.WQ1, and COGS.WQ1. If you type the following spreadsheet link formula into a cell in the current worksheet, Quattro Pro assumes that the [*] filename indicates you want the block A1..A12 summed from each of the other worksheets in the stack:

   @SUM([*]A1..A12)

After you press the Enter key, Quattro Pro changes your entry to the following:

   @SUM([92SALES]A1..A12,[92EXPNS]A1..A12,[COGS]A1..A12)

As another example, if you use the following spreadsheet link formula in a cell in the current worksheet:

   @SUM([92*]A1..A12)

Quattro Pro assumes that the 92* filename indicates you want block A1..A12 summed from each of the worksheets in the stack that start with "92".

After you press the Enter key, Quattro Pro changes your entry to the following:

@SUM([92SALES]A1..A12,[92EXPNS]A1..A12)

Using the ? character. The ? wildcard character works similarly to the * character, except that the ? character stands in for a single character. Suppose, for example, that the current worksheet is named PLAN.WQ1, and the other worksheets in the stack are EXPENSE1.WQ1, EXPENSE2.WQ1, and COGS.WQ1. Now suppose you type the following spreadsheet link formula in a cell in the PLAN.WQ1 worksheet:

@SUM([EXPENSE?]A1..A12)

Quattro Pro assumes that the link formula [EXPENSE?] A1..A12 means that you want block A1..A12 summed from each of the other worksheets in the stack that start with EXPENSE and have any one additional character.

After you press the Enter key, Quattro Pro changes your entry to the following:

@SUM([EXPENSE1]A1..A12,[EXPENSE2]A1..A12)

As another example, consider the following spreadsheet link formula in a cell in the PLAN.WQ1 worksheet:

@SUM([????]A1..A12)

Quattro Pro assumes that the link formula [????]A1..A12 means that you want block A1..A12 summed from each of the worksheets in the stack that have four-character filenames.

After you press the Enter key, Quattro Pro changes your entry to the following:

@SUM([COGS]A1..A12)

Copying spreadsheet link formulas

You cannot create any link formulas by copying a cell or block to another worksheet. However, you can copy existing link formulas with the Edit Copy command. You copy spreadsheet link formulas in the same way as you copy any other cells. The only difference is that when Quattro Pro prompts you for the destination, you must type the name of the worksheet as well as the cell reference. For example, to copy a cell from the current worksheet to cell A5 of the SALES worksheet, type the destination shown below:

[SALES]A5

As usual, with the Copy command, if the cell or block reference is relative, Quattro Pro adjusts the formula when you copy. If the cell or block reference is absolute, Quattro Pro does not adjust the formula when you copy. Finally, if the cell or block reference is mixed, Quattro Pro adjusts the relative portion of the reference.

Retrieving worksheets that have spreadsheet link formulas

A worksheet that is referenced by the current worksheet is called a supporting worksheet. When you retrieve or open a worksheet that has spreadsheet link formulas, Quattro Pro recognizes that the retrieved worksheet relates to other worksheets, and presents a menu listing three choices: Load Supporting, Update Refs, and None. If you choose Load Supporting, Quattro Pro loads the worksheet and opens all of the supporting worksheets. If you select the Update Refs option, Quattro Pro retrieves the necessary values from the supporting worksheets without opening them. For example, if a link formula is +[SALES]A1, the Update Refs option tells Quattro Pro to retrieve the value of cell A1 in the SALES worksheet without actually opening the worksheet. Finally, if you choose the None option, Quattro Pro neither opens the supporting worksheets nor retrieves the necessary values from the supporting worksheets. Because Quattro Pro does not know what value to use for the linked cell or block when you choose the None option, it displays NA in the cells with the link formula and in every cell that references the link formula.

Using the Tools Update Links command

The Tools Update Links command lets you update links and open supporting worksheets after a worksheet is open. When you choose this command, Quattro Pro presents a menu that lists four options: Open, Refresh, Change, and Delete. The Open option lets you open any unopened supporting worksheets (ones that are referenced in spreadsheet link formulas). The Refresh option lets you update the spreadsheet link formulas without opening any supporting worksheets. The Change option lets you substitute one filename for another in all of a worksheet's spreadsheet link formulas. The Delete option erases all references to a specific filename in the current worksheet.

Using the Tools Update Links Open command

If you do not open all of the supporting worksheets when you retrieve or open a worksheet that contains spreadsheet link formulas, you can use the Tools Update Link Open command to do so later. After you choose this command, Quattro Pro displays the prompt *Pick one or more worksheets*, followed by a list of unopened supporting worksheets. Figure 8-17 shows this prompt and list. To open a listed worksheet file, use the direction keys to highlight the filename, and press Shift-F7 to select it. Quattro Pro marks each file you select with a check. To unselect a marked file, press Shift-F7 again. Or, to unselect every marked file in the list, press Alt-F7. After each of the files you want to open is marked, press the Enter key. Quattro Pro opens the marked files and places them on the stack of worksheets stored in memory.

FIGURE 8-17.
The Tools Update Links Open command displays this list.

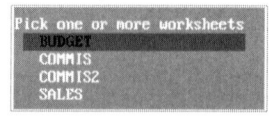

```
Pick one or more worksheets
    BUDGET
    COMMIS
    COMMIS2
    SALES
```

Using the Tools Update Links Refresh command

As mentioned earlier, rather than opening supporting worksheets, Quattro Pro gives you the option of retrieving only the needed values from the supporting worksheets. If the supporting worksheets have changed since you originally retrieved the values, you can use the Tools Update Links Refresh command to retrieve the values again. You can also use this command to retrieve values if you did not retrieve values when you initially opened the worksheet that has the spreadsheet link formulas.

After you choose the Tools Update Links Refresh command, Quattro Pro displays the prompt *Pick one or more worksheets*, followed by a list of unopened worksheet files referenced in link formulas. The prompt and list are the same as the ones Quattro Pro displays when you choose the Tools Update Links Open command. To indicate that you want to update the values from a listed worksheet, use the direction keys to highlight the worksheet file and press Shift-F7 to select it. Quattro Pro marks each file you select with a check. To unselect a marked worksheet, press Shift-F7 again. Or, to unselect all the marked worksheets in the list, press Alt-F7. After each of the files you want to update is marked, press the Enter key. Quattro Pro then retrieves the linked cell or block values from each of the linked files.

Using the Tools Update Links Change command

Because spreadsheet link formulas use filenames, you must update the spreadsheet link formulas if you change a filename. Quattro Pro provides a handy tool for making just these sorts of changes: the Tools Update Links Change command.

Suppose, for example, that you want to change all of the spreadsheet link formula references in a worksheet from SALES.WQ1 to NEWSALES.WQ1, and that both files are in the default directory C:\QPRO. To do so, choose the Tools Update Links Change command. Quattro Pro displays the prompt *Pick a worksheet*, followed by a list of the worksheet files referenced in the current worksheet. Use the direction keys to highlight the worksheet file you want change (for this example, SALES.WQ1) and press the Enter key. Next, Quattro Pro displays the prompt *Change C:\QPRO\SALES.WQ1 to*, followed by the pathname and address *C:\QPRO\SALES.WQ1*. Type the word *NEWSALES* and press the Enter key. Quattro Pro then replaces every occurrence of SALES with NEWSALES.

You do not need to type the complete pathname or the file extension because the new file is in the default directory and the new file's extension is the default (.WQ1). If the new filename is not in the default directory, you need to type the drive letter and pathname. Similarly, if the file extension is an extension other than the default file extension, you also need to type it.

Using the Tools Update Links Delete command

At some point, you may also need to remove spreadsheet links. As a worksheet evolves, for instance, you might find that spreadsheet link formulas become unnecessary, or that they add unnecessary complexity to your worksheet. The Tools Update Links Delete command lets you remove spreadsheet links easily and quickly.

After you choose the Tools Update Links Delete command, Quattro Pro displays the prompt *Pick one or more worksheets*, followed by a list of the worksheet files used in spreadsheet link formulas in the open worksheet files. This prompt and list are the same as the ones Quattro Pro displays when you choose the other Tools Update Links options. Use the direction keys to highlight a worksheet file whose links you want to delete, and press Shift-F7 to select it. Quattro Pro marks each file you select with a check. To unselect a marked worksheet, highlight the worksheet name and press Shift-F7 again. Or, to unselect all the marked worksheets on the list, press Alt-F7. After the worksheets you want to remove from spreadsheet link formulas are marked, press the Enter key. Quattro Pro then displays the prompt *Delete specified links?* followed by two options, Yes and No. To abort the Tools Update Links Delete command, choose the No option. To delete the spreadsheet links to the specified files, choose the Yes option. If you choose Yes, Quattro Pro changes the values of all the cells that reference the worksheets you chose to ERR.

A closer look at spreadsheet links

Despite the obvious benefits spreadsheet links provide, they also present some problems. Be sure to consider these problems before incorporating spreadsheet link formulas into your worksheets.

As mentioned, every time you rename a file you must use the Tools Update Links Change command to modify each of the spreadsheet link formulas for the new filename. This requirement can be time consuming. What's more, the spreadsheet link formulas themselves are longer and more complex than other formulas. For every linked cell or linked block reference, you also have a filename and possibly a pathname and file extension. Using these longer and more complex formulas makes spreadsheet auditing and error-checking more difficult.

Finally, the fewer files you have, the easier they are to manage. For example, imagine the logistical challenge of sharing 10 budgeting worksheet files among four accountants. Unfortunately, by using spreadsheet link formulas, you end up creating and, therefore managing, more files.

9

Working with Windows

Quattro Pro uses windows to display worksheets on your screen. When you stack worksheets in memory, you're actually stacking windows through which you view the worksheets. All this might seem a bit esoteric, but Quattro Pro provides a series of special commands and techniques that make working with these windows easy. The pages that follow describe how to use each of these features.

Freezing labels in view

If you are like most Quattro Pro users, you usually place labels in the first few rows and columns of a worksheet to identify the contents of each cell in the worksheet. For example, rows 1 through 4 and column A in the worksheet shown in Figure 9-1 contain labels that identify the contents of that worksheet. As long as the labels in the first few rows and columns are in view, you'll be able to tell at a glance what each entry in your worksheet represents. When you move the cell selector away from the upper-left corner of the worksheet, however, the labels in the first few rows and columns scroll off the screen, making it difficult, if not impossible, to figure out what the entries on the screen represent.

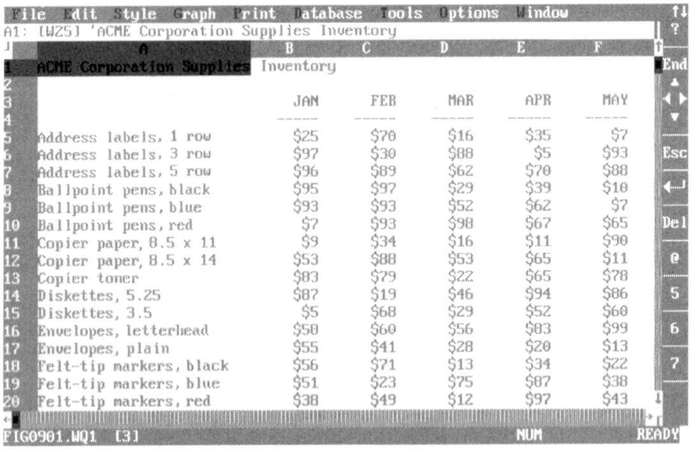

FIGURE 9-1.
You can see the labels in rows 1 through 4 and in column A when you view the upper-left portion of the worksheet.

Fortunately, Quattro Pro provides a command called Window Options Locked Titles that solves this problem. The Window Options Locked Titles command allows you to "freeze" a few rows or columns, or both, on your screen. When you use this command, the labels in those rows and columns always remain in view.

After you choose the Window Options Locked Titles command, Quattro Pro presents a menu that has four options: Horizontal, Vertical, Both, and Clear. The option you choose determines which portion of the worksheet Quattro Pro freezes on the screen. If you choose the Horizontal option, Quattro Pro freezes the rows you specify. If you choose the Vertical option, Quattro Pro freezes the columns you specify. The Both option lets you freeze both rows and columns at one time. The Clear option resets any rows or columns you have frozen previously.

The position of the cell selector determines which rows and columns Quattro Pro freezes on the screen. Consequently, you must move the cell selector to a position that defines the rows or columns, or both, that you want to freeze before you choose the Window Options Locked Titles command. If you choose the Vertical option, Quattro Pro freezes the columns to the left of the column that contains the cell selector. For instance, if the cell selector is in cell D5 when you choose the Window Options Locked Titles command and then the Vertical option, Quattro Pro freezes columns A, B, and C. Likewise, if you choose the Horizontal option, Quattro Pro freezes the rows above the row that contains the cell selector. If you choose the Both option, Quattro Pro freezes both the columns to the left of the cell selector and the rows above it.

An example of freezing labels in view

Suppose you want to freeze rows 1 through 4 and column A in the worksheet shown in Figure 9-1. To begin, press the Home key to move the cell selector to cell

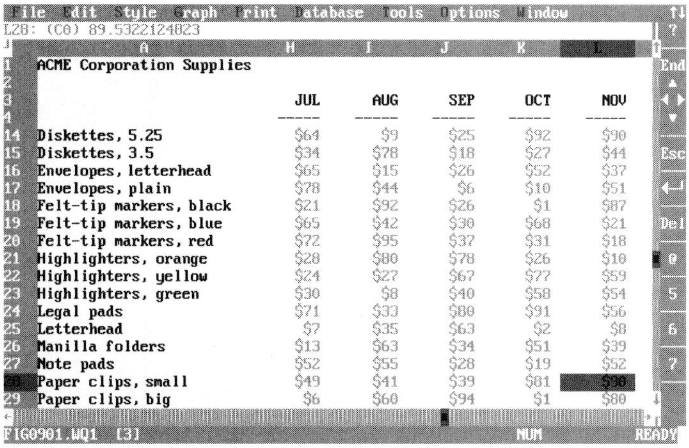

FIGURE 9-2.
The Window Options Locked Titles command freezes your title rows and columns on the screen. In this worksheet rows 1 through 4 and column A are frozen.

A1. Next, move the cell selector to cell B5, which identifies the rows (1 through 4) and the column (A) that you want to freeze. Choose the Window Options Locked Titles command, and choose the Both option. Rows 1 through 4 and column A are now locked on the screen. (If you have a color monitor, the cells in the frozen rows and columns change color.)

After you freeze rows and columns on the screen, those rows and columns are constantly in view. For example, if you move the cell selector in the example worksheet to cell L28, your screen looks like the one shown in Figure 9-2. Notice that the row numbers at the left edge of the screen now read 1, 2, 3, 4, 14, 15, and so on, and that the column letters read A, H, I, J, and so on. As you can see, freezing the labels in rows 1 through 4 and in column A makes the worksheet much easier to read.

A closer look at freezing labels in view

Although you can freeze as many rows and columns on the screen as you want, it's a good idea to keep the frozen area as small as possible. When you freeze more than a few rows and columns, you significantly limit the worksheet's flexibility. You cannot use the direction keys, the Ctrl-direction keys, the Home key, or the PgUp key to move the cell selector into the frozen rows or columns. If you press the Home key, Quattro Pro moves the cell selector to the upper-left cell in the worksheet that is outside the frozen rows and columns. For example, pressing the Home key in the worksheet shown in Figure 9-2 moves the cell selector to cell B5.

Although the direction keys will not move the cell selector into the frozen rows and columns, you can use two techniques to access the frozen area. Use the [Goto] key (F5) to move the cell selector into any cell, including the cells in the frozen area. For example, to move the cell selector to cell A1 in Figure 9-2, press the [Goto] key (F5), type A1, and press the Enter key. Quattro Pro moves the cell selector to cell A1. When the cell selector is in the frozen area, however, rows 1 through 4 and column A are displayed twice, which can be confusing.

The only other time that Quattro Pro allows you to move the cell selector into a frozen area is when you are in POINT mode. Quattro Pro always allows you to point to any cell in a worksheet when you are defining a block. For instance, if you choose the Style Numeric Format Fixed command, Quattro Pro lets you point to any cell in the worksheet to define the block you want to format.

Although your labels are usually in the first few rows and columns of a worksheet, you can freeze any portion of a worksheet that you want. For example, suppose that cells I61 through P80 are in view on your screen and that the cell selector is in cell I63. If you choose the Window Options Locked Titles command at this point and choose the Horizontal option, Quattro Pro locks rows 61 and 62. As you move the cell selector around the worksheet, rows 61 and 62 remain frozen on the screen. Until you choose the Window Options Locked Titles Clear command, you won't be able to move the cell selector above row 63. The Clear option clears the frozen area on your worksheet so you can move freely again around the entire worksheet.

Splitting the screen

As you know, a Quattro Pro worksheet is too large to be displayed fully on the screen at once. Your computer's screen is like a window through which you can view the worksheet. When you first start Quattro Pro, you see 20 rows and eight columns through this window. To view other parts of the worksheet, you must use the cursor-movement keys to move the cell selector and view different parts of the worksheet. Normally, the window you see when you first start Quattro Pro is sufficient. You might encounter times, however, when you need to view two different parts of a worksheet at one time. For example, you might want to edit the entries in one part of a worksheet and observe the effects those changes have on results in another part. In those cases, you can use the Window Options Horizontal and Window Options Vertical commands to split the screen into two independent windows. The Horizontal option tells Quattro Pro to split the screen horizontally. The Vertical option tells Quattro Pro to split the screen vertically.

When you choose the Window Options Horizontal or Window Options Vertical command, the position of the cell selector determines where Quattro Pro splits the screen. Consequently, before you choose the command, you must move the cell selector to a position that defines where you want to split the screen. When you choose the Window Options Horizontal command from the Windows menu, Quattro Pro splits the screen horizontally, immediately above the row that contains the cell selector. If the cell selector is in row 1, Quattro Pro does not split the screen. When you choose the Window Options Vertical command, Quattro Pro splits the

Chapter 9: Working with Windows 289

screen vertically, immediately to the left of the column that contains the cell selector. If the cell selector is in column A, Quattro Pro does not split the screen.

An example of splitting the screen horizontally

Figure 9-1 shows the upper-left corner of a worksheet that occupies columns A through M and rows 1 through 29. Suppose you want to view the information in lower rows of the worksheet while you edit the upper portion of the worksheet. To create a window for this purpose, first move the cell selector to a cell near the bottom of the main window. (For this example, use cell A17.) Next, choose the Window Options Horizontal command, and Quattro Pro splits the screen into two windows immediately above row 17, as shown in Figure 9-3.

The cell selector appears in the upper window after you split the screen. Quattro Pro always places the cell selector in the upper window of a horizontal split and in the left-hand window of vertical split.

Moving the cell selector using the [Window] key (F6)

After you split the screen, you can move the cell selector from one window to the other by pressing the [Window] key (F6). For example, if you press the [Window] key in the previous example, the cell selector moves to cell A17 in the lower window, as shown in Figure 9-3. If you press the [Window] key again, the cell selector returns to the upper window. The [Window] key moves the cell selector to a predictable location in the opposite window, depending on whether the windows are set for synchronized or unsynchronized scrolling. Later in this chapter, "Synchronization and the [Window] Key" explains this concept.

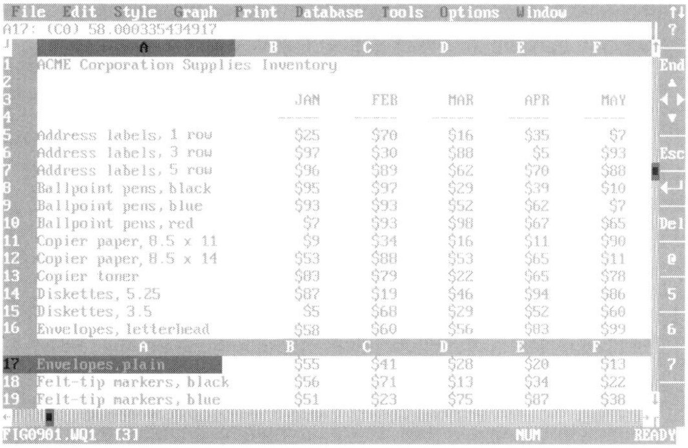

FIGURE 9-3.
The Window Options Horizontal command lets you split the screen horizontally into two windows.

Moving the cell selector inside a split screen

After you split the screen using the Window Options Horizontal or Window Options Vertical command, you can move the cell selector in either window using any of the usual keys or key combinations. As you learned in "Moving the Cell Selector Using Keys" in Chapter 1, the PgUp key, PgDn key, Ctrl-Left direction key, and Ctrl-Right direction keys move the cell selector up, down, left, or right one window at a time. But when you split the screen the effect of these keys changes. If you press the PgUp or PgDn key when the screen is split horizontally, Quattro Pro moves the cell selector up or down within the current window. Similarly, if you press the Ctrl-Left direction key or Ctrl-Right direction key while the screen is split vertically, Quattro Pro moves the cell selector to the left or right within the current window.

Synchronizing windows

The two windows on a split screen scroll in unison by default. If you move the cell selector to the left or right in one window of a screen that is split horizontally, both windows shift to the left or right. If you move the cell selector up or down in one window of a screen that is split vertically, both windows shift up or down. For example, if you press the Right direction key six times while the cell selector is in cell A29 in the lower window in the previous example, the cell selector moves to cell G29. As you can see in Figure 9-4, moving the cell selector in this way brings block B27..I29 into view in the lower window, and shifts the upper window to the right so that cells B1..I16 are in view.

When the two windows are set for synchronous scrolling, they scroll together in one direction. For example, the windows scroll together when you move the cell selector to the left or right if the screen is split horizontally. Similarly, the windows

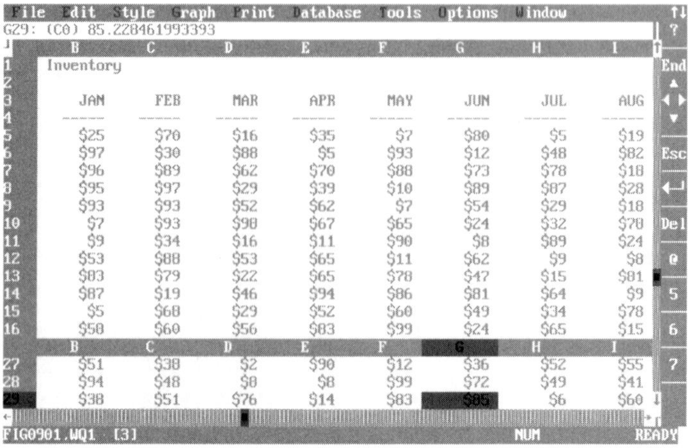

FIGURE 9-4.
When you split the screen, Quattro Pro makes the two windows scroll together.

FIGURE 9-5.
The Window Options Unsync command makes the two windows scroll independently.

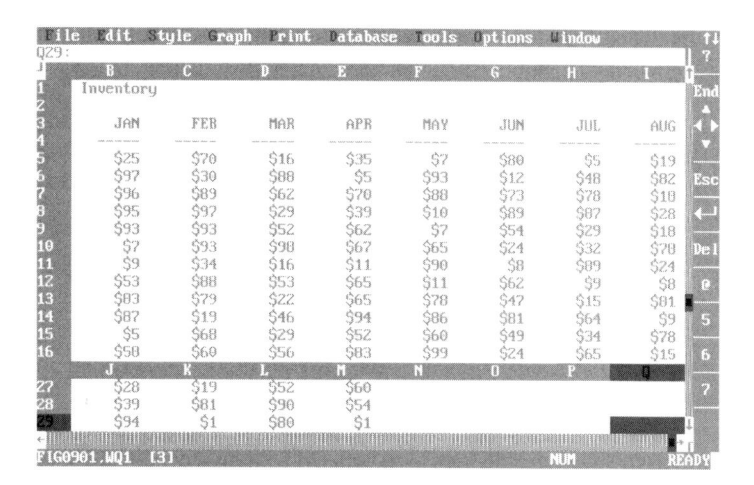

scroll together when you move the cell selector up or down if the screen is split vertically. Even when the windows are synchronized, they scroll independently when you move the cursor in the direction opposite the split. For example, with a horizontal split, the windows do not scroll together when you move the cell selector up and down.

Unsynchronizing windows

The Window Options Unsync command lets you unsynchronize the two windows on a split screen. When the windows are unsynchronized, they scroll independently; moving the cell selector in one window has no effect on the other. For example, suppose you choose the Window Options Unsync command to unsynchronize the windows shown in Figure 9-4. Then suppose you press the Right direction key 10 times. Figure 9-5 shows the result. There, the lower window shows columns J through Q, and the upper window still shows columns B through I.

Resynchronizing windows

To resynchronize two windows, simply choose the Window Options Sync command. The inactive window (the window that does not contain the cell selector) shifts immediately to display the same columns (if the screen is split horizontally) or the same rows (if the screen is split vertically) as the active window. From that point on, the windows again scroll synchronously.

Synchronization and the [Window] key

As mentioned earlier, the effect of the [Window] key (F6) depends in part on whether the windows are synchronized. When the windows are unsynchronized, pressing the [Window] key returns the cell selector to its previous location in the other window. When the windows are synchronized, however, the [Window] key behaves a little differently. If you have split the window horizontally and you press the [Window] key, the cell selector remains in the current column and returns to the row that it last occupied in the other window. If you have split the window vertically and you press the [Window] key, the cell selector remains in the current row and returns to the column that it last occupied in the other window.

For example, suppose the cell selector is in cell G29 in the lower window, as shown in Figure 9-4. Press the [Window] key to move the cell selector to the upper window, and then press the Left direction key four times to move it to column C. If you press the [Window] key again at this point, the cell selector jumps to cell C29 in the lower window, and not to cell G29.

Splitting the screen vertically

So far, you've seen how to split the screen horizontally. As mentioned, you can also split the screen into two vertical windows. To do so, move the cell selector to the column that's to the right of the point at which you want to split the screen, and then choose the Window Options Vertical command.

For example, suppose that you want to split the screen shown in Figure 9-1 so that you can view the values for December at the same time you view the values for January. Move the cell selector to column F, and choose the Window Options Vertical command. Quattro Pro splits the worksheet between columns E and F. To bring December's figures into view (column M), press the [Window] key (F9) to move to the right-hand window, and then press the Right direction key seven times to move the cell selector to column M, as shown in Figure 9-6.

Unsplitting the screen

Use the Window Options Clear command to unsplit a divided screen. As soon as you choose the command, Quattro Pro restores the screen to one window. In

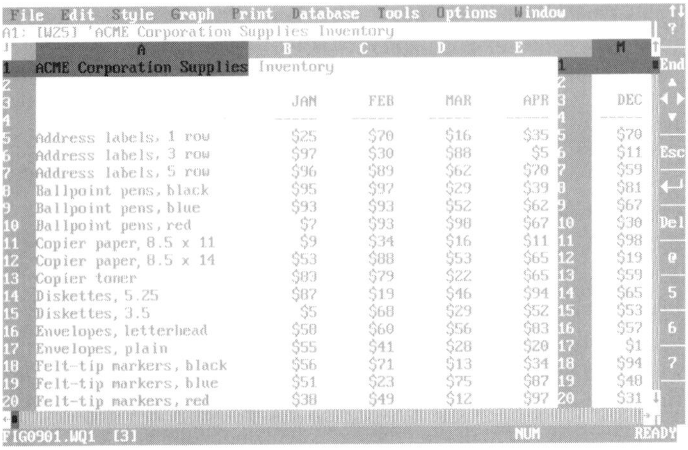

FIGURE 9-6.
The Window Options Vertical command lets you split the screen vertically into two windows.

addition, the cell selector moves to its last position in the upper (or left-hand) window. After you unsplit the screen, you see the same part of the worksheet that you saw in the upper (or left-hand) window of the split screen.

A closer look at splitting screens

After you split a screen into two windows, you can freeze rows and columns in each. To do so, freeze the area in the first window as you normally would, press the [Window] key (F6) to move to the other window, and freeze the area there as well. As you might guess, the Window Options Locked Titles command affects only the current window when the screen is split.

You can have no more than two split windows for a worksheet. To change the location of the split or change the split from horizontal to vertical, choose the Window Options Clear command, move the cell selector to the appropriate location, and split the window again.

More about worksheet windows

In the previous chapter, you read about stacking worksheets in memory by repeatedly choosing the File Open command. When you do so, you actually stack windows through which you view the opened worksheets. Here, you'll learn about a few additional subtleties and nuances of windows.

A definition of a worksheet window

To clarify the following discussion, start by taking a look at the two kinds of windows that Quattro Pro provides: worksheet windows and split windows. Quattro Pro creates a worksheet window whenever you retrieve or open a file or choose the File Manager utility. Quattro Pro creates a split window whenever you use the Window Options Horizontal or Window Options Vertical command to split a worksheet window.

Changing the active worksheet window

Only one worksheet window is active at a time; it's the one displayed on top of the stack. Knowing which worksheet window is active is important because it is the active window that is affected by the commands you choose and where any numbers, labels, or formulas you type are entered. For these reasons, you need to know how to change the active worksheet window. (Earlier in the chapter, you learned how to move between two split windows using the [Window] (F6) key. That method works only for split windows, however, and not for worksheet windows.)

Picking the window you want to make active

The Window Pick command displays a list of open worksheet windows to pick from. To activate one of the worksheet windows listed, select the worksheet name and then press the Enter key. Quattro Pro activates the worksheet window and displays it on top of the stack of windows. You can accomplish the same task by pressing the Alt key and then the number of the window. (Worksheet windows are numbered in the order they are opened.) For example, to activate the second window press Alt-2.

Moving between worksheet windows

Remember that to move between split windows you can simply press the [Window] key (F6). To move between worksheet windows, press Shift-F6. Quattro Pro moves to the next worksheet window in the stack, displays that worksheet window on the top of the stack, and moves the previously displayed worksheet window to the bottom of the stack. You can cycle through all the open worksheets in the stack by pressing Shift+F6 repeatedly.

Using the Window Zoom command

The Window Zoom command changes the size of the active worksheet window. Window Zoom is a toggle command; it alternately shrinks the worksheet window and then expands it. If you have not yet used the Window Move/Size command or the mouse to change the window size, Window Zoom alternately shrinks the window so that it fills half the screen and expands the window so that it fills the full screen. On the other hand, if you have used the Window Move/Size command or the mouse to change the window size, Window Zoom alternately shrinks and expands the window between the size you changed it to and the full screen.

Using the Window Tile command

The Window Tile command reduces the size and position of all the worksheet windows so that they show on the screen at one time. Figure 9-7 shows an example of a tiled screen in which the Window Tile command has been used to display each of the three open worksheet windows.

Using the Window Stack command

At the top of each worksheet window, Quattro Pro provides a title that gives the worksheet filename and the window number. The Window Stack command arranges the worksheet windows so that you can read their window titles, as shown in Figure 9-8.

FIGURE 9-7.
The Window Tile command displays each of the three open windows.

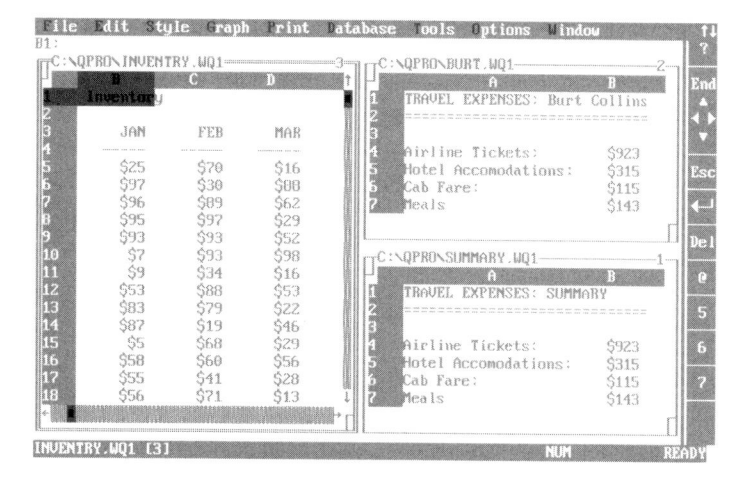

FIGURE 9-8.
The Window Stack command arranges the windows so that you can see the titles of each window.

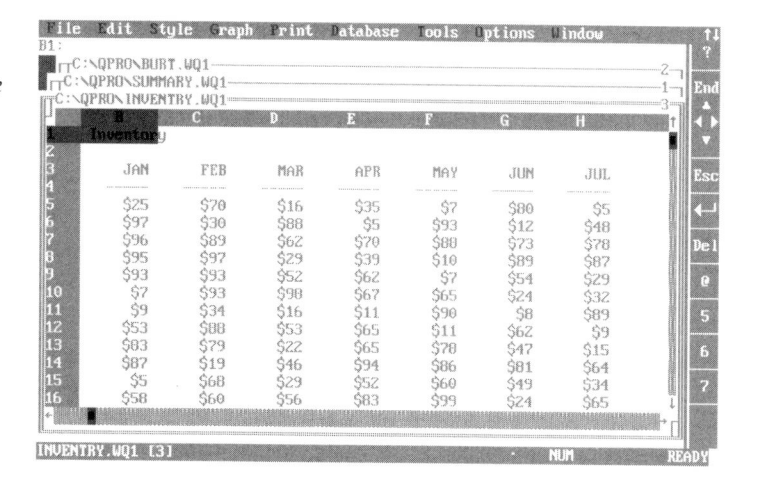

Using the Window Move/Size command

The Window Move/Size command lets you both move and change the size of the active worksheet window. When you choose this command, Quattro Pro displays a small box that inclues the word *move*. You can then use the direction keys to move the active window. You cannot, however, move the window border beyond the edge of the screen. That means you cannot move full-sized windows.

To change the size of the active window, hold down the Shift key and press the direction keys. The Left and Right direction keys control the right edge of the window: The Left direction key decreases the window size by moving the right edge to the left, and the Right direction key increases the window size by moving the right edge to the right. The Up and Down direction keys control the bottom edge of the window: The Up direction key decreases the window size by moving the bottom edge up, and the Down direction key increases the window size by moving the bottom edge down. You cannot resize the window border beyond the edge of the screen.

Using the other Window commands

All of the Window commands have been described earlier in the chapter except the Window Options Row & Col Borders and the Map View commands. Most Quattro Pro users do not need to use these commands. In some special circumstances, however, they can both come in quite handy.

Using the Window Options Row & Col Borders command

The Window Options Row & Col Borders command removes the row numbers and column letters from the active worksheet window, as shown in Figure 9-9. Why would you want to remove the row numbers and column letters? In most cases, you won't. In some worksheets that are controlled by macros, however—worksheets in which all the user does is look at data or enter data only in clearly marked input fields—you do not actually need row numbers or column letters. You can improve the appearance of the worksheet window in these cases by removing rows numbers and column letters.

When you choose the Window Options Row & Col Borders command, Quattro Pro presents a submenu that has two options: Hide and Display. The Hide option removes the row numbers and column letters from the screen. The Display option returns the row numbers and column letters to the screen.

The Window Options Row & Col Borders command affects only the active worksheet window. If other worksheet windows are open, they still show row numbers and column letters.

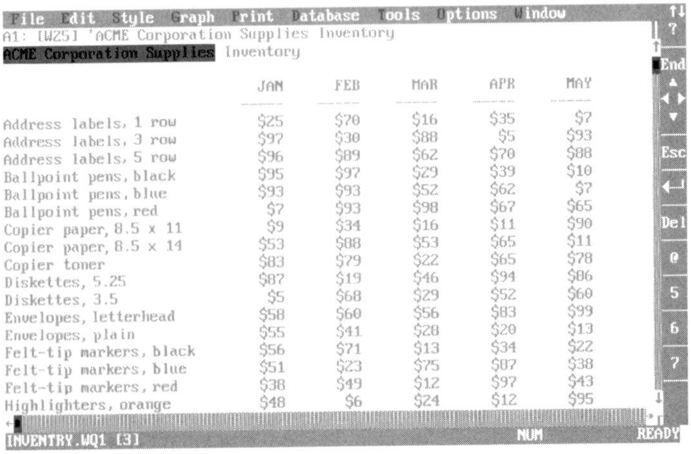

FIGURE 9-9.
Use the Window Options Row & Col Borders command to remove row numbers or column letters.

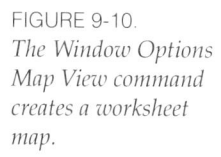

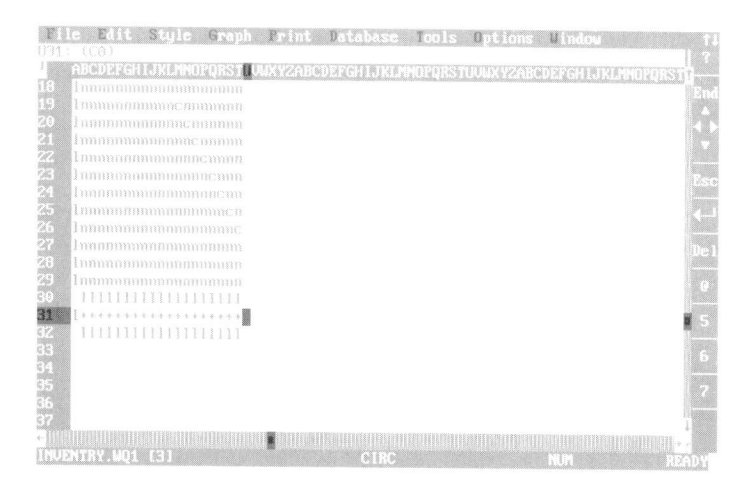

FIGURE 9-10.
The Window Options Map View command creates a worksheet map.

Using the Window Options Map View command

The Window Options Map View command creates, in effect, a map of a worksheet. Figure 9-10 shows an example of a map, which is simply a worksheet window with one-character columns. Rather than displaying or trying to display the contents of cells, however, Quattro Pro displays symbols that indicate the contents of cells. Quattro Pro uses an *l* to show that a cell contains a label, an *n* to show that a cell contains a number, a + to show that a cell contains a formula, a - to show that a cell contains a spreadsheet link formula, a *c* to show that a cell contains a circular reference, and a *g* to indicate that a cell contains a graph insert. (You'll learn more about Quattro Pro graphs in the next chapter.)

Worksheet maps help in several ways. They provide a convenient method to verify quickly that large portions (up to 20-row by 70-column blocks) of a worksheet look right. For example, in a block that is supposed to contain only formulas, you should see only the + symbol. Worksheet maps provide a visual aid for identifying the cells involved in circular references, and can also help you quickly locate special cells such as those that contain spreadsheet link formulas or graph inserts.

Using a mouse to work with worksheet windows

So far, this chapter has explained how to use menu commands and function keys to accomplish such tasks as activating a worksheet window as well as moving, resizing, and closing worksheet windows. Mouse users can perform these tasks more easily and quickly, however, by using a mouse.

Activating a worksheet window using a mouse

To activate a window using a mouse, simply click on the worksheet window. For mouse users, this method of activating a window should prove faster than other methods, including pressing the [Window] key (F6) to move to a split window, pressing Shift-F6 to move to the next worksheet window, or using the Window Pick command.

Zooming a worksheet window using a mouse

To zoom a worksheet window, click on the zoom symbols, which are the up and down arrows in the upper-right corner of the Quattro Pro screen. To increase the size of the worksheet window, click on the arrow that points up. To decrease the size of the worksheet window, click on the arrow that points down.

Moving a worksheet window using a mouse

To move a worksheet window using a mouse, click on the window's title, and then drag the worksheet window in the direction you want to move it. As is the case with the Window Move/Resize command, you cannot move a window border beyond the edge of the screen.

Resizing a worksheet window using a mouse

To resize a worksheet window using a mouse, click on the resize box in the lower-right corner of the window, and then drag the corner to its new position. As you drag the corner, Quattro Pro adjusts the size of the window. Again, you cannot move the window borders beyond the edge of the screen.

Closing a worksheet window using a mouse

To close a worksheet window using a mouse, click on the close box, which is the small box in the upper-left corner of each worksheet window. This action is equivalent to choosing the File Close command. If you've made changes to the worksheet displayed in the window since the last time the worksheet was saved, Quattro Pro displays the prompt *Lose All Changes?* followed by the options Yes and No. To continue with the File Close operation without saving the worksheet, choose the Yes option. To abort the File Close operation so you can save the file using the File Save or File Save As command, choose the No option.

A closer look at worksheet windows

You can have a maximum of 32 worksheet windows open at one time. Keep in mind that Quattro Pro counts the File Manager's window as a worksheet window when determining how many windows are open. Typically, you shouldn't find this limit a problem. Even if your worksheet files are only moderate in size, you might run out of memory long before you approach the 32-window limit anyway.

10
Creating Graphs

So far, you've seen how to create, save, and print worksheets. This chapter explains how to take advantage of another of Quattro Pro's most powerful and useful capabilities: graphing. You begin by exploring the basic commands used to create a graph, and then walk through each of Quattro Pro's graph types, looking at how to enhance and print the graphs you create. Finally, the chapter ends with an explanation of how you can use the Annotator to open the door to great possibilities for enhancing graphs and for drawing pictures.

The basics of creating graphs

Every graph you create in Quattro Pro is based on data in a worksheet. Before you can create a graph, therefore, you must make entries in a new worksheet or open a worksheet file that contains the data you want to graph. You can then create a graph by choosing a few simple commands.

FIGURE 10-1.
Use this spreadsheet to illustrate the Fast Graph option.

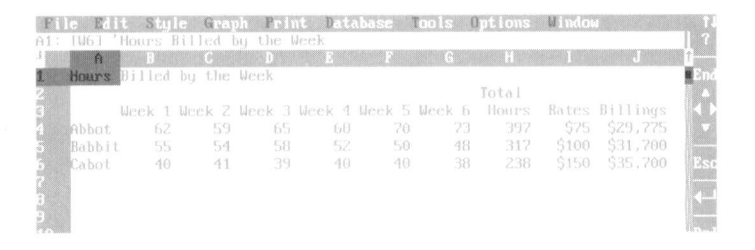

FIGURE 10-2.
The Graph menu includes the Fast Graph option.

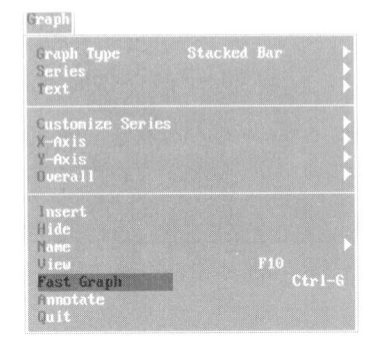

Fast graphs

The easiest way to create a graph is by using the Graph menu's Fast Graph option. In fact if you haven't created graphs before, Fast Graph is the best place to start. To illustrate the Fast Graph command, assume you have a worksheet like the one shown in Figure 10-1, which tracks the weekly billable hours for the law firm of Abbot, Babbit, and Cabot.

To create a graph of the billing data shown in Figure 10-1 in block B4..G6, first choose the Graph command. Quattro Pro presents the Graph menu shown in Figure 10-2. Choose the Fast Graph command, and Quattro Pro displays the prompt *Enter Fast-Graph block* followed by the current address of the cell selector. Define block A3..G6 (include column A because it contains the lawyers' names), and then press the Enter key. Quattro Pro creates a stacked-bar graph like the one shown in Figure 10-3.

On a color monitor, Quattro Pro uses different colors and patterns to identify different data series. On a monochrome monitor, Quattro Pro uses different patterns. Notice in Figure 10-3 that Quattro Pro has added information to both the vertical and horizontal axes to indicate what they measure. For example, the vertical axis identifies the number of hours billed, and the horizontal axis identifies which weeks the stacked-bars represent. Notice also that Quattro Pro has added a legend at the bottom of the screen to indicate which segments of the stacked-bars represent which attorneys. Now, to return from the graph to the worksheet screen, press any key (except F10, F11, or F12).

FIGURE 10-3.
Quattro Pro creates this fast graph, based on the data shown in Figure 10-1.

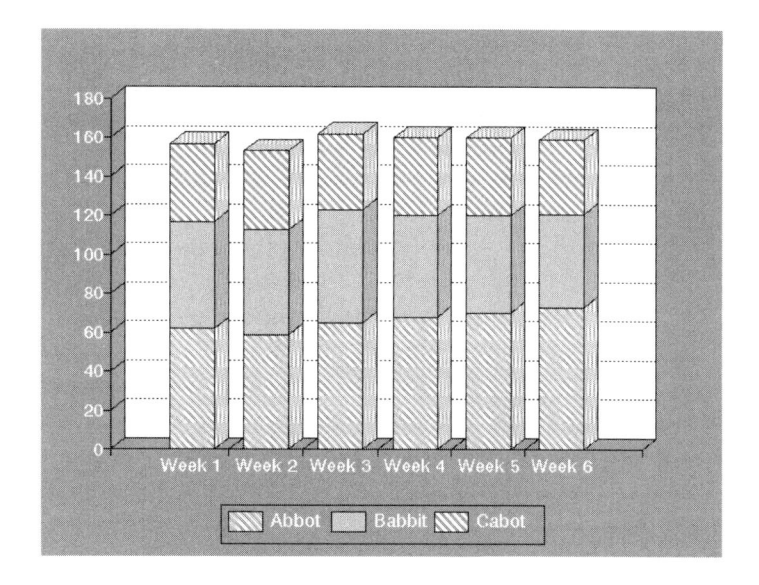

As you can see, Fast Graph is convenient. Using it means you do not have to spend a lot of time defining a graph because Fast Graph uses the default settings, which is especially valuable as you get started with graphing. Because the default graph type is stacked-bar, for instance, the fast graph you created is a stacked-bar graph. Fast Graph's use of default settings, however, is also its major weakness and the reason you'll want to learn about creating graphs from scratch using the other Graph menu options. For example, if you want a different kind of graph or a title that describes the graph and the axes, you'll need to learn about the other graph options.

Creating a simple graph from scratch

When you create a graph from scratch, you can choose from 14 different graph types, as explained later in this chapter in "Quattro Pro's Graph Types." For now, try creating a bar graph. Use the data in the worksheet shown in Figure 10-1 as the basis for creating a bar graph from scratch. To begin, choose the Graph Graph Type Bar command to tell Quattro Pro the type of graph you want to create. Otherwise, Quattro Pro uses its stacked-bar default graph. Next, you identify the data you want to plot in your graph. Before Quattro Pro can create a graph from scratch, you must identify the cells that contain the numbers to be plotted. These cells must be adjacent, and they must contain values. Quattro Pro ignores labels or blanks in a series. For example, in the worksheet shown in Figure 10-1 you can base a graph on the entries in block B4..G6, which is exactly what the Fast Graph option did. Fast Graph assumed that block B4..G6 held the data to be graphed.

Quattro Pro uses the term *data series* to describe the data on which a graph is based. Each graph that you create can contain from one to six data series. The only exceptions to this rule are pie graphs, which can include only one data series, and XY graphs, which must include at least two data series. For most graph types, each data series must contain at least two cells. Although Quattro Pro does not limit the number of cells that you can include in any one data series, a graph can become crowded and virtually unreadable if you try to include too many cells in each data series.

When you create a graph from scratch, you use the Graph Series command to identify the data to be graphed. To do so, choose the Series command from the Graph menu, and the Series menu appears. Select the 1st Series option, then highlight the series of values in cells B4..G4, which tells Quattro Pro to use the values in cells B4, C4, D4, E4, F4, and G4 as one data series in the bar graph you are creating, and then press the Enter key. Then define the second data series as B5..G5 using the 2nd Series option and the third series as B6..G6 using the 3rd Series option. If you have already defined a block for a series, the block is listed to the right of that series option on the Series menu.

For graphs that have multiple data series, you can use another approach to identify the block that contains the data—if the data series is in one contiguous block. Choose the Graph Series Group command, and Quattro Pro presents a menu that lists two options: Columns and Rows. Choose the Columns option if each data series is in a different column, and choose the Rows option if each data series is in a different row. Quattro Pro displays the prompt *Enter block for column/row series* followed by the current address of the cell selector. Define the block that contains the data to be graphed by pointing, and then press the Enter key. For the bar graph, for example, choose the Graph Series Group Rows command and then define block B4..G6. Choose the Quit option to return to the Graph menu.

Viewing graphs

To view the bar graph based on the series you have just defined, choose the View option from the Graph menu. Quattro Pro replaces the worksheet on your screen with the graph image shown in Figure 10-4. To return to the worksheet, press any key (except F10, F11, or F12). Instead of choosing the View option from the Graph menu, you can also press the [Graph] key (F10) to display a graph image on your screen. This key is particularly useful when you want to see how changes to your worksheet data affect the graph image. As you edit the worksheet, you can see instantly how your changes affect the graph by pressing the [Graph] key; you do not need to choose the Graph View command.

Whether you press the [Graph] key or choose the View command, Quattro Pro always displays only one graph. As explained later in this chapter, you can have more than one graph associated with a particular worksheet, but only one graph can be active at any given time; the graph that you see when you choose the View

FIGURE 10-4.
To view a graph that you have created, choose the View option from the Graph menu or press the [Graph] key (F10).

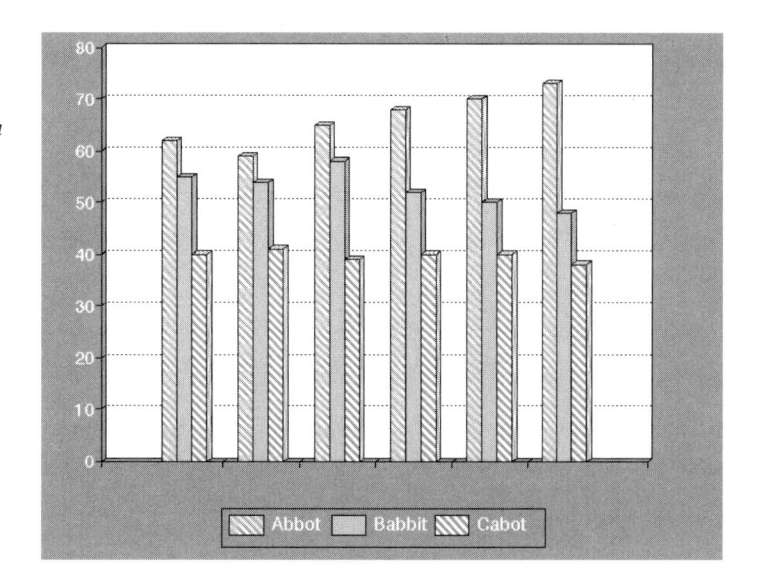

option or press the [Graph] key. If you have not created a graph in the current worksheet, pressing the [Graph] key or choosing the View option displays a blank screen.

Notice that Quattro Pro uses a different pattern for the bars of each data series. The 1st Series bars and the 3rd Series bars are plotted with a diagonal cross hatch pattern, and the 2nd Series bars are solid. If you use a color monitor, you'll also notice that Quattro Pro displays each bar using a separate color. If you want, you can choose a different color or pattern, or both, from the ones Quattro Pro chooses for you, as explained later in the chapter in "Enhancing Graphs."

Editing graphs

After you create a graph, you can edit it in a number of ways. You can add one or more data series to the graph or delete one or more data series. You can also change the graph type. (In addition, you can add titles, x-axis values, y-axis values, interior labels, and many other enhancements to the basic graph. Later in the chapter, "Enhancing Graphs" explains how.)

Adding a data series

As mentioned, graphs in Quattro Pro (except for pie graphs) can contain up to six data series. To add another data series to an existing graph, choose the Graph Series command, define the block that contains the series, and press the Enter key. You will usually add data series to a graph in order, using the 1st Series option to define the first series, the 2nd Series option to define the second series, and so on. You do not have to define the series in order, however. For instance, you could use the 4th Series option to define the graph's second data series. Any enhancements or display options that apply to the 4th Series option would then apply to the second data series.

Changing the graph type

After you create a graph, you can change its type simply by choosing the Graph Graph Type command and then choosing a new type for the graph. Quattro Pro immediately changes the graph into a graph of the type you have chosen.

Managing graphs

As mentioned, you can create more than one graph in a single Quattro Pro worksheet. In fact, a worksheet can contain an unlimited number of graphs, although only one graph in a worksheet is active at any one time. If a worksheet contains more than one graph, all but one are inactive. The active graph is the one you see when you press the [Graph] key (F10) or choose the View option from the Graph menu. When you use the commands on the Graph menu, they affect the active graph. This section shows you how to work with more than one graph in a worksheet.

Naming graphs

If you plan to have more than one graph associated with a worksheet, you must use the Graph Name command to assign a specific name to each graph you create. After you name a graph (which makes its settings permanent) you can create a new graph without losing the original one. To look at the original graph again, simply choose its name to make it the active graph.

After you choose the Graph Name command, Quattro Pro presents the menu shown in Figure 10-5. To name the active graph, choose the Create option from the menu, type the graph's name, and press the Enter key. The name you choose must conform to the same rules that apply to block names—that is, it can contain any alphabetic, numeric, or punctuation character (including spaces) as long as the total length does not exceed 15 characters. For example, you might name the bar graph shown in Figure 10-4 *Billable Hours*.

Creating a second graph

After you name the active graph, you can create a second graph in one of two ways: You can modify the existing graph type and data series settings, or you can use the Graph Customize Series Reset command to reset all of the graph settings

FIGURE 10-5.
The Graph Name command presents this menu.

and then start over from scratch. Essentially, the Graph Customize Series Reset command erases data series settings and resets all the other settings to their default values.

Selecting named graphs

The Graph Name Display command lets you change a worksheet's active graph to activate a graph that you named previously. When you choose this command, Quattro Pro displays a list of the named graphs in the current worksheet. To activate one of these graphs, point to its name in the list and press the Enter key. Quattro Pro then displays the graph you selected. Alternatively, you can type the name of the graph you want to activate, and then press the Enter key, or click on the name.

When you use the Graph Name Display command to activate a named graph, the settings for that graph replace the current graph settings. If you have not named the current graph, its settings are lost, so be careful!

Erasing named graphs

The Graph Name Erase command allows you to erase named graphs selectively. When you choose this command, Quattro Pro displays a list of the named graphs in the current worksheet. To erase one of these graphs, point to its name in the list and press the Enter key. Or, you can type the name of the graph you want to erase, and then press the Enter key. To erase all the named graphs in a worksheet in one step, you can choose the Graph Name Reset command. Quattro Pro presents a menu that has two options: Yes and No. If you choose the Yes option, Quattro Pro erases all named graphs from the worksheet immediately. If you choose the No option, Quattro Pro simply cancels the command. Again, be careful! You can lose a lot of work in a hurry if you make a mistake while using this command.

Creating a slide show using graph names

If you name several graphs, you can direct Quattro Pro to display the graphs like slides in a slide show. To do so, first enter the graph names in consecutive rows in the worksheet in the same order that you want the graphs displayed. For example, if you had three graphs named *Billable Hours*, *Revenues*, and *Rates*, you might enter the label *'Billable Hours* in cell L1, *'Revenues* in cell L2, and *'Rates* in cell L3. Then, choose the Graph Names Slide command. Next, Quattro Pro displays the prompt *Enter block of graph names to show slides* followed by the current address of the cell selector. Define the block that contains the graph names (in this example, L1..L3) and press the Enter key. Quattro Pro displays the graph named *Billable Hours* first. To see the second graph, press a key or click the mouse, and to see the third graph, press a key or click the mouse again. To return to the graph menu, press a key or click the mouse a final time.

Using the Graph Name Slide command along with macros makes it possible to create slide shows using Quattro Pro graphs. In fact, in a macro you can even specify how long a slide should be displayed. Chapter 12, "Macro Basics," explains macros and how you use them.

Copying a graph from one worksheet to another

The Graph Name Graph Copy command lets you copy the graph settings you've named in one worksheet to another worksheet. To use this command, both the worksheet from which you want to copy the graph (called the source worksheet) and the worksheet to which you want to copy the graph (called the target worksheet) must be open. Then, with the source worksheet active, choose the Graph Name Graph Copy command. Quattro Pro displays a list of the named graphs in the active source worksheet. Select the graph you want to copy and then press the Enter key. Next, Quattro Pro displays the prompt *Point to target worksheet*. Select the worksheet you want to copy to by pressing Shift-F6. When the target worksheet is active, press the Enter key. Quattro Pro then copies the graph settings to the target worksheet and makes the source worksheet active again. Although the graph appears in the target worksheet, the data being graphed is still in the source worksheet. The target worksheet uses spreadsheet links to retrieve the data from the source worksheet. (In Chapter 8, "File Management," you'll find a description of spreadsheet links.)

Saving named graphs

Remember that naming a graph does not save it on disk. Naming a graph merely stores the graph's settings within the worksheet. A graph is not saved permanently until you save the worksheet from which it was created. Saving the worksheet saves the data in the worksheet along with all of the worksheet's settings—including graph settings.

Quattro Pro's graph types

Quattro Pro can create 14 different types of graphs, of which this chapter has described two: a stacked-bar graph and a bar graph. This section shows you examples of the other types of Quattro Pro graphs: line, XY, pie, area, rotated bar, column, high-low, text, 3-D bar, 3-D ribbon, 3-D step, and 3-D area.

Line graphs

A line graph is probably the most commonly used business graph. In a line graph, Quattro Pro uses a line to connect the data values in each series, so a line graph is best used to illustrate the trend of data over time. For instance, you might use a line graph to illustrate the growth (or decline) of sales for a company from one month to the next throughout a year or to illustrate the population growth of a country over several years. To define a line graph in Quattro Pro, choose the

FIGURE 10-6.
A line graph is best used to illustrate the trend of data over time.

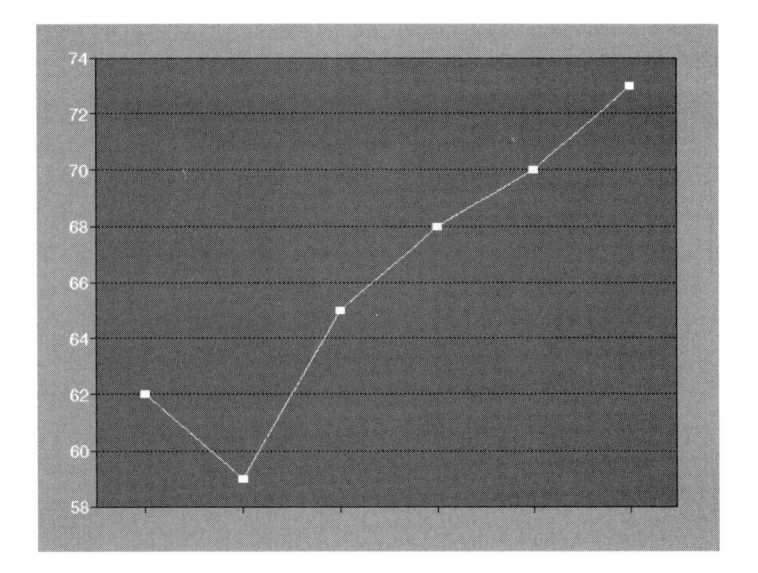

Graph Graph Type command, and then choose the Line option to define the graph as a line graph. Next, choose the Series command to define the graph's series. (You can delete extraneous series from a graph by choosing the Graph Customize Series Reset command and then selecting the series and graphs you want to eliminate from the graph. You can reset all the current graph information by choosing the Graph Customize Series Reset Graph command.) Figure 10-6 shows an example of a line graph based on data from Figure 10-1. It depicts Abbot's hours over a 6-week period of time.

Although all of the data points in this example line graph are positive, you can also plot negative values on a line graph. Negative values on a line graph are represented by lines that dip below the graph's x-axis.

XY graphs

XY graphs, which resemble line graphs, plot the relationship between two quantifiable characteristics of a set of data. XY graphs come in handy when you are using one characteristic (the independent variable) to predict another characteristic (the dependent variable) of a data set. For example, you can use an XY graph to plot the relationship between the independent variable (interest rates) and the dependent variable (home sales). To create an XY graph, choose the Graph Series command to define the data series and the x-series. The values in the two series work together to determine the positions of the points in the graph. The x-series, which determines the horizontal position of each point in the graph, should contain the values for the independent variable. The y–series, which determines the vertical position of each point, should contain the values for the dependent

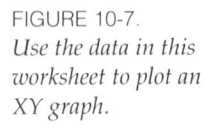

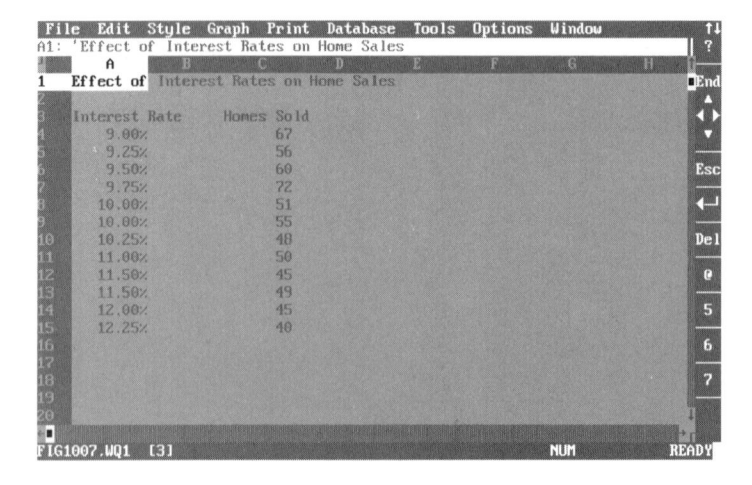

FIGURE 10-7.
Use the data in this worksheet to plot an XY graph.

variable. For example, create an XY graph that depicts the relationship between the interest rates and the home sales in the worksheet shown in Figure 10-7. Use the values for interest rates (the independent variable) in block A4..A15 as the x-axis values and the values for home sales (the dependent variable) in block C4..C15 as the 1st Series.

To begin, choose the Graph Graph Type XY command to define the type of the graph. Next, choose the Series X-Axis Series command, define block A4..A15, and then press the Enter key. Finally, choose the 1st Series option from the Series menu, define block C4..C15, and then press the Enter key.

Choose the Quit option to exit from the Series menu, and then press the [Graph] key (F10) to display the graph shown in Figure 10-8. Notice that Quattro Pro uses the values in the axis series as labels for the x-axis on the graph.

A closer look at XY graphs

Quattro Pro arranges the x-axis labels in ascending order, which makes sense. You probably want to arrange your data in ascending x-value order because Quattro Pro draws lines between the markers; therefore, if you do not arrange your data in ascending x-value order, the line that Quattro Pro draws does not show the ascending x-values. If you choose not to arrange your data in ascending x-value order, you should probably use the Graph Customize Series Markers & Lines command to display only the markers on the graph and not the lines. Later in this chapter, "Enhancing Graphs" explains how to use such enhancements in your graphs.

Pie graphs

Pie graphs are also among the most commonly used types of business graphs. In a pie graph, each value in a series is represented by a segment (slice) of a circle (pie). The entire pie represents the total of the values in the data series. Pie graphs

Chapter 10: Creating Graphs 309

FIGURE 10-8.
XY graphs plot the relationship between two quantifiable characteristics of a set of data.

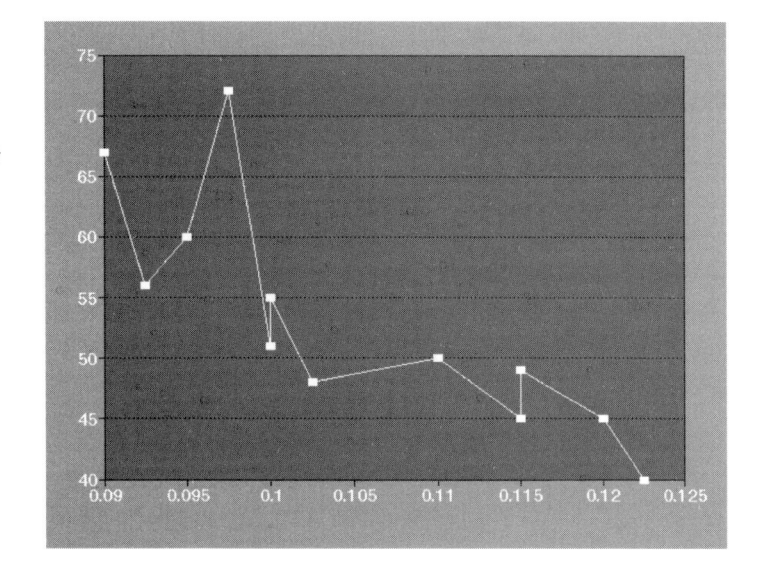

FIGURE 10-9.
Pie graphs illustrate the ratio of the components of a data set to the total of those components.

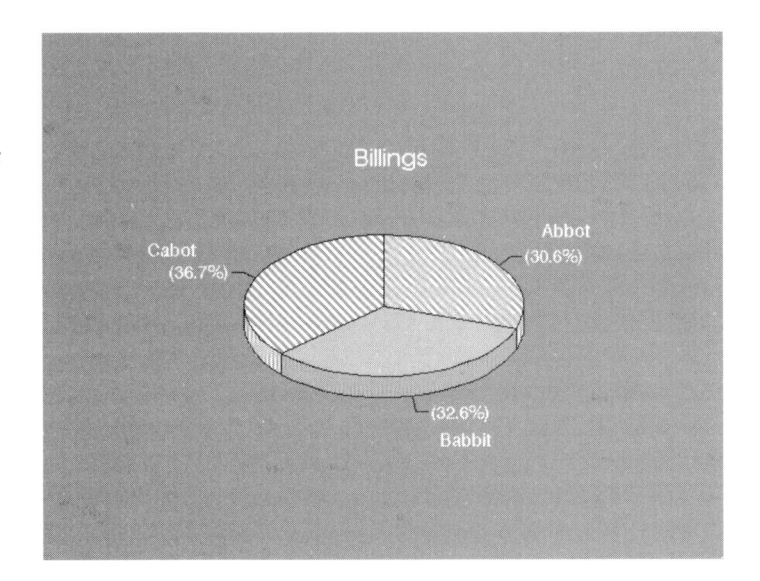

illustrate the ratio of the components of a data set to the total of those components. For this reason, pie graphs can depict only one data series at a time. To create a pie graph in Quattro Pro, first specify the graph type as Pie, and then define the graph's data series. Figure 10-9 shows an example pie chart based on the total billings data in block J4..J6 of the spreadsheet in Figure 10-1.

As you can see, each value in the data series has been plotted as a slice of the pie. The slice for the first value in the series, Abbot's total billings, begins at the 12 o'clock position and wraps around past 3 o'clock. The next slice represents the second value, Babbit's total billings. The third slice represents the third value, Cabot's total billings. Notice the percentage that appears beside each slice in the graph, which indicates the share of the pie that each slice represents. Quattro Pro places percentages on all pie graphs.

If you have a monochrome monitor, Quattro Pro uses only fill patterns to shade the slices in the graph. If you have a color monitor, Quattro Pro uses both colors and fill patterns to distinguish the slices, although you can change the fill patterns and colors that Quattro Pro uses, as described later in this chapter in "Enhancing Graphs."

Area graphs

Area graphs are much like stacked-bar graphs. In a stacked-bar graph, each data series is represented by a series of bar segments. In an area graph, each series is represented by the space, or area, between two lines. The area between the first line and the x-axis represents the first data series, the area between the second line and the first line represents the second series, and so on. Each of the lines represents the cumulative trend of the data series below that line, and the top line represents the sum of all of the data series that make up the graph. Like stacked-bar graphs, area graphs are useful for depicting the relationships between the components of several data series and the totals of those components. Also like line graphs, area graphs depict the trend of the data being graphed. Figure 10-10 shows an example area graph that uses the same data series as does the stacked-bar graph shown in Figure 10-3.

FIGURE 10-10.
In an area graph, each data series is represented by the area between two lines.

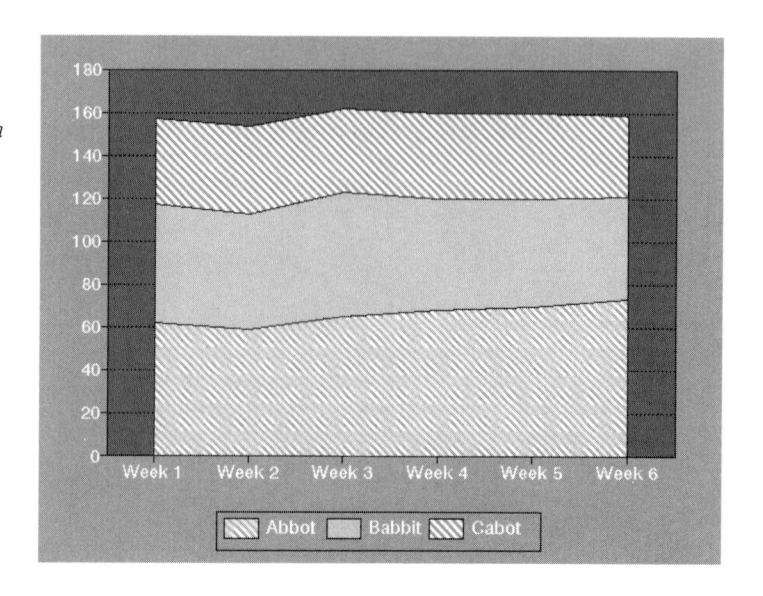

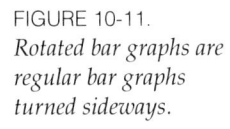

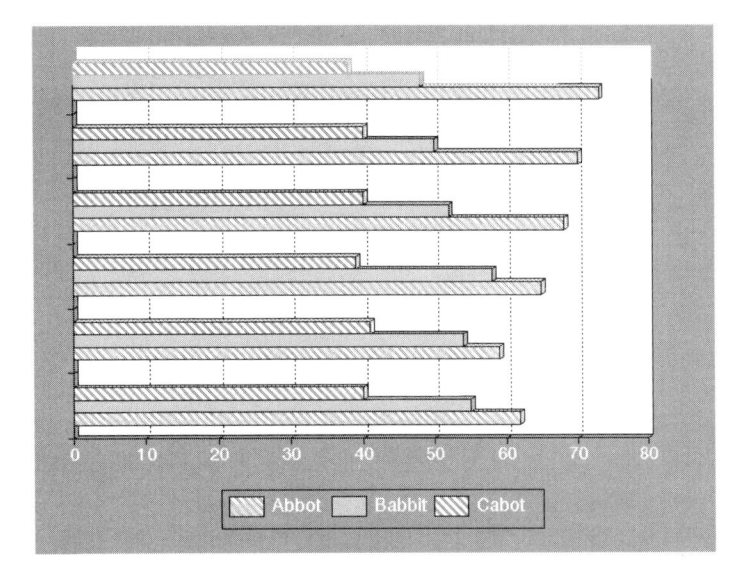

Chapter 10: Creating Graphs

FIGURE 10-11.
Rotated bar graphs are regular bar graphs turned sideways.

Rotated bar graphs

A rotated bar graph is nothing more than a regular bar graph turned on its side. In a rotated bar graph, each data series is plotted as a series of bars along the graph's vertical axis, and each data value is represented by the length of a single bar. In a rotated bar graph, the graph's axes change places: The x-axis becomes a vertical axis, and the y-axis becomes a horizontal axis. Figure 10-11 shows an example of a rotated bar graph.

You can rotate any single data series or clustered bar graph. The only difference between regular bar graphs and rotated bar graphs is their orientation; in every other way, they are identical.

Column graphs

Column graphs resemble pie graphs, because each value in the data series is plotted as a percentage of the total series. Instead of showing values as slices of pie, however, column graphs show values as pieces of a column. The first value in the data series appears as the bottom piece of the column, the second value as the next piece, and so on. As is the case with a pie graph, the percentage that each piece of the column represents appears beside the piece. Figure 10-12 shows an example of a column graph that uses the same data as does the pie graph shown in Figure 10-9.

High-low graphs

High-low graphs are usually used for plotting daily stock prices. The daily high stock prices typically represent one data series and the daily low stock prices

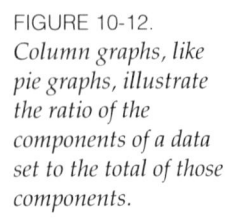

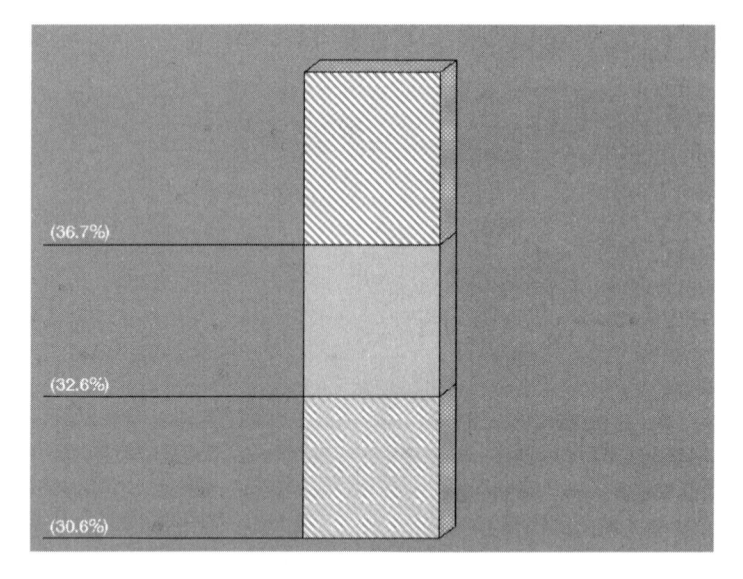

FIGURE 10-12.
Column graphs, like pie graphs, illustrate the ratio of the components of a data set to the total of those components.

another data series. For example, suppose that over a 4-day period the daily high stock prices are $51.00, $53.25, $51.75 and $50.00, and that over the same 4-day period the daily low stock prices are $50.50, $51.25, $50.50 and $49.00. The daily high stock prices represent the first data series, and the daily low stock prices represent the other data series. Given these data series, Quattro Pro draws a high-low graph like the one shown in Figure 10-13. The vertical lines that make up a high-low graph show the differences between the high and low stock prices of the day.

You can plot more than two data series on a high-low graph. For instance, you might also plot the closing and opening prices of a stock using the third and fourth series. The third series, which you might use for the closing price, is plotted as a tick-mark on the right side of the vertical high-low line, and the fourth series, which you might use for an opening price, is plotted as a tick-mark on the left side of the vertical high-low line. You could even use the fifth and sixth data series, which would be plotted as cross marks on the vertical high-low line.

Text graphs

Text graphs are not actually graphs but are instead blank screens that you can add to using the Annotate feature. Later in this chapter, "Using the Annotate Feature" describes the Annotate feature and explains more about the text graph screen.

Three-dimensional graphs

The last option on the Graph Type menu is 3-D Graphs. When you choose this option you see a submenu that lists the three-dimensional graphs that Quattro Pro provides: Bar, Ribbon, Step, and Area. Although several of the graph types

FIGURE 10-13.
High-low graphs are typically used for plotting daily stock prices.

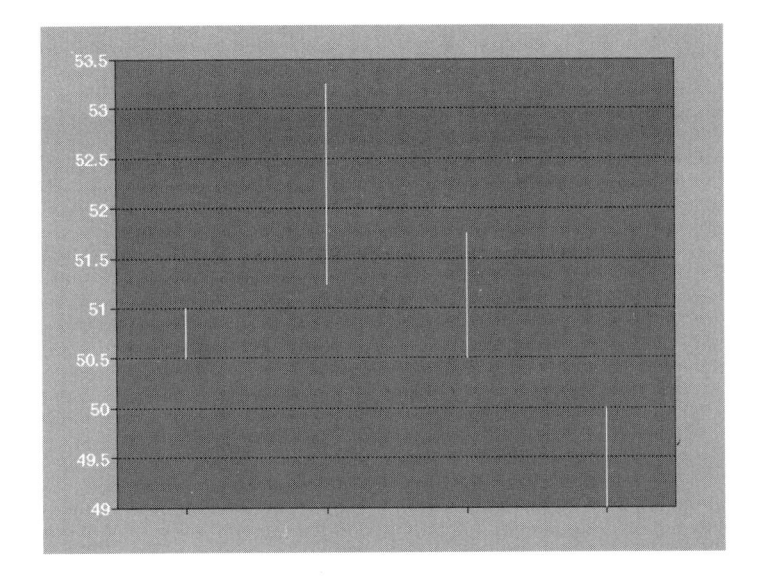

FIGURE 10-14.
This is an example of a 3-D Bar graph.

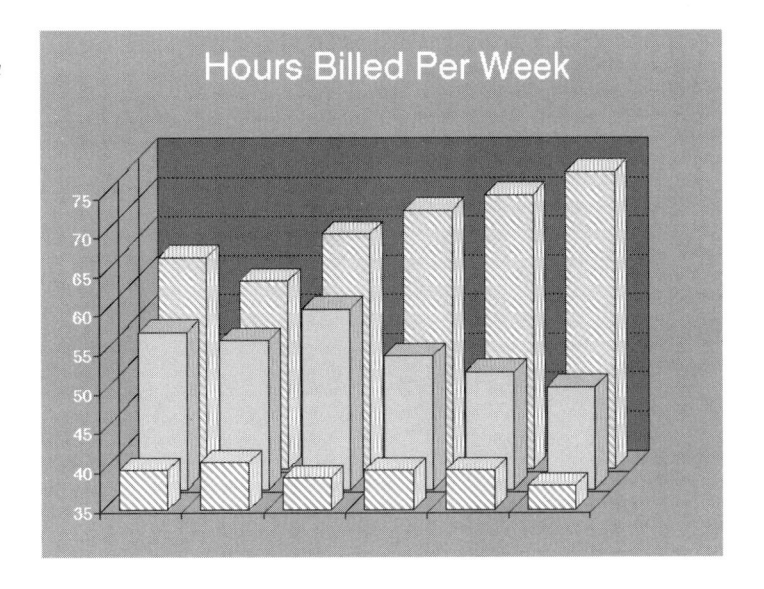

you have already seen look three-dimensional, these four graphs actually show depth in both the graph area and the data series. In addition, the data series tend to be plotted at different depths in the graph area rather than side by side.

Figure 10-14 shows the bar graph from Figure 10-4 redrawn as a 3-D Bar graph. Although both graphs have a three-dimensional look, the 3-D Bar graph makes better use of depth and shading, making the information easier to understand.

FIGURE 10-15.
This is an example of a 3-D Ribbon graph.

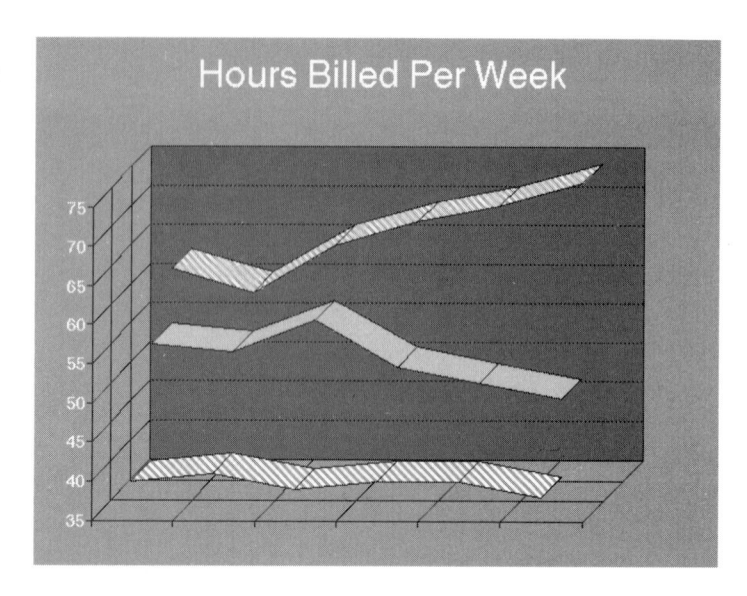

FIGURE 10-16.
This is an example of a 3-D Step graph.

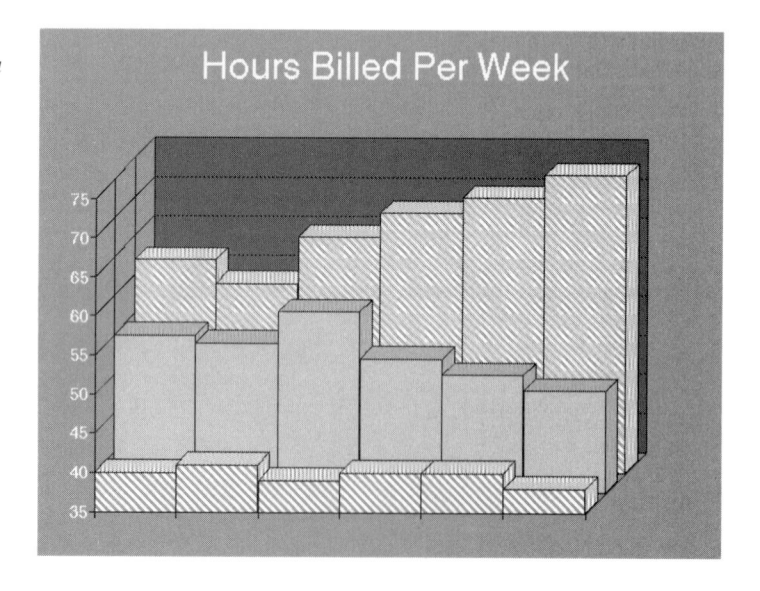

Figure 10-15 shows a 3-D Ribbon graph. A ribbon graph is a line graph drawn in three dimensions. Compare the way the data appears in Figure 10-15 with the way it appears in Figure 10-19.

Figure 10-16 is a 3-D Step graph. This is another variation of the Quattro Pro bar graph, but the bars for each data series are plotted at different depths in the graph.

FIGURE 10-17.
This is an example of a 3-D Area graph.

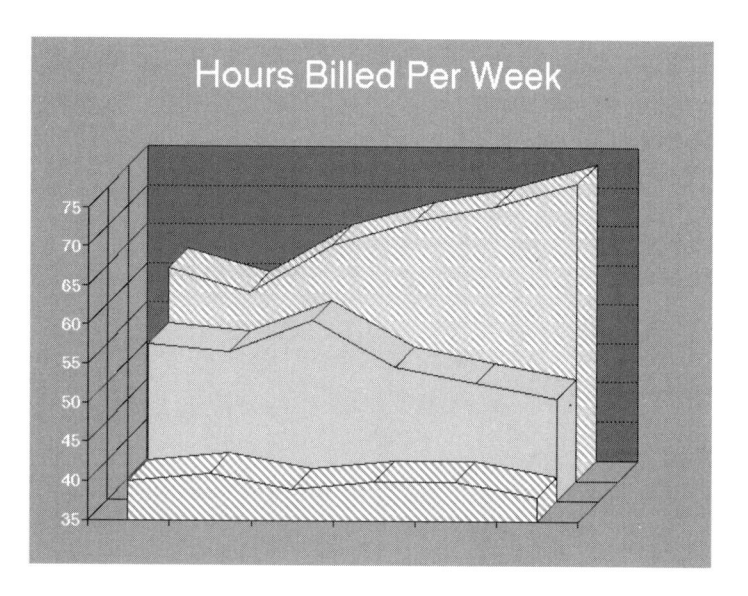

Figure 10-17 is a 3-D Area graph, which resembles the two-dimensional area graph shown in Figure 10-10.

Enhancing graphs

At this point, you've seen how to create the 14 types of graphs that Quattro Pro offers. This section describes how to use graph enhancements, such as titles, legends, interior labels, and color, to make your graphs more attractive and understandable.

Using the Text commands

Quattro Pro provides seven Text commands. The Graph Text 1st Line and Graph Text 2nd Line commands let you add titles that describe the graph. The Graph Text X-Title, Graph Text Y-Title, and Graph Text Secondary Y-Axis commands let you add titles that describe the graph axes. The Graph Text Legends command lets you add a legend to identify the data series. Finally, the Graph Text Font command lets you control which fonts Quattro Pro uses for graph text.

Adding titles to graphs

You can use the Graph Text command to add as many as five titles to a graph; two titles that appear at the top of the graph and three titles for the x-axis, the y-axis, and a second y-axis. To add title lines to the top of a graph, choose the Graph Text command. When the menu shown in Figure 10-18 appears, choose the 1st Line option and type whatever you want to appear at the very top of the graph—for

FIGURE 10-18.
Choosing the Graph Text command presents this menu.

FIGURE 10-19.
You can use the Graph Text command to add as many as five titles to a graph.

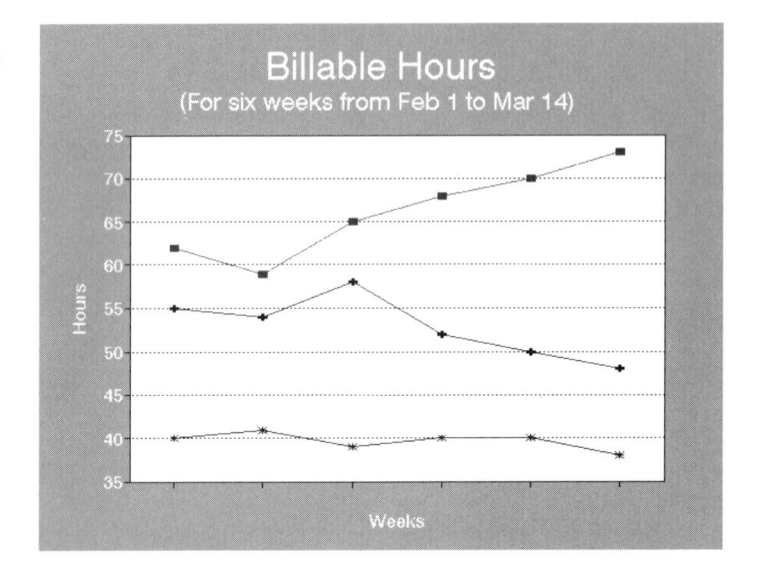

example, a description of what's being depicted in the graph—and then press the Enter key. Choose the 2nd Line option and follow the same process to add a second line of text to the top of the graph.

Quattro Pro also allows you to assign titles to a graph's x-axis and y-axis. To add a title to the x-axis in the example graph, choose the X-Title option from the Graph Text menu, type the text you want to appear beneath the x-axis, and then press the Enter key. Or, to add a title to the y-axis, choose the Y-Title option, type the text you want to appear alongside the y-axis, and then press the Enter key. For graphs that have a second y-axis, use the Secondary Y-Axis option to add a title for the second y-axis. Figure 10-19 shows a line graph that has *Billable Hours* as the first title and *(For the six weeks from Feb 1 to Mar 14)* as the second title. The x-axis title is *Weeks*, and the y-axis title is *Hours*.

A closer look at titles

In some cases, you might want to use entries in your worksheet as titles in your graphs. To use a worksheet entry as a title, choose the Graph Text command and then choose the option for the title that you want to define; 1st Line, 2nd Line, X-Axis, and so forth. Next, type a backslash (\) at the prompt, and then enter the

Chapter 10: Creating Graphs   317

address of the cell that contains the entry you want to use. If you have used the Edit Names Create command to assign a block name to a cell, you can also use that name instead of the cell address to define a title.

To change or delete a title, choose the Graph Text command and then choose the option for the title you want to change. The existing title is displayed on the input line. At this point, you can press the direction keys to move to any character in the title, or use the Del or Backspace key to delete characters. You can insert characters simply by typing those characters. You can also press the Esc key to erase the title completely and then, if you want, type a new title. When you finish, press the Enter key.

Adding legends

To add a legend label to a graph, first choose the Graph Text command, and then choose the Legends option. When Quattro Pro presents the menu shown in Figure 10-20, choose the 1st Series option and type the legend you want for the first series. After you define the legends they appear on the menu. The Position option on the Legends menu lets you specify the position of the legend as Bottom, Right, or None. Bottom indicates that the legend should appear below the graph, Right indicates that the legend should appear to the right of the graph, and None removes the legend. To see an example legend, take another look at Figure 10-3, which is the stacked-bar graph created using the Fast Graph option. Quattro Pro included a legend because the first cells in each of the data series contained labels (as shown in Figure 10-1), and Quattro Pro assumed those labels are legends.

Changing the fonts

To change the font that Quattro Pro uses to display the text in a graph, choose the Graph Text Font command. Quattro Pro displays a list of the graph's text components: 1st Line, 2nd Line, X-Title, Y-Title, Legends, Data Labels, and Tick Labels. To change the font that Quattro Pro uses for a piece of text, select the piece of graph

FIGURE 10-20.
The Graph Text Legends menu lets you define legends.

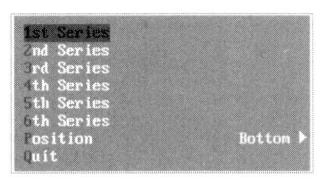

FIGURE 10-21.
Select the graph text you want to change to see this menu.

text you want to change. Quattro Pro presents a menu like that shown in Figure 10-21, which indicates the existing font settings for the piece of graph text.

Use the Font menu to define the typeface, point size, style, and color of a font. After you finish specifying these four font elements, choose the menu's Quit option to return to the menu that lists the graph's text components. To edit another piece of graph text, choose it from the list.

Defining the typeface. To define the typeface, choose the Typeface option from the Graph Text Font menu. Quattro Pro displays a box that lists the available typefaces, including Bitstream Dutch, Bitstream Swiss, Bitstream Courier, Roman, Roman Light, Sans Serif, Sans Serif Light, Script, Old English, Eurostyle, and Monospace. If you use a laser printer that has font cartridges and you have identified to Quattro Pro the font cartridge your printer uses, these fonts are also listed. Choose a typeface, and then press the Enter key.

Defining the point size. To define the point size of the font, choose the Point Size option from the Graph Text Font menu. Quattro Pro displays a box that lists the available point sizes. Each point represents $1/72$ of an inch. The larger the point size number, therefore, the larger the font size.

Defining style. Style refers to whether the font is bold, underlined, or italic. When you choose the Style option from the Graph Text Fonts menu, Quattro Pro displays a box that includes five options: Bold, Italic, Underlined, Reset, and Quit. The first three options—Bold, Italic, and Underlined—represent alternatives to the standard font style. The Reset option returns the font style to regular from Bold, Underlined, or Italic. The Quit option exits from the menu without making a change to the font style.

Defining the color. Quattro Pro also lets you specify the color of a font on the screen. (If you are using a color printer, this choice also determines the color in which the font is printed.) To do so, choose the Color option from the Graph Text Font menu. Quattro Pro displays a box that lists colors; choose from the box and press the Enter key.

Using the Customize Series commands

The Customize Series commands let you change the appearance of the data series and the x-axis and y-axis that appear in a graph. Using the Customize Series commands, for example, you can change the colors used in an area graph, the line styles used for the lines in line and XY graphs, and the widths of the bars in bar graphs.

Changing the colors of data series

To change the default color settings for one of the six data series, choose the Graph Customize Series Colors command. Quattro Pro presents a menu that lists the six data series as options and a seventh option, Quit. If you're working with the

FIGURE 10-22.
Quattro Pro displays a list of fill patterns that you can use in your graphs.

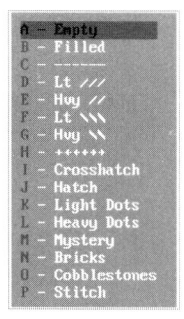

```
A - Empty
B - Filled
C - ------
D - Lt ///
E - Hvy //
F - Lt \\\
G - Hvy \\
H - ++++++
I - Crosshatch
J - Hatch
K - Light Dots
L - Heavy Dots
M - Mystery
N - Bricks
O - Cobblestones
P - Stitch
```

expanded version of the menus (press the plus key (+) on the numeric keypad to do so), you also see the current color style settings for each data series. To change the default color assigned to a data series, choose the option that corresponds to that data series. For example, to change the color assigned to the first data series, choose the 1st Series option. Quattro Pro displays a menu that lists the possible colors. The colors listed depend on your monitor and graphics adapter. From the menu, choose the color you want for the data series.

Changing fill patterns

As mentioned, Quattro Pro uses unique fill patterns to differentiate the data series in many graphs. Although Quattro Pro chooses the pattern, you can override Quattro Pro's choices. To change the pattern that Quattro Pro uses for a data series, choose the Graph Customize Series Fill Patterns command. Quattro Pro presents a menu that lists the data series that appear in the graph. From this menu, choose the data series whose fill pattern you want to modify. Quattro Pro displays a list of patterns, as shown in Figure 10-22. Choose the pattern you want to assign to the chosen series.

Changing the marker symbols and line styles

Both line graphs and XY graphs use lines and symbols to plot data series. Using the Graph Customize Series Markers & Lines command, you can control how Quattro Pro draws these lines and symbols.

Changing line styles. Line styles determine whether a line is solid, dotted, center-lined, or dashed. The default setting is solid. To change this default, choose the Graph Customize Series Markers & Lines command. Quattro Pro presents a menu that has four options: Line Styles, Markers, Formats, and Quit. If you choose the Line Styles option, Quattro Pro displays a list of the data series. If you're working with the expanded version of the menus (press the plus key (+) to do so) you see the current color style setting for each data series. Choose the data series for which you want to specify a line style, and Quattro Pro lists the eight line style choices: Solid, Dotted, Center-Line, Dashed, Heavy Solid, Heavy Dotted, Heavy Centered, and Heavy Dashed. Choose the line style you want, and then press the Enter key.

The different line styles do not show up well in book illustrations, so this section does not try to show them. Instead, it's probably more valuable to describe the line styles. A solid line is an unbroken line. A dotted line is a row of periods. A center-lined line is a row of long and short dashes, and a dashed line is a row of hyphens. The heavy versions of these four line styles simply make them appear thicker and bolder.

Markers. A marker is a symbol Quattro Pro uses to designate a data point. By default, Quattro Pro uses a different marker symbol for each data series: a filled square for the first data series, a plus for the second, an asterisk for the third, an empty square for the fourth, an X for the fifth, and a filled triangle for the sixth. You can change the default settings by using a process that almost that of specifying line styles. Choose the Graph Customize Series Markers & Lines command, and then choose the Markers option. Quattro Pro displays a list of the data series. (As with the Line Styles option, if you're working with the expanded version of the menus, you see the current marker settings for each data series.) Choose the data series for which you want to specify a marker symbol, and Quattro Pro lists the 10 marker symbols that are available, as shown in Figure 10-23. Choose the marker symbol you want and press the Enter key.

Using only lines or only markers. Quattro Pro by default uses both lines and markers to draw the lines on a line graph. To change this default so that Quattro Pro draws only lines or only markers, choose the Formats option from the Graph Customize Series Markers & Lines menu. Quattro Pro displays a list of the data series. Choose the data series for which you want to change the format, and Quattro Pro presents a menu that has four choices: Lines, Symbols, Both, or Neither. To use only lines, choose the Lines option. To use only symbols, choose the Symbols option. To change back to using both lines and markers, choose the Both option. To remove the data series line and markers, choose the Neither option.

Changing bar widths

The Graph Customize Series Bar Width command lets you control the widths of the bars in a bar chart. By default, Quattro Pro uses 60 percent of the space on the x-axis for bars. For example, if the x-axis is 10 centimeters long, the total width of the bars equals 60 percent, or 6 centimeters. If the bar graph has six bars, each bar

FIGURE 10-23.
Quattro Pro displays a list of the marker symbols.

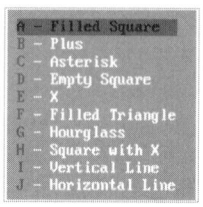

```
A - Filled Square
B - Plus
C - Asterisk
D - Empty Square
E - X
F - Filled Triangle
G - Hourglass
H - Square with X
I - Vertical Line
J - Horizontal Line
```

will be 1 centimeter wide. To change the default bar width, choose the Graph Customize Series Bar Width command. Quattro Pro displays the default bar width setting, 60. To increase the width of the bars, increase the percentage. To decrease the width of the bars, decrease the percentage.

Keep in mind that any increase in the bar width means your bar graph shows less space between the bars. For example, with the bar width settings at 60 percent, 40 percent of the x-axis shows white space. If you increase the bar width setting to 80 percent, only 20 percent of the x-axis shows space.

Adding interior labels

Interior labels are labels that you can place in line, XY, and bar graphs. You cannot add interior labels to an area or pie graph. Unlike titles and axis labels, which appear outside the graph, interior labels appear inside the graph near the data points on the line or bars to which they correspond. You can define an interior label for each data series value that is plotted on a graph.

To add interior labels to a data series in a graph, choose the Graph Customize Series Interior Labels command, and then choose the series to which you want to add the labels. Quattro Pro prompts you to define the block of cells that contains the entries you want to use as interior labels for that series. After you define the block, Quattro Pro presents the Placement menu. Use the options in this menu to determine the positions of the labels in the graph relative to each data point: Center (centered on the data point), Left, Above, Right, or Below. To reset the label setting, choose the None option. Figure 10-24 shows an example bar graph that has interior labels.

FIGURE 10-24.
Quattro Pro allows you to place interior labels in line, XY, and bar graphs.

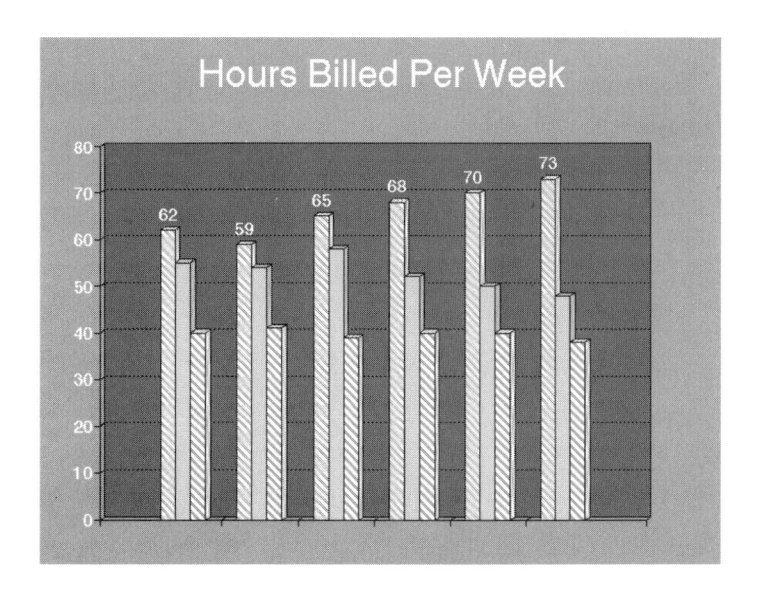

Normally, the block of interior labels you choose for a data series is the same size as the data series block itself. For example, if the data series includes four cells, then the block of interior labels also includes four cells. In many cases, the interior labels block is identical to the data series block. When these two blocks are identical, Quattro Pro uses the values from the data series as labels for the data points on the graph, as is the case in Figure 10-24.

A closer look at interior labels. The entries in the blocks you define as interior labels can be either values or labels. If the entries are values, and if you've given those values a format, the labels in the graph retain that format. If the entries are labels, they should be relatively short or they will overlap.

The position you choose for the interior labels for a data series determines the orientation of the labels relative to the data points that make up the series. In most cases, you'll choose either Above or Below so that the labels appear above or below each data point. For markers and XY graphs, however, you might find it more readable to choose Left or Right. The Center option positions the labels right on the data points.

Erasing interior labels. To erase interior labels from a data series, choose the Graph Customize Series Interior Labels command, and then choose the series whose interior labels you want to erase. When Quattro Pro prompts you to define the interior labels block for the series, press the Enter key. Finally, from the Placement menu, choose the None option to erase the interior labels.

Creating graphs that include both bars and lines

Use the Graph Customize Series Override Type command to create graphs that include both bars and lines. First, choose either a line or bar graph and its series. Then, choose the Graph Customize Series Override Type command. Quattro Pro presents the menu that lists the six possible data series in the graph. Choose the series whose type you want to change. A list of the three graph types for the data series then appears: Default, Bar, and Line. Choose the Default option to use the same graph type for the data series as the graph type you defined using the Graph Type command. (For example, if the graph type is Line, the Default option causes the selected data series to be displayed as a line.) Choose the Bar option to use bars for the data series. Choose the Line option to use a line for the data series. Figure 10-25 shows an example of a bar graph in which the second data series is displayed as a line rather than as a bar.

A closer look at combined bar and line graphs. Quattro Pro plots data series in a graph in order. The first series is plotted first, the second series second, and so on. As a result, you might find that graph lines are hidden by a bar when a bar overlaps a line and the bar is plotted after the line. To avoid this situation, choose the

FIGURE 10-25.
The Graph Customize Series Override Type command lets you put lines on a bar graph and bars on a line graph.

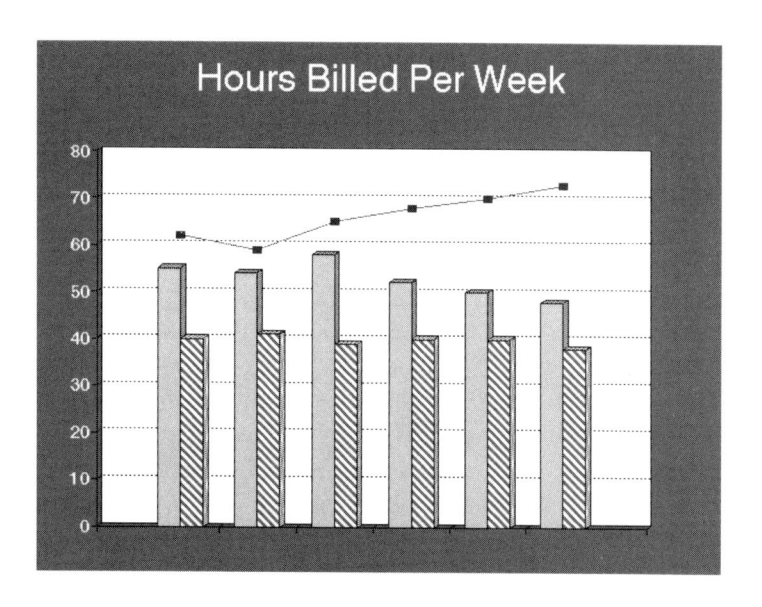

Hours Billed Per Week

series in the order in which you want Quattro Pro to plot them, with the lines following the bars.

Using a second y-axis

Line graphs, XY graphs, and bar graphs initially have two axes: an x-axis and a y-axis. You can, however, use a second y-axis when you want to compare two data series that are not calibrated in the same units. For example, suppose you want to graph ice-cream cone sales and the average daily temperature through July. You can use the x-axis to represent time—the 31 days of July—and the first y-axis to represent the average daily temperature. You cannot, however, show the data series for ice-cream cone sales using the temperature y-axis because doing so does not make sense. Fortunately, Quattro Pro allows you to add a second y-axis that, in this example, can be used to represent ice cream cone sales.

To use a second y-axis, first choose the graph type and series. Then, choose the Graph Customize Series Y-Axis command. Quattro Pro displays a list of the six data series. Choose the series you want to plot against the second y-axis. Quattro Pro presents a submenu that gives you two choices: Primary Y-Axis and Secondary Y-Axis. Choose the Secondary Y-Axis option to plot the data series against a second y-axis, and then press the Enter key. When you next view the graph, Quattro Pro creates a second y-axis based on the values in the data series that you've indicated should be plotted again the second y-axis. If you mistakenly assign a data series to be plotted against the secondary y-axis, choose the Graph Customize Series Y-Axis command again, choose the data series you mistakenly assigned, choose the Primary Y-Axis option, and then press the Enter key. Figure 10-26 shows an example of a line graph with two y-axes.

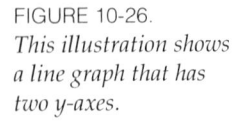

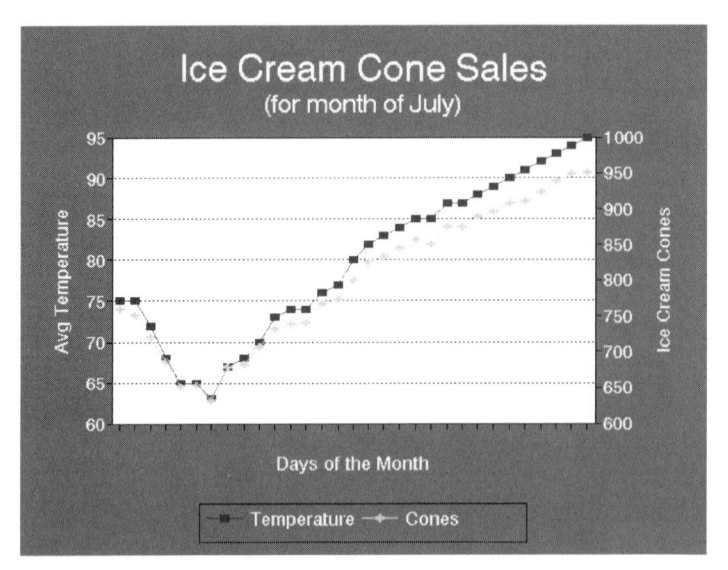

FIGURE 10-26.
This illustration shows a line graph that has two y-axes.

Enhancing a pie graph

Many of the enhancements you use with other graphs also apply to pie graphs. You can add labels to a pie graph, for example. Quattro Pro plots each x-axis value next to the corresponding slice in the pie. Because pie graphs are unlike other graphs, however, Quattro Pro offers several enhancements that apply only to pie graphs. To use these options, choose the Graph Customize Series Pies command, and Quattro Pro presents a menu that lists six options: Label Format, Explode, Patterns, Colors, Tick Marks, and Quit. Using the options in this menu, you can change the various aspects of a pie graph and explode a pie slice to call more attention to it.

Label formats in pie graphs. Quattro Pro places a percentage next to each slice in a pie graph. To change the format of these labels, choose the Graph Customize Series Pies Label Format command. Quattro Pro displays four format options: Value, %, $, and None. The Value option tells Quattro Pro to display next to each slice in the graph the values in the block you defined as the first series. These values replace the percentages that Quattro Pro normally displays next to each slice. The % option, which is the default, tells Quattro Pro to display percentages next to each slice. The $ option tells Quattro Pro to display the values from the first series in currency format next to each slice. The None option tells Quattro Pro to display no labels next to the slices.

Although the labels that Quattro Pro displays next to each pie slice are useful, remember that you can make pie graphs even more informative by adding another label to each slice. You can also use the Graph Series X-Axis Series command to label the slices in a pie graph. When you choose this command, Quattro Pro prompts you to highlight a block of cells. Simply define the block that contains the labels you want to use for the slices in the graph. Quattro Pro displays the contents of the first cell in the block next to the first slice of the pie, the contents of the second cell next to the second slice, and so on.

Exploded pie slices. The Graph Customize Series Pies Explode command lets you explode one or more segments of a pie graph. Exploding a segment draws attention to that segment by separating it slightly from the rest of the graph. When you choose this command, a menu that lists the first slices (up to nine) of the pie appears. Choose the slice you want to explode (or unexplode) from this menu, and Quattro Pro displays another menu that has two options: Don't Explode and Explode. If you choose the Explode option, Quattro Pro explodes, or separates, the selected slice from the other slices. If the selected slice is already exploded, you can choose the Don't Explode option to put it back into the pie. Figure 10-27 shows the same pie graph as shown in Figure 10-9 but with the first slice exploded. (Notice also that the graph has a different title and that the $ format is used rather than the default %.)

Although the series you use to define a pie graph can include more than nine cells, resulting in a pie graph that has more than nine slices, you can explode only the first nine slices.

Pie slice patterns and colors. If you have a color monitor, Quattro Pro fills each slice with a unique pattern and color. If you have a monochrome graphics monitor, Quattro Pro uses a unique pattern for each slice. Quattro Pro chooses the patterns and colors, but you can override Quattro Pro's pattern and color choices.

FIGURE 10-27.
Quattro Pro lets you explode one or more slices of a pie graph.

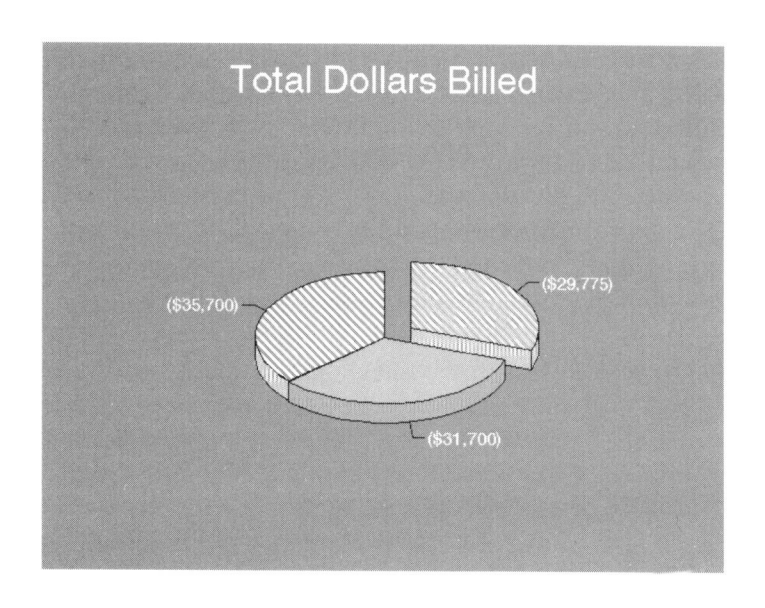

To change the pattern that Quattro Pro assigns to each slice in a pie graph, choose the Graph Customize Series Pies Patterns command. Quattro Pro presents a menu that lists the first nine slices that can appear in a pie graph. Choose the slice whose pattern you want to modify. Quattro Pro displays a list of patterns like the one shown in Figure 10-22. From the list, choose the pattern you want for the selected slice.

To change the colors that Quattro Pro assigns to each slice, use the Graph Customize Series Pies Colors command. When you choose this command, Quattro Pro presents a menu that lists the first nine slices. Choose the slice whose color you want to modify, and Quattro Pro displays a list of colors. (The actual number of colors available depends on the video hardware you use.) Choose the color that you want to assign to the chosen slice. Although a pie graph can have more than nine slices, you can control the colors of only the first nine slices. The colors you choose are reused after the first nine slices have been plotted.

Tick-marks. Quattro Pro by default draws short lines, called tick-marks, from a pie graph label to its pie slice. These tick-marks make it easier to identify which slice goes with which label. If your pie has only a few slices, however, you probably do not need tick-marks. To remove tick-marks from a pie graph, choose the Graph Customize Series Pie Tick Marks command. Quattro Pro presents a menu that lists two choices: Yes and No. Choose the No option to remove the tick-marks. To replace the tick-marks, simply choose the command and then choose the Yes option.

Changing the graph settings

The Customize Series menu contains two more commands: Update and Reset. The Update option saves the current graph settings as the new default values, which means that you can change items such as Quattro Pro's default graph type, colors, fill patterns, line styles, and markers. The Reset option lets you change the current Graph Type, Series, and Customize Series settings back to their original default values. After you choose the Graph Customize Series Reset command, Quattro Pro presents a menu that lists as options the six data series, Graph, and Quit. As mentioned earlier, to erase a data series choose it from the Reset menu. To erase all the data series and change the current Customize Series settings back to their original defaults, choose the Graph option.

Using the Graph X-Axis command

Use the Graph X-Axis command to control the scaling of the x-axis, the tick-marks that appear along the axis, and the labels that identify the tick-marks for XY

FIGURE 10-28.
The Graph X-Axis command displays this menu, from which you can modify a graph's x-axis.

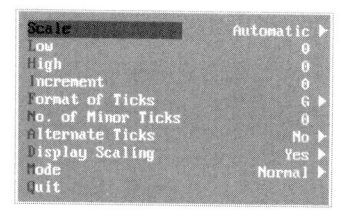

```
Scale              Automatic ▶
Low                        0
High                       0
Increment                  0
Format of Ticks            G ▶
No. of Minor Ticks         0
Alternate Ticks           No ▶
Display Scaling          Yes ▶
Mode                  Normal ▶
Quit
```

graphs. When you choose the Graph X-Axis command, Quattro Pro presents a menu that lists 10 options: Scale, Low, High, Increment, Format Of Ticks, No. Of Minor Ticks, Alternate Ticks, Display Scaling, Mode, and Quit, as shown in Figure 10-28.

Scaling

The scale of the x-axis in the XY graph shown in Figure 10-8 was set by Quattro Pro. In other words, Quattro Pro selected the beginning and ending values that are represented on the axis. Most of the time, you will find that Quattro Pro's scaling is adequate. However, you can adjust the scaling of the x-axis manually. To do so, choose the Graph X-Axis Scale command. Quattro Pro presents a submenu that has two choices: Manual and Automatic. Choose the Manual option to switch from Automatic to Manual scaling. Next, choose the Low option from the Graph X-Axis menu, type the smallest value you want plotted against the x-axis, and then press the Enter key. Similarly, choose the High option, type the biggest value you want plotted against the x-axis, and the press the Enter key. For example, if you want the x-axis to start at 0 and end at 100, set the Low value at 0 and the High value at 100.

Controlling the x-axis tick-marks

Quattro Pro also provides several options on the Graph X-Axis menu that let you control the x-axis tick-marks, including Increment, Format Of Ticks, No. Of Minor Ticks, Alternate Ticks, and Display Scaling.

Increment. To change the increment of the tick-marks on the x-axis, which you usually want to do whenever you set the scaling to manual and specify low and high values, use the Increment option from the Graph X-Axis menu. For example, if you set the low value to 0 and the high value to 100 and you want tick-marks at every 10 units, choose Increment from the Graph X-Axis menu, type 10, and press the Enter key.

Format of ticks. The Format Of Ticks option in the Graph X-Axis menu lets you control the format of the numbers that are displayed next to the tick-marks along the x-axis. When you choose this option, Quattro Pro displays a list of the numeric format options; the same list that Quattro Pro displays when you choose the Style Numeric Format command. From this list, choose the format you want. If you choose a format that allows you to specify the number of decimal places, Quattro Pro prompts you to do so.

Number of minor ticks. Use the No. Of Minor Ticks option to set the interval between the major tick-marks on the graph's x-axis. When you choose this option from the Graph X-Axis menu, Quattro Pro prompts you to enter a number between 0 and 255 to define the number of minor tick-marks between the pairs of major tick-marks. The default setting, 0, tells Quattro Pro to place only major tick-marks and not minor tick-marks on the x-axis. If you change this setting, Quattro Pro adds the specified number of minor tick-marks between the graph's major tick-marks.

Alternate ticks. If not enough room is available under the x-axis to accommodate the x-axis labels, you can use the Alternate Ticks option to tell Quattro Pro to use two lines to display the x-axis labels. Odd-numbered labels—the first, third, fifth, and so on—appear on the first line. Even-numbered labels—the second, fourth, sixth, and so on—appear on the second line. To specify that you want x-axis labels displayed on two lines, choose the Graph X-Axis Alternate Ticks command. Quattro Pro presents a submenu that lists two options: Yes and No. Choose the Yes option to alternate the labels. To reset the labels so that they appear on only one line, choose the command again and choose the No option.

The scale indicator

If the values displayed along the x-axis are large, Quattro Pro divides them by a constant so that they can be displayed without wasting space. In addition, Quattro Pro places a magnitude indicator such as *(Thousands)*, *(Millions)*, or *(1E+10)* next to the y-axis. For example, if the x-axis values in a graph are 1,000,000, 2,000,000, 3,000,000, and so on, Quattro Pro displays the values 1, 2, 3, and so on next to the x-axis and places the magnitude indicator *(Millions)* next to the y-axis.

Although these legends are often quite useful, because they help keep the graph clean and uncluttered, they can also cause a problem. If the values on which the graph is based have already been divided by some constant, Quattro Pro's magnitude indicator might not explain the data in the graph accurately. For example, suppose you have created a worksheet that lists the estimated national debt for each of the next 25 years. The numbers in this worksheet are quite large: 645,921,000,000, 678,553,000,000, and so on. To save space, you decide to divide each number in the worksheet by 1,000,000 so that the numbers in the worksheet are 645,921, 678,553, and so on. In addition, you include an interior label *Numbers in Millions*, as described earlier in "Adding Interior Labels," to let your readers know that the numbers are divided by 1,000,000. After you graph these numbers, Quattro Pro displays the numbers 500, 1000, 1500, 2000, and so on next to the y-axis and places the magnitude indicator *(Thousands)* next to the axis. The problem is that the number 500 along the y-axis can be construed as 500,000 but actually represents 500,000,000.

If you encounter this kind of problem, use the Graph X-Axis Display Scaling option to turn off the magnitude indicator. After you choose this command, you see a menu that has two options: Yes and No. If you choose the Yes option, Quattro Pro displays the magnitude indicator. If you choose the No option, Quattro Pro does not display the magnitude indicator. If you remove the magnitude indicator from a graph, you might want to change the x-axis title to include a magnitude indicator of your own. For instance, in the preceding example you might add the word *(Millions)* to the x-axis title to identify the units of the numbers on the x-axis correctly.

Using logarithmic x-axis scaling

The Graph X-Axis Mode command lets you use logarithmic scaling on the x-axis. To use logarithmic scaling, choose the Graph X-Axis Mode command. Quattro Pro presents a submenu that has two choices: Normal and Log. To tell Quattro Pro to use logarithmic scaling, choose the Log option. If the x-axis already uses logarithmic scaling, you can choose the Normal option to change the scaling back to regular.

Using the Y-Axis commands

The Graph Y-Axis menu shown in Figure 10-29 for the most part mirrors the Graph X-Axis menu, so using the options on the two menus is the same except that the x-axis options affect the x-axis and the y-axis options affect the y-axis. A couple of differences, however, are worth pointing out. First, the Graph Y-Axis menu does not include an Alternate Ticks option. Second, the Graph Y-Axis menu includes a 2nd Y-Axis option. The 2nd Y-Axis option presents a menu that mirrors the y-axis menu, except that its options apply to the second y-axis instead of the first.

Using the Graph Overall options

The Graph Overall command displays a set of options that let you control components of the graph besides the data series, text, and axes. For example, you can change the grid on line graphs, XY graphs, and bar graphs, and draw boxes

FIGURE 10-29.
The Graph Y-Axis menu commands let you modify a graph's y-axes.

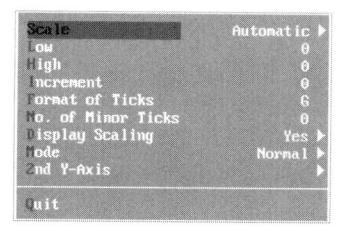

around certain parts of a graph. You can also change the graph's background color and even tell Quattro Pro to display the graph in black and white. You can also control whether Quattro Pro displays graphs using the three-dimensional effect.

Changing a graph's grid

To change the grid in a graph, choose the Graph Overall Grid command. Quattro Pro presents a menu that lists eight options: Horizontal, Vertical, Both, Clear, Grid Color, Line Style, Fill Color, and Quit. The first four options—Horizontal, Vertical, Both, and Clear—control the gridlines displayed for line, XY, and bar graphs. The figures of graphs that appear earlier in this chapter, for example, all show horizontal gridlines drawn from the tick-marks on the y-axis. To replace the horizontal gridlines with vertical gridlines, choose the Vertical option. To use both horizontal and vertical gridlines, choose the Both option. To remove gridlines from the graph, choose the Clear option.

The fifth option, Grid Color, allows you to specify the color of the grid. To do so, choose the Graph Overall Grid Color command. Quattro Pro displays a list of colors from which you can choose the color you want. The list of colors varies depending on the video hardware you use.

The sixth option, Line Style, lets you control how Quattro Pro draws the lines that make up the grid. When you choose this option, Quattro Pro displays a list of the eight line styles available, which are the same as those available for drawing line graphs: Solid, Dotted, Center-Line, Dashed, Heavy Solid, Heavy Dotted, Heavy Centered, and Heavy Dashed. Choose the line style you want to use for the graph's gridlines, and then press the Enter key.

The seventh option, Fill Color, controls the color displayed behind the graph. To change this fill color, choose the Graph Overall Grid Fill Color command. Quattro Pro displays a list of colors, from which you can choose the one you want; after you make your selection, press the Enter key.

Adding outlines

Quattro Pro lets you draw boxes around graph titles, legends, and the graph itself. To do so, choose the Graph Overall Outlines command. Quattro Pro presents a menu that lists the three graph components around which you can draw a box: Titles, Legend, and Graph. Choose the graph component you want and then press the Enter key. Quattro Pro displays a list of the various box types—Box, Double-Line, Thick-Line, Shadow, 3D, Rnd Rectangle, and None—from which you can choose the type of box you want. The Box option draws four lines around the graph component to form a box. The Double-Line option draws the same box but with a double line, and the Thick-Line option draws the same box but with a thick line. The Shadow option draws a box and also the box's shadow, the 3D option draws a cube, the Rnd Rectangle option draws a rectangle with rounded corners, and the None option removes the box.

Changing the background screen color

In addition to being able to change the colors of graph components, you can also change the background screen color by choosing the Graph Overall Background Color command. Quattro Pro displays a list of colors for the background screen color, from which you choose the color you want; after you make your selection, press the Enter key.

Switching between two-dimensional and three-dimensional graphs

By default, Quattro Pro displays the data series components of bar graphs, pie graphs, and 3-D graphs using a three-dimensional effect that gives graphs the illusion of depth. You have the option, however, of forcing Quattro Pro to use only two dimensions. To do so, choose the Graph Overall Three-D command. Quattro Pro presents a menu that lists two options: Yes and No. To force Quattro Pro to display only two dimensions, choose the No option. If you chose the No option previously, you can force Quattro Pro to display three dimensions again by choosing the Yes option.

Displaying a graph in black-and-white

To display a graph in black-and-white on a color monitor, choose the Graph Overall Color/B&W command. Quattro Pro presents a menu that lists two choices: Color and B&W. To display a graph in black-and-white, choose the B&W option. To display the graph in color again, choose the Graph Overall Color/B&W command and choose the Color option.

Printing graphs

Now that you know how to create the various types of Quattro Pro graphs, display them on your monitor, and enhance them, it's time to think about printing them. This section begins by telling you what you need to do before you can print, and continues with a discussion of the process of printing a graph.

Preparing to print. Before you can print a graph, you must configure Quattro Pro for printing, which means telling Quattro Pro what kind of printer you have and how it connects to your printer. Typically, you already have done so, either when you originally installed Quattro Pro or when you first printed a worksheet on your printer. If you have not yet printed a report or configured a new printer, do so now by reading "Hardware Setup" in Chapter 7 and following the steps listed there.

Choosing a destination

Before you print, you also have to tell Quattro Pro where to send the printed graph. To do so, choose the Print Graph Print Destination command. Quattro Pro presents a menu that lists the three graph print destination possibilities: File, Graph Printer, and Screen Preview. To send your graph to the printer or plotter you defined as the first printer, choose the Graph Printer option. To display a printed version of the graph on the screen, choose the Screen Preview option. Finally, to create a print file of the graph that you can print later, choose the File option. (If you choose the File option, Quattro Pro displays the prompt *Enter print file name*, and you must type the filename you want for the file.) The choice you make remains in effect until you make another choice from this menu.

Choosing a graph

When you use the Print Graph Print command to print a graph, Quattro Pro prints the active graph, so before you can print you must activate the graph you want to print if it is not already active. You can activate the graph in one of two ways: by using the Graph Name Display command or by choosing the Print Graph Print Name command, which is equivalent to the Graph Name Display command.

Changing page layout

Although Quattro Pro sizes graphs so that they fit on an 8½-by-11-inch sheet of paper, on occasion you might need to adjust the size of a printed graph. The Print Graph Print Layout command gives you manual control over the dimensions of your printed graphs. To adjust the size of your graph, choose the Print Graph Print Layout command, and Quattro Pro presents the menu shown in Figure 10-30.

The Dimensions option allows you to choose a unit of measure for a page; Quattro Pro's default unit of measure is inches. When you choose this option, Quattro Pro presents a menu that has two options: Inches and Centimeters. To change the setting, choose the option you want to use. All of the settings controlled by the other options in the Print Graph Print Layout menu change to reflect the new settings.

FIGURE 10-30.
To adjust the size of a Quattro Pro graph, use the commands in this menu.

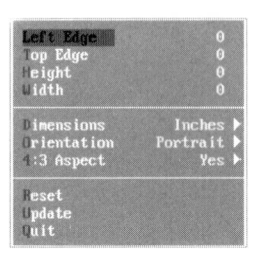

```
Left Edge          0
Top Edge           0
Height             0
Width              0

Dimensions     Inches   ▶
Orientation    Portrait ▶
4:3 Aspect     Yes      ▶

Reset
Update
Quit
```

The Left Edge and Top Edge options let you specify the number of inches or centimeters that Quattro Pro should use as a left and top margin when printing your graph. When you choose either option, Quattro Pro prompts you to enter a new setting. Type the new setting and press the Enter key. The default Left Edge and Top Edge settings are 0.

To specify how tall or wide your graph should be, use the Height and Width options. If you choose either option, Quattro Pro prompts you to enter a new setting. Type the new setting and press the Enter key. The default Height and Width settings are both 0. These settings allow Quattro Pro to print a graph using as much space as possible on an 8½-by-11-inch page. If you do change the Height and Width settings, however, you also need to use the 4:3 Aspect option, which is a Yes-No switch. When the switch is set to Yes, Quattro Pro prints graphs so that their ratio of width to height is 4 to 3, regardless of the height and width settings. The 4:3 ratio, by the way, is the same aspect ratio that Quattro Pro uses to display graphs on the screen. If you want a graph to use your own height and width settings, however, you must switch the 4:3 aspect switch to No. To do so, choose the Print Graph Print 4:3 Aspect command and choose the No option.

The Orientation option in the Print Graph Print Layout menu allows you to specify how your graph should be printed on a page. When you choose this command, Quattro Pro presents a menu that has two options: Portrait and Landscape mode. By default, graphs are printed vertically in portrait mode. To print graphs horizontally, choose the Orientation option, and then choose the Landscape option.

Resetting and saving print settings

The Graph Print Reset command allows you to return all active print settings—Printer Type, Destination, Layout, and so on—to their default values. When you choose this command, Quattro Pro restores all graph print settings to their default values. Be careful, because you can lose a lot of work by using this command hastily.

Use the Update option to save the current graph print settings as defaults. Unless you plan to change your print settings frequently, it's a good idea to choose this command after you adjust all of the graph print settings to suit you. When you choose the Graph Print Update command, Quattro Pro immediately writes the current settings on disk as the new graph print defaults.

Printing

After you choose a destination for graph output, identify the graph to print, and define a page layout, choose the Print Graph Print Go command to print. Quattro Pro begins printing your graph to the printer you selected. If you used the Print Destination menu to specify File, however, you must subsequently use the DOS COPY command to print the file. Type the command *COPY filename.ext >PRN* at the DOS prompt after you choose the Go option from the Print Graph Print menu. (See your DOS manual for information on copying a file to the printer.) If you print to the preview screen, Quattro Pro displays a facsimile of the printed graph page and also provides some special tools. "Previewing Your Worksheets Before Printing" in Chapter 7, explains how to preview.

Writing graph files

The Print Graph Print Write Graph File command makes it possible to write a Quattro Pro graph on disk in one of four formats:

- As a Lotus-compatible pic file that you can print using the Lotus PrintGraph utility
- As an eps (Encapsulated PostScript) file that can be imported into programs that support PostScript, such as Aldus PageMaker
- As an eps file that can be made into a slide
- As a pcx file that can be used by painting or presentation programs that support the pcx file format

To save a graph in one of these four file formats, choose the Print Graph Print Write Graph File command, and then choose the file format. Quattro Pro prompts you to supply the name of the file. Type a filename and press the Enter key. Quattro Pro writes the graph on disk using the file format you chose.

PostScript font compatibility

When you save a graph as an EPS file for use in Aldus PageMaker or another application, Quattro Pro converts all of the patterns in the graph to shades of gray. In addition, because Quattro Pro's fonts do not match PostScript fonts perfectly, the fonts in your graph are also altered.

Using the Annotate feature

The Annotate feature lets you draw arrows, lines, circles, and other shapes on graphs. You can even create a graph that's just a collection of arrows, lines, circles, and other shapes, in which case the graph is not really a graph but a picture.

Modifying a graph using the Annotator

To use the Annotator to modify an existing graph, first display the graph and then press the slash key (/). Quattro Pro redisplays the graph using the Annotator screen. Figure 10-31, for example, shows a bar graph inside an Annotator screen.

FIGURE 10-31.
This illustration shows a bar graph displayed in the Annotator screen.

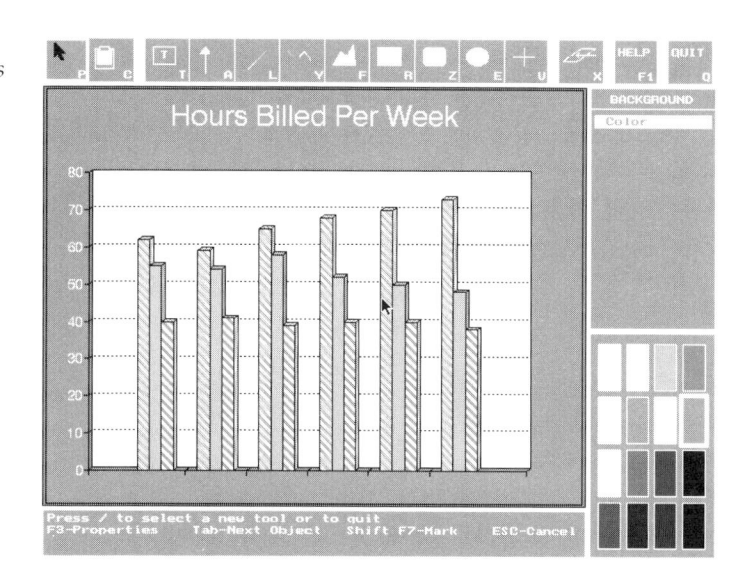

Touring the Annotator screen

The Annotator screen contains five components: the Toolbox, the Draw Area, the Property Sheet, the Gallery, and the Status Area. The Toolbox is the row of squares at the top of the Annotator screen that contains symbols and letters. Each square corresponds to a command that you can use to edit or draw on the graph. The first square, for example, controls the properties of the graph, and such elements as color, fill patterns, and line styles, which are described shortly. The Draw Area is the large rectangle that displays the graph you're modifying or the picture you're drawing. The Property Sheet is the rectangle in the upper-right corner of the screen, directly beneath the Toolbox, that lists the submenu choices or options related to a Toolbox command. When you choose the Property command from the Toolbox, the Property Sheet identifies the selected graph component and lists which properties you can change for that component.

The Gallery is the rectangle in the lower-right corner of the screen directly beneath the Property Sheet. It lists the available options for the property marked on the Property Sheet. For example, if the property color is marked, the Gallery displays a palette of color squares from which you can choose. Alternatively, if the property line style is marked, the Gallery displays a palette of line styles.

The Status Area is at the bottom of the Annotator screen. The Annotator screen's Status Area works exactly like the Status Area of the regular Quattro Pro screen. It describes menu commands, gives instructions, and identifies keyboard shortcuts.

Choosing Toolbox commands

To choose a Toolbox command, press the slash key (/) and the letter of that command or box. For example, to choose the Text command, press /-T. If you're a mouse user, you can simply click on the icon that represents the command. After you choose a Toolbox command, the border of its box becomes a thick line.

Getting help and quitting the Annotator

You can access Quattro's on-line help feature on the Annotator screen by choosing the Help icon. To do so, press F1 or click on the Help icon.

To leave the Annotator screen and return to the regular Quattro Pro worksheet screen, choose the Quit icon by pressing /-Q or clicking on the Quit icon.

Using the Toolbox draw commands

Use the nine command icon boxes that appear in the middle of the Toolbox commands to draw arrows, lines, and other shapes.

Adding text using the Toolbox. To add text to a graph, choose the Text command (/-T) from the Toolbox. Then, move the pointer to the location where you want to start typing text. If you have a mouse, point to the location; if you do not have a mouse, use the direction keys to move the pointer. Now, simply type the text. As you type, you see the letters appear. If you make a mistake, use the Del and Backspace keys to remove unwanted characters. To move the cursor, use the direction keys. To put the text on two lines, press the Ctrl-Enter keys when you reach the end of a line. To later combine the two lines of text on one line, press the Backspace key when the cursor is at the beginning of the second line. Finally, when you're ready to lock in the text, press the Enter key.

Quattro Pro lets you include bullets in the text you add to graphs. Each bullet is designated by a number, and to enter the bullet in a piece of text, type \\bullet #\\ where # is the number of the bullet type. Quattro Pro provides seven types of bullets:

- A box, which is number 0
- A filled box, which is number 1
- A checked box, which is number 2
- A check mark, which is number 3
- A shadowed box, which is number 4
- A checked shadowed box, which is number 5
- A filled circle, which is number 6

FIGURE 10-32.
Quattro Pro provides seven bullets you can use in text that you add to graphs.

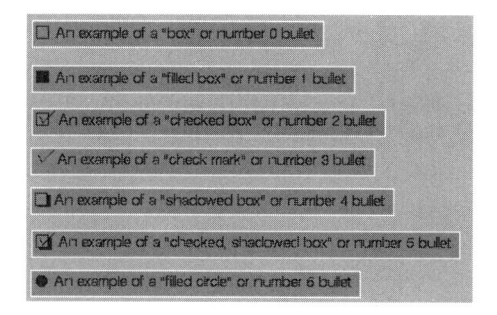

☐ An example of a "box" or number 0 bullet
■ An example of a "filled box" or number 1 bullet
☑ An example of a "checked box" or number 2 bullet
✓ An example of a "check mark" or number 3 bullet
⬜ An example of a "shadowed box" or number 4 bullet
☑ An example of a "checked, shadowed box" or number 5 bullet
● An example of a "filled circle" or number 6 bullet

Figure 10-32 shows examples of the seven bullets you can use in graph text. Although you will probably have fewer occasions to do so, you can also use bullets in worksheets by following the same procedure.

Adding an arrow using the Toolbox. If you have a mouse, follow these steps to add an arrow to a graph: Choose the Arrow command from the Toolbox, and then move the pointer to the location where you want the arrow to start. Click the mouse and then drag the pointer to where you want the arrow to point. As you do so, you see a line drawn between the place where you started the arrow and the pointer's current location. Release the mouse button, and Quattro Pro draws the arrow.

If you do not have a mouse, the process for drawing an arrow is a little more involved. First, choose the Arrow command from the Toolbox. Then, use the direction keys to move the pointer to the place you want the arrow to start. Press the period key (.) to start the arrow. Next, use the direction keys to move the pointer to the location where you want the arrow to point. Press the Enter key, and Quattro Pro draws the arrow.

Adding a line using the Toolbox. The process for adding a line mirrors that of adding an arrow. In fact, the only difference is in the final result: with an arrow of course, you have an arrow, but with a line you do not.

If you have a mouse, first choose the Line command from the Toolbox. Then, move the pointer to the location where you want to the line to start. Click the mouse, and then drag the pointer to where you want the line to end. As you do so, you see a line drawn between the place where you started the line and the pointer's current location. Release the mouse button, and Quattro Pro draws the line.

If you do not have a mouse, choose the Arrow command (/-A). Then use the direction keys to move the pointer to the place you want the line to start. Press the period key (.) to start the line. Next, use the direction keys to move the pointer to the location where you want the line to point. Press the Enter key, and Quattro Pro draws the line.

Adding a polyline using the Toolbox. A polyline is a line that has more than two points. You might think of it as two or more connected straight lines, or line segments. In fact, you can create a polyline that has as many as 999 line segments. Not surprisingly, the process for adding a polyline closely resembles that for adding a line.

If you have a mouse, first choose the Polyline command from the Toolbox. Then, move the pointer to the location where you want to start the first segment of the polyline. Click the mouse, and then drag the pointer to where you want this first segment to end. As you do so, you see a line drawn between the place where you started the line and the pointer's current location. Now move the mouse pointer again, drag the pointer to where you want this second segment to end, and then click the mouse. Quattro Pro draws a line from the end of the last line to the mouse pointer. Move the pointer and click the mouse again to start a third segment, or double-click the mouse to end the polyline.

If you do not have a mouse, choose the Polyline command (/-Y). Then use the direction keys to move the pointer to the place you want the first line segment to start, and then press the period key (.). Next, use the direction keys to move the pointer to the location where you want the first segment to end and the second segment to start. Press the Enter key again. Now, use the direction keys to move the pointer to the place where you want the second segment to end and press the Enter key again. Move the pointer to start a third segment, or press the Enter key twice to end the polyline.

Adding a polygon using the Toolbox. A polygon is a shape that has three or more sides. For example, triangles, trapezoids, pentagons, and octagons are all simple polygons. A polygon, however, can have up to 999 line segments. The process for adding a polygon closely resembles that for adding a polyline.

If you have a mouse, first choose the Polygon command from the Toolbox. Then, move the pointer to the location where you want to start the first segment of the polygon. Click the mouse, and then drag the pointer to where you want this first segment to end and the second segment to begin. As you do so, you see a line drawn between the place where you started the line and the pointer's current location. Click the mouse again, and drag the pointer to where you want the second segment to end and the third segment to start. In a similar fashion, draw any additional line segments. The last line segment, of course, needs to connect to the starting point of the first line segment. Double-click the mouse on this point to complete and fill the polygon.

If you do not have a mouse, choose the Polygon command (/-F). Then, use the direction keys to move the pointer to the place where you want the first line segment of the polygon to start, and then press the period key (.). Next, use the direction keys to move the pointer to the location where you want the first segment to end and the second segment to start. Press the Enter key. Now, use the direction keys to move the pointer to the place where you want the second segment to end and the third segment to start. Draw any additional line segments using the same process. The last line segment needs to connect to the starting point of the first line segment. Press Enter twice to complete and fill the polygon.

If you draw an incomplete polygon, such as two sides of a triangle, and double-click or press Enter twice, Quattro Pro will draw the final line segment between the starting and ending points to complete the polygon, and then fill it in.

Drawing curved lines and shapes using the Toolbox. If you have a mouse, you can also use the Polyline command to draw a curved line and the Polygon command to draw a curved shape. To do so, choose the appropriate command from the Toolbox. Then, when you trace the line or shape using the mouse, hold down the Shift key. In effect, Quattro Pro draws a polyline or polygon that has so many line segments it appears to be curved.

Drawing polygons with empty spaces using the Toolbox. You can use the Polygon command to draw shapes that contain an empty space. For example, you can draw a doughnut with a hole through which you can see. To do so, first draw the line segments that connect to form the outside boundary of the shape. Do not, however, press the Enter key twice or double-click the mouse. Rather, draw a line to where you want the inside boundary of the shape to start. Then, draw the line segments that form the inside boundary. To indicate that you have finished drawing the polygon, press the Enter key twice or double-click the mouse.

Drawing polygons with empty spaces is tricky, but the secret is to pay particular attention to connecting the segments that make up the outside and inside boundaries.

Adding a rectangle using the Toolbox. To add a rectangle to a graph, choose the Rectangle command (/-R). What you do next depends on whether you use a mouse or not.

If you have a mouse, move the pointer to the location where you want one of the rectangle corners. Click the mouse, and then drag the pointer to where you want the the rectangle's opposite corner. As you do this, you see a rectangle drawn based on the two corners: the corner where you started the rectangle and the opposite corner indicated by the current location of the pointer. When the pointer rests where you want the second, opposite corner, release the mouse button. Quattro Pro draws the rectangle.

If you do not have a mouse, use the direction keys to move the pointer to the location where you want one of the rectangle corners. Press the period key (.) to start the rectangle. Next, use the direction keys to move the pointer to the location where you want the rectangle's opposite corner. Press the Enter key, and Quattro Pro draws the rectangle.

Adding a rectangle that has rounded corners using the Toolbox. You can add a rectangle that has rounded corners by using the Rounded Rectangle command (/-Z). The steps for adding a rectangle that has rounded corners mirror those for adding a regular rectangle.

Adding an ellipse using the Toolbox. To add an ellipse to a graph, essentially you draw a temporary rectangle, which Quattro Pro then fills with an ellipse. Choose the Ellipse command (/-E). What you do next depends on whether you use a mouse or not.

If you have a mouse, move the pointer to the location where you want one of the rectangle corners. Click the mouse, and then drag the pointer to where you want the the rectangle's opposite corner. As you do this, you see a rectangle drawn based on the two corners; the corner where you started the rectangle and the opposite corner indicated by the current location of the pointer. Release the mouse button. Quattro Pro removes the rectangle and then draws an ellipse that best fills the space previously filled by the rectangle.

If you do not have a mouse, use the direction keys to move the pointer to the location where you want one of the rectangle corners. Press the period key (.) to start the rectangle. Next, use the direction keys to move the pointer to the location where you want the rectangle's opposite corner. Press the Enter key, and Quattro Pro removes the rectangle and then draws an ellipse that fills the space previously filled by the rectangle.

Adding a perfectly vertical or horizontal line using the Toolbox. If you've tried to draw a perfectly vertical or horizontal line using the mouse, you know it is not easy, exactly as it is not easy to draw a perfectly vertical or horizontal line on a piece of paper. However, Quattro Pro's Annotator provides the Vertical/Horizontal (/-V) command for drawing these sorts of lines.

If you have a mouse, first choose the Vertical/Horizontal command. Then, move the pointer to the location where you want the line to start. Click the mouse. Next, drag the pointer roughly down or up if you want a vertical line, or roughly left or right if you want a horizontal line. As you do so, you see a perfectly vertical or horizontal line drawn between the place where you started the line and the current position of the pointer. When the line is the length you want, release the mouse button and Quattro Pro draws the line.

If you do not have a mouse, choose the Vertical/Horizontal command (/-V). Then, use the direction keys to move the pointer to the place where you want the line to start, and press the period key (.). Next, use the direction keys to move the pointer down or up if you want a vertical line, or left or right if you want a horizontal line. When the line is the length you want, press the Enter key. Quattro Pro draws the line. Note, however, that you shouldn't need to use the Vertical/Horizontal command if you do not have a mouse because pressing the Up or

Down direction key repeatedly draws a perfect vertical line. Similarly, pressing the Right or Left direction key repeatedly draws a perfect horizontal line.

Changing properties

Earlier in the chapter, "Enhancing Graphs" described how to do such tasks as changing the colors used on a graph, the fill patterns used on a bar or pie slice, and the fonts used on graph text. You can accomplish these same tasks from the Annotator screen. What's more, from the Annotator screen you can also change the characteristics of the elements you've added using the Annotator, such as arrows, lines, and other shapes.

This section does not describe every detail regarding changing graph properties but instead describes the general techniques. In addition, the mechanics of changing graph component properties is the same for all of the graph component properties.

What are graph components? You might be wondering which of the elements that appear on the graph screen are graph components. The answer is simple: the graph background, the axes, the bars, the lines, the pie slices, and other elements used to represent the data series are graph components. In addition, all the text on a graph, both that used for titles and legends and text you added using the Toolbox's Text command, are graph components also.

Choosing the Properties command from the Toolbox. Before you begin modifying graph component properties, you must select the Properties command from Toolbox. To do so, either click on the P using the mouse, or press /-P.

Choosing a single graph component. After you choose the Properties command, you must identify the graph component you want to modify. If you have a mouse, click on the object. If you do not have a mouse, select a graph component using the Tab and Shift-Tab keys. The Tab key selects the next graph component, and the Shift-Tab keys select the previous graph component. Pressing the Tab key repeatedly causes Quattro Pro to cycle through selecting each graph component from those created first to those created last. Pressing the Shift-Tab keys repeatedly causes Quattro Pro to cycle through selecting each graph component from those created last to those created first. To indicate that a component has been selected, Quattro Pro marks the component with small squares, called handles. For example, in Figure 10-33, these small squares appear at either end of an arrow that's been selected. Other objects might use more handles. For example, a rectangle that's been selected shows handles on all four corners and all four sides.

Picking the property. After you select a graph component, Quattro Pro lists on the Property Sheet the component properties you can use. For example, in Figure 10-33 the Property Sheet shows three properties: Arrowhead Color, Line Color,

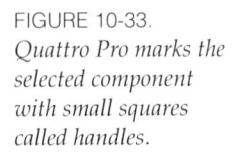

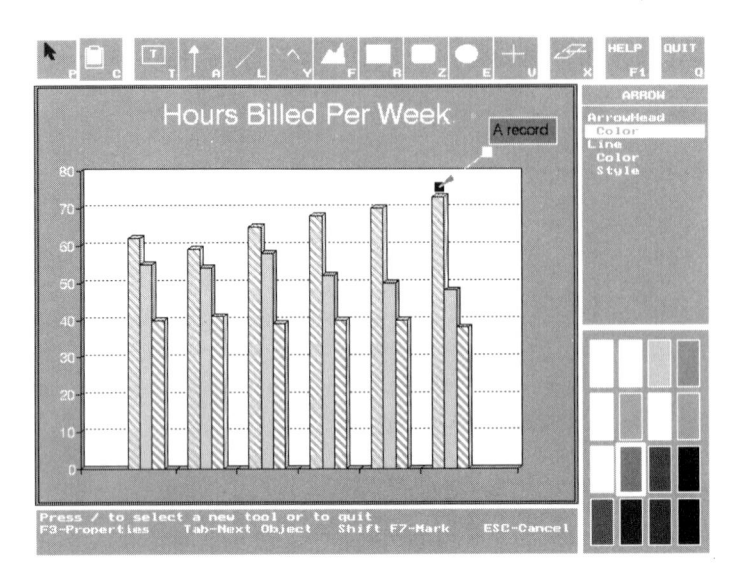

FIGURE 10-33.
Quattro Pro marks the selected component with small squares called handles.

and Line Style (the three elements you can change about an arrow). Of course, other graph components have other properties.

To identify which property you want to change, select that property from the Property Sheet. If you have a mouse, click on the property you want to change. If you do not have a mouse, select a property by pressing F3 to activate the Property Sheet, and then use the Up and Down direction keys to mark the property you want to change. Then, press the Enter key.

Choosing property settings from the Gallery Sheet. After you pick the graph component's property and press the Enter key, the Gallery Sheet displays a list of property settings. For example, if you pick Line Style as the property you want to change, the Gallery Sheet displays samples of line styles. At this point the Gallery Sheet is active, and pressing the direction keys causes different items in the Gallery Sheet to be selected. You can also use the mouse to click on the Gallery Sheet item you want. After you select an item from the Gallery Sheet, Quattro Pro redraws the graph component using the new property.

Some property settings, such as the font for a piece of text, do not lend themselves to being displayed on the Gallery Sheet. In such cases, Quattro Pro presents a menu that lists property settings. For example, if a piece of text in a graph is selected Quattro Pro displays the Font menu; the same menu as shown in Figure 10-21.

Moving graph components. Using the Annotator screen, you can move any graph component. But to do so, you first need to select the component you want to move. After you select a component, how you move it depends on whether you have a mouse. If you have a mouse, click on the component and then drag it in the direction you want it moved. (Do not try to move the object by dragging it by its handles.) If you do not have a mouse, move the graph component up, down, left, or right using the direction keys. To move the graph component in tiny increments, press the direction key that points in the same direction you want the graph component moved. To move the graph component in larger increments, hold down the Shift key and press the direction key that points in the same direction you want the graph component moved.

You can move a graph component diagonally using the Home, End, PgUp, and PgDn keys. The Home key moves the graph component diagonally toward the upper-left corner of the screen. The End key moves the graph component toward the lower-left corner of the screen. The PgUp key moves the graph component toward the upper-right corner of the screen. Finally, the PgDn key moves the graph component toward the lower-right corner of the screen. As is the case with the direction keys, holding down the Shift key and pressing the Home, End, PgUp, or PgDn keys causes Quattro Pro to move the selected graph component in larger increments.

Resizing graph components. You can also resize graph components using the Annotator screen. As is the case with moving graph components, you first need to select the component you want to resize.

If you have a mouse, you can change the size of a graph element by clicking on one of the handles and dragging it. Drag the handle away from the graph component to increase its size and toward the center of the graph component to decrease its size. If you do not have a mouse, resize a graph component using the same keys that you do to move the graph component. The only catch is that before you press any of these keys, you must press the period key (.). Quattro Pro then draws a resize box around the graph component and displays a small square at the lower-right corner of the box. The small square identifies the active corner of the resize box; that is, the corner of the resize box that you move using the direction keys. To move one of the other corners, press the period key to move the small square around the four corners of the box.

To resize the graph component in tiny increments by moving the active corner of the resize box, press the direction key that points in the same direction you want the resize box corner moved. To resize the graph component in larger increments, hold down the Shift key and press the direction key that points in the direction you want the resize box corner moved. To move the active corner of the resize box diagonally, you can also use the Home, End, PgUp, and PgDn keys, which move the corner in the same directions for resizing graph components as they do for moving graph components. Press the Enter key when you have finished.

Selecting more than one graph component. You can select more than one graph component at a time, which is particularly handy when you want to move or resize a group of graph components simultaneously. To do so using the keyboard, select the first graph component by pressing the Tab or Shift-Tab keys, and then pressing Shift-F7. Press the Tab or Shift-Tab keys to select a second graph component. You can continue to press Shift-F7 to select more graph components.

To select more than one graph component using the mouse, hold down the Shift key, point to one of the graph components you want to select, and then drag the pointer to the other graph components you want to select. As you do so, Quattro Pro creates a temporary box called a selection box. When at least part of every graph component you want to select is inside the selection box, release the Shift key. Quattro Pro selects each of the graph components in the box.

After you select multiple graph components, on that set of components you can use any of the techniques described for moving and resizing individual graph components. Here's a warning, however: If you shrink graph components to a much smaller size, you cannot increase their size subsequently and have them look as they did originally, because as Quattro Pro shrinks a set of graph components it loses precision about their relative sizes and positions.

Editing text components. You can edit the text components of graphs right on the Annotator screen. To do so, first select the graph component, and then press F2 to display a cursor at the end of the selected text. You can now edit the text exactly as you would edit a label, number, or formula on the input line of the worksheet screen.

Using the Clipboard

When you choose the Clipboard command from the Toolbox, Quattro Pro replaces the Property Sheet with the Clipboard command list. Figure 10-34 shows this list, which includes commands to move graph components between graphs, make copies of a graph component, and delete graph components. You can even store a graph component in a clip art file so that it can be used by other graphics programs. You can also retrieve a graph component, such as a company logo, from these same sorts of clip art files.

Choosing Clipboard commands. To choose the Clipboard command using the keyboard, select an object on the screen with the Tab and Shift-Tab keys and press

FIGURE 10-34.
Choose the Clipboard command from the Toolbox to display the Clipboard command list.

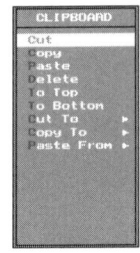

/-C. Then, press F3 to activate the list, use the direction keys to select the command you want, and then press the Enter key. To choose the Clipboard command using the mouse, select an object with the mouse and click on the Clipboard icon. Quattro Pro displays the Clipboard command list, from which you can click on the command you want.

Deleting a graph component. To delete a graph component, first select the component. Next, choose the Clipboard Delete command, and Quattro Pro deletes the selected graph component. Another method of deleting a graph component is to select the component and then press the Del key. You cannot use the Clipboard Delete command to delete graph titles, legends, data series, or the graph itself. To take any of these actions, you must use options in the Graph menu.

Moving or copying a graph component to another graph. To move or copy a graph component to another graph, first select the component you want to move. Next, choose either the Clipboard Cut command or the Clipboard Copy command. The Clipboard Cut command removes the selected graph component from the displayed graph and stores it on the Clipboard so that it can be moved to another graph. The Clipboard Copy command makes a duplicate copy of the selected graph component and stores it on the Clipboard so that it can be duplicated on another graph. The Clipboard is a temporary storage area for graph components. Whenever you cut or copy something new to the Clipboard, Quattro Pro deletes whatever was stored there previously.

Next, display the graph to which you want to move or copy the graph component, and then redisplay the Annotator screen. To do so, you might need to retrieve another worksheet or use the Graph Names Display command. Remember that you display the Annotator screen after the target graph is displayed by pressing the slash key (/). Now, you're ready to place the component on the new graph. Choose the Clipboard Paste command, and Quattro Pro places the graph component that's stored on the Clipboard in the same position it was in the source graph. You can then move the graph component to the location you want. Keep in mind that the graph component you originally cut or copied to the Clipboard is stored there until you cut or copy something else, which makes it possible to paste multiple copies of a graph component into one or more graphs.

Moving and copying graph components from and to clip art files. The Clipboard Cut To, Copy To, and Paste From commands work similarly to the Cut, Copy, and Paste commands. Rather than cutting to, copying to, or pasting from the Clipboard, however, these commands cut to, copy to, and paste from clip art files. This allows you to move and copy graphic images between Quattro Pro and other graphic programs. You can, for instance, include logos and images that were created in another program and stored in a computer graphics metafile (or CGM) format. Quattro Pro also provides over 50 clip art images that you can paste into any Quattro Pro graph.

You can move or copy any graph component except a title, legend, or the actual graph. To move or copy a graph component to a clip art file, first select the component. Next, choose either the Clipboard Cut To or Clipboard Copy To command. The Clipboard Cut To command removes the selected graph component from the displayed graph. The Clipboard Copy To command makes a copy of the selected graph component. After you choose either command, Quattro Pro displays the *Enter File Name* prompt, which is the same prompt that's displayed when you save a regular worksheet file. Either enter a filename for the selected file component or save the graph component using an existing filename. Quattro Pro uses the extension .CLP for clip art files, but you do not have to enter the extension because Quattro Pro enters it for you. For more information about how to save a file, see Chapter 8, "File Management." The process of saving a clip art file mirrors that of saving a regular worksheet file.

To retrieve the images stored in a clip art file, choose the Clipboard Paste From command. Quattro Pro displays the prompt *Enter File Name* followed by a list of clip art files—that is, files with the .CLP extension—stored in the default directory. Select the clip art file that stores the image you want, and then press the Enter key. Quattro Pro retrieves the clip art image from the specified file and pastes it on the graph.

As mentioned, Quattro Pro comes with over 50 clip art files, including a world map, several national and regional maps, symbols for many major currencies, and an assortment of other pictures. Even though DOS allows only eight characters in a filename, most of the clip art files have descriptive names that give you a hint as to what they show. You can also buy additional clip art images. To learn more about doing so, select the clip art file named 1-README.CLP from the list of files that Quattro Pro displays when you choose the Clipboard Paste From command.

Restacking graph components. As you add graph components, you might end up stacking components on top of each other. Doing so does not create a particular problem, although you might end up stacking the components in the wrong order. An arrow, for example, may be on top of instead of underneath a piece of text. To reverse the order of graph components stacked on top of each other, use the Clipboard To Top and To Bottom commands.

The Clipboard To Top command moves the selected graph component so that it is on top of the other components. To use this command, select the graph component, and then choose the command. The Clipboard To Bottom command moves the selected graph component so that it is beneath the other components that appear at the same graph location. To use this command, select the graph component you want to be moved to the bottom of the stack, and then choose the command.

Linking graph elements

Some of the graph components you draw using the Annotator tie specifically to a value in a data series. For example, an arrow might point to a bar graph bar to which you want to draw attention. Or a piece of text might explain a dip in a line or area graph. In these situations, you can tell Quattro Pro that you always want the graph component you've drawn to be located the current distance from the plotted value. That way, even if the value being plotted changes, the component you've drawn moves with the item to which it's attached. Attaching a graph component to a value in a data series is called linking. It's a lot less complicated than you might think.

To link a graph component you've drawn with one of the values in a data series, first select the component. Or, if you want to link several components, select all the components. Then, choose the Link command (/-X) from the Toolbox. Quattro Pro replaces the Property Sheet with the Link Command List, which is shown in Figure 10-35.

To activate the Link Command list, press F3. Then, select the data series to which you want to link the selected graph component. Next, Quattro Pro displays the prompt *Enter link index*. Type the number of the value to which the component should be linked. For example, if you're linking an arrow that points to the third bar in the data series, type 3. Press the Enter key, and Quattro Pro links the graph component to the value in the data series. From this point on, Quattro Pro moves the graph component you drew so that it stays the same distance from the data series point to which it's linked.

Creating graph buttons

Graph buttons are simply pieces of text that you add to a graph using the Annotator. However, graph buttons have a special feature: When you click on a graph button, Quattro Pro either displays another graph or executes a macro. Graph buttons, then, give a mouse user control over which graph is displayed next or the macro that is started next. Chapter 12, "Macro Basics," discusses macros.

To create a graph button, first add the piece of text you want to use for the graph button. Typically, the text describes the graph that the graph button displays or the macro it starts. Then, select the text. One of the properties listed in the

FIGURE 10-35.
Choosing the Link command from the Toolbox displays the Link Command list.

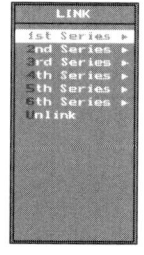

Property Sheet when a text graph component is selected is Graph Button. Activate the Property Sheet by pressing F3 and then select the text property, Graph Button. In a box in the middle of the Annotator screen, Quattro Pro displays a list of graph names and macros for the worksheet with the displayed graph. Using either the direction keys or the mouse, select the graph that should be displayed or the macro that should be started when you click on the graph button. That's all there is to it. Next time you display a full-screen version of the graph—in other words, not the partial, Annotator screen version of the graph—you can click on the graph button. When you do, Quattro Pro either displays the graph or starts the macro you identified.

Drawing a picture from scratch using the Annotator

Although the preceding sections focused on the mechanics of using the Annotator feature to enhance Quattro Pro graphs, you can also draw a freehand picture from scratch using the Annotator. To do so, first reset the current graph settings by choosing the Graph Customize Series Reset Graph command. (If you've displayed the Annotator screen, you need to quit it so that you can choose this command.) Next, choose the Graph Annotator command. Quattro Pro changes the graph type to Text and displays an empty text graph on the Annotator screen. You can then use all of the techniques described thus far to add text, draw arrows, draw lines and shapes, add colors and fill patterns, and so forth. Later, when you leave the Annotator screen, remember to name the text graph you've created and save the worksheet.

11
Database Management

Up to this point, you've seen how Quattro Pro can be used to build worksheets and create graphs. However, you can also use Quattro Pro as a database manager. This chapter explores this third major Quattro Pro function, which is closely related to worksheets. Thus, if you're familiar with worksheets you should have no trouble managing the database environment as well.

What is a database?

A database is simply a collection of information that's arranged in a structured, logical order. The information might include names, telephone numbers, prices, dates, or anything else you need to store and retrieve. Because the information in a database is ordered in a logical manner, a database provides easy access to any individual piece of information. Most people use some kind of database frequently. For example, a telephone book is a database that contains names, addresses, and phone numbers.

The usefulness of a database depends on the organization of the information in that database and how easily it can be retrieved. For example, because a telephone book contains listings arranged in alphabetical order by last name, you can find the phone number of anyone you want, as long as you know that person's last name. Because you cannot change the arrangement of information in a telephone book, however, it would be nearly impossible to find all the listings of people who have the same first name or who live on the same street. In addition, it would be extremely difficult to perform any kind of analysis on the information in the telephone book, such as computing the number of people named Johnson whose phone number begins with 267.

Fortunately, the databases you build in Quattro Pro are far more flexible and easy to analyze than is a printed database such as a telephone book. Using a number of special commands and functions, you can sort the information in a database in different ways; find, extract, or delete information that meets certain conditions; and compute various statistics on the entire database or on a selected part of the database.

This chapter shows you how to build a database in Quattro Pro and then explains each of the tools available for accessing and manipulating the information in a database. It begins by exploring some of the basic concepts and techniques you need to work with databases.

A Quattro Pro database is merely a set of worksheet cell entries organized in a specific way. In fact, creating a database is simply a matter of making certain entries in a worksheet. In the following sections, we'll look at the various rules and techniques you must know and use to build and organize a Quattro Pro database.

The Quattro Pro database structure

A database is simply a collection of structured information. For example, as you thumb through the pages of a telephone book, you see that the database comprises hundreds of individual listings, each occupying a single line. On each line, you find four pieces of information arranged in columns: last name, first name, street address, and phone number. Using database terminology, each listing or line in a telephone book is a record and each piece of information on a line—last name, first name, street address, phone number—is a field. Notice that in each listing, the various fields always occupy the same position, creating a consistent format. This consistent format is fundamental to the usefulness of a database.

All Quattro Pro databases use this structure. Each record occupies an individual row, each field occupies a separate column, and the field order must be the same from one record to another. For example, Figure 11-1 shows a sample Quattro Pro database that contains 15 records that are stored in rows 2 through 16. The database includes four fields in columns A through D: Emp ID, Last Name, First Name, and Salary.

FIGURE 11-1.
This sample database includes four fields and 15 records.

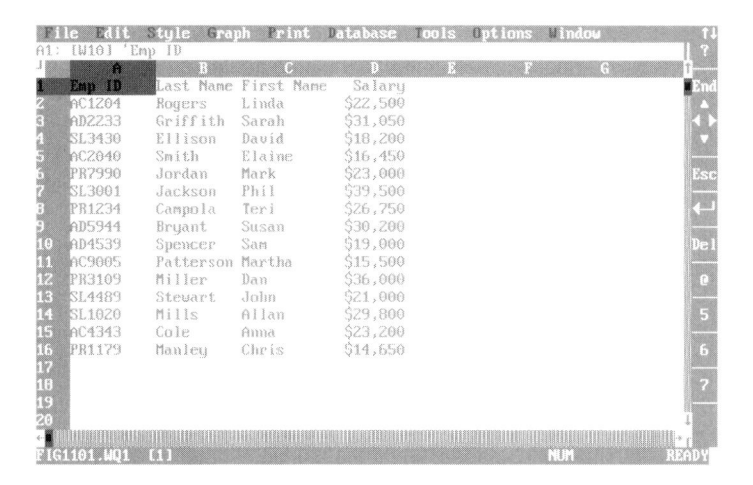

```
File Edit Style Graph Print Database Tools Options Window        ↑↓
A1: [W10] 'Emp ID                                                 ?
       A          B          C         D        E      F     G
1   Emp ID    Last Name  First Name  Salary                      End
2   AC1204    Rogers     Linda       $22,500                      ▲
3   AD2233    Griffith   Sarah       $31,050                     ◄►
4   SL3430    Ellison    David       $18,200                      ▼
5   AC2040    Smith      Elaine      $16,450
6   PR7990    Jordan     Mark        $23,000                     Esc
7   SL3001    Jackson    Phil        $39,500
8   PR1234    Campola    Teri        $26,750                      ↵
9   AD5944    Bryant     Susan       $30,200
10  AD4539    Spencer    Sam         $19,000                     Del
11  AC9005    Patterson  Martha      $15,500
12  PR3109    Miller     Dan         $36,000                      @
13  SL4489    Stewart    John        $21,000
14  SL1020    Mills      Allan       $29,800                      5
15  AC4343    Cole       Anna        $23,200
16  PR1179    Manley     Chris       $14,650                      6
17
18                                                                7
19
20
FIG1101.WQ1  [1]                                       NUM     READY
```

Notice that each of the columns in the database is identified by a field name in row 1. Field names are an essential part of any Quattro Pro database. Not only do these names identify the contents of each field in the database, they are also critical to the process of setting up selection conditions ("criteria") that you use to query a database as discussed later in this chapter in "Querying." Field names are simply labels that you enter in the first row of a database. Although a field name, like any other label, can be up to 240 characters long, you normally want to keep your names relatively short. In addition, you probably want to create descriptive field names that help identify the contents of each field.

Although the sample database shown in Figure 11-1 appears in the upper-left corner of the worksheet, you can position your database entries in any block of cells you choose. You can even create two or more databases in a single worksheet.

The size of a Quattro Pro database

The size of a Quattro Pro database is limited by the size of its worksheet and the amount of available random access memory (RAM) in your computer. A Quattro Pro worksheet contains 8192 rows and 256 columns. Theoretically, then, the maximum size of a database is 8191 records (one row must be reserved for the field-name labels) and 256 fields. In most cases, however, memory constraints limit the maximum size of a database to far fewer records and fields; approximately 5000 records and 6 fields if you have 640 KB memory. Of course, if your computer is fitted with more memory, you can build considerably larger databases. As with worksheets, the type of entries that you make in a database determines how much memory each record consumes and how large the database can be.

Database entries

Entering information in a Quattro Pro database is no different from making any other type of worksheet entry. You simply type the labels, values, formulas, and functions in the appropriate worksheet cells, keeping in mind the same rules that apply to normal worksheet entries. For instance, to enter a label that begins with a number, such as a phone number or zip code, be sure to type a label prefix before the first character in the entry.

Generally, all the entries in a single field are of the same type; a label or value. You usually don't want to mix labels and numbers or labels and formulas in a single field. In most cases, you also want to apply the same format to all the entries in a single field. Although most of your database entries are labels and literal values, you can also enter functions and formulas in a database. Here are a couple of tips to keep in mind whenever you use these types of entries in a database: First, if the function or formula refers to another cell in the same record, be sure to use relative references when creating the formula or function. For example, suppose columns A and B of your database contain the fields Quantity and Unit Price, respectively. In column C, you want to compute the total price by multiplying Unit Price times Quantity. To do so, type a formula like +A2*B2 in column C. (The row references in this formula vary depending on which record you're working with.) When Quattro Pro sorts the database, a topic discussed later in this chapter in "Sorting," the formula references still refer to the proper cells.

On the other hand, if a function or formula refers to a cell outside the database, use an absolute reference. For example, suppose you're building a database in which column A contains the field Quantity. In this case, however, the field Unit Price is stored in a different part of the worksheet outside the database; for the sake of argument, cell Z1. To create a field called Total Price that contains the product of Quantity multiplied by Unit Price, type the formula for that field as +A2*$Z$1. Now, regardless of how often you sort the database, this formula continues to refer to cell Z1.

After you enter some records in a database, you might want to do some editing. The following section explains how.

Editing a database

Editing the contents of a database is no different from editing any other worksheet entries. To edit the contents of any cell in a database, position the cell selector on the entry and press the [Edit] key (F2). When the entry appears in the formula line, add, replace, and delete characters as necessary, and then press the Enter key. To replace an entry, position the cell selector on the cell you want to replace, type the new entry, and press the Enter key. Using Quattro Pro's standard editing commands—Edit Copy, Edit Move, Edit Erase Block, Edit Insert, and Edit Delete—you can copy, move, insert, and delete entries in a database. In addition to changing individual entries, you can manipulate entire database fields or records.

Adding a new field to a database is simply a matter of typing the field name at the top of the database and filling in the field entries in the column below. To add a field to the end of a database, move the cell selector to the first blank column to the right of the database, type a field name in the same row that contains your other field names, and then enter the field data below that. To add a new field to the middle of a database, first open a new column using the Edit Insert Columns command, and then type the field name in the appropriate row of that column. Finally, fill in the field entries below that name.

To add a record to a database, move the cell selector to the first blank row below the database and enter the record data. To insert a new record in the middle of the database, choose the Edit Insert Rows command to open a new row and then fill in the record information in that row. Of course, you can insert several rows if you want to add more than one record to the middle of a database.

Later in this chapter, in "Sorting" and "Querying," you'll learn that you must formally define the boundaries of your database in order to sort or query it. In other words, when you add records or fields to a database, particularly if you make the addition to the end of the database rather than inserting a row or column in the middle of the database, you probably need to redefine the database block before you perform a sort or query operation.

Saving and printing a database

To save a Quattro Pro database, simply save the worksheet in which you created the database. Doing so is no different from saving any other Quattro Pro worksheet. Choose the File Save or File Save As command, choose a name for the worksheet, and press the Enter key to save the file. To retrieve a Quattro Pro database, choose the File Retrieve or File Open command, choose the filename you want to retrieve, and press the Enter key.

Printing a Quattro Pro database is also fairly straightforward. In fact, you print Quattro Pro databases in the same way that you print other worksheets: Choose the Print command, use the Block option to define the block that contains your database information and the field labels, select any other print options you want, adjust the paper in the printer, and choose the Spreadsheet Print command. Quattro Pro then produces a simple tabular listing of the database block.

You can sort or query the database before you print if you want to include only certain records, such as all the records for people whose last names begin with the letters A through D. Later in this chapter, "Sorting" and "Querying" address these techniques.

The Database Restrict Input command

The Database Restrict Input command allows you to create simple input forms for your databases in the cells of your Quattro Pro worksheets. Because this command has applications that go beyond its use with databases, it was explained in Chapter 5, "Worksheet Commands." Turn to that chapter for an explanation and examples of this command.

Sorting

After setting up a database, you might want to sort the records in the database so you can find information more easily. Sorting not only makes it easier to find information, it can also help you compare the entries in one or more fields of different records. When you sort a database, Quattro Pro simply reorders the records based on the information in one or more fields that you specify. You can sort the records into either ascending or descending order, and you can arrange your database records into sorted groups by defining up to five sort key fields.

Basics of sorting

To sort a database, choose the Database Sort command. Quattro Pro presents the Database Sort menu shown in Figure 11-2. Notice that the first option in this menu is Block; typically, the first step in setting up a sort is to choose this option. Quattro Pro then prompts you to specify the block of data that you want to sort. Assuming that you want to sort your entire database, highlight all the records and fields in that database, excluding the field names at the top of the database, and then press the Enter key. (You can also type the block reference instead of highlighting the block.) For example, to sort the sample database shown in Figure 11-1, you would highlight the block A2..D16.

After specifying the block you want to sort, tell Quattro Pro the fields you want to use as the bases of the sort. The sort fields are also referred to as "sort keys," which is why you see the options 1st Key, 2nd Key, 3rd Key, 4th Key, and 5th Key in the Database Sort menu. To specify the first sort key, choose the 1st Key

FIGURE 11-2.
Choosing the Database Sort command displays this menu.

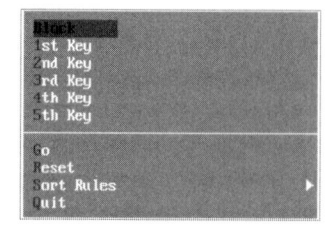

option. When Quattro Pro prompts you to specify the first sort key, point to any cell in the field you want to sort, and press the Enter key. For example, to sort the sample database shown in Figure 11-1 on the basis of the entries in the Salary field, choose the 1st Key option from the Database Sort menu, point to any cell in column D, and press the Enter key.

After you specify the field you want to sort, Quattro Pro prompts you for the order in which to sort the database: descending or ascending. Choose the order you want to use by typing a D or an A or by pointing to the order you want to use and pressing the Enter key. Quattro Pro then returns you to the Database Sort menu. You can define another sort key or go ahead and sort the database. To sort on more than one key, choose the 2nd Key option, point to any cell in the field that you want to use as the secondary sort key, press the Enter key, and then choose either ascending or descending sort order. You can repeat this process for up to five sort keys. Later in this chapter, "Sorting on More Than One Field" explains multiple-field sorts in more detail.

To sort the database, choose Go from the Database sort menu. Quattro Pro then reorders all of the records in the database you specified, based on the entries in the sort key(s) you defined. If you sort the database shown in Figure 11-1 by ascending salary, for example, the sorted database looks like that shown in Figure 11-3.

Editing sort settings

After you define the block you want to sort, your sort keys, and the sort order, Quattro Pro remembers all of these settings. If you save the worksheet after defining the sort block and sort keys, these settings are saved along with your cell entries, which can be a real time-saver if you need to sort your database more than one time. If you need to change one or two of your sort settings, for example, you do not have to start over from scratch. For instance, suppose you have added

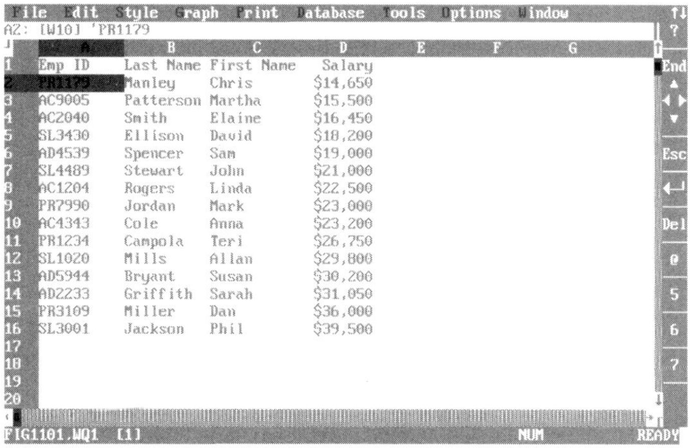

FIGURE 11-3.
This is how the sample database looks after you sort the records into ascending order according to the entries in the Salary field shown in Figure 11-1.

records to a database that you sorted previously. To resort the database, choose the Database Sort Block command and change the parameters of your sort block to include the new records. Then, choose the Go option from the Database Sort menu; you need not redefine your sort keys or sort order. Similarly, to sort a database using a different sort key, simply change the definition of the 1st Key option (and any other sort key options you specified), and then choose the Go option from the Database Sort menu. As long as you have not added any new records or fields, you do not need to redefine the sort block.

Canceling sort settings

You can cancel any of your sort settings at any time. To cancel all of your sort settings, the sort block as well as all the sort keys you defined, choose the Database Sort Reset command. To change several sort keys or sort an entirely different block of data in the same worksheet, using the Database Sort Reset command to define new settings is often faster than changing each setting individually.

Sorting on a text (non-numeric) field

In the preceding example, Quattro Pro sorted the sample database using value entries as the basis of the sort. You also can use text entries. When you specify a field that contains text entries as one of your sort keys, Quattro Pro arranges the entries in the field in alphabetic order. As with numeric sorts, you can choose either ascending or descending order for your sort.

Sort rules

As you have seen, Quattro Pro lets you sort the entries in a field into ascending or descending order. Although the default order is decending, you may use ascending more often. Sorting a field into ascending order arranges the entries in the field into ascending numeric or alphabetic order. If the field contains only numbers, the entries are arranged so that the smallest numbers come first (large negative numbers, followed by small negative numbers, zero, small positive numbers, and large positive numbers). If a cell in the sort key contains a function or formula, the entry in that cell is ranked according to the result of the formula or function. If any of the cells in the sort key are blank, the records that contain those cells will appear first in the sorted database.

If the sort key contains only alphabetic label entries, Quattro Pro by default arranges the entries by ASCII order, which means it arranges alphabetic labels using the ASCII character code of the label's first character. (Capitalized words always come first.) You can also, however, direct Quattro Pro to order alphabetic labels using dictionary order (as explained in the upcoming section, "Changing the Defaults"). In dictionary order, the entries in the sort key are arranged in simple alphabetic order without regard to capitalization. Entries in the sort key that begin with a blank space in dictionary order appear before entries that begin with an alphabetic character. If any of the cells in the sort key are blank, the records that contain those cells appear first in the sorted database.

If a sort key contains mixed label entries (entries like addresses that contain both numbers and labels), in ascending order the entries that begin with an alphabetic character come before entries that begin with a number.

Descending order

Quattro Pro's default is to sort your database into descending order. If the sort key contains only values or numeric labels, the entries are arranged so that the largest values or numeric labels come first, and if the sort key contains only alphabetic labels, by default the entries are sorted into reverse ASCII order. If the sort key contains label entries with letters and numbers, by default the entries that begin with a number will precede entries that begin with a letter. If a sort key contains both values and labels (a rare occurrence) then by default the label entries follow the value entries in the sorted database. Finally, if the sort key contains any blank cells those entries appear last in the sorted database.

Resolving ties

If two or more entries in the sort key begin with the same character, Quattro Pro uses the second character in those entries to arrange them. Quattro Pro then uses the third character, the fourth, the fifth, and so on, to arrange the entries. If two or more entries in the sort key are identical, and both are either numbers or labels, those entries will appear next to one another in the sorted database.

Changing the defaults

As mentioned, in a decending sort Quattro Pro normally arranges a sort key that contains only labels into reverse ASCII order and arranges a sort key that contains labels with letters and numbers so that the numbers come before the labels. You can, however, use the Database Sort Sort Rules command to change both of these defaults. After you choose this command, you see a menu that has three choices: Numbers Before Labels, Label Order, and Quit. The Numbers Before Labels option allows you to determine whether Quattro Pro should place value entries before label entries when sorting a database. After you choose this option, Quattro Pro presents a menu that has two options: Yes and No. Choose the Yes option to place values before labels in an ascending sort. Choose the No option to tell Quattro Pro to place values after labels in an ascending sort.

The Label Order option lets you choose between dictionary and ASCII sort orders for sort keys that contain only labels. As explained, dictionary sort order arranges labels according to alphabetical order, with no regard to capitalization. When sorting a database in ascending dictionary order, Quattro Pro ranks number characters first, followed by the letters of the alphabet from A to Z without regard to uppercase or lowercase. Following the alphabet are all the special punctuation characters on the keyboard. ASCII order arranges labels using the three-digit ASCII codes assigned by your computer to each character. ASCII sort order arranges labels according to alphabetical order, but it places all entries that begin with capital letters before all entries that begin with lowercase letters because the ASCII character codes for uppercase letters range from 65 to 90, and those for lowercase letters range from 97 to 122. For more information about the ASCII sort order, see the ASCII table in your computer's reference manual.

Sorting on more than one field

To further arrange the entries in a grouped database, you sometimes must perform a two-key sort. When you sort using two keys, Quattro Pro reorders the database based on the entry in each record's first key field. Then, any records that have identical entries in the first key field are sorted again according to the entries in the second key field.

To sort using two key fields, first choose the Database Sort Block command to define the Sort block. Then, choose the 1st Key and 2nd Key options from the Database Sort menu to define both a primary and a secondary key field. You define the secondary key field in the same way that you define the first one: Choose the 2nd Key option from the Database Sort menu, point to any cell in the field that you want to use as the secondary key field, press the Enter key, and choose either ascending or descending sort order. Quattro Pro then presents the Database Sort menu, and you can choose the Go option to sort the database.

Sorting on more than two key fields

In Lotus 1-2-3, you are limited to sorting a database on only two key fields at a time. Quattro Pro, however, allows you to sort on up to five key fields. To sort on three or more keys, choose the 3rd Key, 4th Key, and 5th Key options from the Database Sort menu to define the third, fourth, and fifth key fields. You define the third, fourth, and fifth keys in the same way you defined the first and second.

When you sort using three or more key fields, Quattro Pro first reorders the database records based on the entry in each record's first key field. Then, any records that have identical entries in their first key fields are sorted again according to the entries in their second key fields. Next, any records that have identical entries in their second key fields are sorted again according to the entries in their third key fields. Likewise, Quattro Pro uses the fourth key field to arrange any records with identical third key field entries and the fifth key field to arrange records with identical fourth key field entries.

Undoing a sort

Sorting a database changes the order of the records in that database permanently. Unless you plan ahead, it can be difficult to restore the database to its presort order. To "undo" a sort, you can choose from two methods. You can save the worksheet that contains the database you plan to sort immediately before you sort it. Then, when you want to return the database to its original order, you simply retrieve the worksheet. Alternatively, you can include a field in the database that numbers the records in the database in their original order. For example, you might include a customer number field in a database that lists customer names and number the customers in ascending order. To return the database to its original order, sort the database into ascending order using the customer number field as the first key.

Querying

So far, you've seen how to sort your Quattro Pro databases using the Database Sort commands. Quattro Pro lets you do more, however, than just sort a database. The Database Query commands let you locate, extract, and delete specific records, and the database statistical functions let you compute a statistic, such as the sum, average, or count, on the entries in a particular field. This book uses the term "querying" to describe the process of using database statistical functions and Database Query commands to analyze a database.

Before you can query a database, you must specify criteria that define the questions you want to ask. The criteria show Quattro Pro what to look for when scanning your database. When Quattro Pro encounters an entry that matches the criteria you specify, the record that contains that entry is selected for use by the Database Query command or statistical function. The following sections show you how to define criteria that let you select records from a database and how to use Quattro Pro's Database Query commands to find, extract, and delete records. Finally, the sections explain Quattro Pro's database statistical functions.

Criteria

The first step in querying a database is to specify the criteria that define the query you want to perform. The criteria act as filters that select certain records based on the entries in one or more fields of those records. When you use a Database Query command or a database statistical function to query a database, Quattro Pro uses the criteria to select the records that the command or function will act upon.

Specifying criteria

You can specify criteria by creating a criteria table in your worksheet cells. In structure, a criteria table is very similar to a database and, like a database, each column in a criteria table contains one field. The first row of the table contains the names of the individual fields of the table's database. For example, cells A18..D19 in Figure 11-4 contain a criteria table for the sample salary database.

You often define the field names for a criteria table simply by copying the field names from the first row of the database to the location in the worksheet where you want the criteria table to appear. For example, to create the criteria table in Figure 11-4, copy the field names from the block A1..D1 into the block A18..D18. Although you usually include all of the field names from your database in a criteria table, you do not have to. The first row of the table need only include the names of the fields you want to use to query the database. Of course, you can include all of the fields from the database in the criteria table, even if you plan to query on only one or two fields.

You can include up to 45 field names in a criteria table. As long as your database contains fewer than 46 fields (as most do), you can include all of the field names from the database in the criteria table. If the database includes more than 45 fields, you must decide which fields you want to use to query the database and use only those fields in the table.

Although the field names in a criteria table must be spelled exactly like the field names in the database, they can have different label prefixes and can be capitalized differently. In addition, the order of the field names in the criteria table does not have to match the order of the field names in the database.

After you create the table, choose the Database Query Criteria Table command to define the cells that contain the table as the criteria table. The block you select should include all of the field names in the criteria table and at least one row of cells below those names. You enter the actual criteria into the cells below the field names in the criteria table. For example, to define block A18..D19 as the criteria table for the worksheet shown in Figure 11-4, choose the Database Query Criteria Table command. When Quattro Pro asks you to define the criteria table, highlight block A18..D19, and press the Enter key. Notice that this block includes the field names in row 18 and one blank row (row 19).

Most criteria tables include only two rows. As you develop more complex criteria, however, you might have to expand the criteria table to include three, four, or more rows, each of which holds a different criterion. You can define a criteria table anywhere on your worksheet. You might put your criteria table directly below the database, as in Figure 11-4. Placing the criteria table below the database clarifies how the table works with the database but makes it more difficult to add records to the database. Instead of simply moving to the first blank row in the database and entering a new record, you have to use the Edit Insert command to

FIGURE 11-4.

In structure, criteria tables are similar to databases.

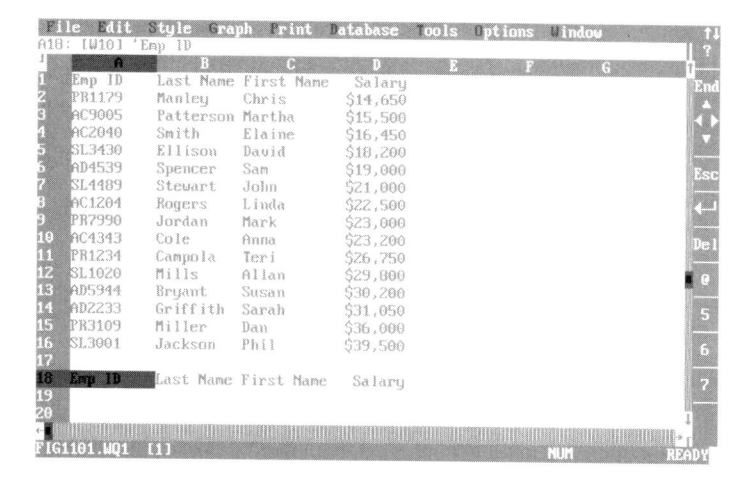

insert one or more new rows for the new records at the bottom of the database. To avoid this problem, you can place the criteria table above or beside the database rather than below it. You can define several criteria tables in a single worksheet, but only one of those tables is active at any time: the table that you defined using the Database Query Criteria Table command.

Entering criteria

After you create a criteria table, you're ready to enter criteria. Quattro Pro lets you specify a wide variety of criteria, ranging from simple, exact-match value or label criteria to complex criteria that search several fields at one time using wildcards (such as ? and *), comparison operators (such as <, >, or =), and special operators (such as #AND# and #NOT#). The following sections look at all the types of criteria you can specify in Quattro Pro.

Exact-match criteria. An exact-match criterion selects records that have specific literal entries in specified fields. You can use this kind of criterion, for example, to find a person in a mailing list database by name or a particular listing in a real estate database by address. You can set up exact-match criteria for labels or values. To specify an exact-match criterion, type the entry you want Quattro Pro to match in the cell of the criteria table below the name of the field that contains the entries you want to match.

Label criteria. To select records that have a particular label entry in a particular field, enter that label in the cell of the criteria table below the name of the field that contains the entries you want to match. For example, suppose you want to query the salary database for records that have a Last Name field entry 'Cole. To do so, position the cell selector in cell B19, the cell directly under the field name Last Name in the criteria table, and enter the label 'Cole in that cell.

FIGURE 11-5.
To select records that have a particular label entry in a particular field, enter that label in the appropriate cell of the criteria table.

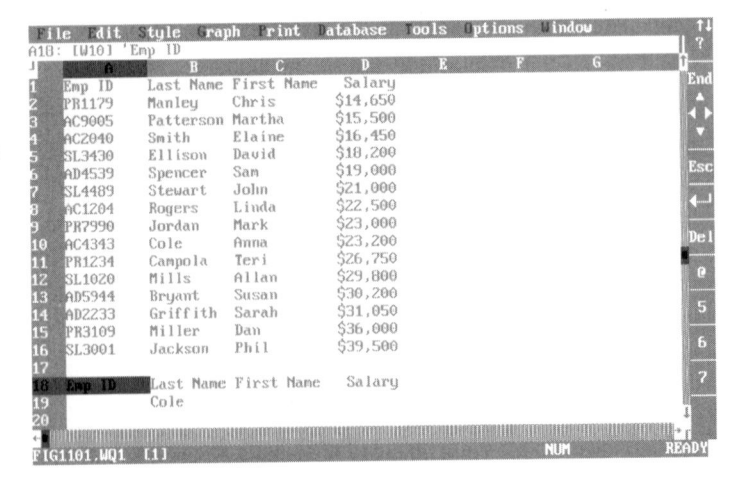

```
A18: [W10] 'Emp ID
         A         B          C          D
1     Emp ID    Last Name  First Name   Salary
2     PR1179    Manley     Chris        $14,650
3     AC9005    Patterson  Martha       $15,500
4     AC2040    Smith      Elaine       $16,450
5     SL3430    Ellison    David        $18,200
6     AD4539    Spencer    Sam          $19,000
7     SL4489    Stewart    John         $21,000
8     AC1204    Rogers     Linda        $22,500
9     PR7990    Jordan     Mark         $23,000
10    AC4343    Cole       Anna         $23,200
11    PR1234    Campola    Teri         $26,750
12    SL1020    Mills      Allan        $29,800
13    AD5944    Bryant     Susan        $30,200
14    AD2233    Griffith   Sarah        $31,050
15    PR3109    Miller     Dan          $36,000
16    SL3001    Jackson    Phil         $39,500
17
18    Emp ID    Last Name  First Name   Salary
19              Cole
20
FIG1101.WQ1  [1]                              NUM    READY
```

Figure 11-5 shows this simple criterion in place. Its position tells Quattro Pro to search each record's Last Name field for the label entry Cole. Quattro Pro will select the record in row 10. Quattro Pro ignores capitalization and label prefixes in exact-match criteria.

Value criteria. You can also specify exact-match criteria for fields that contain values. To select records that have a particular value entry in a particular field, enter that value in the cell of the criteria table below the name of the field that contains the entries you want to match. For example, suppose you want to select the records for those persons who have a salary equal to $23,000. To do so, position the cell selector in cell D19, the cell directly beneath the field name Salary in Figure 11-5, and enter the number 23000. (If the criteria table contains other entries, you must also erase those entries.)

Interestingly, to create an exact-match criterion for a value field, you must enter a literal value in the criteria table. You cannot use a formula or a function that returns the value you want to match. For example, you cannot use the formula +12000+11000 in place of the criterion 23000. Note that this rule has one unfortunate consequence: You cannot use the functions @DATE or @TIME in exact-match criteria for date or time fields.

Blank cells in the criteria table

As you have seen, the entries you make in the cells of a criteria table tell Quattro Pro which records to select from the database. When you use a criteria table with a Database Query command or a database statistical function, Quattro Pro uses all of the entries in the criteria table to select records. If you're defining a simple criterion in a criteria table that already contains entries, you usually want to erase those existing entries before you begin defining the new criterion. Otherwise, Quattro Pro would try to use both the new criterion and the existing criterion together. (Shortly, you'll see how to use multiple criteria to select records that meet any or all of two or more criteria.)

When you use a criteria table Quattro Pro also considers the blank cells in the table. A blank cell under a field name in a criteria table tells Quattro Pro to select records that have any entry at all in that field. For this reason, when you define a query, leave blank those fields you do not want to search. Be sure, however, not to leave blank any entire rows in the criteria table. When Quattro Pro sees a blank field in a criterion row, it considers any entry a match for that field. Therefore, if every field in a criterion row is left blank, Quattro Pro selects every record in the database.

Wildcard characters

Wildcard characters allow you to expand the scope of exact-match criteria. Exactly as wildcards in the game of poker replace any card, wildcards in criteria replace one or more characters. Quattro Pro supports two wildcard characters: the question mark (?), which takes the place of a single character in a criterion, and the asterisk (*), which takes the place of a series of adjacent characters.

The ? wildcard. You can use the ? wildcard at any position in any label criterion. For example, suppose you want to select the record from a database for someone named Andersen but cannot remember whether she spells her name Andersen or Anderson. To make this selection, move the cell selector to cell B19, the cell below the field name Last Name in the criteria table, and type *Anders?n* as the label. (If the criteria table contains other entries, erase them.) This criterion selects records that have the entry Andersen, Anderson, or any other similar variation in the Last Name field.

Although the ? wildcard matches any character in an entry, you cannot use it to match nonexistent characters. For instance, the criterion Joe? matches the entries Joey and Joel, but not the entry Joe.

You can use multiple ? wildcards to match a specific number of unknown characters. For example the criterion *And?????* matches the entries Anderson, Andersen, Andresen, and Andretta. It does not, however, match the entries Anders or Andrews, because these labels are not eight characters long.

Unfortunately, the ? wildcard works only with labels. You cannot use it to make selections from fields that contain value entries. For example, you cannot use the criterion 2? to match the values 21, 22, 23, and so on. You must use comparison operators, such as =, <, and >, which the section "Comparison Criteria" discusses shortly, to make this kind of selection. You can, however, use wildcards to represent numeric characters within labels. For example, suppose you want to select all of the records from the salary database shown in Figure 11-5 that have an Emp ID field entry beginning with the letters AC and followed by any four numbers. To do so, enter the criterion *AC????* in cell A19 of the criteria table.

The * wildcard. You can use the * wildcard in a criterion to take the place of any number of characters at the end of a label. For example, suppose you want to select the record from the salary database shown in Figure 11-5 for someone named Mills or Miller or something like that. To make this selection, move the cell selector to cell B19, the cell below the field name Last Name in the criteria table, and type *'Mill** as the label. (If the criteria table contains other entries, erase them.) This criterion selects records that have the Last Name entry Mills, Miller, Millings, or any other similar entry.

Unlike the ? wildcard, the * wildcard even matches nonexistent characters. The criterion Mill*, for example, would match the entry Mill.

Unfortunately, you can use the * wildcard to match a series of characters only at the end of a criterion. If Quattro Pro encounters the * character within a criterion, it disregards all characters that follow. For example, the criterion *mill, which you might hope would let you find the record for anyone whose name ends with the letters mill, such as Bushmill, Windmill, Sawmill, and so forth, selects every record in the database.

Like the ? wildcard, the * wildcard only works in label criteria. To make selections of ranges of numeric values, you must use comparison operators, which are described in the upcoming section, "Comparison Criteria."

The not-equal-to operator (~). It is sometimes easier to find specific records by querying for characteristics they do not have instead of those they do have. Quattro Pro's not-equal-to operator, the tilde (~), lets you select the records from a database that contain entries that do not match the criterion you specify. You simply precede the criterion with the not-equal-to operator (~).

For example, suppose that you want to query a database that lists employee names and addresses and that you want to find those employees who do not live in Smithtown. To do so, you could use the criterion ~Smithtown. Quattro Pro selects any record whose city field does not contain the entry Smithtown.

You can use the wildcard characters just discussed in combination with the not-equal-to operator. For example, suppose you want to select those records from the salary database example shown in Figure 11-5 that have Emp ID field entries that do not begin with the letters AC. To do so, move the cell selector to cell A19, which is the cell under the field name Emp ID, and type *~AC** as the label. (If the criteria table contains other entries, erase those entries.) Quattro Pro then selects those records with Emp ID field entries that do not begin with the characters AC, regardless of what follows those two characters.

Unfortunately, like wildcards, the tilde character works only with labels. To select records that contain numeric values that do not equal some specific value, use the numeric not-equal comparison operator (<>), which is described later in this chapter in "Using the Not-Equal Comparison Operator (<>)."

Comparison criteria

As you work with Quattro Pro databases, you will often want to select records that contain numeric data that fall within a particular range. For example, you might want to search the salary database in the example shown in Figure 11-5 for people who make less than $20,000. To do so, use a comparison criterion.

Basics of comparison criteria. A comparison criterion is simply a conditional test, not unlike the first argument in an @IF function. Exactly like the conditional test argument of an @IF function, a comparison criterion is either true or false with respect to each record in a database. If the criterion is true, Quattro Pro selects the record. If it is false, Quattro Pro does not select the record. For example, suppose you want to select from the salary database those persons who have salaries less than $20,000. To do so, move the cell selector to cell D19 in the criteria table, which is the cell beneath the field name Salary, and type the comparison criterion +D2<20000. (If the criteria table contains other entries, erase them.) Figure 11-6 shows this criterion in place. Querying with this comparison criterion selects any records that have a Salary entry less than 20000.

Like most comparison criteria, this criterion is made up of a cell reference, a comparison operator, and a fixed value. The cell reference portion is always a relative reference to the first cell below the field name of the field to which the criterion applies. In this case the comparison criterion applies to the Salary field, so the cell reference D2 is used in the criterion. As you can see, cell D2 is the cell below the field name Salary in the database. Although the cell reference in a comparison criterion refers to the first cell under the field name in the appropriate field, Quattro Pro applies the criterion to every record in the database when you query the database. For this process to work correctly, the cell reference must be a relative reference. Because the cell reference of a comparison criterion defines the field to which the criterion applies, you can always place any comparison criterion in any cell in the criteria table. The criterion does not have to appear beneath the field name of the field you want to search. In most cases, however, you'll want to place the criterion under the field name in the usual way.

The comparison operator portion of a comparison criterion defines the relationship between the entries in the field you want to search and the value against which you are comparing those entries. For instance, the comparison operator < is used in the example to select those records that have Salary field entries less than

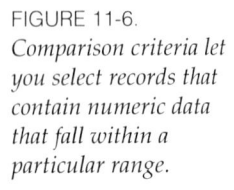

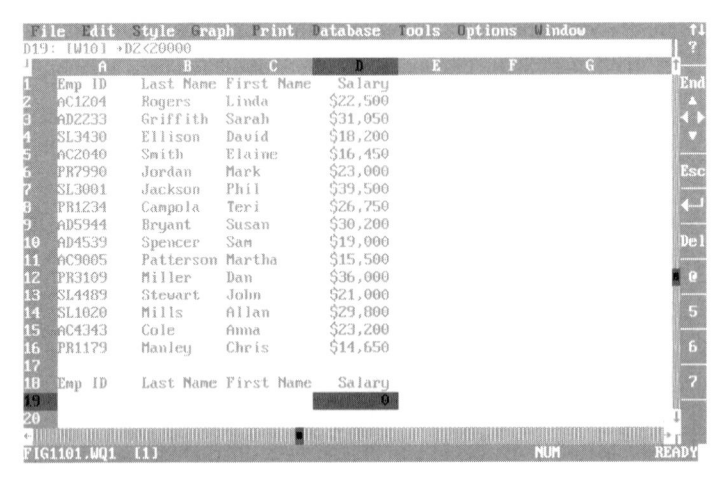

FIGURE 11-6.
Comparison criteria let you select records that contain numeric data that fall within a particular range.

20000. You can use any of the comparison operators explained in Chapter 4, "Functions," in comparison criteria: < (less than), <= (less than or equal to), > (greater than), >= (greater than or equal to), = (equal to), or <> (not equal to).

The fixed value portion of a comparison criterion is the value against which you are comparing the entries in the field. For example, the fixed value in the example criterion, 20000, tells Quattro Pro to compare the database Salary entries to 20000. Notice that the comparison criterion in cell D19 in Figure 11-6 returns the value 0, which indicates that the first entry in the Salary field is not less than 20000 (that is, that the comparison criterion is false with respect to the first record). This result has no impact on the outcome of the criterion, except to indicate that the criterion will not select the first record. Had the first record's Salary field entry been less than 20000, this criterion would have returned the value 1.

Referring to cells outside the database. You'll occasionally want to use a reference to a cell outside the database as the third part (the fixed value) of a comparison criterion. For example, suppose you want to select those records in the salary database that have Salary field entries greater than the value in cell Q20. To create this query, move the cell selector to cell D19, which is the cell below the field name Salary, and type the formula +D2>$Q$20. (If the criteria table contains other entries, erase them.) When you use this criterion with a Database Query command or a statistical function, Quattro Pro selects those records that have a Salary field entry greater than the value in cell Q20. If Q20 were blank, Quattro Pro would select all records with an entry in the Salary field.

As you can see, the reference to cell Q20 in this criterion is an absolute reference. You must use an absolute reference, or a mixed reference that is fixed with respect to the row, when you use a cell reference in a comparison criterion. Otherwise, the criterion does not work properly.

Using the equal-to (=) operator. You usually use the <, >, >=, <=, or <> operators in comparison criteria. You can also use the = operator, however. For example, suppose you want to select the records that have a Salary field entry of 20000. To do so, type the formula *+D2=20000* in cell D19 under the field name Salary. Alternatively, you could simply type the number *20000* in that cell.

Using the not-equal comparison operator (<>). The not-equal operator lets you select records that have entries in a particular field that do not equal a specific value. For example, suppose you want to select those records that do not have a Salary field entry of 23000. Type the formula *+D2<>23000* in cell D19 under the field name Salary. The not-equal operator is similar to the ~ operator, except that the not-equal operator is used only on numbers and the ~ operator is used only on labels.

Using comparison criteria on date fields. You can also use comparison criteria to make selections from fields that contain dates and times. To do so, use a @DATE or @TIME function as the comparison value in a comparison criterion. To select dates after a particular date, use the > operator. To select dates before a particular date, use the < operator. To select dates that match a particular date, use the = operator.

Using comparison criteria on text fields. So far, you've used comparison criteria on values only. You can also use comparison criteria, however, on text entries. For example, you can use the comparison criterion +B2="Jackson" to find the person or persons named Jackson in the salary database. Of course, it would be much simpler, and just as effective, to enter the label 'Jackson in the criteria table. Still, you can use the other comparison operators to match text entries. For example, suppose you want to select every record that has a Last Name field entry that begins with a letter following M in the alphabet. To make this selection, you can use the comparison criterion +B2>"M" in cell B19 of the criteria table. You can also use these operators to work with fields that contain numeric labels, such as telephone numbers, addresses, and zip codes.

Notice that the comparison value in both of these examples is a string enclosed in quotation marks. When you use a literal string as the comparison value in a comparison criterion, you must enclose that string in quotation marks.

Complex comparison criteria. The comparison criteria you've seen so far have been fairly simple. You can, however, use Quattro Pro's powerful calculation functions to develop more complex comparison criteria. For example, you can use the criterion +D2>@AVG(D$2..D$16) to select those records that have a Salary field entry greater than the average of all Salary field entries.

In addition, you can usually choose a number of different ways to state a comparison criterion. For example, the criterion +D2>30000 is equivalent to the criterion 30000<D2, and so is the criterion +D2-30000>0. You are free to state your criteria in any way you want, as long as they follow the basic rules.

Naming cells. As mentioned, comparison criteria always refer to the first cell under the field name of one or more fields in a database. For example, the criterion +D2>20000 refers to the cell immediately below the field name Salary in the salary database. The field name reference in a comparison criterion tells Quattro Pro to which field the criterion applies.

Remembering the exact addresses of the cells below the field names in a database can be difficult. If you plan to create many queries on a database, you can save time by naming the cells immediately below the field names. If the names you give to these cells match the field names themselves, you can refer to the field by name instead of by address in comparison criteria. For example, if you give the name Salary to cell D2, you can use the criterion +Salary>20000 instead of +D2>20000. Quattro Pro offers a command called Database Query Assign Names that you can use to name the cells below the field names in a database quickly and easily. After you choose this command, Quattro Pro simply uses each label in the first row of the Database block you have defined to name the cell immediately below it.

Multiple criteria. You'll often want to select records that meet both of two criteria or that meet any of more than two criteria. For example, you might want to query the salary database for records that have Emp ID field entries that start with the letters AC and Salary field entries below 25000. Or, you might want to query the database for records that have either the Last Name field entry Jackson or the Last Name field entry Jordan. To perform these queries, enter two or more criteria in the criteria table.

Logical AND conditions. If you enter two or more criteria in the same row of the criteria table, Quattro Pro selects only records that match both criteria. This kind of criterion is called an AND criterion because Quattro Pro combines all of the criteria in the table with the word AND when using the criterion, in effect saying "Select the records that meet this condition AND this condition AND this condition...." Quattro Pro then selects only those records that match all of the individual conditions.

Logical OR conditions. In some situations, you'll want Quattro Pro to select records that match one of two or more different criteria. In these cases, use a logical OR criterion which you create by placing each criterion in a separate row of the criteria table. When you use this kind of criterion, Quattro Pro combines the criteria in the rows with the word OR, in effect saying "Select the records that meet this criterion OR this criterion OR this criterion...." Quattro Pro selects any records that match any one of the individual criteria.

Special logical operators. You can use three other operators in a criterion. The #AND# and #OR# operators let you create AND/OR arguments within one cell. The #NOT# operator lets you negate comparison criteria.

The #AND# operator. The #AND# operator allows you to use a logical AND to link two conditions within the same cell. For example, suppose you want to search the salary database for persons with a Salary entry greater than $25,000 and less than $30,000. To do so, first clear all existing criteria from the criteria table. Then, type the formula *+D2>25000#AND#D2<30000 i*n cell D19 of the criteria table. Quattro Pro selects the records in rows 8 and 14.

The #OR# operator. The #OR# operator allows you to create a logical OR criterion in a single cell of the criteria table. For example, suppose you want to query the salary database for persons who have salaries either below $19,000 or above $32,000. To do so, first clear all existing criteria from the criteria table Then, type the formula *+D2<19000#OR#D2>32000* in cell D19 of the criteria table. Quattro Pro selects the records in rows 4, 5, 7, 11, 12, and 16.

The #NOT# operator. The third special operator, #NOT#, lets you negate comparison criteria. For example, the criterion #NOT#B2="Rogers" selects all records that do not have the entry Rogers in the Last Name field. You rarely need to use the #NOT# operator because you can usually find better ways to state a criterion. For example, the following criteria are equivalent:

~Rogers

#NOT#B2="Rogers"

Obviously, the first version is far simpler. The #NOT# operator can also be used to negate compound criteria. For example, the criterion #NOT#(B2="Jordan" #OR#B2="Jackson") selects all the records with Last Name field entries other than Jordan or Jackson.

The advanced Database Query commands

After you specify the query criteria, you're ready to locate database entries using the Database Query Locate, Database Query Extract, Database Query Unique, and Database Query Delete commands. The Database Query Locate command finds, or highlights, those records in your database that match your criteria. Rather than simply highlighting selected records, the Database Query Extract command copies selected records to an output block elsewhere in the worksheet. Likewise, the Database Query Unique command copies selected records to an output block; however, this command copies only one occurrence of any duplicate records to the output block. Finally, the Database Query Delete command removes all records that match the criteria you specify. The sections that follow look at each command in detail.

Defining the blocks before querying

Before you can query a database, you must first use the commands in the Database Query menu to define the blocks Quattro Pro needs to process the query. To use any of these commands, first choose the Database Query Block command to define an input block, which is the block that contains the database you want to query. In addition, if you want to use a criteria table, you must use the Database Query Criteria Table command to define the table in which you've entered the query criteria. Finally, if you intend to use either the Extract or Unique option, use the Database Query Output Block command to tell Quattro Pro where to put the selected records.

Defining the input block. As described earlier in the chapter, before you can query a database, you must use the Database Query Block command to define an input block. This block should include all of the fields and records in the database, and the row that contains the field names. To define the input block, choose the Database Query Block command. Quattro Pro then prompts you to specify the block of cells that contains your database records. Either point to the block or type its coordinates, and press the Enter key.

After you define an input block, be especially careful when inserting and deleting records. As long as you use the Edit Insert Rows and Edit Delete Rows commands to add and remove records, the input block expands and contracts as the size of your database changes. If you simply add a record to the bottom of your database beyond the defined input block, however, you must redefine the input block to include the new record before you query again.

If you use the Edit Delete Row command to delete the last record in the database, Quattro Pro loses your input block definition. Whenever you delete the last record in the database, you must also redefine the input block.

Defining the criteria table. Also as described earlier in the chapter, if you intend to use a criteria table to query your database, you must also define a criteria table. To do so, choose the Database Query Criteria Table command. Quattro Pro prompts you to specify the block of cells for the criteria table. Either point to the block that contains the criteria table or type its coordinates, and press the Enter key. If you want, you can have several criteria tables in a single worksheet. Only one of those tables, however, is active at any time: the table that you defined using the Database Query Criteria Table command.

Defining the output block. Two of Quattro Pro's Database query commands, Database Query Extract and Database Query Unique, copy records that match the criteria you define to another location in the worksheet. Before you can use these commands, you have to use the Database Query Output Block command to tell Quattro Pro where you want the selected records or entries to be copied. This command is discussed in detail later in this chapter in "Extracting Records."

Resetting the settings. The Database Query Reset command lets you reset the input block, criteria table, and output blocks that you defined. After you choose this command, Quattro Pro immediately "forgets" the blocks that you specified as the input block, criteria table, and output block. You can then redefine those blocks from scratch.

Locating records

The Database Query Locate command makes it easy to locate specific records in a database. After you choose this command, Quattro Pro scans the database and highlights the first record that matches the criterion you specified. You can then use the Down and Up direction keys to move the highlight down through the matching records in the database. After you highlight a record, you can edit or replace the entry in any field of that record.

An example of locating a record. Suppose you need to change the Salary field entry for one or two of the persons whose Emp ID field entries begin with the letters AC. (Obviously, with only 15 records you could easily locate and change them. An actual database, however, might contain hundreds of records.)

To locate these records, first erase any existing entries from the criteria table. Next, move the cell selector to cell A19, the cell in the first row of the criteria table under the field name Emp ID, and type *AC** as the criterion. Then, check to be sure that the block A1..D16 is defined as the input block and that block A18..D19 has been defined as the criteria table. To perform the query, choose the Database Query Locate command. Quattro Pro highlights the first record that has an Emp ID field entry that begins with AC.

After Quattro Pro highlights the first matching record, move to the next matching record by pressing the Down direction key. Quattro Pro then moves the highlight bar down the database to the next record that has an Emp ID field entry that begins with AC. Pressing the Up direction key moves the highlight bar up the database to the preceding record that has an Emp ID field entry that begins with AC. If you press the Up direction key while the first matching record is highlighted or the Down direction key while the last matching record is highlighted, Quattro Pro does not move the cell selector.

In addition to using the Up and Down direction keys to move the highlight up and down, you can also move the highlight to the first or last record in the database. If you press the Home key, Quattro Pro highlights the first record in the database even if it does not match the query criteria. Likewise, if you press the End key, Quattro Pro highlights the last record in the database.

Editing entries. After you highlight a record, you can edit the entry in any of its fields by using the Right and Left direction keys to move to the field you want to change. As you do, you'll notice a small underline character moving from field to field in the highlight. This cell selector denotes the currently active field, which is the field that is affected by editing. At the same time, the current field's entry appears in the status line. You can then either make a new entry or edit the existing entry. To make a new entry, type the entry and press the Enter key. To edit the existing entry, press the [Edit] key (F2), and edit the entry just as you would normally edit an entry. If you make an error while editing an entry, press the Esc key to return the previous entry.

Exiting from FIND mode. When you are ready to exit FIND mode, press the Enter key or the Esc key. Quattro Pro then turns off the highlight bar and returns to the Database Query menu. You can then choose another command or back out of the menu structure by pressing the Esc key. If you press the Ctrl-Break keys, Quattro Pro returns to READY mode.

Extracting records

You will often want to copy the information contained in a database block to another location in your worksheet for further processing or printing. Quattro Pro offers two commands that let you copy records that match criteria to another part of the worksheet: Database Query Extract and Database Query Unique. As with the Database Query Locate command, prior to executing these commands, first define an input block and a criteria table. In addition, you must use the Database Query Output Block command to define a block as the output block in which you want Quattro Pro to place the copied data.

The output block. The structure of an output block is like that of a criteria table. The block's first row must contain field names. These names must be identical to the field names in the database, except for label prefixes and capitalization. You can either type the output block field names or copy them from the database block or a criteria table. Although you can place the output block anywhere in the worksheet, you might want to place it somewhere under the database. In this location, the output block can share the column widths and formatting you set up for the database.

The output block can contain as many or as few of the field names from the database as you want. When you use the Database Query Extract and Database Query Unique commands to copy records from the database to the output block, Quattro Pro copies entries from only those fields that are included in the output block. Enter the field names for the output block in any order you want. Quattro Pro simply places the data from the appropriate fields of the database in each field of the output block. In fact, if you enter the same field name twice in the output block, Quattro Pro copies the entries from that field into the output block twice.

Defining the output block. After you enter the field names for which you want to copy data, you're ready to define the output block. To do so, choose the Database Query Output Block command. Quattro Pro prompts you to define a block of cells to serve as the output block. You can choose from two methods to define the output block. You can define a block of cells that contains the field names and is large enough to include one row for each possible selected record. Or, you can define an output block that includes only the one row of field names.

When you define the output block as a multirow block, its size determines how many records Quattro Pro can extract from the database. After Quattro Pro has filled the defined output block, it stops extracting records from the database and displays an error message. For example, if the output block you define is five rows deep (including the row that contains the field names), Quattro Pro places only four matching records from the database in the output block. In many cases, you can avoid this problem by including a large number of rows in the output block.

It is quicker and easier, however, to include only the one row that contains the field names in the output block you define. When you do so, Quattro Pro is free to use all the rows between the field names and the bottom of your worksheet as the output area, which in most cases means that the size of the output block does not restrict the number of records Quattro Pro can extract. Still, this technique is not without its drawbacks. When extracting records from the database to the output block, Quattro Pro also erases all existing entries in that block. If any of the cells between the field names and the last row of the worksheet contain entries, Quattro Pro erases them when you use the Database Query Extract or Database Query Unique commands.

An example of defining an output block

Suppose you want to define an output block based on the worksheet shown in Figure 11-6. To begin, create the row of field names for the output block by choosing the Edit Copy command, selecting the block A1..D1 as the source block, pointing to cell A21, and then pressing the Enter key. Figure 11-7 shows the result. Of course, instead of copying the field names you can type them in cells A21, B21, and so on.

Next, define the output block. Rather than guess how many records might match the criteria, define the output block as a single row by choosing the Database Query Output Block command, and when Quattro Pro prompts you to specify the output block, selecting block A21..D21, and pressing the Enter key.

FIGURE 11-7.
Before you can extract records, you have to set up an output block in the worksheet.

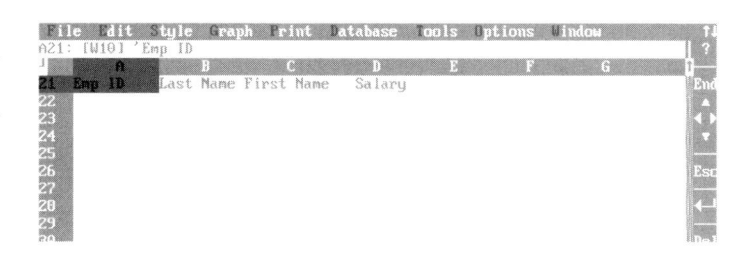

The Database Query Extract command. The Database Query Extract command lets you extract, or copy, records that meet the criteria you specify from the database to the output block. To use this command, first either specify a formula criterion or create and define a criteria table. You must also create and define an output block and define an input block. Then, choose the Database Query Extract command, and Quattro Pro uses the criteria you specified to test each record in the input block. Quattro Pro copies each record that matches the criteria.

An example of extracting. Suppose, for example, that you want to extract each record from the salary database that has a Last Name field entry beginning with the letter J. To begin, erase any existing entries from the criteria table. Next, move the cell selector to cell B19, the cell in the first row of the criteria table under the field name Last Name, and enter J* as the criterion. Then, check to be sure that block A1..D16 is defined as the input block, that block A18..D19 is defined as the criteria table, and that block A21..D21 is defined as the output block.

To execute the query, now choose the Database Query Extract command. Quattro Pro copies the records that have Last Name entries starting with the letter J to the rows below the output block, as shown in Figure 11-8. Any other cell entries between the extracted records and the bottom of the worksheet are erased.

Extracting partial records. As mentioned, the output block can contain as many or as few of the field names from the database as you want. When you use the Database Query Extract command to extract entries from the database to the output block, Quattro Pro copies information only from those fields that are included in the output block. By limiting the number of field names in the output block, you can control the fields of data that Quattro Pro extracts.

The Database Query Unique command. Occasionally, you will need to eliminate duplicate records from those that Quattro Pro copies into the output block. To extract only unique records, use the Database Query Unique command. Like the Database Query Extract command, the Database Query Unique command copies the specified fields in the selected records into the output block. The Database Query Unique command, however, keeps track of those records it has already copied and, if it encounters a record that is identical to a record already extracted, Quattro Pro does not extract the duplicate record. The Database Query Unique

FIGURE 11-8.
The Database Query Extract command lets you copy, from the database into the output block, all records that meet the criteria you defined.

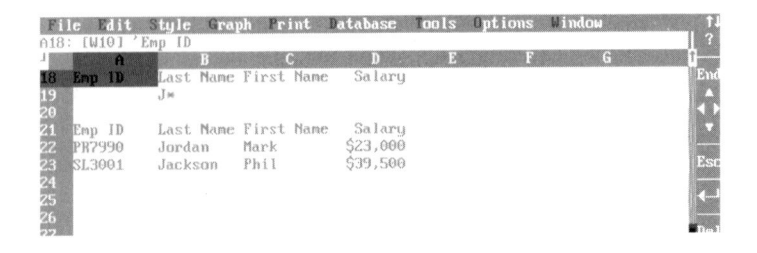

command considers two records to be duplicates if they have identical entries in every field in the output block.

Deleting records

The Database Query Delete command deletes from a database those records that match the criteria you specify. To use this command, first either specify a formula criterion or create and define a criteria table and define the input block. Next, choose the Database Query Delete command. Quattro Pro then uses the criteria you specified to test each record in the input block. Each record that matches the criteria is deleted from the worksheet.

An example of deleting records. Suppose, for example, that an employee whose last name is Spencer resigns and that you want to delete this person's salary record. To begin, check to be sure that the block A1..D16 is defined as the input block. Then, clear any existing criteria from the criteria table. Next, enter the criterion Spencer in cell B2 under the field name Last Name. Finally, check to be sure that block A18..D19 has been defined as the criteria table.

To execute the query, choose the Database Query Delete command. Quattro Pro displays the prompt *Delete Record(s)?* and gives two possible answers: Cancel and Delete. Either choose the Cancel option, in which case Quattro Pro returns to the Database Query Delete menu, or choose the Delete option, in which case Quattro Pro deletes the selected records from the database. Figure 11-9 shows the salary database after the matching records have been deleted. Note that you might want to enable Undo before choosing the Database Query Delete command. Undo allows you replace the records you delete if you choose the Undo command immediately after choosing the Database Query Delete command.

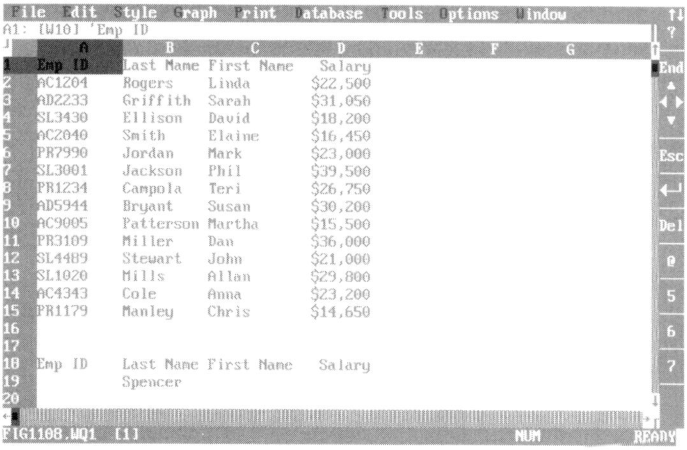

FIGURE 11-9.
The Database Query Delete command deletes from a database those records that match the criteria you define.

Using the [Query] key

The [Query] key (F7) repeats the last Query operation. Accordingly, rather than choosing the Database Query Locate, Database Query Extract, Database Query Unique, or Database Query Delete command over again, you can simply press the [Query] key.

Database statistical functions

Quattro Pro offers nine database statistical functions that you can use to compute statistical information from the entries in your databases. Each of the functions in this group calculates a common statistic, such as the average count, minimum, or maximum, for the entries in a specified field of the records that match your defined criteria. Quattro Pro's statistical functions are @DAVG, @DMAX, @DMIN, @DSUM, @DSTD, @DSTS, @DVAR, @DVARS, and @DCOUNT.

Database statistical functions can be a valuable tool for analyzing Quattro Pro databases. For instance, you could use the @DMAX function when querying a sales staff database to find the top sales achieved in a particular region. Or, you could use the @DCOUNT to find out how many listings in a telephone database have the last name Jones.

Basics of database statistical functions

Although each of Quattro Pro's database statistical functions calculates a different statistic, they all have the same basic form. For example, the form of the @DAVG function is as follows:

@DAVG(*input-block,column-offset,criteria*)

The *input-block* argument defines the block of the worksheet that contains the database you want to analyze. This block should include all of the records in the database and the field names at the top of the database. In most cases, this input block is identical to the input block you define prior to querying a database. If you assigned a name to your database block, you can use that name to define the input block.

The *column-offset* argument determines the field on which you want to compute the statistic and specifies the field's position relative to the leftmost column of the input block. The first column has an offset of 0, the second an offset of 1, and so on. A *column-offset* argument of 2 tells Quattro Pro to compute a statistic on the third field of the database. Because Quattro Pro's database statistical functions compute statistics such as the sum, average, and standard deviation, the field specified by the *column-offset* argument should contain only numeric entries. The one exception to this rule is the @DCOUNT function, which can operate on any type of entry.

The *criteria* argument defines the criteria you want to use to select the records you want to analyze. This argument must be a reference to a block of the worksheet that contains a criteria table you have previously defined.

An example of using database statistical functions

Suppose, for example, that you want to calculate the average salary of employees in the sales department. To do so, type the function *@DAVG(A1..E15,3,E18..E19)* into cell F3, the label *Dept* in cell E18, and the criterion *SALES* in cell E19. Figure 11-10 shows the worksheet after these changes have been added, along with an additional database field that shows the employee's department. Note that this is the same basic worksheet used earlier in the chapter.

Notice that this block includes all of the records in the database as well as the field names. The second argument in the function, 3, is the column offset of the field on which you want to compute the average: the Salary field. If you look at Figure 11-10, you'll see that column D, which contains this field, is three columns to the right of column A, which is the first column in the input block. The third argument, E18..E19, is the criteria table that defines the records for which you want to compute the average. As you can see, this function returns the value 18500, which is the average salary of the employees in the Sales department.

The database statistical functions

Now that you understand the basic form and usage of database statistical functions, take a moment to examine each of the functions individually.

@DAVG

As you have seen, Quattro Pro's @DAVG function computes the average of the values in a specified field of the records that match your specified criteria. For example, in Figure 11-10 the function @DAVG(A1..E15,3,E18..E19) calculates the average salary of employees in the sales department.

@DMAX and @DMIN

Quattro Pro's @DMAX and @DMIN functions return the highest and lowest values, respectively, in a specified field of the records that match your specified criteria. For example, in the worksheet shown in Figure 11-10, the function @DMAX(A1..E15,3,E18..E19) would return the largest value in the Salary field for those records with a Dept field entry of Sales: 23200. The function @DMIN (A1..E15,3,E18..E19) would return the smallest value in the Salary field for those records with a Dept field entry of Sales: 14650.

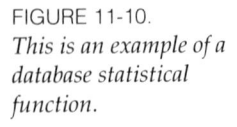

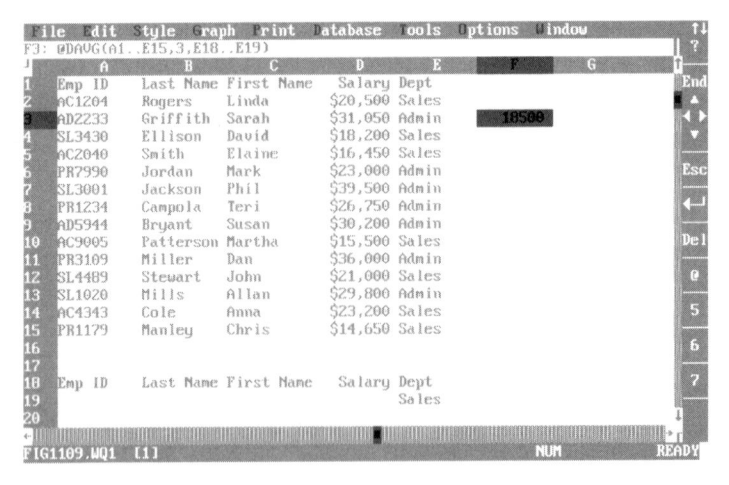

FIGURE 11-10.
This is an example of a database statistical function.

@DSUM

The @DSUM function sums the values in a specific field of those records that match your defined criteria. For example, suppose you need to know the sum of the Salary field entries for all the persons in the sales department. You could use the function @DSUM(A1..E15,3,E18..E19) to compute the correct sum: 129500.

@DSTD, @DSTDS, @DVAR, and @DVARS

The @DSTD and @DVAR functions compute the population standard deviation and variance of the values in a specific field of records that match the criteria you specify. The @DSTDS and @DVARS functions compute the sample standard deviation and variance of the values in a specific field of records that match your specified criteria.

For example, suppose you want to find the population standard deviation and variance of the Salary field entries of the people working in the sales department. You can use the function @DSTD(A1..E15,3,E18..E19) to compute the standard deviation of the entries in the Salary field for the records with the entry Sales in the Dept field, which is 2938.78, and the function @DVAR(A1..E15,3,E18..E19) to compute the population variance of those values, which is 8636429. If you instead wanted to calculate the sample standard deviation and sample variance, you could substitute the @DSTDS and @DVARS functions. See Chapter 4, "Functions," for descriptions of the @STD, @STDS, @VAR, and @VARS functions and a brief discussion of the difference between population and sample statistics.

@DCOUNT

Quattro Pro's @DCOUNT function computes the number of entries in a specified field of the records that match the criteria you have specified. This function stands alone as the one statistical database function that can operate on any kind of entry.

You can use the @DCOUNT function to count the entries in fields that contain values, labels, formulas, or functions. For example, suppose you want to know how many people work in the sales department. You can use the function @DCOUNT(A1..E15,3,E18..E19) to compute the result, which is 7.

Normally, the *column-offset* argument of the @DCOUNT function can refer to any column in the input block. As long as none of the fields in the database contains blank entries, you get the same result no matter which column you refer to. If the database contains blank cells, the *column-offset* argument should refer to the same field that you use to select records. Counting the entries in the field you use to select records helps to ensure a one-to-one relationship between selected records and the count.

Accessing external databases from Quattro Pro

Quattro Pro also allows you execute the Database Query Extract command on external databases in Paradox, Reflex, and dBASE from within Quattro Pro. As a result, even if a database does not fit well into Quattro Pro's worksheet structure, you can still use Quattro Pro's computational power to manipulate data in external databases.

Basic techniques for accessing external databases

The steps you follow to work with an external database closely resemble those you use to work with an internal database; that is, one that's stored in a Quattro Pro worksheet: You must define an input block, a criteria table, and an output block. The steps for defining an output block are the same for external and internal databases. Defining input blocks and criteria tables for external databases, however, differs from defining input blocks and criteria tables for internal databases.

Defining the input block

To access an external database, use worksheet file links, as described in Chapter 8, "File Management." Suppose, for example, that the database filename is EXPENSES.DB and the file is stored in the PARADOX directory on the C drive. In this case, when you choose the Database Query Block command to identify the database, you respond to Quattro Pro's prompt for the database block by entering the following:

+[C:\PARADOX\EXPENSES.DB]A1..A2

The Paradox database contains no columns and rows, so the A1..A2 portion of the input block definition is somewhat nonsensical. You must include a block definition as part of the input block, however, to meet Quattro Pro's syntax requirements. Actually, as long as the database file is not open—and it should not be open—the block definition could be any valid block definition. The only rule you need to remember is that the block must include two rows. Note that if the database file is open, you must specify the entire block to query. For help on how to do so, refer to the documentation that came with the database.

Defining criteria for external databases

When defining the criteria table, you must be careful to use the same field names as appear in the databases to identify the indiviual fields in a record. What's more, the fields you use in your criteria table must include the spreadsheet link formula. For example, suppose you are extracting all the records from the EXPENSES.DB database in which the AMOUNT field is greater than $10,000. In an internal database, the criteria formula might normally look like the following:

    +AMOUNT>10000

In an external database, however, the formula must also include the spreadsheet link portion of the formula. Assuming the database filename is EXPENSES.DB and the file is stored in the PARADOX directory on the C drive, the formula would look like the following:

    +[C:\PARADOX\EXPENSES.DB]AMOUNT>10000

Note that if you have additional questions about worksheet links, you might want to see the section "Linking Spreadsheets Using Formulas" in Chapter 8.

Using the Database Paradox Access commands

The Database Paradox Access commands let you use Quattro Pro with Paradox. Paradox is a separate database program manufactured by Borland. Using the Database Paradox Access commands, you can run Quattro Pro from within Paradox, easily pass data from Paradox to Quattro Pro, and move between Quattro Pro and Paradox using a single keystroke. You do, however, need to learn the basics of working with Paradox.

The options in the Database Paradox Access menu—Go, Load File, Autoload, and Quit—make it possible to work with Quattro Pro in tandem with Paradox. The Go option switches to Paradox. The Load File option names the Paradox file that Quattro Pro can retrieve when you switch to Quattro Pro from Paradox. The Autoload option, which is a Yes-No Switch, specifies whether the Load File you named opens when you switch to Quattro Pro from Paradox. Of course, the Quit option returns you to the worksheet and to READY mode.

To use Paradox and Quattro Pro side by side, you need to buy Paradox version 3.5 or later. You also need a computer that has at least 2 MB of memory and an Intel 80286 or faster processor. You also need to install Paradox following the instructions in the Paradox user documentation.

12

Macro Basics

*P*revious chapters of this book have shown you the variety of tasks that Quattro Pro can perform. As you've seen, each task involves typing. In the course of a typical Quattro Pro session, you're likely to press hundreds of keys. In some cases, you'll press the same keys over and over again as you repeat the same task in different parts of the same worksheet or in different worksheets. To avoid the tedium of pressing the same series of keys repeatedly, you can create a macro that "plays back" a series of keystrokes.

A macro is like a computer program that works within a Quattro Pro worksheet. The simplest macros merely represent the keys that you would press from the keyboard of your computer. The keystrokes can instruct Quattro Pro to make entries in cells, move the cell selector, issue commands, and so forth. More complex macros contain special instructions that allow you to create for/next loops, call subroutines, and solicit user input.

The principal advantage to putting repetitive tasks into macros is that you no longer have to press the keys required to perform the task. Instead, you simply tell Quattro Pro to play the macro, and Quattro Pro executes the keystrokes and commands stored in the macro much faster than you could execute them yourself, even if you are an exceptional typist. Furthermore, Quattro Pro does not make mistakes. When executing a macro, Quattro Pro always presses the exact keys whose representations are stored within that macro.

Although an entire book could be dedicated to Quattro Pro's macro features, this chapter introduces you to macros by showing you how to create, play, and debug macros. Chapter 13, "Programming Command Basics," briefly reviews Quattro Pro's special programming commands, which increase the power of your macros.

The easiest way to use macros is to record them and then play them back. If you want to try recording a macro without learning the details of how they work, turn to "Recording Macros" later in this chapter.

Macro fundamentals

A Quattro Pro macro is a collection of keystrokes and special commands that instruct Quattro Pro to perform one or more tasks. For example, Figure 12-1 contains a Quattro Pro macro that enters and then centers labels. When you tell Quattro Pro to play, or run, this macro (a process that is explained later in this chapter), Quattro Pro enters the labels 'Qtr. 1, 'Qtr. 2, 'Qtr. 3, and 'Qtr. 4 in adjacent cells of a single row, starting in the cell in which the cell selector is currently positioned. Then, Quattro Pro centers each of these labels by choosing the Style Alignment command, choosing the Center option, highlighting the cells into which it just made the entries, and pressing the Enter key. Finally, Quattro Pro sets to 12 spaces the width of each of the four columns into which entries were made.

As you can see in Figure 12-1, a Quattro Pro macro consists of entries in adjacent cells of a single column of a worksheet. In most cases, these entries are labels that are the same as any other labels, except that they represent keystrokes and commands. The cells of a macro, however, can also contain string-producing formulas and functions. In those cases, Quattro Pro executes the result of the formula or function as it would any other macro statement. A macro cell cannot contain a value or a value-producing formula or function. Quattro Pro stops a macro if it encounters a blank cell or a cell that contains a value, a value-producing formula, or a function.

FIGURE 12-1.
This macro enters the labels 'Qtr. 1, 'Qtr. 2, 'Qtr. 3, and 'Qtr. 4 in adjacent cells of a single row, and then centers those labels.

Macro elements

Quattro Pro macros can contain elements: representations of regular keys, representations of special keys, menu-equivalent commands, and programming commands.

Regular keys

A regular key is any of the alphanumeric keys or special symbol keys (such as ? or !) on your keyboard that produces a character on the screen when you press it. This includes the Spacebar, which produces a space character. Within a macro, these keys are represented by the characters they produce. For example, the first six keystrokes in the macro shown in Figure 12-1, cell B1, tell Quattro Pro to type the letters Q, t, and r, followed by a period, a space, and then the digit 1.

Special keys

A special key produces an action instead of a character when you press it. For example, the Enter key, Up direction key, PgDn key, and Esc key are all special keys. These keys must be represented in a macro as listed in Table 12-1. For example, you represent the Right direction key as {Right} or {R}. When recording the representations of these special keys, Quattro Pro uses all lowercase letters. You can, however, use any combination of uppercase and lowercase letters, although capitalizing the first letter of each representation is preferred. For example, you can represent the Up direction key as {Up}, the Right direction key as {Right}, and so forth.

The representations of many special keys accept arguments that multiply their effect. For example, {Down 2} tells Quattro Pro to press the Down direction key two times. You can use value-producing formulas and functions instead of literal values as arguments. For example, if cell A2 contains the value 3 or a formula or function that returns that value, {Esc A2} tells Quattro Pro to press the Esc key three times, and {Abs A2+1} tells Quattro Pro to press the Abs key (F4) four times.

Menu-equivalent commands

Many macros instruct Quattro Pro to choose commands from menus. To do so, include in the macro the keys that you would press to choose that command. For example, the keystrokes /sc in cell B8 of the macro shown in Figure 12-1 tell Quattro Pro to choose the Style Column Width command. Alternatively, you can use special command representations to instruct Quattro Pro to choose commands from menus while a macro runs. These special representations, called menu-equivalent commands, are listed in the documentation that comes with Quattro Pro. The command {/ Publish;AlignCenter} in cell B5 of the macro shown in Figure 12-1 is an example of a menu-equivalent command. This command is equivalent to typing /sac (to choose the Style Alignment Center command).

Key	Macro representation
Enter	~ or {Cr}
Backspace	{Bs} or {Backspace}
Del	{Del} or {Delete}
Esc	{Esc} or {Escape}
Ins	{Ins} or {Insert}
Insert off	{InsOff}
Insert on	{InsOn}
Caps Lock off	{CapOff}
Caps Lock on	{CapOn}
Num Lock off	{NumOff}
Num Lock on	{NumOn}
Scroll Lock off	{ScrollOff}
Scroll Lock on	{ScrollOn}
Home	{Home}
End	{End}
PgUp	{PgUp}
PgDn	{PgDn}
Ctrl-Right direction or Tab	{BigRight}
Ctrl-Left direction or Shift-Tab	{BigLeft}
Up direction	{Up} or {U}
Down direction	{Down} or {D}
Right direction	{Right} or {R}
Left direction	{Left} or {L}
Ctrl-\	{DelEol}
Ctrl-Backspace	{Clear}
Ctrl-Break	{Break}
Ctrl-D	{Date}
F2	{Edit}
F3	{Name}
F4	{Abs}
F5	{Goto}
F6	{Window}
F7	{Query}
F8	{Table}
F9	{Calc} in a worksheet window
F9	{ReadDir} in a File Manager window
F10	{Graph}
Alt-F3	{Functions}
Alt-F5	{Undo}

Key	Macro representation
Alt-F6	{Zoom}
Alt-F7	{MarkAll}
Shift-F2	{Step}
Shift-F3	{Macros}
Shift-F6	{NextWin}
Shift-F7	{Mark}
Shift-F8	{Move}
Shift-F9	{Copy}
Shift-F10	{Paste}
/	/ or {Menu}
{	{{}
}	{}}
~	{~}

TABLE 12-1. *This table shows how the special keys on your computer's keyboard must be represented within Quattro Pro macros.*

All menu-equivalent commands consist of a slash and two words surrounded by braces. The first word specifies the general action of the command; for example, Publish. The second word specifies the specific action; for example, AlignCenter. You must separate the first word from the slash with a single space, and the second from the first with a semicolon; for example, {/ Publish;AlignCenter}.

As you will see in Chapter 13 and Appendix 2, Quattro Pro lets you change the structure of its menus. For example, you can move a command from one menu to another, remove commands entirely, or make Quattro Pro emulate the menu structure of Lotus 1-2-3. The principal advantage of using menu-equivalent commands instead of keystrokes to represent the process of choosing a command in a macro is that, unlike keystrokes, menu-equivalent commands produce the same result under any menu structure. If you use keystrokes to represent the process of choosing a command from a menu, your macro might not work if you subsequently modify the structure of Quattro Pro's menus. The principal disadvantage of using these commands is that it's difficult to remember them or look them up. You'll find out more about the pros and cons of using menu-equivalent commands later in this chapter in "Writing Macros" and "Executing Macros."

Programming commands

The macro programming commands add power to Quattro Pro macros. The command *{For COUNT,1,4,1,SETWIDTH}* in cell B6 of the macro shown in Figure 12-1 and the command *{If COUNT<4}* in cell B9 are examples of programming commands. The *{For}* command instructs Quattro Pro to execute the commands in cells B8 and B9 four times, and the *{If}* command instructs Quattro Pro to press the

Left direction key at the end of the first three passes through this loop. Chapter 13, "Programming Command Basics," covers programming commands in detail.

Macro statements

You can place only a single keystroke or represent only a single command in each cell of a macro. However, macro cells typically contain more than one keystroke or command. A "macro statement" is one or more macro keystrokes or commands. In other words, each cell in a macro contains a single macro statement, and each statement consists of one or more keystrokes or commands.

In general, placing one keystroke or command in each cell wastes space, and entering too many keystrokes and commands in a cell makes a macro difficult to edit. As a general rule, try to group related commands and keystrokes in the same cell, as in the macro shown in Figure 12-1. You can, however, divide a macro in any way you want, with no effect on the way Quattro Pro runs the macro. For example, from the perspective of Quattro Pro, the macro shown in Figure 12-2 is exactly equivalent to the one shown in Figure 12-1.

Special keys, menu-equivalent commands, and programming commands cannot be divided between two or more cells in a macro. For example, Quattro Pro would not recognize the {Right} command if the characters {Ri appeared at the end of the statement in one cell and the characters ght} appeared at the beginning of the next statement. A break of this sort would cause a macro error, as described later in this chapter in "Macro Errors."

Positioning a macro

In general, you can place a macro anywhere within a worksheet. The running of a macro, however, is disturbed when you insert or delete rows above or columns to the left of the macro while Quattro Pro is executing it. Consequently, it is best to place the macro in the upper-left corner of a worksheet, and not use the rows and columns occupied by the macro.

FIGURE 12-2.
This macro is equivalent to the one shown in Figure 12-1.

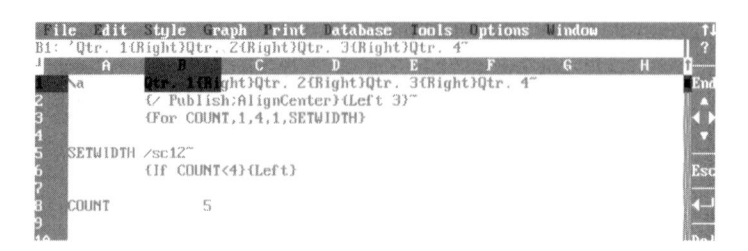

Macro names

You usually assign a block name to the first cell in each of your macros. If you use a name that consists of a backslash and an alphabetic character (for example, \a or \g), you can run the macro simply by holding down the Alt key and pressing that alphabetic character. For example, if you assign the name \z to the first cell in a macro, you can run that macro by pressing Alt-z. Because Quattro Pro does not differentiate between uppercase and lowercase letters in block names, a worksheet cannot contain more than 26 macros of this sort. If you use any other name, you must run the macro by choosing the Tools Macro Excute command.

It's not necessary to name your Quattro Pro macros. Unlike Lotus 1-2-3, Quattro Pro features a command that allows you to run a macro simply by pointing to it. Later in this chapter, "Executing Macros" explains the Tools Macro Execute command and gives a detailed explanation of the other ways in which you can run macros.

Creating macros

You can create a Quattro Pro macro in two ways: by recording it or by writing it. Recording a macro is much easier than writing one, so this section begins by showing you how to record macros. To write a macro, you must be familiar with the layout of Quattro Pro's menus, the representations of special keys, the form of menu-equivalent commands, and so forth. Later in this chapter, "Writing Macros" shows you how to write macros.

Instant replay of recorded keystrokes

The simplest form of a recorded macro is called an "instant replay macro." This is a one-time macro for which you record a series of keystrokes and then direct Quattro Pro to replay those same keystrokes. For example, you might want to enter today's date, format it as a date, and then increase the column width in several places in a worksheet. After the cell selector is in the correct cell, the keystrokes you use to accomplish these tasks are @NOW{Enter}/snd1{Enter}/sc12{Enter}. This sequence of keystrokes enters the @NOW function in the current cell, chooses the Style Numeric Format Date command, and then chooses the Style Column Width command to set the width to 12. (If this sequence seems confusing, try typing these keystrokes with the cell selector located in a blank cell; you'll quickly see what's going on.)

To record this sequence of keystrokes so they can be replayed, first move the cell selector to a blank cell into which you want to enter a date. Then choose the Tools Macro Record command to turn on the macro recorder. Next, type the sequence of keystrokes you want to record: @NOW{Enter}/snd1{Enter}/sc12{Enter}. Quattro Pro records the representation {Enter} but you press the Enter key. Finally, choose the Tools Macro Record command again to turn off the macro recorder. (When you type the keystrokes, you actually enter the date in the current cell, change the format, and increase the column width). To replay these keystrokes, first move the cell selector to another cell in which you want the date entered and formatted, and then choose the Tools Macro Instant Replay command. Quattro Pro enters today's date in the current cell, formats it using the first date format, and then increases the column width to 12 so that the date format fits. To enter the date in other cells, follow the same procedure. You can continue to replay the recorded keystrokes until you replace them by recording a new macro.

Recording macros

To record a macro, first choose the Tools Macro Record command. Quattro Pro clears the prompt from the screen and places the indicator REC at the bottom of the screen. From that point on, Quattro Pro records each key you press. Of course, Quattro Pro also performs the actions that the keys tell it to perform. For example, if you type *123* and then press the Down direction key, Quattro Pro records the characters 123{down} while entering the value 123 in the current cell, and then moves down one cell.

Quattro Pro always records regular keys as you type them. For example, if you type *123*, Quattro Pro records the characters 123. Quattro Pro records special keys as shown in Table 12-1. For example, if you press the Up direction key, Quattro Pro records it as {Up}.

Pasting a recorded macro into a worksheet

Quattro Pro stores a recorded macro in the transcript log. If you want to save a macro you have recorded, you must copy it from the transcript log to a worksheet. To do so, choose the Tools Macro Paste command. Quattro Pro displays the prompt *Enter name of macro to create/modify*, followed by a list of all the named blocks. At this point, you should specify the name (if any) that you want Quattro Pro to assign to the macro you recorded. To specify a new name, type it. To specify the name of an existing block, either choose it from the list or type it. The name you assign to a macro determines how you can start that macro. If you assign a name that consists of a backslash and an alphabetic character, you can start the macro by typing the alphabetic character while you hold down the Alt key. If you assign another name to the macro, you must use the Tools Macro Execute command to run it.

When you press the Enter key after assigning a name to the macro, Quattro Pro displays the prompt *Enter macro block to paste* followed by the current address of the cell selector. In response to this prompt, highlight or type the coordinates of the block into which you want Quattro Pro to paste the macro you have recorded. This block should be a single cell or a block of cells in a single column. If you specify a single cell, Quattro Pro assigns to it the name (if any) that you specified. If you specify a multiple-cell block, Quattro Pro assigns the name to the entire block.

The size of the block you specify determines how many keystrokes Quattro Pro pastes. If you specify a single cell, Quattro Pro fills not only that cell but also the cells below it. If you specify a multiple-cell, single-column block, Quattro Pro stops pasting after it fills the cells of that block.

NOTE: If you choose the Tools Macro Paste command while you are recording a macro, Quattro Pro turns off the recorder.

Recording commands in menu-equivalent form. Unless you specify otherwise, Quattro Pro records menu-equivalent commands in your macros. For example, if you choose the Edit Insert Row command, Quattro Pro records the menu-equivalent command {/ Row;Insert} in the macro.

When set to record the menu-equivalent forms of the commands you choose, Quattro Pro records each command in the same way, no matter how you choose it. For example, regardless of whether you choose the File Save command by pressing the / key, typing *f*, and then typing *s*, or by pressing the / key, pressing the Down direction key three times to move down the File menu, pressing the Enter key, pressing the Down direction key one time to move to the Replace option, and then pressing the Enter key again, Quattro Pro enters the command {/ File;SaveNow} in the macro.

Recording commands in keystroke form. You can also tell Quattro Pro to record the actual keystrokes you press to choose commands, rather than the menu-equivalent form of those commands. To do so, choose the Tools Macro Macro Recording Keystroke command before recording your macro. If you have chosen the Keystroke option, Quattro Pro records the keys you press to choose a command, and not the menu-equivalent form of that command. For example, if you choose the File Save Replace command by pressing /, *f*, *s*, and then *r*, Quattro Pro records */fsr*, and not {/ File;SaveNow}. If you choose the File Save Replace command by pressing /, the Down direction key four times, the Enter key, the Down direction key one more time, and then pressing the Enter key again, Quattro Pro records /{Down4}~{Down}~.

Unlike macros that contain the menu-equivalent forms of commands, macros that contain the keystroke representations of commands do not work if Quattro Pro's menus are modified so that those commands have been removed or are in different locations. If you modify Quattro Pro's menus after recording a macro, as described in Chapter 13 and Appendix B, the commands that the macro is supposed to choose might not be in the same places that they were when you recorded the macro. Consequently, the macro might choose commands other than the ones you intended, or Quattro Pro might beep, indicating an error.

To ensure that you can run your macros under any menu structure and to avoid the necessity of choosing commands only by choosing their first letter while you record your macro, you probably should not record macros in the Keystroke mode. If you have switched to the Keystroke mode, you can return to recording the menu-equivalent form of commands by choosing the Tools Macro Macro Recording Logical command. Unless you choose the Options Update command after setting Quattro Pro to record keystrokes, the next time you start Quattro Pro it will be in the Logical record mode.

An example of recording a macro

As an example of the process of recording a macro, record one that deletes the contents of a current cell. You can name this macro \e and store it in cell A1.

To record this macro, begin by choosing the Tools Macro Record command to turn on the macro recorder. Then, type the keystrokes you want the macro to choose; for this example, choose the Edit Erase Block command and press the Enter key. Next, paste the keystrokes you recorded by choosing the Tools Macro Paste command. When Quattro Pro displays the prompt *Enter name of macro to create/modify*, type \e for the name and press the Enter key. When Quattro Pro displays the prompt *Enter macro block to paste*, move the cell selector to A1 and press the Enter key. Figure 12-3 shows the worksheet with the example macro in cell A1. {/Block;Erase} is the menu-equivalent form of the Edit Erase Block command.

Correcting mistakes

You might make mistakes while you record a macro. For example, you might choose the wrong command from a menu or misspell an entry. If you make such a mistake, you do not need to stop recording the macro. Instead, simply correct the mistake.

After you finish recording, the macro contains the mistake and the keys that you pressed to correct it. When you run the macro, Quattro Pro repeats your mistake and then performs the same actions you performed to correct it. This approach is not elegant, but it works. This problem of mistakes is one reason you might want to try writing macros, which is described in the next section.

FIGURE 12-3.
This example shows a simple macro that erases the contents of the current cell.

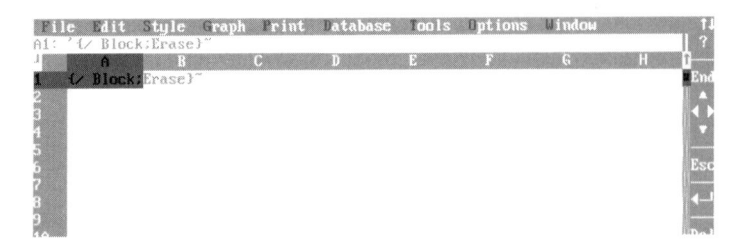

Writing macros

Although recording is the easiest way to create macros, you might also want to write some. To write a macro, type the keystrokes and commands that you want Quattro Pro to execute. Instead of having Quattro Pro record the representations of the keys as you press them, you must type the representations of the keys yourself. For example, instead of pressing the Down direction key, you type {Down}.

Because Quattro Pro does not perform the commands as you write them, you cannot tell if you have made a mistake. This makes writing a macro difficult. Therefore, before you try to write a macro, you should know what keystrokes are required, the layout of the menus that contain the commands you want to use (or the menu-equivalent forms of the commands), and how special keys must be represented in a macro. Writing a macro is a job only for experienced Quattro Pro users.

General rules about writing macros

As explained at the beginning of this chapter, macros are keystrokes and commands stored as labels in a single column of a Quattro Pro worksheet. Like any label, the macro statement in a cell can contain up to 254 characters. You'll probably want to divide your macros, however, into smaller statements that group related commands. Never divide a macro in the middle of a menu-equivalent command or within the representation of a special key.

By necessity, all macro statements (except ones that are the result of string formulas or functions) must begin with a label prefix. Quattro Pro, however, ignores those prefixes when executing the statements in a macro. For example, when executing the commands in the first cell in the macro shown in Figure 12-1, Quattro Pro does not type a single quotation mark (') before typing the characters Qtr. 1 and pressing the Right direction key.

The statements in your macros usually begin with non-numeric characters. In those situations, you do not need to type a label prefix at the beginning of the statement because Quattro Pro supplies the prefix for you. If the first character in the statement is a digit, however, you must type a label prefix at the beginning of that entry. If you don't begin such an entry with a label, Quattro Pro will read it as a value rather than as a macro command. For example, if you want a macro to begin by entering the value 123 in a cell, type '123~, "123~, or ^123~ in its first cell. When executing this statement, Quattro Pro ignores the label prefix, types 123, and then presses the Enter key. This series of keystrokes enters the value 123 in the cell in which the cell selector is currently positioned.

If a macro statement begins with a digit, and you intend the digit to be a label, you must precede that digit with two label prefixes. The first label prefix tells Quattro Pro that what follows is a macro statement, and the second prefix tells Quattro Pro that what follows is a label. For example, suppose you want a macro to begin by entering the centered label 123 Main Street in the current cell. To accomplish this task, enter the label '^123 Main Street~ in the first cell in the macro. When executing this statement, Quattro Pro ignores the first label prefix ', uses the second label prefix ^ to center the label 123 Main Street, and then presses the Enter key. If the first cell in the macro had contained the statement '123 Main Street~, Quattro Pro would have beeped because after the label prefix is ignored, it looks as if you want to enter 123 Main Street as a value.

Representing menu commands

When you write a macro, you can represent the process of choosing a menu command either with the keystrokes required to choose that command or with the menu-equivalent form of that command. For example, you can represent the Tools Advanced Math Multiply command either with the character sequence /tam or the menu-equivalent command {/ Math;MultiplyMatrix }.

Representing menu commands with keystrokes. If you choose to use the keystroke form of menu commands in your macros, you will occasionally need to begin a statement with the slash (/) key. To do so, type a label prefix before you press the / key. If you press the key without first typing a label prefix, Quattro Pro displays its main menu instead entering the / character in the second cell.

In most cases, the keystroke representation of a command is shorter than the menu-equivalent form. Also, you probably will be more familiar with the keystrokes required to choose a command than with the menu-equivalent form of that command. In spite of these apparent advantages, you'll probably want to use menu-equivalent commands whenever possible. By doing so, you ensure that Quattro Pro is able to run your macro no matter how you have arranged its menus. What's more, you'll find that the menu-equivalent commands are much easier to read.

Representing menu commands with menu-equivalent commands. Unfortunately, it's almost impossible to memorize the menu-equivalent forms of each of Quattro Pro's commands and is often useless to guess. Help, however, is available. You can look up the menu-equivalent form of the command that you want Quattro Pro to choose in the documentation that comes with Quattro Pro. Alternatively, you can use the [Macros] key (Shift-F3) to display a list that contains seven choices: Keyboard, Screen, Interactive, Program Flow, Cells, File, and / Commands. The first five choices display a list of programming commands, which are explained in Chapter 13, "Programming Command Basics." But, if you choose the final option, / Commands, Quattro Pro displays a list like the one shown in Figure 12-4.

The items in this list are the words that describe the general action of each command. From this list, choose the general action of the menu command you want to represent. Quattro Pro then displays a list of specific actions for the general action you selected. For example, if you choose the Basics option, Quattro Pro

FIGURE 12-4.
Quattro Pro displays this list when you choose the / Commands option.

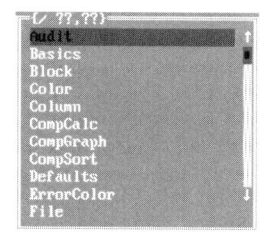

displays a list that contains the choices Close, Erase, OS, Quit, and so forth. When you choose an item from this list, Quattro Pro types the menu-equivalent form of the command in the input line. For example, if you choose the Column option from the list of general actions and the Hide option from the list of specific actions, Quattro Pro types {/ Column;Hide} in the input line. If the input line already contains characters when you make your choices, Quattro Pro inserts the menu-equivalent command at the position of the cursor.

Choose items from the lists of general and specific actions by moving the highlight to them and pressing the Enter key. Although you can choose items from these lists by typing the first letters of those items, many of the lists contain multiple items that share the same first letter. If you type a letter that begins more than one item in a list, Quattro Pro selects the item closest to the top of the list.

Quattro Pro does not type anything in the input line until you choose an item from both the list of general actions and the list of specific actions. If you choose an incorrect general action, you can return to the list of general actions by pressing the Esc key. If you press the Esc key while viewing the list of general actions, Quattro Pro returns to the original list of choices.

Naming a macro

You'll want to name most of the macros that you write because naming a macro makes it easier to run. The name of a macro is simply a block name. You can name a macro in the same way that you name any other block; by using the Edit Names Create command. Or, you can use the Macro Name command. To name a macro using either of these commands, choose it, type the name that you want to assign to the macro, highlight or type the coordinates of the first cell of that macro, and press the Enter key. Like any block name, the name of a macro can contain up to 15 characters. To run a macro by pressing the Alt key and a single letter, give it a name that consists of a backslash (\) followed by that letter. Otherwise, you have to use the Tools Macro Execute command to run the macro.

Note that instead of assigning a name to only the first cell in a macro, you can assign a name to any block that has that cell in its upper-left corner. As long as the first cell in the macro is in the upper-left corner of the block, you can use the name of that block to run the macro.

Combining recording and writing techniques

If you want, you can use a combination of recording and writing to create a macro. For most macros that do not contain programming commands, you'll record more often than you'll write. But, because you cannot record programming commands, you'll write most portions of the macros that contain those commands. Chapter 13, "Programming Command Basics," covers programming commands in detail.

Editing macros

Because your macro statements are labels, you can edit them in the same way you do other labels; by moving the cell selector to the cell that contains the statement you want to edit, pressing the [Edit] key (F2), and revising the entry in the input line. To move or copy macro statements from one place to another, use the Edit Move and Edit Copy commands. To erase a macro statement, use the Edit Erase Block command. Likewise, you can use the Edit Insert Row command to insert a new row in a macro and the Edit Delete Row command to delete a row from a macro.

Documenting your macros

You might want to annotate your macros in case you forget how they work or someone else has to use them. One approach is to enter explanatory labels in the cells to the right of the macro statements that you want to explain. For example, you might enter the labels 'Enters column heading labels, 'Centers labels in cells, and 'Sets column widths to 12 as explanations of the statements in the macro shown in Figure 12-5, which is an annotated version of the macro shown in Figure 12-1.

You can also document a macro by using Quattro Pro's {; comment} form to embed comments. When encountering a statement in a macro that begins with an opening brace and a semicolon, Quattro Pro skips that statement and proceeds to

FIGURE 12-5.
You can annotate a macro by placing explanatory labels in the cells to its right.

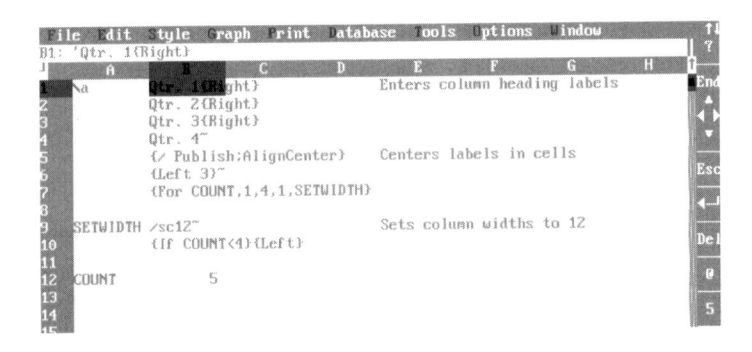

FIGURE 12-6.
You can also annotate a macro by using {;comment}.

the next one. Figure 12-6 shows the same macro as shown in Figure 12-5 but with the annotations shown in {; *comment*} form.

Another command that is useful for documenting macros is { }, which is the null command. Instead of telling Quattro Pro to do a task, { } simply occupies space in a macro. When encountering a { } command, Quattro Pro proceeds to the next statement in the macro. The { } command lets you put empty lines in a macro to break up the sections of a macro, exactly as blank lines separate the paragraphs of text.

Executing macros

The ways you can run a Quattro Pro macro depend on whether you have assigned it a name, and, if so, what name you used. The following sections show you the various ways in which you can run macros and how Quattro Pro executes them.

Running instant macros

If you have assigned a block name that consists of a backslash (\) and an alphabetic character either to the first cell in a macro or to a block that has the first cell in its upper-left corner, you can tell Quattro Pro to run that macro simply by typing that alphabetic character while holding down the Alt key. Quattro Pro calls macros with backslash-letter names "instant macros." Because Quattro Pro does not differentiate between uppercase and lowercase in block names, you can have a maximum of 26 instant macros in any Quattro Pro worksheet.

Executing unnamed macros

The Tools Macro Execute command lets you run macros that you have not named. After you choose this command, Quattro Pro displays the prompt *Enter a block of macros to execute* in the input line, followed by the address of the current cell. To run an unnamed macro, move the cell selector to its first cell or type the address of that cell, and then press the Enter key.

You also can use the Tools Macro Execute command to run named macros. To do so, choose the Tools Macro Execute command and point to the first cell of the macro, type the address of the first cell in the macro, or type the name of the macro. After you press the Enter key, Quattro Pro runs the macro that you specified.

Macro speed considerations

As mentioned, you can represent the process of choosing a command either with the keystrokes required to choose the command or with the menu-equivalent form of the command. In addition to the advantages described earlier in the chapter, you should also know that Quattro Pro processes commands faster when you use their menu-equivalent forms. When encountering the keystroke form of a command, Quattro Pro presses each key required to choose that command. When encountering the menu-equivalent form of a command, Quattro Pro chooses that command in a single step. For example, when executing the keystrokes /fs, Quattro Pro presses the slash key (/), which displays the main menu, and then presses the F key, which chooses the File command and displays the File menu. Then, Quattro Pro presses the S key, which chooses the Save command and displays the *Enter save file name* prompt. When executing the {/ File;SaveNow} command, however, Quattro Pro displays the *Enter save file name* prompt immediately, without working through the intermediate steps.

Ending the running of a macro

Quattro Pro continues executing the statements in a macro until one of three situations occurs:

- Quattro Pro encounters a blank cell or a cell that contains an entry other than a label or a string-producing formula or function
- Quattro Pro encounters a macro error
- You tell Quattro Pro to stop executing the macro

In most cases, you use a blank cell to signal the end of a macro. When encountering a blank cell, a cell that contains a value, or a cell that contains a value-producing formula or function, Quattro Pro ends the running of the macro and clears the MACRO indicator from the status line. At that point, the worksheet reflects the changes that the macro made to it.

Quattro Pro also stops the running of a macro if it encounters an error; for example, the misspelled representation of a special key or a command that cannot be executed under the current circumstances. In those cases, Quattro Pro stops running the macro and displays an error message. Press the Enter key, and Quattro Pro removes the message and the MACRO indicator from the status line and cancels the macro. Later in this chapter, "Macro Errors" explains more about canceling a macro.

Quattro Pro allows you to cancel the running of a macro manually by pressing the Ctrl-Break keys. Quattro Pro stops running the macro and displays a message in the form *Break: ([Filename])XX* in a pop-up window in the middle of the screen, where *[Filename]* is the name of the worksheet that contains the macro and *XX* is the address of the statement Quattro Pro was executing when you pressed Ctrl-Break. Press the Enter key, and Quattro Pro clears this message and the MACRO indicator from the bottom of the screen and cancels the macro. In Chapter 13, the section "Descriptions of the Programming Commands" shows you how to disable the Ctrl-Break combination.

Autoexecuting macros

In some cases you might want Quattro Pro to run a macro automatically when you retrieve the worksheet in which it's contained. To make Quattro Pro do so, you must assign that macro a special name. When retrieving a worksheet, Quattro Pro looks for a macro that has been assigned the special name, and runs it. If the worksheet does not contain a macro with the special name, Quattro Pro simply opens the worksheet. A macro that Quattro Pro runs automatically is called an "autoexecuting macro."

Unless you specify otherwise, \0 (zero) is the special name that identifies an autoexecuting macro. You can change the name, however, by choosing the Options Startup Startup Macro command. Quattro Pro displays the prompt *Startup Macro* in a pop-up window, followed by the current autoexecuting macro name. To specify a different name, type that name and press the Enter key. Unless you choose the Options Update command, the change lasts only for the duration of the current Quattro Pro session.

Starting macros from DOS

As explained in Chapter 8, "File Management," you can direct Quattro Pro to retrieve a specific file as part of starting Quattro Pro. Suppose, for example, that you want to retrieve the file EXPENSES.WQ1 from the default directory. To do so, you start Quattro Pro by typing *q EXPENSES* at the DOS prompt. If that file also has a macro named \z that you want to run as soon as Quattro Pro retrieves the worksheet, you can direct Quattro Pro to do so by typing *q EXPENSES \z* at the DOS prompt.

Debugging macros

No matter how experienced you are at creating macros, some of your macros will contain errors ("bugs"). However, Quattro Pro has excellent debugging features that allow you to find and correct any errors in your macros. This section describes the causes of macro errors, explains what happens when a macro error occurs, and shows you how to use Quattro Pro's debugging feature to locate and correct macro errors.

Macro errors

If you write your macros or edit them after you record them, they might contain errors. Some errors cause Quattro Pro to cancel the running of a macro; others simply cause Quattro Pro to perform actions other than the ones you intended. In either case, you will want to identify the errors and correct them.

The list of potential macro errors is virtually unlimited. Most macro errors, however, are caused by one of the following mistakes:

- Omitting keystrokes and commands from a macro
- Supplying invalid responses to command prompts
- Using the incorrect representations of special keys, menu-equivalent commands, and programming commands (in other words, syntax errors)

Omitted keystrokes and commands

Many macro errors are caused when you accidentally omit keystrokes and commands from your macros. Although errors of this sort usually do not cause Quattro Pro to cancel the running of a macro, they do cause the macro to take actions other than what you intended. For example, suppose you want a macro to move the cell selector down four rows but, instead of including four {Down} commands in the macro, you include only three. In this case, Quattro Pro moves the cell selector down only three times when you run the macro.

You also might omit characters from a series of keystrokes that is designed to choose a menu command. For example, suppose you include the statement *'/eA1..B2~* in a macro, intending to erase the entries in cells A1..B2. Because you omitted the second e for Edit Erase Block, however, Quattro Pro chooses only the Edit command instead of the full Edit Erase Block command. Consequently, Quattro Pro ignores the keystrokes as it types the characters A, 1, ., ., B, and 2. The final keystroke, ~, chooses the first option in the Edit menu, which is Copy.

Invalid responses to command prompts

Another leading cause of macro errors is supplying invalid responses to the prompts that Quattro Pro displays when a macro selects a command from a menu. Most errors of this sort cancel the running of a macro. For example, suppose that Quattro Pro executed the statement {/ File;Directory}C:\EXAMPLES~ in cell B1 of a worksheet when a directory named C:\EXAMPLES did not exist. Instead of changing the default directory, Quattro Pro cancels the running of the macro, beeps, displays the error message *Directory does not exist*, and flashes ERROR at the right edge of the status line. Press the Enter key, and Quattro Pro cancels the macro and clears all messages.

Syntax errors

Misspelling the representations of special keys, menu-equivalent commands, or programming commands causes Quattro Pro to cancel the running of a macro. For example, suppose you enter the representation of the Down direction key as {Dwon} instead of {Down} in cell B3 of a macro. When encountering this command in a macro, Quattro Pro stops the running of the macro and displays the message *Unknown key or block name: ([filename]B3)* in a pop-up window. The filename portion names the worksheet that has the macro error, and B3 tells you where the error was found. Press the Enter key, and Quattro Pro clears the word MACRO from the status line and cancels the running of the macro.

Errors in the spelling or punctuation of menu-equivalent commands and programming commands also cause Quattro Pro to cancel the running of a macro. For example, suppose you enter {/ Block;Name} into cell B5 of a worksheet, intending to instruct Quattro Pro to choose the Edit Names Create command. Because the menu-equivalent form of the Edit Names Create command is {/ Name;Create}, however, Quattro Pro does not recognize this command, cancels the running of the macro, and displays an error message in a pop-up window. Press the Enter key, and Quattro Pro clears this message, removes the word MACRO from the status line, and returns to the worksheet.

Other causes of errors

A number of other factors can cause macro errors. For example, invalid arguments in programming commands (a subject covered in Chapter 13, "Programming Command Basics") cancel the running of a macro, as does any condition that causes an error message box to appear on the screen outside the context of a macro. For example, if the door of your computer's A drive is open when a macro executes the statement {/ File;Save}A:\BACKUP~, Quattro Pro beeps, displays an error message on the screen, flashes ERROR, and, after you press the Enter key, cancels the running of the macro.

Debugging basics

Whether an error cancels the running of a macro or causes the macro to take actions other than those intended, you will want to correct the error. Doing so is called "debugging." In many cases, you can identify errors from the messages that Quattro Pro displays. When an error does not produce a message, you might have a more difficult time tracking down its source. In these more difficult cases, you can use Quattro Pro's debugging functions to track the error down.

To access Quattro Pro's macro debugging functions, choose the Tools Macro Debugger command. Quattro Pro presents a submenu that lists two options: Yes and No. If you choose the Yes option, Quattro Pro enters debug mode and displays the word DEBUG in the status line. Note that you can also press the Shift-F2 keys to toggle the debugger off and on. If you run a macro while Quattro Pro is in debug mode, Quattro Pro displays the macro in a special Debug window, like the one shown in Figure 12-7.

While you view a macro in a Debug window, you can tell Quattro Pro to run the macro step by step, set breakpoints that pause the running of the macro when it reaches a certain statement or when a certain condition is true, and trace the effect of each command in the macro on the worksheet. To use many of these features, choose commands from the Debug menu, which is shown in Figure 12-8. To access this menu, press the / key while Quattro Pro is displaying a macro in the Debug window.

To exit from debug mode, choose the Abort option from the Debug menu. Quattro Pro closes the Debug window, removes the DEBUG indicator from the status line, and stops executing the macro.

FIGURE 12-7.
If Quattro Pro is in Debug mode when you run a macro, the macro is displayed in a Debug window.

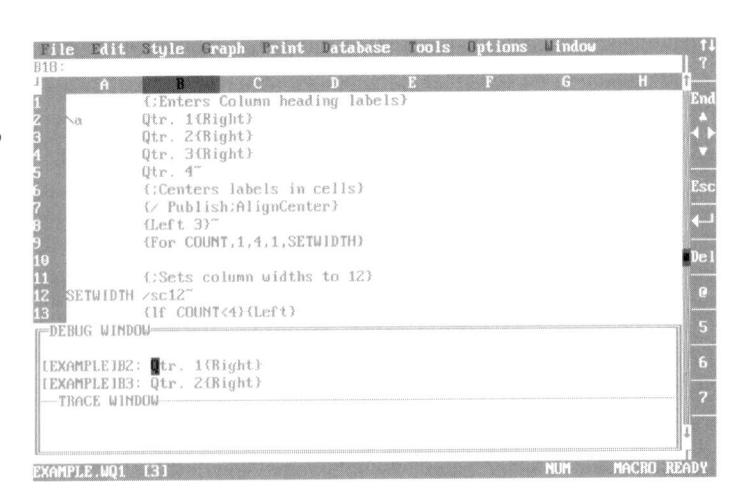

FIGURE 12-8.
Quattro Pro displays this menu when you press the / key while Quattro Pro is displaying a macro in the Debug window.

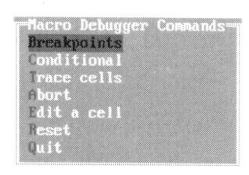

```
=Macro Debugger Commands=
Breakpoints
Conditional
Trace cells
Abort
Edit a cell
Reset
Quit
```

Executing a macro step by step

If you run a macro while Quattro Pro is in debug mode, Quattro Pro displays the first two lines of the macro in the Debug window, highlighting the first keystroke in the first line. At that point, you can run the macro one step at a time simply by pressing the Spacebar. Each time you press the Spacebar, Quattro Pro executes the highlighted keystroke or command and then moves the highlight to the next keystroke or command. As soon as Quattro Pro finishes executing all of the commands in the macro's first line, the highlight moves to the first command in the second line in the macro and shifts the third line of the macro into view within the Debug window. From that point on, three lines in the macro are visible within the Debug window, and the highlight is always on a command in the second of the three lines.

Stepping through the macro one command at a time makes it easy to find the keystroke or command that is causing a macro error. Unless the screen is frozen (a subject that discussed in Chapter 13, "Programming Command Basics"), you can see the effect of each command on the worksheet as Quattro Pro executes it. If a command affects a cell that is obscured by the Debug window, you can remove the Debug window temporarily by pressing the Esc key. As soon as you press any other key, Quattro Pro returns the Debug window to the screen and executes the next command in the macro.

After you locate the error-causing keystroke, you can cancel the execution of the macro either by pressing the Ctrl-Break keys or by choosing the Abort command from the Debug menu. At that point, you can press the Esc key to clear the Debug window from the screen. Then, use normal editing techniques to correct the error.

If you press the Enter key while you are executing a macro step by step, Quattro Pro closes the Debug window and begins executing the macro at full speed. Quattro Pro remains in debug mode, however. Because of the effect of the Enter key, you might have trouble debugging macros that contain programming commands that solicit input from the user. You'll read more about this trouble and how to avoid it in "Descriptions of the Programming Commands," in Chapter 13.

Editing within the Debugger

You usually cancel the running of a macro as soon as you identify the location of an error, and then exit from the Debugger and use standard editing techniques to correct the mistake. You can, however, edit a macro statement from within the Debugger. To do so, press the / key to display the Debug menu, and then choose the Edit A Cell option. Quattro Pro displays the prompt *Enter cell to edit* in the input line. Type the address or name of the cell or point to the cell you want to edit. Quattro Pro displays the contents of that cell in the input line, exactly as if you had moved the cell selector to that cell and pressed the [Edit] key (F2). At that point, you can edit the entry in the same way you would edit any entry in the input line.

After you correct the error, press the Enter key to lock the revised statement back into the worksheet. Quattro Pro returns you to the Debug menu. To clear the menu from the screen, choose the Quit option, or press Esc. You can then press the Spacebar to run the next command in the macro, or press the Enter key to run the remaining commands in the macro at full speed.

You might run into trouble if you use the Edit A Cell option from the Debug menu to edit the statement in which the highlight is currently positioned. If the change you make to that statement shortens or lengthens the command on which the highlight is positioned or the commands (if any) to the left of it, Quattro Pro might become confused when trying to execute the current command. Editing the current statement, however, does not cause problems if you edit a command to the right of the one that is marked by the highlight.

Standard breakpoints

When you know the approximate location of an error within a macro, it wastes time to step through all the keystrokes from the beginning up to the point of the error, unless the error occurs near the beginning of the macro. Instead of stepping through the macro, you can set what's called a "standard breakpoint" at a cell immediately ahead of the statement that contains the error. If, after setting the breakpoint, you run the macro within debug mode and press the Enter key, Quattro Pro runs the macro at full speed until reaching the breakpoint. Quattro Pro then pauses the execution of the macro and allows you to run it step by step.

Setting standard breakpoints

To set a standard breakpoint, enter debug mode and run the macro in which you want to set the breakpoint. Then, press the / key to display the Debug menu and choose the Breakpoints option. Quattro Pro presents the menu shown in Figure 12-9. The first four commands in this menu allow you to set standard breakpoints

FIGURE 12-9.
The Breakpoints option displays this menu.

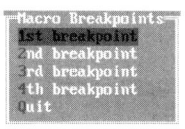

```
Macro Breakpoints
1st breakpoint
2nd breakpoint
3rd breakpoint
4th breakpoint
Quit
```

(up to four per worksheet, not necessarily per macro). The last command removes the menu from the screen.

To set a standard breakpoint, choose one of the first four items from the Breakpoints menu. Quattro Pro presents a submenu that has three options: Block, Pass Count, and Quit. Choose the Block option. Quattro Pro displays the prompt *Enter breakpoint cell* in the input line followed by the current address of the cell selector. Point to the cell at which you want to set the breakpoint or type the address or name of that cell, and then press the Enter key. Finally, choose the Quit option three times to clear the Debugger menus from the screen and return to the Debug window.

After you set a breakpoint at one of the cells in a macro, you can press the Enter key to begin running the macro at full speed. When Quattro Pro reaches the breakpoint, it pauses the execution of the macro, and you can then press the Spacebar to run the macro one command at a time. If you press the Enter key, Quattro Pro resumes executing the macro at full speed until reaching the next breakpoint, if one exists.

Setting multiple-cell breakpoints

In most cases, you specify single-cell breakpoints. You can, however, assign a breakpoint to a block of cells if you want. If you do so, Quattro Pro runs the macro at full speed until reaching the block. At that point, Quattro Pro executes one command each time you press either the Spacebar or the Enter key. Quattro Pro does not resume executing the macro at full speed until all of the commands in the block have been executed and you press the Enter key.

Multiple breakpoints

To set a new breakpoint without clearing one already set, choose an option other than the one(s) you chose previously from the Breakpoints menu. For example, if you used the 1st Breakpoint option to set the first breakpoint in a worksheet, choose the 2nd Breakpoint, 3rd Breakpoint, or 4th Breakpoint option to set the second one. If you choose the same option that you used to set a previous breakpoint in its place, Quattro Pro deletes the previous breakpoint and sets a new one. Later in this chapter, "Resetting Breakpoints and Trace Cells" explains how to clear breakpoints without setting new ones.

The Pass Count option

When you choose one of the four breakpoint options from the Breakpoints menu, Quattro Pro presents a menu that has the Block, Pass Count, and Quit options. As explained, the Block option allows you to specify where you want to set a breakpoint, and the Quit option removes the menu from the screen. The remaining option, Pass Count, allows you to tell Quattro Pro how many times to execute the cell(s) to which you assigned the breakpoint before it starts to single-step. This feature is handy for debugging macros that have programming loops, which are discussed in Chapter 13.

To set a pass count for a breakpoint, choose the Pass Count option for the breakpoint to which you want to assign it, type the number of times you want Quattro Pro to execute commands at the breakpoint before pausing, and then press the Enter key. The default value, which is 1, tells Quattro Pro to pause each time it passes through the breakpoint. A pass count of 2 tells Quattro Pro to pause after every second pass, a pass count of 3 tells Quattro Pro to pause after every third pass, and so forth.

A closer look at breakpoints

Breakpoints are active only when Quattro Pro is executing a macro in debug mode. If you run a macro when Quattro Pro is not in debug mode, Quattro Pro does not stop and enter debug mode when it encounters a breakpoint. Instead, it runs the macro from beginning to end, as if the breakpoint did not exist.

Conditional breakpoints

In addition to standard breakpoints, Quattro Pro allows you to set "conditional breakpoints." A conditional breakpoint causes Quattro Pro to enter single-step mode when the condition you specify becomes true. For example, you might want Quattro Pro to pause the running of a macro when the value in a cell becomes greater than a certain value, after the macro has been executing for a certain period of time, and so forth. You can set up to four conditional breakpoints per worksheet.

To set a conditional breakpoint, enter a logical expression that specifies the condition that you want to use in one of the worksheet cells. A logical expression is an expression that is either true or false. Most logical expressions include one of Quattro Pro's conditional operators: =, >, <, >=, and <=. A logical expression, however, can be a function like @ISERR or @ISNA. Logical expressions can also contain the operators #AND#, #OR#, and #NOT#. For example, +COUNT>5, @ISERR(TEST) and A1<B1#AND#C1<=D1 are all logical expressions. A logical expression that is false returns the value 0; one that is true returns the value 1.

After you enter a logical expression in a cell, choose the Tools Macro Debugger Yes command to enter debug mode. Then, run the macro for which you want to set the conditional breakpoint. Next, press the / key to display the Debug

FIGURE 12-10.
You see this menu when you choose the Conditional option from the Debug menu.

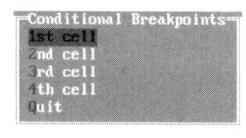

```
─Conditional Breakpoints─
 1st cell
 2nd cell
 3rd cell
 4th cell
 Quit
```

menu, and choose the Conditional option. Quattro Pro presents the menu shown in Figure 12-10. The first four commands in this menu allow you to set conditional breakpoints. The last command, Quit, removes the Conditional menu from the screen.

To set a conditional breakpoint, choose one of the first four options from the menu shown in Figure 12-10. When you do so, Quattro Pro displays the prompt *Enter condition cell* followed by the current address of the cell selector. Point to or type the address of the cell that contains your logical expression, and then press the Enter key. Finally, choose the Quit option two times to clear the Debugger menus from the screen and return to the Debug window.

After you set a conditional breakpoint, you can press the Enter key to begin running the macro. Quattro Pro runs the macro at full speed until the logical expression for the breakpoint you set becomes true. At that point, Quattro Pro pauses the macro and starts to single-step. Quattro Pro remains in single step mode until the logical expression becomes false again, even if you press the Enter key.

Trace cells

Quattro Pro allows you to monitor the contents and appearance of up to four cells while Quattro Pro runs a macro in debug mode. To do so, specify those cells as trace cells. While Quattro Pro runs a macro in debug mode, the contents of the trace cells appear in the lower half of the Trace window. Specifying one or more cells as trace cells allows you to monitor cells that you normally would not see on the screen during the running of the macro or two or more cells that would not fit on the screen at the same time. Quattro Pro updates the copies of the trace cells that appear in the Debug window after each keystroke or command the macro executes, even if the screen is frozen at the time. You'll read about freezing and unfreezing the screen in "Descriptions of the Programming Commands" in Chapter 13.

To specify a cell as a trace cell, enter debug mode, and then run the macro that you want to debug. Next, press the slash key (/) to access the Debug menu, and choose the Trace Cells option. Quattro Pro presents the menu shown in Figure 12-11. The first four items in this menu allow you to set trace cells (up to four per worksheet). The final option, Quit, clears the Trace Cells menu from the screen.

From the Trace Cells menu shown in Figure 12-11, choose one of the first four options. Quattro Pro displays the prompt *Enter trace cell* in the input line. Point to or type the address of the cell you want to monitor, and then press the Enter key.

FIGURE 12-11.
You see this menu when you choose the Trace Cells option from the Debug menu.

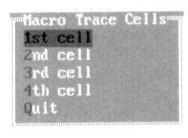

FIGURE 12-12.
If you specify one or more cells as trace cells, Quattro Pro displays the contents of those cells in the bottom portion of the Debug window.

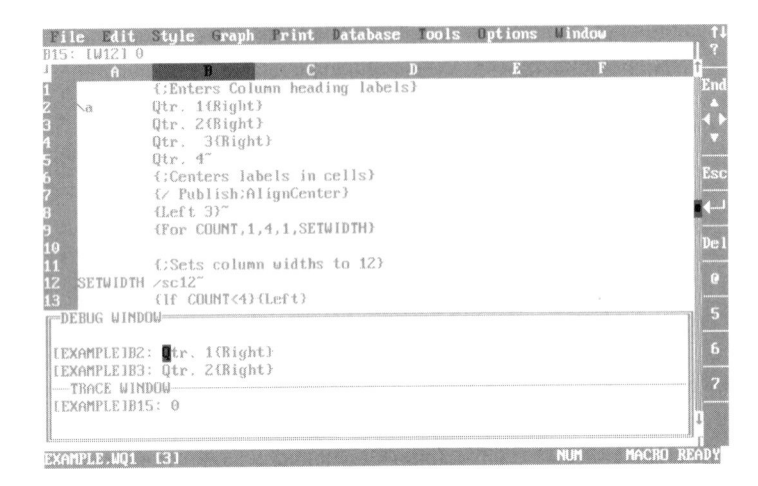

After you set one or more trace cells, choose the Quit option two times to remove the Debugger menus from the screen. Then, press the Spacebar to begin executing the macro step by step. As soon as Quattro Pro executes a command, it displays the address and contents of each trace cell you specified in the Trace window. For example, Figure 12-12 shows how your screen might look if you specified cell B15 in the macro shown in Figure 12-6 as a trace cell. Each time Quattro Pro executes a command, it updates the contents of the trace cell(s) in the Trace window.

Resetting breakpoints and trace cells

After you set one or more standard breakpoints, conditional breakpoints, or trace cells in a worksheet, they remain in effect until you reset, respecify, or clear them. To change the location of a breakpoint or respecify a trace cell, use the same command you used to set it the first time, but choose a different cell. To clear a breakpoint or a trace cell, choose either the Reset option from the Debug menu or the Tools Macro Clear Breakpoints command. Quattro Pro then clears all standard breakpoints, conditional breakpoints, and trace cells in the worksheet. Unfortunately, you cannot clear breakpoints or trace cells individually.

As mentioned, breakpoints and trace cells apply to an entire worksheet, and not only to an individual macro. Consequently, if you want to debug one macro after debugging another one in the same worksheet, you probably want to clear any breakpoints and trace cells that you used to debug the first macro. Otherwise, they are active when you debug the other macro.

Saving and retrieving macros

Because a macro is a series of label entries stored in the cells of a worksheet, Quattro Pro saves your macros when you save the worksheets in which they're contained. Consequently, to save a macro you simply choose the File Save or File Save As command. When you retrieve a worksheet that contains a macro, you also retrieve that macro. If you want to save a macro independently from the worksheet in which you created it, you can do so by using the Tools Xtract command.

Macro libraries

Again, Quattro Pro stores macros in a worksheet. When you try to run a macro, Quattro Pro looks for it in the active worksheet. Of course, if Quattro Pro cannot find the macro in the active worksheet, it does not run the macro. Normally, this approach works fine. With Quattro Pro, however, you also have the ability to create a macro library worksheet, which is simply a regular worksheet that you designate as a macro library worksheet by choosing the Tools Macro Library Yes command. (To save this setting, of course, you also need to save the worksheet after you choose the command.) When a worksheet has been designated a macro library worksheet, Quattro Pro looks in it for a macro if the macro has not already been found in the active worksheet.

As an example, suppose that the worksheet BUDGET.WQ1 is currently active, and that you want to run the \A macro. Normally, the \A macro would need to be in the BUDGET.WQ1 worksheet file and BUDGET.WQ1 would need to be the active worksheet. You could, however, also create and store the macro in a worksheet named MACROS.WQ1 and then designate MACROS.WQ1 as a macro library worksheet. If MACROS.WQ1 is open but inactive, you can still run the \A macro. For example, if BUDGET.WQ1 is active and MACROS.WQ1, the macro library worksheet, is open but inactive, running the \A macro causes Quattro Pro to look in BUDGET.WQ1 for the \A macro. When Quattro Pro does not find the \A macro, it begins looking in any of the other open inactive worksheets that you designated as macro library worksheets. When it finds the \A macro in MACROS.WQ1, Quattro Pro runs it.

A closer look at macro libraries

You'll want to remember a few points about macro library worksheets. First, even though a macro is from a macro library worksheet, it behaves in most ways as if it were in the active worksheet. For example, Quattro Pro interprets the block definition the macro gives in response to a menu command prompt as referring to the active worksheet. If the macro chooses the command for erasing a block or copying a block, Quattro Pro assumes that the block coordinates refer to the active worksheet, and not to the macro library worksheet.

Second, Quattro Pro assumes that block definitions used in programming commands refer to the macro library. This point will make more sense after you read Chapter 13, "Programming Command Basics," but the programming commands often use block definitions to specify which part in the macro should be executed next. For example, the {Branch} command specifies the next line in the macro that should be executed. Quattro Pro assumes that the cell or block that {Branch} refers to is in the macro library worksheet, and not in the active worksheet.

Identifying the worksheet to which a block definition refers can be confusing. For this reason, you might want to include the filename as part of block definitions, using the same spreadsheet linking capability described in Chapter 8, "File Management." For example, rather than specify the block to be erased as A1..A1, you could specify the block as (BUDGET.WQ1)A1..A1.

Using Transcript to record keystrokes and commands

Transcript is essentially a computerized eavesdropping device; it records all of the keystrokes and commands entered during a session and saves them in a disk file called QUATTRO.LOG. You can play back this record to recover from mistakes or system crashes. You can also copy the record to a worksheet and run it as a macro. You can also use the list of commands stored by Transcript as an audit trail to track changes made to a worksheet.

The QUATTRO.LOG file

Transcript begins recording commands as soon as you start Quattro Pro. To view the transcript, run Transcript by choosing the Tools Macro command and choosing the Transcript option. A window labeled Transcript appears, which displays the contents of the QUATTRO.LOG file. Figure 12-13 shows an example of the Transcript window.

The QUATTRO.LOG file by default can be up to 2000 lines long. Each line represents one command you chose or one action you performed while working with Quattro Pro. If you want, you can increase or decrease the size of the transcript, as described later in the section "The Transcript and Settings Menus."

After the size limit is reached, Transcript renames the current QUATTRO.LOG file QUATTRO.BAK, and creates a new QUATTRO.LOG file. Subsequently, each time the limit is reached, Quattro Pro repeats this process and overwrites the existing

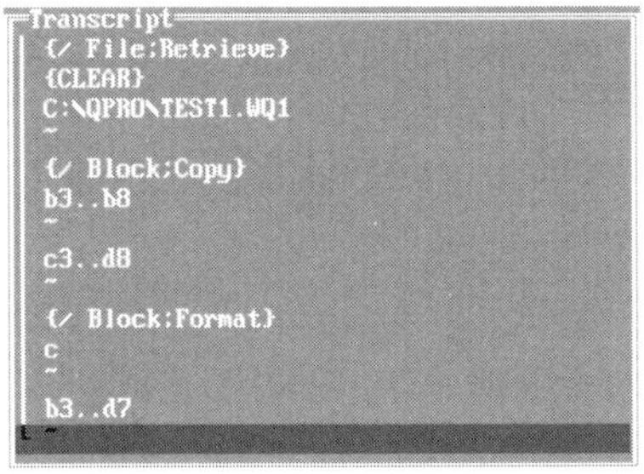

FIGURE 12-13.
The Transcript window contains a record of all the commands and keystrokes you have entered in the current session.

```
┌─Transcript─────────────────────
│ {/ File;Retrieve}
│ {CLEAR}
│ C:\QPRO\TEST1.WQ1
│ 
│ {/ Block;Copy}
│ b3..b8
│ ~
│ c3..d8
│ ~
│ {/ Block;Format}
│ c
│ ~
│ b3..d7
```

QUATTRO.BAK file. Therefore, if you have important information stored in a QUATTRO.BAK file, be sure to rename it or make a copy of it in case Transcript overwrites it.

Quattro Pro does not empty the QUATTRO.LOG file when you exit from Quattro Pro. If you used Transcript during previous Quattro Pro sessions, the QUATTRO.LOG file contains commands and keystrokes used during those sessions. Quattro Pro adds all of the commands recorded during the current session to the end of those that were previously stored in the QUATTRO.LOG file. The commands that were recorded during the current session are enclosed in a long, thin bracket. The bracket looks like an extra line to the left of the lines of the transcript.

Transcript does not update the QUATTRO.LOG file each time you press a key or choose a command. Instead, it waits until it has recorded five lines, and then adds all five lines to the QUATTRO.LOG file at once. If you want, you can increase or decrease the number of commands Transcript will buffer in memory before updating QUATTRO.LOG.

If you scroll to the top of the transcript file, you'll notice the lines *{Break} {/ Basics;Erase}{HOME}{DOWN}*. Transcript inserts this command to reset the worksheet to its original state in case you run the Transcript as a macro. It also inserts this command whenever you open a new worksheet.

The Transcript and Settings menus

To access the features that make Transcript's record of keystrokes and commands really useful, choose the Tools Macro Transcript command to display the Transcript window, and then press the / key to display the Transcript menu shown in Figure 12-14. From this menu, you can:

- Negate the effects of your most recent command
- Restore a worksheet to a point before a series of commands were chosen
- Play back a block of commands
- Copy a block of commands to a worksheet, where it can be printed or used as a macro

FIGURE 12-14.
You can reuse the commands stored in Transcript from the Transcript menu.

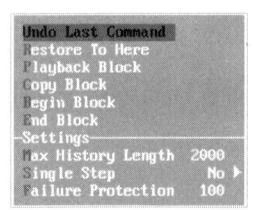

```
Undo Last Command
 estore To Here
 layback Block
 opy Block
 egin Block
 nd Block
─Settings─
 ax History Length    2000
 ingle Step             No ▶
 ailure Protection     100
```

- Define the maximum number of commands Transcript will store in QUATTRO.LOG and the number of commands that should be buffered in memory before Transcript adds them to QUATTRO.LOG

- Choose the Single Step command that allows Transcript to play back a series of commands one at a time, pausing after each until you press a key confirming that Transcript should continue

Perhaps Transcript's most useful feature is its ability to negate the effects of your most recent command. For example, suppose you accidentally choose the Graph Customize Series Reset Graph command and want to recover the graph settings lost as a result. Start by choosing the Tools Macro Transcript command. When the Command History window appears, press the / key to display the Transcript menu. From that menu, choose the Undo Last Command option, and Transcript replays all of the commands you entered since the last time you saved or opened the file, excluding the Graph Customize Series Reset Graph command.

If you choose more than one command by accident before deciding that you want to use Transcript to restore a worksheet to a previous state, you can use the Transcript menu's Restore To Here option. First, choose the Tools Macro Transcript command, and use the direction keys to scroll back through the commands until the highlight is positioned on the command immediately preceding the commands you want to negate. As you move the highlight over a command, notice that it is displayed in the input line, along with a line number indicating its position in the QUATTRO.LOG file. Press the / key to activate the Transcript menu, and then choose the Restore To Here option. Transcript replays commands from the time you last saved or opened the worksheet to the command you highlighted, restoring the worksheet in the process.

Transcript can also play back a block of commands whose starting and ending points you define. To do so, run Transcript, and then use the direction keys to scroll through the list of commands until the highlight is positioned on the first command you want to play back. Press the / key to activate the Transcript menu, and then choose the Begin Block option. Transcript places a marker on this command, indicating that it is the first in a block. Next, use the direction keys again to position the highlight on the last command you want to replay. Choose the End Block option from the Transcript menu, and Quattro Pro places a marker to the left of all the commands in the block. You are now ready to replay the block. To do so, choose the Playback Block option from the Transcript menu, and Transcript replays all of the commands within the block you have defined. You can now copy the block of commands to a worksheet, where it can be printed or used as a macro. To do so, choose the Copy Block option from the Transcript menu. Transcript prompts you to name the block as a macro. Type a name or choose one from the list of existing names, and press the Enter key. Transcript then prompts you to select a cell address in which the block should be placed. Use the cursor-movement keys to select a cell, or type an address at the prompt. Press the Enter key, and Transcript copies the block of commands to the worksheet.

As mentioned, when you initially start Transcript, the maximum number of lines that it will store in QUATTRO.LOG before creating a new file is 2000. You can raise this limit to 25,000 or lower it to 0 using the Transcript menu's Max History Length option. To change this setting, choose the Max History Length option, type a number between 0 and 25,000, and press the Enter key. (A setting of 0 turns off Transcript.)

The Single Step option in the Transcript menu works with the Playback command in the same menu. If you toggle the Single Step option to ON, Transcript plays back the transcript one command at a time. When you choose one of the playback options, Transcript plays back only the first command in the group you have specified, and then pauses and waits for you to press any key. When you do, Transcript moves on to the second command and pauses again. If you leave the Single Step option set to OFF, Transcript plays back commands one after the other without pausing.

Finally, the Transcript menu's Failure Protection option allows you to specify the number of command lines Transcript buffers in memory before saving them on disk. This number can be as low as 1 or as high as the Max History Length setting allows. The default setting of 100 seems satisfactory on systems equipped with a fast hard disk, but if you have a slower system you might want to increase this number. Also, if you do not plan to use Transcript as protection against a power failure or system crash, you might want to use an extremely large number. To change the number of commands Transcript buffers in memory, choose the Failure Protection option, type a value at the prompt, and press the Enter key.

Managing Transcript LOG files

If you use Transcript all the time, you might find it useful to maintain individual log files for individual worksheets. For example, you could maintain a LOG file for a worksheet called PAYROLL and another for a worksheet called SALES. To create separate LOG files for each worksheet, first delete or rename the LOG file (QUATTRO.LOG) that is currently present. Next, create the PAYROLL worksheet while Transcript is active, exit to DOS, and change the name of QUATTRO.LOG to PAYROLL.LOG. Next, start Quattro Pro again, create the SALES worksheet while

Transcript is active, exit to DOS, and change the name of QUATTRO.LOG to SALES.LOG. If you want to use a worksheet-specific LOG file, change its name to QUATTRO.LOG, and then run Quattro Pro and open your worksheet. When you finish, exit from Quattro Pro, and change the name of the QUATTRO.LOG file back to SALES.LOG, PAYROLL.LOG, or whatever you want.

13

Programming Command Basics

*I*n addition to containing keystrokes and commands, Quattro Pro macros can contain special programming commands to add power and versatility. These commands allow you to accomplish such tasks as soliciting input from the user during the running of a macro, performing conditional tests, branching from one macro to another, calling subroutines, setting up For/Next loops, and creating custom menus. This chapter describes each of Quattro Pro's programming commands and gives examples of how you can use them.

Programming command basics

Quattro Pro offers 56 programming commands. The pages that follow describe and illustrate each of these commands, but first you'll find it helpful to understand a few basics about these commands.

Braced commands and /x commands

Quattro Pro has two types of programming commands: commands that are surrounded by braces (braced commands) and commands that are preceded by a slash and an x (/x commands).

Braced commands

The majority of Quattro Pro's programming commands are braced commands, which consist of a command name (such as Quit or GetNumber) surrounded by braces (curly brackets). Most, but not all, braced commands require one or more arguments. {Branch A5} is an example of a braced command that requires an argument; {Quit} is an example of one that does not.

/x commands

Quattro Pro's eight /x commands duplicate the functions of eight of the most useful braced commands. As their name implies, all /x commands begin with the characters /x. These characters are followed by a single letter that identifies the command. Like most braced commands, most /x commands require one or more arguments. For example, /xgA5~ is an example of an /x command that requires an argument; /xq is an example of one that does not. Quattro Pro includes these commands to be compatible with macros created in early releases of Lotus 1-2-3.

Arguments to programming commands

Many of Quattro Pro's programming commands require one or more arguments, and different programming commands require different types of arguments. Most programming commands that require an argument require a location argument, which tells the command what to act upon or where to place a result. A location argument can be the name or address of a cell or block or, in some cases, a function that returns a cell or block reference.

Other programming commands require string arguments, which usually serve as prompts and, in most cases, must be literal strings. Unlike the string arguments to functions, the string arguments to programming commands need not be enclosed in quotation marks unless they contain an argument separator, a semicolon, a colon, or a closing brace.

Some programming commands require value arguments, which can be literal values, formulas and functions that return values, or references to cells that contain or return values. Other programming commands require conditional text arguments (expressions that are either true or false). For example, the first argument to the {If} and /xi commands must be a conditional test.

Many programming commands require a single argument; others require more than one. Separate the first (or only) argument to a braced command from the name of that command by a single space; however, do not separate the first argument to an /x command from the name of that command. The arguments to braced commands that require more than one argument must be separated from each other by the default argument separator (usually a comma). Each argument to an /x command must end with a tilde (~), which separates multiple arguments.

Using programming commands

Because programming commands do not represent keys that you can press from the keyboard of your computer, you cannot record them. To enter a programming command in a macro, you must either type it or choose it from a list. Typing a programming command is exactly like typing any other macro statement; you move the cell selector to the cell in which you want to enter the command, and then type it. For example, to enter the command {Quit} in cell B3, move the cell selector to cell B3 and type *{Quit}*.

Like other macro commands, programming commands are label entries. Because braced commands begin with a { character, you can enter them simply by typing them and pressing the Enter key. The /x commands, however, begin with a slash, and if you type a slash while Quattro Pro is in READY mode, the main Quattro Pro menu is displayed. Therefore, to enter a slash character at the beginning of a cell you must first type a label prefix. For example, to enter the command /xq in a cell, type ', ", or ^, then type */xq*, and press the Enter key.

If you want, you can combine programming commands with keystrokes and menu-equivalent commands in the same worksheet cell. In most cases, however, keep them separate so that the macro is easier to understand when you view it.

Instead of typing programming commands, you can choose them from a list. When you press the [Macros] key (Shift-F3), Quattro Pro displays a list like the one shown in Figure 13-1. The first six items in this list are categories of programming commands. As you learned in Chapter 12, "Macro Basics," Quattro Pro displays a list of menu-equivalent commands when you choose the last option from this list.

After you choose one of the options from the menu shown in Figure 13-1, Quattro Pro presents another menu, as shown in Figure 13-2. After you choose an option from that menu, Quattro Pro adds the name of the command, enclosed in braces, to the input line. Quattro Pro also adds the command to the input line at the cursor position if you press the [Macros] key (Shift-F3) and choose an option

FIGURE 13-1.
Quattro Pro displays this list when you press the [Macros] key (Shift-F3).

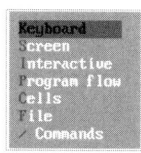

FIGURE 13-2.
Quattro Pro presents this menu after you choose the Screen option from the list shown in Figure 13-1.

while making or editing an entry in insert mode. If Quattro Pro is in overwrite mode, it enters the command at the position of the cursor but overwrites the text to the right of the cursor.

After you choose an option from one of these lists, Quattro Pro enters only the name of the command you selected and the braces that surround it. You must then fill in the arguments yourself. Because Quattro Pro does not insert placeholders for the arguments (if any) that are required by the command or provide you with any clue as to what arguments are needed, you must either remember them, look them up, or press the [Help] key (F1) to access Quattro Pro's built-in Help facility.

Descriptions of the programming commands

This chapter presents Quattro Pro's 56 programming commands within the context of 11 programming techniques: stopping macros, soliciting input, making entries in cells, doing conditional testing, branching, calling subroutines, looping, creating custom menus, controlling the user interface, controlling recalculation, and using file input/output commands.

Stopping macros using programming commands

As explained in Chapter 12, "Macro Basics," Quattro Pro ends the running of a macro when it encounters a cell that either is blank or contains a value. In most cases, you use this technique to mark the end of a macro. You can also, however, use the {Quit} or /xq command to cancel the running of a macro. Although you can use the {Quit} or /xq command at the end of a macro, these commands are most useful for stopping the running of a macro prior to that point. For example, you can use one of these commands in conjunction with an {If} or /xi command to stop the macro when a certain condition is met. You'll read about the use of the {Quit} command in conjunction with the {If} command in the discussions of the {If} and /xi commands later in this chapter.

The {Quit} command

{Quit} is one of the simplest programming commands. The form of this command is simply {Quit}. It accepts no arguments. After executing a {Quit} command, Quattro Pro cancels the running of the macro immediately, exactly as if it had encountered a blank cell or a cell that contained a value.

The /xq command

The /xq command is also a simple command. Like {Quit}, it does not accept arguments; its syntax is simply /xq. After executing this command, Quattro Pro cancels the running of the macro immediately, exactly as if it had encountered a {Quit} command, a blank cell, or a value.

Soliciting input using programming commands

Quattro Pro features seven programming commands that allow you to solicit input from the keyboard during the running of a macro. This section explores each of these commands.

The {?} command

The {?} command is the simplest of Quattro Pro's input-soliciting commands. When encountering this command in a macro, Quattro Pro pauses the running of that macro until the user presses the Enter key. During the pause, the user can take any action that is appropriate in the current situation, such as typing an entry in a cell or choosing an item from a menu.

For example, the one-line macro {/ Name;Create}TEMP~{?}~ instructs Quattro Pro to choose the Edit Names Create command, specify the name TEMP, and press the Enter key. When executing this command, Quattro Pro displays the prompt *Enter block* in the input line and, if TEMP is the name of an existing block, highlights that block. At this point, Quattro Pro executes the {?} command, which instructs it to pause until you press the Enter key. During this pause, highlight or type the coordinates of the block of cells to which you want to assign the name TEMP, and then press the Enter key. Contrary to what you might expect, pressing the Enter key after you highlight or type the address of the block does not complete the Edit Names Create command. Instead, pressing the Enter key signals the end of the pause, telling Quattro Pro to execute the next command in the macro: ~. This command, which is the representation of the Enter key, locks in those coordinates you specified, completing the command. Quattro Pro then assigns the name TEMP to the block you specified.

The {GetNumber} command

Quattro Pro's {GetNumber} command allows you to solicit numeric values from a user during the running of a macro. The form of this command is as follows:

{GetNumber *prompt,destination*}

The *prompt* argument is a string argument, and the *destination* argument is the name or address of a cell or block. If the *prompt* argument contains a semicolon, colon, command, or closing brace (}) or if it has the same spelling as the name of a named block, you must enclose it in quotation marks. The length of the prompt is limited to 70 characters.

When executing a {GetNumber} command, Quattro Pro displays the first argument at the top of the screen and waits for your reply. During this pause, type a value or a value-producing formula or function, and press the Enter key. Quattro

Pro locks the value (or, if you typed a formula or function, the result of that formula or function) into the cell specified by the *destination* argument. If the *destination* argument specifies a block of cells, Quattro Pro places the value in the upper-left cell of that block.

For example, the one-line macro {GetNumber "Enter the value to square:", RESPONSE} tells Quattro Pro to display the prompt *Enter the value to square*, and waits for your reply. In response, type a value, and it appears to the right of the prompt at the top of the screen. (If you make a mistake while typing, you can edit your input using the same techniques you use to edit an entry in the input line.) Now, press the Enter key, and Quattro Pro enters that value in the cell specified by the *destination* argument (in this case, the cell named RESPONSE). If you type a formula or function, Quattro Pro calculates it, and then enters the result in the specified cell.

Invalid responses. Although you should always enter a value or value-producing formula or function in response to a {GetNumber} prompt, you can also enter a string or a string-producing formula or function. If you do, however, Quattro Pro places the function @ERR in the *destination* cell. As explained in Chapter 4, "Functions," this function returns the value ERR. Quattro Pro enters this same result if you type an invalid value-producing formula or function in response to the {GetNumber} prompt or if you press the Enter key without typing anything.

The /xn command

Quattro Pro provides a second command that allows you to solicit values: /xn. The form of this command is shown below:

/xn*prompt~destination~*

Like the arguments to the {GetNumber} command, the *prompt* argument to the /xn command must be a literal string of 70 characters or less, and the *destination* argument must be the name or address of a cell or block. Because pressing the slash (/) key normally accesses the main Quattro Pro menu, type a label prefix before you type the slash (/) that begins this command.

Despite their difference in form, the /xn command and the {GetNumber} commands work identically. When encountering an /xn command in a macro, Quattro Pro displays the *prompt* argument at the top of the screen and waits for your reply. In response, type either a value or a formula or function that returns a value, and press the Enter key. Quattro Pro enters the value (or the result of the formula or function) in the cell specified by the *destination* argument. If you type an invalid numeric formula or function, a string, a string-producing formula or function, or nothing, Quattro Pro locks the function @ERR into the destination cell after you press the Enter key.

Entering a response into the current cell. The /xn command makes it easy to enter the user's response in the cell on which the cell selector is positioned when Quattro Pro executes that command. To do so, omit the *destination* argument from the command. (You must, however, retain the ending ~.) For example, the statement /xnEnter a value: ~~ causes Quattro Pro to enter the user's response in the current cell. If the cell selector is on cell B5 when Quattro Pro executes this command, it enters the user's response in cell B5; if the cell selector is on cell Z100, Quattro Pro enters the response in cell Z100; and so forth. To use a {GetNumber} command in this way, you must use what's called a "calculated macro statement." Later in this chapter, "Advanced Macro Techniques" demonstrates the use of calculated macro statements.

Soliciting labels using the {Get Label} and /xl commands

Quattro Pro's {GetLabel} and /xl commands allow you to solicit labels from the user during the running of a macro in much the same way that the {GetNumber} and /xn commands allow you to solicit values. The form of the {GetLabel} command is shown below:

{GetLabel *prompt,destination*}

The form of the /xl command is as follows:

/xl*prompt~destination~*

In both cases, the *prompt* argument must be a literal string of 70 characters or less, and the *destination* argument must be the name or address of the cell into which you want to place the user's response to the prompt. If the /xl command is to be the first command in a cell, you must type a label prefix before typing the / that begins the command. Otherwise, Quattro Pro displays its main menu when you press the slash key (/).

When executing a {GetLabel} or /xl command, Quattro Pro places the prompt argument to that command at the top of the screen, and then waits for your response. Type a response and press the Enter key. Quattro Pro then enters that response in the destination cell in the form of a label. For example, if you type *test*, Quattro Pro enters the label 'test in the destination cell. If you type *123*, Quattro Pro enters the label '123. Unlike the {GetNumber} and /xn commands, the {GetLabel} and /xl commands enter formulas and functions as labels rather than calculating them and entering their results. For example, if you type +A1+101 in response to a {GetLabel} prompt, Quattro Pro enters the label '+A1+101 into the destination cell. If you type +"*Jane*"&" "&"*Doe*", Quattro Pro enters the label '+"Jane"&" "&"Doe". If you press the Enter key without typing anything, Quattro Pro enters a null label in the destination cell.

The {Get} command

Quattro Pro's {Get} command pauses the running of a macro until you press any key. At that point, Quattro Pro enters the macro representation of the key you pressed in the cell specified by the argument to the {Get} command, and then continues running the macro. The form of this command is shown below:

{Get *destination*}

The *destination* argument is the name or address of the cell in which you want Quattro Pro to place the macro representation of the key that you press. If this argument is the name or address of a multiple-cell block, Quattro Pro places the representation of the key you press in the upper-left cell of that block.

The keyboard buffer. Although you usually press keys during the running of a macro only when Quattro Pro prompts you for input, you can press them anytime. If Quattro Pro is not expecting input, it stores your keystrokes in what's called the "keyboard buffer." This buffer can hold up to 15 characters.

If Quattro Pro executes a {Get} command while the keyboard buffer contains one or more characters, it does not pause. Instead, Quattro Pro retrieves the first character from the buffer, enters the representation of that key in the cell specified by the {Get} command, and continues running the macro. If you know ahead of time what key to type in response to an upcoming {Get} command, you can type that key in advance. If you type the wrong key, however, you cannot correct your mistake.

The {Look} command

The final input-soliciting command, {Look}, instructs Quattro Pro to check the keyboard buffer to see if it contains any characters. If the keyboard buffer contains one or more characters, Quattro Pro enters the representation of the first (or only) character in the cell specified by the argument to the {Look} command. Quattro Pro does not remove that character from the buffer, however, as the {Get} command does. If the keyboard buffer is empty, Quattro Pro enters a null label in the cell specified by the {Look} command's argument. In either case, Quattro Pro continues running the macro as soon as it executes the {Look} command.

Debugging macros that solicit input

Exercise special care when you single step through a macro that contains a {?}, {GetNumber}, /xn, {GetLabel}, /xl, {Get}, or {Look} command. When encountering one of these commands in a macro, Quattro Pro pauses the running of that macro, regardless of whether Quattro Pro is single stepping. During the pause, provide the appropriate information or perform the appropriate action, whether Quattro Pro is running the macro step by step or at full speed. If Quattro Pro is running the macro step by step, stop pressing the Spacebar as soon as Quattro Pro executes the input-soliciting command. Otherwise, Quattro Pro enters space characters in response to the command. Fortunately, you can use the Backspace key to delete any unwanted space characters.

Now, press the Enter key to complete the command. Unfortunately, if Quattro Pro is in single-step mode pressing the Enter key in these situations does not simply complete the command; it causes Quattro Pro to resume running the macro at full speed. As explained in Chapter 12, "Macro Basics," this is the normal function of the Enter key when Quattro Pro is in single-step mode. After Quattro Pro starts running a macro at full speed, it continues to do so until it reaches the end of the macro or a breakpoint.

Fortunately, you can prevent Quattro Pro from resuming the running of a macro at full speed after you press the Enter key to complete a {GetNumber}, {GetLabel}, or {?} command. To do so, set a breakpoint at the cell that follows the one that contains the input-soliciting command. Then, although Quattro Pro begins running the macro at full speed as soon as you press the Enter key to end the pause caused by an input-soliciting command, Quattro Pro resumes running the macro step by step as soon as it executes all of the commands in the cell that contains that command. To ensure that every command in the macro is executed step by step, edit the macro so that the command that solicits input from the user is the last one in its cell.

Making entries in cells using programming commands

Quattro Pro provides four programming commands for entering data directly in the cells of a worksheet: {Let}, {Put}, {Blank}, and {Contents}.

The {Let} command

Quattro Pro's {Let} command allows you to place values, labels, and the results of calculations in cells of the worksheet without moving the cell selector to those cells. The form of this command is as follows:

{Let *destination,value or string*}

The *destination* argument to this command must be the name or address of a cell or block. The *value or string* argument can be a value, a string, a formula, or a function. If this second argument is a string or a value, Quattro Pro places it in the cell specified by the *destination* argument. For example, the command {Let A1,123} instructs Quattro Pro to place the value 123 in cell A1. Likewise, the command {Let B2, "John Smith"} instructs Quattro Pro to place the label 'John Smith in cell B2. If the *value or string* argument is a formula or a function, Quattro Pro evaluates it and places the result in the cell specified by *destination*. For example, the command {Let LENGTH,@LENGTH(A1)} instructs Quattro Pro to enter the length of the label in cell A1 in the cell named LENGTH. If the *destination* argument specifies a block of cells, Quattro Pro makes an entry in the upper-left cell of that block. For example, if the name BLOCK applies to the block A1..B2, Quattro Pro places the value 15 in cell A1 when it evaluates the command {Let BLOCK,10+5}.

Optional suffixes in the {Let} command. Unless you specify otherwise, the type of entry that Quattro Pro places in the destination cell of a {Let} command depends on the form of the second argument to that command. If this argument contains only digits (for example, 123), Quattro Pro enters a value into the destination cell. If the second argument contains only letters (for example, abc) or both digits and letters (for example, 123 Main Street), Quattro Pro enters a label into the destination cell. If the argument is a formula or function, Quattro Pro enters the result (either a value or a label) in the destination cell. If the second argument is an invalid formula or function, Quattro Pro enters it in the destination cell in the form of a label. For example, suppose one of your macros contains the command {Let A1,Z100+ZZ101}. Because cell ZZ101 does not exist, Quattro Pro enters the label 'Z100+ZZ101 in cell A1 when evaluating this command.

You can override Quattro Pro's decision about what type of entry to enter in the destination cell. To do so, follow the second argument with the suffix :*string* or :*value*. The :*string* suffix tells Quattro Pro to treat the second argument as a label. For example, the command {Let A1,123} tells Quattro Pro to enter the value 123 in cell A1. The command {Let A1,123:string}, however, tells Quattro Pro to enter the label '123 into that cell.

Similarly, the :*value* suffix tells Quattro Pro to treat the second argument as a value, formula, or function. The principal use of this suffix is to override the {Let} command's default treatment of invalid formulas and functions. Normally, Quattro Pro enters an invalid formula or function in the *destination* cell as a label. If you follow the formula or function argument to a {Let} command with a :value suffix, however, a macro error results when Quattro Pro executes that command. Consequently, Quattro Pro stops the running of the macro at that point. Following a literal string or a valid string-producing formula or function with a :*value* suffix also causes a macro error. Following a literal value or a valid formula or function with a :*value* suffix has no effect; Quattro Pro enters in the destination cell the value or result of the formula or function, exactly as it would if you did not include the :*value* suffix.

An alternative to the {Let} command. As explained, the {Let} command provides a way to enter the result of a calculation in a cell during the running of a macro without moving the cell selector to that cell. If you do not mind moving the cell selector to the destination cell, however, you can use an alternative technique, which consists of two steps. First, use a statement in the form {Goto}*destination*~ to move the cell selector to the destination cell. Then, use a statement with the form '*formula*{Calc}~ to enter the result of *formula* in that cell. (Be sure to give the formula a label prefix.) The first part of this statement enters the formula in the input line. The second part presses the [Calc] key (F9), which replaces the formula with its result. The final part of the statement (~) locks that result into the current cell.

The {Put} command

Like the {Let} command, Quattro Pro's {Put} command allows you to place a label or value (usually the result of a calculation) in a worksheet cell without moving the cell selector to that cell. However, while the {Let} command uses an address or name to specify the cell into which Quattro Pro should place that value, the {Put} command specifies the destination in terms of a row and column offset within a block.

The form of the {Put} command is shown below:

{Put *block,column-offset,row-offset,calculation*}

Block is the name or address of a block of cells. The *column-offset* and *row-offset* arguments are literal values or formulas or functions that return integer values, and the *calculation* argument is a literal string, a literal value or, more commonly, a formula or function that returns a string or value.

The {Put} command's first three arguments specify the cell into which Quattro Pro places the result of the fourth argument, *calculation*. The *block* argument specifies the block of potential destinations for the result of the calculation. The *column-offset* argument identifies which column of the block contains the destination cell. A column offset of 0 identifies the first column of the block, a column offset of 1 identifies the second column of the block, an offset of 2 identifies the third column of the block, and so forth. The *row-offset* argument identifies which row of the block contains the destination cell. A row offset value of 0 identifies the first row of the block, a row offset of 1 identifies the second row of the block, a row offset of 2 identifies the third row of the block, and so forth.

Together, the {Put} command's arguments tell Quattro Pro which cell to place information in and what information to place in that cell. For example, the command {Put A1..C3,1,2,@SQRT(9)} instructs Quattro Pro to place the value 3 (the result of the function @SQRT(9)) in cell B3, the cell at the intersection of the second column and third row of the block A1..C3.

The {Blank} command

Quattro Pro's {Blank} command gives you an alternative to the {/ Block;Erase} command for erasing the entries in a block. The form of this command is shown below:

{Blank *location*}

The *location* argument is the name or address of the block of cells that you want to erase. When executing a {Blank} command, Quattro Pro erases the entries from all the cells in the block specified by the *location* argument. Quattro Pro, however, does not alter the formats, widths, or protection attributes of those cells.

Two factors distinguish the {Blank} command from the {/ Block;Erase} command. First, the {Blank} command is slightly faster than the {/ Block;Erase} command, but this difference is often not significant. Second, you can use the {Blank} command anywhere within a macro, even when Quattro Pro is in the middle of choosing a command from a menu. For example, the following is a valid series of commands that instructs Quattro Pro to erase cells A1..B5 while it is assigning the name TEMP to cells C10..D15:

{/ Name;Create}{Blank A1..B5}TEMP~C10..D15~

The {Contents} command

The {Contents} command is a special copying command that makes a copy of what is displayed in one cell and places it in another cell in the form of a label. The basic form of this command is as follows:

{Contents *destination,source*}

The *destination* argument is the cell you want to copy to, and the *source* argument is the cell you want to copy from. Both arguments should specify a single cell, either by name or address. If you specify a multiple-cell block, Quattro Pro acts only upon the upper-left cell of that block. When executing a {Contents} command, Quattro Pro copies what you see on the screen when you look at the source cell, complete with formats, alignments, and so forth, and places it in the *destination* cell in the form of a label.

The resulting table is exactly what you saw on the screen for the source cell. For example, if the source cell contains the number 123, centered with two spaces on either side, the destination cell contains the label ' 123 . If the source cell contains the label 'Main Street, but only *Main S* shows on the screen, then the destination cell contains the label 'Main S. Finally, if the source cell shows ***** because it is too narrow to show the actual contents, the destination cell contains the label '*****. You can override this default behavior of the {Contents} command with the optional arguments described in the next section.

Optional arguments to the {Contents} command. You can choose to override the default length and format of the {Contents} command. To do so, use one or both of these optional arguments: *width* and *format*. These must be the third and fourth arguments to the {Contents} command, as shown below:

{Contents *destination,source,width,format*}

These optional arguments must be literal values or formulas or functions that return values. The *width* argument controls the width of the resulting label. For example, a *width* argument of 15 tells Quattro Pro to return a 15-character-long

Code	Format
0-15	Fixed, 0 to 15 digits to the right of the decimal point
16-31	Scientific, 0 to 15 digits to the right of the decimal point
32-47	Currency, 0 to 15 digits to the right of the decimal point
48-63	Percentage, 0 to 15 digits to the right of the decimal point
64-79	Comma, 0 to 15 digits to the right of the decimal point
112	+/- (Bar graph)
113	General
114	Date 1 (DD-MMM-YY)
115	Date 2 (DD-MMM)
116	Date 3 (MMM-YY)
117	Text (display formulas)
118	Hidden
119	Time 1 (HH:MM:SS AM/PM)
120	Time 2 (HH:MM AM/PM)
121	Date 4 (Long International Date)
122	Date 5 (Short International Date)
123	Time 3 (Long International Time)
124	Time 4 (Short International Time)
127	Default format for worksheet

TABLE 13-1. *This table lists the possible options for the format argument to a {Contents} command.*

label just as if the source cell had a width of 15. The *format* argument specifies the numeric format the resulting label should have. The *format* argument must be one of the codes listed in Table 13-1. For example, the value 34 specifies the Currency format, with two digits to the right of the decimal point. You can specify a *width* argument without specifying a *format* argument; however, you must specify a *width* argument if you specify a *format* argument.

When you specify a *width* argument and, optionally, a *format* argument, Quattro Pro produces a label that shows what the entry in the source cell would look like if the source cell had been assigned that width and format. For example, if cell A1 contains the value 123, Quattro Pro enters the label '*** in cell B2 when executing the command {Contents B2,A1,3,34}, because the value 123 appears as three asterisks in a three-space-wide cell that is assigned the Currency 2 format. The command {contents B2,A1,8,34} produces the label '$123.00 in cell B2.

Conditional testing

Quattro Pro's {If}, {Ifkey}, and /xi commands allow you to perform conditional testing during the running of a macro. The outcome of the test determines which set of commands Quattro Pro executes. If the conditional test is true, Quattro Pro executes one set of commands; if the conditional test is false, Quattro Pro executes another.

The {If} command

The {If} command is the most commonly used of Quattro Pro's conditional testing commands. The form of this command is shown below:

{If *condition*}

The *condition* argument is a conditional test, which is an expression that is either true or false. Most conditional tests consist of two values or strings separated by one of the following conditional operators: =, <, >, <=, >=, or <>. For example, A1=5, @SUM(A1..A5)<500, and FIRST<>SECOND are all conditional tests. You can also, however, use logical functions like @ISERR and @ISSTRING as conditional tests. For a complete discussion of conditional tests, see Chapter 4, "Functions."

When an {If} command's conditional test is true, Quattro Pro executes the remaining commands in the cell that contains the {If} command before executing the commands in the cells below. If the conditional test is false, Quattro Pro skips the remaining commands in the {If} cell and continues with the commands in the cell below it. For example, the following command tests the value in INPUT:

{If INPUT<1#OR#INPUT>100}{Quit}

If INPUT contains a value that is less than 1 or greater than 100, the conditional test INPUT<1#OR#INPUT>100 is true. In that case, Quattro Pro executes the next command in the cell, {Quit}, which cancels the running of the macro. If the value in INPUT is 1 through 100, the {If} command's conditional test is false. In that case, Quattro Pro skips the {Quit} command and instead executes the command in the next cell.

The {Ifkey} command

The {Ifkey} command tests whether a string is a valid macro name for a key. ("Macro Fundamentals" in Chapter 12 describes the requirements for macro names.) If the conditional test is true, Quattro Pro executes the remaining commands in the cell that contains the {Ifkey} command. If the conditional test is false, Quattro Pro skips the remaining commands in the cell that contains the {Ifkey} command and continues running the macro using the commands in the cell below it. For example, consider the one-line macro shown below:

{Ifkey "home"}{Quit}

When this macro runs it executes {Quit} because the string "home" is the macro name for the Home key.

The /xi command

Quattro Pro's /xi command is equivalent to the {If} command. The form of this command is as follows:

/xi*condition*~

The *condition* argument is a conditional test. If the conditional test is true, Quattro Pro continues running the commands in the cell containing /xi. If the conditional test is false, Quattro Pro skips the remaining commands in the cell that contains the /xi command and continues with the commands in the next cell. For example, the command /xiINPUT<1#OR# INPUT>100~{Quit} is equivalent to the earlier {If} command. The command tests the value in INPUT. If INPUT contains a value that is less than 1 or greater than 100, the conditional test is true. In that case, Quattro Pro executes the next command in the cell, {Quit}.

A closer look at conditional tests

Often, you want Quattro Pro to do more than simply cancel the running of a macro when a conditional test is true. In some cases, you can fit all of the commands that you want Quattro Pro to execute in the same cell as the {If} or /xi commands. In other cases, you might not be able to (or want to) enter all of the commands in that cell. In such situations, you can enter the commands in another part of the worksheet and then use Quattro Pro's {Branch} or /xg commands to route the macro to them. The next section explains these commands.

Branching using programming commands

After executing all the commands in one cell of a macro, Quattro Pro normally begins executing the commands in the cell immediately below it. For example, if a macro occupies cells B1..B3, Quattro Pro begins executing the commands in cell B2 after executing all of the commands in cell B1. After executing all of the commands in cell B2, Quattro Pro begins executing the commands in cell B3.

Quattro Pro, however, features two commands that allow you to redirect the running of a macro: {Branch} and /xg. These commands instruct Quattro Pro to route the running of a macro to the cell specified by their arguments.

The {Branch} command

Quattro Pro's {Branch} command is the principal command you use to redirect the flow of a macro. The form of this command is as follows:

{Branch *location*}

The *location* argument is the name or address of a cell or block. When encountering a {Branch} command in a macro, Quattro Pro stops running the macro at that point and immediately resumes the running of the macro using the first command in the cell specified by the *location* argument. For example, the command {Branch A1} causes the macro to jump to the first command in cell A1. If the {Branch} command's argument specifies a multiple-cell block, Quattro Pro resumes the running of the macro using the first command in the upper-left cell of that block. After executing all of the commands in the cell specified by {Branch}, Quattro Pro executes all of the instructions in the cell below that cell, and then in the cell below that cell, and so forth. Quattro Pro continues in this fashion until it encounters a blank cell, a {Quit} command, or another {Branch} command. If Quattro Pro encounters a {Quit} command or a blank cell, it cancels the running of the macro at that point; Quattro Pro does not branch back to the command (if any) that follows the original {Branch} command. If Quattro Pro encounters another {Branch} command, it branches to the cell specified by that command.

The /xg command

Quattro Pro's /xg command provides an alternative way to redirect the running of a macro. Although the action of this command is identical to that of the {Branch} command, its form is different, as shown below:

/xglocation~

The *location* argument is the name or address of the cell to which you want Quattro Pro to route the running of the macro. When executing a /xg command, Quattro Pro immediately branches the running of the macro to the cell specified by the *location* argument. If the argument specifies a multiple-cell block, Quattro Pro branches the macro to the upper-left cell of that block. In either case, Quattro Pro continues running the macro from the new cell down, until it reaches a blank cell or a {Quit} command. At that point, Quattro Pro cancels the running of the macro and does not route the macro back to the command that followed the /xg command.

Calling subroutines using programming commands

As explained, the {Branch} and /xg commands cause a one-way rerouting of the running of a macro. If Quattro Pro encounters a blank cell or a {Quit} command after executing a {Branch} or /xg command, it stops running the macro. Quattro Pro does not return to the command that follows the {Branch} or /xg command.

Fortunately, Quattro Pro provides two commands that do allow the two-way rerouting of the running of a macro: {Subroutine} and /xc. When executing either of these commands, Quattro Pro routes the running of the macro to the cell specified by the command's argument, exactly as it does when encountering a {Branch} or /xg command. Quattro Pro, however, does not end the running of the macro when it subsequently encounters a blank cell. Instead, Quattro Pro routes the running of the macro back to the command that follows the {Subroutine} or /xc command. The command to which Quattro Pro routes the running of the macro is called a "subroutine." The {Subroutine} and /xc commands are "subroutine calls," because they call (route the running of the macro through) a subroutine.

Subroutines are most useful for storing sets of commands that Quattro Pro executes several times during the running of a macro. That way, instead of repeating the series of commands at several places within the macro, you can enter those commands only one time, and then use a subroutine call whenever you want Quattro Pro to execute them.

The {Subroutine} command

The most common way to call a subroutine is to enclose its name or address in braces. For example, to call a subroutine whose first cell is named TEST, use the command {TEST}. If the name TEST is assigned to cell B27, you can also use the command {B27} to call this subroutine. If you want, you can use the name or address of a multiple-cell block. For example, if the name TEST applies to cells B27..B32, the subroutine call {TEST} is a valid macro command, as is the command {B27..B32}. When you enclose the name or address of a multiple-cell block within braces, Quattro Pro routes the running of the macro to the upper-left cell of that block. (Unlike Quattro Pro, Lotus 1-2-3 does not allow you to call a subroutine by address. Therefore, if you want your Quattro Pro macros to be compatible with 1-2-3, call subroutines by name.)

Whether you reference a single cell or a block, Quattro Pro executes the commands in the first cell of the subroutine, and then the commands in the cell below that cell, and so forth, until encountering a blank cell or a {Return} command. When either of these situations occurs, Quattro Pro routes the running of the macro back to the command that follows the subroutine call. If Quattro Pro encounters a {Quit} command before a blank cell, it cancels the running of the macro, exactly as it does when it encounters a {Quit} command after executing a {Branch} or /xg command.

The {Return} and /xr commands

As mentioned, the {Return} command lets you end a subroutine. When it encounters a {Return} command, Quattro Pro immediately routes the running of the macro back to the command that follows the one that called the subroutine.

If you want, you can use a blank cell instead of a {Return} command at the end of a subroutine. In most cases, however, you want to use the {Return} command to end the execution of a subroutine prematurely. To do so, you can preface the {Return} command with an {If} command. If the conditional test of the {If} command is true, Quattro Pro executes the {Return} command, which routes the running of the macro to the command that follows the subroutine call. If the conditional test is false, Quattro Pro skips the {Return} command and continues executing the subroutine at the next cell.

The /xr command performs exactly the same function as the {Return} command in exactly the same way.

Passing arguments to subroutines

Programming languages like BASIC and Pascal allow you to pass arguments to subroutines when you call them. Passing an argument to a subroutine provides the subroutine with the values it needs to perform a calculation. Consequently, passing an argument eliminates the necessity of assigning values to variables before you call the subroutine. You also can pass information to subroutines that you call within a Quattro Pro macro. To do so, include the information that you want to use as arguments to the subroutine call, as shown below:

{subroutine *arg1,arg2,...*}

The arguments to a subroutine call can be values, labels, formulas, or functions. Separate each argument from the preceding one with a comma. For example, {TEST B3*10,A1,"Hello",@SUM(A1..A5),1} is a valid subroutine call that passes five pieces of information to the subroutine that begins at the cell named TEST.

Including the {Define} command in a subroutine. Any subroutine to which you pass information should contain a {Define} command. This command tells Quattro Pro how to interpret and distribute the information passed to the subroutine; its form is shown below:

{Define *location1:type1,location2:type2,...*}

Each *location:type* pair tells Quattro Pro where to place one of the pieces of information passed to the subroutine and whether the information is a value or label. The first *location:type* pair provides instructions for the first argument to the subroutine call, the second *location:type* pair provides instructions for the second argument to the subroutine call, and so forth. The {Define} command should have as many *location:type* pairs as there are arguments in the subroutine call.

The *location* portion of each *location:type* pair tells Quattro Pro in what cell to place the information specified by the argument with which it is paired. This argument should be either the name or address of a single cell (preferably a name); however, it can be the name or the address of a block. If *location* specifies a single cell, Quattro Pro places the information specified by the argument in that cell. If *location* specifies a block, Quattro Pro places the information in the upper-left cell of that block.

The *type* portion of each *location:type* pair tells Quattro Pro how to interpret each argument. This portion is optional. If you specify a *type*, however, it must be one of these two: *:string* or *:value*. If you use the *:string*, or if you do not include a *type*, Quattro Pro treats the argument as a label. If you include the *:value*, Quattro Pro treats the argument either as a value or as a formula or function, whichever is appropriate.

For example, suppose you use the command {TEST A1} to call a subroutine named TEST. If the subroutine contains the command {Define ONE} or the command {Define ONE:string}, Quattro Pro places the label 'A1 in the cell named ONE. If, however, the subroutine contains the command {Define ONE:value}, Quattro Pro interprets the argument A1 as a reference to cell A1. If cell A1 contains a value, Quattro Pro enters that value in the cell named ONE. If cell A1 contains a label, Quattro Pro enters that label in ONE. If cell A1 contains a formula or function, Quattro Pro enters the result of that formula or function in the cell named ONE.

The /xc command

Quattro Pro's /xc command provides an alternative way to call subroutines. The form of this command is shown below:

   /xc*subroutine*~

The *subroutine* argument is the name or address of the cell or block to which you want to route the running of the macro. If the argument to an /xc command specifies a single cell, Quattro Pro routes the running of the macro to that cell. If the argument is the name or address of a multiple-cell block, Quattro Pro routes the macro to the cell in the upper-left corner of that block. After executing the commands in the first cell of the subroutine, Quattro Pro executes the commands (if any) in the cell below. Quattro Pro continues in this fashion until encountering a blank cell, a cell that contains a {Return} command, or a cell that contains a {Quit} command. In the first two cases, Quattro Pro returns the running of the macro to the command that follows the /xc command. If Quattro Pro encounters a {Quit} command, it cancels the running of the macro.

The only difference between the {Subroutine} and /xc forms of a subroutine call is that you cannot pass arguments when you use the /xc form. Otherwise, the action of the two forms is identical. Consequently, you can use these two commands interchangeably when you do not need to pass arguments to the subroutine.

A closer look at subroutines

When you call a subroutine that has a multiple-word name, enclose that name in quotation marks or use the /xc form. Otherwise, Quattro Pro assumes that the first word of the name is the name of the subroutine and the remaining words are arguments. For example, suppose you want to call a subroutine whose first cell is named SUB ONE. If you use the command {SUB ONE}, Quattro Pro assumes you are calling a subroutine named SUB and passing the argument ONE to it. As SUB probably is not a valid block name, the subroutine call fails. To call this subroutine successfully, use either the command {"SUB ONE"} or the command /xcSUB ONE~.

If you want, you can call one subroutine within another, which is called nesting. Each time you call a subroutine, Quattro Pro drops down to a new level of the macro. As soon as it finishes executing the subroutine, Quattro Pro goes back up to the previous level. Nesting subroutines does not cause a problem until Quattro Pro reaches the thirty-second level. If you call a subroutine while the macro is in the thirty-second level, Quattro Pro cancels the running of the macro. This is a minor problem because you rarely need more than a few levels of subroutines.

Looping using the {For} programming command

The {For} command allows you to set up For/Next loops within your macros, making it easy to program Quattro Pro to execute a subroutine a set number of times, one right after the other. Its form is as follows:

{For *counter,start,stop,step,subroutine*}

The *subroutine* argument tells Quattro Pro what subroutine to execute, and the *counter, start, stop,* and *step* arguments tell Quattro Pro how many times to execute the commands in that subroutine. The *counter* and *subroutine* arguments should be the names or addresses of cells or blocks; the *start, stop,* and *step* arguments should be literal values, formulas or functions that return values, or references to cells that contain either literal values or value-producing formulas or functions.

When executing a {For} command, Quattro Pro proceeds like this: First, Quattro Pro enters the value specified by the *start* argument (the *start* value) in the cell specified by the *counter* argument. If the value in the *counter* cell (the *counter* value) does not exceed the value specified by the *stop* argument (the *stop* value), Quattro Pro executes the commands in the subroutine specified by the *subroutine* argument. This process is called "making a pass through the subroutine." After Quattro Pro completes the first pass through the subroutine (that is, when it encounters a blank cell or a {Return} command), Quattro Pro increases the *counter* value by the amount specified by the *step* argument (the *step* value). If the *counter* value still does not exceed the *stop* value, Quattro Pro executes the commands in the subroutine again (that is, makes a second pass through the subroutine). After completing the second pass, Quattro Pro again increases the *counter* value by the *step* value and, if the *counter* value does not exceed the *stop* value, makes another pass through the subroutine. Quattro Pro continues in this fashion until the *counter* value exceeds the *stop* value. At that point, Quattro Pro breaks from the {For} command and executes the next command in the macro.

The {Return} command in {For} loops

You use a blank cell in most cases to mark the end of a subroutine that is called by a {For} command. You can also, however, use a {Return} command. When encountering a {Return} command while making a pass through a subroutine, Quattro Pro ends that current pass and returns to the top of the {For} command. At that point, Quattro Pro adds the *step* value to the *counter* value, and, if the result is not greater than the *stop* value, makes another pass through the subroutine. If the *counter* value does exceed the *stop* value, of course, Quattro Pro ends the {For} command and goes on.

Although you can use a {Return} command at the end of a subroutine called by a {For} loop, you usually use it in conjunction with an {If} command to end a pass prematurely.

The {ForBreak} command

The {ForBreak} command, which uses no arguments, allows users to cancel the execution of a {For} command before Quattro Pro has made the full number of passes through the subroutine specified by that command. When encountering a {ForBreak} command during a pass through a {For} loop, Quattro Pro cancels the execution of the {For} command, and then continues on to the command that follows the {For} command. Unlike the {Return} command, the {ForBreak} command does not simply end the current pass through the loop; it cancels that pass and all passes that follow it. Unlike the {Quit} command, the {ForBreak} command does not cancel the running of the entire macro; it cancels only the {For} command that Quattro Pro is executing at the time.

Use the {ForBreak} command in conjunction with an {If} command to cancel the execution of a {For} command when a certain condition is true.

Debugging {For} loops

As you have seen, the {For} command instructs Quattro Pro to execute a subroutine multiple times. If you specify the cell that contains a {For} command as a breakpoint and you run that macro while Quattro Pro is in DEBUG mode, Quattro Pro pauses the running of the macro before beginning each new pass through the loop. If you specify one of the cells within the subroutine as a breakpoint, Quattro Pro pauses the running of the macro during each pass through the loop before implementing the commands in that cell.

In many cases, you do not want Quattro Pro to pause the running of the macro during each pass through a {For} loop. For example, suppose you know that an error occurs in the running of a macro at some point after Quattro Pro has made the tenth pass through a {For} loop. In that case, you want Quattro Pro to run the macro at full speed until completing 10 passes through the loop, and then begin running the macro one step at a time. Alternatively, you might want to check the entries in various worksheet cells after every five passes through the loop.

The Pass Count option makes these actions possible. As mentioned in "Debugging Macros" in Chapter 12, you set a pass count by choosing the / Breakpoints #Breakpoint Pass Count command while you are running a macro in Debugging mode. If you assign a pass count to a breakpoint that is set for a {For} command or a cell within a subroutine, Quattro Pro pauses the running of the macro after making the number of passes specified by that pass count. (Of course, you must run the macro in debug mode.) For example, if you specify a pass count of 5, Quattro Pro pauses the running of the macro after making five passes through the loop before executing the commands in the break cell for the sixth time. After Quattro Pro pauses, you can press the Spacebar to run the macro one step at a time. Alternatively, you can press the Enter key to resume the running of the macro at full speed. If you do so, Quattro Pro pauses again after executing the loop the number of times specified by the pass count. For information about how to set breakpoints and specify pass counts, see "Debugging Macros" in Chapter 12.

A closer look at the {For} command

As explained earlier, the *start*, *stop*, and *step* arguments to a {For} command can be formulas or functions. When encountering a {For} command that includes formula or function arguments, Quattro Pro calculates those formulas or functions and uses the results as the *start*, *stop*, or *step* values for the duration of the execution of the {For} command. Quattro Pro does not recalculate these formulas and functions at the beginning of each new pass through the loop. Consequently, any changes that the commands in the loop might make to the cells referenced by these formulas and functions have no effect on the number of passes Quattro Pro makes through the {For} loop.

You should not use negative *step* values in your {For} commands. A negative *step* value, which causes Quattro Pro to reduce the *counter* value after each pass through a {For} loop, should signal Quattro Pro to cancel the execution of the {For} command after the *counter* value becomes less than the *stop* value. Unfortunately, it does not work that way. Whether the *step* value is positive or negative, Quattro Pro cancels the execution of the {For} loop when the *counter* value exceeds the *step* value. Because the *start* value of a {For} command with a negative *step* value is greater than the *stop* value, Quattro Pro does not make any passes through the specified subroutine.

Quattro Pro's {For} command also does not react to negative *counter* values in the way you might expect. If the initial *counter* value (the *start* value) is negative, or if the *counter* value becomes negative at some point during the execution of the {For} command, Quattro Pro cancels the execution of the {For} command. For example, suppose that Quattro Pro encounters {For COUNT,-100,-1,1,LOOP} in a macro. Because the initial *counter* value (the *start* value) is negative, Quattro Pro cancels the execution of the {For} command before making any passes through the loop, and continues running the macro using the statement that follows the {For} command.

Other methods of controlling program flow

You've already read about 13 commands that allow you to control the flow of a Quattro Pro macro. In addition to these commands, Quattro Pro features eight others that allow you to control the flow of a macro: {OnError}, {Wait}, {BreakOff}, {BreakOn}, {Dispatch}, {Restart}, {StepOn}, and {StepOff}. Collectively, these commands are called the program flow commands, and they appear under the Program Flow option in the list that Quattro Pro displays when you press the [Macro] key (Shift-F3).

The {OnError} command

Usually, when Quattro Pro encounters an error in your macro, it displays an error message and terminates the macro. When you "trap" an error, you take care of it before Quattro Pro encounters it. In this way, you can recover from an error without terminating the macro.

The {OnError} command allows you to trap a number of errors that otherwise would cancel the running of a macro. If an {OnError} command is in effect when Quattro Pro encounters a trapable error, Quattro Pro routes the running of the macro to the cell specified by the command's first argument and, optionally, enters the error message Quattro Pro would normally display in the cell specified by the command's second argument and the address of the error in the cell specified by the third argument. The form of this command is shown below:

{OnError *location1,location2,location3*}

The *location1* argument is the name or address of the cell to which the macro branches if it encounters a trapable error. *Location2* (which is optional) specifies the cell in which Quattro Pro should enter the error message. *Location3* specifies a cell in which Quattro Pro should enter the address of the macro cell that caused the error.

Trapable errors. As explained in Chapter 12, "Macro Basics," a number of situations cause macro errors, including omitted or incorrect characters in keystrokes; misspellings or incorrect syntax in programming commands, menu-equivalent commands, and the macro representations of special keys; and invalid or inappropriate responses to the prompts that Quattro Pro displays when you choose many commands. Unfortunately, the {OnError} command does not trap all of these errors. It traps only errors that are caused by Quattro Pro's inability to execute a command that has been chosen from one of Quattro Pro's menus, either as the result of a valid sequence of keystrokes or a valid menu-equivalent command. For example, the {OnError} command traps the error caused when a macro chooses the File Retrieve command and specifies an invalid name.

The lifespan of an {OnError} command. After Quattro Pro reads an {OnError} command, the error-trapping condition specified by that command remains in effect until one of three situations occurs: a trapable error occurs, Quattro Pro reads another {OnError} command, or Quattro Pro ends the running of the macro.

If a trapable error occurs, the {OnError} command gets used up. If you want error-trapping to remain in effect, include an {OnError} command in the statements that Quattro Pro executes when the first {OnError} command is tripped.

If Quattro Pro encounters one {OnError} command while another is still in effect, the error-trapping condition specified by the new {OnError} command replaces the error-trapping condition specified by the old one. To cancel one {OnError} condition without imposing a new one, simply use an {OnError} command without any arguments. An {OnError} command of this sort cancels any existing error-trapping condition, but does not set another one.

Quattro Pro cancels any active {OnError} command when ending the running of a macro. Consequently, you need not end your macros with a null {OnError} command.

The {Wait} command

The {Wait} command pauses the running of a macro until the date and time specified by its argument. During the pause, Quattro Pro flashes the word WAIT at the right side of the status line. The form of this command is shown below:

{Wait *dateandtime*}

The *dateandtime* argument specifies the date and time at which you want Quattro Pro to resume the running of the macro. The argument to a {Wait} command can be a literal date and time value or a formula or function that returns a combined date and time value. The simplest use of the {Wait} command is to pause the running of a macro until a particular time on a particular day. For example, the following command pauses the running of a macro until 12:30 PM on July 4, 1991:

{Wait @DATE(91,7,4)+@TIME(12,30,0)}

Because Quattro Pro compares the date and time specified by a {Wait} command's argument to the date and time specified by your computer's system clock, this form of the {Wait} command does not work correctly unless your computer's clock is set properly. In most cases, however, use the {Wait} command to pause the running of a macro for a particular span of time. To do so, include a @NOW function in the command's argument. For example, the following command pauses the running of a macro for thirty seconds:

{Wait @NOW+@TIME(0,0,30)}

Because this form of the {Wait} command specifies a relative date and time, it works correctly regardless of whether your computer's clock is set correctly.

The {BreakOff} and {BreakOn} commands

Although Quattro Pro normally cancels the running of a macro when you press the Ctrl-Break key combination, you can use the {BreakOff} command to prevent a user from canceling the running of a macro in this way. The form of this command is simply {BreakOff}; it accepts no arguments. When executing a {BreakOff} command, Quattro Pro immediately disables the Ctrl-Break combination. From that point until you specify otherwise, Quattro Pro does not respond when the user presses the Ctrl and Break keys simultaneously.

After you disable the Ctrl-Break key combination, it remains that way until one of two situations occurs: Quattro Pro executes a {BreakOn} command, or it ends the running of the macro that contains the {BreakOff} command. Like the {BreakOff} command, the {BreakOn} command does not accept any arguments. If a {BreakOff} command is active when Quattro Pro executes a {BreakOn} command, Quattro Pro restores the normal function of the Ctrl-Break key combination. If no {BreakOff} command is currently active, Quattro Pro ignores a {BreakOn} command. Quattro Pro restores the normal function of the Ctrl-Break key combination when it ends the running of a macro. Consequently, you need not end your macros with a {BreakOn} command.

The principal reason for including a {BreakOff} command in a macro is to prevent a user other than yourself from canceling the running of a macro. Before you add a {BreakOff} command to a macro, you probably want to debug that macro completely. Otherwise, if the macro does not do what you want it to do, you have to let it run to completion or stop it by rebooting your computer.

The {Dispatch} command

The {Dispatch} command provides you with an alternative way to branch the running of a macro. As explained earlier, both the {Branch} and /xg commands instruct Quattro Pro to branch the running of a macro to the cell specified by the argument. For example, the command {Branch B5} instructs Quattro Pro to route the running of a macro to cell B5. Unlike the {Branch} and /xg commands, which specify the destination of a branch directly, the {Dispatch} command specifies the destination indirectly. The form of this command is shown below:

{Dispatch *location*}

The *location* argument is the name or address of a cell that contains or returns the name or address of the cell to which you want to branch the running of the macro. For example, if cell A1 contains the label 'B5, the command {Dispatch A1} branches the running of the macro to cell B5, and not to cell A1. In order for Quattro Pro to execute a {Dispatch} command properly, the argument must be a literal string that specifies the name or address of a cell or block. If the argument specifies a cell, Quattro Pro looks in that cell for the name or address of the cell to branch to. If the argument specifies a block, Quattro Pro looks in the cell at the upper-left corner of that block for the name of the cell to branch to.

The cell referenced by the argument to a {Dispatch} command must contain the label form of the name or address of the cell or block or a formula or function that returns the name or address of that cell or block. If the referenced cell contains or returns the name or address of a cell, Quattro Pro branches the running of the macro to that cell. If the referenced cell contains or returns the name or address of a block, Quattro Pro branches the running of the macro to the upper-left cell of that block.

Quattro Pro does not recalculate the formula or function in the referenced cell when executing a {Dispatch} command. Consequently, if your worksheet is set for Manual recalculation, the {Dispatch} command might not produce the result you intend.

If the cell specified by the argument to a {Dispatch} command contains or returns an invalid address or a nonexistent block name, Quattro Pro cancels the running of the macro.

The {Restart} command

The {Restart} command converts a subroutine call (by a {Subroutine} command, an /xc command, or a {For} command) to a branch. When encountering a {Restart} command in a subroutine, Quattro Pro breaks the connection with the command that called the subroutine. After the {Restart} command, Quattro Pro ends the running of the macro as soon as it encounters a blank cell or {Return} command. Subsequent {ForBreak} commands cause a macro error.

The {StepOn} and {StepOff} commands.

The {StepOn} and {StepOff} commands instruct Quattro Pro to enter and exit debug mode during the running of a macro. The forms of these commands are simply {StepOn} and {StepOff}; they do not accept any arguments. When encountering a {StepOn} command during the running of a macro, Quattro Pro pauses the running of the macro and enters debug mode exactly as if you had set a breakpoint at that point. Consequently, Quattro Pro displays the macro within a Debug window, highlights the current command, and runs one step of the macro each time you press the Spacebar.

Quattro Pro continues running the macro in this fashion until one of three situations occurs: Quattro Pro encounters a {StepOff} command, you press the Enter key, or Quattro Pro ends the running of the macro. If Quattro Pro encounters a {StepOff} command, it exits from debug mode, closes the Debug window, and resumes running the macro at full speed. Quattro Pro also resumes running the macro at full speed if you press the Enter key, but leaves the Debug window on the screen. If Quattro Pro reaches the end of the macro before either of these other two situations occurs, it closes the Debug window and cancels the running of the macro.

Creating custom menus

One of Quattro Pro's most useful programming features is the ability it gives you to create custom menus. These menus look exactly like Quattro Pro's regular menus, and work like them in almost every way. You can, however, control the options that appear in the menus, the prompts that correspond to those options, and the actions that Quattro Pro performs when you choose those options. Three commands give you the ability to create custom menus: {MenuBranch}, /xm, and {MenuCall}. The forms of these commands are shown below:

{MenuBranch *location*}

/xm*location*~

{MenuCall *location*}

In most cases, the *location* argument is the name or address of the upper-left cell of the area of the worksheet that contains the options, prompts, and commands for the menu; this is called the menu area. The *location* argument, however, can specify any block of cells that has the upper-left cell of the menu area at its upper-left corner.

When executing any of these three commands, Quattro Pro builds a menu from the entries in the menu area, displays that menu on the screen, and pauses. During the pause, you can choose an option from the menu in the same way you can from a regular Quattro Pro menu. After you make a choice, Quattro Pro executes the commands that correspond to that choice. The difference among these three commands is what Quattro Pro does when it finishes executing the commands that correspond to the option you chose.

The {MenuBranch} and /xm commands branch the running of the macro to the custom menu. Consequently, Quattro Pro ends the running of the macro after executing all of the commands that correspond to the option you chose from the custom menu. The {MenuCall} command calls the menu as a subroutine. As a result, after Quattro Pro executes all of the commands that correspond to the option you choose from the custom menu, it returns to the statement that follows the {MenuCall} command.

The structure of the menu area

The entries in the menu area—the block that is referenced by the argument to the {MenuBranch}, /xm, and {MenuCall} commands—determine the appearance and action of a custom menu. For Quattro Pro to be able to produce a custom menu, this block must be arranged as follows:

- The first row of the block must contain the options that appear in the menu.
- The second row must contain the descriptions that will be displayed in the status line for each option.

- The rows below these two rows must contain the commands that correspond to the menu options and prompts.

In other words, each column of the menu area contains the definition of an option on your custom menu. The first row names the option, the second row describes the option, and the subsequent rows define the action that the option performs.

Menu options. The first row of the menu area must contain the options that you want Quattro Pro to list in the custom menu. The entries in this row can be labels, values, formulas, or functions. If a cell contains a label or a value, Quattro Pro displays that label or value in the menu. If the cell contains a formula or function that returns a string, Quattro Pro displays the result of that formula in the menu. If the cell contains a formula or function that returns a value, Quattro Pro displays the character 0 in the menu. The formats and alignments of the entries in this row do not affect the appearance of the options in the menu.

Menu options appear in the order in which they are listed in the first row of the menu area. The label in the upper-left corner of the menu area appears at the top of the custom menu, the label in the cell to the right of that cell appears immediately below the first option in the custom menu, and so forth. A value entry or a blank cell marks the end of the menu. Options to the right of a blank cell do not appear in the custom menu. If at all possible, each option in a custom menu should begin with a different letter, which allows you to choose any option from a custom menu simply by typing the first character of that option. Capitalization is irrelevant. For example, you can choose the Test option by typing *t* or *T*.

The entries in the first row of the menu area can contain up to 254 characters (the maximum length of an entry in a Quattro Pro worksheet cell). Quattro Pro, however, displays only the first 55 characters of any entry in a custom menu. Consequently, the practical limit on the length of the entries in the first row of the menu area is 55 characters. Any custom menu can include up to 256 options (the number of columns in a Quattro Pro worksheet). Quattro Pro, however, can display a maximum of 13 options in a menu at one time. As explained later in "Choosing an Option from a Custom Menu," Quattro Pro shifts new options into view as you use the direction keys to move the highlight within the menu.

Descriptions of menu options. The second row of the menu area should contain explanatory descriptions of the corresponding options in the first row. Quattro Pro displays these descriptions in the status line as you move the highlight to the various options. The description for each menu option should appear in the cell immediately below the one that contains that option. For example, the description for the first option in the menu should be situated in the leftmost cell of the second row of the menu area, the description for the second option should appear in the cell to the right of the one that contains the first description, and so forth.

Like the cells in the first row of the menu area, the cells in the second row can contain labels, values, formulas, or functions. If a cell in the second line contains a label or a value, Quattro Pro displays that label or value in the input line. If the cell contains a string-producing formula, Quattro Pro displays the result of that formula. If the cell contains a value-producing formula, Quattro Pro displays the character 0 in the prompt line. Unlike the cells in the first row of the menu area, the cells in the second row can be blank. If a cell in the second row is blank, Quattro Pro does not display a prompt for the menu option to which that cell corresponds. The formats or alignments assigned to the cell in the second row of the menu area do not affect the appearance of the descriptions in the input line.

Like the entries in any Quattro Pro worksheet cell, the cells in the second row of the menu area can contain up to 254 characters. Quattro Pro, however, displays only the first 72 characters of any of these entries in the input line. Consequently, the practical limit for the descriptions of the options in a custom menu is 72 characters.

Custom menu commands. The cells below the cell that contains the description for each option in the custom menu should contain one or more commands. In most cases, these cells contain a series of commands. However, you might enter a single {Branch} or /xg command that directs Quattro Pro to another place in the worksheet.

How custom menus work

When executing a {MenuBranch}, /xm, or {MenuCall} command, Quattro Pro creates a custom menu from the entries in the menu area specified by that command, displays that menu near the right edge of the screen, and then pauses. The options in the menu are arranged one on top of the other, exactly as they are in a regular Quattro Pro menu. The first character of each option is bright or displayed in a different color. The first choice in the custom menu is highlighted, and the description for that option appears in the input line. If the menu contains more than 13 options, only the first 13 are visible within the menu box.

Choosing an option from a custom menu. You can choose options from custom menus in the same way you choose options from standard Quattro Pro menus. First, type the first letter of the option you want. Quattro Pro erases the custom menu and executes the commands that correspond to the option you chose. If you have designed your custom menu well, each option begins with a different character. If more than one option begins with the character you type, Quattro Pro executes the commands that correspond to whichever of those options is closest to the top of the menu. If none of the options begin with the character you press, Quattro Pro simply beeps.

Alternatively, you can choose an option from a custom menu by moving the highlight to that option and then pressing the Enter key. Move the highlight to the various options in a custom menu in the same way you move it in a standard

Quattro Pro menu. Only 13 options are visible on the screen at one time. You can use the End, PgDn, and Down direction keys to reveal options that are hidden below the bottom border of the menu box and the Home, PgUp, and Up direction keys to reveal options that are hidden above the top border. Each time you move the highlight to a new option in the menu, the description for that option appears on the status line. When you press the Enter key, Quattro Pro erases the custom menu and executes the commands that correspond to the option that was highlighted at the time.

Completing a command. Quattro Pro continues to execute the commands that correspond to the options you chose until encountering one of the following: a blank cell, a {Return} command, or a {Quit} command. How Quattro Pro reacts to a blank cell or a {Return} command depends on which command created the custom menu. If it was created by a {MenuBranch} or /xm command, Quattro Pro ends the running of the macro at that point. If the menu was created by a {MenuCall} command, Quattro Pro routes the running of the macro back to the command that follows that {MenuCall} command. If Quattro Pro encounters a {Quit} command, it cancels the running of the macro, no matter which of the three commands created the menu.

Pressing the Esc key. Instead of choosing an option from a custom menu, you can press the Esc key. Quattro Pro then erases the custom menu and routes the running of the macro back to the command that follows the one that called the menu (either {MenuBranch}, /xm, or {MenuCall}). If the menu-creating command is not the last command in the macro, Quattro Pro executes the remaining commands.

You might, in some cases, want to force the user to make a choice from a custom menu. Later in this chapter, "Forcing the User to Choose an Option from a Custom Menu" explains how to do so.

Using {MenuBranch} /xm, and {MenuCall} commands

As you create macros, you'll find a number of situations in which you want to present the user with a custom menu. In most cases, it's best to branch the running of a macro to a custom menu. To do so, use either the {MenuBranch} or /xm command. In cases in which you want to use the same macro more than one time, or you simply want to return the running of the macro to the command following the one that created the menu, use the {MenuCall} command. The following demonstrates the uses of each command.

The {MenuBranch} command. The macro shown in Figure 13-3 contains a simple use of the {MenuBranch} command. This macro streamlines the process of entering a group of entries in the cells of a column or row. The first statement in this

Chapter 13: Programming Command Basics   443

FIGURE 13-3.
*The {MenuBranch}
command in this
macro creates the
custom menu shown
in Figure 13-4.*

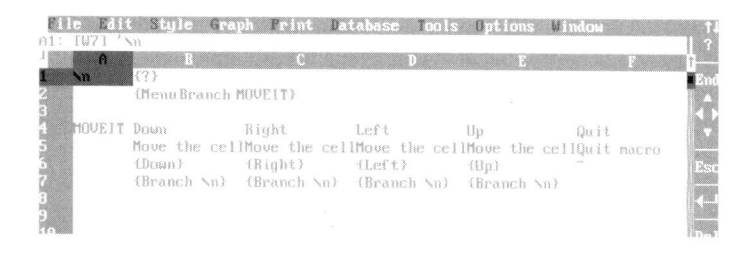

```
File  Edit  Style  Graph  Print  Database  Tools  Options  Window
A1: [W7] '\n
        A            B              C              D              E              F
1  \n           {?}
2               {MenuBranch MOVEIT}
3
4  MOVEIT  Down         Right          Left           Up             Quit
5          Move the cell Move the cell Move the cell Move the cell Quit macro
6          {Down}       {Right}        {Left}         {Up}
7          {Branch \n}  {Branch \n}   {Branch \n}   {Branch \n}
8
9
```

FIGURE 13-4.
*Quattro Pro presents
this menu when
executing
{MenuBranch}.*

```
Down
Right
Left
Up
Quit
```

macro, which is {?}, commands Quattro Pro to pause until you press the Enter key. During this pause, type the value, label, formula, or function that you want to enter in the current cell. Press the Enter key, and Quattro Pro executes the second command in the macro, which is {MenuBranch MOVEIT}. This command, which references the cell named MOVEIT (B4), tells Quattro Pro to display the custom menu shown in Figure 13-4. The first four options in this menu control the direction in which Quattro Pro moves the cell selector. If you choose Down, Quattro Pro executes the command in cell B6, which instructs it to press the Down direction key. This key causes Quattro Pro to lock your entry into the current cell, and move the cell selector down one cell. Then, Quattro Pro executes the command in cell B7, which instructs it to branch back to the beginning of the macro. Quattro Pro then pauses for you to make another entry.

As you would expect, the Right, Left, and Up options tell Quattro Pro to move the cell selector one cell to the right, to the left, or up, respectively. If you choose the Right option, Quattro Pro executes the commands in cells C6 and C7, which tell Quattro Pro to lock your entry into the current cell, move the cell selector one cell to the right, then branch back to the beginning of the macro. If you choose the Left option, Quattro Pro executes the commands in cells D6 and D7, which tell Quattro Pro to lock your entry into the current cell and move the cell selector one cell to the left before branching back to the beginning of the macro. If you choose the Up option, Quattro Pro executes the commands in cells E6 and E7, which tell Quattro Pro to branch back to the beginning of the macro after locking your entry into the current cell and moving the cell selector up one cell. Quattro Pro continues cycling through this macro until you choose the Quit option from the custom menu. After you do so, Quattro Pro executes the command in cell F6, which locks your entry into the current cell. Because cell F7 is blank, Quattro Pro ends the running of the macro at that point.

Because the actions of Quattro Pro's {MenuBranch} and /xm commands are identical, you can use them interchangeably within your Quattro Pro macros. The only difference between the macro above and one that uses the /xm command is the substitution of the command /xmMOVEIT~ for the {MenuBranch MOVEIT} command.

The {MenuCall} command. Unlike the {MenuBranch} and /xm commands, the {MenuCall} command routes the running of a macro back to the command that follows it after Quattro Pro executes the commands that correspond to whichever option you chose from the custom menu. Consequently, {Menu Call} is well suited for use in macros that access the same custom menu multiple times. In fact, you can use a {MenuCall} command to streamline the macro shown in Figure 13-3, as shown in Figure 13-5. As you can see, the {MenuBranch} command in cell B2 of this macro is replaced with the commands {MenuCall MOVEIT} and {Branch \n}, the {Branch \n} commands in cells B7..E7 are erased, and the command {Quit} is entered in cell F7.

Exactly like the {MenuBranch} command in cell B2 of the macro shown in Figure 13-3, the {MenuCall} command in cell B2 of this macro instructs Quattro Pro to display the custom menu shown in Figure 13-4. If you choose any of the first four options from this menu, Quattro Pro locks your entry into the current cell, and then moves the cell selector one cell in the indicated direction. For example, if you choose the Down option, Quattro Pro executes the {Down} command in cell B6, which locks your entry into the current cell and moves the cell selector down one cell.

As you can see, cells B7..E7 of this macro are blank. Because a {MenuCall} command was used to create the custom menu, Quattro Pro does not end the macro after moving the cell selector in the direction you indicate. Instead, Quattro Pro routes the macro back to the command that follows the {MenuCall} command, {Branch \n}. This command tells Quattro Pro to branch back to the beginning of the macro and run it again. Quattro Pro continues looping through this macro until you choose the Quit option from the custom menu. After you do so, Quattro Pro executes the command in cell F6, which locks your entry into the current cell, and then executes the command in cell F7, {Quit}, which cancels the running of

FIGURE 13-5.
This macro uses a {MenuCall} command to streamline the macro shown in Figure 13-3.

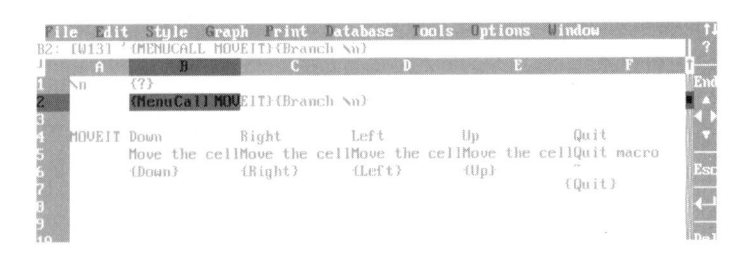

the macro. Without the {Quit} command, Quattro Pro routes the running of the macro back to the {Branch \n} command in cell B2, which, in turn, routes Quattro Pro back to the beginning of the macro.

Forcing the user to choose an option from a custom menu

If you press the Esc key instead of choosing an option from a custom menu, Quattro Pro routes the running of a macro to the command that follows the one that created the menu. If you use a {MenuBranch} or /xm command with no commands following it to create the menu, Quattro Pro ends the running of the macro at that point. For example, because the {MenuBranch} command in the macro shown in Figure 13-3 is the only command in cell B2, and because cell B3 is blank, Quattro Pro ends the running of that macro if you press the Esc key while viewing the custom menu created by that macro.

In many situations, you want to force the user of a macro to choose an option from a custom menu. You can do so by making Quattro Pro redisplay the custom menu if the user presses the Esc key instead of choosing an option; simply follow the {MenuBranch} command with a {Branch} command that routes the macro back to the {MenuBranch} command. However, if you do so, be sure to provide another way out of the macro; for example, by entering a {Quit} command at the end of each menu action.

Multiple-level custom menus

After you choose commands from many of Quattro Pro's menus, Quattro Pro presents another menu. For example, after you choose the File command from the main Quattro Pro menu, Quattro Pro presents a menu that contains 12 options. If you want, you can program Quattro Pro to create multiple-level custom menus. To do so, enter a menu-producing command in the cell below the one that contains the description for a choice on another menu. That way, Quattro Pro presents the custom menu referenced by that command after you choose the corresponding option from the previous menu.

Controlling the user interface using programming commands

Quattro Pro features six programming commands that allow you to control the user interface. These commands are called "system commands." Quattro Pro lists them after you choose the Screen option from the list that appears when you press the [Macros] key (Shift-F3). The following sections describe these six commands.

The {WindowsOff} and {WindowsOn} commands

The {WindowsOff} and {WindowsOn} commands control whether Quattro Pro updates the screen during the running of a macro. The {WindowsOff} command, which accepts no arguments, instructs Quattro Pro to freeze the window portion of the screen; the area below the top border of the worksheet. Freezing the screen means that Quattro Pro does not display any changes that the macro makes to the worksheet. For example, while the screen is frozen, you do not see the results of:

- Erase, move, or copy operations
- Making entries into the worksheet
- Moving the cell selector

Because Quattro Pro does not have to update the screen after each change when the screen is frozen, it is able to run a macro faster than when the screen is not frozen. Freezing the screen also eliminates the irritating flicker that is caused by the rapid execution of the commands in a macro.

After the window portion of the screen has been frozen by a {WindowsOff} command, it remains frozen until Quattro Pro cancels the running of the macro or encounters a {WindowsOn} command. After unfreezing the screen, Quattro Pro updates it. Consequently, after being unfrozen, the screen reflects the changes that Quattro Pro made to the worksheet while the screen was frozen. Because Quattro Pro unfreezes the screen at the end of a macro, you need not end your macros with a {WindowsOn} command. Use this command only to unfreeze the screen during the running of a macro. The form of this command is simply {WindowsOn}; it accepts no arguments.

Soliciting user input while the window area is frozen. Because the {WindowsOn} command freezes the window area of the screen, it should not be active when Quattro Pro executes a {?} command designed to allow the user to highlight a block or make an entry in a cell. If the screen is frozen when Quattro Pro executes a {?} command, the user cannot see the movement or expansion of the cell selector or what entry he or she has made in the current cell. To avoid these problems, precede the {?} command with a {WindowsOn} command.

The {PanelOff} and {PanelOn} commands

Exactly as the {WindowsOff} and {WindowsOn} commands freeze and unfreeze the window area of the screen, the {PanelOff} and {PanelOn} commands freeze and unfreeze the input line and menu areas of the screen. The {PanelOff} command, which accepts no arguments, instructs Quattro Pro to freeze the input line of the screen and prevent the display of menus. While a {PanelOff} command is in effect, Quattro Pro does not display the prompts that it normally displays in the input line. Instead, you see whatever was visible in that portion of the screen when Quattro Pro executed the {PanelOff} command. Also, Quattro Pro does not present menus when the macro chooses commands. Again, you see whatever was visible when Quattro Pro executed the {PanelOff} command.

After Quattro Pro executes a {PanelOff} command, the input line of the screen remains frozen until Quattro Pro reaches the end of the macro, cancels the running of the macro, or encounters a {PanelOn} command. When any of these situations occur, Quattro Pro unfreezes and updates the input line. Because Quattro Pro unfreezes the input line at the end of a macro, you need not end your macros with a {PanelOn} command. You will, however, need to use this command when you want to unfreeze the input line during the running of a macro after you execute a {PanelOff} command. The form of this command is simply {PanelOn}; it accepts no arguments.

Soliciting user input while the control panel is frozen. Because the {PanelOff} command freezes the input line and prevents menus from being displayed, it should not be active when Quattro Pro executes a {?} command that is designed to allow the user to type an entry, edit an entry, or choose an option from a Quattro Pro menu. If a {PanelOff} command is active in these situations, the user cannot to see what he or she is doing. To avoid these problems, precede the {?} command with a {PanelOn} command.

Fortunately, Quattro Pro's {GetNumber}, {GetLabel}, /xn, /xl, {MenuBranch}, /xm, and {MenuCall} commands override the {PanelOff} command. Even if Quattro Pro executes a {GetNumber}, {GetLabel}, /xn, or /xl command while a {PanelOff} command is active, the prompts for those commands and your responses to them appear in the control panel. Similarly, the custom menus produced by the {MenuBranch}, /xm, and {MenuCall} commands appear on the screen, and the highlight moves within them when you press the direction keys.

The {Beep} command

The {Beep} command instructs Quattro Pro to sound a tone of the pitch you specify. The form of this command is as follows:

{Beep *pitch*}

The *pitch* argument specifies the tone Quattro Pro sounds and is optional. If you specify an argument, however, it must be a literal value, a formula or function that returns a value, or the name or address of a cell that contains a value or a value-producing formula or function. The value 1 specifies a low tone, the value 2 a slightly higher tone, the value 3 an even higher tone, and the value 4 the highest tone. A {Beep} command without an argument produces the same tone as does a {Beep} command that includes 1 as the *pitch* argument.

The {Indicate} command

Quattro Pro's {Indicate} command allows you to replace the mode indicator (READY, EDIT, POINT, and so forth) with a custom message.

The form of this command is shown below:

{Indicate *message*}

The *message* argument is the message that you want Quattro Pro to place in the mode indicator, and must be a literal string. If you use a formula as the argument to an {Indicate} command, Quattro Pro treats it as a literal string. Quattro Pro can display only five characters of your custom message in this area of the screen. If the argument to an {Indicate} command contains more than five characters, Quattro Pro displays only the first five characters.

You'll typically want to replace the mode indicator with a message that tells the user what the macro is doing at the time. For example, you might want to display the message *SORT* while a macro is sorting a database, or display the name of the macro that Quattro Pro is currently running.

Restoring the mode indicator. Unfortunately, Quattro Pro does not clear the custom message produced by an {Indicate} command after ending the running of a macro. To clear this message, you must use a null {Indicate} command without an argument. When Quattro Pro executes a command of this sort, it clears the custom message from the screen, revealing the normal mode indicator. If you ever find a stray message obscuring the mode indicator after the running of the macro, you can clear it simply by creating and running a macro that consists only of a null {Indicate} command.

The {Message} command

The {Message} command lets you use pop-up messages in a macro. The following shows the form of the command:

{Message *location,left,top,dateandtime*}

The *location* argument is the block that is displayed inside the message box, and the *left* and *top* arguments specify how many characters from the left and top edges of the screen the upper-left corner of the message box should be. The *dateandtime* argument indicates when the message is removed.

For example, the one-line macro {Message A1..B15,15,5,@NOW+@TIME0,0,30)} displays the contents of the block A1..B15 just as you see it on the screen (cells A1..A15 on the first line and cells B1..B15 on the second line). The upper-left corner of the message box is located 15 characters from the left edge of the screen and 5 characters from the top edge. The message is displayed for 30 seconds. Note that if you set the *dateandtime* argument to 0, Quattro Pro displays the message until the user presses a key.

Controlling recalculation using programming commands

Quattro Pro features two programming commands that let you control recalculation: {Recalc} and {RecalcCol}. The basic forms of these commands are shown below:

{Recalc *location*}

{RecalcCol *location*}

The *location* argument is the name or address of the block that you want to recalculate. When executing either of these commands, Quattro Pro recalculates the formulas and functions in the block specified by the argument to that command. For example, the command {Recalc A1..B5} instructs Quattro Pro to recalculate the formulas and functions in cells A1..B5. The command {RecalcCol TEST} commands Quattro Pro to recalculate the formulas and functions in the block named TEST.

The difference between the {Recalc} and {RecalcCol} commands is the order in which they instruct Quattro Pro to recalculate the specified block. The {Recalc} command instructs Quattro Pro to recalculate the block one row at a time, starting with the top row of the block and working left to right across each row. The {RecalcCol} command, on the other hand, instructs Quattro Pro to recalculate the block column by column. For example, when executing the command {Recalc A1..B2}, Quattro Pro recalculates the cells in block A1..B2 in the following order: A1, B1, A2, and then B2. When executing the command {RecalcCol A1..B2}, however, Quattro Pro recalculates the cells in this order: A1, A2, B1, and then B2.

Potential problems with {Recalc} and {RecalcCol}

Because the {Recalc} and {RecalcCol} commands recalculate in order by rows or columns, they do not completely recalculate a block that contains forward references. As you recall, a forward reference is a reference to a cell that is not recalculated until after the cell containing the reference is recalculated. With the {Recalc} command, a forward reference is any reference to a cell in the same row and to the right of the cell that contains that reference (or to any cell in a row below the row that contains the reference). With the {RecalcCol} command, a forward reference is any reference to a cell in the same column and below the cell that contains that reference (or to any cell in a column to the right of the column that contains the reference).

In either case, Quattro Pro does not recalculate any formulas or functions outside the block specified by the {Recalc} or {RecalcCol} commands. Consequently, if your worksheet is set for Manual recalculation, some of the formulas and functions within the block specified by the {Recalc} or {RecalcCol} command might not return the correct answer. Remember that you can use the {Calc} function key macro name, which is equivalent to pressing the [Calc] key (F9).

Extra arguments for {Recalc} and {RecalcCol}

In most cases, you use the {Recalc} and {RecalcCol} commands in their basic form. If you want, however, you can embellish them with one or both of the extra arguments shown below:

{Recalc *location,condition,iterations*}

{RecalcCol *location,condition,iterations*}

These arguments tell Quattro Pro to recalculate the block specified by the {Recalc} or {RecalcCol} command more than one time, allowing you to resolve many forward and circular references. The first optional argument, *condition*, should be a conditional test (an expression that is either true or false) or a reference to a cell that contains a conditional test. If you include this argument in a {Recalc} or {RecalcCol} command, Quattro Pro continues to recalculate the specified block until the conditional test is true. For example, the command {Recalc TEST,A1-B1<.001} instructs Quattro Pro to recalculate the block named TEST until the difference between the values in cells A1 and B1 is less than .001. The second optional argument, *iterations*, is a value that specifies the number of times you want Quattro Pro to recalculate the block specified by *location*. Although you cannot use this argument without also including a *condition* argument, you can eliminate the effect of the *condition* argument by making it an expression that is always false, such as 1>2. For example, the command {RecalcCol TEMP,1>2,100} instructs Quattro Pro to recalculate the block named TEMP 100 times.

Using file input/output programming commands

In addition to its other programming commands, Quattro Pro features nine commands that allow you to write information to and read information from files during the running of a macro: {Open}, {SetPos}, {GetPos}, {FileSize}, {Read}, {ReadLn}, {Write}, {WriteLn}, and {Close}. These commands do not open or close files in the same sense that the commands in the File menu do. They do not load worksheet files onto the stack or close currently open worksheet files. Rather, you use them to input and output information to and from ASCII text files.

These commands appear after you choose the File I/O option from the list that Quattro Pro displays when you press the [Macros] key (Shift-F3). The following sections describe these nine commands.

The {Open} command

Quattro Pro's {Open} command opens the file specified by its filename argument. The form of this command is:

{Open *filename,mode*}

The *filename* argument is the name of the file you want to open, and the *mode* argument specifies the mode in which you want to access that file. The *filename* argument can be a literal string, a string-producing formula or function, or a reference to a cell that contains one of those types of entries. Unless the file that you want to access is in the current default directory, you must also specify the complete path to the file. Suppose, for example, that C:\QUATTRO\EXAMPLES is the current directory and that you want to open a file named STUFF.WQ1, which is stored in the C:\QUATTRO\OTHER directory. To do so, you can use the string C:\QUATTRO\OTHER\STUFF.WQ1 as the *filename* argument. In all cases, you must specify the file's name and extension (if any).

The second argument to the {Open} command, *mode*, determines what you can do with the file specified by the first argument. This argument must be one of the following: R, M, or W. It can be a literal string or a formula or function that returns one of these strings.

After Quattro Pro successfully executes an {Open} command, the file opened by that command remains open until Quattro Pro encounters a {Close} command, encounters another valid {Open} command, or ends the running of the macro.

The Read-only and Modify modes. The *mode* arguments R and M allow you to access existing files. The R argument opens the file in Read-only mode. While a file is open in this mode, you can read information from it but not write information to it. The M argument opens the file in the Modify mode. While a file is open in this mode, you can both read information from it and write information to it.

If Quattro Pro is able to locate the file specified by the *filename* argument and the command has either R or M as its second argument, it opens that file, skips any remaining commands in the cell that contains the {Open} command, and continues running the macro using the first command in the next cell. If unable to locate the file specified by the first argument to the {Open} command, Quattro Pro does not open that file. Instead, Quattro Pro executes any remaining commands in the cell that contains the {Open} command before executing the commands in the next cell(s) of the macro.

The Write mode. The W argument tells Quattro Pro to create a new file and assign it the name specified by the *filename* argument to the {Open} command. If a file with the same name already exists, Quattro Pro overwrites that file. You can both write information to and read information from the new file. As long as Quattro Pro is able to execute a {Write} command that has a second argument of W, it skips the remaining commands in the cell that contains the {Open} command and continues the running of the macro using the first command in the cell below that cell. If unable to execute the {Open} command, Quattro Pro executes the remaining commands in the cell that contains the command before executing the commands in the cells that follow it. Quattro Pro is unable to execute the {Open} command if the name or path specified by the *filename* argument to the {Open} command is invalid.

Controlling the file pointer

When a file is open, DOS uses a marker called a "file pointer" to keep track of its position within that file. After opening a file in Read-only, Modify, or Write mode, Quattro Pro places the file pointer at the beginning of that file. You can, however, move the file pointer around within the file easily. You can also determine the position of the file pointer within the file and calculate the size of the file. The following sections show you the commands that perform these tasks.

The {SetPos} command. Use the {SetPos} command when you want to move the file pointer around within an open file. The form of this command is as follows:

{SetPos *position*}

The *position* argument specifies the position to which you want to move the file pointer within the open file. This argument can be a literal value or a value-producing formula or function. Quattro Pro begins numbering the characters in a file with the number 0, not the number 1. Consequently, the command {SetPos 0} moves the file pointer to the beginning of the open file, the command {SetPos 1} moves the pointer to the second character in the file, and so forth. If the *position* argument is a value that exceeds the number of bytes in a file, Quattro Pro moves the file pointer immediately to the right of the final character in that file. Furthermore, if the *position* argument is a negative value or a label, Quattro Pro moves the file pointer to the first character in the open file. If no file is open when Quattro Pro executes a {SetPos} command, it ignores that command and executes any remaining commands in the cell that contains the {SetPos} command. If a file is open, Quattro Pro skips the commands that follow {SetPos} in the same cell.

The {GetPos} command. Quattro Pro's {GetPos} command finds the current position of the file pointer within an open file and enters that position in the cell specified by the command's argument. The form of this command is as follows:

{GetPos *location*}

The *location* argument is the name or address of a cell or block. If the *location* argument is the name or address of a single cell, Quattro Pro places the position of the file pointer in that cell. If the *location* argument is the name or address of a multiple-cell block, Quattro Pro enters the position of the file pointer in the upper-left cell of that block. Again, Quattro Pro begins numbering the positions of the characters in a file with the value 0. Consequently, if the file pointer is at the beginning of a file, the command {GetPos POS} enters the value 0 in the cell named POS. If the file pointer is on the fifth character in the file, Quattro Pro enters the value 4 in that cell. If no file is open when Quattro Pro executes a {GetPos} command or if the argument to the {GetPos} command is invalid, Quattro Pro skips the {GetPos} command and executes any remaining commands in the same cell as that command. Quattro Pro skips these commands if it is able to execute the {GetPos} command.

The {FileSize} command. Quattro Pro's {FileSize} command finds the size of the currently open file and enters it in the cell specified by the *location* argument. The form of this command is shown below:

{FileSize *location*}

The *location* argument is the name or address of a cell or block. If *location* specifies a single cell, Quattro Pro places the size of the open file (a value) in that cell. If *location* specifies a multiple-cell block, Quattro Pro enters the size of the open file in the upper-left cell of that block. As you would expect, the size of a file is the number of bytes stored in that file. Quattro Pro enters this count in the form of a value in the cell specified by the argument. For example, if the open file contains 545 bytes of information, the statement {FileSize SIZE} enters the value 545 in the cell named SIZE.

Ordinarily, Quattro Pro skips any commands that follow a {FileSize} command in the same cell that contains that command. If unable to execute a {FileSize} command, however, Quattro Pro executes those commands. Quattro Pro is unable to execute the command if it encounters {FileSize} when no file is open, or when the *location* argument is invalid.

Reading information from an open file

While a file is open in any mode, you can read information from it in the cells of the current worksheet. To do so, use the {Read} and {ReadLn} commands. The following sections show you how to use these commands to extract information from an open file.

The {Read} command. The {Read} command copies the number of characters specified by its first argument in the cell specified by its second argument, starting with the character on which the file pointer is currently positioned. The form of this command is shown below:

{Read *count,location*}

The *count* argument is a value or value-producing formula or function, and the *location* argument is the name or address of a cell or block. The *count* argument tells Quattro Pro how many characters to read from the open file. The *location* argument tells Quattro Pro where to store those characters. If *location* specifies a single cell, Quattro Pro enters the characters that it reads from the open file in that cell. If the location argument specifies a multiple-cell block, Quattro Pro enters the characters into the upper-left cell of that block. In either case, Quattro Pro enters the characters in the form of a label.

Because Quattro Pro allows a maximum of 254 characters in any cell, the *count* argument to any {Read} command should be 254 or less. If you specify a value greater than 254, Quattro Pro reads only 254 characters from the file. And, if the *count* argument specifies more characters than are between the current position of the file pointer and the end of the file, Quattro Pro reads only to the end of the file. After reading each character from an open file, Quattro Pro advances the file pointer to the next character in that file. Consequently, at the end of a {Read} operation, the file pointer is on the character following the last one that Quattro Pro read.

The {ReadLn} command. Like the {Read} command, the {ReadLn} command copies information from the open file into a worksheet cell. Unlike the {Read} command, however, which reads the number of characters you specify, {ReadLn} reads from the position of the file pointer until encountering a carriage return and line feed combination. The form of this command is as follows:

{ReadLn *location*}

The *location* argument is the name or address of a cell or block. If *location* specifies a single cell, Quattro Pro enters the characters it has read in that cell. If *location* specifies a multiple-cell block, Quattro Pro enters the characters into the upper-left cell of that block.

When encountering a {ReadLn} command in a macro, Quattro Pro begins reading characters, starting with the one on which the file pointer is currently positioned. Quattro Pro continues until it encounters a carriage return and line feed combination, until it has read 254 characters, or until it reaches the end of the file, whichever comes first. If Quattro Pro encounters a carriage return and line feed combination before reading 254 characters or reaching the end of the file, it enters the characters that it has read—but not the carriage return and line feed characters—in the cell specified by the *location* argument. After Quattro Pro completes this command, the file pointer is positioned on the character that follows the line feed character. If Quattro Pro reads 254 characters without encountering a carriage return and line feed combination or the end of the file, it enters those characters in the specified cell and then ends the command. And, if Quattro Pro encounters the end of the file before encountering a carriage return and line feed combination or reading 254 characters from the file, it enters the characters that it has read and then ends the command.

Quattro Pro ordinarily skips any commands that follow a {Read} or {ReadLn} command in the same cell that contains that command. Quattro Pro executes those commands, however, if it is unable to execute the {Read} or {ReadLn} command that precedes them. Quattro Pro is unable to execute the command if it encounters {Read} or {ReadLn} when no file is open or when the *location* argument specifies an invalid block.

Writing information to an open file

While a file is open in either the Modify or Write modes, you can use the {Write} and {WriteLn} commands to write information to that file. This section explains the forms and actions of these two commands.

The {Write} command. Quattro Pro's {Write} command writes the characters specified by its argument in the open file, starting at the current position of the file pointer. The form of this command is shown below:

{Write *string*}

The *string* argument is a literal string or a string-producing formula or function. For example, {Write This is a test.} is a valid command, as is {Write TEST}, if TEST is the name of the cell that contains a label or a string-producing formula or function. It's not necessary to enclose a string in quotation marks unless the string contains the argument separator or is the name of a block.

When executing a {Write} command, Quattro Pro writes the string specified by its argument in the open file, starting at the position of the file pointer. Unless the file pointer is at the end of the file, the characters that Quattro Pro writes in that file overwrite existing characters in the file. At the end of the {Write} operation, the file pointer is positioned immediately after the last character that was written to the file. Quattro Pro can write a maximum of 254 characters to any file using a single {Write} command.

The {WriteLn} command. You also can use the {WriteLn} command to write information to an open file. The form of this command is shown below:

{WriteLn *string*}

The *string* argument is a literal string or a string-producing formula or function. It's not necessary to enclose a string in quotation marks unless it contains the argument separator or is the name of a block. When executing a {WriteLn} command, Quattro Pro writes the string specified by the argument to that command to the open file, starting at the position of the file pointer. Quattro Pro then writes a carriage return and a line feed. At the end of the {WriteLn} operation, the file pointer is positioned immediately after the line feed character. If the file pointer is positioned anywhere other than at the end of the file when Quattro Pro executes the {WriteLn} command, the characters that Quattro Pro writes to the file overwrite existing characters in the file. Quattro Pro can write a maximum of 254 characters to any file using a single {WriteLn} command.

Quattro Pro ordinarily skips any commands that follow a {Write} or {WriteLn} command in the same cell that contains that command. Quattro Pro executes those commands, however, if it is unable to execute the {Write} or {WriteLn} command that precedes them. Quattro Pro is unable execute the command if it encounters {Write} or {WriteLn} when no file is open or when the argument to the command returns a value.

Closing an open file

When encountering a {Close} command in a macro, Quatto Pro immediately closes whatever file is currently open. The form of this command is simply {Close}; it accepts no arguments. If no file is open when Quattro Pro reads a {Close} command, it skips that command. Quattro Pro never executes commands that follow the {Close} command in a cell, even if unable to execute the {Close} command. If Quattro Pro encounters an {Open} command while another file is open, it closes the open file; this situation occurs even if Quattro Pro is not able to open the file specified by the new {Open} command.

When ending the running of a macro, Quattro Pro closes any file that is currently open at the time. Consequently, you need not end a macro with a {Close} command unless you want to do so. In fact, the only time you might want to include a {Close} command is when you open a file and work with it only near the beginning of a long macro. If your computer crashes or is rebooted before Quattro Pro completes the running of the macro, the file you accessed is unusable unless you used a {Close} command to close it beforehand.

Advanced macro techniques

In Chapter 12, "Macro Basics," you saw how to record, write, and debug macros. In this chapter, you've explored each of Quattro Pro's programming commands. Before leaving the topic, however, you might want to look at two additional topics: self-modifying macros and calculated macro statements.

Self-modifying macros

As explained in Chapter 12, "Macro Basics," the commands in a Quattro Pro macro are simply label entries in the cells of a worksheet. In most cases, all of the cells in your macros contain one or more commands before you execute them. In some cases, however, you might leave cells blank and let the macro fill them in during the course of its running. The entries are usually the result of a {GetNumber}, {GetLabel}, or {Let} command. As long as the entries are valid macro commands, Quattro Pro executes them as soon as it reaches the cells in which they are entered.

The macro shown in Figure 13-6 uses this technique. This macro sets the global column width to the value you specify. The first command, {GetNumber"Global column width? ",WIDTH}, instructs Quattro Pro to present the prompt

FIGURE 13-6.
This example shows a self-modifying macro.

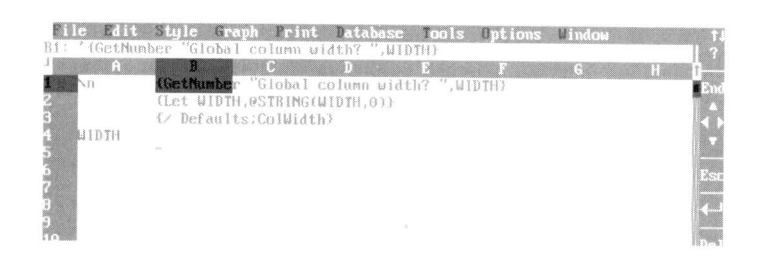

```
B1: '{GetNumber "Global column width? ",WIDTH}
      A        B            C            D          E       F       G      H
1              {GetNumber "Global column width? ",WIDTH}
2              {Let WIDTH,@STRING(WIDTH,0)}
3              {/ Defaults;ColWidth}
4     WIDTH
```

Global column width? at the top of the screen. In response, type the width you want Quattro Pro to assign to all the columns in the worksheet, and then press the Enter key. Quattro Pro then enters the value you typed in the cell named WIDTH (B4). For example, if you type 15, Quattro Pro enters the value 15 in cell B4.

The next command in this macro, {Let WIDTH,@STRING(WIDTH,0)}, converts the value in WIDTH to a label. For example, if WIDTH contains the value 15, this command replaces it with the label '15. Because macro commands must be labels, this step is crucial to the successful execution of the remainder of this macro.

The third command in this macro, {/ Defaults;ColWidth}, instructs Quattro Pro to choose the Column Set Global command. Because this is the last (in fact, the only) command in cell B3, Quattro Pro will look to cell B4 (WIDTH) for the next command. Although this cell was blank when the macro began, at this point it contains the label form of the width you specified. Consequently, Quattro Pro enters that width in response to the prompt. For example, if WIDTH contains the label '15, Quattro Pro enters the digits 15. Because these digits are the only characters in cell B4, Quattro Pro then looks to cell B5. The single command in this cell, ~, instructs Quattro Pro to press the Enter key. Doing so completes the command, changing the global column width to the width you specified.

Calculated macro statements

As an alternative to the self-modifying technique described above, you can use calculated macro statements. Although the statements in your macros are usually labels, they can be formulas and functions that, when recalculated, return strings. As long as the string results of these formulas and functions are valid macro statements, Quattro Pro executes them in the same way it would if they were part of a label.

Use the macro shown in Figure 13-7 to demonstrate the use of a calculated macro statement. This macro achieves the same result as the one shown in Figure 13-6; it sets the global column width to the value you specify. This macro, however, uses a calculated macro statement instead of modifying itself.

The first command in this macro, {GetNumber"Global column width?5", WIDTH}, solicits a value from the user. After the user types a value and presses

FIGURE 13-7.
This macro demonstrates the use of a calculated macro statement.

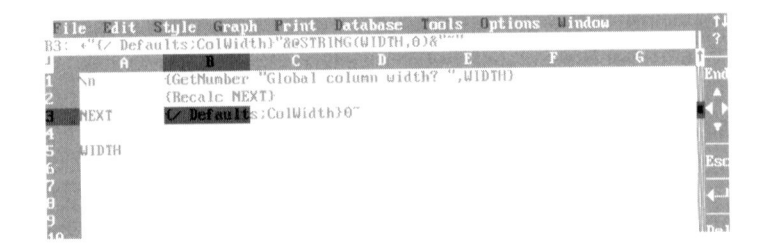

the Enter key, Quattro Pro enters that value in the cell named WIDTH (in this case, cell B5). For example, if the user types 20, Quattro Pro enters the value 20 in this cell.

The next statement in this macro, {Recalc NEXT}, tells Quattro Pro to recalculate the formula in the cell named NEXT (in this case, cell B3 is the next cell in the macro). When recalculated, the formula in this cell, shown below, returns a macro command that instructs Quattro Pro to set the global column width to the value contained in WIDTH:

+"{/ Defaults;Colwidth}"&@STRING(WIDTH,0)&"~"

This formula tells Quattro Pro to concatenate the string "{/ Defaults; Colwidth}" with the string form of WIDTH and the ~ character. For example, if WIDTH contained the value 20 when Quattro Pro recalculated this formula, it would return the string {/ Defaults;ColWidth}20~. Because the {Recalc} command is the final one in cell B2, and because the next cell in this macro contains the formula that Quattro Pro just recalculated, Quattro Pro next executes the result of that formula. When Quattro Pro does so it sets the global column width to the width you entered in response to the {GetNumber} command. Then, because cell B4 is blank, Quattro Pro ends the running of the macro.

Appendix A

Exchanging Data with Other Programs

The vast majority of PC users use more than one software program. Most use a spreadsheet (such as Quattro Pro) and a word processor, as well as database and other software. As a result, one of the most significant concerns users have is file compatibility; everyone wants to use files created with one application in other applications. Fortunately, Quattro Pro can read and write data files that are compatible with many of the most popular PC applications and can exchange files with several popular database packages. It can also import and export ASCII data that can be used by most word processors. Quattro Pro can read and write files in Lotus 1-2-3 format.

Importing data

One of Quattro Pro's unique features is its ability to import files created by Lotus 1-2-3, Symphony, dBASE, Paradox, and Reflex. The heart of this capability is the File Retrieve command in combination with a filename extension. For example, if you use the File Retrieve or File Open command to open a file that has the extension

.WK1, Quattro Pro assumes that it is a Lotus 1-2-3 version 2 worksheet and translates the data found in that file to Quattro Pro format as it is opened.

Quattro Pro can also import ASCII files created by word processors, such as Borland's Sprint or Microsoft Word. The following sections show you how to import ASCII files and those files created by each of the applications mentioned above. Along the way, you'll learn about compatibility issues that might arise when Quattro Pro imports a particular file.

Importing Lotus 1-2-3 worksheets into Quattro Pro

You can open worksheets created in Lotus 1-2-3 versions 1A, 2, and in the educational version directly in Quattro Pro by choosing the File Retrieve or File Open command and specifying the name of the 1-2-3 file. Quattro Pro imports the 1-2-3 file, making the adjustments that are necessary. Quattro Pro translates all of the settings associated with that worksheet to the equivalent Quattro Pro settings, including graph settings and block names. All formulas and functions in the 1-2-3 worksheet are also imported correctly.

To execute a Lotus 1-2-3 macro in an imported Lotus 1-2-3 worksheet, you must run Quattro Pro using the Lotus 1-2-3 menu tree. Otherwise, the menu commands that the 1-2-3 macro uses do not match the commands in the Quattro Pro menu. You'll read about how to switch menu trees in Appendix B, "Customizing Quattro Pro," where 1-2-3 macro compatibility is also discussed.

Importing Lotus Symphony worksheets into Quattro Pro

The process of importing a worksheet created by Lotus Development Corporation's Symphony is automatic and transparent. To import a .WRK file created by Symphony version 1.2, or a .WR1 file created by version 2.0, choose the File Retrieve command and specify the name of the Symphony file. Quattro Pro then imports the Symphony file. Quattro Pro translates all of the settings associated with that worksheet to the equivalent Quattro Pro settings.

The Symphony menu structure is different from both the Quattro Pro and 1-2-3 menu trees. Therefore, you cannot use Symphony macros in Quattro Pro unless you use the Menu Builder add-in to modify the Quattro Pro menu structure so that it emulates the Symphony menu structure, as described in "Startup Defaults" in Appendix B.

Importing dBASE worksheets into Quattro Pro

To import a file created by dBASE II (.DB2) or a file created by dBASE III, dBASE III Plus, or dBASE IV (.DBF) into Quattro Pro, choose the File Retrieve command, press the Esc key to clear the edit line, type the name and extension of the dBASE file, and then press the Enter key. Quattro Pro translates the dBASE file into a Quattro Pro database.

Quattro Pro uses the data type, width, and decimal settings of fields in the dBASE database to set the display formats and column widths of the columns in the Quattro Pro worksheet. The entries from each of the fields of the dBASE database become columns in the worksheet, and the records from the dBASE database become rows. The field names from the dBASE database appear as column headings in the Quattro Pro worksheet.

Importing Paradox worksheets into Quattro Pro

Quattro Pro can also import files from Paradox, Borland's own PC database manager. To import a Paradox database, choose the File Retrieve command, press the Esc key to clear the edit line, type the name of the file (including the .DB file extension), and then press the Enter key. Quattro Pro then translates the Paradox file into a Quattro Pro database. Quattro Pro uses the field type and width of fields in the Paradox database to set the display formats and column widths of the columns in the Quattro Pro worksheet. The fields of the Paradox database become columns in the Quattro Pro worksheet, and the records from the Paradox database become rows. The field names from the Paradox database appear as column headings in the Quattro Pro worksheet.

Importing Reflex worksheets into Quattro Pro

Quattro Pro also has the ability to import files from Reflex; the Analyst version 1 (.RXD) and version 2 (.R2D). To import a Reflex file into Quattro Pro, choose the File Retrieve command, press the Esc key to clear the edit line, type the name and extension of the Reflex file, and press the Enter key. Quattro Pro translates the Reflex file into a Quattro Pro database. Quattro Pro uses the field types and formats of fields in the Reflex database to set the formats of the columns in the Quattro Pro worksheet. The fields of the Reflex database become columns, and the records become rows. The field names from the Reflex database appear as column headings in row 1 of the worksheet. Quattro Pro recognizes the types and the formats of the entries in the fields of the Reflex database.

Importing text files into Quattro Pro

Quattro Pro can import data from any ASCII text file, which is a file that contains only the ASCII codes 9 (Tab), 10 (Linefeed), 13 (Carriage Return), and 32 through 127 (the alphabetic, numeric, and punctuation characters you can type from your keyboard). Quattro Pro's ability to read ASCII files is particularly handy if you need to use data created by a word processor or downloaded from an on-line information service.

FIGURE A-1.
You can import unformatted and delimited text files.

```
ASCII Text File
Comma & "" Delimited File
Only Commas
```

To import an ASCII file into Quattro Pro, first move the cell selector to the spot on the worksheet in which you want the data to be placed, and choose the Tools Import command. Quattro Pro presents a menu that has three options, as shown in Figure A-1: ASCII Text File, Comma & "" Delimited File, and Only Commas. The ASCII Text File option allows you to import a plain ASCII text file into Quattro Pro. The Comma & "" Delimited File option lets you import a text file delimited by commas and quotation marks, and the Only Commas File option lets you import a text file delimited by commas, with quotation marks optional. The appropriate option depends on the format of the file you want to import. You can usually find this format information in the documentation that describes the program that created the text file.

Importing ASCII files into Quattro Pro

When you import a text file into Quattro Pro using the ASCII Text File option, Quattro Pro treats each line ending with a carriage return and line feed in the file as a single label and stores it in a separate row of the worksheet. After you choose this option, Quattro Pro displays a list of files stored in the data directory that have the extension .PRN (the extension often given to ASCII text files). Choose the name of the file you want to import, or, if the file you want to import does not appear in this list, type its name at the prompt and press the Enter key. Quattro Pro places the file in the worksheet at the point marked by the cell selector.

Parsing to divide long labels

The Tools Parse command lets you divide long labels, like those that result from importing a file using the Tools Import ASCII Text File command, into separate labels and value entries. After you choose the Tools Parse command, Quattro Pro presents the menu shown in Figure A-2. Use the options in this menu to create a format line, and then use that line to parse the labels.

To parse a set of labels, first create a format line by moving the cell selector to the first cell that contains a label you want to parse, and choose the Tools Parse Create command. Quattro Pro creates and inserts a format line in the row above the row that contains the cell selector. The format line begins with the pipe symbol (|), as shown in Figure A-4. The other symbols that appear in the line represent Quattro Pro's best guess at the divisions you'll want to make in the labels when you parse them. Table A-1 lists the characters that can appear in a format line.

FIGURE A-2.
After you choose the Tools Parse command you see this menu.

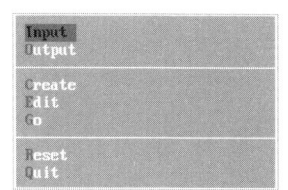

After you create a format line, choose the Tools Parse Edit command to modify the format line so that it defines the proper divisions for the label you want to parse. Quattro Pro then places the cell selector at the beginning of the active format line, and you can use the standard edit keys to insert or delete any of the characters listed in Table A-1. Continue to make changes until the format line indicates the divisions you want Quattro Pro to make in the labels when parsing them. Press the Enter key to return to the Tools Parse menu.

After you are satisfied with the format line, use the Tools Parse Input command to mark the block of data that you want to parse. The first row in this block must contain the format line you have defined. The block should also include one or more rows that contain the labels you want to parse.

Next use the Tools Parse Output command to choose the area of the worksheet in which Quattro Pro should place the parsed data; you can choose any area of the worksheet, including the area presently occupied by the input block. If the output block and input block are identical, Quattro Pro overwrites the long labels with the parsed entries.

After you define an output block, you are ready to parse the Input block. To do so, choose the Tools Parse Go command.

If you want to change the input or output blocks that you have defined, you can clear them by choosing the Tools Parse Reset command.

Symbol	Meaning
¦	Represents the first character in every format line
V	Indicates the starting position of a numeric block
L	Indicates the starting position of a label block
T	Indicates the starting position of a time block
D	Indicates the starting position of a date block
>	Marks space occupied by an entry
*	Represents a blank
S	Marks a character that should be skipped (deleted)

TABLE A-1. *This table lists the format characters that can appear on a format line.*

FIGURE A-3.
This worksheet shows a group of long labels in column A, which you parse into separate columns.

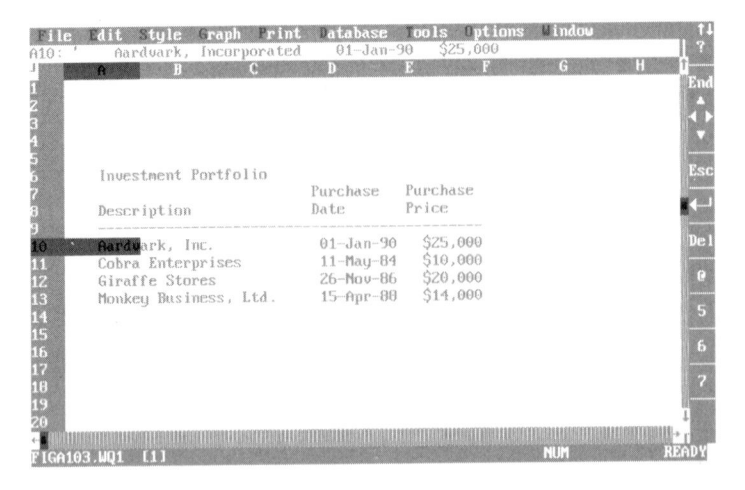

FIGURE A-4.
The format line in cell A10 describes the labels stored in cells A11..A14.

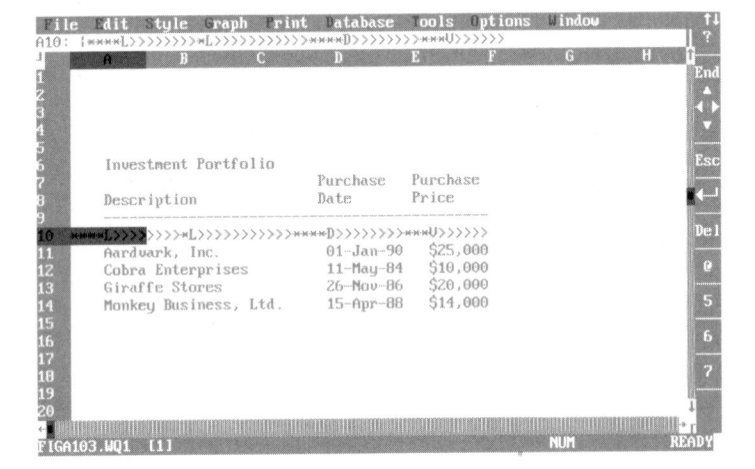

An example of parsing labels

Use the Tools Parse command to split the labels stored in cells A10..A13 in the worksheet shown in Figure A-3 into separate label and value entries. To begin, move the cell selector to cell A10, and then choose the Tools Parse Create command, which creates the format line shown in Figure A-4. Notice that this line appears in row 10 and that the labels are shifted down one row. Also notice that the format line Quattro Pro has created describes the data contained in the label in cell A11. Because the labels stored in the block A12..A14 are essentially identical to the label in cell A11, the format line also describes them.

As mentioned earlier, format lines are templates that describe the format of the data within a label or a series of labels. For example, the format line in cell A10 of the worksheet shown in Figure A-4 contains symbols that describe the labels in cells A11..A14. The * symbols indicate a blank space, L marks the beginning of a label block, the > symbols each represent one character within a block, D represents the start of a date block, and V shows the start of a value block. Therefore, if the label stored in cell A11 is parsed using the format line in cell A10, the result would be the two separate labels 'Aardvark, and 'Inc., a date value (January 1, 1990), and an integer (25000).

Most of the time, the default format line that Quattro Pro creates when you choose the Tools Parse Create command breaks a piece of text into the appropriate labels and values. If the format line is not correct, however, you can choose the Tools Parse Edit command to change it.

After you choose this command, Quattro Pro places the cursor at the beginning of the format line. (In Figure A-4, this position is the first character in cell A10.) Use the direction keys to move the cursor to the portion of the format line that's incorrect and replace the incorrect symbol with the correct one. In this case, Quattro Pro suggests breaking Aardvark, Inc. into two separate labels, which is incorrect. Delete the *L that appears above Inc. so that Aardvark, Inc. is parsed as a single label. When the format line is correct, choose the Input option from the Parse menu, and select the block that should be parsed; A11..A14 as shown in Figure A-4. Then, choose the Output option from the Tools Parse menu, and again choose A11..A14 so that the parsed entries replace the unparsed labels, and press the Enter key. Finally, to parse the data defined within the input block using the format line stored in cell A10, choose the Go option. Figure A-5 shows the result.

As you can see in Figure A-5, information from cells A11..A14 has been divided into three columns. Column A contains the descriptions from the original labels. Notice that the leading blanks have been deleted. Column B contains the date values from the original labels. Notice that they have been converted into date values. Similarly, column C contains the purchase prices, converted into integer

FIGURE A-5.
Quattro Pro used the format line in cell A10 to parse the labels in cells A11..A14.

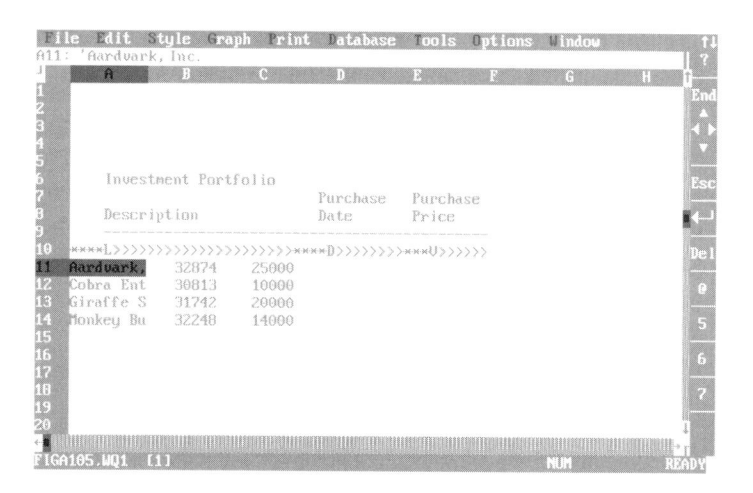

values. It is now possible to use formulas or functions to act on the values in columns B and C. To remove the format line, choose the Edit Delete Rows command, select cell A10, and press the Enter key.

Delimited files

You can use the Tools Import Comma & "" Delimited File command and the Tools Import Only Commas Command to import files that contain information that is delimited, or separated, by commas and quotation marks. Some programs, such as dBASE, have the ability to create delimited files. After you choose this option, Quattro Pro uses the commas in the file to divide each line of the file into the cells in one row of the worksheet. If you use the Tools Import Comma & "" Delimited File command, any text that is enclosed in quotation marks is imported as a label, any numbers are imported as values, and any text that is not enclosed in quotation marks is not imported.

If you use the Tools Import Only Commas command, any text in the file is imported as a label (whether or not it is in quotation marks), and any numbers are imported as values. After you choose either command, Quattro Pro displays a list of files stored in the data directory that have the extension .PRN. Choose the name of the file you want to import from this list, or, if the file you want does not appear in this list, type its name at the prompt and press the Enter key. Quattro Pro places the file in the worksheet at the point marked by the cell selector. Quattro Pro puts each line from the imported file into a separate worksheet row and each field within a line into a separate cell.

Exporting data

Exactly as Quattro Pro can import data from files created by other programs, it can also export data in formats that can be read by Lotus 1-2-3, Symphony, dBASE, Paradox, and Reflex, as well as in an ASCII format that most popular word processing packages can use.

Exporting data to Lotus 1-2-3

To save a Quattro Pro worksheet in a format that Lotus 1-2-3 can use, all you have to do is save the worksheet with the proper file extension. To save a worksheet in the .WKS format used by Lotus 1-2-3 version 1A, choose the File Save As command and save the worksheet with the filename extension .WKS. Likewise, to save a worksheet in the .WK1 format used by version 2, choose the File Save As command and save the worksheet with the filename extension .WK1.

Lotus 1-2-3 and Quattro Pro compatibility issues

The following sections point out the incompatibilities that might crop up when you try to use a Quattro Pro worksheet in Lotus 1-2-3. You'll find solutions or advice concerning each incompatibility.

Macros and compatibility. The only Quattro Pro macros that work properly in Lotus 1-2-3 are those that you created using keystroke-equivalent commands. Although you can export worksheets that contain command-equivalent macro commands, you cannot use those macros in 1-2-3. For more information, see Appendix B, "Customizing Quattro Pro."

Functions and compatibility. Lotus 1-2-3 offers many of the functions Quattro Pro supports. Some functions, however, are unique to Quattro Pro. After you export a Quattro Pro worksheet that contains one of these functions, the function is converted to a label. For example, if a cell in your Quattro Pro worksheet contains the function @FVAL, which 1-2-3 does not support, that same cell in the 1-2-3 worksheet contains the label '@FVAL.

In some cases, you might be able to use a 1-2-3 function to emulate a Quattro Pro function that 1-2-3 does not support. For example, neither versions 1A nor 2 of 1-2-3 supports Quattro Pro's @TODAY function. Therefore, this function is treated as a label after a Quattro Pro worksheet is saved in .WK1 or .WKS format. Because 1-2-3's @NOW function is quite similar to the @TODAY function, however, it is possible to manually substitute @NOW for @TODAY. Unfortunately, you'll find no quick and easy way to overcome the problems created by Quattro Pro functions that are not supported by 1-2-3. Therefore, if you use a large number of functions specific to Quattro Pro in your worksheets, expect to run into difficulty when exporting the worksheets to Lotus 1-2-3.

Worksheet size and compatibility. Lotus 1-2-3 version 1A worksheets are limited to 256 columns and 2048 rows. If you export a Quattro Pro worksheet that contains entries in rows below 2048 into a Lotus 1-2-3 version 1A file, you will see the message *Worksheet full* after you try to open the file in 1-2-3. The only way to avoid this problem is to change your worksheets in Quattro Pro so that they do not contain any entries below row 2048.

Memory allocation and compatibility. You should be able to open most worksheets that you have created in Quattro Pro in Lotus 1-2-3 version 2. Because 1-2-3 version 1A uses a different (and less efficient) memory management scheme than Quattro Pro or 1-2-3 version 2, however, you might not be able to open all Quattro Pro worksheets in 1-2-3 version 1A. Both versions of 1-2-3 display the message *Memory Full* if you attempt to load a worksheet that does not fit into available memory.

You can, in many cases, overcome the memory limitations of 1-2-3 version 1A by reworking your worksheet within Quattro Pro before saving it in the Lotus format. To do so, change your worksheet so that all of the entries are as close as possible to the upper-left corner of the worksheet. It's also important to limit the number of blank rows and columns in the worksheet.

Finally, if you are not able to import an entire Quattro Pro worksheet into 1-2-3 version 1A because of a lack of memory, use Quattro Pro's Tools Xtract command to save smaller portions of the worksheet as .WKS files, and open smaller portions in version 1A.

Special characters and compatibility. If your Quattro Pro worksheet contains any special characters, such as the currency symbols £ and ¥, those characters are not translated properly when the worksheet is written to .WKS or .WK1 format. After you open the exported worksheet in Lotus 1-2-3, you have to translate those characters manually to the appropriate Lotus International Character Set (LICS) character. Appendix C, "Using Special Characters," gives a more detailed explanation of how to use special characters in Quattro Pro.

Exporting data to Symphony

To save a worksheet in the .WRK format of Symphony version 1.2, save the file by choosing the File Save As command and using the extension .WRK. Likewise, to save a worksheet in the .WR1 format of Symphony 2.0, save the file by choosing the File Save As command and using the extension .WR1.

Symphony and Quattro Pro compatibility issues

You need to be aware of a number of incompatibilities when you export Quattro Pro files to Symphony. The following sections point out the incompatibilities and offer a solution or advice concerning each incompatibility.

Macros and compatibility. Because Symphony's command structure is completely different from that of Quattro Pro (and from that of Lotus 1-2-3), most Quattro Pro macros do not work properly in Symphony. If the macro includes only command-language commands, such as {Branch} and {Let}, and keystroke representations such as {GoTo}, the macro might work in Symphony.

Functions and compatibility. Symphony offers most of the same functions as Quattro Pro. Quattro Pro, however, offers a few functions that are not found in Symphony. After you export a Quattro Pro worksheet that contains one of these functions, the function is converted to a label. For example, if a cell in your Quattro Pro worksheet contains the function @FVAL, which is not supported by Symphony, that same cell in the Symphony worksheet contains the label '@FVAL.

Memory allocation and compatibility. Symphony 1.1 and later versions should be able to open most worksheets that you have created in Quattro Pro. Because Symphony 1.0 uses a different (and less efficient) memory management scheme than does Quattro Pro, however, you might not be able to open all Quattro Pro worksheets in Symphony 1.0. Either version of Symphony displays the message *Memory Full* if you try to open a worksheet that does not fit into available memory.

You can often overcome Symphony's memory limitations by reworking your worksheet within Quattro Pro before saving it in .WRK format. To overcome this limitation, change your worksheet so that all of the entries are as close as possible to the upper-left corner of the worksheet. It's also important to limit the number of blank rows and columns in the worksheet.

Special characters and compatibility. If your Quattro Pro worksheet contains any special characters, such as the currency symbols £ and ¥, those characters are not translated properly when the worksheet is written to .WRK or .WR1 format. After you open the exported worksheet in Symphony, you have to translate those characters manually to the appropriate Lotus International Character Set (LICS) character. Appendix C, "Using Special Characters," gives a more detailed explanation of how to use special characters in Quattro Pro.

Exporting data to dBASE

If you use a Quattro Pro database to manage lists of data, at some point you might need to export information to Ashton-Tate's dBASE. (For more information on the structure of Quattro Pro databases, see Chapter 11, "Database Management.") If the Quattro Pro worksheet you are saving contains only a database, and the field names for the database are in row 1, you can save the entire worksheet as a dBASE file. To do so, choose the File Save As command and save the worksheet with the appropriate filename extension: .DB2 for dBASE II and .DBF for dBASE III, dBASE III Plus, and dBASE IV. If the worksheet also contains other information, choose the Tools Xtract command and save only the portion of the worksheet that contains the database in a file with the proper filename extension.

After you choose either command and specify a filename and an extension, Quattro Pro presents the menu shown in Figure A-6. The first option in this menu,

FIGURE A-6.
This menu lets you change the structure of a Quattro Pro database before you export it to dBASE.

View Structure, lets you view and change the structure of the database that Quattro Pro will create from your worksheet. You can delete fields or change their names, widths, and type settings and then choose the Write dBASE File option to save the database on disk.

Key concepts of exporting to dBASE

When you save a Quattro Pro worksheet in dBASE format, Quattro Pro treats each column that contains data as a field. If the first cell in a column contains a label, as is usual, that label is used as a field name for that column. Otherwise, the column letter for the column is used as a field name. (You will see how to change the names that Quattro Pro assigns to fields in a later section.) If any of the labels in the first row contain spaces, Quattro Pro substitutes an underline character for the space because spaces and periods are not allowed in dBASE field names.

Quattro Pro uses the entries in each column (field) of a Quattro Pro worksheet to determine the field types of the fields in the dBASE database. For example, if a column of data in a Quattro Pro worksheet contains only character data, Quattro Pro makes that field a Character field in the dBASE file. If a column contains only numbers, the corresponding field in the dBASE database becomes a Numeric field. On the other hand, if a column contains a combination of data types, it is treated as a Character field when in dBASE format. As a result, you might in some cases find it necessary to specify a field's data type manually, which you'll see how to do shortly.

Quattro Pro also uses the entries in the columns of the Quattro Pro worksheet to determine the widths of the fields in the dBASE database. For example, the width of a Character field is determined by the width of the widest entry in a column that contains character data. On the other hand, the width of a Numeric field is determined by the format of the numeric data that is stored in a column. The width of Date fields is fixed. As you will see in a later section, it's possible to change the widths of Character and Numeric fields manually.

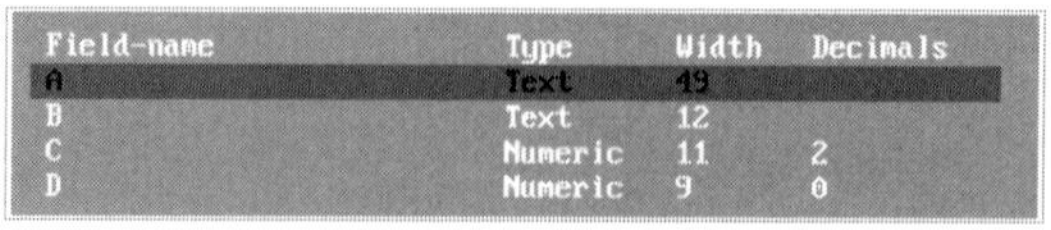

FIGURE A-7.
If you choose the View Structure option you see this menu.

Field-name	Type	Width	Decimals
A	Text	49	
B	Text	12	
C	Numeric	11	2
D	Numeric	9	0

FIGURE A-8.
The Field menu lets you change the name or type of the field.

FIGURE A-9.
The Field Type menu lets you specify what a field contains.

Changing the structure of a Quattro Pro database exported to dBASE

If you choose the View Structure option from the menu shown in Figure A-6, Quattro Pro displays a structure window like the one shown in Figure A-7. This window shows the structure of the database that Quattro Pro creates when the worksheet is saved with a .DBF or .DB2 extension.

While the structure window is in view, you can move through the list of fields by pressing the Down and Up direction keys. You can also change the structure of the database by highlighting a field and then pressing the Enter key. After you do so, Quattro Pro presents the menu shown in Figure A-8. You can use the options in this menu to change the name and type of field. To change the type, choose Type from the menu and Quattro Pro presents a submenu, shown in Figure A-9, which lets you specify whether a field should be a text, numeric, logical, or date field.

Changing a field's name. After you instruct Quattro Pro to save a file in dBASE format, Quattro Pro uses the labels in the first row of the worksheet (or the first row of the block you are extracting) as field names. To change the name that Quattro Pro has assigned to a field, highlight that field in the structure window, press the Enter key, and then choose the Name option from the menu shown in Figure A-8. Quattro Pro then prompts you for a new name; type the new name and press the Enter key. The name you type must conform to all of the rules for dBASE field names.

Changing a field's type. When you instruct Quattro Pro to save a file in dBASE format, Quattro Pro selects an appropriate data type based on the data that it finds in a particular column. dBASE supports four different field types: Character, Numeric, Date, and Logical. To change the data type that Quattro Pro has assigned to a field, highlight that field in the structure window, press the Enter key, and then choose the Type option from the menu shown in Figure A-8. Quattro

Pro then presents the menu shown in Figure A-9. If you choose the Text or Numeric option as the new field type, Quattro Pro prompts you to enter a field width. Press the Enter key to accept the default width, or type a new width. If you choose the Numeric field type, Quattro Pro first prompts you for the field width and then prompts you to specify the number of decimal places that should be reserved within the field. Press the Enter key to accept the default, which is 0, or type a new number, and then press the Enter key.

If you change a field's type to Numeric, you tell Quattro Pro not to save any character data that might exist in the worksheet column that corresponds to that field. As a result, zeros are placed in fields that contain non-numeric data. If you change a field's type to Date, Quattro Pro replaces any character data in the field with the null date 01/01/00 and converts numeric values to date values. For example, if the value 12345 appears in a field whose data type has been specified as Date, it is saved on disk as 10/18/33. Finally, if you change a field's type to Logical, any non-numeric data in the field is replaced with the character ?, every 0 in the field is replaced with the character F, and every value other than 0 is replaced with the character T.

Deleting a field. To delete a field, highlight that field in the structure window, and press the Delete key. Quattro Pro places asterisks in the structure window next to the field name. Fields marked with an asterisk are not saved.

If, after deleting a field, you decide you do want to include it in a file after all, highlight the field name with the cell selector, and then press the Delete key again. Doing so removes the asterisk, and the field is saved when you save the file on disk.

Exporting a file to dBASE

After you have made any necessary changes to the structure of a file, you're ready to export it. To do so, choose the Write dBASE File option from the dBASE III File Save menu. Quattro Pro creates a dBASE database from your Quattro Pro worksheet with the structure you've defined.

A closer look at exporting to dBASE. After you save a Quattro Pro file on disk in dBASE format, only the current values of any formulas or functions in the worksheet are saved, and not the formulas or functions themselves. The formulas or functions that might be used to generate a value on the worksheet are ignored. For example, if a cell contains the function @TRUE, Quattro Pro saves the number 1. By default, dBASE treats this number as a numeric value. If you change the data type, however, to Logical, it is saved in dBASE format as T.

You can include a maximum of 128 fields in dBASE III Plus; dBASE II databases are limited to 32 fields. If a Quattro Pro worksheet contains more than 128

FIGURE A-10.
You can change the structure of a Quattro Pro database before you export it to Paradox.

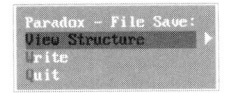

```
Paradox - File Save:
View Structure    ▶
Write
Quit
```

columns of data, only the first 128 columns can be exported to dBASE III Plus. Likewise, only 32 columns of data can be exported to dBASE II.

Exporting data to Paradox

Quattro Pro also has the ability to save databases in Paradox format. This process is almost identical to the process of exporting to dBASE. (For more information on the structure of Quattro Pro databases, see Chapter 11, "Database Management.") If the Quattro Pro worksheet you are saving contains only a database and the field names for the database are in row 1, you can save the entire worksheet as a Paradox file. To do so, choose the File Save As command and save the worksheet with the filename extension .DB. If the worksheet also contains other information, choose the Tools Xtract command and save only the portion with the database in a file with the appropriate filename extension.

After you choose either command and specify a filename and an extension, Quattro Pro presents the menu shown in Figure A-10. The first option in this menu, View Structure, lets you view and change the structure of the database that Quattro Pro will create from your worksheet. You can delete fields or change their names and type settings and then choose the Write option to save the database on disk.

Key concepts of exporting to Paradox

When you save a Quattro Pro worksheet in Paradox format, Quattro Pro treats each column that contains data as a field. If the first cell in a column contains a label, as is usual, that label is used as a field name for that column. Otherwise, the column letter for the column is used as a field name. (You'll learn how to change the names that Quattro Pro assigns to fields in a later section.) Because Paradox field names cannot be more than 25 characters long, any labels in the first row that are longer than 25 characters are truncated. In addition, the labels cannot include quotation marks (""), brackets ([]), braces ({}), or the character combination ->. Because these characters cannot be used in Paradox field names, Quattro Pro ignores cells in which they are found.

Quattro Pro uses the entries in each column (field) of a Quattro Pro worksheet to determine the field types of the fields in the Paradox database. For example,

FIGURE A-11.
The View Structure option lets you change the structure of a Paradox database.

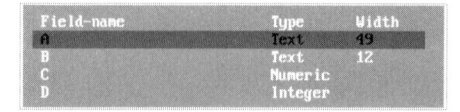

Field-name	Type	Width
A	Text	49
B	Text	12
C	Numeric	
D	Integer	

if a column of data in a Quattro Pro worksheet contains nothing but text, Quattro Pro makes that field an Alphabetic field in the Paradox file. If a column contains only numbers, the corresponding field in the Paradox database becomes a Numeric field. On the other hand, if a column contains a combination of data types, it is treated as an Alphanumeric field when saved in Paradox format. As a result, you might find it necessary to specify a field's data type manually, which you'll see how to do shortly.

Quattro Pro also uses the entries in the columns of the Quattro Pro worksheet to determine the widths of the fields in the Paradox database. For example, the width of a Character field is determined by the width of the widest entry that contains data in a column. On the other hand, the width of a Numeric field is determined by the format of the numeric data that is stored in a column. The width of Date fields is fixed. As you'll see in a later section, it's possible to change the width of Alphanumeric fields manually.

Changing the structure of a Quattro Pro database exported to Paradox

If you choose the View Structure option from the menu shown in Figure A-10, Quattro Pro displays a structure window like the one shown in Figure A-11. This window shows the structure of the database that Quattro Pro creates when the worksheet is saved with a .DB extension.

While the structure window is in view, you can move through the list of fields by pressing the Down and Up direction keys. You can change the structure of the database by highlighting a field, and then pressing the Enter key. After you do so, Quattro Pro presents the menu shown in Figure A-8. You can use the options in this menu to change the name and type of a field.

Changing a field's name. After you instruct Quattro Pro to save a file in Paradox format, Quattro Pro uses the labels in the first row of the worksheet (or the first row of the block you are extracting) as field names. To change the name that Quattro Pro has assigned to a field, highlight that field in the structure window, press the Enter key, and then choose the Name option from the menu shown in Figure A-8. Quattro Pro then prompts you for a new name; type the name and press the Enter key. The field name can be from 1 to 25 characters long and can include spaces, but it cannot begin with a space. In addition, the field name cannot include quotation marks (""), brackets ([]), braces ({}), or the character combination ->.

FIGURE A-12.
When you modify a field's data type, this menu is displayed.

```
Text
Numeric
Integer
Date
$ Dollar
```

Changing a field's type. After you instruct Quattro Pro to save a file in Paradox format, Quattro Pro selects an appropriate data type based on the data that it finds in a particular column. Paradox supports five different field types: Text, Numeric, Integer, Date, and $ Dollar. To change the data type that Quattro Pro has assigned to a field, highlight that field in the structure window, press the Enter key, and then choose the Type option from the menu shown in Figure A-8. Quattro Pro then presents the menu shown in Figure A-12. Choose the new type for the field. If you choose the Text option as the new field type, Quattro Pro prompts you to enter a field width. Press the Enter key to accept the default width, or type a new width.

Deleting a field. To delete a field, highlight that field in the structure window and press the Delete key. Quattro Pro places an asterisk in the structure window next to the field name. Fields marked with asterisks are not saved. If, after deleting a field, you decide you do want to include it in a file after all, highlight the field name and then press the Delete key again. Doing so removes the asterisk, and the field is saved when you save the file.

Exporting a file to Paradox

After you have made any necessary changes to the structure of a file, you're ready to export it. To do so, choose the Write option from the Paradox File Save menu. Quattro Pro creates a Paradox database from your Quattro Pro worksheet with the structure you defined. Quattro Pro then returns you to the worksheet.

A closer look at exporting to Paradox. After you save a Quattro Pro file in Paradox format, only the current values of any formulas or functions in the worksheet are saved; the formulas or functions themselves are ignored. Paradox databases can contain a maximum of 128 fields. If a Quattro Pro worksheet contains more than 128 columns, only the first 128 columns can be exported to Paradox.

Exporting data to Reflex

Quattro Pro can save databases in a Reflex format. (For more information on the structure of Quattro Pro databases, see Chapter 11, "Database Management.") If the Quattro Pro worksheet you are saving contains only a database and the field names for the database are in row 1, you can save the entire worksheet as a Reflex file. To do so, choose the File Save As command and save the worksheet with the

FIGURE A-13.
This menu lets you change the structure of a Quattro Pro database before you export it to Reflex.

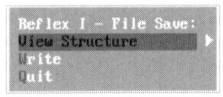

filename extension .RXD for Reflex version 1 and .R2D for Reflex version 2. If the worksheet contains other information as well, choose the Tools Xtract command and save only the portion containing the database in a Reflex file.

After you choose either command and specify a filename, Quattro Pro presents the menu shown in Figure A-13. The first option in this menu, View Structure, lets you view and change the structure of the database that Quattro Pro will create from your worksheet. You can delete fields or change their names, widths, and type settings and then choose the Write option to save the database to disk.

Key concepts of exporting to Reflex

When you save a Quattro Pro worksheet in Reflex format, Quattro Pro treats each column that contains data as a field. If the first cell in a column contains a label, as is usual, that label is used as a field name for that column. Otherwise, the column letter for the column is used as a field name. (You'll see how to change the names Quattro Pro assigns to fields in a later section.) Because Reflex field names cannot be more than 25 characters long, any labels in the first row that are longer than 25 characters are truncated. In addition, the labels cannot include quotation marks (""), brackets ([]), braces ({}), or the character combination ->. Because these characters cannot be used in Reflex field names, Quattro Pro ignores cells in which they are found. The name of the column is substituted for invalid field names.

Quattro Pro uses the entries in each column (field) of a Quattro Pro worksheet to determine the field types of the fields in the Reflex database. For example, if a column of data in a Quattro Pro worksheet contains nothing but text, Quattro Pro makes that field a Text field in the Reflex file. If a column contains only numbers, the corresponding field in the Reflex database is a Numeric or Integer field. On the other hand, if a column contains a combination of data types, it is treated as a Text field in the Reflex file. As a result, you might find it necessary to specify a field's data type manually, which you'll see how to do shortly.

Quattro Pro assigns widths to the fields as follows: The width of Text fields is 18; the width of Integer fields is 7; and the width of Date fields is 12. The width of Numeric fields varies according to the actual width and the display format of that value.

FIGURE A-14.
The View Structure option lets you view and change the structure of the Reflex database.

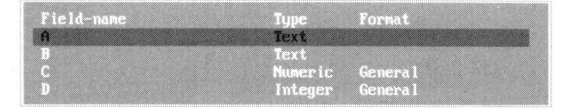

FIGURE A-15.
When you choose to modify a field's data type, this menu is displayed.

Changing the structure of a Quattro Pro database exported to Reflex

If you choose the View Structure option from the menu shown in Figure A-13, Quattro Pro displays a structure window like the one shown in Figure A-14. This window shows the structure of the database that Quattro Pro will create when the worksheet is saved with an .RXD or .R2D extension.

While the structure window is in view, you can move through the list of fields by pressing the Down and Up direction keys. You can change the structure of the database by highlighting a field and then pressing the Enter key. After you do so, Quattro Pro presents the menu shown in Figure A-8. You can use the options in this menu to change the name and type of a field.

Changing a field's name. After you instruct Quattro Pro to save a file in Reflex format, Quattro Pro uses the labels in the first row of the worksheet (or the first row of the block you are extracting) as field names. To change the name that Quattro Pro has assigned to a field, highlight that field in the structure window, press the Enter key, and then choose the Name option from the menu shown in Figure A-8. Quattro Pro then prompts you for a new name; type the new name and press the Enter key. The name you type must conform to all of the rules for Reflex field names.

Changing a field's type. When you instruct Quattro Pro to save a file in Reflex format, Quattro Pro selects an appropriate data type based on the data that it finds in a particular column. Reflex supports four different field types: Text, Numeric, Integer, and Date. To change the data type that Quattro Pro has assigned to a field, highlight that field in the structure window, press the Enter key, and then choose the Type option from the menu shown in Figure A-8. Quattro Pro then presents the menu shown in Figure A-15. Choose the new type for the field.

FIGURE A-16.
Save fields containing numeric or integer data using any of these display formats.

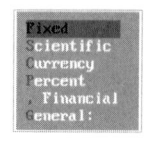

```
Fixed
Scientific
Currency
Percent
, Financial
General:
```

If you choose the Text option, Quattro Pro changes the field type to Text and returns to the structure window. If you choose any other field type, Quattro Pro displays another menu where you can choose the specific format for the type you chose. For example, you can format numeric values using Fixed, Scientific, General, Currency, or Financial formats. To do so, highlight the field you want to format in the structure window, press the Enter key, and choose the Numeric option from the menu shown in Figure A-15. When you do so, Quattro Pro presents the menu shown in Figure A-16. Choose the format you want to use.

After you choose one of the formats in the menu shown in Figure A-16 (except General), Quattro Pro prompts you to enter the number of decimal places that should be displayed in the field. Type a value between 1 and 15, and press the Enter key.

Deleting a field. To delete a field, highlight that field in the structure window and press the Delete key. Quattro Pro places an asterisk in the structure window next to the field name. Fields marked with asterisks are not saved. If, after deleting a field, you decide you want to include it after all, highlight the field name and press the Delete key again. Doing so removes the asterisk, and the field is saved when you save the file.

Exporting a file to Reflex

After you have made any necessary changes to the structure of a file, you're ready to export it. To do so, choose the Write option from the Reflex File Save menu. Quattro Pro creates a Reflex database from your Quattro Pro worksheet with the structure you defined. Quattro Pro then returns you to the worksheet.

A closer look at exporting to Reflex. After you save a Quattro Pro file on disk in Reflex format, only the current values of any formulas or functions in the worksheet are saved; the formulas or functions themselves are ignored. Reflex databases can contain a maximum of 128 fields. If a Quattro Pro worksheet contains more than 128 columns of data, only the first 128 columns can be exported to Reflex.

Exporting data as text files

Although Quattro Pro can save worksheets in formats that several major applications can use, you might need to export data to an application whose format Quattro Pro does not support. When you encounter this situation, your best option is to save the data in ASCII format. You can also use ASCII format files to export worksheets into most word processors. A file stored in ASCII format is essentially a mirror image of the raw data as it might appear on your monitor or in a printout. ASCII files contain no control codes or format sequences and can be read by most PC software packages that work with text.

To store a Quattro Pro worksheet in ASCII format, print it to your disk. To do so, first choose the Print Block command to define the block of data that you want to print. Next, choose the Print Layout Margins command to set the top, bottom, and left margins to 0 and the right margin to 80. Then, choose the Print Destination File command to set the destination to Disk and to define the filename to which ASCII data will be written. Quattro Pro then displays a list of the files in your data directory that have the extension .PRN (the extension often given to ASCII files). Choose a filename from this list or type a new name. If you choose a filename from the list, Quattro Pro presents a menu with four options: Cancel, Replace, Backup, and Append. To cancel the command, choose the Cancel option. To replace the existing file, choose the Replace option. To store the old version as a backup, choose the Backup option. To append the data in the worksheet to the data in the file, choose the Append option. Then, use the Print Spreadsheet Print command to print the worksheet to the disk file you specified. The disk file now contains the ASCII representation of the portion of your worksheet that you selected.

Appendix B
Customizing Quattro Pro

Although the nature of personal computing encourages individualism, many software applications have been designed in a way that would make Henry Ford proud. "You can get it in any color you want as long as it's black" seems to be their theme. Such is not the case with Quattro Pro, however. As you have seen throughout this book, it's possible to change the default setting of almost any cosmetic or functional aspect of the program. You can alter menu structures, specify the type of display and printer you use, choose colors for every part of the screen display, and much more.

To change Quattro Pro's default settings, choose the Options command, which presents the Options menu shown in Figure B-1. The commands in this menu let you change colors, formats, recalculation settings, and so on. You've already read about many of these commands. This appendix further examines the Options menu, discussing all of the customizing options not mentioned earlier. You'll see how to change the colors Quattro Pro uses for various parts of the screen, how to change the symbol Quattro Pro uses to represent monetary values, and much more.

FIGURE B-1.
The Options command displays this menu, which lets you change a variety of Quattro Pro settings.

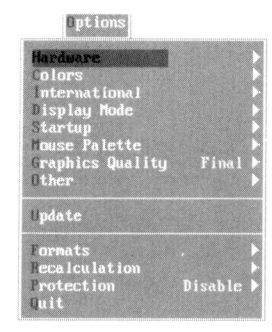

Changing Quattro Pro's default hardware settings

Use the Options Hardware command when you want to change several of Quattro Pro's default hardware settings. After you choose this command, Quattro Pro presents the menu shown in Figure B-2. From this menu, you can specify the video system that is installed in your computer and set communications parameters for a text printer. This menu also displays the amount of normal and expanded memory that is available and lets you know whether a math coprocessor is installed in your computer.

Chapter 7, "Printing," covers the Printers option, so it is not explained here. Instead, the following sections take an in-depth look at the Screen option.

Screen settings

Quattro Pro was designed to configure itself for the particular monitor that you happen to be using. For example, if you're using a Compaq portable, Quattro Pro uses the IBM Monochrome Display Adaptor (MDA) mode to display text and the IBM Color Graphics Adaptor (CGA) mode to display graphs.

Specifying the correct video hardware

You might find in some cases that Quattro Pro is unable to detect and install itself correctly to make use of your video hardware. When this situation occurs, choose the Options Hardware Screen command to override Quattro Pro's automatic video driver. Quattro Pro presents the Options Hardware Screen menu shown in Figure B-3.

FIGURE B-2.
Use the Options Hardware menu to alter printer and screen settings.

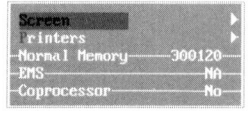

FIGURE B-3.
This is the Options Hardware Screen menu.

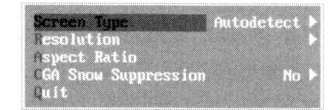

```
Screen Type              Autodetect ▶
Resolution                          ▶
Aspect Ratio
CGA Snow Suppression            No  ▶
Quit
```

Choose Screen Type, the first option in the Options Hardware Screen menu. Quattro Pro displays a list of screen types: CGA, MCGA, 256 KB EGA, and so on. Choose the correct screen type from the list, and press the Enter key.

Now, return to the Options menu and choose the Update option, which locks in your changes, making them a part of Quattro Pro's default driver. Because Quattro Pro configures itself as it starts, you must then choose the Quit command to leave Quattro Pro. Then, run the program again. As Quattro Pro starts, it uses the new screen settings.

Setting display resolution

The Options Hardware Screen menu's Resolution option lets you choose the video mode that Quattro Pro uses to display graphs. After you choose this option, Quattro Pro presents a menu that lists the various resolutions supported by the graphic device currently installed. Simply choose the resolution you want to use. Quattro Pro by default uses the highest resolution mode that your hardware supports. Because the number and types of resolution modes available depend on the graphics hardware you use, it's a good idea to take a moment to experiment with this command to find the mode that best suits your needs. Again, after you change this setting, choose the Options Update command if you want to make the change permanent.

Adjusting the aspect ratio

To draw a perfect circle when displaying a pie chart, Quattro Pro has to know the precise aspect ratio of your screen. (The aspect ratio is the ratio of the screen's width to its height.) Quattro Pro usually does a good job of selecting an appropriate aspect ratio. If your pie charts are not round, however, you might need to specify the correct aspect ratio. To do so, choose the Options Hardware Screen Aspect Ratio command, and Quattro Pro displays the screen shown in Figure B-4. Use the Up and Down direction keys to adjust the circle until it is round, and then press the Enter key. To make the change permanent, choose the Options Update command.

Suppressing CGA snow

If you use a CGA monitor and you see "snow" on the screen (flecks of white) you can choose the Options Hardware Screen CGA Snow Suppression Yes command to eliminate the snow. Turning on Quattro Pro's CGA Snow Suppression option slows Quattro Pro down considerably, so you do not want to use this option

FIGURE B-4.
Use the Options Hardware Screen Aspect Ratio command to ensure that circles are actually round.

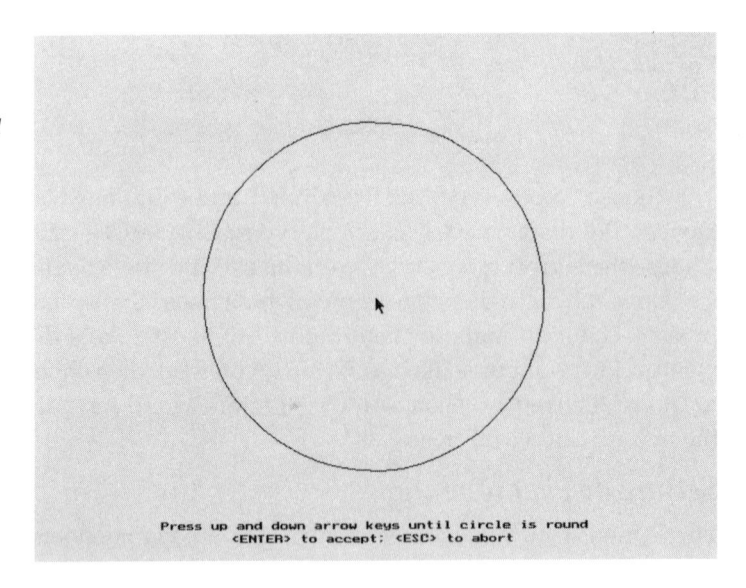

FIGURE B-5.
If you do not like Quattro Pro's default color scheme, you can use the Options Colors command to change it.

unless necessary. To make the change permanent, choose the Options Update command.

Changing default screen colors

The Options Colors command lets you change Quattro Pro's default color scheme. After you choose this command, Quattro Pro presents the menu shown in Figure B-5. This menu lets you change the colors that Quattro Pro uses to display menus, cells, the cell selector, and every other screen element. You can also choose the colors Quattro Pro uses to indicate errors and the colors Quattro Pro uses to represent values that fall within a specified range.

An example of changing menu colors

The Options Colors Menu command presents the menu shown in Figure B-6, which lets you control the colors used to display each element of Quattro Pro's menus. Each of the options in this menu lets you control one aspect of Quattro

Appendix B: Customizing Quattro Pro

FIGURE B-6.
The Options Colors Menu command presents this menu, which lets you control the colors that Quattro Pro uses to display each element of Quattro Pro's menus.

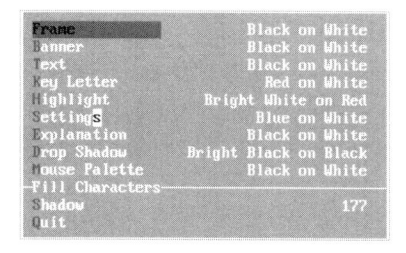

```
Frame                    Black on White
Banner                   Black on White
Text                     Black on White
Key Letter                 Red on White
Highlight         Bright White on Red
Settings                  Blue on White
Explanation              Black on White
Drop Shadow       Bright Black on Black
Mouse Palette            Black on White
─Fill Characters─
Shadow                              177
Quit
```

FIGURE B-7.
As you can see in this Quattro Pro help screen, you can change the colors used to display any menu element.

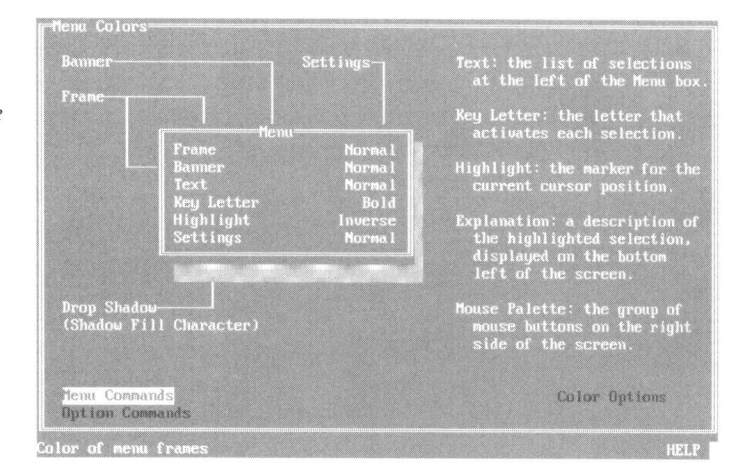

```
┌Menu Colors─────────────────────────────────────────────────┐
│  Banner─────────────       Settings─┐   Text: the list of selections
│                                          at the left of the Menu box.
│   Frame─┐
│         │                                Key Letter: the letter that
│         │    ┌Menu──────────────┐         activates each selection.
│         │    │ Frame      Normal│
│         │    │ Banner     Normal│        Highlight: the marker for the
│         │    │ Text       Normal│         current cursor position.
│         │    │ Key Letter   Bold│
│         │    │ Highlight Inverse│        Explanation: a description of
│         │    │ Settings   Normal│         the highlighted selection,
│         │    └──────────────────┘         displayed on the bottom
│                                           left of the screen.
│
│   Drop Shadow─┐                          Mouse Palette: the group of
│   (Shadow Fill Character)                 mouse buttons on the right
│                                           side of the screen.
│
│   Menu Commands                                      Color Options
│   Option Commands
└────────────────────────────────────────────────────────────┘
 Color of menu frames                                         HELP
```

Pro's menus. Figure B-7, which Quattro Pro displays if you press the [Help] key (F1) when the menu shown in Figure B-6 is displayed, shows the part of the menu each of these options affects.

Although each of the options in this menu controls the color of a different element of the menu area, all of the options work in the same way. After you choose an option, you see one of two menus, depending on the video hardware you use to display text. If you use a monochrome monitor, you see a menu that has these options: Normal, Bold, Underlined, Inverse, and Empty. These options allow you to display the selected element as normal text, bold text, underlined text, or inverse text. The Empty option lets you to turn off the display of the selected element. When you see this menu, choose the option you want to use for the selected element. If you have a color monitor, you see a pop-up box. This box, which appears in color on your screen, displays each background and foreground color combination your video hardware supports. When you see this box, use the direction keys to choose the color combination you want to use and press the Enter key.

Changing colors of other screen components

The remaining Options Colors commands let you control the colors used to display the other screen components. Use the Options Colors Desktop command to specify the colors that Quattro Pro uses to display the background desktop and the desktop pattern. The Options Colors Spreadsheet command lets you specify the colors that Quattro Pro uses to display each element of the worksheet, and the Options Colors Conditional command lets you assign colors to cells based on the entries they contain. Choose the Options Colors Help command to specify the colors Quattro Pro uses on Help screens. The Options Colors File Manager command allows you to specify the colors that Quattro Pro uses on the File Manager screen. In each of these cases, however, the steps for changing the color of the screen component closely resemble those for changing the color of a menu, so that discussion is not repeated here.

Resetting the default text screen colors

The Options Colors Palettes command lets you reset all of Quattro Pro's text screen colors to their default state in one step. You can also use this command to tell Quattro Pro that you do not want to display color or that you want to display colors as shades of gray. After you choose the Options Colors Palettes command, you see a menu that lists three color scheme choices: Color, Monochrome, and Black & White. If you want your text screen to display color using Quattro Pro's default color scheme, choose the Color palette. If you do not want to display any color on the text screen, choose the Monochrome palette. Finally, to display shades of gray in place of color on your text screen, choose the Black & White palette, and Quattro Pro allows you to assign shades of gray to components of a worksheet. Use the Black & White palette if you use a composite monochrome monitor with a CGA or EGA system, or an LCD-equipped laptop computer such as the Toshiba 1100 or the Tandy 1400 LT.

Configuring international settings

The Options International command lets you configure Quattro Pro for use around the world. After you choose the Options International command, the menu shown in Figure B-8 appears. The Currency option in this menu lets you change the symbol that Quattro Pro uses in the Currency format from $ to ¥, £, or one of several other available options. Use the Punctuation option when you want to change the punctuation conventions that Quattro Pro uses when displaying numeric values to conform to accepted international standards. The Date and Time options allow you to change the form of Quattro Pro's international date and time formats, as explained in Chapter 6, "Dates and Times." The Use Sort Table option controls the sorting rules that Quattro Pro follows, and the LICS

FIGURE B-8.
The Options International command displays this menu.

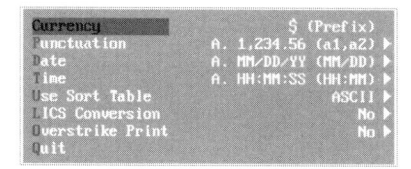

Currency	$ (Prefix)
Punctuation	A. 1,234.56 (a1,a2)
Date	A. MM/DD/YY (MM/DD)
Time	A. HH:MM:SS (HH:MM)
Use Sort Table	ASCII
LICS Conversion	No
Overstrike Print	No
Quit	

Conversion option determines whether Quattro Pro converts Lotus International Character Set characters in Lotus .WK1 files to their equivalent ASCII characters when you retrieve .WK1 files. The Overstrike Print option tells Quattro Pro to print accented characters.

Changing the currency symbols

The Options International Currency command allows you to change the currency symbol that Quattro Pro uses when displaying monetary values. After you choose this command, Quattro Pro prompts you to define the new currency symbol. The current symbol (usually $) appears after the prompt. Press the Esc key to erase the current symbol, and then define the new symbol. You can use any character (or group of characters up to 10) as the currency symbol in the PC character set. To use a symbol that does not appear on the keyboard, such as ¥ or £, press the Alt key and type the numeric code to create the character.

After you define the new symbol and press the Enter key, Quattro Pro presents a menu that lists two choices: Prefix and Suffix. This menu allows you to display the currency symbol before or after the formatted value. Choose the Prefix option if you want the currency symbol displayed before the number or choose Suffix if you want the currency symbol displayed after the number. After you change the currency symbol, any monetary values that appear in your worksheet are updated to reflect that change. It is not possible, therefore, to use more than one currency symbol in the same worksheet.

Changing punctuation defaults

Use the Options International Punctuation command to change three loosely related settings. First, you can use this command to tell Quattro Pro whether to use a period, a comma, or a space to represent the decimal points in values. Second, you can use it to tell Quattro Pro if thousands should be separated from the rest of a numeric value by a comma, period, or space. Finally, you can use this command to change the character that Quattro Pro uses to separate arguments in functions or macros. After you choose this command, you see the menu shown in Figure B-9.

FIGURE B-9.
The Options International Punctuation command displays this menu.

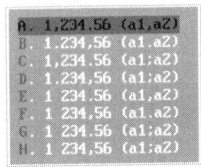

```
A. 1,234.56 (a1.a2)
B. 1.234,56 (a1;a2)
C. 1,234.56 (a1;a2)
D. 1.234,56 (a1;a2)
E. 1 234.56 (a1,a2)
F. 1 234,56 (a1,a2)
G. 1 234.56 (a1;a2)
H. 1 234,56 (a1;a2)
```

An example of changing punctuation defaults

The Options International Punctuation menu, shown in Figure B-9, lists the various combinations of decimal points and separators from which you can choose to change the punctuation settings. For example, if you choose option H, which is 1 234,56 (a1;a2), Quattro Pro uses a space to separate hundreds from thousands, a comma as the decimal point, and a semicolon as the argument separator in macros and functions. Because you can change three different settings by choosing only one option from this menu, be careful to choose the option that changes only the setting or settings that you actually want to change. After you change the punctuation setting, Quattro Pro updates your worksheet instantly to reflect the setting. For example, suppose that cell A1 of your worksheet contains the function @SUM(B1,B2). If you choose the Options International Punctuation command and then choose option C, which is 1,234.56 (a1;a2), the character used to separate arguments in the function changes. In other words, cell A1 will contain @SUM(B1;B2).

Specifying the sort table used

As mentioned, the Use Sort Table settings control the sorting rules that Quattro Pro follows. After you choose the Options International Use Sort Table command, Quattro Pro presents a submenu that gives you the four sort orders you can use:

- In order of ASCII character codes
- Using the International sort sequence, which is essentially alphabetic
- Using a Norwegian/Danish sort, much like the International sort sequence except it includes special characters used in Denmark and Norway
- Using a Swedish/Finnish sort, much like the International sort sequence except that it includes special characters used in Sweden and Finland

Controlling LICS character conversions

Lotus 1-2-3 versions through 2.01 use a special character set called the Lotus International Character Set, or LICS. Much of the LICS character set mirrors the regular ASCII Character set. You'll find some differences between the character codes for LICS and the character codes for ASCII, however, especially when you start working with international and graphics character codes. Because of these

Appendix B: Customizing Quattro Pro

differences, Quattro Pro needs to know if you want LICS character codes converted when you retrieve .WK1 files. Choose the Options International LICS Conversion command, and Quattro Pro presents a submenu that has two options: Yes and No. By default, Quattro Pro does not convert LICS character codes to their equivalent ASCII character codes. If you want to change this setting, however, choose the Yes option.

Overstrike printing

Quattro Pro provides the Overstrike Print option so that you can create accented characters using a seven-bit printer. If you have a seven-bit printer, set the Overstrike Print option to Yes to print characters like an accented e (é).

Display mode

Quattro Pro, by default, uses a text display mode that is 80 characters wide and 25 characters high when displaying the worksheet screen. You can specify, however, that Quattro Pro use another display mode that packs more information onto the screen. After you choose the Options Display Mode command, Quattro Pro presents the menu shown in Figure B-10. The first option listed, 80 × 25, is the default setting.

The Graphics Mode option directs Quattro Pro to display the screen in graphics mode. In graphics mode, Quattro Pro displays the mouse pointer as an arrowhead and certain menus as galleries (graphic representations of the options). It also displays any graphs that you inserted in your worksheet. The EGA: 80 × 43 and VGA: 80 × 50 options let you display more lines on a screen. If you have an EGA graphics card, you can use the third option, for example, to display 43 lines on a screen instead of the standard 25 lines. Or, if you have a VGA graphics card, you can use the fourth option to display 50 lines on a screen instead of 25 lines. (Note that if you have a VGA card, you can probably choose either option.)

The remaining options in the Options Display Mode menu provide 132 character screen widths for specific VGA cards. For example, the fifth option, Ahead Systems VGA Wizard, works if you have an Ahead Systems VGA Wizard graphics card. If you do have this card, you can choose this option to display 132 characters across the width of the screen rather than the standard 80 characters. If you do not

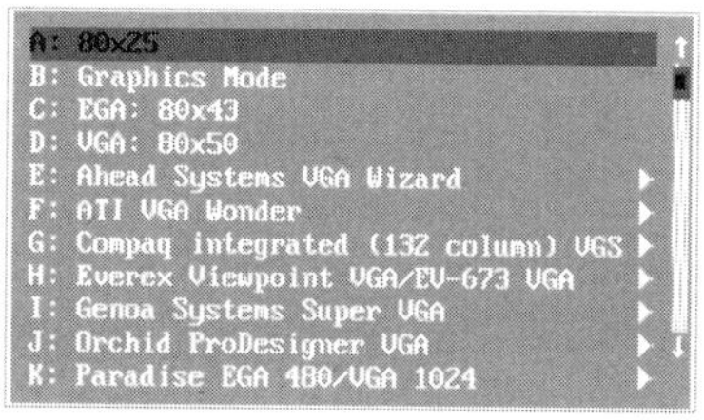

FIGURE B-10.
The Options Display Mode menu lets you pack more information onto a screen, and display worksheets and graphs.

```
A: 80x25
B: Graphics Mode
C: EGA: 80x43
D: VGA: 80x50
E: Ahead Systems VGA Wizard      ▶
F: ATI VGA Wonder                ▶
G: Compaq integrated (132 column) VGS ▶
H: Everex Viewpoint VGA/EV-673 VGA ▶
I: Genoa Systems Super VGA       ▶
J: Orchid ProDesigner VGA        ▶
K: Paradise EGA 480/VGA 1024     ▶
```

see your VGA card listed, you can try each of the listed display modes to find one that works with your particular VGA card. You can tell whenever you find a display mode that does not work because your screen becomes illegible. When this situation occurs, press Ctrl-Break to cancel the menu, choose the Options Display Mode command again, and press the Enter key to choose the 80 × 25 mode again.

Startup defaults

The Options Startup command lets you change a number of system settings that are used by Quattro Pro each time you run the program. After you choose this command, you see the menu shown in Figure B-11. The options in this menu let you specify an autoload worksheet, a startup macro, the default extension for Quattro Pro worksheet files, the default help access method, any default add-ins that should be loaded, and the menu tree to use. If you are concerned about Quattro Pro's Lotus 1-2-3 compatibility, you can turn on or off several compatibility options with the Startup menu.

Automatic worksheet starting

The Options Startup menu's Autoload File option lets you specify the name of a worksheet that Quattro Pro should open each time you run Quattro Pro. If you always use a particular worksheet with Quattro Pro, you can use this feature to bypass the File Retrieve or File Open command. After you choose the Autoload File option from the Startup menu, Quattro Pro prompts you to enter the name of a worksheet. Press the the Esc key to clear any previously defined filename, type the name of the worksheet that you want Quattro Pro to open, and then press the Enter key.

Using a startup macro

Use the Options Startup menu's Startup Macro command to specify the name of a macro that you want Quattro Pro to execute each time a worksheet is retrieved from disk. By default, the startup macro is \0. Until you specify another macro name, therefore, Quattro Pro always looks for the macro \0 each time it retrieves a worksheet. If such a macro is present, Quattro Pro executes it. After you choose

FIGURE B-11.
The Options Startup command allows you to configure several system settings.

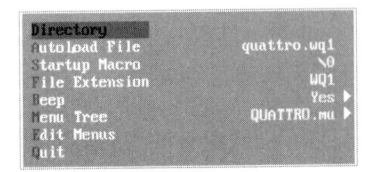

the Startup Macro option, Quattro Pro prompts you to enter the name of the macro that it will attempt to execute each time a worksheet is retrieved. If a macro name has been specified previously, that name appears after the prompt. Press the Esc key to erase the name, type the name of the macro you want, and press the Enter key.

Worksheet file extensions

As you learned in Appendix A, "Exchanging Data with Other Programs," one of Quattro Pro's most useful features is its ability to read and write data files in formats that a number of other applications use, based on the extension that a filename carries. For example, Quattro Pro saves a file in Paradox format if you save it with the extension .DB. Likewise, if you want to import a Paradox file into Quattro Pro, simply open it using the File Retrieve or File Open command.

Whenever you choose a File Save As command and type a filename at the prompt (without an extension), Quattro Pro saves the file using the extension (and the associated file format) that is specified with the Options Startup menu's File Extension option. After you choose this option, Quattro Pro prompts you to enter a new extension. Press the Esc key to erase the currently defined extension, type the extension you want to use, and press the Enter key.

Although the Options Startup File Extension command does change the default extension Quattro Pro uses when saving files, this command does not affect the extension Quattro Pro uses when opening files. In other words, when you choose the File Retrieve or File Open command, Quattro Pro searches for files in the data directory using the *.W?? file specification. You cannot permanently change the wildcard that Quattro Pro uses to search for data files when the File Retrieve and File Open commands are chosen.

Turning Quattro Pro's beep off and on

Quattro Pro normally beeps whenever an error occurs. The Beep option in the Options Startup menu allows you to turn this beeping off. After you choose the Beep option, choose the Yes option if you want Quattro Pro to beep when errors occur, or choose the No option if you do not want Quattro Pro to beep when errors occur.

Choosing a menu tree

Use the Options Startup Menu Tree command to tell Quattro Pro which menu tree structure to use. After you choose this command, Quattro Pro presents a menu that lists three options: Q1, QUATTRO, and 123. The menu structure described in this book, which is the default, is QUATTRO. The Q1 option makes Quattro Pro look like Quattro Pro version 1. The 123 option makes Quattro Pro look like Lotus

1-2-3. If you do not want to use the default Quattro Pro menus, use one of these other menu tree options.

Editing the menu tree

As you use Quattro Pro on a day-to-day basis, you might find that some of the commands you use most often are buried several levels in the menu tree. For example, each time you run a macro, you must choose the File Utilities DOS Shell command to display a list of current directories. It would be better if you could simply choose a DOS Shell command instead. Fortunately, Quattro Pro includes the Edit Menu command, which accesses the Menu Builder feature. The purpose of the Menu Builder is simple: It allows you to redesign Quattro Pro's menu structure according to your own tastes and needs.

Before you can use the Menu Builder effectively, you must understand the difference between commands and actions. Commands are the options that appear in the Quattro Pro menus. For example, Edit Copy and Print Block are commands. Actions, on the other hand, are the tasks that commands perform. For example, choosing the Edit Copy command tells Quattro Pro to copy a block of cells. In Quattro Pro, each action is defined by two words. The first describes the type of action, and the second describes the specific action. For example, Quattro Pro uses the words Edit and Copy to describe the action that Quattro Pro takes when you choose the Edit Copy command. As explained in Chapter 12, "Macro Basics," this is the same form that Quattro Pro uses to describe commands in macros.

Every action in Quattro Pro is linked to one of the commands you see in the basic Quattro Pro menu structure. For example, the {/ Block;Copy} action is linked to the Edit Copy command. Quattro Pro can perform only a limited number of actions: Quattro Pro's basic menu tree includes one command for every possible Quattro Pro action. Short of writing an add-in, you cannot add actions to Quattro Pro.

Commands, on the other hand, are completely flexible. If you want, you can use the Menu Builder to change the command that you use to execute a given action. For instance, you can change the command that executes the Block;Copy action from Edit Copy to Edit Duplicate. You can also use the Menu Builder to delete a command from Quattro Pro's menu tree or to move a command from one place in the tree to another. This ability to manipulate commands gives you the power to customize Quattro Pro for your own needs.

To use Quattro Pro's Menu Builder, choose the Options Startup Edit Menu command. Quattro Pro presents the Menu Builder screen shown in Figure B-12. The box at the top of the screen, called the "current item pane," describes the current menu item. The box in the middle of the screen, called the "menu tree pane," shows the menu being modified. The box at the bottom of the screen, called the

Appendix B: Customizing Quattro Pro 493

FIGURE B-12.
After you choose the Options Startup Edit Menu command, you see the Menu Builder screen, which you use to modify existing menu trees or to create new menu trees.

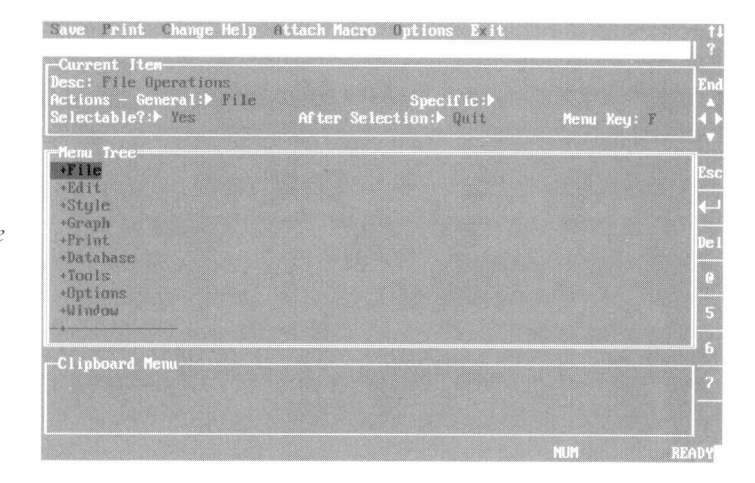

"clipboard menu pane," shows menu commands that have been deleted from the menu tree pane.

Navigating in the Menu Builder screen

Before you see how to use the Menu Builder screen to modify menus or create other menus from scratch, you need some information about navigating on the screen. To move between the panes, press F6. When the cursor is in the current item pane, use the Tab and Shift-Tab keys to move between that pane's fields. Or, you can use use the direction keys to move to the field in the direction in which the direction key points. When the cursor is in the menu tree pane, use the direction keys to move between the menu options listed. The Up and Down direction keys move between individual menus. As you point to a menu, the current item pane displays information about that menu.

To see the options in the highlighted menu, press the plus key (+). For example, if you press + when the File menu is highlighted, the screen looks like Figure B-13. To collapse the menu so that it does not show, press the minus key (-) on the numeric keypad.

To move between the different menu levels, use the Right and Left direction keys. Quattro Pro also provides shortcuts for moving around in the menu tree pane. Pressing Ctrl-PgUp moves the cursor to the menu above the currently selected option. Pressing Ctrl-Home moves the cursor to the first menu or menu option in the menu tree. Pressing Ctrl-End moves the cursor to the last menu or option in the menu tree.

Editing commands

Use the current item pane to change the name and location of a command in the Quattro Pro menu structure. You can change the name of the command you want to perform a particular action or the action that Quattro Pro executes when you

FIGURE B-13.
Press the plus key (+) when a menu item is highlighted to see the commands in the menu.

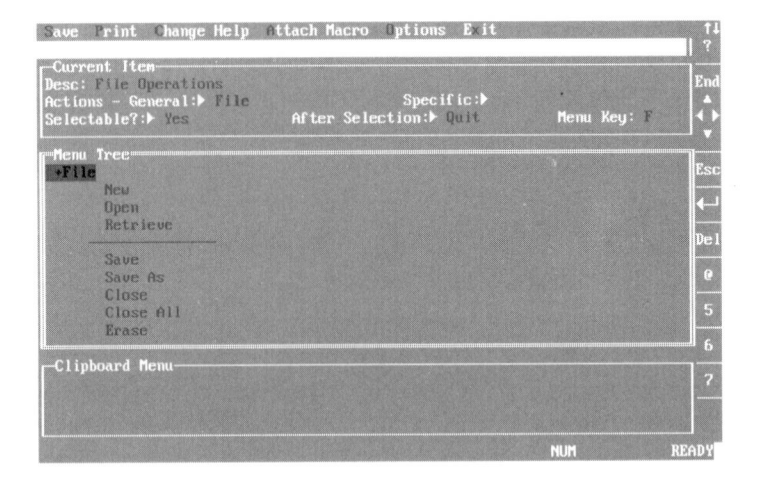

choose a particular command. In addition, you can move a command from one menu to another or delete it from the menu structure altogether.

To change a command, first highlight it in the menu tree pane, and then press F6. The current item pane is then activated. By changing the settings in this pane, you can edit a command in a number of ways. The first option in the current item pane, Desc, shows the name of the current command. For example, in Figure B-13, the command name *File* is highlighted, and the Desc field contains the text *File Operations,* which is displayed in the control panel whenever that command is highlighted.

The Actions-General and Actions-Specific options define the action that Quattro Pro takes if you choose the highlighted command. Use these options when you create a new command in Quattro Pro or when you move a command from one place to another in the menu structure. The Actions-General option identifies the type or class of command that Quattro Pro performs when you choose the highlighted command. If you point to this option and press the Enter key, the menu shown in Figure B-14 appears. This menu lists all of the possible types of actions that a command can perform in Quattro Pro.

The Actions-Specific option identifies the specific commands Quattro Pro performs when the highlighted menu command is executed. If you point to this option and press the Enter key, a menu appears that lists the specific commands that are available, given the current Actions-General setting. For example, if the Actions-General option is currently defined as File, the menu shown in Figure B-15 appears when you point to the Actions-Specific field and press the Enter key.

The Selectable? option determines whether you can choose the item from the menu or whether the item is merely displayed. The After Selection option specifies what Quattro Pro will do after executing the action described by the Actions-General and Actions-Specific options. If you point to this option and press the

FIGURE B-14.
This menu shows actions that a command can perform in Quattro Pro.

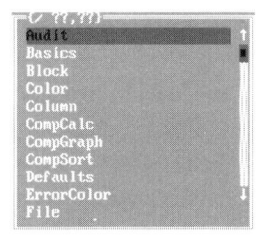

FIGURE B-15.
This menu shows the various types of specific actions that a command can perform, given an Actions-General setting of File.

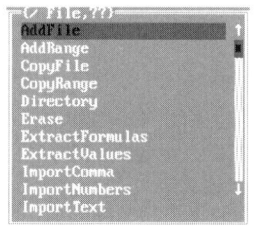

Enter key, Quattro Pro presents a menu that has three options: Stay, Quit, and Go To Parent. The Stay option tells Quattro Pro to remain in the currently active menu after executing the command. The Quit option tells Quattro Pro to return to the worksheet after a command has been executed. The Go to Parent option tells Quattro Pro to return to the parent menu of the command after executing it.

The final option in the current item pane is Menu Key. This option specifies the key to press to choose this command. The Menu Key typically is the first letter of the command name. It can, however, be any letter that's used in the command name.

Changing the name of a command. To change the name of a command, activate the menu tree pane if it is not already active, and then highlight the command name. If the command name is not on the main menu, choose the menu option the command is under, and press the plus key (+) on the numeric keypad. If the command is buried deep within the Quattro Pro menu tree, you might need to repeat this process several times. After the command is highlighted, press F2. Quattro Pro then displays the cursor at the end of the command name. Using the same editing techniques as you would to edit a cell formula or label, change the command name, and then press the Enter key.

Changing a command's description. To change the description of a menu command, activate the menu tree if it is not already active, and then highlight the command name for which you want to change the description. If the name is not in the main menu, choose the menu option the command is under, and press the plus (+) key on the numeric keypad. You might need to repeat this process several times. Next, press F6 to activate the current item pane. Press the Esc key to erase the current description, and then type a new description and press the Enter key.

Changing the After Selection option. To change the action Quattro Pro takes after performing a command, change that command's After Selection option. To do so, highlight the command you want to change, and then press F6 to activate the current item pane. Next, move down to the After Selection option, and press the Enter key. Quattro Pro presents a menu that has three options: Stay, Quit, and Go To Parent. Choose the option you want to use for this command, and press the Enter key.

Adding commands

Although Quattro Pro's menu tree contains a command for every action that Quattro Pro supports, you might want to add a command or two to the menu structure. For instance, you might want to duplicate at another location higher in the menu tree a command that is buried deep in the Quattro Pro menus.

To add a command, use the direction keys to move through the menu tree until you reach the point at which you want to insert a new command, and press the Enter key. Quattro Pro inserts a blank line in the menu tree. Next, type the name of the command you want to add, and press the Enter key. The new selection appears in the current menu. In addition, a blank current item pane appears at the top of the screen. To define the effect of that command, fill in the current item pane.

Adding a display-only command

To add a display-only command to a menu, use the direction keys to move through the menu tree until you reach the point at which you want to insert a new command, and press the Enter key. Quattro Pro inserts a blank line at that position in the menu tree. Next, type the name of the command you want to add, and press the Enter key. The new selection appears in the current menu, and a blank current item pane appears at the top of the screen. To define the new command as a display-only command, activate the current item pane, move to the Selectable? option, press the Enter key, choose the No option, and press the Enter key again.

Adding a menu

You can also add a new menu to the Quattro Pro menu tree. To do so, move the highlight to the point in the menu tree at which you want the new menu to appear, press the Enter key, and type the name of the menu in the blank line that Quattro Pro creates. Next, activate the current item pane, and define the description for the new menu. Highlight the Actions-General option, and choose the type of command(s) you want to place in the new menu. Then, highlight the Actions-Specific option, and press the Del key to ensure that the option is set to None. Finally, highlight the After Selection option, and choose the Stay option. To add commands under the menu, insert a blank line by pressing Enter and then press the Tab key. The Tab key indents the cursor to indicate that the subsequent menu commands you add are at a lower menu level. Other than pressing the Tab key, the steps for adding menu commands under the menu you have created are the same as those already discussed. When you add a command to the Quattro Pro menu tree that calls a submenu, Quattro Pro includes a Quit command in the submenu. Note that if you want to move a command out from under a menu to a higher level in the menu tree, highlight the item and press Shift-Tab.

Deleting commands

The Menu Builder also allows you to delete menu commands. To do so, use the direction keys to move through the menu tree until you reach the command you want to delete, and press the Del key. Quattro Pro erases the command from the current menu, positions the highlight on the command immediately preceding the deleted command, updates the current item pane, and displays the command in the clipboard pane. After a command is deleted, you can no longer perform the action that was associated with that command unless you either create a new command to perform that action or assign the action to another existing command.

Although a deleted command disappears from the menu tree, it is not deleted immediately. Instead, the command is stored on the clipboard pane, so it is possible to restore the command from the clipboard. To do so, first highlight the command you want to restore in the clipboard pane by activating the clipboard pane and using the direction keys. Next, activate the menu tree pane, and highlight the menu command where you want the command you are replacing to be inserted, and then press the Ins key.

Moving commands

To move a command, first highlight it, then press the Del key. Next, move the highlight to the point in the menu tree in front of which you want the command to appear, and then press the Ins key.

Saving changes made to a menu tree

After you have made all of your changes to the menu tree, it's time to save the menu on disk. To do so, press the slash key (/) to activate the menu bar that appears along the top row of the Menu Builder screen. Then, choose the Save option. Quattro Pro displays a prompt that resembles the prompt that's displayed when you choose the File Save As command. Type the name you want to assign to the new menu tree, and press the Enter key. Quattro Pro does not allow you to overwrite the current menu tree. You do not have to specify a file extension because Quattro Pro adds the extension for you; Quattro Pro uses the file extension .MU for menu tree files. The menu tree name you enter must be a valid DOS filename.

To use the new menu tree, choose the Options Startup Menu Tree command. Quattro Pro lists the menu tree you created along with the other menu trees. To use the menu tree, choose it from the list.

Printing a menu tree

The Print option that appears on the Menu Builder screen lets you print a copy of a menu tree either on your printer or as a text file on disk. To print the menu tree, activate the menu bar by pressing the slash key (/). Next press the P key, or use the direction keys to highlight the Print option, and then press the Enter key. After you use either approach, Quattro Pro presents a menu that has two choices: Printer and File. To print a copy of the menu tree, choose the Print option. To create a text file that you can print later or retrieve in another software program, choose the File option.

Changing Quattro Pro's help

Quattro Pro supplies a default help screen for each menu command. To change the help screen displayed for a command or to specify which help screens should be displayed for the menu commands you add, choose the menu command for which you want to change the Help screen. Next, press the slash key (/) to activate the menu bar. Then, press the C key or use the direction keys to highlight the Change Help option, and then press the Enter key. Quattro Pro displays the Help Index, which you can use to display the help screen you want. Then, press the Esc key, and Quattro Pro presents the Change Help Screen menu. If the last help screen displayed is the one you want for the menu command, choose the Attach To Last Screen Shown option. If it is not, choose the Cancel option.

Adding macros to menus

You can also add macros to menus so that they execute as menu commands. As noted in Chapter 12, "Macro Basics," to execute a macro that macro must be in the active worksheet or in an open macro library. Add a new menu command to represent the macro, and then activate the current item pane. Set the Actions-General option to Name and the Actions-Specific option to Attach. Then, press the slash key (/) to activate the menu, and choose the Attach Macro option. After Quattro Pro prompts you for the macro name, type it enclosed in braces, and then press the Enter key.

Using the other Menu Builder options

Quattro Pro includes several additional options in the Menu Builder's menu bar that let you specify general characteristics of a menu tree. These options appear in this menu to make it easier to create menu trees that mimic another product, such as Lotus 1-2-3. To access these other options, first choose Options from the Menu Builder menu by pressing the slash key (/) and then pressing the O key. Quattro Pro presents the menu shown in Figure B-16.

You might already be familiar with the first three options in the Menu Builder's Options menu—Autoload File, File Extension, and Macro Recording—because equivalent commands appear in other menus. The Autoload File option

FIGURE B-16.
This is the Menu Builder's Options menu.

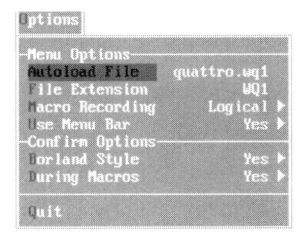

specifies what the default autoload file should be with this menu tree. The File Extension option specifies which file extension Quattro Pro should use if you do not specify one when you choose the File Save As command. The Macro Recording option specifies whether Quattro Pro records keystrokes as menu-equivalent commands, such as {/ File;Save}, or as the actual keystrokes, such as /fs.

The Use Menu Bar option controls the orientation of menus. The default setting, which is Yes, directs Quattro Pro to present the main menu on a bar across the top of the screen and submenus in pop-up boxes, as shown throughout this book. If you do not want Quattro Pro to use a menu bar, even for the main menu, you can change the Use Menu Bar setting to No. All menus, even the main menu, are then displayed in pop-up boxes that appear only when you activate the menu by pressing the slash key (/).

The last two items, listed under Borland Style and During Macros, relate to the confirmation messages that Quattro Pro displays before executing a command that erases data. The Borland Style option controls whether confirmation messages warn you whenever you attempt an operation that erases data. If you instead want to use the Lotus 1-2-3 method, which always warns you during a File Erase or File Quit operation, even if you will not lose any data, set this option to No. The During Macros option controls the display of confirmation messages during macro execution. By default, this option is set to Yes for both the standard Quattro Pro menu and the menu that mimics Lotus 1-2-3. If you want to suppress the confirmation during macro execution, however, set this option to No.

Exiting from the Menu Builder

To leave the Menu Builder screen and return to the regular Quattro Pro worksheet screen, choose the Exit command. To do so, press the slash key (/) and then press the E key.

A closer look at menu trees

Using the techniques described in the preceding pages, you can create custom menu trees. You can, for instance, create a menu tree that resembles Microsoft Excel. If you want to do so, however, you need to consider a few issues. First, you need to include a command equivalent to File Exit so that you can leave Quattro Pro. If you do not, you must reset your computer to quit Quattro Pro. Second, if you or someone else switch menu trees in the future, you also need to include a menu command equivalent to Options Startup Menu Tree. Third, if you want your menu tree to be displayed as the default, name your menu tree QUATTRO.MU. If you do so, however, it's probably a good idea to save the original QUATTRO.MU file in case you ever want to reuse it.

Changing the mouse palette

Mouse users see a mouse palette on the right side of the Quattro Pro screen. This palette lets mouse users use keys, such as End, the direction keys, Esc, Enter, Del, and @, by clicking on a palette button. You can use the Options Mouse Palette command to change the keys that Quattro Pro types for you when you click on one of the mouse palette buttons.

After you choose the Options Mouse Palette command, Quattro Pro presents a menu that lists the seven user-definable buttons: 1st Button, 2nd Button, 3rd Button, and so forth. By default, the first four user-definable buttons are set as Esc, Enter, Del, and @. The last three are set to the macro command {Beep} so that they beep when you click on them. To change any of the buttons, choose the button you want to change from the Options Mouse Palette menu. Quattro Pro then displays a prompt with several choices. To specify the text that should appear on the button as a description, choose the Text option, and Quattro Pro displays a pop-up window into which you can type up to three characters of text. To specify the action you want Quattro Pro to take when you click the mouse button, choose the Macro option. Quattro Pro displays another pop-up window with the prompt *Macro to execute when button is pressed* followed by the current key or macro command that Quattro Pro executes after the button is clicked. If you want Quattro Pro to type a letter or number, such as *W* or *4*, simply enter that character. You can also type the macro command for a key, such as {Home} or {Menu}, or you can enter a macro name. If you enter a macro name, the macro must be in the active worksheet or in an open macro library worksheet to be executed.

Other customization options

The two additional options in the Options menu are Graphics Quality and Other. The Options Graphics Quality command lets you specify whether Quattro Pro uses either the Bitstream fonts you specify or the fonts that Quattro Pro uses by default. The default setting is Final, which directs Quattro Pro to use the Bitstream fonts. This setting, however, initially slows down your printing, screen previewing

FIGURE B-17.
Choose the Options Other command to display this menu.

Undo	Disable ▶
Macro	Both ▶
Expanded Memory	Spreadsheet Data ▶
Clock	None ▶
Paradox	▶

of reports, and use of the Annotator, because Quattro Pro needs to build a Bitstream font the first time you use it. The Bitstream fonts are of higher quality. If you cannot afford to slow down your printing, screen previewing, and Annotator, however, you can set the Graphic Quality to Draft. If you do so, Quattro Pro uses Hershey fonts in place of the Bitstream fonts. The Hershey fonts are crude approximations of the equivalent Bitstream fonts. Experiment with changing the two font settings. You'll probably find that the crisper, cleaner appearance of the Bitstream fonts outweigh their initial cost in printing and previewing time.

The Options Other command presents the menu shown in Figure B-17, which lists a set of assorted settings, some of which have already been described earlier in the book.

The Undo option lets you enable or disable Quattro Pro's Undo feature. The Macro option allows you to specify the screen components that Quattro Pro updates during the execution of a macro: the input line, the worksheet window, both the input line and the worksheet window, or neither the input line nor the worksheet window.

The Expanded Memory setting lets you control what Quattro Pro stores in expanded memory. After you choose the Options Other Expanded Memory command, Quattro Pro presents a menu that has four options: Both, Spreadsheet Data, Format, and None. By default, Quattro Pro stores only the spreadsheet data in expanded memory; the rest of the information in the spreadsheet is stored in system memory (the first 640 KB). If you're running out of system memory, however, you can choose the Both option to tell Quattro Pro to also store the formatting information in expanded memory. Or, if you have plenty of system memory and want to speed up Quattro Pro's performance, choose the Format option, which tells Quattro Pro to store only format information in expanded memory; or choose the None option, which tells Quattro Pro to store neither worksheet data nor formatting information in expanded memory.

Use the Clock option to control whether Quattro Pro displays the date and time at the bottom of the screen in the status line. If you choose the Options Other Clock command, Quattro Pro presents a menu that has three options: Standard, International, and None. The Standard option causes the date and time to be displayed in the format DD-MMM-YY HH:MM xx. Using the Standard format, the date November 16, 1992, and the time 10 o'clock at night is displayed as 16-NOV-92 10:00 PM. The International option causes the date and time to be displayed in the format MM-DD-YY HH:MM. For example, 11-16-92 22:00 represents the date November 16, 1992, and the time 10 o'clock at night. The None option removes the date and time from the status line.

The Paradox option lets you more easily exchange data with Paradox. After you choose this option, Quattro Pro display a menu that has four options: Network Type, Directory, Retries, and Quit. If you choose the Network Type option, Quattro Pro presents a menu that lists the various network types. If you're trying to access Paradox files on a network, simply identify the type of network you use. The Directory option lets you identify the directory in which the PARADOX.NET file is stored; information Quattro Pro needs to find the Paradox files. Finally, the Retries option lets you control how many seconds Quattro Pro waits before attempting a second time to access a Paradox file that is locked because someone else is using it. The default Retries setting is 300 seconds, but you can increase this setting if a five-minute wait is insufficient.

Appendix C
Using Special Characters

*I*n Chapter 4, "Functions," you saw how you can use the @CHAR function to enter into a worksheet characters that do not appear on a standard PC keyboard. This appendix shows you how to enter these characters using the Alt key and the numeric keypad.

An IBM PC, PS/2, or compatible system can display a total of 256 different alphanumeric characters, each of which is identified by a unique three-digit ASCII (American Standard Code for Information Interchange) code. When Quattro Pro or any other PC application displays a character on your screen, it does so by telling the PC to display the character represented by a particular ASCII code. For example, when Quattro Pro displays the letter A on your monitor, it has told your PC to display ASCII character 065. Although you can enter the majority of the characters available in the PC character set using your keyboard, you can enter many of them using only the @CHAR function or the Alt key. To enter a character in a cell using the @CHAR function, enter the function in a cell using the character's three-digit ASCII code as the function's argument. For example, the function @CHAR(156) returns the character £. To enter a character using the Alt key, hold down the Alt key while you type the character's three-digit ASCII code using your computer's numeric keypad. For example, to enter the character £ in a cell, move the cell selector to that cell, hold down the Alt key, and type *156* on the numeric keypad. When you release the Alt key, the character £ is displayed in the edit line. Press the Enter key to lock in the character.

Table C-1 lists a number of commonly used currency symbols, along with their corresponding decimal ASCII codes. Use the @CHAR function or the Alt key to enter any of these characters—as well as any other character in the PC character set—into a Quattro Pro worksheet. A complete listing of the characters available in the PC character set and their corresponding ASCII codes is available in the *Quattro Pro 2.0 Users Guide*.

ASCII Code	Character	Description
155	¢	U.S. cent symbol
156	£	British pound sign
157	¥	Japanese yen symbol
159	ƒ	Dutch guilder symbol

TABLE C-1. *You can generate each of the characters listed in this table by typing its ASCII code on the numeric keypad while pressing the Alt key.*

Index

Special characters

~ (not-equal-to) operator 364–65
+/- (plus/minus) format 51–52
* (asterisk) wildcard 364
= (equal sign) operator 367
? (question mark) wildcard 363–64
{?} (question mark) command 417
@@ function 139–40
<> (not-equal) operator 367

A

@ABS function 88
absolute references 21, 79–80. *See also* cells, references
@ACOS function 91
addition 93–94, 378. *See also* recalculation
aligning labels and values 56–57
amortization 102–4
#AND# operator 122, 369
angles, measuring 90–91
Annotate feature
  arrows 337
  clip art 345–46
  graph buttons 347–48
  lines 337–38, 339, 340–41
  linking elements 347
  moving and editing components 342–46
  overview 334–36
  pictures 348
  property settings 341–44
  shapes 338–41
  text 336–37
area graphs 310, 315
arrows 337
ASCII
  characters 125–26, 133, 356–57, 503–4
  files 450–56, 461–62, 479

@ASIN function 91
aspect ratio 483
asterisk (*) wildcard 363–64
art, clip 345–46
@ATAN functions 91
automatic-load worksheets 251–52
averaging values 95, 377
@AVG 95

B

backup, automatic 408–12
bar graphs 51–52, 311, 312–14, 320–21
bar/line graphs 322–23
baud rate, printing and 208
beep 447, 491
{Blank} command 423–24
blocks
  of cells (*see also* cells)
    changing coordinates of 41
    combining 276
    copying and rotating 82–84
    copying entries between 78
    defining 27–28
    erasing 66–67
    extracting 266–70
    filling 141–44
    font assignment for 234
    formatting 47–49, 184
    moving 72–74
    names of 36–41, 74
    referencing in link formulas 277, 278
  of columns 60–61
  database 370–75, 379–80
  of labels 56–57
  print 211–13
borders 231–33, 330
boxes 336–37
braced commands 413–14. *See also* programming commands

505

{Branch} command 427–28
{BreakOff} and {BreakOn} commands 437
breakpoints, in macros 402–5, 406–7
bullets 336–37
buttons, graph 347–48

C

calculating worksheets 7, 32–36, 152, 449–50
case, searching by 179–80
cash flow, present value 97–101
@CELL function 135–36
@CELLINDEX function 136
@CELLPOINTER function 134
cell selector
  defined 4
  moving 7–13, 181, 289, 290
cells. See also blocks, of cells
  adding notes to 22
  counting 95
  database (see database)
  editing 7
  entering data with programming commands to 421–25
  entries to
    canceling 14
    copying 75–84
    editing 23–25
    erasing 423–24
    formula (see formulas)
    function (see functions)
    hiding 52
    label (see labels)
    locking in 13–14, 23–24
    moving 71–74
    notes in 22
    numbers in 14–16
    types of 13
  erasing 66
  formatting 47–49
  moving to create links 278–79
  naming 41–42
  protecting 173–75

cells, continued
  references
    copying and 78–80
    effect of moving entries 73–74
    effect of row and column changes 69, 70–71
    in formulas 19–20, 21
    indirect 139–40
    in link formulas 277
  status functions 134–37
CGA snow 483–84
characters. See also fonts
  accented 488–89
  ASCII 125–26, 133, 356–57, 503–4
  LICS conversions 488–89
  program compatibility and 468, 469
  string (see strings)
  value 15
  wildcard 363–65
@CHAR function 126, 503–4
[Choices] key 38, 39
@CHOOSE function 112–13
CIRC indicator 34
circular bullets 336–37
circular references 34–36
@CLEAN function 133
clip art 345–46
Clipboard commands 344–46
clock 501–2
@CODE function 125–26
color
  font 236, 318
  in graphs 318–19, 325
  screen 217, 331, 484–86
@COLS function 137
column graphs 311, 312
columns
  copying entries between 77, 78
  deleting 70–71
  determining number of 137
  freezing in view 285–88
  hiding 63–65
  inserting 68, 69
  printing headings for 229–31

Index 507

columns, *continued*
  removing letters in 296
  width of
    adjusting 59–63
    dates and 188–89
    formats and 48–49, 196
Comma format 50
commands. *See also particular command or function*
  adding 496
  deleting 497
  editing 493–96
  macro (*see* macros)
  moving 497
  overview of 25–28
  programming (see programming commands)
compressing worksheet files 247–49
computer requirements 1–2
concatenation in formulas 21–22
conditional testing 120–23, 425–27
{Contents} command 424–25
[Contract] keys 6
Control Pane 259–61
@COS function 91
@COUNT function 95
criteria, query. *See* querying database, criteria used in
@CTERM function 107–8
currency symbols 487
cursor movement, while editing entries 23. *See also* cell selector
@CURVALUE function 137

D

daisy-wheel printers 213. *See also* printer; printing
data, exchanging. *See* exchanging data
Database Restrict Input command 180–83
database
  accessing external 379–80
  defined 349–50
  deleting records from 375–76
  editing 352–53

database, *continued*
  entering data into 352
  exchanging data between programs (*see* exchanging data)
  extracting records from 372–75
  input forms for 354
  locating records 371–72
  printing 353
  querying (*see* querying databases)
  saving 353
  size 351
  sorting 354–59
  statistical functions 376–79
  structure 350–51
data series
  adding to graph 303–4
  colors 318–19
  defined 301–2
@DATE function 186, 190
dates
  comparison criteria and 367
  entering 186–87
  formatting 187–89, 200
  functions 186, 190–91, 200–202
  in headers and footers 228
  series 191–94
  times combined with 199–201
  working with 189–94
@DATEVALUE function 201–2
@DAVG function 377
@DAY function 191
dBASE, exchanging data with 379–80, 460–61, 469–73
debugging macros
  basics 390, 400
  breakpoints 402–5, 406–7
  editing 402
  [For] loops 433–34
  function key 7
  programming command for 420–21
  step-by-step execution 401
  trace cells 405–7
  trapping errors 435–36
  types of errors 398–99
decimal places, adjusting 89–90

@DCOUNT function 378–79
@DDB function 111–12
default directory, changing 252–55
Defaults Formats Hide Zeros command 54-55
@DEGREES function 90
deleting worksheets. *See* erasing worksheets
delimited files 466
depreciation functions 110–12
direction keys, moving cell selector with 8
directories. *See also* files
   changing 252–55, 259–60
   creating 261
   reading 261
   searching for files 260–61
   specifying in link formulas 278
disk, printing graphs to 334
disk drives
   changing 259–60
   requirements 1–2
disk-full errors 246
{Dispatch} command 437–38
display, changing defaults 489–90. *See also* screens
@DMAX and @DMIN functions 377–78
DOS
   MODE command 208
   requirements 1–2
   starting macros from 397–98
dot-matrix printers 213. *See also* printers; printing
draw commands 336–341
drawing pictures in graphs 348
@DSTD, @DSTDS, @DVAR, and @DVARS functions 378
@DSUM function 378

E

Edit Copy command 75–80, 262
Edit Delete command 69–71
Edit Duplicate command 263

Edit Erase command 66–67, 262–63
Edit Fill command 141–44
Edit Insert command 67–68
Edit key, editing entries with 23–25
Edit Move command 71–74, 262
Edit Names command 36–42
Edit Paste command 262
Edit Rename command 263
Edit Search And Replace command 175–80
Edit Select command 262
Edit Transpose command 82–84
Edit Values command 81–82
ellipses, in graphs 340
End key, moving cell selector with 9, 11
EPS (encapsulated PostScript) files, saving graphs as 334
equal sign (=) operator 367
erasing worksheets 65–67
@ERR function 138
error messages
   disk-full 246
   formulas and 22
   macros and 435–36
   memory-full 31
   overview 6
errors, in macros. *See* debugging macros
Esc key, changing directory with 253
@EXACT function 127–28
exchanging data
   with ASCII files 450–56, 461–62, 479
   with dBASE 379–80, 460–61, 469–73
   with Lotus 1-2-3 460, 466–68
   with Lotus Symphony 460, 468–69
   with Paradox 7, 379–80, 461, 473–75, 502
   with Reflex 379–80, 461, 475–78
exiting Quattro Pro 43, 265
Expanded Memory setting 501
[Expand] keys 6
@EXP function 92

Index 509

exploded pie graphs 325
exporting data. *See* exchanging data

F
@FALSE function 125
Fast Graph option 300–1
fields, in databases. *See* database
File Close command 255–57
File Directory command 254
File Erase command 65–67
@FILEEXISTS function 125
File List Pane 258, 260–61
File Make Dir command 261
File Manager
  accessing 258
  arranging files 263
  changing drive, directory, or filter 259–60
  directory trees 263–64
  editing files 262–63
  function key commands 7
  overview 258–59
  printing 264–65
  reading and creating directories 261
  retrieving files 260
File Open command 249–52, 255
File Read Dir command 261
File Retrieve command 248, 249–52
File Save commands 43, 243–48, 407
{FileSize} command 453
File Utilities commands 249, 265–66
File Workspace commands 256–57
files. *See also* directories; File Manager
  database (*see* database)
  delimited 466
  determining existence of 124–25
  importing and exporting (*see* exchanging data)
  managing with programming commands 450–56
  worksheet (*see* worksheets)
fill patterns, in graphs 319
filters, changing 259–60
financial functions, 97–112

@FIND function 127
Fixed format 50
fonts. *See also* characters
  cartridges 209
  changing 234–36
  color 318
  in graph text 317–18
  PostScript 334
footers and headers 225–29
{ForBreak} command 433
{For} command 432–34
For/Next loops 432–34
foreign currency symbols 487
format indicators 49
formatting, worksheet
  aligning labels and values 56–57
  cells and blocks 47–49
  changing label prefix 57
  format options 45–47, 50–54
  global format 46–47
  hiding zeros 54–55
  indicator 49
  unformatting 49
forms, input 180–83
formulas. *See also* functions
  circular references 34–36
  copying 78–80, 81–82, 275
  dates and 190
  displaying in cell 53
  editing 25
  entering 18–22
  in extracted blocks 267–69
  filling blocks and 144
  linking worksheets with 276–83
  references to cells (*see* cells, references)
  transposing 83–84
frequency distributions 144–46
function keys 6, 7
functions. *See also particular function*
  arguments 86–87
  cell status 134–37
  copying 78–80
  database statistical 376–79
  date 186, 190–91

functions, *continued*
  entering in worksheet 87–88
  filling blocks and 144
  financial 97–112
  list of 7
  logical 120–25
  lookup 112–20
  mathematical 88–92, 133
  names 86
  program compatibility and 468
  statistical 92–97
  string 125–33
  time 195–96, 198–99, 202–3
@FV function 105–6
@FVAL function 106–7

G

General format 46–47, 53–54
{Get} command 420
{Get Label} command 419
{Get Number} command 417–18
{GetPos} command 452–53
global format 46–47, 53–54
[Go To] key, moving cell selector with 11
graphics 231–36. *See also* Annotate feature
graphics display adapters 2
graph
  area 310, 315
  bar 320–21
  bar/line 322–23
  black-and-white display 331
  borders 330
  buttons 347–48
  changing settings 326
  changing type 304
  color in 318–19, 325, 331
  column 311, 312
  copying 306, 341–46
  creating 300–302, 304–5
  displaying 7
  editing 303–4, 341–46
  erasing 305
  fast 300–301

graph, *continued*
  file formats 334
  fill patterns in 319
  graphic devices in (*see* Annotate feature)
  grids 330
  high-low 311–12
  interior labels 321–22
  legends 317
  line 306–7
  line styles in 319–20
  linking elements 347
  marker symbols 319–21
  moving components 341–46
  naming 304
  page layout 332–33
  pie 308–10, 324–26
  printing 331–34
  rotated bar 311
  saving 306
  second y-axis 323–24
  selecting 305
  slide shows and 305–6
  text in 315–18, 336–37
  three-dimensional 312–15, 331
  tick marks 326, 327–28
  titles 315–17
  viewing 302–3
  x-axis control 326–29
  XY 307–8, 309
  y-axis control 323, 329
grids 330

H

hardware
  changing default settings 482–84
  requirements 1–2, 205–10
headers and footers 225–29
help 7, 217, 498
@HEXTONUM function 133
hiding
  columns 63–65
  entries 52
  zeros 54–55
high-low graphs 311–12

@HLOOKUP function 118–20
Home key, moving cell selector with 11
@HOUR function 198

I

{If} command 426
@IF functions 120–23
{Ifkey} command 426
importing data. *See* exchanging data
@INDEX function 113–14
{Indicate} command 448
input forms 180–83, 354
input line 4
interest 104–5, 109–10
interior labels 321–22
international settings 189, 197, 486–89
investments
    future value of 105–9
    interest on 109–10
    rate of return on 101–2
@INT function 89–90
@IPAYMT and @PPAYMT functions 104–5
@IRATE function 109–10
@IRR function 101–2
@ISERR function 123–24
@ISNA function 124–25

K

keyboard, function keys 6, 7
keys, representation in macros 384–85

L

labels
    aligning 56–57
    changing default prefix, 57
    converting to dates and times 201–3
    in databases (*see* database)
    determining existence of 124–25
    entering 16–18, 421–25

labels, *continued*
    freezing in view 285–88
    graph 321–22, 324–25
    hiding 52
    looking up 112–20
    naming cells with 41–43
    parsing 462–66
    removing spaces from 132
    soliciting 419
landscape orientation 222–23
laser printers 209, 214. *See also* printer; printing
layout, report 223–24, 241
legends, in graphs 317
@LEFT function 129
@LENGTH function 130
{Let} command 421–23
line feeds 210
line graphs 306–7, 322–23
linear programming 162–64
linear regression 153–59
lines
    in graphs 337–41
    styles 319–20
    in worksheets 231–33
linked worksheets
    copying formulas 280
    overview of 276–78
    retrieving 281
    stacked worksheets 278–80
    updating 281–83
    wildcards and 279–80
listings, worksheet 240–41
@LN function 92
loan payments 102–5
LOG files 411–12
logarithmic functions 92
logarithmic scaling, in graphs 329
logical functions 120–25
logical operators 368–69
{Look} command 420
lookup functions 112–20
loops, For/Next 432–34

Lotus
  1-2-3, exchanging data with 460, 466–68
  International Character Set (LICS) character conversions 488–89
  PIC files, saving graphs as 334
  Symphony, exchanging data with 460, 468–69
@LOWER function 130

M

macros
  adding to menus 498
  automatic backup 408–12
  calculated statements 457–58
  conditional testing during 425–27
  controlling flow 434–38
  creating 388–90, 391–94, 408–12
  debugging (see debugging macros)
  displaying menu 7
  documenting 394–95
  editing 394, 402
  elements 383–86
  executing 387–88, 395–98, 401
  For/Next loops in 432–34
  libraries 407–8
  messages in 448, 499
  naming 387, 393
  overview of 381–82
  pasting into worksheet 388–90
  positioning 386
  program compatibility and 467, 468
  programming commands (see programming commands)
  redirecting 427–28
  saving and retrieving 407
  self-modifying 456–57
  simple form 387–88
  soliciting input for 417–21
  startup 490–91
  statements 386
  stopping 396–97, 416–17
  Transcript and 408–12

main menu 25–26
map view 297
margins 219–21, 223–24
markers
  graph 320
  scroll bar 12
mathematical operators, dates and 190
mathematics. *See also particular operation*
  formulas 18–22
  functions 88–92
matrices, manipulating 159–64
@MAX function 96
mean 95
@MEMAVAIL and MEMEMSAVAIL functions 138
memory
  available 138
  databases and 351
  expanded 32, 501
  managing 30–32
  program compatibility and 469
  requirements 1–2
memory-full errors 31
menu bars 4, 499
{MenuBranch} and {MenuCall} commands 439–45
Menu Builder 492–500
menu commands, representation in macros 392–93
menu trees 263–64, 491–500
menus. *See also particular menu or function*
  adding 496–97
  color of 484–85
  custom 439–45, 491–500
  main 25–26
  submenus 26–27
{Message} command 448
@MID function 129–30
@MIN function 95–96
@MINUTE function 198

Index   513

mixed references 80. *See also* cells, references
@MOD function 88
MODE command (DOS) 208
mode indicator, changing 448
monochrome monitors 486. *See also* screen
@MONTH function 191
mouse
   moving cell selector with 12–13
   palette 5, 13, 500
   using Quattro Pro with 2, 5
   window operation 297–98
multiple regression 157–58
multiplication in matrices 159–61

N

@N function 138–39
@NA function 138
#NOT# operator 123, 369
not-equal (<>) operator 367
not-equal-to (~) operator 364–65
notes, adding to cells 22
@NOW function 199–200
@NPER function 108–9
@NPV function 100–101
Num Lock key, moving cell selector with 9
numbers. *See also* values
   absolute value of 88
   random 89
   in worksheets 16–18
numeric conversion functions 133
numeric labels 18. *See also* labels
numeric lookups 115, 119
@NUMTOHEX function 133

O

{OnError} command 435–36
{Open} command 450–52
operators in formulas 19
optimization problems 164–72
Options Colors commands 484–86
Options Display Mode command 489–90

Options Formats commands 54–55, 57, 63
Options Graphic Quality command 501–2
Options Hardware commands 30, 482–84
Options International commands 486–89
Options Mouse Palette command 500
Options Protection commands 174–75
Options Recalculation commands 32–36
Options Startup commands 251, 254–55, 397, 490–500
#OR# operator 122, 369
orientation, page 222–23

P

page
   breaks 214–16, 225, 236–37
   layout 223–24, 241, 332–33
   numbering 227–28
   orientation 222–23
   rulers 217–18
   settings 219–25
{PanelOff} and {PanelOn} commands 446–47
paper alignment 213–14
Paradox
   exchanging data with 7, 461, 473–75, 502
   running Quattro Pro within 379–80
parity, printing and 208
parsing labels 462–66
Pass Count option 404
passwords 246–47, 251
@PAYMT function 103–4
PCX files, saving graphs as 334
Percent format 50
PIC files, saving graphs as 334
pictures, drawing in graphs 348
pie graphs 308–10, 324–26
@PI function 90
plotters 209

plus/minus (+/-) format 51–52
@PMT function 102–3
point size 235, 318
polygons 338–39
polylines 338
portrait orientation 222–23
PostScript compatibility 334
present value 97–101
previewing worksheets 216–18
Print Layout Reset command 241
printer. *See also* printing
  requirements 2
  setup 205–10, 213–14
  seven-bit 489
printing. *See also* printer
  databases 353
  via File Manager 264–65
  fonts (*see* fonts)
  graphs 331–34
  menu trees 498
  overstrike 489
  with two printers 209
  worksheets
    aborting 216
    column and row headings 229–31
    example 211
    format settings 219–25, 241
    hardware setup 205–10
    headers and footers 225–29
    lines and shading 231–34
    page breaks 214–16, 225, 236–37
    page numbering 227–28
    paper alignment 213–14
    previewing 216–18
    print blocks 211–13
    setup strings 238–40
    listings 240–41
programming, linear 162–64
programming commands. *See also particular command*
  arguments to 414
  braced and /x commands 413–14
  calling subroutines with 428–32

programming commands, *continued*
  conditional testing with 425–27
  controlling macro flow with 434–38
  controlling recalculation with 449–50
  controlling user interface with 445–48
  creating custom menus with 439–45
  described 385–86, 413
  entering cell data with 421–25
  file input/output with 450–56
  looping with 432–34
  redirecting macros with 427–28
  soliciting keyboard input with 417–21
  stopping macros with 416–17
  using 415–16
@PROPER function 130
punctuation defaults 487–88
{Put} command 423
@PV function 97–98
@PVAL function 98–99

Q

QUATTRO.LOG file 408–12
Quattro Pro
  accessing version number 139
  customizing (*see particular item*)
  use with Paradox 379–80
querying databases. *See also* databases
  criteria used in
    comparison 365–69
    entering 361–63
    specifying 360–61
  defining blocks 370–71
  locating records 371–72
  logical operators 368–69
  referencing cells outside database 366
  wildcard characters 363–65
[Query] key 376
question mark {?} command 417

question mark (?) wildcard 364
{Quit} command 416
quitting Quattro Pro 43, 265

R
@RADIANS function 90
RAM 1–2, 30
@RAND function 89
@RATE function 109
rate of return 101–2
{Read} command 453–54
{ReadLn} command 454–55
recalculation 7, 32–36, 152, 449–50
records. *See* database
rectangles, in graphs 339–40
references, cell
  copying and 78–80
  effect of moving entries 73–74
  effect of row and column changes
      69, 70–71
  in formulas 19–20, 21
  indirect 139–40
  in link formulas 277
Reflex, exchanging data with 379–80,
    461, 475–78
regression, linear 146–53
relative references 21, 78–79. *See also*
    cells, references
remainders 88
@REPEAT function 132
replace, search and 175–180
@REPLACE function 128
reports. *See* printing, worksheets
requirements, hardware 1–2
{Restart} command 438
{Return} command 429–30, 432–33
ribbon graphs 314
@RIGHT function 129
rotated bar graphs 311
round bullets 336–37
@ROUND function 89
rows
  copying entries between 77
  database (*see* database)
  deleting 69–71

rows, *continued*
  determining number of 137
  freezing in view 285–88
  inserting 67–68, 69
  printing headings 229–31
  removing numbers 296
rulers 217–18

S
@S function 138–39
Scientific format 50–51
screen
  changing settings 482–86, 489–90
  colors on 217, 331, 484–86
  requirements 2
  splitting 288–93
scroll bars 5, 12–13
search and replace 175–80
@SECOND function 199
security 246–47, 251
serial printers 208. *See also* printer;
    printing
{SetPos} command 452
setup strings 237–40
shading 233–34
shapes 339–40
@SIN function 91
slide shows 305–6
@SLN function 111
sorting
  databases 354–59
  specifying tables 488
  worksheets 263
sound 447, 491
splitting screen 288–93
spreadsheet programs, exchanging
    data with. *See* exchanging data
spreadsheets. *See* worksheet
square bullets 336–37
square root 89
SQZ! program 247–49
stacks
  graph components 346
  window 294, 295
  worksheet 255–57, 265, 278–80

standard deviation 378
start, stop, and step values 142–44
startup
  automatic worksheet loading at 251–52
  customizing 490–500
  described 2–3
  macros and 397, 490–91
statistical functions 92–97
status line 4, 5
@STD and STDS functions 96–97
step graphs 314
{StepOn} and {StepOff} commands 438
stop bits, printing and 208
string formulas 21–22
@STRING function 130–31
strings
  in conditional tests 122
  functions 125–33
  looking up 112–20
  setup 237–40
  as true and false results 121
Style Alignment command 56–57
Style Block Widths command 61–62
Style Column Width command 60–61
Style Font command 234–36
Style Hide Column command 63–65
Style Insert Break command 236–37
Style Line Drawing command 231–33
Style Protection commands 174–75
Style Reset Width command 61, 63
Style Shading command 233–34
submenus 26–27
subroutines, calling 428–32
summing values 93–94, 378. *See also* recalculation
@SYD function 112
Symphony, exchanging data with 460, 468–69
system commands 445–48

T

tables
  block name 39–40

tables, *continued*
  lookup 112–20
  sort 488
  what-if 146–43
@TAN function 91
@TERM function 107
text
  comparison criteria and 367
  in graphs 315–18, 336–37, 344–46
  looking up 117–18, 120
  sorting databases by 356
Text format 53
text graphs. *See* Annotate feature
text-only files, exchanging data with 450–56, 461–62, 479
three-dimensional graphs 312–15, 331
tick marks 326, 327–28
tilde (~) operator 364–65
@TIME function 195, 198, 200–201
@TIMEVALUE function 202–3
time
  clock 501
  dates combined with 199–201
  entering 195
  formatting 196–97, 200
  functions 195–96, 198–99, 202–3
  working with 197–99
titles, in graphs 315–17
Toolbox draw commands 336–41
Tools Advanced Math Invert commands 161–64
Tools Advanced Math Regression commands 153–59
Tools Advanced Math Multiply commands 159–61
Tools Advanced Math Optimization commands 164–72
Tools Combine commands 270–76
Tools Frequency command 144–46
Tools Macro commands. *See* macros
Tools Parse command 462–66
Tools Reformat command 183–84
Tools Solve For command 172–73
Tools Update Links commands 281–83

Tools What-If command 146–53
Tools Xtract command 266–70
trace cells, in macros 405–7
Transcript 408–12
trees, menu 263–64, 491–500
triangles 338–39
trigonometric functions 90–92
@TRIM function 132
@TRUE function 125
typefaces. *See* fonts

U

Undo command 7, 29, 501
Unzoom command 218
@UPPER function 130
user interface, controlling 445–48

V

value characters 15
@VALUE function 130–32
values. *See also* cells, entries
   adding to worksheet file 273–75
   aligning 56–57
   averaging 377
   converting strings to 131–32
   converting to strings 130–31
   copying and editing 81–82
   in databases (*see* database)
   deleting from worksheet file 275–76
   determining 137
   determining existence 124–25
   entering with programming commands 421–25
   error 138
   in extracted blocks 269–70
   frequency distributions for 144–46
   hiding 52
   looking up 112–20
   maximum 96
   mean 95
   minimum 95–96
   multiplying 94
   rounding 89
   square root of 89

values, *continued*
   standard deviation 96–97, 378
   start, stop, and step 142–44
   summing 93–94, 378
   variance 97
@VAR and VARS functions 97
@VERSION function 139
viewing, graphs 302–3
@VLOOKUP function 114–18

W

{Wait} command 436
what-if tables 146–53
wildcards 279–80, 363–65
[Window] key 289, 291–92, 294
Window Options Locked Titles command 285–88
Window Pick command 265
windows
   activating 293–94, 297–98
   changing size 294, 295–96, 298
   cell selector movement with 289, 290
   defined 293
   displaying list of 7
   enlarging or shrinking 7
   File Manager 258–59
   freezing 446–47
   mouse and 297–98
   moving 295–96
   removing row and column borders 296
   splitting screen with 288–93
   stacking 294, 295
{WindowsOff} and {WindowsOn} commands 446
word processing 183–84
worksheet
   ASCII files and 450–56
   automatic-load 251–52
   automatic opening 490
   cells (*see* cells)
   changing default directory 252–55
   columns (*see* columns)
   combining 270–76

worksheet, *continued*
  components 3–6
  compressing files 247–49
  copying 262, 271–76
  database (*see* database)
  duplicating 263
  entering functions in 87–88
  entries (*see* cells, entries)
  erasing 65–67, 262–63
  exchanging data between programs
      (*see* exchanging data)
  file extensions 251, 491
  fonts in 234–36
  formatting
    aligning labels and values 56–57
    cells and blocks 47–49
    changing label prefix 57
    format options 45–47, 50–54
    global format 46–47
    hiding zeros 54–55
    indicator 49
    unformatting 49
  grouping 256–57
  lines and borders 231–33
  linked (*see* linked worksheets)
  listings 240–41
  map view of 297
  matrices in 159–64
  moving 262
  naming 244–46, 263
  pasting macros into 388–90
  previewing 216–18
  printing (*see* printing, worksheets)
  protecting 173–75, 246–47, 251
  recalculating 7, 32–36
  retrieving 249–52, 260–61, 280–81
  rows (*see* rows)

worksheet, *continued*
  saving 243–49, 266–70
  selecting 262
  shading 233–34
  size, program compatibility and
      467–68
  sorting 263
  stacks of 255–57, 265, 278–80
  windows (*see* windows)
  word processing 183–84
workspaces 256–57
{Write} and {WriteLn} commands
    455–56

X

/x commands 414. *See also* programming commands
x-axis 316, 326–29. *See also* graphs
/xc command 431
/xg command 428
/xi command 427
/xl command 419
/xm command 439–42
/xn command 418–19
/xq command 416–17
/xr command 429–30
XY graphs 307–8

Y

y-axis 316, 329. *See also* graphs
@YEAR function 191

Z

zeros, hiding 54–55
zooming
  windows 7, 294, 298
  worksheets 218

Stephen L. Nelson

Stephen L. Nelson, a CPA and former senior consultant with the systems consulting group of Arthur Andersen & Co., provides financial and personal computer applications consulting to businesses in a variety of industries.

Nelson has written more than 50 articles on spreadsheet applications for national publications such as *LOTUS Magazine* and *PC Computing*. He is the author and architect of the *Microsoft Excel Small Business Consultant*, *Microsoft Excel Money Manager*, and *Lotus 1-2-3 Money Manager*, collections of worksheet templates published by Microsoft Press. Nelson's best-selling computer tutorials include *Using 1-2-3 Release 3* and *Using Quicken*, published by Que.

Nelson holds a bachelor of science degree in accounting from Central Washington University and a master's degree in business administration from the University of Washington.

Douglas F. Cobb

Douglas F. Cobb, president and founder of The Cobb Group, Inc., is the author or co-author of many best-selling computer books, including *Using 1-2-3*. Microsoft Press titles by Doug include *Running Microsoft Excel*, *Excel in Business*, and *Putting Works to Work*. Doug earned a B.S., magna cum laude, from Williams College, and an M.S. in accounting from New York University.

Mark W. Crane

Mark W. Crane is an author and editor for the Cobb Group. Mark holds a B.S. in Electrical Engineering from Purdue University, where he graduated with highest distinction. He has served as a PC Specialist with IBM and with the Citizens Fidelity Corporation in Louisville, Kentucky.

The manuscript for this book was prepared and submitted in electronic form. Text files were formatted and processed using Microsoft Word.

Principal Word Processor: Lise Kreps
Principal Proofreader: Ward Webber
Principal Typographers: David Blatner and Valerie Brewster
Cover color separator: Wescan Color Corporation

Text composition by Parallax Productions in Palatino with display type in Palatino Italic, using QuarkXPress desktop publishing software and a Linotronic 330 laser imagesetter.

Printed on recycled paper stock.